THE NATIONAL
FOOTBALL LEAGUE

PETE ROZELLE, *Commissioner*

American Football Conference
LAMAR HUNT, *President*

D1066334

OFFICIAL
RECORD BOOK

51st SEASON

League Office
410 Park Avenue
New York, N.Y. 10022
PLaza 8-1500

Compiled by Don Weiss, Seymour Siwoff, Jim Heffernan and Harold
    Rosenthal
Statistics by Elias Sports Bureau, Inc.
Library of Congress Catalog Card Number: 75-128760
Copyright © 1970 by The National Football League
Production by Rutledge Books, Inc., in association with
The Benjamin Company
485 Madison Avenue, New York, New York 10022
Distributed by Fawcett World Library
Printed in the United States of America
SBN 87502-011-9

FOREWORD

BY
PETE ROZELLE, COMMISSIONER

The decade of 1960–69 was one of expansion and great change in professional football. As the National Football League begins its 51st season under still another change— a merged, 26-team league composed of the 10 former members of the American Football League and the 16 NFL teams—our special goal is to make the next decade the Stabilizing Seventies.

Paramount in that stabilization is getting our main emphasis away from the meeting room that produced the great new franchises, the merger agreement, and realignment, and back to the playing of the game, to the on-the-field competition that has always brought so much enjoyment to so many millions of our fans.

We feel that with our realignment into two 13-team conferences—the American Football Conference, made up of the 10 AFL teams plus Baltimore, Cleveland and Pittsburgh, and the National Football Conference, which includes the remaining 13 NFL teams of the pre-1970 era— we will not only maintain but increase the high caliber of play and strong rivalries that have developed in past years. This year, for the first time, teams that existed for 10 years in the American Football League will be playing regular season games against clubs from the old NFL. In the new NFL, we want to continue as many of the old rivalries as we can but we also look ahead with considerable anticipation to the beginnings of new ones like Kansas City vs. St. Louis, Dallas vs. Houston, Jets vs. Giants, Miami vs. Atlanta, Cleveland vs. Cincinnati, Oakland vs. San Francisco, and Los Angeles vs. San Diego.

We look forward to a post-season schedule that each year will be climaxed by the Super Bowl, which in just four years has established itself as one of the world's foremost sports events. Last year, the game in New Orleans' Tulane Stadium was played before a record crowd of 80,562 and set an alltime record gate of some $3.8 millions for a single-day team sports event. Did you know more people watched the Super Bowl on television than watched man's first walk on the moon?

We expect the response for the next Super Bowl to be no less enthusiastic.

When the agreement was made to merge the AFL and the NFL in the summer of 1966, we allowed ourselves four years to implement the actual merger. We felt at the time that it gave us a chance to put professional football on a foundation that would carry it for many years. We hope 1970 and the decade ahead shows we have taken advantage of that opportunity.

THE NATIONAL FOOTBALL LEAGUE

Pete Rozelle, *Commissioner*
Jim Kensil, *Executive Director*
Mark Duncan, *Director of Personnel*
Don Weiss, *Director of Public Relations*
Bill Ray, *Treasurer*
Bob Cochran, *Broadcast Coordinator*
Jack Danahy, *Director of Security*
Bill Granholm, *Player Relations*
Buddy Young, *Player Relations*
Peter Hadhazy, *Player Personnel*
Bernard Jackson, *Security*
Joe Browne, *Public Relations*

NATIONAL FOOTBALL CONFERENCE

George Halas, *Chicago Bears, President*
John Thompson, *Assistant to President*
Jim Heffernan, *Director of Information*
Art McNally, *Supervisor of Officials*

AMERICAN FOOTBALL CONFERENCE

Lamar Hunt, *Kansas City Chiefs, President*
Val Pinchbeck, Jr., *Assistant to President*
Harold Rosenthal, *Director of Information*
Mel Hein, *Supervisor of Officials*

410 Park Avenue
New York, N.Y. 10022
PLaza 8-1500

THE NATIONAL FOOTBALL LEAGUE

AMERICAN FOOTBALL CONFERENCE

CENTRAL DIVISION

CINCINNATI
CLEVELAND
HOUSTON
PITTSBURGH

WESTERN DIVISION

DENVER
KANSAS CITY
OAKLAND
SAN DIEGO

EASTERN DIVISION

BALTIMORE
BOSTON
BUFFALO
MIAMI
NEW YORK JETS

NATIONAL FOOTBALL CONFERENCE

CENTRAL DIVISION

CHICAGO
DETROIT
GREEN BAY
MINNESOTA

WESTERN DIVISION

ATLANTA
LOS ANGELES
NEW ORLEANS
SAN FRANCISCO

EASTERN DIVISION

DALLAS
NEW YORK GIANTS
PHILADELPHIA
ST. LOUIS
WASHINGTON

Contents

PREVIEW OF THE SEASON

The start of the second fifty years of the National Football League means new rivalries through inter-conference play and realignment, new chapters added to old rivalries, a new playoff system that should stimulate more fan interest than ever, and hopefully, continued growth in the sport.

In the four years since the 1966 agreement to merge the American Football League and the National Football League into a single, expanded 26-team league, there have been many additions to professional football—the Super Bowl, the combined draft, pre-season inter-league competition, restructuring of the league administrative offices among them. But none carries the impact of the new look for 1970. Since so much has happened and will happen, it would seem that a review would be in order.

Beginning with this season, the National Football League is made up of the 26 teams of major professional football, divided into two 13-team conferences, with each conference further broken down into three divisions.

Denver's Floyd Little (44) takes Tensi handoff and heads for a hole.

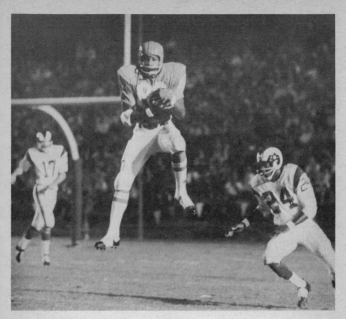

Otis Taylor of the Chiefs goes high for a catch before Williams rams him.

The 10 former American Football League teams—Boston, Buffalo, Cincinnati, Denver, Houston, Kansas City, Miami, New York Jets, Oakland and San Diego—have been joined by Baltimore, Cleveland and Pittsburgh from the pre-1970 NFL to form the American Football Conference (AFC). They've been realigned in this manner:

Eastern Division—Baltimore, Boston, Buffalo, Miami and New York Jets.

Central Division—Cincinnati, Cleveland, Houston and Pittsburgh.

Western Division—Denver, Kansas City, Oakland and San Diego.

The 13 remaining teams from the pre-1970 NFL now form the National Football Conference (NFC). They've also been realigned into one five-team division and two four-team divisions:

Eastern Division—Dallas, New York Giants, Philadelphia, St. Louis and Washington.

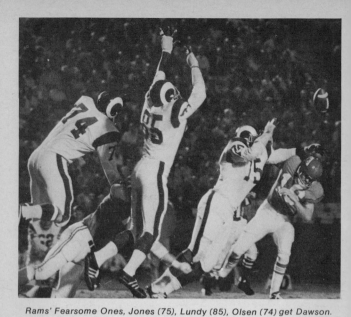

Rams' Fearsome Ones, Jones (75), Lundy (85), Olsen (74) get Dawson.

Newly acquired Junior Coffey of the Giants takes it through the Cards.

Central Division—Chicago, Detroit, Green Bay and Minnesota.

Western Division—Atlanta, Los Angeles, New Orleans and San Francisco.

During the 1970 regular season, each of the teams in a four-team division will play six games within their division (home-and-home with the three other teams), five games with the teams of the two other divisions in their conference, and three games with teams from the other conference. Each of the teams in a five-team division (the Eastern in each conference) will play eight games within its division (home-and-home with the four other teams), three games with teams in the other two divisions of their conference, and three games with teams in the other conference.

There are two exceptions to this pattern. Under the re-alignment agreement, Denver receives a fourth inter-conference game and, to accommodate the Broncos, a team from one of the NFC's four-team divisions also must play a fourth inter-conference game. In 1970, that NFC team is San Francisco.

During the 14-week regular season, 182 games will be played. Of these, 88 are intra-divisional, 54 are inter-divisional, and 40 are inter-conference. Thirty-one of the 40 games represent pairings that for the first time match teams from the old AFL and NFL in regular season competition, and adding in the new foes for the three teams that moved—Baltimore, Cleveland and Pittsburgh—the number of games between old AFL and NFL teams on the 1970 schedule totals 60, or nearly a third of the total schedule.

For instance, Kansas City's Super Bowl champions in 1970 will play Minnesota (in a Super Bowl rematch), Dallas and St. Louis from the pre-1970 NFL. Oakland will play Washington, Detroit and San Francisco. Denver—which has an extra inter-conference game—will play Atlanta, San Francisco, Washington and New Orleans.

But Baltimore, which now is in the AFC, will have 11 of its games against former AFL teams. And Cleveland and Pittsburgh, the two others that moved, will have nine of their games against former AFL foes—two fewer than Baltimore because the Browns and Steelers play each other twice.

The inter-conference pairings thus permit the start of new "natural" rivalries like New York Giants vs. New York Jets, Houston vs. Dallas, Kansas City vs. St. Louis, Oakland vs. San Francisco, Los Angeles vs. San Diego, Atlanta vs. Miami, but there still will be plenty of the old, traditional games—Chicago vs. Green Bay and Detroit, Los Angeles vs. San Francisco, Giants vs. Washington, Cleveland vs. Pittsburgh, and a continuance of the more recent rivalries like Oakland and Kansas City, Boston and Buffalo, Jets and Oakland, Dallas and St. Louis, New Orleans and Atlanta, Denver and San Diego.

At the end of the regular season, the three divisional winners plus the non-winning team with the best won-lost percentage will qualify in each conference for post-season competition.

The divisional playoff games will be played two on Saturday, December 26, and two on Sunday, December 27. The four winners will advance to the AFC and NFC championship games on Sunday, January 3, and the AFC and NFC champions will then meet for the Super Bowl championship at Miami's Orange Bowl stadium on Sunday, January 17. The post-season schedule ends a week later with the playing of the All-Star Game, matching the best of the AFC against the best of the NFC.

Under the rotation established, the Eastern and Western Division champions of the AFC and the Eastern and Central Division champions of the NFC will be the home teams for the 1970 divisional playoff games.

The drawings also involved Conference championship game sites for the next three seasons, each of which will depend upon the results of the divisional playoff games. The rotation was established as follows:

DIVISIONAL PLAYOFF GAMES

American Football Conference	National Football Conference
A—Eastern	A—Eastern
B—Western	B—Central
C—Central	C—Western

Boston's Rookie of the Year Carl Garrett gains against the Bengals.

Adrian Young (35), Eagle linebacker, lines up the 49ers' Jim Thomas.

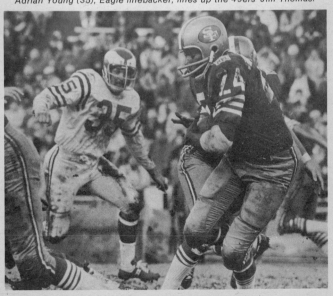

CONFERENCE CHAMPIONSHIP GAMES

1970—Eastern (A)	1970—Western (C)
1971—Western (B)	1971—Eastern (A)
1972—Central (C)	1972—Central (B)

Under the divisional playoff game formula adopted, A and B will be the home teams for 1970 and C and D, the latter being the second-place team with the best percentage in the conference, will be the visitors. C will be at A and D at B unless D is from B's division. In that event, D will be at A and C will be at B.

Second year 1971:	B and C home teams.
	A at B and D at C, unless D is from C division.
	In that event, D at B and A at C.
Third year 1972:	C and A home teams.
	B at C and D at A, unless D from A division.
Fourth year 1973:	Rotation is recycled.

In the conference championship games, the rotation for home sites for the first three years was drawn as follows:

American Conference—A, B, C

National Conference—C, A, B

If the designated division representative should lose in the divisional playoffs, the next division in the rotation would become the home site. If both the designated division and the next division should lose in the divisional playoffs, the third division in the rotation would become the home site. An example: If in the American Football Conference, A is beaten in the divisional playoffs, then B would be the home site. If both A and B are beaten C will be the home site.

In no case will D, the best percentage second-place team, be the home team—either in the divisional or the conference championship games.

If in the example above, C becomes the home site for the American Football Conference championship game in 1970, then A would be the original designated site for 1971. If B becomes the home site in 1970, then C would be the original designated site for 1971.

Three clubs—Cincinnati (Riverfront), Philadelphia (Philadelphia Veterans), and Pittsburgh (Three Rivers)—will be playing in new stadiums in 1970, bringing to 15 the number of NFL clubs who play in stadiums that have either been built or considerably enlarged in the last 10 years. Next year, new stadiums will open in Dallas and Kansas City and planning is underway for new structures in Boston (Foxboro), Buffalo and New Orleans.

The 1970 season brings professional football one more first as it becomes the only sport ever to be under contract to all three major television networks at the same time. For the next four years, CBS has the broadcasting rights to NFC games, NBC has rights to AFC games, and ABC will televise nationally a 13-week series of Monday night games.

Bob Griese of Miami had a good year as the Dolphins' quarterback.

Charlie Sanders (88) and Ed Flanagan (54) block for Lions' Nick Eddy.

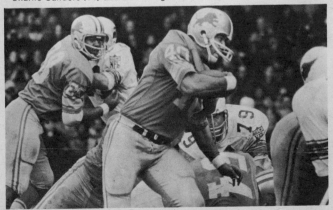

NFL 1969
PRE-SEASON
RECAP

EASTERN CONFERENCE

Capitol Division

	W	L	T	Pct.	Pts.	O.P.
Dallas	4	2	0	.667	114	97
Philadelphia	3	2	0	.600	92	80
Washington	2	4	0	.333	101	102
New Orleans	2	4	0	.333	101	155

Century Division

	W	L	T	Pct.	Pts.	O.P.
St. Louis	4	2	0	.667	132	132
Cleveland	3	2	1	.600	106	101
Pittsburgh	2	3	0	.400	99	118
New York	0	5	0	.000	92	128

WESTERN CONFERENCE

Coastal Division

	W	L	T	Pct.	Pts.	O.P.
Baltimore	6	0	0	1.000	159	89
Los Angeles	4	2	0	.667	146	131
Atlanta	2	4	0	.333	105	120
San Francisco	0	6	0	.000	117	157

Central Division

	W	L	T	Pct.	Pts.	O.P.
Minnesota	5	1	0	.833	184	96
Detroit	5	1	0	.833	145	104
Green Bay	4	2	0	.667	140	131
Chicago	3	3	0	.500	113	104

TEAM VS. TEAM

ATLANTA (2-4)

13	Philadelphia	7
34	Boston (AFL)	16
7	Washington	24
17	New Orleans	21
10	Kansas City (AFL)	14
24	Green Bay	38
105		120

BALTIMORE (6-0)

26	San Diego (AFL)	6
34	Oakland (AFL)	30
33	Houston (AFL)	29
20	Buffalo (AFL)	7
23	Miami (AFL)	10
23	Dallas	7
159		89

CHICAGO (3-3)

7	Washington	13
16	Miami (AFL)	10
19	Green Bay	9
17	Houston (AFL)	19
23	Buffalo (AFL)	16
31	St. Louis	37
113		104

CLEVELAND (3-2-1)

24	San Francisco	19
10	Los Angeles	3
19	San Diego (AFL)	19
17	Green Bay	27
20	Washington	10
16	Minnesota	23
106		101

DALLAS (4-2)

17	Los Angeles	24
20	San Francisco	17
31	Green Bay	13
14	Houston (AFL)	11
25	New York (AFL)	9
7	Baltimore	23
114		97

DETROIT (5-1)

13	Kansas City (AFL)	38
24	Buffalo (AFL)	12
22	Boston (AFL)	6
21	Washington	20
23	Philadelphia	21
42	New Orleans	7
145		104

GREEN BAY (4-2)

22	New York	21
9	Chicago	19
13	Dallas	31
27	Cleveland	17
31	Pittsburgh	19
38	Atlanta	24
140		131

LOS ANGELES (4-2)

24	Dallas	17
3	Cleveland	10
14	Kansas City (AFL)	42
24	San Diego (AFL)	14
50	Buffalo (AFL)	20
31	San Francisco	28
146		131

MINNESOTA (5–1)

45	Miami (AFL)	10
26	Denver (AFL)	6
41	St. Louis	13
21	New York (AFL)	24
28	New York	27
23	Cleveland	16
184		96

NEW ORLEANS (2–4)

7	San Diego (AFL)	10
28	Denver (AFL)	22
24	Pittsburgh	34
21	Atlanta	17
14	Houston (AFL)	30
7	Detroit	42
101		155

NEW YORK (0–5)

21	Green Bay	22
14	New York (AFL)	37
17	Philadelphia	24
27	Minnesota	28
13	Pittsburgh	17
92		128

PHILADELPHIA (3–2)

7	Atlanta	13
14	Miami (AFL)	10
24	New York	17
21	Detroit	23
26	Washington	17
92		80

PITTSBURGH (2–3)

13	St. Louis	27
34	New Orleans	24
16	Cincinnati (AFL)	23
19	Green Bay	31
17	New York	13
99		118

ST. LOUIS (4–2)

13	New York (AFL)	6
27	Pittsburgh	13
13	Minnesota	41
21	Kansas City (AFL)	31
21	San Francisco	10
37	Chicago	31
132		132

SAN FRANCISCO (0–6)

19	Cleveland	24
17	Dallas	20
15	Denver (AFL)	19
28	Oakland (AFL)	42
10	St. Louis	21
28	Los Angeles	31
117		157

WASHINGTON (2–4)

13	Chicago	7
17	Buffalo (AFL)	21
24	Atlanta	7
20	Detroit	21
10	Cleveland	20
17	Philadelphia	26
101		102

Browns' Walter Johnson (71) is too late as Joe Kapp plunges for score.

Calvin Hill, Dallas' big rookie sensation, stampedes against St. Louis.

1969 STATISTICS
NFL FINAL
STANDINGS
EASTERN CONFERENCE

Capitol Division

	W	L	T	Pct.	Pts.	O.P.
Dallas	11	2	1	.846	369	223
Washington	7	5	2	.583	307	319
New Orleans	5	9	0	.357	311	393
Philadelphia	4	9	1	.308	279	377

Century Division

	W	L	T	Pct.	Pts.	O.P.
Cleveland	10	3	1	.769	351	300
New York	6	8	0	.429	264	298
St. Louis	4	9	1	.308	314	389
Pittsburgh	1	13	0	.071	218	404

WESTERN CONFERENCE

Coastal Division

	W	L	T	Pct.	Pts.	O.P.
Los Angeles	11	3	0	.785	320	243
Baltimore	8	5	1	.615	279	268
Atlanta	6	8	0	.429	276	268
San Francisco	4	8	2	.333	277	319

Central Division

	W	L	T	Pct.	Pts.	O.P.
Minnesota	12	2	0	.857	379	133
Detroit	9	4	1	.692	259	188
Green Bay	8	6	0	.571	269	221
Chicago	1	13	0	.071	210	339

WESTERN CONFERENCE CHAMPIONSHIP
Minnesota 23, Los Angeles 20

EASTERN CONFERENCE CHAMPIONSHIP
Cleveland 38, Dallas 14

PLAYOFF BOWL
Los Angeles 31, Dallas 0

NFL CHAMPIONSHIP
Minnesota 27, Cleveland 7

AFL-NFL CHAMPIONSHIP GAME
Kansas City (AFL) 23, Minnesota (NFL) 7

PRO BOWL
West 16, East 13

OFFENSE

	Atl.	Balt.	Chi.	Clev.	Dall.	Det.	G.B.	L.A.	Minn.	N.O.	N.Y.	Phil.	Pitt.	St.L.	S.F.	Wash.	Total	Lg. Avg.
First Downs	209	255	237	250	275	198	242	209	239	282	235	231	210	224	253	256	3805	237.8
Rushing	97	99	120	97	133	83	95	75	102	93	91	83	81	83	84	84	1500	93.8
Passing	89	140	97	138	125	93	122	114	117	158	133	132	115	125	153	149	2000	125.0
Penalty	23	16	20	15	17	22	25	20	20	31	11	16	14	16	16	23	305	19.0
Rushes	455	417	462	447	532	474	432	382	489	399	397	395	400	382	391	377	6831	426.9
Yds. Gained (Net)	2058	1490	2078	1788	2276	1755	1692	1413	1850	1705	1593	1563	1542	1446	1536	1532	27,317	1707.3
Avg. Gain	4.5	3.6	4.5	4.0	4.3	3.7	3.9	3.7	3.8	4.3	4.0	4.0	3.9	3.8	3.9	4.1	—	4.0
Passes Att.	282	429	384	378	355	329	319	416	346	453	435	458	391	430	496	444	6345	396.6
Completed	149	225	193	199	189	165	182	222	176	245	234	216	176	216	278	275	3340	208.8
% Completed	52.8	52.4	50.3	52.6	53.2	50.2	57.1	53.4	50.9	54.1	53.8	47.2	45.0	50.2	56.0	61.9	52.6	52.6
Tot. Yds. Gained	2230	3143	1929	2830	3212	1958	2678	2650	2498	3215	3076	3022	2458	2940	3379	3106	44,324	2770.3
Passer Tackled	63	19	55	20	44	42	34	17	34	27	37	29	52	21	27	40	561	35.1
Yds. Lost	477	156	439	190	366	358	302	129	252	241	301	240	374	201	221	322	4569	285.6
Net Yds. Gained	1753	2987	1490	2640	2846	1600	2376	2521	2246	2974	2775	2782	2084	2739	3158	2784	39,755	2484.7
Yds. Gained (Net) per Pass Play	5.08	6.67	3.39	6.63	7.13	4.31	6.73	5.82	5.91	6.20	5.88	5.71	4.70	6.07	6.04	5.75	—	5.76
Yds. Gained per Comp.	14.97	13.97	9.99	14.22	16.99	11.87	14.71	11.94	14.19	13.12	13.15	13.99	13.97	13.61	12.15	11.29	—	13.27
Net Yards Gained Rushing and Passing	3811	4477	3568	4428	5122	3355	4068	3934	4096	4679	4368	4345	3626	4185	4694	4316	67,072	4192.0
% Tot. Yds. — Rushing	54.00	33.28	58.24	40.38	44.44	52.31	41.59	35.92	45.17	36.44	36.47	35.97	42.53	34.55	32.72	35.50	—	40.73
% Tot. Yds. — Passing	46.00	66.72	41.76	59.62	55.56	47.69	58.41	64.08	54.83	63.53	63.53	64.03	57.47	65.45	67.28	64.50	—	59.27
Ball Control Plays	800	865	901	845	931	845	785	815	869	879	869	882	843	833	914	861	13,737	858.6
Avg. Gain (Net)	4.8	5.2	4.0	5.2	5.5	4.0	5.2	4.8	4.7	5.3	5.0	4.9	4.3	5.0	5.1	5.0	—	4.9
Interceptions																		
Had Intercepted	12	27	21	21	18	18	17	7	18	20	8	28	29	25	26	16	311	19.4
Yds. Opp. Ret.	233	394	271	275	167	168	256	40	208	265	78	343	535	202	304	188	3927	245.4
Ret. by Opp. for TD	2	3	0	1	1	1	1	0	2	0	0	3	3	0	1	1	19	1.2

	Atl.	Balt.	Chi.	Clev.	Dall.	Det.	G.B.	L.A.	Minn.	N.O.	N.Y.	Phil.	Pitt.	St.L.	S.F.	Wash.	Total	Lg. Avg.
Punts	69	57	76	60	63	74	59	80	67	49	73	74	77	73	71	70	1092	68.3
Yds. Punted	2846	2580	2964	2250	2729	2510	2363	3259	2680	2031	2744	2942	3254	2746	2874	2957	43,729	2733.1
Avg. Yds. per Punt	41.2	45.3	39.0	37.5	43.3	33.9	40.1	40.7	40.0	41.4	37.6	39.8	42.3	37.6	40.5	42.2	—	40.0
Punt Returns	26	37	30	32	38	21	32	58	45	34	15	36	37	38	22	26	523	32.7
Yds. Returned	82	192	164	183	273	230	287	556	266	217	50	219	165	201	63	190	3338	208.6
Avg. Yds. per Ret.	3.2	5.2	5.5	5.7	7.2	11.0	9.0	9.6	5.9	6.4	3.3	6.1	4.5	5.3	2.9	7.3	—	6.4
Ret. for TD	0	0	0	0	0	1	0	0	0	0	0	0	0	0	0	1	3	0.2
Kickoff Returns	52	51	52	46	36	42	50	53	33	62	56	63	60	68	47	60	831	51.9
Yds. Returned	1104	1290	1132	985	718	1017	1165	1107	774	1455	1075	1258	1241	1507	908	1268	18,004	1125.3
Avg. Yds. per Ret.	21.2	25.3	21.8	21.4	19.9	24.2	23.3	20.9	23.5	23.5	19.2	20.0	20.7	22.2	19.3	21.1	—	21.7
Ret. for TD	1	1	0	0	0	1	2	0	0	0	0	0	1	1	0	0	7	0.4
Penalties	63	62	89	58	81	71	63	95	67	83	70	80	67	72	85	74	1180	73.8
Yds. Penalized	601	561	940	603	840	734	602	994	744	943	777	843	659	765	845	756	12,207	762.9
Fumbles	37	23	27	26	28	18	31	23	17	20	22	18	36	24	25	23	398	24.9
Own Rec.	15	10	9	11	15	6	10	11	5	7	7	7	16	14	13	13	169	10.6
TDs on Own Rec.	0	0	0	0	0	0	0	0	1	0	0	0	0	0	0	0	2	0.1
Opp. Rec.	27	10	11	22	11	21	7	12	12	10	14	14	16	12	11	10	220	13.8
Opp. Rec. for TD	2	0	0	1	1	0	0	0	0	0	0	0	0	2	2	2	10	0.6
Total Points Scored	276	279	210	351	369	259	269	320	379	311	264	279	218	314	277	307	4682	292.6
Touchdowns (Total)	33	34	26	45	44	26	36	36	43	35	33	33	26	40	37	37	564	35.3
TDs Rushing	9	16	14	17	17	11	11	8	15	12	8	10	8	17	13	11	197	12.3
TDs Passing	20	17	11	24	24	12	20	25	24	22	24	20	17	19	22	22	323	20.2
TDs on Ret. and Rec.	4	1	1	4	3	3	5	3	4	1	1	3	1	4	2	4	44	2.8
Extra Points	33	33	26	45	43	26	35	36	43	33	33	31	26	38	35	34	551	34.4
Safeties	0	0	0	0	1	1	0	1	0	2	0	0	0	0	1	1	9	0.6
Field Goals	15	14	8	12	20	25	6	22	26	22	11	16	12	12	6	16	243	15.2
F. G. Att.	30	31	21	23	36	37	22	34	37	41	21	30	26	24	21	27	461	28.8
% Successful	50.0	45.2	38.1	52.2	55.6	67.6	27.3	64.7	70.3	53.7	52.4	53.8	46.2	50.0	28.6	59.3	—	52.7

DEFENSE

	Att.	Balt.	Chi.	Clev.	Dall.	Det.	G.B.	L.A.	Minn.	N.O.	N.Y.	Phil.	Pitt.	St.L.	S.F.	Wash.	Total	Lg. Avg.
First Downs	254	256	208	257	203	182	224	242	158	242	243	268	260	289	242	277	3805	237.8
Rushing	120	70	89	120	52	64	103	84	55	88	120	111	101	83	91	149	1500	93.8
Passing	120	164	98	121	141	101	107	125	88	131	103	136	142	185	128	110	2000	125.0
Penalty	14	22	21	16	10	17	14	33	15	23	20	21	17	21	23	18	305	19.0
Rushes	475	399	440	417	313	372	485	415	337	419	466	467	455	438	422	511	6831	426.9
Yds. Gained (Net)	2032	1400	1900	1990	1050	1223	1982	1475	1089	1835	2053	1909	1732	1644	1704	2299	27,317	1707.3
Avg. Gain	4.3	3.5	4.3	4.8	3.4	3.3	4.1	3.6	3.2	4.4	4.4	4.1	3.8	3.8	4.0	4.5	—	4.0
Passes Att.	383	459	296	387	458	350	360	430	410	382	340	444	410	465	402	369	6345	396.6
Completed	225	271	150	202	235	167	177	202	213	200	171	243	227	260	205	192	3340	208.8
% Completed	58.7	59.0	50.7	52.2	51.3	47.7	49.2	47.0	52.0	52.4	50.3	54.7	55.5	55.9	51.0	52.0	—	52.6
Tot. Yds. Gained	2536	3499	2239	2787	3109	2238	2133	2919	2035	3382	2430	3250	2973	3752	2726	2316	44,324	2770.3
Passer Tackled	30	33	33	37	55	46	36	50	21	21	32	25	33	33	30	18	561	35.1
Yds. Lost	251	250	258	323	452	377	288	393	199	199	275	181	304	220	255	139	4569	285.6
Net Yds. Gained	2285	3249	1981	2464	2657	1861	1845	2526	1631	3183	2155	3069	2669	3532	2471	2177	39,755	2484.7
Yards Gained (Net) per Pass Play	5.53	6.60	6.02	5.81	5.18	4.70	4.66	5.26	3.55	7.90	5.79	6.54	6.02	7.09	5.72	5.63	—	5.76
Yds. Gained per Comp.	11.27	12.91	14.93	13.80	13.23	13.40	12.05	14.45	9.55	16.91	14.21	13.37	13.10	14.43	13.30	12.06	—	13.27
Net Yds. Gained																		
Rushing and Passing	4317	4649	3881	4454	3707	3084	3827	4001	2720	5018	4208	4978	4401	5176	4175	4476	67,072	4192.0
% Tot. Yds.—Rushing	47.07	30.11	48.96	44.68	28.32	39.66	51.79	36.87	40.04	36.57	48.79	38.35	39.35	31.76	40.81	51.36	—	40.73
% Tot. Yds.—Passing	52.93	69.89	51.04	55.32	71.68	60.34	48.21	63.13	59.96	63.43	51.21	61.65	60.65	68.24	59.19	48.64	—	59.27
Ball Control Plays	888	891	769	841	826	768	881	895	796	822	838	936	898	982	854	898	13,737	858.6
Avg. Gain (Net)	4.9	5.2	5.0	5.3	4.5	4.0	4.3	4.5	3.4	6.1	5.0	5.3	4.9	5.5	4.9	5.0	—	4.9
Intercepted By	19	15	16	19	24	21	19	26	30	12	19	15	25	15	20	16	311	19.4
Yds. Returned	200	106	132	217	339	207	428	424	459	73	221	179	257	245	194	246	3927	245.4
Ret. for TD	0	0	1	3	1	0	2	3	2	0	1	3	0	1	1	1	19	1.2

	Atl.	Balt.	Chi.	Clev.	Dall.	Det.	G.B.	L.A.	Minn.	N.O.	N.Y.	Phil.	Pitt.	St.L.	S.F.	Wash.	Total	Lg. Avg.
Punts	56	69	63	64	82	70	72	77	100	58	53	69	65	67	65	62	1092	68.3
Yds. Punted	2171	2647	2607	2593	3463	2798	2855	3154	3680	2410	2062	2819	2608	2710	2629	2523	43,729	2733.1
Avg. Yds. per Punt	38.8	38.4	41.4	40.5	42.2	40.0	39.7	41.0	36.8	41.6	38.9	40.9	40.1	40.4	40.4	40.7	—	40.0
Punt Returns	38	35	28	20	43	31	18	36	34	27	41	21	41	35	39	36	523	32.7
Yds. Returned	171	182	106	72	305	133	62	181	237	176	449	93	396	158	293	324	3338	208.6
Avg. Yds. per Ret.	4.5	5.2	3.8	3.6	7.1	4.3	3.4	5.0	7.0	6.5	11.0	4.4	9.7	4.5	7.5	9.0	—	6.4
Ret. for TD	0	0	0	0	0	0	0	0	1	1	0	0	1	0	0	0	3	0.2
Kickoff Returns	52	55	38	56	64	59	51	56	70	48	45	51	46	49	43	48	831	51.9
Yds. Returned	1132	1135	917	1166	1242	1242	1078	1208	1453	935	1100	1043	962	1007	1186	1198	18,004	1125.3
Avg. Yds. per Ret.	21.8	20.6	24.1	20.8	19.4	21.0	21.1	21.6	20.8	14.5	24.4	20.5	20.9	20.6	27.6	25.0	—	21.7
Ret. for TD	2	1	1	0	0	0	1	1	1	0	0	0	0	0	0	0	7	0.4
Penalties	73	74	66	72	58	90	65	88	69	81	62	79	79	71	70	83	1180	73.8
Yds. Penalized	762	848	612	746	680	857	733	709	795	773	601	950	793	773	671	904	12,207	762.9
Fumbles	37	18	21	32	23	24	23	33	24	20	23	31	25	19	26	19	398	24.9
Own Rec.	9	8	10	10	12	2	16	19	12	9	9	14	9	7	14	9	169	10.6
TDs on Own Rec.	0	0	0	1	0	0	0	0	0	0	0	0	1	0	0	0	2	0.1
Opp. Rec.	19	12	17	14	12	12	21	11	12	12	15	23	27	10	12	17	220	13.8
Opp. Rec. for TD	1	1	0	1	0	1	1	0	1	1	0	2	0	0	1	0	10	0.6
Total Points Scored	268	268	339	300	223	188	221	243	133	393	298	377	404	389	319	319	4682	292.6
Touchdowns (Total)	32	32	43	38	28	23	23	26	16	49	35	44	50	48	39	38	564	35.3
TDs Rushing	14	8	17	18	3	7	7	8	4	31	14	15	17	10	14	10	197	12.3
TDs Passing	13	20	23	19	23	15	13	18	8	17	18	23	27	38	22	26	323	20.2
TDs on Ret. and Rec.	5	4	3	1	2	1	3	0	4	1	3	6	6	0	3	2	44	2.8
Extra Points	32	31	42	36	28	23	23	25	16	47	32	44	49	47	38	38	551	34.4
Safeties	1	0	0	0	0	0	0	1	0	2	1	0	2	0	1	1	9	0.6
Field Goals	14	15	13	12	9	9	20	20	7	16	18	23	17	18	15	17	243	15.2
F. G. Att.	27	34	31	22	25	29	34	26	18	29	29	37	26	31	36	27	461	28.8
% Successful	51.9	44.1	41.9	54.5	36.0	31.0	58.8	76.9	38.9	55.2	62.1	62.2	65.4	58.1	41.7	63.0	—	52.7

PASSING

TEAM CHAMPION—The Dallas Cowboys, who finished first in only one of the four categories on which the title is based, edged the Los Angeles Rams, who led in two rating categories. Dallas was first in average gain per pass play (7.13 yards), tied for second in touchdown passes (24), sixth in lowest percentage of interceptions (5.1), and seventh in percentage of completions (53.2). Thus, on a basis of one point for first place, two for second, three for third, etc., the Cowboys accumulated 17½ points, the lowest total of the 16 teams. Los Angeles had the most TD passes (25) and the lowest interception percentage (1.7), was sixth in percentage of completions (53.4), and 10th in average gain per pass play (5.82 yards). Washington had the highest completion percentage (61.9).

INDIVIDUAL CHAMPION—Sonny Jurgensen of Washington, who previously won in 1967. Jurgensen was second in completion percentage (62.0), third in percentage of interceptions (3.4), fourth in touchdown passes (22), and 11th in average gain (7.02 yards). Roman Gabriel of Los Angeles led in TD passes (24) and lowest percentage of interceptions (1.8). Bart Starr of Green Bay led in completion percentage (62.2), and Don Horn of Green Bay led in average gain (8.96 yards).

LONGEST COMPLETION—Roman Gabriel of Los Angeles, 93 yards to Wendell Tucker for a touchdown on first play from scrimmage in 41–30 victory over San Francisco on November 9.

A recharged Sonny Jurgensen gave the Redskins a winning season.

1969 PASSING—TEAM

	Atts.	Comp.	Pct. Comp.	Gross Yards	Yds. Lost	Net Yards	Tds.	Long.	Had Int.	Pct. Int.	Gain per Comp.	Gain per Pass Play
Dallas	355	189	53.2	3212	44/366	2846	24	†75	18	5.1	*17.00	*7.13
Los Angeles	416	222	53.4	2650	*17/129*	2521	*25	*†93	*7	*1.7	11.94	5.82
New York	435	234	53.8	3076	37/301	2775	24	65	8	1.8	13.15	5.88
New Orleans	453	245	54.1	3215	27/241	2974	22	70	20	4.4	13.12	6.20
Washington	444	275	*61.9	3106	40/322	2784	22	†88	16	3.6	11.29	5.75
Green Bay	319	182	57.1	2678	34/302	2376	20	†60	17	5.3	14.71	6.73
San Francisco	*496	*278	56.0	*3379	27/221	*3158	22	†80	26	5.2	12.15	6.04
†Cleveland	378	199	52.6	2830	20/190	2640	24	†82	21	5.6	14.22	6.63
Minnesota	346	176	50.9	2498	34/252	2246	24	†83	18	5.2	14.19	5.91
Atlanta	282	149	52.8	2230	63/477	1753	20	†88	12	4.3	14.97	5.08
Baltimore	429	225	52.4	3143	19/156	2987	17	†52	27	6.3	13.97	6.67
St. Louis	430	216	50.2	2940	21/201	2739	19	84	25	5.8	13.61	6.07
Philadelphia	458	216	47.2	3022	29/240	2782	20	†80	28	6.1	13.99	5.71
Chicago	384	193	50.3	1929	55/439	1490	11	48	21	5.5	9.99	3.39
Detroit	329	165	50.2	1958	42/358	1600	12	†62	18	5.5	11.87	4.31
Pittsburgh	391	176	45.0	2458	52/374	2084	17	63	29	7.4	13.97	4.70
League Total	6345	3340	—	44,324	561/4569	39,755	323	—	311	—	13.27	5.76
League Average	396.6	208.8	52.6	2770.3	35.1/285.6	2484.7	20.2	—	19.4	4.9		

*—High for 1969
†—1968 Leader
†—Touchdown
NOTE: Standing based on percent of completions, touchdown passes, percent of interceptions and average gain per pass play.

1969 PASSING—INDIVIDUAL

	Std.	Att.	Com.	Pct. Com.	Yds. Gain.	Td.	Lng.	Int.	Pct. Int.	Avg. Gain
JURGENSEN, WASH	1	*442	*274	62.0	*3102	22	t88	15	3.4	7.02
Starr, G.B.	2	148	92	*62.2	1161	9	51	*6	4.1	7.84
Tarkenton, N.Y.	3	409	220	53.8	2918	23	65	8	2.0	7.13
Gabriel, L.A.	4	399	217	54.4	2549	*24	*t93	7	*1.8	6.39
Morton, Dall.	5	302	162	53.6	2619	21	t67	15	5.0	8.67
Nelsen, Clev.	6	352	190	54.0	2743	23	t82	19	5.4	7.79
Brodie, S.F.	7	347	194	55.9	2405	16	t80	15	4.3	6.93
Kilmer, N.O.	8	360	193	53.6	2532	20	52	17	4.7	7.03
Unitas, Balt.	9	327	178	54.4	2342	12	t52	20	6.1	7.16
Kapp, Minn.	10	237	120	50.6	1726	19	t83	13	5.5	7.28
Horn, G.B.	11	168	89	53.0	1505	11	t60	11	6.5	*8.96
Snead, Phil.	12	379	190	50.1	2768	19	t80	23	6.1	7.30
Johnson, St.L.	13	260	131	50.4	1847	13	t84	13	5.0	7.10
Munson, Det.	14	166	84	50.6	1062	7	t62	8	4.8	6.40
Shiner, Pitt.	15	209	97	46.4	1422	7	63	10	4.8	6.80
Concannon, Chi.	16	160	87	54.4	783	4	38	8	5.0	4.89
Spurrier, S.F.	17	146	81	55.5	926	5	t75	11	7.5	6.34
Hart, St.L.	18	169	·84	49.7	1086	6	t60	12	7.1	6.43
Douglass, Chi.	19	148	68	45.9	773	5	48	8	5.4	5.22
Landry, Det.	20	160	80	50.0	853	4	43	10	6.3	5.33
Berry, Atl	—	124	71	57.3	1087	10	t88	2	1.6	8.77
Hanratty, Pitt.	—	126	52	41.3	716	8	41	13	10.3	5.68
Johnson, Atl.	—	93	51	54.8	788	8	t65	5	5.4	8.47
Cuozzo, Minn.	—	98	49	50.0	693	4	50	5	5.1	7.07
†Morrall, Balt.	—	99	46	46.5	755	5	t42	7	7.1	7.63
Carter, Chi.	—	71	36	50.7	343	2	t41	5	7.0	4.83
Hargett, N.O.	—	52	31	59.6	403	0	32	0	0.0	7.75
Nix, Pitt.	—	53	25	47.2	290	2	t47	6	11.3	5.47
Lemmerman, Atl.	—	62	25	40.3	330	1	57	4	6.5	5.32
Mira, Phil.	—	76	25	32.9	240	1	35	5	6.6	3.16
Staubach, Dall.	—	47	23	48.9	421	1	t75	2	4.3	8.96
Ninowski, N.O.	—	34	17	50.0	227	1	70	2	5.9	6.68
Wood, N.Y.	—	16	10	62.5	106	1	25	0	0.0	6.63
Lee, Minn.	—	11	7	63.6	79	1	30	0	0.0	7.18
Rhome, Clev.	—	19	7	36.8	35	0	22	2	10.5	1.84
Sweetan, L.A.	—	13	5	38.5	101	1	t67	0	0.0	7.77
Cunningham, S.F.	—	3	3	100.0	48	1	31	0	0.0	16.00
Hill, Dall.	—	3	3	100.0	137	2	t59	0	0.0	45.67
Livingston, N.O.	—	4	3	75.0	38	1	14	1	25.0	9.50
Plum, N.Y.	—	9	3	33.3	37	0	23	0	0.0	4.11
Green, Chi.	—	2	2	100.0	30	0	19	0	0.0	15.00
Hoak, Pitt.	—	3	2	66.7	30	0	16	0	0.0	10.00
Hill, St.L.	—	1	1	100.0	7	0	7	0	0.0	7.00
Koy, N.Y.	—	1	1	100.0	15	0	15	0	0.0	15.00
Lothridge, Atl.	—	1	1	100.0	9	0	9	0	0.0	9.00
Morrison, Clev.	—	1	1	100.0	16	0	16	0	0.0	16.00
Ryan, Wash.	—	1	1	100.0	4	0	4	0	0.0	4.00
Wages, Atl.	—	1	1	100.0	16	0	t16	0	0.0	16.00
L. Walton, Det.	—	1	1	100.0	43	1	t43	0	0.0	43.00
Barrington, N.O.	—	2	1	50.0	15	0	15	0	0.0	7.50
Keyes, Phil.	—	2	1	50.0	14	0	14	0	0.0	7.00
Matte, Balt.	—	3	1	33.3	46	0	46	0	0.0	15.33
Reeves, Dall.	—	3	1	33.3	35	0	35	1	33.3	11.67
Stevens, G.B.	—	3	1	33.3	12	0	12	0	0.0	4.00
Kelly, Clev.	—	5	1	20.0	36	1	t36	0	0.0	7.20
Barton, Det.	—	1	0	00.0	0	0	0	0	0.0	0.00
Bradley, Phil.	—	1	0	00.0	0	0	0	0	0.0	0.00
Bull, Chi.	—	1	0	00.0	0	0	0	0	0.0	0.00
Farr, Det.	—	1	0	00.0	0	0	0	0	0.0˙	0.00

	Std.	Att.	Com.	Pct. Com.	Yds. Gain.	Td.	Lng.	Int.	Pct. Int.	Avg. Gain
Gipson, Atl.	—	1	0	00.0	0	0	0	1	100.0	0.00
R. Johnson, Clev.	—	1	0	00.0	0	0	0	0	0.0	0.00
Knight, Wash.	—	1	0	00.0	0	0	0	1	100.0	0.00
Looney, N.O.	—	1	0	00.0	0	0	0	0	0.0	0.00
Meador, L.A.	—	1	0	00.0	0	0	0	0	0.0	0.00
L. Smith, L.A.	—	1	0	00.0	0	0	0	0	0.0	0.00
Ellison, L.A.	—	2	0	00.0	0	0	0	0	0.0	0.00
Sayers, Chi.	—	2	0	00.0	0	0	0	0	0.0	0.00

*—High for 1969
†—1968 Leader
t —Touchdown
NOTE: Standing based on percent of completions, touchdown passes, percent of interceptions and average yards gained. To qualify for championship rating a player must throw at least 140 passes.

PUNT RETURNS

TEAM CHAMPION—The Detroit Lions, with 21 returns for 230 yards and an 11.0 average. The Dallas Cowboys led in 1968 with a 13.5 average on 30 returns for 405 yards.

INDIVIDUAL CHAMPION—Alvin Haymond of the Los Angeles Rams, with a 13.2 average on 33 returns for 435 yards. Haymond finished second with a 13.4 average in 1968 when Bob Hayes of Dallas won the title with a 20.8 average for 15 returns for 312 yards. Hayes was third in 1969.

MOST YARDS GAINED—Haymond's 435 yards led the league and topped every other team total in the league. The league record is 555 yards by Bill Grimes of Green Bay in 1950.

LONGEST RETURN—Rickie Harris of the Washington Redskins, 86 yards for the winning touchdown in 20–14 victory over New York on October 19.

1969 PUNT RETURNS—TEAM

	No.	F.C.	Yds. Ret.	Avg. Ret.	Long.	Tds.
Detroit	21	23	230	*11.0	t74	*1
Los Angeles	*58	14	*556	9.6	52	0
Green Bay	32	17	287	9.0	t83	*1
Washington	26	11	190	7.3	*t86	*1
†Dallas	38	15	273	7.2	50	0
New Orleans	30	12	217	7.2	30	0
Philadelphia	36	10	219	6.1	37	0
Minnesota	45	*26	266	5.9	55	0
Cleveland	32	15	183	5.7	21	0
Chicago	30	9	164	5.5	27	0
St. Louis	38	11	201	5.3	35	0
Baltimore	37	15	192	5.2	14	0
Pittsburgh	37	13	165	4.5	23	0
New York	15	22	50	3.3	11	0
Atlanta	26	12	82	3.2	15	0
San Francisco	22	22	63	2.9	18	0
League Total	523	247	3338	—	t86	3
League Average	32.7	15.4	208.6	6.4	—	0.2

*—High for 1969
†—1968 Leader
t —Touchdown
NOTE: Standing based on average return.

1969 PUNT RETURNS—INDIVIDUAL

	Stdg.	No.	F.C.	Yards	Avg.	Long.	Tds.
HAYMOND, L.A.	1	33	8	*435	*13.2	52	0
Harris, Wash.	2	14	2	158	11.3	*t86	*1
†Hayes, Dall.	3	18	5	179	9.9	50	0
Dodd, N.O.	4	15	9	106	7.1	21	0
Bradley, Phil.	5	28	5	181	6.5	37	0
West, Minn.	6	*39	*19	245	6.3	55	0
Renfro, Dall.	7	15	7	80	5.3	34	0
R. Smith, L.A.	8	23	6	122	5.3	21	0
B. Campbell, Pitt.	9	28	7	133	4.8	23	0
Pitts, G.B.	10	16	8	60	3.8	10	0
Wehrli, St. L.	—	13	4	65	5.0	25	0
Havrilak, Balt.	—	13	7	56	4.3	13	0
Mallory, Atl.	—	13	6	42	3.2	15	0
Lyle, Chi.	—	12	1	78	6.5	27	0
Roberts, Wash.	—	12	9	32	2.7	25	0
Morrison, Clev.	—	11	3	49	4.5	15	0
Volk, Balt.	—	10	6	58	5.8	14	0
Roland, St. L.	—	10	4	53	5.3	8	0
Smith, S.F.	—	10	4	46	4.6	18	0
Lockhart, N.Y.	—	10	14	29	2.9	11	0
Barney, Det.	—	9	5	191	21.2	t74	*1
Sumner, Clev.	—	9	11	88	9.8	21	0
Howard, N.O.	—	9	0	73	8.1	30	0
Shivers, St. L.	—	9	2	44	4.9	9	0
Piccolo, Chi.	—	9	5	43	4.8	15	0
L. Walton, Det.	—	9	10	24	2.7	20	0
T. Williams, G.B.	—	8	3	189	23.6	t83	*1
Logan, Balt.	—	8	2	41	5.1	11	0
Wood, G.B.	—	8	6	38	4.8	13	0
Turner, Chi.	—	8	2	32	4.0	12	0
Kelly, Clev.	—	7	0	28	4.0	13	0
T. Brown, St. L.	—	6	1	39	6.5	35	0
Pearson, Balt.	—	6	0	37	6.2	11	0
Leigh, Clev.	—	5	1	18	3.6	14	0
Fuller, S.F.	—	5	4	12	2.4	7	0
Freeman, Atl.	—	4	0	30	7.5	12	0
Thompson, N.O.	—	4	1	25	6.3	12	0
Jefferson, Pitt.	—	4	2	23	5.8	9	0
Wright, Atl.	—	4	0	21	5.3	11	0
Rentzel, Dall.	—	4	3	14	3.5	11	0
Grim, Minn.	—	4	2	12	3.0	8	0
Scarpati, Phil.	—	4	1	6	1.5	2	0
McCauley, Atl.	—	4	6	−11	−2.8	0	0
Alexander, S.F.	—	4	3	−18	−4.5	0	0
Cunningham, S.F.	—	3	11	23	7.7	14	0
Minniear, N.Y.	—	3	2	15	5.0	9	0
Martha, Pitt.	—	3	2	0	0.0	0	0
Lawrence, Phil.	—	2	2	26	13.0	18	0
Vaughn, Det.	—	2	2	10	5.0	6	0
Bryant, Minn.	—	2	5	9	4.5	9	0
Brenner, N.Y.	—	2	4	6	3.0	3	0
Gordon, Chi.	—	1	0	11	11.0	11	0
Hoak, Pitt.	—	1	1	9	9.0	9	0
Barrington, N.O.	—	1	0	8	8.0	8	0
Hawkins, Phil.	—	1	2	6	6.0	6	0
Eddy, Det.	—	1	6	5	5.0	5	0
Ward, N.O.	—	1	1	5	5.0	5	0
Cahill, Atl.	—	1	0	0	0.0	0	0
Davis, Pitt.	—	1	0	0	0.0	0	0

	Stdg.	No.	F.C.	Yards	Avg.	Long.	Tds.
Hughes, Phil.	—	1	0	0	0.0	0	0
Johnson, Dall. ,	—	1	0	0	0.0	0	0
Pergine, L.A.	—	1	0	0	0.0	0	0
Meador, L.A.	—	1	0	—1	—1.0	—1	0
Beatty, Pitt.	—	0	1	0	0.0	0	0
Lorick, N.O.	—	0	1	0	0.0	0	0
Sayers, Chi.	—	0	1	0	0.0	0	0
Longo, N.Y.	—	0	2	0	0.0	0	0

*—High for 1969
†—1968 Leader
t —Touchdown
NOTE: Standing based on average return. To qualify for championship
rating a player must return at least 14 punts.

SCORING

TEAM CHAMPION—The Minnesota Vikings, for the first time in their nine-year history, with 379 points. The record is 466 by Los Angeles in 1950. Cleveland had the most touchdowns, 45.

INDIVIDUAL CHAMPION—Fred Cox of the Minnesota Vikings, with 121 points, the most ever solely by kicking in a single NFL season. Cox made 43 extra points without a miss and was successful on 26 of 37 field goals. The record is 176 by Paul Hornung of Green Bay in 1960.

MOST TOUCHDOWNS—Tom Matte of the Baltimore Colts and Lance Rentzel of the Dallas Cowboys each scored 13. Matte scored 11 TDs rushing and two on pass receptions; Rentzel scored 12 on pass receptions and one on a fumble recovery. Leroy Kelly of the Cleveland Browns led in 1968, with 20. The record is 22, by Gale Sayers of the Chicago Bears as a rookie in 1965.

MOST POINTS AFTER TOUCHDOWN—Don Cockroft of the Cleveland Browns, with 45 in 45 attempts. Mike Clark of the Dallas Cowboys led last year with 54. The record is 56 by Danny Villanueva of the Dallas Cowboys in 1966.

MOST FIELD GOALS—Fred Cox of the Minnesota Vikings, 26 in 37 attempts. Mac Percival of the Chicago Bears led in 1968, with 25. The record is 28 (in 49 attempts) by Bruce Gossett of the Los Angeles Rams in 1966.

BEST ONE-GAME PERFORMANCE—Ben Hawkins of the Philadelphia Eagles, 24 points on four touchdown pass receptions in 41–24 victory over Pittsburgh on September 28; and Davey Williams of the St. Louis Cardinals, 24 points on four touchdown pass receptions in 51–42 loss to New Orleans on November 2.

TEAM LEADERS—Atlanta, Bob Etter, 78; Baltimore, Tom Matte, 78; Chicago, Mac Percival, 50; Cleveland, Don Cockroft, 81; Dallas, Mike Clark, 103; Detroit, Errol Mann, 101; Green Bay, Travis Williams, 54; Los Angeles, Bruce Gossett, 102; Minnesota, Fred Cox, 121; New Orleans, Tom Dempsey, 99; New York, Pete Gogolak and Joe Morrison, 66 each; Philadelphia, Sam Baker, 79; Pittsburgh, Gene Mingo, 62; St. Louis, Jim Bakken, 74; San Francisco, Ken Willard, 60; Washington, Curt Knight, 83.

1969 SCORING—TEAM

	Tot. Tds.	Tds. R.	Tds. P.	Tds. Rb.	XP	XPM	FG	FGA	Saf.	Tot. Pts.
Minnesota	43	15	24	4	43	0	*26	37	0	*379
†Dallas	44	*17	24	3	43	1	20	36	1	369
Cleveland	*45	*17	24	4	*45	0	12	23	0	351
Los Angeles	36	8	*25	3	36	0	22	34	1	320
St. Louis	40	*17	19	4	38	*2	12	24	0	314
New Orleans	35	12	22	1	33	*2	22	*41	1	311
Washington	37	11	22	4	35	*2	16	27	1	307
Baltimore	34	16	17	1	33	1	14	31	0	279
Philadelphia	33	10	20	3	31	*2	16	30	1	279
San Francisco	37	13	22	2	35	*2	6	21	1	277
Atlanta	33	9	20	4	33	0	15	30	0	276
Green Bay	36	11	20	*5	35	1	6	22	0	269
New York	33	8	24	1	33	0	11	21	0	264
Detroit	26	11	12	3	26	0	25	37	1	259
Pittsburgh	26	8	17	1	26	0	12	26	0	218
Chicago	26	14	11	1	26	0	8	21	*2	210
League Total	564	197	323	44	551	13	243	461	9	4682
League Average	35.3	12.3	20.2	2.8	34.4	0.8	15.2	28.8	0.6	292.6

*—High for 1969
†—1968 Leader

1969 SCORING—INDIVIDUAL

	Tot. Tds.	Tds. R.	Tds. P.	Tds. Rb.	XP	XPM	FG	FGA	Tot. Pts.
COX, MINN.	0	0	0	0	43	0	*26	37	*121
M. Clark, Dall.	0	0	0	0	43	1	20	36	103
Gossett, L.A.	0	0	0	0	36	0	22	34	102
Mann, Det.	0	0	0	0	26	0	25	37	101
Dempsey, N.O.	0	0	0	0	33	*2	22	*41	99
Knight, Wash.	0	0	0	0	35	1	16	27	83
Cockroft, Clev.	0	0	0	0	*45	0	12	23	81
Baker, Phil.	0	0	0	0	31	0	16	30	79
Etter, Atl.	0	0	0	0	33	0	15	30	78
Matte, Balt.	*13	*11	2	0	0	0	0	0	78
Rentzel, Dall.	*13	0	*12	1	0	0	0	0	78
Michaels, Balt.	0	0	0	0	33	1	14	31	75
Bakken, St. L.	0	0	0	0	38	*2	12	24	74
Collins, Clev.	11	0	11	0	0	0	0	0	66
Gogolak, N.Y.	0	0	0	0	33	0	11	21	66
Morrison, N.Y.	11	4	7	0	0	0	0	0	66
Mingo, Pitt.	0	0	0	0	26	0	12	26	62
Gilliam, St. L.	10	0	9	1	0	0	0	0	60
†Kelly, Clev.	10	9	1	0	0	0	0	0	60
Warfield, Clev.	10	0	10	0	0	0	0	0	60
Willard, S.F.	10	7	3	0	0	0	0	0	60
Harraway, Wash.	9	6	3	0	0	0	0	0	54
Jackson, Phil.	9	0	9	0	0	0	0	0	54
Jefferson, Pitt.	9	0	9	0	0	0	0	0	54
Smith, Wash.	9	0	9	0	0	0	0	0	54
Washington, Minn.	9	0	9	0	0	0	0	0	54
T. Williams, G.B.	9	4	3	*2	0	0	0	0	54
Percival, Chi.	0	0	0	0	26	0	8	21	50
Hawkins, Phil.	8	0	8	0	0	0	0	0	48
Hill, Dall.	8	8	0	0	0	0	0	0	48

	Tot. Tds.	Tds. R.	Tds. P.	Tds. Rb.	XP	XPM	FG	FGA	Tot. Pts.
Livingston, N.O.	8	5	3	0	0	0	0	0	48
Osborn, Minn.	8	7	1	0	0	0	0	0	48
Sayers, Chi.	8	8	0	0	0	0	0	0	48
Taylor, Wash.	8	0	8	0	0	0	0	0	48
Abramowicz, N.O.	7	0	7	0	0	0	0	0	42
Gros, Pitt.	7	4	3	0	0	0	0	0	42
Hampton, G.B.	7	4	2	1	0	0	0	0	42
R. Johnson, Clev.	7	7	0	0	0	0	0	0	42
Tucker, L.A.	7	0	7	0	0	0	0	0	42
D. Williams, St. L.	7	0	7	0	0	0	0	0	42
Mercer, G.B.	0	0	0	0	23	0	5	17	38
Dale, G.B.	6	0	6	0	0	0	0	0	36
Flatley, Atl.	6	0	6	0	0	0	0	0	36
Koy, N.Y.	6	2	4	0	0	0	0	0	36
Roland, St. L.	6	5	1	0	0	0	0	0	36
Snow, L.A.	6	0	6	0	0	0	0	0	36
Thomas, S.F.	6	1	5	0	0	0	0	0	36
Gavric, S.F.	0	0	0	0	22	*2	3	11	31
Beasley, Minn.	5	0	4	1	0	0	0	0	30
Butler, Atl.	5	3	2	0	0	0	0	0	30
Cogdill, Atl.	5	0	5	0	0	0	0	0	30
Coffey, Atl.-N.Y.	5	2	3	0	0	0	0	0	30
Gabriel, L.A.	5	5	0	0	0	0	0	0	30
Henderson, Minn.	5	0	5	0	0	0	0	0	30
Herrmann, N.Y	5	0	5	0	0	0	0	0	30
McCullouch, Det	5	0	5	0	0	0	0	0	30
Reeves, Dall.	5	4	1	0	0	0	0	0	30
Truax, L.A.	5	0	5	0	0	0	0	0	30
Wallace, Chi.	5	0	5	0	0	0	0	0	30
Wheelwright, N.O.	5	4	1	0	0	0	0	0	30
L. Brown, Wash.	4	4	0	0	0	0	0	0	24
Dowler, G.B.	4	0	4	0	0	0	0	0	24
Farr, Det.	4	4	0	0	0	0	0	0	24
Gordon, Chi.	4	0	4	0	0	0	0	0	24
Hayes, Dall.	4	0	4	0	0	0	0	0	24
Mitchell, Atl.	4	0	4	0	0	0	0	0	24
Poage, N.O.	4	0	4	0	0	0	0	0	24
Triplett, Det.	4	3	1	0	0	0	0	0	24
Tucker, S.F.	4	2	2	0	0	0	0	0	24
Woodeshick, Phil.	4	4	0	0	0	0	0	0	24
Davis, S.F.	0	0	0	0	13	0	3	10	22
Brown, Minn.	3	3	0	0	0	0	0	0	18
Cole, Balt.	3	2	1	0	0	0	0	0	18
Crenshaw, St. L.	3	3	0	0	0	0	0	0	18
Cunningham, S.F.	3	3	0	0	0	0	0	0	18
Ditka, Dall.	3	0	3	0	0	0	0	0	18
Eddy, Det.	3	2	1	0	0	0	0	0	18
Edwards, St. L.	3	3	0	0	0	0	0	0	18
Henderson, Pitt.	3	0	3	0	0	0	0	0	18
Hoak, Pitt.	3	2	1	0	0	0	0	0	18
Jones, Minn.	3	3	0	0	0	0	0	0	18
Keyes, Phil.	3	3	0	0	0	0	0	0	18
McNeil, S.F.	3	0	3	0	0	0	0	0	18
Mitchell, Balt.	3	0	3	0	0	0	0	0	18
Norman, Dall.	3	0	3	0	0	0	0	0	18
Parks, N.O.	3	0	3	0	0	0	0	0	18
Perkins, Balt.	3	0	3	0	0	0	0	0	18
Piccolo, Chi.	3	2	1	0	0	0	0	0	18

	Tot. Tds.	Tds. R.	Tds. P.	Tds. Rb.	XP	XPM	FG	FGA	Tot. Pts.
Reed, Minn.	3	1	2	0	0	0	0	0	18
Richardson, Balt.	3	0	3	0	0	0	0	0	18
Sanders, Det.	3	0	3	0	0	0	0	0	18
Shivers, St. L.	3	2	1	0	0	0	0	0	18
L. Smith, L.A.	3	1	2	0	0	0	0	0	18
Thomas, N.Y.	3	0	3	0	0	0	0	0	18
Wages, Atl.	3	2	1	0	0	0	0	0	18
Washington, S.F.	3	0	3	0	0	0	0	0	18
Witcher, S.F.	3	0	3	0	0	0	0	0	18
Wright, Det.	3	0	2	1	0	0	0	0	18
Lusteg, G.B.	0	0	0	0	12	0	1	5	15
Anderson, G.B.	2	1	1	0	0	0	0	0	12
Baker, N.O.	2	1	1	0	0	0	0	0	12
Ballman, Phil.	2	0	2	0	0	0	0	0	12
Douglass, Chi.	2	2	0	0	0	0	0	0	12
Ellison, L.A.	2	1	1	0	0	0	0	0	12
Fleming, G.B.	2	0	2	0	0	0	0	0	12
Garrison, Dall.	2	2	0	0	0	0	0	0	12
Glass, Clev.	2	0	2	0	0	0	0	0	12
Grabowksi, G.B.	2	1	1	0	0	0	0	0	12
Hart, St. L.	2	2	0	0	0	0	0	0	12
Hill, Balt.	2	2	0	0	0	0	0	0	12
Josephson, L.A.	2	0	2	0	0	0	0	0	12
Lindsey, Minn.	2	1	1	0	0	0	0	0	12
Mackey, Balt.	2	0	2	0	0	0	0	0	12
Mason, L.A.	2	1	1	0	0	0	0	0	12
Meador, L.A.	2	0	0	*2	0	0	0	0	12
Orr, Balt.	2	0	2	0	0	0	0	0	12
Shy, N.O.	2	1	1	0	0	0	0	0	12
Shy, Dall.	2	1	1	0	0	0	0	0	12
Snead, Phil.	2	2	0	0	0	0	0	0	12
Windsor, S.F.	2	0	2	0	0	0	0	0	12
Acks, Atl.	1	0	0	1	0	0	0	0	6
Adderley, G.B.	1	0	0	1	0	0	0	0	6
Bankston, Pitt.	1	1	0	0	0	0	0	0	6
Barnes, Clev.	1	0	0	1	0	0	0	0	6
Barney, Det.	1	0	0	1	0	0	0	0	6
Barrington, N.O.	1	1	0	0	0	0	0	0	6
Bradley, Phil.	1	0	0	1	0	0	0	0	6
Cole, Dall.	1	0	0	1	0	0	0	0	6
Concannon, Chi.	1	1	0	0	0	0	0	0	6
Denney, Chi.	1	0	1	0	0	0	0	0	6
Dodd, N.O.	1	0	1	0	0	0	0	0	6
Duncan, Balt.	1	0	0	1	0	0	0	0	6
Dyer, Wash.	1	0	1	0	0	0	0	0	6
Eaton, N.Y.	1	0	0	1	0	0	0	0	6
Frederickson, N.Y.	1	0	1	0	0	0	0	0	6
Gipson, Atl.	1	1	0	0	0	0	0	0	6
Grim, Minn.	1	0	1	0	0	0	0	0	6
Hanburger, Wash.	1	0	0	1	0	0	0	0	6
Harris, Wash.	1	0	0	1	0	0	0	0	6
Hart, G.B.	1	0	0	1	0	0	0	0	6
Havrilak, Balt.	1	1	0	0	0	0	0	0	6
Hester, N.O.	1	0	1	0	0	0	0	0	6
Hill, Phil.	1	0	1	0	0	0	0	0	6
Hinton, Balt.	1	0	1	0	0	0	0	0	6
Hoffman, Wash.	1	0	0	1	0	0	0	0	6
Horn, G.B.	1	1	0	0	0	0	0	0	6

	Tot. Tds.	Tds. R.	Tds. P.	Tds. Rb.	XP	XPM	FG	FGA	Tot. Pts.
Huff, Wash.	1	0	0	1	0	0	0	0	6
Hull, Chi.	1	1	0	0	0	0	0	0	6
Humphrey, Atl.	1	0	0	1	0	0	0	0	6
Johnson, St. L.	1	1	0	0	0	0	0	0	6
Johnson, Atl.	1	1	0	0	0	0	0	0	6
W. Johnson, Clev.	1	0	0	1	0	0	0	0	6
Jones, N.Y.	1	0	1	0	0	0	0	0	6
Jurgensen, Wash.	1	1	0	0	0	0	0	0	6
Kellermann, Clev.	1	0	0	1	0	0	0	0	6
Klein, L.A.	1	0	1	0	0	0	0	0	6
Kotite, N.Y.	1	0	1	0	0	0	0	0	6
Kramer, Minn.	1	0	1	0	0	0	0	0	6
Krause, Minn.	1	0	0	1	0	0	0	0	6
Kwalick, S.F.	1	0	1	0	0	0	0	0	6
Lakes, S.F.	1	0	0	1	0	0	0	0	6
Landry, Det.	1	1	0	0	0	0	0	0	6
Lane, St. L.	1	1	0	0	0	0	0	0	6
Lemmerman, Atl.	1	1	0	0	0	0	0	0	6
Lilly, Dall.	1	0	0	1	0	0	0	0	6
Long, Wash.	1	0	1	0	0	0	0	0	6
McCall, Pitt.	1	0	0	1	0	0	0	0	6
Minniear, N.Y.	1	1	0	0	0	0	0	0	6
Morrison, Clev.	1	1	0	0	0	0	0	0	6
Morton, Dall.	1	1	0	0	0	0	0	0	6
Page, Minn.	1	0	0	1	0	0	0	0	6
Pinder, Phil.	1	1	0	0	0	0	0	0	6
Pitts, G.B.	1	0	1	0	0	0	0	0	6
Preece, N.O.	1	0	0	1	0	0	0	0	6
Ramsey, Phil.	1	0	0	1	0	0	0	0	6
Reilly, Minn.	1	0	0	1	0	0	0	0	6
Rowe, St. L.	1	0	0	1	0	0	0	0	6
Scarpati, Phil.	1	0	0	1	0	0	0	0	6
Shiner, Pitt.	1	1	0	0	0	0	0	0	6
Smith, St. L.	1	0	1	0	0	0	0	0	6
R. Smith, L.A.	1	0	0	1	0	0	0	0	6
Snider, Atl.	1	0	0	1	0	0	0	0	6
Stallings, St. L.	1	0	0	1	0	0	0	0	6
Staubach, Dall.	1	1	0	0	0	0	0	0	6
Sumner, Clev.	1	0	0	1	0	0	0	0	6
Watkins, Det.	1	1	0	0	0	0	0	0	6
Weatherford, Atl.	1	0	0	1	0	0	0	0	6
White, N.Y.	1	0	1	0	0	0	0	0	6
Williams, Det.	1	0	0	1	0	0	0	0	6
E. Williams, Pitt.	1	0	1	0	0	0	0	0	6
L. Wilson, St. L.	1	0	0	1	0	0	0	0	6
Woitt, S.F.	1	0	0	1	0	0	0	0	6
Youngblood, Chi.	1	0	0	1	0	0	0	0	6

*—High for 1969
†—1968 Leader
SAFETIES SCORED BY: Butkus & O'Bradovich, Chi.; Andrie, Dall.; Tom, Phil. (Detroit, Los Angeles, New Orleans, San Francisco and Washington scored one team safety each.)

INTERCEPTIONS

TEAM CHAMPION—The Minnesota Vikings, who had only 16 in 1968, with 30. The Cleveland Browns led in 1968, with 32. Minnesota had the most yards returned, 459. Los Angeles, Cleveland and Philadelphia each returned three interceptions for touchdowns.

INDIVIDUAL CHAMPION—Mel Renfro of the Dallas Cowboys, with 10 for 118 yards. Ten has been the leading total in each of the last four seasons. The record is 14 by Dick (Night Train) Lane of the Los Angeles Rams in 1952.

MOST TOUCHDOWNS ON INTERCEPTIONS—Eddie Meador of the Los Angeles Rams, two. The record is three shared by Dick Lynch, New York, 1963; Herb Adderley, Green Bay, 1965; Lem Barney, Detroit, 1967.

LONGEST RETURN—Doug Hart of the Green Bay Packers, 85 yards for a touchdown in 9–7 loss to Minnesota on November 16. The record is 102 by Bob Smith, Detroit, 1949, and Erich Barnes, New York, 1961.

MOST YARDS RETURNED—Herb Adderley of the Green Bay Packers, 169 yards on five interceptions. The record is 301 by Don Doll, Detroit, 1949.

TEAM LEADERS—Atlanta, Rudy Redmond, 5; Baltimore, Rick Volk, 4; Chicago, Dick Daniels, Joe Taylor and George Youngblood, 3 each; Cleveland, Mike Howell, 6; Dallas, Mel Renfro, 10; Detroit, Lem Barney, 8; Green Bay, Herb Adderley, 5; Los Angeles, Eddie Meador and Richie Petitbon, 5 each; Minnesota, Bobby Bryant, 8; New Orleans, Elijah Nevett and Dave Whitsell, 3 each; New York, Bruce Maher, 5; Philadelphia, Joe Scarpati, 4; Pittsburgh, Bob Hohn and Paul Martha, 5 each; St. Louis, Bob Atkins and Roger Wehrli, 3 each; San Francisco, Kermit Alexander and Jim Johnson, 5 each; Washington, Rickie Harris, 4.

1969 INTERCEPTIONS—TEAM

	No.	Yds. Ret.	Avg. Ret.	Long.	Tds.
Minnesota	*30	*459	15.3	t77	2
Los Angeles	26	424	16.3	40	*3
Pittsburgh	25	257	10.3	26	0
Dallas	24	339	14.1	t41	1
Detroit	21	207	9.9	32	0
San Francisco	20	194	9.7	t57	1
Green Bay	19	428	*22.5	*t85	2
New York	19	221	11.6	48	1
†Cleveland	19	217	11.4	t55	*3
Atlanta	19	200	10.5	40	0
Washington	16	246	15.4	47	1
Chicago	16	132	8.3	32	1
St. Louis	15	245	16.3	44	1
Philadelphia	15	179	11.9	t56	*3
Baltimore	15	106	7.1	23	1
New Orleans	12	73	6.1	24	0
League Total	311	3927	—	t85	19
League Average	19.4	245.4	12.6	—	1.2

---

*—High for 1969
†—1968 Leader
t —Touchdown
NOTE: Standing based on most interceptions.

1969 INTERCEPTIONS—INDIVIDUAL

	No.	Yards	Avg.	Long.	Tds.
RENFRO, DALL.	*10	118	11.8	41	0
Barney, Det.	8	126	15.8	32	0
Bryant, Minn.	8	97	12.1	56	0
Mackbee, Minn.	6	100	16.7	38	0
Howell, Clev.	6	21	3.5	11	0
LeBeau, Det.	6	15	2.5	8	0
Adderley, G.B.	5	*169	33.8	t80	1
Maher, N.Y.	5	112	22.4	48	0
Meador, L.A.	5	97	19.4	t38	*2
Krause, Minn.	5	82	16.4	t77	1
Hohn, Pitt.	5	64	12.8	24	0
Redmond, Atl.	5	50	10.0	32	0
Petitbon, L.A.	5	46	9.2	25	0
Alexander, S.F.	5	39	7.8	22	0
Martha, Pitt.	5	37	7.4	15	0
J. Johnson, S.F.	5	18	3.6	18	0
Williams, L.A.	4	97	24.3	40	0
Sumner, Clev.	4	82	20.5	t40	1
Harris, Wash.	4	81	20.3	47	0
Scarpati, Phil.	4	54	13.5	t34	1
Warwick, Minn.	4	46	11.5	19	0
Volk, Balt.	4	36	9.0	23	0
Woodlief, L.A.	4	29	7.3	10	0
†Williams, N.Y.	4	19	4.8	19	0
Hart, G.B.	3	156	52.0	*t85	1
Atkins, St. L.	3	74	24.7	42	0
Gaechter, Dall.	3	72	24.0	37	0
R. Smith, L.A.	3	70	23.3	t24	1
Huff, Wash.	3	65	21.7	32	1
Shorter, Pitt.	3	47	15.7	23	0
Weger, Det.	3	44	14.7	25	0
Wehrli, St. L.	3	44	14.7	44	0
Kellermann, Clev.	3	40	13.3	t40	1
Wood, G.B.	3	40	13.3	21	0
Daniels, Chi.	3	37	12.3	32	0
Maxwell, Balt.	3	37	12.3	22	0
J. Taylor, Chi.	3	37	12.3	23	0
Stenger, Pitt.	3	36	12.0	19	0
Bass, Wash.	3	31	10.3	31	0
Jeter, G.B.	3	30	10.0	30	0
Owens, Wash.	3	24	8.0	15	0
Youngblood, Chi.	3	22	7.3	t22	1
Nevett, N.O.	3	20	6.7	20	0
Winston, Minn.	3	17	5.7	17	0
Reaves, Atl.	3	14	4.7	14	0
Whitsell, N.O.	3	14	4.7	11	0
Nelson, Phil.	3	10	3.3	10	0
Grant, Balt.	3	0	0.0	0	0
Hansen, Atl.	2	51	25.5	40	0
Russell, Pitt.	2	48	24.0	26	0
Wright, St. L.	2	41	20.5	21	0
Jordan, Dall.	2	38	19.0	38	0
Howley, Dall.	2	37	18.5	28	0
Nettles, L.A.	2	37	18.5	25	0
Kassulke, Minn.	2	36	18.0	20	0
Nitschke, G.B.	2	32	16.0	20	0
Heck, N.Y.	2	31	15.5	20	0
Longo, N.Y.	2	31	15.5	26	0
Fischer, Wash.	2	28	14.0	27	0

	No.	Yards	Avg.	Long.	Tds.
Ramsey, Phil.	2	26	13.0	t26	1
Eaton, N.Y.	2	23	11.5	t23	1
Lloyd, Phil.	2	22	11.0	14	0
Zook, Atl.	2	22	11.0	15	0
Rowe, St. L.	2	19	9.5	t18	1
Wilcox, S.F.	2	17	8.5	17	0
Taylor, S.F.	2	15	7.5	15	0
L. Wilson, St. L.	2	15	7.5	15	0
Butkus, Chi.	2	13	6.5	11	0
Buffone, Chi.	2	12	6.0	12	0
Austin, Balt.	2	10	5.0	10	0
Randolph, S.F.	2	10	5.0	5	0
Garlington, Clev.	2	4	2.0	4	0
May, Pitt.	2	4	2.0	4	0
P. Clark, Dall.	2	2	1.0	2	0
Caffey, G.B.	2	1	0.5	1	0
Calland, Pitt.	2	0	0.0	0	0
Green, Dall.	2	0	0.0	0	0
Howard, N.O.	2	0	0.0	0	0
Lavan, Atl.	2	0	0.0	0	0
Lockhart, N.Y.	2	0	0.0	0	0
Vaughn, Det.	2	0	0.0	0	0
Woitt, S.F.	1	57	57.0	t57	1
Bradley, Phil.	1	56	56.0	t56	1
Barnes, Clev.	1	55	55.0	t55	1
Cole, Dall.	1	41	41.0	t41	1
Sharockman, Minn.	1	36	36.0	36	0
Brown, Dall.	1	31	31.0	31	0
Fuller, S.F.	1	31	31.0	31	0
Marshall, Minn.	1	30	30.0	30	0
Stovall, St. L.	1	28	28.0	28	0
Burris, N.O.	1	24	24.0	24	0
Karras, Det.	1	22	22.0	22	0
Mallory, Atl.	1	22	22.0	22	0
T. Brown, St. L.	1	21	21.0	21	0
Pardee, L.A.	1	19	19.0	19	0
Weatherford, Atl.	1	18	18.0	18	0
Pottios, L.A.	1	16	16.0	16	0
Hillebrand, Pitt.	1	14	14.0	14	0
Daniel, L.A.	1	13	13.0	13	0
Gregory, Clev.	1	12	12.0	12	0
Colman, Phil.	1	11	11.0	11	0
Gaubatz, Balt.	1	11	11.0	11	0
Lyle, Chi.	1	10	10.0	10	0
Absher, N.O.	1	7	7.0	7	0
Hinton, Pitt.	1	7	7.0	7	0
Nunley, S.F.	1	7	7.0	7	0
Allen, Atl.	1	6	6.0	6	0
Logan, Balt.	1	6	6.0	6	0
Preece, N.O.	1	6	6.0	6	0
Stukes, Balt.	1	6	6.0	6	0
Holifield, N.Y.	1	5	5.0	5	0
Lindsey, Clev.	1	3	3.0	3	0
McKeever, Wash.	1	3	3.0	3	0
Rosema, St. L.	1	3	3.0	3	0
Brezina, Atl.	1	2	2.0	2	0
Thompson, N.O.	1	2	2.0	2	0
Pride, Chi.	1	1	1.0	1	0
Cross, Phil.	1	0	0.0	0	0

	No.	Yards	Avg.	Long.	Tds.
Crutcher, N.Y.	1	0	0.0	0	0
Davis, G.B.	1	0	0.0	0	0
Edwards, Dall.	1	0	0.0	0	0
Krueger, S.F.	1	0	0.0	0	0
McRae, Chi.	1	0	0.0	0	0
Nobis, Atl.	1	0	0.0	0	0
Upshaw, Clev.	1	0	0.0	0	0
Walker, Det.	1	0	0.0	0	0
Woodson, Pitt.	1	0	0.0	0	0
Young, Phil.	1	0	0.0	0	0
Acks, Atl.	0	15L	—	15	0
Page, Minn.	0	15L	—	t15	1
Wade, Wash.	0	14L	—	14	0

---

* —High for 1969
† —1968 Leader
t —Touchdown
L —Lateral

PASS RECEIVING

INDIVIDUAL CHAMPION—Dan Abramowicz of the New Orleans Saints, with 73 receptions, two more than the total that won in 1968 for Clifton McNeil of the San Francisco 49ers. Abramowicz is New Orleans' first departmental champion. The record is 93 by Johnny Morris of the Chicago Bears in 1964.

MOST YARDS GAINED—Harold Jackson of the Philadelphia Eagles, with 1,116 yards on 65 receptions, in his first full NFL season. Two other players exceeded 1,000 yards in 1969: Roy Jefferson of the Pittsburgh Steelers, 1,079, and Dan Abramowicz of the New Orleans Saints, 1,015. The record is 1,495 by Elroy Hirsch of the Los Angeles Rams in 1951.

MOST TOUCHDOWNS—Lance Rentzel of the Dallas Cowboys, with 12. The record is 17 by Don Hutson, Green Bay, 1942, and Elroy Hirsch, Los Angeles, 1951.

HIGHEST AVERAGE GAIN—On the basis of 35 or more receptions, Lance Rentzel of the Dallas Cowboys, 22.3 yards per catch. Homer Jones of the New York Giants led the previous three seasons.

BEST ONE-GAME PERFORMANCE—Seven players had 10 receptions in one game: John Gilliam and Davey Williams, St. Louis; Bob Long and Charley Taylor, Washington; Dick Gordon and Bob Wallace, Chicago; and Mel Farr, Detroit.

LONGEST RECEPTION—Wendell Tucker of the Los Angeles Rams, 93 yards on a touchdown pass from Roman Gabriel on the first play from scrimmage in 41–30 victory over San Francisco on November 9.

TEAM LEADERS—Atlanta, Paul Flatley, 45; Baltimore, Willie Richardson, 43; Chicago, Bob Wallace, 47; Cleveland, Gary Collins, 54; Dallas, Lance Rentzel, 43; Detroit, Charlie Sanders, 42; Green Bay, Carroll Dale, 45; Los Angeles, Jack Snow, 49; Minnesota, Gene Washington, 39; New Orleans, Dan Abramowicz, 73; New York, Joe Morrison, 44; Philadelphia, Harold Jackson, 65; Pittsburgh, Roy Jefferson, 67; St. Louis, Davey Williams, 56; San Francisco, Gene Washington and Doug Cunningham, 51 each; Washington, Charley Taylor, 71.

1969 PASS RECEIVING—INDIVIDUAL

	No.	Yards	Avg.	Long.	Tds.
ABRAMOWICZ, N.O.	*73	1015	13.9	t49	7
Taylor, Wash.	71	883	12.4	t88	8
Jefferson, Pitt.	67	1079	16.1	63	9
Jackson, Phil.	65	*1116	17.2	t65	9
D. Williams, St. L.	56	702	12.5	61	7
Harraway, Wash.	55	489	8.9	t64	3
Collins, Clev.	54	786	14.6	t48	11
Smith, Wash.	54	682	12.6	28	9
Gilliam, St. L.	52	997	19.2	t84	9
Washington, S.F.	51	711	13.9	52	3
Cunningham, S.F.	51	484	9.5	58	0
Snow, L.A.	49	734	15.0	t74	6
Windsor, S.F.	49	597	12.2	32	2
Long, Wash.	48	533	11.1	52	1
Wallace, Chi.	47	553	11.8	45	5
L. Smith, L.A.	46	300	6.5	38	2
Dale, G.B.	45	879	19.5	48	6
Flatley, Atl.	45	834	18.5	t71	6
Morrison, N.Y.	44	647	14.7	65	7
Rentzel, Dall.	43	960	*22.3	t75	*12
Hawkins, Phil.	43	761	17.7	58	8
Richardson, Balt.	43	646	15.0	39	3
Smith, St. L.	43	561	13.0	34	1
Matte, Balt.	43	513	11.9	49	2
Warfield, Clev.	42	886	21.1	t82	10
Jones, N.Y.	42	744	17.7	t54	1
Sanders, Det.	42	656	15.6	47	3
Hayes, Dall.	40	746	18.7	t67	4
Washington, Minn.	39	821	21.1	t83	9
Tucker, L.A.	38	629	16.6	*t93	7
Dodd, N.O.	37	600	16.2	52	1
Morin, Clev.	37	495	13.4	35	0
Truax, L.A.	37	431	11.6	49	5
Gordon, Chi.	36	414	11.5	t41	4
Willard, S.F.	36	326	9.1	36	3
Henderson, Minn.	34	553	16.3	t47	5
Mackey, Balt.	34	443	13.0	t52	2
Baker, N.O.	34	352	10.4	35	1
L. Brown, Wash.	34	302	8.9	31	0
McCullouch, Det.	33	529	16.0	45	5
Witcher, S.F.	33	435	13.2	49	3
Herrmann, N.Y.	33	423	12.8	62	5
Beasley, Minn.	33	361	10.9	32	4
Josephson, L.A.	32	295	9.2	t51	2
Ballman, Phil.	31	492	15.9	t80	2
Dowler, G.B.	31	477	15.4	45	4
Parks, N.O.	31	.439	14.2	40	3
White, N.Y.	29	315	10.9	t23	1
Keyes, Phil.	29	276	9.5	35	0
Perkins, Balt.	28	391	14.0	t47	3
Livingston, N.O.	28	278	9.9	t51	3
T. Williams, G.B.	27	275	10.2	t60	3
Orr, Balt.	25	.474	19.0	47	2
Cogdill, Atl.	24	374	15.6	52	5
R. Johnson, Clev.	24	164	6.8	18	0
Edwards, St. L.	23	309	13.4	37	0
Thomas, N.Y.	22	348	15.8	37	3
Mitchell, Atl.	22	339	15.4	t42	4
Osborn, Minn.	22	236	10.7	31	1

	No.	Yards	Avg.	Long.	Tds.
Wages, Atl.	22	228	10.4	t88	1
Denney, Chi.	22	203	9.2	29	1
Woodeshick, Phil.	22	177	8.0	15	0
Brown, Minn.	21	183	8.7	27	0
Wilburn, Pitt.	20	373	18.7	53	0
Kelly, Clev.	20	267	13.4	36	1
Hill, Dall.	20	232	11.6	28	0
Hoak, Pitt.	20	190	9.5	26	1
Koy, N.Y.	19	152	8.0	41	4
Thomas, S.F.	18	364	20.2	t75	5
Poage, N.O.	18	236	13.1	29	4
Fleming, G.B.	18	226	12.6	23	2
Reeves, Dall.	18	187	10.4	29	1
Butler, Atl.	17	297	17.5	t65	2
Ditka, Dall.	17	268	15.8	51	3
†McNeil, S.F.	17	255	15.0	t80	3
Piccolo, Chi.	17	143	8.4	t25	1
Gros, Pitt.	17	131	7.7	20	3
Sayers, Chi.	17	116	6.8	25	0
Hampton, G.B.	15	216	14.4	50	2
Anderson, G.B.	14	308	22.0	51	1
Simmons, Atl.-Chi.	14	182	13.0	48	0
Tucker, S.F.	14	104	7.4	t18	2
Frederickson, N.Y.	14	95	6.8	16	1
Bull, Chi.	14	91	6.5	17	0
Coffey, Atl.-N.Y.	14	89	6.4	28	3
Hinton, Balt.	13	269	20.7	46	1
Norman, Dall.	13	238	18.3	t31	3
Triplett, Det.	13	141	10.8	t62	0
Garrison, Dall.	13	131	10.1	25	0
Farr, Det.	13	94	7.2	24	0
Watkins, Det.	13	87	6.7	20	0
Taylor, Det.	13	86	6.6	20	0
Homan, Dall.	12	240	20.0	66	0
Hilton, Pitt.	12	231	19.3	34	0
Henderson, Pitt.	12	188	15.7	45	3
Roland, St. L.	12	136	11.3	23	1
Wright, Det.	12	130	10.8	t26	2
L. Walton, Det.	12	109	9.1	16	0
Grabowski, G.B.	12	98	8.2	25	1
Pinder, Phil.	12	77	6.4	20	0
Hull, Chi.	12	63	5.3	29	0
Mason, L.A.	11	185	16.8	t67	1
Crenshaw, St. L.	11	94	8.5	31	0
Hill, Balt.	11	44	4.0	12	0
Grim, Minn.	10	155	15.5	44	1
Wilson, N.Y.	10	132	13.2	33	0
Eddy, Det.	10	78	7.8	t14	1
Mitchell, Balt.	9	199	22.1	t51	3
Shy, N.O.	9	141	15.7	70	1
Cropper, Pitt.	9	116	12.9	19	0
Cole, Balt.	9	65	7.2	t18	1
Lane, St. L.	9	61	6.8	14	0
Pitts, G.B.	9	47	5.2	t21	1
Shy, Dall.	8	124	15.5	t49	1
Wheelwright, N.O.	8	68	8.5	t20	1
Ogden, Chi.	7	100	14.3	21	0
Spilis, G.B.	7	89	12.7	16	0
Shivers, St. L.	7	61	8.7	26	1

	No.	Yards	Avg.	Long.	Tds.
Reed, Minn.	7	59	8.4	16	2
Adams, Pitt.	6	80	13.3	19	0
Morrison, Clev.	6	71	11.8	26	0
Minniear, N.Y.	6	68	11.3	21	0
Hill, Phil.	6	64	10.7	23	1
Kopay, Wash.	6	60	10.0	18	0
Scott, Clev.	6	25	4.2	14	0
Bankston, Pitt.	6	6	1.0	8	0
Dunn, Balt.	5	30	6.0	10	0
Glass, Clev.	4	91	22.8	40	2
Conrad, Dall.	4	74	18.5	34	0
Roberts, Wash.	4	66	16.5	22	0
Pearson, Balt.	4	64	16.0	37	0
P. Williams, G.B.	4	63	15.8	24	0
Barrington, N.O.	4	42	10.5	15	0
L. Johnson, S.F.	4	42	10.5	14	0
Gipson, Atl.	4	33	8.3	18	0
Ellison, L.A.	4	31	7.8	t14	1
Kurek, Chi.	4	30	7.5	13	0
Hester, N.O.	3	44	14.7	22	1
Hughes, Phil.	3	29	9.7	15	0
Studstill, L.A.	3	28	9.3	11	0
Jones, Minn.	3	23	7.7	9	0
E. Williams, Pitt.	3	14	4.7	t6	1
Fuqua, N.Y.	3	11	3.7	6	0
Dyer, Wash.	2	86	43.0	t69	1
Houston, N.Y.	2	69	34.5	46	0
Lindsey, Minn.	2	45	22.5	30	1
Dunaway, N.Y.	2	37	18.5	25	0
Kramer, Minn.	2	37	18.5	24	1
Jones, Clev.	2	33	16.5	22	0
Kwalick, S.F.	2	32	16.0	31	1
Moore, S.F.	2	28	14.0	24	0
Malinchak, Det.	2	24	12.0	21	0
Odle, Det.	2	24	12.0	14	0
Hooker, Clev.	2	21	10.5	12	0
Klein, L.A.	2	17	8.5	16	1
Smith, Atl.	2	17	8.5	10	0
Bryant, Atl.	2	15	7.5	9	0
Harris, Minn.	2	13	6.5	10	0
Daanen, St. L.	2	12	6.0	7	0
Montgomery, Chi.	2	8	4.0	6	0
McCall, Pitt.	2	2	1.0	5	0
Blye, Phil.	2	−6	−3.0	1	0
Leigh, Clev.	2	−9	−4.5	−4	0
B. Campbell, Pitt.	1	32	32.0	32	0
Brown, Phil.	1	20	20.0	20	0
Turner, Chi.	1	19	19.0	19	0
Alley, Pitt.	1	16	16.0	16	0
Ledbetter, Atl.	1	16	16.0	16	0
Hall, Minn.	1	12	12.0	12	0
Wright, Dall.	1	12	12.0	12	0
Lyle, Chi.	1	11	11.0	11	0
Lawrence, Phil.	1	10	10.0	10	0
Brezina, Atl.	1	9	9.0	9	0
Young, N.Y.	1	8	8.0	8	0
T. Brown, St. L.	1	7	7.0	7	0
Wilson, Phil.	1	6	6.0	6	0
Allen, Wash.	1	5	5.0	5	0

	No.	Yards	Avg.	Long.	Tds.
Havrilak, Balt.	1	5	5.0	5	0
Kotite, N.Y.	1	2	2.0	t2	1
Edwards, S.F.	1	1	1.0	1	0

*—High for 1969
†—1968 Leader
t—Touchdown

RUSHING

TEAM CHAMPION—The Dallas Cowboys, for the first time in the club's 10-year history, with 2,276 yards. The record of 2,885 was set by Detroit in 1936. Dallas is the first team since Chicago in 1956 to be top-rated in team passing and also gain the most yards rushing. With 2,846 net yards gained passing, the Cowboys repeated as overall offensive leader, with 5,122 yards; it was Dallas' third overall title in four years.

INDIVIDUAL CHAMPION—Gale Sayers of the Chicago Bears, with 1,032 yards, ending the two-year reign of Cleveland's Leroy Kelly, who had 1,239 yards in 1968 and 1,205 in 1967. Sayers also won the title in 1966, with 1,231 yards. The record is 1,863 yards by Jim Brown, Cleveland, in 1963.

BEST AVERAGE—Tony Baker of the New Orleans Saints, with 4.8 for 642 yards on 134 attempts. Sayers led in 1968, with 6.2. The record is 9.9 by Beattie Feathers of the Chicago Bears in 1934.

MOST TOUCHDOWNS—Tom Matte of the Baltimore Colts, with 11, breaking Leroy Kelly's three-year hold on the title. The record is 19, by Jim Taylor, Green Bay, in 1962.

MOST ATTEMPTS—Gale Sayers of the Chicago Bears, with 236. Kelly led last season, with 248. The record is 305 by Jim Brown, Cleveland, in 1961.

BEST ONE-GAME PERFORMANCE—Leroy Kelly of the Cleveland Browns, 151 yards on 22 attempts in 20–7 victory over Green Bay on December 7. It was Kelly's 20th 100-yards-or-more performance. Sayers also has 20 100-yard rushing games. Only Jim Brown (58), Jim Taylor (26) and Joe Perry (22) have more. The record for one game is 237 by Jim Brown in 1957 and again in 1961.

LONGEST RUN—Clint Jones of the Minnesota Vikings, 80 yards for a touchdown in 31–14 victory over Chicago on November 2. It was the longest run from scrimmage in the NFL since Green Bay's Jim Taylor ran 84 yards on November 8, 1964. The record is 97 yards by Andy Uram, Green Bay, 1939, and Bob Gage, Pittsburgh, 1949.

TEAM LEADERS—Atlanta, Jim Butler, 655; Baltimore, Tom Matte, 909; Chicago, Gale Sayers, 1,032; Cleveland, Leroy Kelly, 817; Dallas, Calvin Hill, 942; Detroit, Bill Triplett, 377; Green Bay, Travis Williams, 536; Los Angeles, Larry Smith, 599; Minnesota, Dave Osborn, 643; New Orleans, Andy Livingston, 761; New York, Joe Morrison, 387; Philadelphia, Tom Woodeshick, 831; Pittsburgh, Dick Hoak, 531; St. Louis, Cid Edwards, 504; San Francisco, Ken Willard, 557; Washington, Larry Brown, 888.

1969 RUSHING—TEAM

	Atts.	Net Yds. Gained	Avg.	Long. Gain	Tds
Dallas	*532	*2276	4.3	55	*17
†Chicago	462	2078	*4.5	t39	14
Atlanta	455	2058	*4.5	t66	9
Minnesota	489	1850	3.8	*t80	15
Cleveland	447	1788	4.0	54	*17
Detroit	474	1755	3.7	52	11
New Orleans	399	1705	4.3	54	12
Green Bay	432	1692	3.9	53	11
New York	397	1593	4.0	35	8
Philadelphia	395	1563	4.0	50	10
Pittsburgh	400	1542	3.9	35	8
San Francisco	391	1536	3.9	t75	13
Washington	377	1532	4.1	57	11
Baltimore	417	1490	3.6	29	16
St. Louis	382	1446	3.8	48	*17
Los Angeles	382	1413	3.7	46	8
League Total	6831	27,317	—	t80	197
League Average	426.9	1707.3	4.0	—	12.3

*—High for 1969
†—1968 Leader
t —Touchdown

1969 RUSHING—INDIVIDUAL

	Atts.	Yards	Avg.	Long.	Tds.
SAYERS, CHI.	*236	*1032	4.4	28	8
Hill, Dall.	204	942	4.6	55	8
Matte, Balt.	235	909	3.9	26	*11
L. Brown, Wash.	202	888	4.4	57	4
Woodeshick, Phil.	186	831	4.5	21	4
Garrison, Dall.	176	818	4.6	21	2
†Kelly, Clev.	196	817	4.2	31	9
Livingston, N.O.	181	761	4.2	18	5
Butler, Atl.	163	655	4.0	39	3
Osborn, Minn.	186	643	3.5	t58	7
Baker, N.O.	134	642	*4.8	54	1
L. Smith, L.A.	166	599	3.6	46	1
Willard, S.F.	171	557	3.3	18	7
Cunningham, S.F.	147	541	3.7	33	3
T. Williams, G.B.	129	536	4.2	t39	4
Hoak, Pitt.	151	531	3.5	13	2
Coffey, Atl.-N.Y.	131	511	3.9	20	2
Edwards, St. L.	107	504	4.7	48	3
Roland, St. L.	138	498	3.6	21	5
R. Johnson, Clev.	137	471	3.4	t48	7
Josephson, L.A.	124	461	3.7	17	0
Brown, Minn.	126	430	3.4	30	3
Harraway, Wash.	141	428	3.0	17	6
Douglass, Chi.	51	408	8.0	t39	2
Reed, Minn.	83	393	4.7	23	1
Morrison, N.Y.	107	387	3.6	13	4
Triplett, Det.	111	377	3.4	33	3
Wages, Atl.	72	375	5.2	t66	2
Hampton, G.B.	80	365	4.6	53	4
Keyes, Phil.	121	361	3.0	28	3

	Atts.	Yards	Avg.	Long.	Tds.
Taylor, Det.	118	348	2.9	26	0
Gros, Pitt.	116	343	3.0	t16	4
Pinder, Phil.	60	309	5.2	50	1
Gipson, Atl.	62	303	4.9	33	1
Morrison, Clev.	60	301	5.0	54	1
Koy, N.Y.	76	300	3.9	24	2
Anderson, G.B.	87	288	3.3	t16	1
Eddy, Det.	78	272	3.5	26	2
Grabowski, G.B.	73	261	3.6	22	1
Bankston, Pitt.	62	259	4.2	15	1
Bryant, Atl.	50	246	4.9	41	0
Farr, Det.	58	245	4.2	52	4
Landry, Det.	33	243	7.4	26	1
Jones, Minn.	54	241	4.5	*t80	3
Cole, Balt.	73	204	2.8	27	2
Watkins, Det.	62	201	3.2	12	1
Thomas, S.F.	23	190	8.3	t75	1
Bull, Chi.	44	187	4.3	16	0
Reeves, Dall.	59	173	2.9	12	4
Tarkenton, N.Y.	37	172	4.6	21	0
Crenshaw, St. L.	55	172	3.1	t26	3
Scott, Clev.	44	157	3.6	20	0
Jurgensen, Wash.	17	156	9.2	33	1
Gabriel, L.A.	35	156	4.5	22	5
Shy, Dall.	42	154	3.7	23	1
Piccolo, Chi.	45	148	3.3	15	2
Hill, Balt.	49	143	2.9	14	2
Minniear, N.Y.	35	141	4.0	16	1
Frederickson, N.Y.	33	136	4.1	19	0
Mason, L.A.	33	135	4.1	17	1
Pitts, G.B.	35	134	3.8	13	0
Shivers, St. L.	27	115	4.3	17	2
Hanratty, Pitt.	10	106	10.6	31	0
Kapp, Minn.	22	104	4.7	18	0
McCall, Pitt.	30	98	3.3	14	0
Lane, St. L.	25	93	3.7	13	1
Fuqua, N.Y.	20	89	4.5	35	0
Wheelwright, N.O.	25	85	3.4	17	4
Pearson, Balt.	24	81	3.4	10	0
Hull, Chi.	29	81	2.8	14	1
Mitchell, Atl.	5	77	15.4	40	0
Shy, N.O.	21	75	3.6	22	1
Tucker, S.F.	20	72	3.6	t24	2
Nix, Pitt.	10	70	7.0	20	0
Berry, Atl.	20	68	3.4	30	0
Brodie, S.F.	11	62	5.6	15	0
Morton, Dall.	16	62	3.9	15	1
Concannon, Chi.	22	62	2.8	30	1
Abramowicz, N.O.	3	61	20.3	28	0
Starr, G.B.	7	60	8.6	18	0
Staubach, Dall.	15	60	4.0	19	1
Lemmerman, Atl.	10	57	5.7	20	1
Ellison, L.A.	20	56	2.8	15	0
Johnson, Atl.	11	55	5.0	13	1
Shiner, Dall.	14	55	3.9	t18	1
P. Williams, G.B.	18	55	3.1	13	0
Montgomery, Chi.	15	52	3.5	6	0
Johnson, St. L.	17	51	3.0	15	1
McCauley, Atl.	2	49	24.5	32	0

	Atts.	Yards	Avg.	Long.	Tds.
Havrilak, Balt.	5	49	9.8	29	1
Spurrier, S.F.	5	49	9.8	29	0
Jefferson, Pitt.	4	46	11.5	22	0
Dunn, Balt.	13	45	3.5	11	0
Windsor, S.F.	5	39	7.8	13	0
Barney, Det.	3	36	12.0	27	0
Perkins, Balt.	3	36	12.0	18	0
Barrington, N.O.	7	33	4.7	17	1
Munson, Det.	7	31	4.4	13	0
Morin, Clev.	2	30	15.0	22	0
Wilburn, Pitt.	2	29	14.5	35	0
Gordon, Chi.	2	28	14.0	22	0
Blye, Phil.	8	25	3.1	11	0
Taylor, Wash.	3	24	8.0	18	0
Kurek, Chi.	8	24	3.0	6	0
Warfield, Clev.	2	23	11.5	16	0
Unitas, Balt.	11	23	2.1	13	0
Davis, S.F.	2	21	10.5	16	0
Lindsey, Minn.	6	21	3.5	10	1
Welch, Dall.	6	21	3.5	6	0
Norman, Dall.	5	20	4.0	21	0
Carter, Chi.	4	19	4.8	11	0
Dyer, Wash.	6	18	3.0	9	0
Kilmer, N.O.	11	18	1.6	12	0
Green, Chi.	1	17	17.0	17	0
Hayes, Dall.	4	17	4.3	8	0
Mira, Phil.	3	16	5.3	6	0
Wallace, Chi.	4	16	4.0	15	0
Hart, St. L.	7	16	2.3	10	2
Hargett, N.O.	5	15	3.0	11	0
Harris, Minn.	6	13	2.2	5	0
Dodd, N.O.	3	12	4.0	9	0
Houston, N.Y.	1	11	11.0	11	0
Rentzel, Dall.	2	11	5.5	14	0
Lorick, N.O.	5	11	2.2	6	0
Jackson, Phil.	2	10	5.0	6	0
Lee, Minn.	3	9	3.0	7	0
Jones, N.Y.	3	8	2.7	9	0
Smith, Wash.	3	8	2.7	6	0
Wilson, Phil.	4	7	1.8	4	0
L. Walton, Det.	2	6	3.0	17	0
McDermott, Atl.	7	6	0.9	3	0
Bradley, Phil.	1	5	5.0	5	0
B. Campbell, Pitt.	1	5	5.0	5	0
Meador, L.A.	1	5	5.0	5	0
Lewis, S.F.	4	5	1.3	4	0
Denney, Chi.	1	4	4.0	4	0
Dunaway, N.Y.	1	4	4.0	4	0
McCullouch, Det.	1	4	4.0	4	0
Moore, S.F.	2	4	2.0	2	0
Kopay, Wash.	3	4	1.3	3	0
Allen, Wash.	1	3	3.0	3	0
Bragg, Wash.	1	3	3.0	3	0
Wood, N.Y.	1	3	3.0	3	0
Mackey, Balt.	2	3	1.5	7	0
Snead, Phil.	8	2	0.3	t5	2
Bass, L.A.	1	1	1.0	1	0
Lang, L.A.	1	1	1.0	1	0
D. Williams, St. L.	1	1	1.0	1	0

	Atts.	Yards	Avg.	Long.	Tds.
Conjar, Balt.	1	0	0.0	0	0
Jones, Phil.	1	0	0.0	0	0
Rhome, Clev.	1	0	0.0	0	0
Smith, St. L.	4	0	0.0	9	0
Stanceil, Atl.	4	—1	—0.3	4	0
Plum, N.Y.	1	—1	—1.0	—1	0
Sweetan, L.A.	1	—1	—1.0	—1	0
Baynham, Dall.	3	—2	—0.7	2	0
Hawkins, Phil.	1	—3	—3.0	—3	0
Hinton, Balt.	1	—3	—3.0	—3	0
Poage, N.O.	1	—3	—3.0	—3	0
Cuozzo, Minn.	3	—4	—1.3	2	0
Gilliam, St. L.	1	—4	—4.0	—4	0
Washington, S.F.	1	—4	—4.0	—4	0
Looney, N.O.	3	—5	—1.7	4	0
Horn, G.B.	3	—7	—2.3	t2	1
Sanders, Det.	1	—8	—8.0	—8	0
Nelsen, Clev.	5	—11	—2.2	3	0

---

*—High for 1969
†—1968 Leader
t —Touchdown

KICKOFF RETURNS

TEAM CHAMPION—The Baltimore Colts, for the second straight season, with 51 returns for 1,290 yards and a 25.3 average. Baltimore won last season with a 26.4 average. The record is 28.9, by Pittsburgh in 1952.

INDIVIDUAL CHAMPION—Bobby Williams of the Detroit Lions, with a 33.1 average for 563 yards on 17 returns. He scored one touchdown on a 96-yard return. The record return average is 41.1 by Travis Williams, Green Bay, in 1967.

MOST YARDS—Bo Scott of the Cleveland Browns, with 722 yards on 25 returns. The record is 1,237 yards by Chuck Latourette, St. Louis, in 1968.

MOST RETURNS—Preston Pearson of the Baltimore Colts, 1968's average leader, with 31 returns. The record is 46 by Latourette in 1968.

LONGEST RETURN—Don McCall of the Pittsburgh Steelers, 101 yards for a touchdown in 52–14 loss to Minnesota on November 23. The record is 106 yards by Al Carmichael, Green Bay, in 1956.

1969 KICKOFF RETURNS—TEAM

	No.	Yds. Ret.	Avg. Ret.	Long.	Tds.
†Baltimore	51	1290	*25.3	t92	1
Detroit	42	1017	24.2	t96	1
New Orleans	62	1455	23.5	86	0
Minnesota	33	774	23.5	78	0
Green Bay	50	1165	23.3	t96	*2
St. Louis	*68	*1507	22.2	t100	1
Chicago	52	1132	21.8	74	0
Cleveland	46	985	21.4	65	0
Atlanta	52	1104	21.2	61	1
Washington	60	1268	21.1	54	0
Los Angeles	53	1107	20.9	37	0
Pittsburgh	60	1241	20.7	*t101	1
Philadelphia	63	1258	20.0	42	0
Dallas	36	718	19.9	46	0
San Francisco	47	908	19.3	60	0
New York	56	1075	19.2	33	0
League Total	831	18,004	—	t101	7
League Average	51.9	1125.3	21.7	—	0.4

*—High for 1969
†—1968 Leader
t—Touchdown
NOTE: Standing based on average return.

1969 KICKOFF RETURNS—INDIVIDUAL

	Stdg.	No.	Yds.	Avg.	Long.	Tds.
WILLIAMS, DET.	1	17	563	*33.1	t96	*1
Duncan, Balt.	2	19	560	29.5	t92	*1
Scott, Clev.	3	25	*722	28.9	65	0
Shy, N.O.	4	16	447	27.9	57	0
Hampton, G.B.	5	22	582	26.5	t87	*1
Lane, St. L.	6	20	523	26.2	69	0
Jones, Minn.	7	17	444	26.1	71	0
McCall, Pitt.	8	21	532	25.3	*t101	*1
T. Williams, G.B.	9	21	517	24.6	t96	*1
Sayers, Chi.	10	14	339	24.2	52	0
Harris, Wash.	11	19	458	24.1	54	0
Haymond, L.A.	12	16	375	23.4	36	0
Barrington, N.O.	13	17	394	23.2	54	0
†Pearson, Balt.	14	*31	706	22.8	51	0
Roberts, Wash.	15	17	383	22.5	42	0
Smith, S.F.	16	14	315	22.5	60	0
Bradley, Phil.	17	21	467	22.2	42	0
R. Smith, L.A.	18	27	585	21.7	37	0
T. Brown, St. L.	19	15	320	21.3	28	0
B. Campbell, Pitt.	20	26	522	20.1	46	0
Fuqua, N.Y.	21	20	399	20.0	31	0
Blye, Phil.	22	19	370	19.5	35	0
Bryant, Atl.	23	21	407	19.4	39	0
Butler, Atl.	—	13	405	31.2	61	0
Houston, N.Y.	—	12	252	21.0	33	0
L. Walton, Det.	—	12	230	19.2	35	0
Gilliam, St. L.	—	11	339	30.8	t100	*1
Lyle, Chi.	—	11	248	22.5	32	0
Flowers, Dall.	—	11	238	21.6	30	0

1969 KICKOFF RETURNS—INDIVIDUAL (Cont'd)

	Stdg.	No.	Yds.	Avg.	Long.	Tds.
Dyer, Wash.	—	11	207	18.8	25	0
Turner, Chi.	—	10	326	32.6	74	0
Shivers, St. L.	—	10	205	20.5	35	0
West, Minn.	—	9	240	26.7	78	0
Howard, N.O.	—	9	227	25.2	86	0
Cunningham, S.F.	—	9	207	23.0	30	0
Keyes, Phil.	—	9	200	22.2	34	0
Kopay, Wash.	—	9	187	20.8	27	0
Morrison, Clev.	—	9	155	17.2	31	0
Gipson, Atl.	—	9	145	16.1	27	0
Dodd, N.O.	—	8	171	21.4	28	0
Holifield, N.Y.	—	8	156	19.5	28	0
Fuller, S.F.	—	8	155	19.4	28	0
Barney, Det.	—	7	154	22.0	32	0
Baynham, Dall.	—	6	114	19.0	29	0
Gordon, Chi.	—	6	105	17.5	27	0
Williams, N.Y.	—	6	96	16.0	21	0
Wages, Atl.	—	6	76	12.7	23	0
Lewis, S.F.	—	5	155	31.0	54	0
Welch, Dall.	—	5	112	22.4	35	0
Thompson, N.O.	—	5	101	20.2	26	0
Lawrence, Phil.	—	5	97	19.4	24	0
Minniear, N.Y.	—	5	83	16.6	27	0
Hill, Dall.	—	4	125	31.3	46	0
Bankston, Pitt.	—	4	89	22.3	41	0
Jefferson, Pitt.	—	4	80	20.0	27	0
Lang, L.A.	—	4	70	17.5	25	0
Kurek, Chi.	—	4	66	16.5	20	0
M. Wilson, St. L.	—	4	66	16.5	24	0
Pinder, Phil.	—	4	56	14.0	19	0
Cranshaw, St. L.	—	4	34	8.5	18	0
Hayes, Dall.	—	3	80	26.7	46	0
Nelson, Phil.	—	3	63	21.0	27	0
Ward, N.O.	—	3	58	19.3	21	0
Alexander, S.F.	—	3	47	15.7	24	0
Shy, Dall.	—	3	47	15.7	26	0
Robinson, G.B.	—	3	31	10.3	15	0
Butkus, Chi.	—	3	28	9.3	28	0
Edwards, S.F.	—	3	3	1.0	3	0
Davis, Pitt.	—	3	0	0.0	0	0
Nevett, N.O.	—	2	53	26.5	37	0
Brown, Clev.	—	2	45	22.5	24	0
Vaughn, Det.	—	2	44	22.0	25	0
Brenner, N.Y.	—	2	39	19.5	21	0
Ellison, L.A.	—	2	38	19.0	22	0
Longo, N.Y.	—	2	31	15.5	17	0
McKeever, Wash.	—	2	31	15.5	21	0
Curran, L.A.	—	2	28	14.0	22	0
Kelly, Clev.	—	2	26	13.0	14	0
Lindsey, Minn.	—	2	26	13.0	16	0
Seals, Chi.	—	2	20	10.0	20	0
Mooney, Det.	—	2	12	6.0	12	0
Leigh, Clev.	—	2	6	3.0	6	0
Graham, Phil.	—	2	5	2.5	5	0
Olerich, St. L.	—	2	2	1.0	2	0
Green, Dall.	—	2	0	0.0	0	0
Snider, Atl.	—	1	48	48.0	t48	*1
Reed, Minn.	—	1	38	38.0	38	0
R. Johnson, Clev.	—	1	31	31.0	31	0

	Stdg.	No.	Yds.	Avg.	Long.	Tds.
Hinton, Balt.	—	1	24	24.0	24	0
Harris, Minn.	—	1	23	23.0	23	0
Pitts, G.B.	—	1	22	22.0	22	0
Lockhart, N.Y.	—	1	19	19.0	19	0
Wehrli, St. L.	—	1	18	18.0	18	0
Woodson, Pitt.	—	1	18	18.0	18	0
Taylor, S.F.	—	1	16	16.0	16	0
Nowatzke, Det.	—	1	14	14.0	14	0
Gillingham, G.B.	—	1	13	13.0	13	0
Kunz, Atl.	—	1	13	13.0	13	0
Burman, L.A.	—	1	11	11.0	11	0
Stanceil, Atl.	—	1	10	10.0	10	0
Wilcox, S.F.	—	1	10	10.0	10	0
Hester, N.O.	—	1	4	4.0	4	0
Smith, Minn.	—	1	3	3.0	3	0
Garrison, Dall.	—	1	2	2.0	2	0
Snowden, Wash.	—	1	2	2.0	2	0
Alderman, Minn.	—	1	0	0.0	0	0
Holman, Chi.	—	1	0	0.0	0	0
Howell, Clev.	—	1	0	0.0	0	0
Hyland, G.B.	—	1	0	0.0	0	0
Jenkins, Clev.	—	1	0	0.0	0	0
Johnson, Dall.	—	1	0	0.0	0	0
Kanicki, Clev.	—	1	0	0.0	0	0
Klein, L.A.	—	1	0	0.0	0	0
Kolb, Pitt.	—	1	0	0.0	0	0
Kuechenberg, Chi.	—	1	0	0.0	0	0
Kwalick, S.F.	—	1	0	0.0	0	0
Matheson, Clev.	—	1	0	0.0	0	0
Mitchell, Clev.	—	1	0	0.0	0	0
Preece, N.O.	—	1	0	0.0	0	0
Richter, Wash.	—	1	0	0.0	0	0
Sniadecki, S.F.	—	1	0	0.0	0	0
Sunde, Minn.	—	1	0	0.0	0	0
Tucker, S.F.	—	1	0	0.0	0	0
C. Williams, St. L.	—	1	0	0.0	0	0
P. Williams, G.B.	—	1	0	0.0	0	0
Yarbrough, Det.	—	1	0	0.0	0	0

*—High for 1969
†—1968 Leader
t—Touchdown

PUNTING

TEAM CHAMPION—The Baltimore Colts, with a 45.3 average for 2,580 yards on 57 punts. The Atlanta Falcons led in 1968, with a 44.3 average, and in 1967, with a 43.7 average. The record is 47.6 by Detroit in 1961.

INDIVIDUAL CHAMPION—David Lee of the Baltimore Colts, with a 45.3 average for 2,580 yards on 57 punts. Lee also led in his rookie season, 1966, with a 45.6 average for 49 punts. Billy Lothridge of the Atlanta Falcons led in 1967 and 1968.

LONGEST PUNT—Tom McNeill of the New Orleans Saints, 81 yards against Dallas on September 28. The record is 94 yards by Wilbur (Fats) Henry, Canton, in 1923.

MOST PUNTS—Pat Studstill of the Los Angeles Rams, 80, one less than his league-leading total in 1968. The record is 92 by Howard Maley of the Boston Yanks in 1947.

1969 PUNTING—TEAM

	No.	Yards	Avg. Dist.	Long.	Blkd.
Baltimore	57	2580	*45.3	66	0
Dallas	63	2729	43.3	62	0
Pittsburgh	77	3254	42.3	61	0
Washington	70	2957	42.2	63	*2
New Orleans	49	2031	41.4	*81	1
†Atlanta	69	2846	41.2	57	0
Los Angeles	*80	*3259	40.7	60	0
San Francisco	71	2874	40.5	72	0
Green Bay	59	2363	40.1	58	0
Minnesota	67	2680	40.0	56	0
Philadelphia	74	2942	39.8	60	0
Chicago	76	2964	39.0	59	1
St. Louis	73	2746	37.6	57	1
New York	73	2744	37.6	66	*2
Cleveland	60	2250	37.5	59	1
Detroit	74	2510	33.9	53	1
League Total	1092	43,729	—	81	9
League Average	68.3	2733.1	40.0	—	0.6

*—High for 1969
†—1968 Leader
NOTE: Standing based on average distance.

1969 PUNTING—INDIVIDUAL

	Stdg.	No.	Yards	Avg. Dist.	Long.	Blkd.
LEE, BALT.	1	57	2580	*45.3	66	0
Widby, Dall.	2	63	2729	43.3	62	0
Walden, Pitt.	3	77	3254	42.3	61	0
Bragg, Wash.	4	70	2957	42.2	63	2
†Lothridge, Atl.	5	69	2846	41.2	57	0
Cordill, N.O.	6	42	1719	40.9	58	1
Studstill, L.A.	7	*80	*3259	40.7	60	0
Kilgore, S.F.	8	36	1451	40.3	72	0
Anderson, G.B.	9	58	2329	40.2	58	0
Lee, Minn.	10	67	2680	40.0	56	0
Bradley, Phil.	11	74	2942	39.8	60	0
Green, Chi.	12	76	2964	39.0	59	1
Hill, St. L.	13	73	2746	37.6	57	1
Cockroft, Clev.	14	57	2138	37.5	55	1
Barney, Det.	15	66	2249	34.1	53	1
Koy, N.Y.	—	26	933	35.9	54	0
Davis, S.F.	—	23	955	41.5	55	0
C. Johnson, N.Y.	—	22	823	37.4	66	2
Dunaway, N.Y.	—	13	497	38.2	52	0
Gogolak, N.Y.	—	12	491	40.9	61	0
Spurrier, S.F.	—	12	468	39.0	57	0
McNeill, N.O.	—	7	312	44.6	*81	0
Malinchak, Det.	—	5	184	36.8	47	0
Collins, Clev.	—	3	112	37.3	59	0
Duncan, Det.	—	3	77	25.7	29	0
Dowler, G.B.	—	1	34	34.0	34	0

*—High for 1969
†—1968 Leader
NOTE: Standing based on average distance. To qualify for championship
rating a player must punt at least 35 times.

1969 FUMBLES—TEAM

	Fum.	Own Rec.	Yds.	Tds.	Opp. Rec.	Yds.	Long	Tds.	Tot. Rec.
Minnesota	*17	5	*60	*1	12	11	8	0	17
Detroit	18	6	—9	0	21	51	t26	1	27
Philadelphia	18	7	—34	0	14	32	24	0	21
New Orleans	20	7	—25	0	10	8	6	0	17
†New York	22	7	—10	0	14	23	10	0	21
Washington	23	13	0	0	10	30	t19	*2	23
Los Angeles	23	11	—4	0	12	4	4	0	23
Baltimore	23	10	1	0	10	5	5	0	20
St. Louis	24	14	—5	0	12	*156	*t88	*2	26
San Francisco	25	13	—11	0	11	2	t2	1	24
Cleveland	26	11	—36	0	22	17	t12	1	33
Chicago	27	9	—11	0	11	0	0	0	20
Dallas	28	15	4	*1	11	22	t9	1	26
Green Bay	31	10	0	0	7	0	0	0	17
Pittsburgh	36	*16	0	0	16	53	50	0	32
Atlanta	37	15	—29	0	*27	119	t74	*2	*42
League Total	398	169	—109	2	220	533	t88	10	389
League Average	24.9	10.6	—6.8	0.1	13.8	33.3	—	0.6	24.3

*—High for 1969.
†—1968 Leader.
t —Touchdown.

1969 FUMBLES—INDIVIDUAL

	No.	Own Rec.	Yds.	Long	Opp. Rec.	Yds.	Long	Total Rec.
Absher, N.O.	0	0	0	0	1	0	0	1
Acks, Atl.	0	0	0	0	1	0	0	1
Adams, Pitt.	0	0	0	0	1	0	0	1
Aldridge, G.B.	0	0	0	0	1	0	0	1
Alexander, S.F.	3	2	0	0	0	0	0	2
Allen, Atl.	0	0	0	0	2	0	0	2
Amsler, Chi.	0	0	0	0	1	0	0	1
Anderson, G.B.	4	2	0	0	0	0	0	2
Andrews, Clev.	0	0	0	0	2	0	0	2
Atkins, N.O.	0	0	0	0	1	0	0	1
Baker, N.O.	2	2	0	0	0	0	0	2
Ball, Balt.	0	1	0	0	0	0	0	1
Ballman, Phil.	0	1	0	0	0	0	0	1
Bankston, Pitt.	6	0	0	0	0	0	0	0
Barnes, Clev.	1	0	0	0	0	0	0	0
Barney, Det.	3	1	0	0	1	25	25	2
Bass, Wash.	0	0	0	0	1	0	0	1
Baughan, L.A.	0	0	0	0	2	0	0	2
Baynham, Dall.	1	0	0	0	0	0	0	0
Beasley, Minn.	1	1	*60	*t60	1	0	0	2
Berry, Atl.	6	1	—5	0	0	0	0	1
Blue, S.F.	1	1	—11	0	0	0	0	1
Blye, Phil.	0	0	0	0	1	0	0	1
Boston, N.Y.	0	0	0	0	1	0	0	1
Bradley, Phil.	2	0	0	0	0	0	0	0
Brewer, N.O.	0	0	0	0	1	0	0	1
Brezina, Atl.	0	0	0	0	*5	0	0	*5
Brodie, S.F.	1	0	0	0	0	0	0	0

	No.	Own Rec.	Yds.	Long	Opp. Rec.	Yds.	Long	Tot. Rec.
Brown, Minn.	3	1	0	0	0	0	0	1
L. Brown, Wash.	6	2	0	0	0	0	0	2
Brown, Dall.	0	0	0	0	1	6	6	1
T. Brown, St. L.	2	1	0	0	1	0	0	2
Bryant, Minn.	0	0	0	0	1	8	8	1
Bryant, Atl.	2	0	0	0	2	0	0	2
Buffone, Chi.	0	0	0	0	1	0	0	1
Bull, Chi.	1	1	0	0	0	0	0	1
Butkus, Chi.	0	0	0	0	2	0	0	2
Butler, Atl.	3	2	0	0	0	0	0	2
Cadile, Chi.	0	1	0	0	0	0	0	1
Caffey, G.B.	0	0	0	0	1	0	0	1
B. Campbell, Pitt.	5	3	0	0	0	0	0	3
Campbell, Balt.	0	0	0	0	1	0	0	1
Carroll, Wash.	0	0	0	0	1	0	0	1
Carrolo, Phil.	0	1	0	0	0	0	0	1
Clark, Clev.	0	2	0	0	0	0	0	2
Coffey, N.Y.	4	0	0	0	0	0	0	0
Cogdill, Atl.	0	2	0	0	0	0	0	2
Cole, Dall.	0	0	0	0	2	7	7	2
Cole, Balt.	2	1	0	0	0	0	0	1
Collett, S.F.	0	0	0	0	1	0	0	1
Colman, Phil.	0	1	0	0	0	0	0	1
Concannon, Chi.	2	0	0	0	0	0	0	0
Crenshaw, St. L.	1	0	0	0	0	0	0	0
Cropper, Pitt.	0	2	0	0	0	0	0	2
Cross, Phil.	0	0	0	0	1	8	8	1
Cunningham, S.F.	5	1	0	0	0	0	0	1
Cuozzo, Minn.	2	0	0	0	0	0	0	0
Curry, Balt.	0	1	0	0	0	0	0	1
Daniel, L.A.	0	0	0	0	1	0	0	1
Davis, N.Y.	0	0	0	0	1	9	9	1
Davis, Pitt.	2	0	0	0	0	0	0	0
Davis, S.F.	0	1	0	0	0	0	0	1
Davis, G.B.	0	0	0	0	2	0	0	2
Demarie, Clev.	0	0	0	0	1	0	0	1
Denney, Chi.	0	1	0	0	0	0	0	1
Dirks, Phil.	0	0	0	0	1	0	0	1
Ditka, Dall.	0	1	0	0	0	0	0	1
Douglass, Chi.	7	2	1	1	0	0	0	2
Dryer, N.Y.	0	0	0	0	2	0	0	2
Duncan, Balt.	1	0	0	0	0	0	0	0
Dunn, Balt.	1	1	0	0	0	0	0	1
Dyer, Wash.	1	0	0	0	0	0	0	0
East, Dall.	0	0	0	0	2	0	0	2
Eaton, N.Y.	0	0	0	0	1	0	0	1
Eddy, Det.	1	0	0	0	0	0	0	0
Edwards, St. L.	3	3	0	0	0	0	0	3
Edwards, S.F.	1	1	0	0	1	0	0	2
Enderle, Atl.	0	1	0	0	0	0	0	1
Evey, Chi.	0	0	0	0	1	0	0	1
Farr, Det.	2	0	0	0	0	0	0	0
Ferguson, Atl.	1	0	−24	0	0	0	0	0
Fischer, Wash.	0	0	0	0	1	11	11	1
Flanagan, Det.	0	1	0	0	1	0	0	2
Flatley, Atl.	1	0	0	0	0	0	0	0
Fleming, G.B.	0	1	0	0	0	0	0	1
Freeman, Atl.	0	1	0	0	1	0	0	2
Fuller, S.F.	1	1	0	0	0	0	0	1

1969 FUMBLES—INDIVIDUAL (Cont'd)

	No.	Own Rec.	Yds.	Long	Opp. Rec.	Yds.	Long	Total Rec.
Fuqua, N.Y.	2	0	0	0	0	0	0	0
Gabriel, L.A.	7	*5	—4	0	0	0	0	*5
Garlington, Clev.	0	0	0	0	2	0	0	2
Garrison, Dall.	4	1	0	0	0	0	0	1
Gilliam, St. L.	1	0	0	0	0	0	0	0
Gillingham, G.B.	0	1	0	0	0	0	0	1
Gipson, Atl.	*8	4	0	0	0	0	0	4
Goich, Det.	0	0	0	0	4	0	0	4
Goode, St. L.	0	2	0	0	0	0	0	2
Grabowski, G.B.	2	0	0	0	0	0	0	0
Gregory, Clev.	0	0	0	0	1	0	0	1
Grim, Minn.	1	0	0	0	1	0	0	1
Grimm, Balt.	0	1	1	1	0	0	0	1
Gros, Pitt.	4	1	0	0	0	0	0	1
Hackbart, Minn.	0	0	0	0	1	0	0	1
Hampton, G.B.	7	2	0	0	0	0	0	2
Hanburger, Wash.	0	0	0	0	3	19	t19	3
Hanratty, Pitt.	3	0	0	0	0	0	0	0
Harraway, Wash.	7	2	0	0	0	0	0	2
Harris, Wash.	0	0	0	0	1	0	0	1
Hart, St. L.	1	0	0	0	0	0	0	0
Hauss, Wash.	0	2	0	0	0	0	0	2
Havrilak, Balt.	4	0	0	0	0	0	0	0
Hawkins, Phil.	1	0	0	0	0	0	0	0
Hayes, Dall.	2	2	0	0	0	0	0	2
Haymond, L.A.	3	1	0	0	0	0	0	1
Heck, N.Y.	0	0	0	0	1	0	0	1
Herrmann, N.Y.	1	0	0	0	0	0	0	0
Hill, Dall.	7	2	0	0	0	0	0	2
Hill, Balt.	3	0	0	0	0	0	0	0
Hillebrand, Pitt.	0	0	0	0	1	0	0	1
Hilton, Balt.	0	0	0	0	1	0	0	1
Hinton, N.Y.	1	0	—10	0	0	0	0	0
Hinton, Pitt.	1	0	0	0	3	0	0	3
Hoaglin, Clev.	1	0	—41	0	1	0	0	1
Hoak, Pitt.	4	0	0	0	0	0	0	0
Hobbs, Phil.	0	0	0	0	1	0	0	1
Hoffman, Wash.	0	0	0	0	1	0	t0	1
Hohn, Pitt.	0	0	0	0	3	3	3	3
Holifield, N.Y.	1	1	0	0	0	0	0	1
Horn, G.B.	6	1	0	0	0	0	0	1
Houston, Clev.	0	0	0	0	1	0	0	1
Howard, N.O.	2	0	0	0	0	0	0	0
Howley, Dall.	0	0	0	0	1	0	0	1
Hughes, Phil.	1	1	0	0	0	0	0	1
Hull, Chi.	1	0	0	0	0	0	0	0
Humphrey, Atl.	0	0	0	0	1	24	t24	1
Iman, L.A.	0	1	0	0	0	0	0	1
Jackson, Phil.	0	1	0	0	0	0	0	1
Jefferson, Pitt.	3	1	0	0	0	0	0	1
Jenkins, Clev.	1	0	0	0	0	0	0	0
Johnson, St. L.	4	1	—5	0	0	0	0	1
C. Johnson, N.Y.	0	1	0	0	0	0	0	1
Johnson, Dall.	2	1	0	0	0	0	0	1
Johnson, Atl.	3	0	0	0	0	0	0	0
R. Johnson, Clev.	4	2	0	0	0	0	0	2
W. Johnson, Clev.	0	0	0	0	2	12	t12	2
Jones, L.A.	0	0	0	0	1	0	0	1

	No.	Own Rec.	Yds.	Long	Opp. Rec.	Yds.	Long	Total Rec.
Jordan, Dall.	0	0	0	0	2	0	0	2
Josephson, L.A.	4	2	0	0	0	0	0	2
Jurgensen, Wash.	2	1	0	0	0	0	0	1
Kanicki, Clev.	0	0	0	0	1	0	0	1
Kapp, Minn.	1	1	0	0	0	0	0	1
Karras, Det.	0	0	0	0	2	0	0	2
Kelly, Clev.	1	1	0	0	0	0	0	1
Keyes, Phil.	3	1	0	0	1	0	0	2
Kilmer, N.O.	5	1	0	0	0	0	0	1
Klein, L.A.	0	0	0	0	2	0	0	2
Kolb, Pitt.	0	1	0	0	0	0	0	1
Koy, N.Y.	1	0	0	0	0	0	0	0
Krause, Minn.	0	0	0	0	1	3	3	1
Kunz, Atl.	0	1	0	0	1	0	0	2
Lakes, S.F.	0	0	0	0	4	2	t2	4
Landry, Det.	2	1	0	0	0	0	0	1
Lane, St. L.	2	1	0	0	2	2	2	3
Larsen, Minn.	0	0	0	0	1	0	0	1
Lavan, Atl.	1	0	0	0	1	0	0	1
Lee, Minn.	2	0	0	0	0	0	0	0
Leigh, Clev.	2	0	0	0	1	0	0	1
Lemmerman, Atl.	4	2	0	0	0	0	0	2
Lilly, Dall.	0	0	0	0	2	9	t9	2
Lindsey, Minn.	0	1	0	0	0	0	0	1
Livingston, N.O.	2	0	0	0	0	0	0	0
Lockhart, N.Y.	2	0	0	0	1	0	0	1
Logan, Balt.	1	2	0	0	2	0	0	4
Long, Wash.	0	1	0	0	0	0	0	1
Longo, N.Y.	0	0	0	0	3	0	0	3
Lorick, N.O.	1	0	0	0	0	0	0	0
Lucci, Det.	0	0	0	0	1	0	0	1
Lueck, G.B.	0	1	0	0	0	0	0	1
Lyle, Chi.	2	0	0	0	1	0	0	1
Mackbee, Minn.	0	0	0	0	1	0	0	1
Mackey, Balt.	1	0	0	0	0	0	0	0
Mallory, Atl.	1	0	0	0	2	14	14	2
Mansfield, Pitt.	0	1	0	0	0	0	0	1
Marshall, Minn.	0	0	0	0	2	0	0	2
Martha, Pitt.	3	0	0	0	1	0	0	1
Matte, Balt.	4	0	0	0	0	0	0	0
McCall, Pitt.	1	1	0	0	0	0	0	1
McCauley, Atl.	1	0	0	0	0	0	0	0
McKeever, Wash.	0	0	0	0	1	0	0	1
McNeil, S.F.	1	0	0	0	0	0	0	0
McRae, Chi.	0	0	0	0	1	0	0	1
Meador, L.A.	0	0	0	0	1	0	0	1
Minniear, N.Y.	2	0	0	0	0	0	0	0
Mitchell, Clev.	0	0	0	0	1	0	0	1
Mitchell, Atl.	1	0	0	0	0	0	0	0
Molden, N.Y.	0	0	0	0	2	10	10	2
Mooney, Det.	0	0	0	0	1	0	0	1
Moore, Det.	0	0	0	0	2	0	0	2
Moore, G.B.	0	0	0	0	1	0	0	1
Morin, Clev.	1	0	0	0	0	0	0	0
Morrison, N.Y.	0	1	0	0	1	0	0	2
Morrison, Clev.	2	3	5	5	0	0	0	3
Morton, Dall.	4	1	0	0	0	0	0	1
Munson, Det.	3	2	−9	0	0	0	0	2

	No.	Own Rec.	Yds.	Long	Opp. Rec.	Yds.	Long	Total Rec.
Nelsen, Clev.	*8	3	0	0	0	0	0	3
Nevett, N.O.	1	0	0	0	2	2	2	2
Niland, Dall.	0	1	0	0	0	0	0	1
Nix, Pitt.	1	0	0	0	0	0	0	0
Nobis, Atl.	0	0	0	0	1	0	0	1
Nordquist, Phil.	0	0	0	0	1	0	0	1
Norman, Dall.	1	1	0	0	0	0	0	1
Nunley, S.F.	0	0	0	0	2	0	0	2
O'Bradovich, Chi.	0	0	0	0	1	0	0	1
Ogden, Chi.	0	0	0	0	1	0	0	1
Olerich, St. L.	1	0	0	0	0	0	0	0
Oliver, Pitt.	0	0	0	0	1	0	0	1
Osborn, Minn.	3	0	0	0	0	0	0	0
Page, Minn.	0	0	0	0	1	0	0	1
Pearson, Balt.	2	1	0	0	0	0	0	1
Pergine, L.A.	1	0	0	0	0	0	0	0
Petitbon, L.A.	0	0	0	0	1	4	4	1
Piccolo, Chi.	2	1	8	8	0	0	0	1
Pinder, Phil.	1	0	0	0	0	0	0	0
Pitts, G.B.	2	1	0	0	0	0	0	1
Plum, N.Y.	1	1	0	0	0	0	0	1
Poage, N.O.	1	0	0	0	1	6	6	1
Porter, Phil.	0	0	0	0	3	0	0	3
Preece, N.O.	0	0	0	0	2	0	0	2
Pugh, Dall.	0	0	0	0	1	0	0	1
Purnell, L.A.	0	0	0	0	2	0	0	2
Pyle, Chi.	2	0	−20	0	0	0	0	0
Randolph, S.F.	0	0	0	0	2	0	0	2
Rasmussen, Det.	0	0	0	0	1	0	0	1
Raye, Phil.	0	0	0	0	1	0	0	1
Reaves, Atl.	0	0	0	0	1	0	0	1
Redmond, Atl.	0	0	0	0	2	0	0	2
Reed, Minn.	1	0	0	0	0	0	0	0
Reeves, Dall.	2	0	0	0	0	0	0	0
Renfro, Dall.	2	0	0	0	0	0	0	0
Rentzel, Dall.	0	1	4	t4	0	0	0	1
Reynolds, Clev.	0	0	0	0	3	0	0	3
Rhome, Clev.	1	0	0	0	0	0	0	0
Richardson, Balt.	2	1	0	0	0	0	0	1
Rivers, St. L.	0	0	0	0	1	0	0	1
Robb, Det.	0	0	0	0	2	0	0	2
Roberts, Wash.	6	*5	0	0	0	0	0	*5
Robinson, G.B.	0	0	0	0	1	0	0	1
Rohde, S.F.	0	1	0	0	0	0	0	1
Roland, St. L.	4	4	0	0	0	0	0	4
Rossovich, Phil.	0	0	0	0	2	0	0	2
Roussel, Wash.	0	0	0	0	1	0	0	1
Rowe, St. L.	0	0	0	0	1	4	4	1
Rowe, N.O.	0	0	0	0	1	0	0	1
Rush, Det.	0	0	0	0	1	0	0	1
Sayers, Chi.	7	2	0	0	0	0	0	2
Scott, Clev.	1	0	0	0	2	0	0	2
Shay, Atl.	0	0	0	0	1	0	0	1
Shiner, Pitt.	3	1	0	0	0	0	0	1
Shivers, St. L.	2	1	0	0	0	0	0	1
Shorter, Pitt.	0	0	0	0	2	50	50	2
Shy, N.O.	2	2	0	0	0	0	0	2
Shy, Dall.	1	0	0	0	0	0	0	0

	No.	Own Rec.	Yds.	Long	Opp. Rec.	Yds.	Long	Total Rec.
B. Smith, Balt.	0	0	0	0	2	0	0	2
B. R. Smith, Balt.	0	0	0	0	2	0	0	2
Smith, St. L.	1	0	0	0	0	0	0	0
L. Smith, L.A.	1	1	0	0	0	0	0	1
Smith, S.F.	4	3	0	0	0	0	0	3
R. Smith, L.A.	3	0	0	0	0	0	0	0
Snead, Phil.	4	0	−34	0	0	0	0	0
Sniadecki, S.F.	0	0	0	0	1	0	0	1
Snidow, Clev.	0	0	0	0	2	0	0	2
Snow, L.A.	3	1	0	0	0	0	0	1
Spurrier, S.F.	2	0	0	0	0	0	0	0
Stallings, St. L.	0	0	0	0	1	62	t62	1
Stanceil, Atl.	1	0	0	0	0	0	0	0
Starr, G.B.	4	0	0	0	0	0	0	0
Staubach, Dall.	2	1	0	0	0	0	0	1
Sturm, N.O.	1	1	−25	0	0	0	0	1
Sumner, Clev.	3	0	0	0	0	0	0	0
Talbert, L.A.	0	0	0	0	1	0	0	1
Tarkenton, N.Y.	7	2	0	0	0	0	0	2
Taylor, Det.	4	0	0	0	0	0	0	0
Taylor, Wash.	1	0	0	0	0	0	0	0
Taylor, Pitt.	0	2	0	0	0	0	0	2
Thompson, N.O.	1	1	0	0	1	0	0	2
Triplett, Det.	1	0	0	0	0	0	0	0
Truax, L.A.	1	0	0	0	0	0	0	0
Turner, Chi.	2	0	0	0	0	0	0	0
Unitas, Balt.	2	1	0	0	0	0	0	1
Upshaw, Clev.	0	0	0	0	2	5	5	2
Van Dyke, Pitt.	0	3	0	0	0	0	0	3
Vaughn, Det.	0	0	0	0	1	0	0	1
Vellone, Minn.	0	1	0	0	0	0	0	1
Volk, Balt.	0	0	0	0	2	5	5	2
Voss, Pitt.	0	0	0	0	2	0	0	2
Wages, Atl.	3	0	0	0	0	0	0	1
Walker, St. L.	0	0	0	0	*5	0	0	*5
Walker, Dall.	0	2	0	0	0	0	0	2
Walker, Det.	0	0	0	0	1	0	0	1
Wallace, Chi.	1	0	0	0	0	0	0	0
Ward, N.O.	1	0	0	0	0	0	0	0
Warwick, Minn.	0	0	0	0	2	0	0	2
Washington, Pitt.	0	0	0	0	1	0	0	1
Washington, Minn.	1	0	0	0	0	0	0	0
Waskiewicz, Atl.	0	0	0	0	2	0	0	2
Weatherford, Atl.	0	0	0	0	3	74	t74	3
Weger, Det.	0	0	0	0	2	0	0	2
Welch, Dall.	0	1	0	0	0	0	0	1
West, Minn.	2	0	0	0	0	0	0	0
Wetoska, Chi.	0	1	0	0	0	0	0	1
Wheelwright, N.O.	1	0	0	0	0	0	0	0
Willard, S.F.	6	1	0	0	0	0	0	1
Williams, Det.	1	1	0	0	0	0	0	1
Williams, L.A.	0	0	0	0	1	0	0	1
D. Williams, St. L.	1	0	0	0	0	0	0	0
P. Williams, G.B.	1	0	0	0	0	0	0	0
T. Williams, G.B.	5	1	0	0	0	0	0	1
Williams, N.Y.	0	1	0	0	1	4	4	2
L. Wilson, St. L.	0	0	0	0	1	*88	*t88	1
M. Wilson, St. L.	1	1	0	0	0	0	0	1

	No.	Own Rec.	Yds.	Long	Opp. Rec.	Yds.	Long	Total Rec.
Woitt, S.F.	0	1	0	0	0	0	0	1
Wood, G.B.	0	0	0	0	1	0	0	1
Woodeshick, Phil.	6	0	0	0	0	0	0	0
Woodson, Pitt.	0	0	0	0	1	0	0	1
Wright, Det.	0	0	0	0	1	26	t26	1
Wright, Atl.	1	0	0	0	0	0	0	0
Yarbrough, Det.	1	0	0	0	0	0	0	0
Young, Phil.	0	1	0	0	2	24	24	3
Youngblood, Chi.	0	0	0	0	2	0	0	2
Zook, Atl.	0	0	0	0	1	7	7	1

TOUCHDOWNS: Humphrey & Weatherford, Atl.; W. Johnson, Clev.; Lilly & Rentzel, Dall.; Wright, Det.; Beasley, Minn.; Stallings & L. Wilson, St. L.; Lakes, S.F.; Hanburger & Hoffman, Wash.

---

*—High for 1969.
t—Touchdown.

1969 FIELD GOALS—TEAM

	Made	Attempts	Percentage	Long
Minnesota	*26	37	*.703	48
Detroit	25	37	.676	50
Los Angeles	22	34	.647	44
Washington	16	27	.593	38
Dallas	20	36	.556	47
New Orleans	22	*41	.537	*55
Philadelphia	16	30	.533	47
New York	11	21	.524	45
Cleveland	12	23	.522	45
Atlanta	15	30	.500	34
St. Louis	12	24	.500	46
Pittsburgh	12	26	.462	41
Baltimore	14	31	.452	49
Chicago	8	21	.381	38
San Francisco	6	21	.286	32
Green Bay	6	22	.273	48
League Total	243	461	—	55
League Average	15.2	28.8	.527	—

*—High for 1969.
†—1968 Leader.

1969 FIELD GOAL ANALYSIS

	1-19	20-29	30-39	40-49	50-over	Total	Avg. Yds. Att.	Avg. Yds. Made	Avg. Yds. Missed	Long
Cox, Minn.	7-7 1.000	7-7 1.000	8-11 .727	4-10 .400	0-2 .000	26-37 .703	32.2	27.3	43.8	48
Mann, Det.	5-6 .833	9-10 .900	7-11 .636	3-8 .375	1-2 .500	25-37 .676	31.2	27.9	38.1	50
Gossett, L.A.	7-7 1.000	8-8 1.000	6-7 .857	1-11 .091	0-1 .000	22-34 .647	32.4	25.6	44.7	44
Knight, Wash.	7-8 .875	4-5 .800	5-7 .714	0-5 .000	0-2 .000	16-27 .593	30.9	24.1	40.8	38
M. Clark, Dall.	7-8 .875	6-7 .857	4-6 .667	3-11 .273	0-4 .000	20-36 .556	32.9	25.6	42.0	47
Dempsey, N.O.	5-6 .833	6-7 .857	3-6 .500	7-11 .636	1-11 .091	22-41 .537	38.1	30.8	46.6	55
Baker, Phil.	4-7 .571	2-3 .667	4-5 .800	6-13 .462	0-2 .000	16-30 .533	34.6	31.3	38.4	47
Gogolak, N.Y.	3-3 1.000	4-5 .800	1-4 .250	3-8 .375	0-1 .000	11-21 .524	33.4	27.7	39.7	45
Cockroft, Clev.	0-0 .000	7-8 .875	3-8 .375	2-6 .333	0-1 .000	12-23 .522	34.4	30.0	39.2	45
Etter, Atl.	6-6 1.000	5-5 1.000	4-8 .500	0-9 .000	0-2 .000	15-30 .500	32.4	23.3	41.6	34
Bakken, St. L.	2-2 1.000	4-8 .500	3-4 .750	3-7 .429	0-3 .000	12-24 .500	34.7	30.3	39.1	46
Mingo, Pitt.	5-6 .833	1-4 .250	4-7 .571	2-9 .222	0-0 .000	12-26 .462	32.2	27.3	36.4	41
Michaels, Balt.	5-5 1.000	3-3 1.000	3-9 .333	3-11 .273	0-3 .000	14-31 .452	35.3	26.9	42.2	49
Percival, Chi.	1-2 .500	3-6 .500	4-8 .500	0-3 .000	0-2 .000	8-21 .381	33.2	28.4	36.2	38
Davis, S.F.	2-2 1.000	1-2 .500	0-2 .000	0-4 .000	0-0 .000	3-10 .300	33.6	21.3	38.9	29
Mercer, G.B.	2-2 1.000	1-3 .333	1-7 .143	1-5 .200	0-0 .000	5-17 .294	32.8	27.2	35.1	48
Gavric, S.F.	0-0 .000	2-3 .667	1-2 .500	0-5 .000	0-1 .000	3-11 .273	37.6	25.3	42.3	32
Lusteg, G.B.	0-0 .000	1-1 1.000	0-1 .000	0-2 .000	0-1 .000	1-5 .200	40.4	28.0	43.5	28
Totals	68-77 .883	74-95 .779	61-113 .540	38-138 .275	2-38 .053	243-461 .527	33.6	27.4	40.6	

57

1969 NFL TEAM SUMMARY
LEAGUE GAMES

ATLANTA (6-8)

24	*San Francisco	12
7	Los Angeles	17
14	*Baltimore	21
17	*Dallas	24
21	San Francisco	7
10	Green Bay	28
6	*Los Angeles	38
21	Detroit	27
48	*Chicago	31
20	Washington	27
6	Baltimore	13
45	*New Orleans	17
27	Philadelphia	3
10	*Minnesota	3
276		268

BALTIMORE (8-5-1)

20	*Los Angeles	27
14	Minnesota	52
21	Atlanta	14
24	*Philadelphia	20
30	New Orleans	10
21	*San Francisco	24
41	*Washington	17
14	*Green Bay	6
17	San Francisco	20
24	Chicago	21
13	*Atlanta	6
17	*Detroit	17
10	Dallas	27
13	Los Angeles	7
279		268

CHICAGO (1-13)

0	Green Bay	17
17	St. Louis	20
24	New York	28
0	*Minnesota	31
7	Detroit	13
7	*Los Angeles	9
14	Minnesota	31
38	*Pittsburgh	7
31	Atlanta	48
21	*Baltimore	24
24	*Cleveland	28
21	San Francisco	42
3	*Green Bay	21
3	*Detroit	20
210		339

CLEVELAND (10-3-1)

27	Philadelphia	20
27	*Washington	23
21	*Detroit	28
27	New Orleans	17
42	*Pittsburgh	31
21	*St. Louis	21
42	*Dallas	10
3	Minnesota	51
24	Pittsburgh	3
28	*New York	17
28	Chicago	24
20	*Green Bay	7
27	St. Louis	21
14	New York	27
351		300

DALLAS (11-2-1)

24	*St. Louis	3
21	New Orleans	17
38	Philadelphia	7
24	Atlanta	17
49	*Philadelphia	14
25	*New York	3
10	Cleveland	42
33	*New Orleans	17
41	Washington	28
23	Los Angeles	24
24	*San Francisco	24
10	Pittsburgh	7
27	*Baltimore	10
20	*Washington	10
369		223

DETROIT (9-4-1)

13	Pittsburgh	16
24	*New York	0
28	Cleveland	21
17	*Green Bay	28
13	*Chicago	7
10	Minnesota	24
26	San Francisco	14
27	*Atlanta	21
20	*St. Louis	0
16	Green Bay	10
0	*Minnesota	27
17	Baltimore	17
28	*Los Angeles	0
20	Chicago	3
259		188

*Home Game

58

GREEN BAY (8–6)			LOS ANGELES (11–3)	
17	*Chicago	0	27	Baltimore	20
14	*San Francisco (M)	7	17	*Atlanta	7
7	Minnesota	19	36	*New Orleans	17
28	Detroit	17	27	San Francisco	21
21	Los Angeles	34	34	*Green Bay	21
28	*Atlanta	10	9	Chicago	7
38	Pittsburgh	34	38	Atlanta	6
6	Baltimore	14	41	*San Francisco	30
7	*Minnesota (M)	9	23	*Philadelphia	17
10	*Detroit	16	24	*Dallas	23
20	*New York (M)	10	24	Washington	13
7	Cleveland	20	13	*Minnesota	20
21	Chicago	3	0	Detroit	28
45	*St. Louis	28	7	*Baltimore	13
269		221	320		243

MINNESOTA (12–2)			NEW ORLEANS (5–9)	
23	New York	24	20	*Washington	26
52	*Baltimore	14	17	*Dallas	21
19	*Green Bay	7	17	Los Angeles	36
31	Chicago	0	17	*Cleveland	27
27	St. Louis	10	10	*Baltimore	30
24	*Detroit	10	10	Philadelphia	13
31	*Chicago	14	51	St. Louis	42
51	*Cleveland	3	17	Dallas	33
9	Green Bay (M)	7	25	New York	24
52	*Pittsburgh	14	43	*San Francisco	38
27	Detroit	0	26	*Philadelphia	17
20	Los Angeles	13	17	Atlanta	45
10	*San Francisco	7	14	Washington	17
3	Atlanta	10	27	*Pittsburgh	24
379		133	311		393

NEW YORK (6–8)			PHILADELPHIA (4–9–1)	
24	*Minnesota	23	20	*Cleveland	27
0	Detroit	24	41	*Pittsburgh	27
28	*Chicago	24	7	*Dallas	38
10	*Pittsburgh	7	20	Baltimore	24
14	Washington	20	14	Dallas	49
3	Dallas	25	13	*New Orleans	10
20	*Philadelphia	23	23	New York	20
17	St. Louis	42	28	Washington	28
24	*New Orleans	25	17	*Los Angeles	23
17	Cleveland	28	34	St. Louis	30
10	Green Bay (M)	20	17	New Orleans	26
49	*St. Louis	6	29	*Washington	34
21	Pittsburgh	17	3	*Atlanta	27
27	*Cleveland	14	13	San Francisco	14
264		298	279		377

*Home Game
(M) Milwaukee

PITTSBURGH (1–13)			ST. LOUIS (4–9–1)		
16	*Detroit	13	3	Dallas	24
27	Philadelphia	41	20	*Chicago	17
14	*St. Louis	27	27	Pittsburgh	14
7	New York	10	17	Washington	33
31	Cleveland	42	10	*Minnesota	27
7	*Washington	14	21	Cleveland	21
34	*Green Bay	38	42	*New Orleans	51
7	Chicago	38	42	*New York	17
3	*Cleveland	24	0	Detroit	20
14	Minnesota	52	30	*Philadelphia	34
10	St. Louis	47	47	*Pittsburgh	10
7	*Dallas	10	6	New York	49
17	*New York	21	21	*Cleveland	27
24	New Orleans	27	28	Green Bay	45
218		404	314		389

SAN FRANCISCO (4–8–2)			WASHINGTON (7–5–2)		
12	Atlanta	24	26	New Orleans	20
7	Green Bay (M)	14	23	Cleveland	27
17	*Washington	17	17	San Francisco	17
21	*Los Angeles	27	33	*St. Louis	17
7	*Atlanta	21	20	*New York	14
24	Baltimore	21	14	Pittsburgh	7
14	*Detroit	26	17	Baltimore	41
30	Los Angeles	41	28	*Philadelphia	28
20	*Baltimore	17	28	*Dallas	41
38	New Orleans	43	27	*Atlanta	20
24	Dallas	24	13	*Los Angeles	24
42	*Chicago	21	34	Philadelphia	29
7	Minnesota	10	17	*New Orleans	14
14	*Philadelphia	13	10	Dallas	20
277		319	307		319

*Home Game

Alvin Haymond, great return specialist, in action against the Vikings.

All-Pro Gale Sayers (40) comes back after knee surgery.

Jan Stenerud (3), with Len Dawson holding, leads the Chiefs to victory.

AFL 1969 PRE-SEASON RECAP

Eastern Division

	W	L	T	Pct.	Pts.	O.P.
Houston	3	2	0	.600	113	85
*New York	3	3	0	.500	108	121
Boston	2	3	0	.400	72	92
Buffalo	1	5	0	.167	83	158
Miami	1	5	0	.167	74	126

*—Includes victory over College All-Stars

Western Division

	W	L	T	Pct.	Pts.	O.P.
Kansas City	6	0	0	1.000	171	82
Cincinnati	3	2	0	.600	84	89
San Diego	2	2	1	.500	59	83
Oakland	2	3	0	.400	120	101
Denver	1	4	0	.200	68	108

TEAM VS. TEAM

BOSTON (2–3–0)
21	Cincinnati	13
16	Atlanta (NFL)	34
9	Detroit (NFL)	22
26	Denver	10
0	Miami	13
72		92

BUFFALO (1–5–0)
7	Houston	24
21	Washington (NFL)	17
12	Detroit (NFL)	24
7	Baltimore (NFL)	20
16	Chicago (NFL)	23
20	Los Angeles (NFL)	50
83		158

CINCINNATI (3–2–0)
13	Boston	21
7	Kansas City	23
28	Miami	21
23	Pittsburgh (NFL)	13
13	Denver	11
84		89

DENVER (1–4–0)
6	Minnesota (NFL)	26
22	New Orleans (NFL)	28
19	San Francisco (NFL)	15
10	Boston	26
11	Cincinnati	13
68		108

HOUSTON (3–2–0)
24	Buffalo	7
29	Baltimore (NFL)	33
19	Chicago (NFL)	17
11	Dallas (NFL)	14
30	New Orleans (NFL)	14
113		85

KANSAS CITY (6–0–0)
23	Oakland	17
38	Detroit (NFL)	13
23	Cincinnati	7
42	Los Angeles (NFL)	14
31	St. Louis (NFL)	21
14	Atlanta (NFL)	10
171		82

MIAMI (1–5–0)
10	Minnesota (NFL)	45
10	Chicago (NFL)	16
10	Philadelphia (NFL)	14
21	Cincinnati	28
10	Baltimore (NFL)	23
13	Boston	0
74		126

NEW YORK (3–3–0)
26	College All-Stars	24
6	St. Louis (NFL)	13
37	New York (NFL)	14
6	Oakland	24
24	Minnesota (NFL)	21
9	Dallas (NFL)	25
108		121

OAKLAND (2–3–0)
17	Kansas City	23
30	Baltimore (NFL)	34
7	San Diego	10
24	New York	6
42	San Francisco	28
120		101

SAN DIEGO (2–2–1)
6	Baltimore (NFL)	26
10	New Orleans (NFL)	7
10	Oakland	7
19	Cleveland (NFL)	19
14	Los Angeles (NFL)	24
59		83

Mike Garrett tackled by Dave Grayson during AFL Championship.

1969 STATISTICS
AFL FINAL STANDINGS

EASTERN DIVISION

	W	L	T	Pct.	Pts.	O.P.
New York	10	4	0	.714	353	269
Houston	6	6	2	.500	278	279
Boston	4	10	0	.286	266	316
Buffalo	4	10	0	.286	230	359
Miami	3	10	1	.231	233	332

WESTERN DIVISION

	W	L	T	Pct.	Pts.	O.P.
Oakland	12	1	1	.923	377	242
Kansas City	11	3	0	.786	359	177
San Diego	8	6	0	.571	288	276
Denver	5	8	1	.385	297	344
Cincinnati	4	9	1	.308	280	367

INTER-DIVISIONAL PLAYOFFS

Kansas City 13, New York 6
Oakland 56, Houston 7

AFL CHAMPIONSHIP GAME

Kansas City 17, Oakland 7

AFL-NFL CHAMPIONSHIP GAME

Kansas City (AFL) 23, Minnesota (NFL) 7

AFL ALL-STAR GAME

West 26, East 3

Purple people eater Carl Eller (81) goes after morsel Jerry Rhome.

OFFENSE

	Bos.	Buff.	Cin.	Den.	Hou.	K.C.	Miami	N.Y.	Oak.	S.D.	Total	Lg. Avg.
First Downs	166	224	172	243	256	258	224	252	261	275	2331	233.1
Rushing	64	83	66	87	95	129	73	98	84	119	898	89.8
Passing	87	122	95	130	146	125	131	130	153	131	1250	125.0
Penalty	15	19	11	26	15	4	20	24	24	25	183	18.3
Rushes	367	384	363	394	440	522	401	469	459	455	4254	425.4
Yds. Gained (Net)	1489	1522	1523	1637	1706	2220	1513	1782	1765	1985	17,142	1714.2
Avg. Gain	4.1	4.0	4.2	4.2	3.9	4.3	3.8	3.8	3.8	4.4	—	4.0
Passes Att.	338	442	308	403	489	351	424	394	439	444	4032	403.2
Completed	162	215	163	192	239	196	201	203	227	208	2006	200.6
% Completed	47.9	48.6	52.9	47.6	48.9	55.8	47.4	51.5	51.7	46.8	—	49.8
Tot. Yds. Gained	2191	2716	2720	2835	3147	2638	2558	2939	3375	2927	28,046	2804.6
Passer Tackled	24	42	57	44	36	26	53	16	12	33	343	34.3
Yds. Lost	261	371	375	311	322	251	481	138	104	301	2915	291.5
Net Yds. Gained	1930	2345	2345	2524	2825	2387	2077	2801	3271	2626	25,131	2513.1
Yards Gained (Net) per Pass Play	5.33	4.85	6.42	5.65	5.38	6.33	4.35	6.83	7.25	5.51	—	5.74
Yds. Gained per Comp.	13.52	12.63	16.69	14.77	13.17	13.46	12.73	14.48	14.87	14.07	—	13.98
Net Yards Gained												
Rushing and Passing	3419	3867	3868	4161	4531	4607	3590	4583	5036	4611	42,273	4227.3
% Tot. Yds.—Rushing	43.56	39.35	39.37	39.34	37.65	48.19	42.14	38.88	35.05	43.05	—	40.55
% Tot. Yds.—Passing	56.44	60.65	60.63	60.66	62.35	51.81	57.86	61.12	64.95	56.95	—	59.45
Ball Control Plays	729	868	728	841	965	899	878	879	910	932	8629	862.9
Avg. Gain (Net)	4.7	4.5	5.3	4.9	4.7	5.1	4.1	5.2	5.5	4.9	—	4.9
Interceptions												
Had Intercepted	18	30	15	23	31	20	29	20	26	21	233	23.3
Yds. Opp. Ret.	225	449	239	421	441	325	596	380	349	265	3690	369.0
Ret. by Opp. for TD	1	2	0	4	3	3	3	2	1	0	19	1.9

	Bos.	Buff.	Cin.	Den.	Hou.	K.C.	Miami	N.Y.	Oak.	S.D.	Total	Lg. Avg.
Punts	70	78	85	72	70	68	85	56	69	71	724	72.4
Yds. Punted	2903	3471	3295	2889	2722	3022	3451	2482	2944	3169	30,348	3034.8
Avg. Yds. per Punt	41.5	44.5	38.8	40.1	38.9	44.4	40.6	44.3	42.7	44.6	—	41.9
Punt Returns	23	31	23	37	43	32	45	39	39	31	343	34.3
Yds. Returned	212	187	135	450	391	251	266	256	225	300	2673	267.3
Avg. Yds. per Return	9.2	6.0	5.9	12.2	9.1	7.8	5.9	6.6	5.8	9.7		7.8
Ret. for TD	0	0	0	0	0	0	0	0	0	0	0	0.0
Kickoff Returns	54	62	55	56	49	41	60	46	42	39	504	50.4
Yds. Returned	1247	1475	1165	1323	1141	1090	1383	985	996	842	11,647	1164.7
Avg. Yds. per Return	23.1	23.8	21.2	23.6	23.3	26.6	23.1	21.4	23.7	21.6	—	23.1
Ret. for TD	0	0	0	0	0	1	1	0	0	0	2	0.2
Penalties	77	67	50	80	70	62	53	61	100	63	683	68.3
Yds. Penalized	837	632	556	753	730	757	631	725	1274	731	7626	762.6
Fumbles	15	35	30	15	24	34	27	19	17	27	243	24.3
Own Rec.	5	14	5	6	5	12	13	4	0	14	88	8.8
TDs on Own Rec.	0	0	0	0	0	0	1	0	0	0	1	0.1
Opp. Rec.	14	18	15	14	17	15	13	16	16	6	144	14.4
Opp. Rec. for TD	1	1	0	0	2	2	0	0	1	1	8	0.8
Total Points Scored	266	230	280	297	278	359	233	353	377	288	2961	296.1
Touchdowns (Total)	32	26	33	37	31	40	28	37	45	35	344	34.4
TDs Rushing	11	7	10	12	12	19	12	14	4	18	119	11.9
TDs Passing	19	17	22	23	15	16	12	21	36	13	194	19.4
TDs on Ret. and Rec.	2	2	1	2	4	5	4	2	5	4	31	3.1
*Extra Points	28	23	32	36	33	38	26	35	45	33	329	32.9
Safeties	2	0	1	0	1	0	0	0	1	0	5	0.5
Field Goals	14	17	16	13	19	27	13	32	20	15	186	18.6
F. G. Att.	34	26	24	29	40	35	22	47	37	28	322	32.2
%Successful	41.2	65.4	66.7	44.8	47.5	77.1	59.1	68.1	54.1	53.6	—	57.8

*Includes 2-pt. conversions.

DEFENSE

	Bos.	Buff.	Cin.	Den.	Hou.	K.C.	Miami	N.Y.	Oak.	S.D.	Total	Lg. Avg.
First Downs	278	236	278	276	183	181	206	229	232	232	2331	233.1
Rushing	142	106	135	95	77	53	66	63	90	71	898	89.8
Passing	115	118	130	151	93	111	126	151	107	148	1250	125.0
Penalty	21	12	13	30	13	17	14	15	35	13	183	18.3
Rushes	528	454	523	436	430	314	422	343	438	366	4254	425.4
Yds. Gained (Net)	2359	1858	2651	1709	1556	1091	1489	1326	1661	1442	17,142	1714.2
Avg. Gain	4.5	4.1	5.1	3.9	3.6	3.5	3.5	3.9	3.8	3.9	—	4.0
Passes Att.	348	368	396	437	371	426	404	437	422	423	4032	403.2
Completed	203	175	205	223	167	200	196	232	164	241	2006	200.6
% Completed	58.3	47.6	51.8	51.0	45.0	46.9	48.5	53.1	38.9	57.0	49.8	49.8
Tot. Yds. Gained	2610	2772	2866	3295	2495	2491	2845	3086	2511	3075	28,046	2804.6
Passer Tackled	22	31	16	45	32	48	25	42	47	35	343	34.3
Yds. Lost	159	296	180	363	278	419	208	330	402	280	2915	291.5
Net Yds. Gained	2451	2476	2686	2932	2217	2072	2637	2756	2109	2795	25,131	2513.1
Yards Gained (Net)												
per Pass Play	6.62	6.21	6.52	6.08	5.50	4.37	6.15	5.75	4.50	6.10	—	5.74
Yds. Gained per Comp.	12.86	15.84	13.98	14.78	14.94	12.46	14.52	13.30	15.31	12.76	—	13.98
Net Yards Gained												
Rushing and Passing	4810	4334	5337	4641	3773	3163	4126	4082	3770	4237	42,273	4227.3
% Tot. Yds.—Rushing	49.04	42.87	49.67	36.82	41.24	34.49	36.09	32.48	44.06	34.03	—	40.55
% Tot. Yds.—Passing	50.96	57.13	50.33	63.18	58.76	65.51	63.91	67.52	55.94	65.97	—	59.45
Ball Control Plays	898	853	935	918	833	788	851	822	907	824	8629	862.9
Avg. Gain (Net)	5.4	5.1	5.7	5.1	4.5	4.0	4.8	5.0	4.2	5.1	—	4.9
Interceptions												
Intercepted By	20	19	21	14	23	32	18	29	26	31	233	23.3
Yds. Returned	326	251	362	228	335	595	317	348	484	444	3690	369.0
Ret. for TD	1	1	1	2	2	2	2	1	4	3	19	1.9

	Bos.	Buff.	Cin.	Den.	Hou.	K.C.	Miami	N.Y.	Oak.	S.D.	Total	Lg. Avg.
Punts	55	62	55	71	85	84	80	69	87	76	724	72.4
Yds. Punted	2123	2647	2275	3059	3660	3612	3526	2748	3639	3059	30,348	3034.8
Avg. Yds. per Punt	38.6	42.7	41.4	43.1	43.1	43.0	44.1	39.8	41.8	40.3	—	41.9
Punt Returns	19	45	39	35	37	43	30	28	37	30	343	34.3
Yds. Returned	114	466	297	246	196	502	130	280	151	291	2673	267.3
Avg. Yds. per Return	6.0	10.4	7.6	7.0	5.3	11.7	4.3	10.0	4.1	9.7	—	7.8
Ret. for TD	0	0	0	0	0	0	0	0	0	0	0	0.0
Kickoff Returns	56	55	39	21	38	59	47	72	64	53	504	50.4
Yds. Returned	1068	1322	1065	471	792	1431	1073	1669	1518	1238	11,647	1164.7
Avg. Yds. per Return	19.1	24.0	27.3	22.4	20.8	24.3	22.8	23.2	23.7	23.4	—	23.1
Ret. for TD	0	0	1	1	0	0	0	0	0	0	2	0.2
Penalties	69	71	72	84	61	39	66	69	81	71	683	68.3
Yds. Penalized	810	719	824	901	592	443	840	788	918	791	7626	762.6
Fumbles	33	25	19	24	27	25	27	25	25	13	243	24.3
Own Rec.	18	0	3	0	9	0	12	9	8	6	88	8.8
TDs on Own Rec.	1	0	0	0	0	0	0	0	0	0	1	0.1
Opp. Rec.	10	21	23	8	17	19	13	13	7	13	144	14.4
Opp. Rec. for TD	0	0	3	1	2	0	0	1	0	1	8	0.8
Total Points Scored	316	359	367	344	279	177	332	269	242	276	2961	296.1
Touchdowns (Total)	38	40	42	40	33	19	37	32	29	34	344	34.4
TDs Rushing	18	17	13	15	10	6	9	7	13	11	119	11.9
TDs Passing	18	21	24	19	18	10	25	22	15	22	194	19.4
TDs on Ret. and Rec.	2	2	5	6	5	3	3	3	1	1	31	3.1
*Extra Points	37	39	41	38	33	16	34	32	26	33	329	32.9
Safeties	0	0	1	0	0	2	2	0	0	0	5	0.5
Field Goals	17	26	24	22	16	15	24	15	14	13	186	18.6
F. G. Att.	28	41	46	32	30	27	36	27	30	25	322	32.2
% Successful	60.7	63.4	52.2	68.8	53.3	55.6	66.7	55.6	46.7	52.0	—	57.8

*Includes 2-pt. conversions.

RUSHING

TEAM CHAMPION—The Kansas City Chiefs, who gained 2,220 yards in winning the title for the third time in four years. The record is 2,480 by the Buffalo Bills in 1962.

INDIVIDUAL CHAMPION—Dick Post of the San Diego Chargers with 873 yards. The record was set by Jim Nance of Boston in 1966 with 1,458 yards gained. Nance finished runner-up to Post with 750; 1968 champion Paul Robinson of Cincinnati was 16th with 489.

BEST AVERAGE—Rookie Carl Garrett of Boston with a 5.04-yard average that edged Floyd Little of Denver. The record is 6.45 by Keith Lincoln of San Diego in 1963.

MOST TOUCHDOWNS—Jim Kiick of Miami with 9, two more than Warren McVea of Kansas City. The record for touchdowns rushing is 13 by Cookie Gilchrist of Buffalo and Abner Haynes of Dallas, both in 1962.

MOST ATTEMPTS—Jim Nance of Boston with 193. Nance holds the record, 299, set in 1966.

BEST ONE GAME PERFORMANCE—Floyd Little of Denver vs. Cincinnati, October 19. He gained 166 yards in 29 carries in a 30–23 victory. The record is 243 yards by Cookie Gilchrist of Buffalo in 1963.

LONGEST RUN—Jesse Phillips, of Cincinnati, 83 yards vs Oakland, November 2, in a game which Cincinnati won 31–17.

TEAM LEADERS—Boston, Jim Nance, 750 yards; Buffalo, O. J. Simpson, 697; Cincinnati, Jesse Phillips, 578; Denver, Floyd Little, 729; Houston, Hoyle Granger, 740; Kansas City, Mike Garrett, 732; Miami, Jim Kiick, 575; New York, Matt Snell, 695; Oakland, Charlie Smith, 600; San Diego, Dick Post, 873.

1969 RUSHING—TEAM

	Atts.	Net Yds. Gained	Avg.	Long. Gain	Tds.
†Kansas City	*522	*2220	4.3	t80	*19
San Diego	455	1985	*4.4	60	18
New York	469	1782	3.8	50	14
Oakland	459	1765	3.8	51	4
Houston	440	1706	3.9	t43	12
Denver	394	1637	4.2	54	12
Cincinnati	363	1523	4.2	*83	10
Buffalo	384	1522	4.0	72	7
Miami	401	1513	3.8	54	12
Boston	367	1489	4.1	t80	11
League Total	4254	17142	..	83	119
League Average	425.4	1714.2	4.0	..	11.9

*—High for 1969
†—1968 Leader
t—Touchdown

1969 RUSHING—INDIVIDUAL

	Atts.	Yards	Avg.	Long.	Tds.
POST, S.D.	182	*873	4.8	60	6
Nance, Bos.	*193	750	3.9	43	6
Granger, Hou.	186	740	4.0	23	3
Garrett, K.C.	168	732	4.4	t34	6
Little, Den.	146	729	*5.0	t48	6
Simpson, Buff.	181	697	3.9	t32	2

1969 RUSHING—INDIVIDUAL (Cont'd)

	Atts.	Yards	Avg.	Long.	Tds.
Snell, N.Y.	191	695	3.6	34	4
Garrett, Bos.	137	691	*5.0	t80	5
Holmes, K.C.	150	612	4.1	25	2
Boozer, N.Y.	130	604	4.6	50	4
Smith, Oak.	177	600	3.4	26	2
Phillips, Cin.	118	578	4.9	*83	3
Kiick, Mia.	180	575	3.2	27	*9
Csonka, Mia.	131	566	4.3	t54	2
McVea, K.C.	106	500	4.7	t80	7
†Robinson, Cin.	160	489	3.1	24	4
Hopkins, Hou.	131	473	3.6	t43	4
Lynch, Den.	96	407	4.2	54	2
Dixon, Oak.	107	398	3.7	19	0
Banaszak, Oak.	88	377	4.3	40	0
Patrick, Buff.	83	361	4.3	72	3
Mathis, N.Y.	96	355	3.7	27	4
Hubbert, S.D.	94	333	3.5	24	4
Foster, S.D.	64	236	3.7	24	0
Smith, S.D.	51	211	4.1	16	2
Hayes, K.C.	62	208	3.4	11	4
Todd, Oak.	47	198	4.2	51	1
Enyart, Buff.	47	191	4.1	26	1
Quayle, Den.	57	183	3.2	17	0
Smiley, Den.	56	166	3.0	26	3
Cook, Cin.	25	148	5.9	30	1
Burrell, Hou.	41	147	3.6	19	0
Domres, S.D.	19	145	7.6	22	4
Kemp, Buff.	37	124	3.4	13	0
Hubbard, Oak.	21	119	5.7	18	0
Morris, Mia.	23	110	4.8	37	1
Hadl, S.D.	26	109	4.2	17	2
Wyche, Cin.	12	107	8.9	22	1
Turner, Cin.	23	105	4.6	34	0
Livingston, K.C.	15	102	6.8	39	0
Griese, Mia.	21	102	4.9	22	0
Campbell, Hou.	28	98	3.5	10	1
Beathard, Hou.	19	89	4.7	16	2
White, N.Y.	28	88	3.1	10	0
Mitchell, Mia.	28	80	2.9	12	0
Anderson, Buff.	13	74	5.7	16	1
Tensi, Den.	12	63	5.3	17	0
Milton, Mia.	7	62	8.9	27	0
E. Johnson, Cin.	15	54	3.6	13	0
Sayers, S.D.	14	53	3.8	8	0
Richardson, Hou.	5	51	10.2	28	0
Liske, Den.	10	50	5.0	19	0
Johnson, Hou.	11	42	3.8	9	0
Lamonica, Oak.	13	36	2.8	12	1
Gamble, Bos.	16	35	2.2	9	0
Lowe, K.C.	10	33	3.3	18	0
Namath, N.Y.	11	33	3.0	16	2
Blanks, Bos.	7	30	4.3	12	0
Pitts, K.C.	5	28	5.6	11	0
Ridlehuber, Buff.	4	25	6.3	11	0
Alworth, S.D.	5	25	5.0	16	0
Trull, Hou.	8	25	3.1	7	2
Harris, Buff.	10	25	2.5	9	0
Wells, Oak.	3	24	8.0	17	0
Haik, Hou.	2	21	10.5	11	0
Livingston, Cin.	1	18	18.0	18	0

	Atts.	Yards	Avg.	Long.	Tds.
Levias, Hou.	6	18	3.0	10	0
Williams, Den.	10	18	1.8	8	1
Thomas, Cin.	4	16	4.0	t16	1
Norton, Mia.	8	16	2.0	9	0
Sherman, Buff.	2	14	7.0	10	0
Darragh, Buff.	6	14	2.3	8	0
Woodall, N.Y.	4	13	3.3	14	0
Eischeid, Oak.	1	10	10.0	10	0
Denson, Den.	1	9	9.0	9	0
Burnett, Den.	5	9	1.8	5	0
Lamb, Cin.	5	8	1.6	7	0
Hines, Mia.	1	7	7.0	7	0
Seiple, Mia.	1	6	6.0	6	0
Sauer, N.Y.	1	5	5.0	5	0
Parilli, N.Y.	3	4	1.3	2	0
Dawson, K.C.	1	3	3.0	3	0
Hagberg, Oak.	1	3	3.0	3	0
Jones, Den.	1	3	3.0	3	0
Lee, K.C.	1	3	3.0	3	0
Davis, Hou.	3	2	0.7	4	0
Arbanas, K.C.	1	1	1.0	1	0
Blanda, Oak.	1	0	0.0	0	0
Flores, K.C.	1	0	0.0	0	0
Frazier, Bos.	2	—1	—0.5	9	0
Taylor, K.C.	2	—2	—1.0	10	0
Masters, Buff.	1	—3	—3.0	—3	0
B. Turner, N.Y.	1	—4	—4.0	—4	0
Nock, N.Y.	3	—5	—1.7	4	0
Maynard, N.Y.	1	—6	—6.0	—6	0
Noonan, Mia.	1	—11	—11.0	—11	0
Taliaferro, Bos.	12	—16	—1.3	4	0

*—High for 1969
†—1968 Leader
t—Touchdown

KICKOFF RETURNS

TEAM CHAMPION—Kansas City replaced Houston as team champion with 26.6 average on 41 returns for 1,090 yards. Houston led in 1968 with a 23.3 average on 53 returns for 1,235 yards.

INDIVIDUAL CHAMPION—Bill Thompson, Denver rookie, topped Boston's Carl Garrett, another first-year performer, by 28.5 to 28.3. Thompson has 18 returns for 513 yards. The 1968 leader was George Atkinson of Oakland with 32 returns for 802 yards and a 25.1 average. The record is 31.3 yards by Ken Hall of Houston in 1960.

MOST YARDS—Eugene Morris of Miami led with 1,136 on 43 returns. The 1968 leader was Max Anderson of Buffalo with 971 yards on 39 returns. The record is 1,317 by Bobby Jancik of Houston on 45 returns in 1963.

MOST RETURNS—Eugene Morris' 43 returns were 4 less than the record by Odell Barry of Denver in 1964.

LONGEST RETURN—Eugene Morris, 105 yards for a touchdown in a 27–21 loss to Cincinnati, September 14. The record is 106 by Noland Smith of Kansas City against Denver in 1967.

1969 KICKOFF RETURNS—TEAM

	No.	Yds. Ret.	Avg. Ret.	Long.	Tds.
Kansas City	41	1090	*26.6	t53	*1
Buffalo	*62	*1475	23.8	73	0
Oakland	42	996	23.7	41	0
Denver	56	1323	23.6	63	0
†Houston	49	1141	23.3	87	0
Boston	54	1247	23.1	63	0
Miami	60	1383	23.1	*t105	*1
San Diego	39	842	21.6	52	0
New York	46	985	21.4	45	0
Cincinnati	55	1165	21.2	74	0
League Total	504	11647	—	t105	2
League Average	50.4	1164.7	23.1	—	0.2

*—High for 1969
†—1968 Leader
t—Touchdown
NOTE: Standing based on average return.

1969 KICKOFF RETURNS—INDIVIDUAL

	Stdg.	No.	Yds.	Avg.	Long.	Tds.
THOMPSON, DEN.	1	18	513	*28.5	63	0
Garrett, Bos.	2	28	792	28.3	63	0
Duncan, S.D.	3	21	587	28.0	52	0
Morris, Mia.	4	*43	*1136	26.4	*t105	*1
Simpson, Buff.	5	21	529	25.2	73	0
Thornton, Buff.	6	30	749	25.0	58	0
Williams, Den.	7	23	574	25.0	38	0
Levias, Hou.	8	38	940	24.7	87	0
Battle, N.Y.	9	31	750	24.2	45	0
†Atkinson, Oak.	10	16	382	23.9	39	0
Riley, Cin.	11	14	334	23.9	40	0
E. Johnson, Cin.	12	16	362	22.6	51	0
McVea, K.C.	—	13	318	24.5	40	0
Sherman, Oak.	—	12	300	25.0	31	0
Smith, Oak.	—	10	247	24.7	41	0
Guillory, Cin.	—	8	170	21.3	28	0
Milton, Mia.	—	8	166	20.8	37	0
Mitchell, K.C.	—	7	178	25.4	36	0
Podolak, K.C.	—	7	165	23.6	28	0
Leonard, N.Y.	—	7	120	17.1	23	0
Smith, S.D.	—	6	138	23.0	27	0
Marsh, Bos.	—	6	136	22.7	41	0
Blanks, Bos.	—	6	131	21.8	25	0
Burrell, Den.	—	6	108	18.0	30	0
Scott, Bos.	—	6	43	7.2	14	0
Robinson, Cin.	—	5	168	33.6	74	0
Lowe, K.C.	—	5	116	23.2	30	0
Burrell, Hou.	—	5	101	20.2	32	0
Lamb, Cin.	—	5	64	12.8	19	0
Smith, K.C.	—	4	125	31.3	37	0
Anderson, Buff.	—	4	86	21.5	28	0
Post, S.D.	—	4	74	18.5	27	0
Gladieux, Bos.	—	4	61	15.3	20	0
Beier, Mia.	—	4	58	14.5	17	0
Little, Den.	—	3	81	27.0	30	0
Crawford, Buff.	—	3	74	24.7	31	0
B. Turner, N.Y.	—	3	74	24.7	28	0
Joiner, Hou.	—	3	73	24.3	28	0
Allen, Oak.	—	3	67	22.3	38	0

1969 KICKOFF RETURNS—INDIVIDUAL (Cont'd)

	Stdg.	No.	Yds.	Avg.	Long.	Tds.
Phillips, Cin.	—	3	52	17.3	29	0
Criter, Den.	—	3	31	10.3	14	0
Turner, Cin.	—	3	15	5.0	13	0
Fetherston, S.D.	—	3	0	0.0	0	0
Reed, Hou.	—	3	0	0.0	0	0
Hayes, K.C.	—	2	81	40.5	45	0
Holmes, K.C.	—	2	54	27.0	36	0
Sayers, S.D.	—	2	42	21.0	21	0
Richards, N.Y.	—	2	36	18.0	20	0
Collins, Buff.	—	2	14	7.0	14	0
Mertens, Mia.	—	2	1	0.5	1	0
Bell, K.C.	—	1	53	53.0	t53	*1
Carwell, Bos.	—	1	28	28.0	28	0
Gamble, Bos.	—	1	23	23.0	23	0
Hines, Mia.	—	1	22	22.0	22	0
Berger, Bos.	—	1	20	20.0	20	0
Barnes, Den.	—	1	16	16.0	16	0
Schottenheimer, Bos.	—	1	13	13.0	13	0
Enyart, Buff.	—	1	12	12.0	12	0
Harvey, Buff.	—	1	11	11.0	11	0
White, N.Y.	—	1	5	5.0	5	0
Foster, S.D.	—	1	1	1.0	1	0
Benson, Oak.	—	1	0	0.0	0	0
Briggs, S.D.	—	1	0	0.0	0	0
Carroll, N.Y.	—	1	0	0.0	0	0
Gunner, Cin.	—	1	0	0.0	0	0
Hollomon, Den.	—	1	0	0.0	0	0
Huey, S.D.	—	1	0	0.0	0	0
Mumphord, Mia.	—	1	0	0.0	0	0
Myrtle, Den.	—	1	0	0.0	0	0
Sauer, N.Y.	—	1	0	0.0	0	0
Warren, Mia.	—	1	0	0.0	0	0
Houston, Hou.	—	0	27L	—	20	0
James, Buff.	—	0	0L	—	0	0

*—High for 1969
†—1968 Leader
t —Touchdown
L—Lateral
NOTE: Standing based on average return. To qualify for championship
rating a player must return at least 14 kickoffs.

PASS RECEIVING

INDIVIDUAL CHAMPION—Lance Alworth of San Diego repeated with 64 receptions, compared with his 68 in 1968. The record is 101 by Charley Hennigan of Houston in 1964.

MOST YARDS GAINED—Warren Wells of Oakland with 1,260. Alworth was the 1968 leader with 1,312. The record is 1,746 by Charley Hennigan of Houston in 1961. Alworth was the only other receiver to top 1,000 yards with 1,003. Don Maynard of New York had 938 to boost his all-pro record to 10,373.

MOST TOUCHDOWNS—Warren Wells with 14, two more than teammate Fred Biletnikoff. Wells shared the 1968 lead with Karl Noonan of Miami with 11. The record is 17 by Bill Groman of Houston in 1961.

HIGHEST AVERAGE GAIN—Warren Wells with 26.8 on 47 receptions. Don Maynard led in 1968 with 22.8 yards on 57 receptions.

BEST ONE GAME PERFORMANCE—Gary Garrison of San Diego with 10 receptions for 188 yards and two touchdowns against New York, September 28 in a 34–27 victory. Don Maynard was the only receiver to top 200 yards in one game (7 for 212 and 2 touchdowns) against Houston, October 20. The record number of receptions for one game is 13 by Charley Hennigan of Houston in 1961, Alworth in 1963 and Lionel Taylor of Denver and Sid Blanks of Houston in 1964.

LONGEST RECEPTION—Jerry Levias of Houston, 86 yards for a touchdown from Pete Beathard against Denver, November 16, in a 20–20 tie. The record is 98 yards by Willard Dewveall of Houston, from Jacky Lee, in 1962.

TEAM LEADERS—Boston, Carl Garrett, Jim Nance, 29 receptions; Buffalo, Haven Moses, 39; Cincinnati, Eric Crabtree, 40; Denver, Al Denson, 53; Houston, Alvin Reed, 51; Kansas City, Mike Garrett, 43; Miami, Larry Seiple, 41; New York, Don Maynard, 47; Oakland, Fred Biletnikoff, 54; San Diego, Lance Alworth, 64.

1969 PASS RECEIVING—INDIVIDUAL

	No.	Yards	Avg.	Long.	Tds.
†ALWORTH, S.D.	*64	1003	15.7	t76	4
Biletnikoff, Oak.	54	837	15.5	t53	12
Denson, Den.	53	809	15.3	t62	10
Reed, Hou.	51	664	13.0	t43	2
Wells, Oak.	47	*1260	*26.8	t80	*14
Maynard, N.Y.	47	938	20.0	t60	6
Sauer, N.Y.	45	745	16.6	t40	8
Garrett, K.C.	43	432	10.0	41	2
Levias, Hou.	42	696	16.6	*t86	5
Beirne, Hou.	42	540	12.9	t37	4
Taylor, K.C.	41	696	17.0	79	7
Seiple, Mia.	41	577	14.1	t41	5
Crabtree, Cin.	40	855	21.4	t73	7
Garrison, S.D.	40	804	20.1	50	7
Moses, Buff.	39	752	19.3	t55	5
Trumpy, Cin.	37	835	22.6	t80	9
Haffner, Den.	35	563	16.1	46	5
Patrick, Buff.	35	229	6.5	19	0
Thomas, Cin.	33	481	14.6	62	3
Lammons, N.Y.	33	400	12.1	25	2
Masters, Buff.	33	387	11.7	31	1
Dixon, Oak.	33	275	8.3	t37	1
Briscoe, Buff.	32	532	16.6	t50	5

	No.	Yards	Avg.	Long.	Tds.
Pitts, K.C.	31	470	15.2	51	2
Simpson, Buff.	30	343	11.4	t55	3
Smith, Oak.	30	322	10.7	32	2
Embree, Den.	29	469	16.2	t79	5
Kiick, Mia.	29	443	15.3	t53	1
Hopkins, Hou.	29	338	11.7	56	1
Noonan, Mia.	29	307	10.6	27	3
Garrett, Bos.	29	267	9.2	34	2
Nance, Bos.	29	168	5.8	27	0
Sellers, Bos.	27	705	26.1	77	6
Haik, Hou.	27	375	13.9	42	1
Granger, Hou.	27	330	12.2	53	1
Holmes, K.C.	26	266	10.2	t33	3
Post, S.D.	24	235	9.8	46	0
Richardson, K.C.	23	381	16.6	39	2
Snell, N.Y.	22	187	8.5	54	1
Clancy, Mia.	21	289	13.8	50	1
Cannon, Oak.	21	262	12.5	t53	2
Csonka, Mia.	21	183	8.7	42	1
Boozer, N.Y.	20	222	11.1	29	0
Robinson, Cin.	20	104	5.2	25	0
Frazier, Bos.	19	306	16.1	t50	7
Little, Den.	19	218	11.5	t67	1
Enyart, Buff.	19	186	9.8	t32	2
Mathis, N.Y.	18	183	10.2	35	1
Rademacher, Bos.	17	217	12.8	40	3
Frazier, S.D.	17	205	12.1	50	0
Banaszak, Oak.	17	119	7.0	19	3
Arbanas, K.C.	16	258	16.1	44	0
Whalen, Bos.	16	235	14.7	47	1
Todd, Oak.	16	149	9.3	t48	1
Thornton, Buff.	14	134	9.6	21	0
Foster, S.D.	14	83	5.9	28	1
Phillips, Cin.	13	128	9.8	31	0
Milton, Mia.	12	179	14.9	49	0
B. Turner, N.Y.	11	221	20.1	t54	3
Quayle, Den.	11	167	15.2	71	0
Hubbert, S.D.	11	43	3.9	18	0
Myers, Cin.	10	205	20.5	50	2
Twilley, Mia.	10	158	15.8	33	1
Queen, S.D.	10	148	14.8	42	0
Smith, S.D.	10	144	14.4	55	0
Mitchell, Mia.	10	125	12.5	34	0
Moreau, Mia.	10	136	13.6	35	0
Beer, Den.	9	200	22.2	48	0
Eber, S.D.	9	141	15.7	43	1
Pivec, Den.	9	117	13.0	18	0
Lynch, Den.	9	86	9.6	19	0
Hayes, K.C.	9	64	7.1	17	0
Marsh, Bos.	8	108	13.5	21	0
Campbell, Hou.	7	82	11.7	37	0
MacKinnon, S.D.	7	82	11.7	23	0
Joiner, Hou.	7	77	11.0	16	0
Gamble, Bos.	7	74	10.6	20	0
McVea, K.C.	7	71	10.1	22	0
Anderson, Buff.	7	65	9.3	22	0
Hagberg, Oak.	6	84	14.0	20	1
Brown, Bos.	6	69	11.5	15	0
Morris, Mia.	6	65	10.8	29	0
Williams, Den.	5	56	11.2	14	0

	No.	Yards	Avg.	Long.	Tds.
Stewart, N.Y.	5	39	7.8	9	0
Burrell, Hou.	5	28	5.6	8	0
Smiley, Den.	5	23	4.6	t17	1
Turner, Cin.	5	14	2.8	8	0
Crockett, Buff.	4	50	12.5	19	0
Buckman, Den.	4	48	12.0	20	1
Boutwell, Mia.	4	29	7.3	12	0
Van Heusen, Den.	3	64	21.3	36	0
Trapp, S.D.	2	39	19.5	24	0
Hubbard, Oak.	2	30	15.0	20	0
Mertens, Mia.	2	26	13.0	15	0
Hines, Mia.	2	23	11.5	22	0
Johnson, Hou.	2	17	8.5	16	1
Blanks, Bos.	2	16	8.0	13	0
Riley, Cin.	2	15	7.5	17	0
Pryor, Mia.	2	−3	−1.5	0	0
T. Smith. Cin.	1	41	41.0	41	0
Coslet, Cin.	1	39	39.0	t39	1
Buie, Oak.	1	37	37.0	37	0
Cappelletti, Bos.	1	21	21.0	21	0
Grate, Buff.	1	19	19.0	t19	1
James, Buff.	1	19	19.0	19	0
Pastrana, Den.	1	15	15.0	15	0
Darnall, Mia.	1	13	13.0	13	0
Anderson, Mia.	1	8	8.0	8	0
Dockery, N.Y.	1	6	6.0	6	0
Richardson, Bos.	1	5	5.0	5	0
E. Johnson, Cin.	1	3	3.0	3	0
White, N.Y.	1	−2	−2.0	−2	0

*—High for 1969
†—1968 Leader
t—Touchdown

PUNTING

TEAM CHAMPION—The San Diego Chargers with 44.6 yards average on 71 punts totaling 3,169 yards. Kansas City led in 1968 with 45.26 yards average on 65 punts totaling 2,942 yards. The record is 45.28 by New York in 1965.

INDIVIDUAL CHAMPION—Dennis Partee of San Diego with 44.6 average on 71 punts for 3,169 yards. Only three-tenths of a yard separated the first four. Jerrel Wilson of Kansas City led in 1968 with a 45.1 average. Wilson set the record with 45.4 in 1965.

LONGEST PUNT—Steve O'Neal of New York, 98 yards against Denver, September 21, a record. Bob Scarpitto of Boston had set the former record in 1968, 87 yards against Denver.

MOST PUNTS—Larry Seiple of Miami, 80. The record of 105 was set by Bob Scarpitto for Denver in 1967.

1969 PUNTING—TEAM

	No.	Yards	Avg. Dist.	Long.	Blkd.
San Diego	71	3169	*44.6	62	0
Buffalo	78	*3471	44.5	78	1
†Kansas City	68	3022	44.4	62	0
New York	56	2482	44.3	*98	0
Oakland	69	2944	42.7	58	0
Boston	70	2903	41.5	56	0
Miami	*85	3451	40.6	66	*2
Denver	72	2889	40.1	61	1
Houston	70	2722	38.9	70	0
Cincinnati	*85	3295	38.8	55	*2
League Total	724	30,348	—	98	6
League Average	72.4	3034.8	41.9	—	0.6

*—High for 1969
†—1968 Leader
NOTE: Standing based on average distance.

1969 PUNTING—INDIVIDUAL

	Stdg.	No.	Yards	Avg. Dist.	Long.	Blkd.
PARTEE, S.D.	1	71	3169	*44.6	62	0
Maguire, Buff.	2	78	*3471	44.5	78	1
†Wilson, K.C.	3	68	3022	44.4	62	0
O'Neal, N.Y.	4	54	2393	44.3	*98	0
Eischeid, Oak.	5	69	2944	42.7	58	0
Janik, Bos.	6	70	2903	41.5	56	0
Seiple, Mia.	7	*80	3263	40.8	66	2
Gerela, Hou.	8	41	1656	40.4	70	0
Hollomon, Den.	9	47	1868	39.7	57	1
Livingston, Cin.	10	70	2769	39.6	55	1
Burrell, Hou.	—	29	1066	36.8	56	0
Van Heusen, Den.	—	25	1021	40.8	61	0
Swanson, Cin.	—	12	459	38.3	55	0
Anderson, Mia.	—	5	188	37.6	49	0
B. Turner, N.Y.	—	2	89	44.5	46	0
Muhlmann, Cin.	—	2	38	19.0	38	1
Lamb, Cin.	—	1	29	29.0	29	0

*—High for 1969
†—1968 Leader
NOTE: Standing based on average distance. To qualify for championship rating a player must punt at least 35 times.

INTERCEPTIONS

TEAM CHAMPION—Kansas City with 32, champions for the fourth straight year. The record is 49 by San Diego in 1961. Kansas City also led in yardage (595) and shared with Oakland the lead in average return (18.6). Oakland led with 4 touchdown returns.

INDIVIDUAL CHAMPION—Emmitt Thomas of Kansas City with 9, one more than teammate Johnny Robinson and Dave Grayson of Oakland, who led in 1968 with 10. The record is 12 by Fred Glick of Houston in 1963 and Dainard Paulson of New York in 1964.

MOST TOUCHDOWNS ON INTERCEPTIONS—Kenny Graham of San Diego and Bill Stanfill, rookie lineman from Miami, tied with 2. The record is 3 shared by Miller Farr of Houston, 1967 and Dick Harris of San Diego, 1961. Farr shared the 1968 title with three others at 2.

MOST YARDS RETURNED—Johnny Robinson of Kansas City with 158 yards on 8 returns. Dick Anderson of Miami led with 230 on 8 in 1968. The record is 349 on 9 returns by Charles McNeil of San Diego in 1961.

LONGEST RETURN—Dave Grayson of Oakland, 76 yards against Miami September 20 for a touchdown in a game Oakland won 20–17. Speedy Duncan of San Diego set the record, 100 yards in 1967 against Kansas City, and it was tied by Tom Janik of Buffalo against New York in 1968.

TEAM LEADERS—Boston, Larry Carwell, John Charles, Ed Philpott, all 4; Buffalo, Butch Byrd, 7; Cincinnati, Bill Peterson, Fletcher Smith, Bobby Hunt and Ken Riley, all 4; Denver, Bill Thompson, 3; Houston, Miller Farr, 6; Kansas City, Emmitt Thomas, 9; Miami, Lloyd Mumphord, 5; New York, Bill Baird and John Dockery, 5; Oakland, Dave Grayson, 8; San Diego, Jim Hill, 7.

1969 INTERCEPTIONS—TEAM

	No.	Yds. Ret.	Avg. Ret.	Long.	Tds.
†Kansas City	*32	*595	*18.6	t60	2
San Diego	31	444	14.3	t72	3
New York	29	348	12.0	37	1
Oakland	26	484	*18.6	*t76	*4
Houston	23	335	14.6	t51	2
Cincinnati	21	362	17.2	t70	1
Boston	20	326	16.3	38	1
Buffalo	19	251	13.2	39	1
Miami	18	317	17.6	51	2
Denver	14	228	16.3	t57	2
League Total	233	3690	—	t76	19
League Average	23.3	369.0	15.8	—	1.9

*—High for 1969
†—1968 Leader
t—Touchdown
NOTE: Standing based on most interceptions.

1969 INTERCEPTIONS—INDIVIDUAL

	No.	Yards	Avg.	Long.	Tds.
THOMAS, K.C.	*9	146	16.2	t45	1
Robinson, K.C.	8	*158	19.8	33	0
†Grayson, Oak.	8	132	16.5	*t76	1
Byrd, Buff.	7	95	13.6	32	1
Hill, S.D.	7	92	13.1	42	0
Duncan, S.D.	6	118	19.7	t72	1
Howard, S.D.	6	50	8.3	19	0
Farr, Hou.	6	48	8.0	35	0
Kearney, K.C.	5	143	28.6	t60	1
Brown, Oak.	5	111	22.2	30	0
Mumphord, Mia.	5	102	20.4	51	0
Dockery, N.Y.	5	98	19.6	35	0
Barnes, S.D.	5	64	12.8	25	0
Baird, N.Y.	5	10	2.0	7	0
Carwell, Bos.	4	114	28.5	38	0
Graham, S.D.	4	112	28.0	t65	*2
Houston, Hou.	4	87	21.8	t51	1
Moore, Hou.	4	71	17.8	t51	1
Lanier, K.C.	4	70	17.5	44	0
F. Smith, Cin.	4	67	16.8	29	0
Hunt, Cin.	4	66	16.5	27	0
Riley, Cin.	4	66	16.5	66	0
Charles, Bos.	4	46	11.5	t25	1
Philpott, Bos.	4	37	9.3	16	0
Hicks, Hou.	4	36	9.0	20	0
Gordon, N.Y.	4	23	5.8	20	0
Peterson, Cin.	4	23	5.8	17	0
Anderson, Mia.	3	106	35.3	40	0
Thompson, Den.	3	92	30.7	t57	1
Laskey, Oak.	3	66	22.0	32	0
Crane, N.Y.	3	63	21.0	27	1
Richards, N.Y.	3	48	16.0	37	0
Saimes, Buff.	3	47	15.7	28	0
Buoniconti, Mia.	3	27	9.0	24	0
Lynch, K.C.	3	18	6.0	14	0
Weisacosky, Mia.	3	10	3.3	7	0
Burrell, Den.	2	65	32.5	t38	1
Bergey, Cin.	2	62	31.0	58	0
Peacock, Hou.	2	56	28.0	39	0
Pitts, Buff.	2	40	20.0	38	0
Guidry, Buff.	2	39	19.5	39	0
Atkinson, Oak.	2	38	19.0	t22	1
Beverly, N.Y.	2	37	18.5	37	0
Webster, Hou.	2	35	17.5	26	0
Marsalis, K.C.	2	33	16.5	28	0
Stanfill, Mia.	2	32	16.0	t17	*2
Webb, Bos.	2	32	16.0	32	0
Cavness, Den.	2	30	15.0	29	0
Wilson, Oak.	2	25	12.5	22	0
Johnson, Bos.	2	23	11.5	23	0
Hudson, N.Y.	2	22	11.0	22	0
Huard, Den.	2	18	9.0	18	0
Richardson, Buff.	2	17	8.5	17	0
Greer, Den.	2	13	6.5	13	0
Jacobs, Buff.	2	13	6.5	12	0
Cunningham, Den.	2	10	5.0	5	0
Atkinson, N.Y.	2	4	2.0	4	0
G. Otto, Oak.	2	4	2.0	4	0
Williams, Oak.	2	4	2.0	2	0
Conners, Oak.	1	75	75.0	t75	1

	No.	Yards	Avg.	Long.	Tds.
Gunner, Cin.	1	70	70.0	t70	1
Cheyunski, Bos.	1	37	37.0	37	0
Petrella, Mia.	1	33	33.0	33	0
Oliver, Oak.	1	29	29.0	t29	1
Mitchell, K.C.	1	27	27.0	27	0
Bramlett, Bos.	1	26	26.0	26	0
Battle, N.Y.	1	25	25.0	25	0
Philbin, N.Y.	1	18	18.0	18	0
Beauchamp, Cin.	1	8	8.0	8	0
Janik, Bos.	1	8	8.0	8	0
Beier, Mia.	1	7	7.0	7	0
Bruggers, S.D.	1	5	5.0	5	0
Redman, S.D.	1	3	3.0	3	0
Schottenheimer, Bos.	1	3	3.0	3	0
Underwood, Hou.	1	2	2.0	2	0
Baker, N.Y.	1	0	0.0	0	0
Campbell, S.D.	1	0	0.0	0	0
Edgerson, Buff.	1	0	0.0	0	0
Guillory, Cin.	1	0	0.0	0	0
Hollomon, Den.	1	0	0.0	0	0

*—High for 1969
†—1968 Leader
t—Touchdown

PASSING

TEAM CHAMPION—The Cincinnati Bengals, who led in gain per pass play (8.83), one of the four categories on which the title is based. Leaders in the other contributing categories were Kansas City, percentage of completions, 55.8; Oakland, touchdown passes, 36; and San Diego, percentage of interceptions, 4.7. Oakland netted the greatest yardage, 3,271 and lost the least yards, 104 on the fewest tackles of its passers, 12. Cincinnati had the fewest number of passes intercepted, 15, and had the greatest average gain per completion, 16.69.

INDIVIDUAL CHAMPION—Greg Cook of Cincinnati, the first rookie passer to win the title. He led in one of four title-contributing categories, average yards gained, 9.41. Other category leaders were Daryle Lamonica of Oakland, 34 touchdowns; Len Dawson of Kansas City, percentage of completions, 59.0; and John Hadl, of San Diego, percentage of interceptions, 3.4. Lamonica also was the yardage leader, 3,302, and had the most attempts, 426 and the most completions, 221.

LONGEST COMPLETION—Mike Livingston of Kansas City, 93 yards (Otis Taylor 79 yards, lateral to Robert Holmes 14 yards for touchdown), October 19 against Miami, in 17–10 victory. The record is 98 yards by Jacky Lee of Houston to Willard Dewveall in 1962.

1969 PASSING—TEAM

	Atts.	Comp.	Pct. Comp.	Gross Yards	Yds. Lost	Net Yards	Tds.	Long.	Had Int.	Pct. Int.	Gain per Pass Comp.	Gain per Pass Play
Cincinnati	308	163	52.9	2720	57/375	2345	22	t80	*15	4.9	*16.69	*8.83
Oakland	439	227	51.7	*3375	*12/104*	*3271	*36	t80	26	5.9	14.87	7.69
New York	394	203	51.5	2939	16/138	2801	21	t60	20	5.1	14.48	7.46
†Kansas City	351	196	*55.8	2638	26/251	2387	16	*t93	20	5.7	13.46	7.52
Denver	403	192	47.6	2835	44/311	2524	23	t79	23	5.7	14.77	7.03
Boston	338	162	47.9	2191	24/261	1930	19	77	18	5.3	13.52	6.48
San Diego	444	208	46.8	2927	33/301	2626	13	t86	21	*4.7	14.07	6.59
Houston	*489	*239	48.9	3147	36/322	2825	15	t86	31	6.3	13.17	6.44
Buffalo	442	215	48.6	2716	42/371	2345	17	t55	30	6.8	12.63	6.14
Miami	424	201	47.4	2558	53/481	2077	12	t53	29	6.8	12.73	6.03
League Total	4032	2006	—	28,046	343/2915	25,131	194	t93	233	—	—	—
League Average	403.2	200.6	49.8	2804.6	34.3/291.5	2513.1	19.4	—	23.3	5.8	13.98	5.74

*—High for 1969
†—1968 Leader
t—Touchdown
NOTE: Standing based on percent of completions, touchdown passes, percent of interceptions and average gain per pass play.

82

1969 PASSING—INDIVIDUAL

	Std.	Att.	Com.	Pct. Com.	Yds. Gain	Td.	Lng.	Int.	Pct. Int.	Avg. Gain
COOK, Cin.	1	197	106	53.8	1854	15	t78	11	5.6	*9.41
Namath, N.Y.	2	361	185	51.2	2734	19	t60	17	4.7	7.57
Lamonica, Oak.	3	*426	*221	51.9	*3302	*34	t80	25	5.9	7.75
Livingston, K.C.	4	161	84	52.2	1123	4	*t93	*6	3.7	6.98
Hadl, S.D.	5	324	158	48.8	2253	10	t76	11	*3.4	6.95
†Dawson, K.C.	6	166	98	*59.0	1323	9	t55	13	7.8	7.97
Tensi, Den.	—	286	131	45.8	1990	14	t79	12	4.2	6.96
Beathard, Hou.	8	370	180	48.6	2455	10	t86	21	5.7	6.64
Kemp, Buff.	9	344	170	49.4	1981	13	t55	22	6.4	5.76
Griese, Mia.	10	252	121	48.0	1695	10	t53	16	6.3	6.73
Taliaferro, Bos.	11	331	160	48.3	2160	19	77	18	5.4	6.53
Norton, Mia.	12	148	65	43.9	709	2	29	11	7.4	4.79
Liske, Den.	—	115	61	53.0	845	9	71	11	9.6	7.35
Wyche, Cin.	—	108	54	50.0	838	7	t80	4	3.7	7.76
Domres, S.D.	—	112	47	42.0	631	2	55	10	8.9	5.63
Trull, Hou.	—	75	34	45.3	469	3	57	6	8.0	6.25
Davis, Hou.	—	42	25	59.5	223	2	22	4	9.5	5.31
Darragh, Buff.	—	52	24	46.2	365	1	53	6	11.5	7.02
Harris, Buff.	—	36	15	41.7	270	1	55	1	2.8	7.50
Stofa, Mia.	—	23	14	60.9	146	0	42	2	8.7	6.35
Parilli, N.Y.	—	24	14	58.3	138	2	29	1	4.2	5.75
Lee, K.C.	—	20	12	60.0	109	1	31	1	5.0	5.45
Blanda, Oak.	—	13	6	46.2	73	2	20	1	7.7	5.62
Woodall, N.Y.	—	9	4	44.4	67	0	35	2	22.2	7.44
Flores, Buff.-K.C.	—	6	3	50.0	49	1	t33	0	0.0	8.17
Foster, S.D.	—	5	2	40.0	39	1	t30	0	0.0	7.80
Hammond, Bos.	—	6	2	33.3	31	0	18	0	0.0	5.17
McVea, K.C.	—	3	1	33.3	50	1	t50	0	0.0	16.67
Livingston, Cin.	—	2	2	100.0	15	0	17	0	0.0	7.50
Sherman, Buff.	—	2	2	100.0	20	1	t19	0	0.0	10.00
Gehrke, Cin.	—	1	1	100.0	13	0	13	0	0.0	13.00
Maguire, Buff.	—	1	1	100.0	19	0	19	0	0.0	19.00
Ridlehuber, Buff.	—	1	1	100.0	45	1	t45	0	0.0	45.00
Seiple, Mia.	—	1	1	100.0	8	0	8	0	0.0	8.00
Post, S.D.	—	2	1	50.0	4	0	4	0	0.0	2.00
Briscoe, Buff.	—	1	0	00.0	0	0	0	1	100.0	0.00
Hubbert, S.D.	—	1	0	00.0	0	0	0	0	0.0	0.00
Garrett, Bos.	—	1	0	00.0	0	0	0	0	0.0	0.00
Levias, Hou.	—	2	0	00.0	0	0	0	0	0.0	0.00
Little, Den.	—	2	0	00.0	0	0	0	0	0.0	0.00

* —High for 1969
† —1968 Leader
t —Touchdown
NOTE: Standing based on percent of completions, touchdown passes,
     percent of interceptions and average gain per attempt. To qualify
     for championship rating a player must throw at least 140 passes.

PUNT RETURNS

TEAM CHAMPION—Denver Broncos, who returned 37 punts for 450 yards and a 12.2 average. Kansas City led in 1968 with 31 punts for 450 yards and a 14.5 average, including two touchdowns. For the only time in league history there were no punt returns for a touchdown. The record is 17.8 yards by New York on 26 returns for 463 yards in 1961.

INDIVIDUAL CHAMPION—Bill Thompson of Denver (also the kickoff return champion) with 25 returns for 288 yards and an average of 11.5. The 1968 champion was Noland Smith of Kansas City who returned 18 punts for 270 yards and a 15.0 average including one touchdown. The record is 21.3 by Dick Christy of New York in 1961.

MOST YARDS GAINED—Jerry Levias of Houston with 292 yards on 35 returns. The record is 612 by Rodger Bird of Oakland in 1967.

MOST RETURNS—Jerry Levias with 35. The 1968 leader was George Atkinson of Oakland with 36. The record is 46 by Rodger Bird in 1967.

LONGEST RETURN—Noland Smith of Kansas City, 64 yards, against Boston, September 21. The record is 95 yards for a touchdown by Speedy Duncan of San Diego against New York, 1968.

1969 PUNT RETURNS—TEAM

	No.	F.C.	Yds. Ret.	Avg. Ret.	Long.	Tds.
Denver	37	9	*450	*12.2	52	0
San Diego	31	*32	300	9.7	38	0
Boston	23	6	212	9.2	45	0
Houston	43	18	391	9.1	46	0
†Kansas City	32	17	251	7.8	*64	0
New York	39	6	256	6.6	22	0
Buffalo	31	8	187	6.0	32	0
Miami	*45	14	266	5.9	38	0
Cincinnati	23	10	135	5.9	35	0
Oakland	39	28	225	5.8	30	0
League Total	343	148	2673	—	64	0
League Average	34.3	14.8	267.3	7.8	—	0.0

*—High for 1969
†—1968 Leader
NOTE: Standing based on average return.

1969 PUNT RETURNS—INDIVIDUAL

	Stdg.	No.	F.C.	Yards	Avg.	Long.	Tds.
THOMPSON, DEN.	1	25	4	288	*11.5	40	0
Duncan, S.D.	2	27	7	280	10.4	38	0
Levias, Hou.	3	*35	11	*292	8.3	46	0
Anderson, Buff.	4	19	4	142	7.5	30	0
Battle, N.Y.	5	34	4	235	6.9	22	0
Morris, Mia.	6	25	3	172	6.9	38	0
Atkinson, Oak.	7	25	8	153	6.1	30	0
E. Johnson, Cin.	8	17	6	85	5.0	17	0
Mitchell, K.C.	—	13	7	101	7.8	35	0
Garrett, Bos.	—	12	0	159	13.3	45	0
Anderson, Mia.	—	12	3	82	6.8	29	0
†Smith, K.C.	—	9	2	107	11.9	*64	0
Sherman, Oak.	—	9	16	46	5.1	14	0
Garrett, K.C.	—	8	1	28	3.5	10	0
Richardson, Hou.	—	7	7	93	13.3	27	0
Byrd, Buff.	—	7	2	37	5.3	32	0
Little, Den.	—	6	3	70	11.7	52	0
Burrell, Den.	—	5	2	56	11.2	42	0
Carwell, Bos.	—	5	0	43	8.6	13	0
Blanks, Bos.	—	5	2	10	2.0	12	0
Beier, Mia.	—	5	5	8	1.6	9	0
Grayson, Oak.	—	4	0	28	7.0	12	0
Baird. N.Y.	—	4	2	21	5.3	7	0
Thomas, Cin.	—	4	3	15	3.8	12	0
Graham, S.D.	—	3	*24	15	5.0	9	0
Sellers, K.C.	—	2	1	15	7.5	8	0
Reeves, Buff.	—	2	2	3	1.5	3	0
Greer, Den.	—	1	0	36	36.0	36	0
Burrell, Hou.	—	1	0	6	6.0	6	0
Smith, S.D.	—	1	0	5	5.0	5	0
Milton, Mia.	—	1	0	4	4.0	4	0
Ridlehuber, Buff.	—	1	0	3	3.0	3	0
James, Buff.	—	1	0	2	2.0	2	0
Coleman, Cin.	—	1	0	0	0.0	0	0
Guillory, Cin.	—	1	0	0	0.0	0	0
Janik, Bos.	—	1	0	0	0.0	0	0
Leonard, N.Y.	—	1	0	0	0.0	0	0
McCullers, Mia.	—	1	0	0	0.0	0	0
Richardson, Buff.	—	1	0	0	0.0	0	0
Twilley, Mia.	—	1	3	0	0.0	0	0
Allen, Oak.	—	1	4	—2	—2.0	—2	0
Gamble, Bos.	—	0	1	0	0.0	0	0
Gehrke, Cin.	—	0	1	0	0.0	0	0
Trapp, S.D.	—	0	1	0	0.0	0	0
Gladieux, Bos.	—	0	3	0	0.0	0	0
Podolak, K.C.	—	0	6	0	0.0	0	0
King, Cin.	—	0	0	35L	—	35	0

*—High for 1969
†—1968 Leader
L—Lateral
NOTE: Standing based on average return. To qualify for championship
rating a player must return at least 14 punts.

SCORING

TEAM CHAMPION—The Oakland Raiders for the third straight year, with 377 points. Oakland led in 1968 with 453. The record is 513 by Houston in 1961.

INDIVIDUAL CHAMPION—Jim Turner of New York repeated with 129 points on 32 field goals and 33 extra points. Turner led in 1968 with 145 points on 34 field goals and 43 extra points. The scoring record is 155 by Gino Cappelletti of Boston in 1964.

MOST TOUCHDOWNS—Warren Wells of Oakland with 14 (all receiving). Wells was the 1968 leader with 12 (11 receiving, 1 rushing). The record is 19 (13 rushing, 6 receiving) by Abner Haynes of Dallas in 1962.

MOST POINTS AFTER TOUCHDOWN—George Blanda of Oakland with 45 of 45 attempts. Blanda led in 1968 with 54 of 54. He also led in 1967 with 56 of 57 and in 1961 established the record, 64, with Houston.

MOST FIELD GOALS—Jim Turner with 32 in a record 47 attempts. Turner led in 1968 with 34 of 46 attempts.

BEST ONE-GAME PERFORMANCE—Six players tied with 18 points: Brad Hubbert, San Diego; Bob Trumpy, Cincinnati; Fred Biletnikoff, Oakland; Otis Taylor, Kansas City; Dick Post, San Diego and Warren Wells, Oakland. Lance Alworth of San Diego led in 1968 with 24 points. The record, 30, is shared by Abner Haynes of Dallas, 1961; Billy Cannon of Houston, 1961 and Cookie Gilchrist of Buffalo, 1963.

TEAM LEADERS—Boston, Gino Cappelletti, 68; Buffalo, Bruce Alford, 74; Cincinnati, Horst Muhlmann, 80; Denver, Bobby Howfield, 75; Houston, Roy Gerela, 86; Kansas City, Jan Stenerud, 119; Miami, Karl Kremser, 65; New York, Jim Turner, 129; Oakland, George Blanda, 105; San Diego, Dennis Partee, 78.

1969 SCORING—TEAM

	Tot. Tds.	Tds. R.	Tds. P.	Tds. Rb.	Kicks XP	XPM	2-Pt. Made	2-Pt. Miss	FG	FGA	Saf.	Tot. Pts.
†Oak.	*45	4	*36	*5	*45	0	0	0	20	37	1	*377
K.C.	40	*19	16	*5	38	0	0	2	27	35	0	359
N.Y.	37	14	21	2	33	0	1	*3	*32	*47	0	353
Den.	37	12	23	2	36	1	0	0	13	29	0	297
S.D.	35	18	13	4	33	1	0	1	15	28	0	288
Cin.	33	10	22	1	32	1	0	0	16	24	1	280
Hou.	31	12	15	4	29	0	*2	0	19	40	1	278
Bos.	32	11	19	2	26	*3	1	2	14	34	*2	266
Mia.	28	12	12	4	26	1	0	1	13	22	0	233
Buff.	26	7	17	2	23	1	0	2	17	26	0	230
Lg. Total	344	119	194	31	321	8	4	11	186	322	5	2961
Lg. Avg.	34.4	11.9	19.4	3.1	32.1		0.8	1.1	18.6	32.2	0.5	296.1

*—High for 1969
†—1968 Leader

1969 SCORING—INDIVIDUAL

	Tot. Tds.	Tds. R.	Tds. P.	Tds. Rb.	XP	XPM	2-Pt. XP	FG	FGA	Tot. Pts.
†J. TURNER, N.Y.	0	0	0	0	33	0	0	*32	*47	*129
Stenerud, K.C.	0	0	0	0	38	0	0	27	35	119
Blanda, Oak.	0	0	0	0	*45	0	0	20	37	105
Gerela, Hou.	0	0	0	0	29	0	0	19	40	86
Wells, Oak.	*14	0	*14	0	0	0	0	0	0	84
Muhlmann, Cin.	0	0	0	0	32	*1	0	16	24	80
Partee, S.D.	0	0	0	0	33	0	0	15	28	78
Howfield, Den.	0	0	0	0	36	*1	0	13	29	75

	Tot. Tds.	Tds. R.	Tds. P.	Tds. Rb.	XP	XPM	2-Pt. XP	FG	FGA	Tot. Pts.
Alford, Buff.	0	0	0	0	23	*1	0	17	26	74
Biletnikoff, Oak.	12	0	12	0	0	0	0	0	0	72
Cappelletti, Bos.	0	0	0	0	26	*1	0	14	34	68
Kremser, Mia.	0	0	0	0	26	*1	0	13	22	65
Denson, Den.	10	0	10	0	0	0	0	0	0	60
Kiick, Mia.	10	*9	1	0	0	0	0	0	0	60
Trumpy, Cin.	9	0	9	0	0	0	0	0	0	54
Garrett, K.C.	8	6	2	0	0	0	0	0	0	48
Sauer, N.Y.	8	0	8	0	0	0	0	0	0	48
Crabtree, Cin.	7	0	7	0	0	0	0	0	0	42
Frazier, Bos.	7	0	7	0	0	0	0	0	0	42
Garrett, Bos.	7	5	2	0	0	0	0	0	0	42
Garrison, S.D.	7	0	7	0	0	0	0	0	0	42
Little, Den.	7	6	1	0	0	0	0	0	0	42
McVea, K.C.	7	7	0	0	0	0	0	0	0	42
Taylor, K.C.	7	0	7	0	0	0	0	0	0	42
Maynard, N.Y.	6	0	6	0	0	0	*1	0	0	38
Nance, Bos.	6	6	0	0	0	0	0	0	0	36
Post, S.D.	6	6	0	0	0	0	0	0	0	36
Sellers, Bos.	6	0	6	0	0	0	0	0	0	36
Briscoe, Buff.	5	0	5	0	0	0	0	0	0	30
Embree, Den.	5	0	5	0	0	0	0	0	0	30
Haffner, Den.	5	0	5	0	0	0	0	0	0	30
Holmes, K.C.	5	2	3	0	0	0	0	0	0	30
Hopkins. Hou.	5	4	1	0	0	0	0	0	0	30
Levias, Hou.	5	0	5	0	0	0	0	0	0	30
Mathis, N.Y.	5	4	1	0	0	0	0	0	0	30
Moses, Buff.	5	0	5	0	0	0	0	0	0	30
Seiple, Mia.	5	0	5	0	0	0	0	0	0	30
Simpson, Buff.	5	2	3	0	0	0	0	0	0	30
Snell, N.Y.	5	4	1	0	0	0	0	0	0	30
Beirne, Hou.	4	0	4	0	0	0	*1	0	0	26
Alworth, S.D.	4	0	4	0	0	0	0	0	0	24
Boozer, N.Y.	4	4	0	0	0	0	0	0	0	24
Domres, S.D.	4	4	0	0	0	0	0	0	0	24
Granger, Hou.	4	3	1	0	0	0	0	0	0	24
Hayes, K.C.	4	4	0	0	0	0	0	0	0	24
Hubbert, S.D.	4	4	0	0	0	0	0	0	0	24
Robinson, Cin.	4	4	0	0	0	0	0	0	0	24
Smiley, Den.	4	3	1	0	0	0	0	0	0	24
Smith, Oak.	4	2	2	0	0	0	0	0	0	24
Thomas, Cin.	4	1	3	0	0	0	0	0	0	24
Banaszak, Oak.	3	0	3	0	0	0	0	0	0	18
Csonka, Mia.	3	2	1	0	0	0	0	0	0	18
Enyart, Buff.	3	1	2	0	0	0	0	0	0	18
Noonan, Mia.	3	0	3	0	0	0	0	0	0	18
Patrick, Buff.	3	3	0	0	0	0	0	0	0	18
Phillips, Cin.	3	3	0	0	0	0	0	0	0	18
Rademacher, Bos.	3	0	3	0	0	0	0	0	0	18
B. Turner, N.Y.	3	0	3	0	0	0	0	0	0	18
Beathard, Hou.	2	2	0	0	0	0	0	0	0	12
Cannon, Oak.	2	0	2	0	0	0	0	0	0	12
Conners, Oak.	2	0	0	*2	0	0	0	0	0	12
Crane, N.Y.	2	0	0	*2	0	0	0	0	0	12
Graham, S.D.	2	0	0	*2	0	0	0	0	0	12
Hadl, S.D.	2	2	0	0	0	0	0	0	0	12
Lammons, N.Y.	2	0	2	0	0	0	0	0	0	12
Lynch, Den.	2	2	0	0	0	0	0	0	0	12
Morris, Mia.	2	1	0	1	0	0	0	0	0	12

1969 SCORING—INDIVIDUAL (Cont'd)

	Tot. Tds.	Tds. R.	Tds. P.	Tds. Rb.	XP	XPM	2-Pt. XP	FG	FGA	Tot. Pts.
Myers, Cin.	2	0	2	0	0	0	0	0	0	12
Namath, N.Y.	2	2	0	0	0	0	0	0	0	12
Pitts, K.C.	2	0	2	0	0	0	0	0	0	12
Reed, Hou.	2	0	2	0	0	0	0	0	0	12
Richardson, K.C.	2	0	2	0	0	0	0	0	0	12
Smith, S.D.	2	2	0	0	0	0	0	0	0	12
Stanfill, Mia.	2	0	0	*2	0	0	0	0	0	12
Todd, Oak.	2	1	1	0	0	0	0	0	0	12
Trull, Hou.	2	2	0	0	0	0	0	0	0	12
Johnson, Bos.	1	0	0	1	0	0	0	0	0	8‡
Anderson, Buff.	1	1	0	0	0	0	0	0	0	6
Atkinson, Oak.	1	0	0	1	0	0	0	0	0	6
Bell, K.C.	1	0	0	1	0	0	0	0	0	6
Briggs, S.D.	1	0	0	1	0	0	0	0	0	6
Buckman, Den.	1	0	1	0	0	0	0	0	0	6
Burrell, Den.	1	0	0	1	0	0	0	0	0	6
Byrd, Buff.	1	0	0	1	0	0	0	0	0	6
Campbell, Hou.	1	1	0	0	0	0	0	0	0	6
Charles, Bos.	1	0	0	1	0	0	0	0	0	6
Clancy, Mia.	1	0	1	0	0	0	0	0	0	6
Cook, Cin.	1	1	0	0	0	0	0	0	0	6
Coslet, Cin.	1	0	1	0	0	0	0	0	0	6
Daney, K.C.	1	0	0	1	0	0	0	0	0	6
Dixon, Oak.	1	0	1	0	0	0	0	0	0	6
Domres, Hou.	1	0	0	1	0	0	0	0	0	6
Duncan, S.D.	1	0	0	1	0	0	0	0	0	6
Eber, S.D.	1	0	1	0	0	0	0	0	0	6
Edgerson, Buff.	1	0	0	1	0	0	0	0	0	6
Foster, S.D.	1	0	1	0	0	0	0	0	0	6
Grate, Buff.	1	0	1	0	0	0	0	0	0	6
Grayson, Oak.	1	0	0	1	0	0	0	0	0	6
Gunner, Cin.	1	0	0	1	0	0	0	0	0	6
Hagberg, Oak.	1	0	1	0	0	0	0	0.	0	6
Haik, Hou.	1	0	1	0	0	0	0	0	0	6
Houston, Hou.	1	0	0	1	0	0	0	0	0	6
Johnson, Hou.	1	0	1	0	0	0	0	0	0	6
Kearney, K.C.	1	0	0	1	0	0	0	0	0	6
Lamonica, Oak.	1	1	0	0	0	0	0	0	0	6
Masters, Buff.	1	0	1	0	0	0	0	0	0	6
Milton, Mia.	1	0	0	1	0	0	0	0	0	6
Moore, Hou.	1	0	0	1	0	0	0	0	0	6
Oliver, Oak.	1	0	0	1	0	0	0	0	0	6
Peacock, Hou.	1	0	0	1	0	0	0	0	0	6
Sellers, K.C.	1	0	0	1	0	0	0	0	0	6
Thomas, K.C.	1	0	0	1	0	0	0	0	0	6
Thompson, Den.	1	0	0	1	0	0	0	0	0	6
Twilley, Mia.	1	0	1	0	0	0	0	0	0	6
Whalen, Bos.	1	0	1	0	0	0	0	0	0	6
Williams, Den.	1	1	0	0	0	0	0	0	0	6
Wyche, Cin.	1	1	0	0	0	0	0	0	0	6
Hammond, Bos.	0	0	0	0	0	0	*1	0	0	2
Richardson, Hou.	0	0	0	0	0	0	*1	0	0	2

SAFETIES: Johnson and Jones, Bos.; Bethea, Hou.; Dotson, Oak. Team: Cin.

*—High for 1969
†—1968 Leader
‡—Includes safety

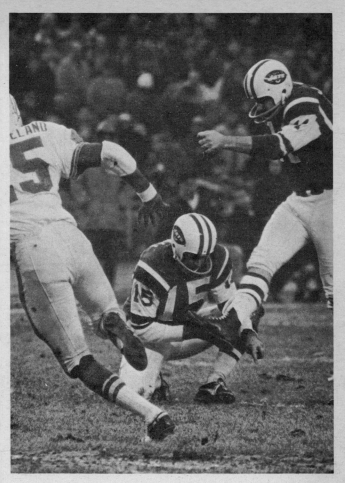

AFL's leading scorer Jim Turner kicks one from Babe Parilli's hold.

1969 FUMBLES—TEAM

	Fum.	Own Rec.	Yds.	Tds.	Opp. Rec.	Yds.	Long	Tds.	Tot. Rec.
Boston	*15	5	—4	0	14	70	t32	1	19
Denver	*15	6	7	0	14	23	17	0	20
Oakland	17	10	—13	0	16	53	t25	1	26
New York	19	4	—13	0	16	13	13	0	20
Houston	24	5	—10	0	17	72	*t38	*2	22
†Miami	27	13	—26	*1	13	0	0	0	26
San Diego	27	*14	—5	0	6	21	21	1	20
Cincinnati	30	5	*32	0	15	36	36	0	20
Kansas City	34	12	8	0	15	42	t19	*2	27
Buffalo	35	*14	18	0	*18	*130	33	1	*32
League Total	243	88	6	1	144	460	t38	8	232
League Average	24.3	8.8	0.6	0.1	14.4	46.0	—	0.8	23.2

*—High for 1969.
†—1968 Leader.
t —Touchdown

1969 FUMBLES—INDIVIDUAL

	No.	Own Rec.	Yds.	Long	Opp. Rec.	Yds.	Long	Tot. Rec.
Allen, S.D.	0	0	0	0	1	0	0	1
Allen, Oak.	1	0	0	0	0	0	0	0
Anderson, Mia.	1	1	0	0	2	0	0	3
Anderson, Buff.	1	0	0	0	0	0	0	0
Autry, Hou.	1	0	0	0	1	0	0	1
Avery, Cin.	0	0	0	0	2	0	0	2
Banaszak, Oak.	0	1	0	0	0	0	0	1
Barnes, S.D.	0	0	0	0	1	0	0	1
Battle, N.Y.	3	0	0	0	0	0	0	0
Beathard, Hou.	2	0	0	0	0	0	0	0
Beauchamp, Cin.	0	0	0	0	1	36	36	1
Beier, Mia.	1	0	0	0	1	0	0	1
Bell, K.C.	0	0	0	0	3	0	0	3
Belser, K.C.	0	0	0	0	1	0	0	1
Bemiller, Buff.	0	0	0	0	1	0	0	1
Benson, Oak.	0	0	0	0	1	0	0	1
Berger, Bos.	0	0	0	0	1	0	0	1
Berry, Cin.	0	0	0	0	1	0	0	1
Biggs, N.Y.	0	0	0	0	3	0	0	3
Biletnikoff, Oak.	1	0	0	0	0	0	0	0
Bishop, Hou.	0	0	0	0	1	0	0	1
Blanda, Oak.	1	1	—7	0	0	0	0	1
Blanks, Bos.	1	1	0	0	0	0	0	1
Boozer, N.Y.	3	1	0	0	0	0	0	1
Boyette, Hou.	0	0	0	0	1	0	0	1
Bramlett, Bos.	0	0	0	0	0	17L	17	0
Briggs, S.D.	0	0	0	0	1	0	t0	1
Briscoe, Buff.	1	1	0	0	0	0	0	1
Brown, K.C.	0	0	0	0	3	12	12	3
Buoniconti, Mia.	0	0	0	0	1	0	0	1
Burrell, Hou.	2	0	0	0	0	0	0	0
Byrd, Buff.	1	0	0	0	1	26	26	1
Campbell, Hou.	1	1	0	0	0	0	0	1

	No.	Own Rec.	Yds.	Long	Opp. Rec.	Yds.	Long	Tot. Rec.
Carroll, N.Y.	1	0	0	0	0	0	0	0
Cavness, Den.	0	1	0	0	1	17	17	2
Chandler, Buff.	0	0	0	0	1	0	0	1
Charles, Bos.	0	0	0	0	1	0	0	1
Cheyunski, Bos.	0	0	0	0	3	21	18	3
Coleman, Cin.	0	0	0	0	3	0	0	3
Conners, Oak.	0	0	0	0	3	31	t25	3
Cook, Cin.	*10	0	—2	0	0	0	0	0
Crane, N.Y.	0	0	0	0	1	0	0	1
Crawford, Buff.	1	1	7	7	0	0	0	1
Csonka, Mia.	1	0	0	0	0	0	0	0
Daney, K.C.	0	1	0	0	1	5	t5	2
Darragh, Buff.	2	0	0	0	0	0	0	0
Davis, Hou.	3	0	0	0	0	0	0	0
Dickey, Den.	0	0	0	0	1	0	0	1
Dixon, Oak.	4	2	3	3	0	0	0	2
Domres, S.D.	0	1	0	0	0	0	0	1
Domres, Hou.	0	0	0	0	1	38	*t38	1
Drungo, Hou.	0	0	0	0	1	0	0	1
Duncan, S.D.	4	1	0	0	0	0	0	1
Duranko, Den.	0	0	0	0	3	0	0	3
Edgerson, Buff.	0	0	0	0	*4	*39	22	4
Edmunds, Mia.	0	0	0	0	1	0	0	1
Edwards, Oak.	0	0	0	0	2	0	0	2
Eischeid, Oak.	0	0	0	0	1	0	0	1
Elliott, N.Y.	0	0	0	0	1	0	0	1
Emanuel, Mia.	0	0	0	0	1	0	0	1
Enyart, Buff.	2	0	0	0	0	0	0	0
Fernandez, Mia.	0	0	0	0	1	0	0	1
Foster, S.D.	3	0	0	0	0	0	0	0
Frazier, Bos.	2	0	0	0	0	0	0	0
Frazier, S.D.	1	0	0	0	0	0	0	0
Gamble, Bos.	1	0	0	0	0	0	0	0
Garrett, Bos.	6	2	0	0	0	0	0	2
Garrett, K.C.	4	0	0	0	0	0	0	0
Garrison, S.D.	1	0	0	0	0	0	0	0
Gehrke, Cin.	0	0	0	0	1	0	0	1
Gerela, Hou.	1	0	—10	0	0	0	0	0
Goode, Mia.	0	1	0	0	0	0	0	1
Gordon, N.Y.	1	0	0	0	0	0	0	0
Graham, S.D.	4	4	2	2	0	0	0	4
Granger, Hou.	1	0	0	0	0	0	0	0
Grantham, N.Y.	0	0	0	0	2	0	0	2
Grayson, Oak.	0	0	0	0	1	15	15	1
Greer, Den.	0	0	0	0	1	0	0	1
Griese, Mia.	5	2	0	0	0	0	0	2
Guillory, Cin.	2	0	0	0	1	0	0	1
Gunner, Cin.	1	0	0	0	0	0	0	0
Hadl, S.D.	3	2	—7	0	0	0	0	2
Haik, Hou.	1	0	0	0	0	0	0	0
Harris, Buff.	3	1	0	0	0	0	0	1
Hayes, K.C.	2	1	0	0	0	0	0	1
Hill, S.D.	0	1	0	0	1	0	0	2
Hines, Mia.	1	0	0	0	0	0	0	0
Hollomon, Den.	2	0	0	0	2	6	6	2
Holmes, K.C.	9	2	0	0	0	0	0	2
Hopkins, Hou.	2	0	0	0	0	0	0	0
Houston, Hou.	1	0	0	0	3	7	7	3

	No.	Own Rec.	Yds.	Long	Opp. Rec.	Yds.	Long	Tot. Rec.
Howard, S.D.	1	1	0	0	1	0	0	2
Hubbard, Oak.	1	1	0	0	0	0	0	1
Hubbert, S.D.	5	3	0	0	0	0	0	3
Hunt, Cin.	0	0	0	0	1	0	0	1
Hunt, Bos.	0	0	0	0	1	0	0	1
Inman, Den.	0	0	0	0	1	0	0	1
Jackson, Den.	0	0	0	0	1	0	0	1
Jacobs, Buff.	0	0	0	0	1	0	0	1
Jacobs, Bos.	0	0	0	0	2	0	0	2
James, Buff.	0	0	0	0	2	0	0	2
Jaquess, Den.	0	0	0	0	1	0	0	1
B. Johnson, Cin.	1	0	0	0	0	0	0	0
Johnson, Bos.	0	0	0	0	1	32	t32	1
E. Johnson, Cin.	1	0	0	0	0	0	0	0
Jones, Bos.	0	0	0	0	1	0	0	1
Jones, N.Y.	0	0	0	0	1	0	0	1
Kearney, K.C.	2	0	0	0	0	0	0	0
Keating, Oak.	0	0	0	0	1	0	0	1
Kemp, Buff.	8	*5	0	0	0	0	0	*5
Kiick, Mia.	2	1	0	0	0	0	0	1
Lamb, Cin.	0	1	*34	*34	0	0	0	1
Lammons, N.Y.	1	0	0	0	0	0	0	0
Lamonica, Oak.	1	0	−9	0	0	0	0	0
Lanier, K.C.	0	0	0	0	1	5	5	1
Lassiter, Oak.	0	0	0	0	2	3	3	2
Leonard, N.Y.	0	0	0	0	1	13	13	1
Levias, Hou.	5	2	0	0	0	0	0	2
Liske, Den.	1	0	0	0	0	0	0	0
Little, Den.	2	0	0	0	0	0	0	0
Livingston, K.C.	4	2	0	0	0	0	0	2
Long, Bos.	0	1	0	0	0	0	0	1
Loukas, Buff.	0	0	0	0	1	5	5	1
Lowe, K.C.	1	0	0	0	0	0	0	0
Lynch, Den.	1	0	0	0	0	0	0	0
Lynch, K.C.	0	0	0	0	1	0	0	1
Maples, Hou.	0	1	0	0	0	0	0	1
Masters, Buff.	1	0	0	0	0	0	0	0
McBath, Buff.	0	0	0	0	1	10	10	1
McCullers, Mia.	1	2	0	0	0	0	0	2
McVea, K.C.	1	1	0	0	0	0	0	1
Mikolajewski, S.D.	1	0	0	0	0	0	0	0
Milton, Mia.	2	2	1	t1	0	0	0	2
Mitchell, Mia.	1	0	0	0	0	0	0	0
Mitchell, K.C.	4	2	0	0	1	1	1	3
Moore, Hou.	0	0	0	0	2	0	0	2
Morris, Mia.	4	0	0	0	0	0	0	0
Moses, Buff.	0	1	11	11	0	0	0	1
Mumphord, Mia.	0	0	0	0	2	0	0	2
Myrtle, Den.	0	0	0	0	1	0	0	1
Namath, N.Y.	3	1	−13	−4	0	0	0	1
Nance, Bos.	1	0	0	0	0	0	0	0
Neidert, N.Y.	0	1	0	0	1	0	0	2
Nock, N.Y.	1	0	0	0	0	0	0	0
Norton, Mia.	6	3	−27	0	0	0	0	3
Nunnamaker, Buff.	0	0	0	0	1	33	33	1
Oats, Oak.	0	0	0	0	1	0	0	1
Oberg, Den.	0	1	7	7	0	0	0	1
Ogas, Buff.	0	0	0	0	1	0	0	1

	No.	Own Rec.	Yds.	Long	Opp. Rec.	Yds.	Long	Tot. Rec.
Oliver, Oak.	0	0	0	0	2	0	0	2
Park, Cin.	0	2	0	0	0	0	0	2
Parker, Hou.	0	0	0	0	1	0	0	1
Patrick, Buff.	6	1	0	0	0	0	0	1
Peacock, Hou.	0	0	0	0	1	27	t27	1
Pearson, Mia.	0	1	0	0	0	0	0	1
Petrella, Mia.	0	0	0	0	1	0	0	1
Philbin, N.Y.	0	0	0	0	3	0	0	3
Phillips, Cin.	4	1	0	0	0	0	0	1
Philpott, Bos.	0	0	0	0	1	0	0	1
Pitts, Buff.	0	0	0	0	1	17	17	1
Podolak, K.C.	3	0	0	0	0	0	0	0
Post, S.D.	3	0	0	0	0	0	0	0
Powell, Mia.	0	0	0	0	1	0	0	1
Pritchard, Hou.	0	0	0	0	1	0	0	1
Pryor, Mia.	0	0	0	0	1	0	0	1
Quayle, Den.	1	0	0	0	0	0	0	0
Redman, S.D.	0	1	0	0	0	0	0	1
Reed, Hou.	2	0	0	0	0	0	0	0
Rice, Cin.	0	0	0	0	2	0	0	2
John Richardson, Mia.	0	0	0	0	1	0	0	1
Richardson, Hou.	1	0	0	0	0	0	0	0
Richardson, Buff.	1	1	0	0	1	0	0	2
Richardson, Bos.	0	1	0	0	0	0	0	1
Richey, Buff.	0	2	0	0	0	0	0	2
Riley, Cin.	1	0	0	0	2	0	0	2
Robinson, Cin.	4	0	0	0	0	0	0	0
Sayers, S.D.	1	0	0	0	0	0	0	0
Scott, Bos.	1	0	0	0	2	0	0	2
Seiple, Mia.	1	0	0	0	0	0	0	0
Sellers, K.C.	1	0	0	0	2	19	t19	2
Shaw, Buff.	0	1	0	0	0	0	0	1
Sherman, Oak.	1	1	0	0	0	0	0	1
Simpson, Buff.	6	0	0	0	0	0	0	0
Smiley, Den.	3	1	0	0	0	0	0	1
Smith, Oak.	3	0	0	0	0	0	0	0
Smith, K.C.	2	1	0	0	0	0	0	1
P. Smith, Den.	0	0	0	0	1	0	0	1
Snell, N.Y.	5	1	0	0	0	0	0	1
Staggs, S.D.	0	0	0	0	1	21	21	1
Stein, K.C.	0	0	0	0	1	0	0	1
Stewart, N.Y.	0	0	0	0	1	0	0	1
Stith, Hou.	0	0	0	0	1	0	0	1
Stratton, Buff.	0	0	0	0	1	0	0	1
Suggs, Hou.	0	1	0	0	0	0	0	1
Svihus, Oak.	0	1	0	0	0	0	0	1
Taliaferro, Bos.	3	0	−4	0	0	0	0	0
Taylor, K.C.	1	1	8	8	0	0	0	1
Tensi, Den.	1	1	0	0	0	0	0	1
Thomas, K.C.	0	1	0	0	1	0	0	2
Thomas, Cin.	1	0	0	0	0	0	0	0
Thompson, Den.	4	2	0	0	1	0	0	3
Thompson, N.Y.	0	0	0	0	1	0	0	1
Thornton, Buff.	2	0	0	0	1	0	0	1
Todd, Oak.	1	1	0	0	0	0	0	1
Trull, Hou.	1	0	0	0	0	0	0	0
Trumpy, Cin.	2	1	0	0	0	0	0	1
B. Turner, N.Y.	1	0	0	0	0	0	0	0

	No.	Own Rec.	Yds.	Long	Opp. Rec.	Yds.	Long	Tot. Rec.
Turner, Cin.	2	0	0	0	1	0	0	1
J. Turner, N.Y.	0	0	0	0	1	0	0	1
Twilley, Mia.	1	0	0	0	0	0	0	0
Underwood, Hou.	0	0	0	0	1	0	0	1
Upshaw, Oak.	0	1	0	0	0	0	0	1
Webster, Hou.	0	0	0	0	1	0	0	1
Wells, Oak.	3	1	0	0	0	0	0	1
Williams, Oak.	0	0	0	0	1	4	4	1
Williamson, Bos.	0	0	0	0	1	0	0	1
Wilson, Oak.	0	0	0	0	1	0	0	1
Woods, Hou.	0	0	0	0	1	0	0	1
Wyche, Cin.	1	0	0	0	0	0	0	0

TOUCHDOWNS: Johnson, Bos.; Edgerson, Buff.; Domres & Peacock, Hou.; Daney & Sellers, K.C.; Milton, Mia.; Conners, Oak.; Briggs, S.D.

*—High for 1969
t —Touchdown
L—Lateral

1969 FIELD GOALS—TEAM

	Made	Attempts	Pct.	Long
†Kansas City	27	35	*.771	*54
New York	*32	*47	.681	50
Cincinnati	16	24	.667	50
Buffalo	17	26	.654	44
Miami	13	22	.591	39
Oakland	20	37	.541	46
San Diego	15	28	.536	50
Houston	19	40	.475	50
Denver	13	29	.448	51
Boston	14	34	.412	43
League Total	186	322	—	54
League Average	18.6	32.2	.578	—

*—High for 1969.
†—1968 Leader.

1969 FIELD GOAL ANALYSIS

	1–19	20–29	30–39	40–49	50–over	Total	Avg. Yds. Att.	Avg. Yds. Made	Avg. Yds. Missed	Long
Stenerud, K.C.	9-9	4-6	6-8	6-9	2-3	27-35	31.5	29.4	38.6	54
	1.000	.667	.750	.667	.667	.771				
J. Turner, N.Y.	10-11	7-8	7-10	7-15	1-3	32-47	32.8	28.8	41.3	50
	.909	.875	.700	.467	.333	.681				
Muhlmann, Cin.	6-6	5-5	3-4	1-3	1-6	16-24	33.3	25.3	49.3	50
	1.000	1.000	.750	.333	.167	.667				
Alford, Buff.	6-7	6-9	4-5	1-5	0-0	17-26	27.0	23.4	33.9	44
	.857	.667	.800	.200	.000	.654				
Kremser, Mia.	4-4	4-4	5-9	0-5	0-0	13-22	31.4	25.1	40.4	39
	1.000	1.000	.556	.000	.000	.591				
Blanda, Oak.	4-5	8-12	6-8	2-12	0-0	20-37	32.3	27.9	37.6	46
	.800	.667	.750	.167	.000	.541				
Partee, S.D.	4-4	5-8	3-9	2-5	1-2	15-28	32.0	28.5	36.1	50
	1.000	.625	.333	.400	.500	.536				
Gerela, Hou.	9-9	5-6	3-12	1-8	1-5	19-40	33.2	23.7	41.8	50
	1.000	.833	.250	.125	.200	.475				
Howfield, Den.	4-5	4-8	0-2	4-11	1-3	13-29	33.3	27.8	37.8	51
	.800	.500	.000	.364	.333	.448				
Cappelletti, Bos.	6-7	1-4	6-12	1-9	0-2	14-34	32.9	25.6	38.1	43
	.857	.250	.500	.111	.000	.412				
Totals	62-67	49-70	43-79	25-82	7-24	186-322	32.1	26.9	39.3	
	.925	.700	.544	.305	.292	.578				

1969 AFL TEAM SUMMARY
LEAGUE GAMES

BOSTON (4–10)

7	Denver	35
0	*Kansas City	31
23	*Oakland	38
14	*New York	23
16	Buffalo	23
10	*San Diego	13
17	New York	23
24	*Houston	0
16	*Miami	17
25	Cincinnati	14
35	*Buffalo	21
38	Miami (Tampa)	23
18	San Diego	28
23	Houston	27
266		316

BUFFALO (4–10)

19	*New York	33
3	*Houston	17
41	*Denver	28
14	Houston	28
23	*Boston	16
21	Oakland	50
6	Miami	24
7	*Kansas City	29
6	New York	16
28	*Miami	3
21	Boston	35
16	*Cincinnati	13
19	Kansas City	22
6	San Diego	45
230		359

CINCINNATI (4–9–1)

27	*Miami	21
34	*San Diego	20
24	*Kansas City	19
14	San Diego	21
7	*New York	21
23	*Denver	30
22	Kansas City	42
31	*Oakland	17
31	Houston	31
14	*Boston	25
7	New York	40
13	Buffalo	16
17	Oakland	37
16	Denver	27
280		367

DENVER (5–8–1)

35	*Boston	7
21	*New York	19
28	Buffalo	41
13	*Kansas City	26
14	*Oakland	24
30	Cincinnati	23
21	Houston	24
13	*San Diego	0
10	Oakland	41
20	*Houston	20
24	San Diego	45
17	Kansas City	31
24	Miami	27
27	*Cincinnati	16
297		344

HOUSTON (6–6–2)

17	Oakland	21
17	Buffalo	3
22	*Miami	10
28	*Buffalo	14
0	Kansas City	24
17	New York	26
24	*Denver	21
0	Boston	24
31	*Cincinnati	31
20	Denver	20
32	Miami	7
17	*San Diego	21
26	*New York	34
27	*Boston	23
278		279

KANSAS CITY (11–3)

27	San Diego	9
31	Boston	0
19	Cincinnati	24
26	Denver	13
24	*Houston	0
17	*Miami	10
42	*Cincinnati	22
29	Buffalo	7
27	*San Diego	3
34	New York	16
24	*Oakland	27
31	*Denver	17
22	*Buffalo	19
6	Oakland	10
359		177

MIAMI (3–10–1)			NEW YORK (10–4)		
21	Cincinnati	27	33	Buffalo	19
17	Oakland	20	19	Denver	21
10	Houston	22	27	San Diego	34
20	*Oakland	20	23	Boston	14
14	*San Diego	21	21	Cincinnati	7
10	Kansas City	17	26	*Houston	17
24	*Buffalo	6	23	*Boston	17
31	New York	34	34	*Miami	31
17	Boston	16	16	*Buffalo	6
3	Buffalo	28	16	*Kansas City	34
7	*Houston	32	40	*Cincinnati	7
23	*Boston (Tampa)	38	14	*Oakland	27
27	*Denver	24	34	Houston	26
9	*New York	27	27	Miami	9
233		332	353		269

OAKLAND (12–1–1)			SAN DIEGO (8–6)		
21	*Houston	17	9	*Kansas City	27
20	*Miami	17	20	Cincinnati	34
38	Boston	23	34	*New York	27
20	Miami	20	21	*Cincinnati	14
24	Denver	14	21	Miami	14
50	*Buffalo	21	13	Boston	10
24	San Diego	12	12	*Oakland	24
17	Cincinnati	31	0	Denver	13
41	*Denver	10	3	Kansas City	27
21	*San Diego	16	16	Oakland	21
27	Kansas City	24	45	*Denver	24
27	New York	14	21	Houston	17
37	*Cincinnati	17	28	*Boston	18
10	*Kansas City	6	45	*Buffalo	6
377		242	288		276

*Home Game

O. J. Simpson (32) takes Jack Kemp handoff and follows blocking.

1969 OFFICIAL ALL-PRO TEAM

(First annual team selected by Pro Football Hall of Fame
Selection Committee)

OFFENSE

FIRST TEAM	Position	SECOND TEAM
Lance Alworth, San Diego	WIDE RECEIVER	Fred Biletnikoff, Oakland
Paul Warfield, Cleveland	WIDE RECEIVER	Don Maynard, N.Y. Jets
Bob Trumpy, Cincinnati	TIGHT END	Charlie Sanders, Detroit
Bob Brown, Los Angeles	TACKLE	Ralph Neely, Dallas
Jim Tyrer, Kansas City	TACKLE	Harry Schuh, Oakland
Tom Mack, Los Angeles	GUARD	Gene Upshaw, Oakland
Gene Hickerson, Cleveland	GUARD	Gale Gillingham, Green Bay
Mick Tingelhoff, Minnesota	CENTER	Jim Otto, Oakland
Roman Gabriel, Los Angeles	QUARTERBACK	Daryle Lamonica, Oakland
Gale Sayers, Chicago	RUNNING BACK	Floyd Little, Denver
Calvin Hill, Dallas	RUNNING BACK	Leroy Kelly, Cleveland
Jan Stenerud, Kansas City	PLACEKICKER	Jim Turner, New York Jets
David Lee, Baltimore	PUNTER	Paul Maguire, Buffalo

DEFENSE

FIRST TEAM	Position	SECOND TEAM
Dave Jones, Los Angeles	END	Rich Jackson, Denver
Carl Eller, Minnesota	END	Gerry Philbin, New York Jets
Merlin Olsen, Los Angeles	TACKLE	Alan Page, Minnesota
Bob Lilly, Dallas	TACKLE	Buck Buchanan, Kansas City
Bobby Bell, Kansas City	OUTSIDE LB	George Webster, Houston
Chuck Howley, Dallas	OUTSIDE LB	Dave Robinson, Green Bay
Dick Butkus, Chicago	MIDDLE LB	Willie Lanier, Kansas City
Lem Barney, Detroit	CORNERBACK	Herb Adderley, Green Bay
Willie Brown, Oakland	CORNERBACK	Jim Johnson, San Francisco
Larry Wilson, St. Louis	SAFETY	Mel Renfro, Dallas
Johnny Robinson, Kansas City	SAFETY	Dave Grayson, Oakland
Bud Grant, Minnesota	COACH	George Allen, Los Angeles

1969 ALL-NFL SELECTIONS

Selected by Associated Press, United Press International and Newspaper
Enterprises Association)

OFFENSE

Roy Jefferson, Pittsburgh (AP, UPI, NEA)	Wide Receiver
Gary Collins, Cleveland (AP, UPI)	Wide Receiver
Dan Abramowicz, New Orleans (AP)	Wide Receiver
Paul Warfield, Cleveland (NEA)	Wide Receiver
Jerry Smith, Washington (AP, UPI, NEA)	Tight End
Bob Brown, Los Angeles (AP, UPI, NEA)	Tackle
Ralph Neely, Dallas (AP, UPI, NEA)	Tackle
Gene Hickerson, Cleveland (AP, UPI)	Guard
Tom Mack, Los Angeles (UPI, NEA)	Guard
John Niland, Dallas (AP)	Guard
Gale Gillingham, Green Bay (NEA)	Guard
Mick Tingelhoff, Minnesota (AP, UPI, NEA)	Center
Roman Gabriel, Los Angeles (AP, UPI)	Quarterback
Sonny Jurgensen, Washington (NEA)	Quarterback
Gale Sayers, Chicago (AP, UPI, NEA)	Running Back
Calvin Hill, Dallas (AP, UPI)	Running Back
Leroy Kelly, Cleveland (NEA)	Running Back

DEFENSE

Deacon Jones, Los Angeles (AP, UPI, NEA)	End
Carl Eller, Minnesota (AP, UPI, NEA)	End
Merlin Olsen, Los Angeles (AP, UPI, NEA)	Tackle
Bob Lilly, Dallas (AP, NEA)	Tackle
Alan Page, Minnesota (UPI)	Tackle
Dick Butkus, Chicago (AP, UPI, NEA)	Linebacker
Chuck Howley, Dallas (AP, UPI, NEA)	Linebacker
Dave Robinson, Green Bay (AP, UPI, NEA)	Linebacker
Lem Barney, Detroit (AP, UPI, NEA)	Cornerback
Herb Adderley, Green Bay (AP)	Cornerback
Cornell Green, Dallas (UPI)	Cornerback
Jim Johnson, San Francisco (NEA)	Cornerback
Larry Wilson, St. Louis (AP, UPI, NEA)	Safety
Eddie Meador, Los Angeles (AP, UPI)	Safety
Mel Renfro, Dallas (NEA)	Safety

1969 ALL-AFL SELECTIONS

(Selected by Associated Press, United Press International and Newspaper
Enterprises Association)

OFFENSE

Fred Biletnikoff, Oakland (AP, NEA)	Wide Receiver
(*) Lance Alworth, San Diego (UPI, NEA)	Wide Receiver
Don Maynard, New York (AP)	Wide Receiver
Warren Wells, Oakland (UPI)	Wide Receiver
Bob Trumpy, Cincinnati (AP, UPI, NEA)	Tight End
(*) Jim Tyrer, Kansas City (AP, UPI, NEA)	Tackle
Harry Schuh, Oakland (AP, UPI)	Tackle
Winston Hill, New York (NEA)	Tackle
Ed Budde, Kansas City (AP, NEA)	Guard
(*) Gene Upshaw, Oakland (AP, UPI)	Guard
(*) Walt Sweeney, San Diego (UPI, NEA)	Guard
(*) Jim Otto, Oakland (AP, UPI, NEA)	Center
Daryle Lamonica, Oakland (AP, UPI)	Quarterback
(*) Joe Namath, (NEA)	Quarterback
Floyd Little, Denver (AP, UPI, NEA)	Running Back
Matt Snell, New York (AP, UPI, NEA)	Running Back

DEFENSE

(*) Rich Jackson, Denver (AP, UPI, NEA)	End
(*) Gerry Philbin, New York (AP, UPI)	End
(*) Ron McDole, Buffalo (NEA)	End
John Elliott, New York (AP, UPI, NEA)	Tackle
(*) Buck Buchanan, Kansas City (AP, UPI)	Tackle
Tom Keating, Oakland (NEA)	Tackle
Nick Buoniconti, Miami (AP, UPI, NEA)	Middle Linebacker
(*) George Webster, Houston (AP, UPI, NEA)	Outside Linebacker
(*) Bobby Bell, Kansas City (AP, UPI, NEA)	Outside Linebacker
(*) Willie Brown, Oakland (AP, UPI, NEA)	Cornerback
Butch Byrd, Buffalo (AP, UPI, NEA)	Cornerback
(*) Dave Grayson, Oakland (AP, UPI, NEA)	Safety
(*) Johnny Robinson, Kansas City (AP, UPI, NEA)	Safety

(*) Repeaters from last year.

NATIONAL PROFESSIONAL FOOTBALL HALL OF FAME

The National Professional Football Hall of Fame is located in Canton, Ohio, site of the organizational meeting in 1920 from which the National Football League grew.

The League recognized Canton as the Hall of Fame site on April 27, 1961, and ground was broken for the Hall on August 11, 1962. Dedication ceremonies were held Sept. 7, 1963.

The National Board of Selectors, consisting of representatives from professional football cities, elected 17 charter members to the Hall. The selections were announced on January 29, 1963.

Subsequent selections were announced on Feb. 28, 1964, Jan. 19, 1965, March 23, 1966, Feb. 8, 1967, Feb. 19, 1968, Feb. 6, 1969 and Feb. 2, 1970.

ROSTER OF MEMBERS (63)

CLIFF BATTLES (West Virginia Wesleyan), 1968, halfback-quarterback, Boston Braves, Boston Redskins, Washington Redskins (1932–37).

SAMMY BAUGH (Texas Christian), Charter 1963, quarterback, Washington Redskins (1937–52).

CHUCK BEDNARIK (Pennsylvania), 1967, center and linebacker, Philadelphia Eagles (1949–62).

BERT BELL (Pennsylvania), Charter 1963, NFL Commissioner (1946–59).

CHARLES W. BIDWILL (Loyola), 1967, owner, Chicago Cardinals (1933–47).

PAUL BROWN (Miami, Ohio), 1967, coach, Cleveland Browns (1946–62), Cincinnati Bengals (1968–69).

JOE CARR, Charter 1963, NFL President (1921–39).

GUY CHAMBERLIN (Nebraska), 1965, player-coach, Canton Bulldogs, Cleveland, Frankford Yellowjackets, Chicago Bears, and Chicago Cardinals (1919–28).

JACK CHRISTIANSEN (Colorado State), 1970, defensive back, punt returner, Detroit Lions (1951–58).

DUTCH CLARK (Colorado College), Charter 1963, quarterback, Portsmouth Spartans and Detroit Lions (1931–38).

JIMMY CONZELMAN (Washington, Mo.), 1964, halfback, coach, executive, Decatur, Rock Island, Milwaukee, Detroit, Providence, Chicago Cardinals (1920–48).

ART DONOVAN (Boston College), 1968, defensive tackle, Baltimore Colts, New York Yanks, Dallas Texans, Baltimore Colts (1950–61).

PADDY DRISCOLL (Northwestern), 1965, player-coach, Chicago Cardinals and Chicago Bears (1919–31, 1941–68).

BILL DUDLEY (Virginia), 1966, halfback, Pittsburgh Steelers, Detroit Lions and Washington Redskins (1942–53).

TURK EDWARDS (Washington State), 1969, tackle, Boston Braves, Boston Redskins, Washington Redskins (1932–40).

TOM FEARS (Santa Clara, UCLA), 1970, end, Los Angeles Rams (1948–56).

DANNY FORTMANN, M.D. (Colgate), 1965, guard, Chicago Bears (1936–43).

OTTO GRAHAM (Northwestern), 1965, quarterback, Cleveland Browns (1946–55).

RED GRANGE (Illinois), Charter 1963, halfback, Chicago Bears (1925–34).

JOE GUYON (Carlisle, Georgia Tech), 1966, halfback, Canton Bulldogs, Cleveland Indians, Oorang Indians, Rock Island Independents, Kansas City Cowboys and New York Giants (1918–27).

GEORGE HALAS (Illinois), Charter 1963, player, coach, founder, Chicago Bears (1920–68).

ED HEALEY (Dartmouth), 1964, tackle, Rock Island and Chicago Bears (1920–27).

MEL HEIN (Washington State), Charter 1963, center, New York Giants (1931–45).

PETE (FATS) HENRY (Washington & Jefferson), Charter 1963, tackle, Canton Bulldogs, Akron Indians, New York Giants, Pottsville Maroons, Pittsburgh Steelers (1920–30).

ARNIE HERBER (Regis), 1966, halfback, Green Bay Packers and New York Giants (1930–45).

CLARKE HINKLE (Bucknell), 1964, fullback, Green Bay Packers (1932–41).

ELROY (CRAZYLEGS) HIRSCH (Wisconsin), 1968, end-halfback, Chicago Rockets, Los Angeles Rams (1946–57).

CAL HUBBARD (Centenary, Geneva), Charter 1963, tackle and end, New York Giants, Green Bay Packers, and Pittsburgh Steelers (1927–36).

DON HUTSON (Alabama), Charter 1963, end, Green Bay Packers (1935–45).

WALTER KIESLING (St. Thomas), 1966, player-coach, Duluth Eskimos, Pottsville Maroons, Boston Braves, Chicago Cardinals, Chicago Bears, Green Bay Packers and Pittsburgh Steelers (1926–56).

CURLY LAMBEAU (Notre Dame), Charter 1963, founder, player, coach, Green Bay Packers (1919–49).

BOBBY LAYNE (Texas), 1967, quarterback, Chicago Bears, New York Bulldogs, Detroit Lions, Pittsburgh Steelers (1948–62).

SID LUCKMAN (Columbia), 1965, quarterback, Chicago Bears (1939–50).

ROY (LINK) LYMAN, 1964, tackle, Canton Bulldogs, Cleveland, Chicago Bears (1922–34).

TIM MARA, Charter 1963, founder, New York Giants (1925–65).

GEORGE PRESTON MARSHALL, Charter 1963, founder, Washington Redskins (1932–1965).

GEORGE McAFEE (Duke), 1966, halfback, Chicago Bears (1940–41, 1945–50).

HUGH McELHENNY (Washington), 1970, halfback, San Francisco 49ers, Minnesota Vikings, New York Giants, Detroit Lions (1952–64).

JOHN "BLOOD" McNALLY (St. John's, Minn.), Charter 1963, halfback, Milwaukee Badgers, Duluth Eskimos, Pottsville Maroons, Green Bay Packers, Pittsburgh Steelers (1925–39).

AUGUST (MIKE) MICHALSKE (Penn State), 1964, guard, New York Yankees and Green Bay Packers (1927–37).

WAYNE MILLNER (Notre Dame), 1968, end, Boston Redskins, Washington Redskins (1936–41, 1945).

MARION MOTLEY (Nevada), 1968, fullback-linebacker, Cleveland Browns, Pittsburgh Steelers (1946–1955).

BRONKO NAGURSKI (Minnesota), Charter 1963, fullback and tackle, Chicago Bears (1930–37, 1943).

EARLE (GREASY) NEALE (West Virginia Wesleyan), 1969, coach, Philadelphia Eagles (1941–50).

ERNIE NEVERS (Stanford), Charter 1963, fullback, Duluth Eskimos and Chicago Cardinals (1926–37).

LEO NOMELLINI (Minnesota), 1969, defensive tackle, San Francisco 49ers (1953–63).

STEVE OWEN (Phillips), 1966, player-coach, Kansas City Cowboys and New York Giants (1924–53).

JOE PERRY (Compton J.C.), 1969, fullback, San Francisco 49ers, Baltimore Colts (1948–62).

PETE PIHOS (Indiana), 1970, end, Philadelphia Eagles (1947–55).

HUGH (SHORTY) RAY (Illinois), 1966, NFL technical advisor and supervisor of officials (1938–56).

DANIEL F. REEVES (Georgetown), 1967, founder, Los Angeles Rams 1941–68).

ARTHUR J. ROONEY (Georgetown), 1964, founder, Pittsburgh Steelers 1933–68).

ERNIE STAUTNER (West Virginia), 1969, defensive tackle, Pittsburgh Steelers (1950–63).

KEN STRONG (New York U.), 1967, halfback-placekicker, Staten Island Stapletons, New York Yankees and New York Giants (1929–39, 1944–47).

JOE STYDAHAR (West Virginia), 1967, tackle, Chicago Bears (1936–42, 1945–46).

JIM THORPE (Carlisle), Charter 1963, halfback, Canton Bulldogs, Oorang Indians, Cleveland Indians, Toledo Maroons, Rock Island Independents, New York Giants (1915–26, 1929).

GEORGE TRAFTON (Notre Dame), 1964, center, Chicago Bears (1920–32).

CHARLIE TRIPPI (Georgia), 1968, halfback, Chicago Cardinals (1947–55).

EMLEN TUNNELL (Iowa), 1967, defensive back, New York Giants and Green Bay Packers (1948–61).

CLYDE (BULLDOG) TURNER (Hardin-Simmons), 1966, center-linebacker, Chicago Bears (1940–52).

STEVE VAN BUREN (Louisiana State), 1965, halfback, Philadelphia Eagles (1944–52).

BOB WATERFIELD (UCLA), 1965, quarterback, Cleveland Rams and Los Angeles Rams (1945–52).

ALEX WOJCIECHOWICZ (Fordham), 1968, center-linebacker, Detroit Lions, Philadelphia Eagles (1938–50).

Lance Alworth (19), breaker of Don Hutson's catch record.

CHRONOLOGY

1895—Aug. 31: First professional football game, at Latrobe, Pa., sponsored by Y.M.C.A. Latrobe 12 vs Jeannette 0.

1902—Nov. 21: First night game, Philadelphia Athletics, (39), vs. Kanaweola A. C., (0), at Elmira, N.Y.

 Nov. 26: Connie Mack organized Philadelphia Athletics (with Rube Waddell in lineup). Claimed professional football championship of the United States after defeating Pittsburgh (with Christy Mathewson at fullback) 12–6.

 Dec. 28: First indoor football game, Syracuse (with Glenn Warner at guard) 6 vs. Philadelphia Nationals, 0 in Madison Square Garden. Attendance, 3,000.

1905— : Charles (Cy) Rigler organized Massillon Tigers (Charlie Moran in lineup).

 : Organization of Canton Bulldogs.

1920—Sept. 17: American Professional Football Association formed at Canton O. Membership: Canton Bulldogs, Cleveland Indians, Dayton Triangles, Akron Professionals, Massillon Tigers, Rochester (N.Y.); Rock Island (Ill.); Muncie (Ind.); Staley's of Decatur (Ill.); Chicago Cardinals and Hammond (Ind.).

 : Jim Thorpe (Canton) elected president; Stan Cofall (Massillon) vice-president; A. F. Ranney (Akron) secretary and treasurer.

 : Membership set at $100.

 : First pro player deal—Bob Nash purchased from Akron by Buffalo for $300.00.

1921—April 30: American Professional Football Association reorganized at Akron, O. Joe F. Carr (Columbus) elected president; M. O'Brien (Decatur) vice-president; and Carl L. Storck (Dayton) secretary and treasurer.

 Aug. 27: J. E. Clair of Acme Packing Company granted franchise for Green Bay, Wis.

1922—Jan. 28: Franchise of George Halas (Staley A. C., Decatur, Ill.) transferred to Chicago, renamed Chicago Bears.

 : J. E. Clair turned Green Bay franchise back to league following discussion over alleged use of ineligible players.

 June 24: Earl Lambeau granted franchise for Green Bay, Wis.

 : American Professional Football Association renamed National Football League.

1924— : Frankford (Pa.) Yellow Jackets awarded franchise.

1925—Aug. 1: Timothy J. Mara and Will Gibson granted franchise for New York for $500.

 : Jimmy Conzelman granted franchise for Detroit.

 Nov. 22: Red Grange signed with Chicago Bears.

1926—Feb. 6: Adoption of rule making all players ineligible for National League competition until their college classes have graduated.

 July 10: Milwaukee fined $500 for using four high school boys against Chicago Cardinals and A. L. McGurk ordered to dispose of franchise within 90 days.

1927—July 27: National League re-organized with withdrawal of Brooklyn, Detroit and nine other clubs.

1928—Aug. 12: Detroit's application for re-instatement approved; Cleveland withdrew.

1929—July 27: Sale of Chicago Cardinal franchise by Chris O'Brien to Dr. David J. Jones.
July 28: Adoption of rule to employ fourth official, a field judge.
Aug. 21: Chicago Cardinals become first professional team to go to an out-of-town training camp (Coldwater, Mich.).

1930—July 12: Portsmouth franchise granted to Harold Griffen.
: Detroit franchise declared inactive.
: Dayton franchise sold by Carl L. Storck to William B. Dwyer and John Depler who transferred it to Brooklyn, N.Y.

1931—July 11: Chicago Bears, Green Bay and Portsmouth fined $1,000 each for having players on their rosters whose college classes had not been graduated.

1932—July 9: Inactive Boston franchise transferred to new syndicate composed of Geo. P. Marshall. Vincent Bendix, Jay O'Brien and M. Dorland Doyle.
Dec. 18: Chicago Bears defeated Portsmouth Spartans 9–0 for championship (indoor) in Chicago Stadium.

1933—Feb. 25: Goal posts returned to goal line.
: Forward passing legalized from any spot behind line of scrimmage
July 8: Resolution by George P. Marshall setting up a divisional system and a championship playoff adopted.
: A. J. Rooney and A. McCool awarded franchise for Pittsburgh.
July 9: Frankford Yellow Jackets franchise declared forfeited and awarded to Bert Bell and Lud Wray of Philadelphia.
Oct. 24: Chicago Cardinal franchise sold to Charles Bidwill by Dr. David J. Jones.
Dec. 17: First World Championship game between divisional winners played at Wrigley Field, Chicago. The Chicago Bears defeated the New York Giants 23–21.

1934—June 30: G. A. Richards purchased Portsmouth franchise and moved team to Detroit.
Dec. 10: Player waiver rule adopted.

1935—May 19: Selection of players proposed by Bert Bell, Philadelphia Eagles, and adopted.

1936—Feb. 8: Jay Berwanger, University of Chicago halfback, first player selected in first National League draft. Chosen by Philadelphia.

1937—Feb. 12: Homer Marshman granted franchise for Cleveland.
13: Boston franchise transferred to Washington.

1939—May 20: Joe F. Carr, National League president since 1921, died at Columbus, O.
May 25: Carl L. Storck named president of National League.

1940—Feb. 2: Detroit Lions fined $5,000 for tampering with Bulldog Turner, Hardin-Simmons center, drafted by Chicago Bears.
Feb. 10: Fred L. Mandel, Jr., purchased Detroit Lions and franchise from G. A. Richards.

April 12:	Clipping penalty reduced from 25 to 15 yards.
:	All distance penalties enforced from spot on field of play limited to half the distance to the goal.
Dec. 9:	Alexis Thompson of New York purchased Pittsburgh Steeler franchise from Arthur J. Rooney, who purchased half interest in Philadelphia Eagles.
1941—March 1:	Elmer F. Layden, head coach and athletic director at the University of Notre Dame, named commissioner of professional football for five years.
April 5:	Carl L. Storck resigned as president-secretary.
:	Elmer F. Layden elected president for five years.
:	Philadelphia franchise transferred to Pittsburgh and Pittsburgh franchise transferred to Philadelphia.
June 1:	Cleveland franchise transferred from Homer Marshman and associates to Daniel F. Reeves and Frederick Levy, Jr.
1943—April 6:	Cleveland Rams, granted permission to suspend operations for one season.
April 7:	Free-substitution rule adopted for duration.
April 16:	Maj. Fred Levy transferred his stock in Cleveland Rams to Lt. Dan Reeves.
June 19:	Philadelphia Eagles and Pittsburgh Steelers granted permission to merge under name of Phil-Pitt Eagles.
June 20:	Ted Collins granted franchise for Boston (Yanks).
Dec. 5:	Philadelphia Eagles and Pittsburgh Steelers merger automatically dissolved on last day of season.
1944—April 19:	Boston Yanks activated franchise
:	Cleveland Rams resumed operations.
April 20:	Adoption of rule assessing five-yard penalty for kick-offs out of bounds, obligating kicking team to re-kick after each offense.
:	Coaching from bench legalized.
April 21:	Chicago Cardinals and Pittsburgh Steelers requested by league to merge for one year under the name of Card-Pitt.
Dec. 3:	Card-Pitt merger dissolved automatically on last day of season.
1945—April 9:	Wearing of socks in league games made mandatory.
:	Rule regarding attempts to consume or conserve time at the end of the second and fourth periods extended to include first and third periods also.
April 10:	Brooklyn Tigers and Boston Yanks merged for one year under name of The Yanks.
:	By V-J day (Aug. 14), the National League's service roster for World War II, limited to men who had participated in league games, totaled 638 men, 355 of whom were commissioned, 69 were decorated and 21 had lost their lives.
1946—Jan. 11:	Elmer F. Layden resigned as commissioner.
:	Bert Bell of Philadelphia, co-owner of Pittsburgh Steelers named to succeed Layden and given three-year contract.
:	Substitutions limited to no more than three men at one time.
:	Forward passes made incomplete automatically upon striking either team's goal post.
Jan 12:	Cleveland Ram franchise and club transferred to Los Angeles

1947—Jan. 1: Bert Bell's contract as Commissioner of the National Football League renewed for five years.

  : An amendment to the constitution imposing a major penalty for anyone not reporting the offer of a bribe, an attempt to fix a game or any other infraction of the rules having to do with gambling.

Jan. 24: A fifth official, with primary duties as prescribed, is to be used on the field. He is known as Back Judge.

  : Sudden death method of deciding tie game in divisional playoff or championship game adopted.

1948—Jan. 14: A clarification of the clipping rule, permission to use an artificial tee at the kickoff, and the equipping of all officials with whistles were among the important items passed by the Rules Committee and approved at the annual meeting.

Jan. 15: A syndicate headed by D. Lyle Fife purchased the Detroit franchise from Fred L. Mandel, Jr.

1949—Jan. 15: A syndicate headed by James P. Clark purchased the franchise of the Philadelphia Eagles from Lex Thompson.

Jan. 20: Bert Bell, as commissioner-president, and Dennis J. Shea, as vice-president and treasurer, appointed for ten-year terms.

  : For one year only the league adopted the free substitution rule.

Jan. 21: Unanimous consent of the league given for the cancellation of the Boston franchise and a new franchise awarded to Ted Collins in New York City under the name of the New York Bulldogs.

Dec. 9: Bert Bell, Commissioner of the National Football League and J. Arthur Friedlund, representing the All-America Conference, announced a merger of the two leagues. Baltimore, Cleveland and San Francisco joined the ten teams in the National Football League.

1950—Jan. 23: The free substitution rule was readopted for an indefinite term.

  : A backward pass going out of bounds between the goal lines shall belong to the team last in possession.

March 3: Upon the advice of counsel and unanimous consent of member clubs the Commissioner announced that the league would use the name National Football League divided into American and National Conferences. The American Conference includes Chicago Cardinals, Cleveland, New York Giants, Philadelphia, Pittsburgh and Washington. The National Conference includes Baltimore, Chicago Bears, Detroit, Green Bay, Los Angeles, New York Yanks and San Francisco.

March 13: Carl L. Storck, secretary-treasurer of the National Football League from 1921 until 1939 and president from 1939 until 1941, died in Dayton, Ohio.

1951—Jan. 14: The first Pro Bowl game played under the auspices of the Los Angeles Publishers' Association was won by the American Conference All-Stars over the National Conference All-Stars 28 to 27 before 53,676 spectators.

Jan. 18: Abraham Watner returned Baltimore franchise to league and was voted $50,000 for Colt players.

  : No tackle, guard or center may become eligible for a forward pass. Adopted for one year.

1952—Jan. 19: The assets and franchise of the New York Yanks were purchased by the National Football League.

Jan. 24: A new franchise was awarded the Dallas Texans after they purchased the assets of the New York Yanks from the National Football League.

1953—Jan. 23: New franchise awarded to Baltimore.

Jan. 24: Permanent Conferences, Eastern and Western were established.

March 28: James Thorpe, famous Indian athlete, brilliant professional football player and first president of the American Professional Football Association, died in Lomita, Cal.

June 10: Arthur B. McBride, original owner of the Cleveland Browns, sold the club franchise to a syndicate headed by Dave R. Jones.

Nov. 12: Judge Allan K. Grim, of the United States District Court for the Eastern District of Pennsylvania, has rendered his decision on the Anti-Trust case which was brought by the Government against the National Football League and its members. The primary effect of the decision was to uphold the restrictions on telecasts into the home territory of a club on the day that such club was playing at home.

1954—Jan. 29: Commissioner-President Bert Bell was given a new twelve year appointment.

1955—Jan. 27: Joseph A. Donoghue elected assistant treasurer.

Aug. 28: Los Angeles defeated New York 23 to 17 in first sudden death game played in Portland, Oregon, in pre-season.

1956—Jan. 16: Dennis J. Shea, treasurer since 1940 and associated with the league since 1932, retired on pension.

: Austin H. Gunsel elected treasurer of the league.

1957—Feb. 2: Waivers may not be recalled on the same player more than once in any one year by the same club.

1958—Jan. 29: The bonus pick started in 1947 eliminated.

Nov. 2: For the second year in succession the paid attendance record for a regular season game was broken in the Los Angeles Coliseum where the Los Angeles Rams and the Chicago Bears drew 90,833 spectators.

Dec. 28: Baltimore defeated New York 23 to 17 in the first use of the sudden death method of deciding a championship game. The Colts scored a touchdown after 8 minutes, 15 seconds of overtime play.

1959—Jan. 22: For the first time since 1933 no changes were made in the playing rules.

Jan. 23: The annual selection meeting shall be held prior to the end of the season. Twenty (20) selections shall be made by each club, a reduction of ten from previous selection meetings.

Aug. 14: First organizational meeting of AFL held in Chicago under leadership of Lamar Hunt, league founder from Dallas. Member teams and principal owners: New York, Harry Wismer; Dallas, Lamar Hunt; Los Angeles, Barron Hilton; Minneapolis, Max Winter and William Boyer; Denver, Bob Howsam; Houston, K. S. (Bud) Adams. Plans made for start of league play in 1960.

Aug. 22: American Football League name adopted in meeting in Dallas. Six members represented.

Oct. 11: Bert Bell, Commissioner of the National Football League since 1946, died after a heart attack suffered in Franklin Field during the last two minutes of the Philadelphia Eagles-Pittsburgh Steelers game. Age 65.

Oct. 14: Austin H. Gunsel, league treasurer, was named President in the office of the Commissioner until the annual NFL meeting in January 1960.

Oct. 28: Buffalo admitted to AFL membership in meeting in New York, with Ralph C. Wilson, Jr., of Detroit, the principal owner.

Nov. 22: In meeting in Minneapolis, Boston admitted as eighth AFL club, filling out first year complement, with William H. Sullivan, Jr., heading 10-man ownership syndicate.

: First AFL draft selection was made through first 33 rounds. Draft was by position (11 offensive positions) with first order of selection drawn for, then alternated. First-round selections announced in team alphabetical order: Boston—Gerhard Schwedes, hb, Syracuse; Buffalo—Richie Lucas, qb, Penn State; Dallas—Don Meredith, qb, SMU; Denver—Roger LeClerc, c, Trinity; Houston—Billy Cannon, hb, LSU; Los Angeles—Monty Stickles, e, Notre Dame; Minneapolis—Dale Hackbart, qb, Wisconsin; New York—George Izo, qb, Notre Dame.

Nov. 23: AFL adopted co-operative TV plan, with league negotiating contract and dividing proceeds equally among member clubs.

Nov. 30: Joe Foss, Congressional Medal of Honor winner, World War II Marine flying ace and former Governor of South Dakota, named AFL Commissioner for 3-year term.

Dec. 2: AFL completed initial draft with 20 rounds, making 53 rounds overall for first year.

1960—Jan. 26: Pete Rozelle named commissioner, succeeding Bert Bell.

: Lamar Hunt, Dallas, named first AFL president for 1-year term.

Jan. 27: AFL adopted 14-game home-and-home schedule and approved withdrawal of Minneapolis because of stadium problems.

Jan. 28: Two-point option on points-after-touchdown adopted by AFL. Scoring team awarded one point on successful kick, or two points for successful run or pass across the goal line from two-yard line.

: NFL awarded Dallas a 1960 franchise and Minnesota a 1961 franchise in expansion to 14 teams.

Jan. 30: Oakland completed eight-team lineup for AFL's first season. Teams divided into Eastern Division (Boston, Buffalo, Houston, New York) and Western Division (Dallas, Denver, Los Angeles, Oakland).

Feb. 9: "No tampering" verbal pact, relative to players' contracts, agreed to between NFL and AFL.

: Eddie Erdelatz named Oakland coach. Others: Lou Saban (Boston); Buster Ramsey (Buffalo); Hank Stram (Dallas); Frank Filchock (Denver); Lou Rymkus (Houston); Sid Gillman (Los Angeles); Sammy Baugh (New York).

March 13: Chicago Cardinals (NFL) transferred to St. Louis.

June 9: AFL signed 5-year contract with American Broadcasting Company for network televising of games. First year revenue set at $1,785,000 to league with graduating increases each succeeding year.

Aug. 25: Lettering of players' names on the backs of their jerseys adopted by AFL.

Sept. 9: Denver defeated Boston 13–10, before 21,597 fans at Boston, in first AFL regular season game.

1961—Jan. 1: Houston's Oilers won the first AFL championship, defeating Los Angeles 24–16 before 32,183 at Houston.

Jan. 7: Detroit defeated Cleveland 17–16 in inaugural NFL Playoff Bowl between second place teams in each conference. Nationally televised game was played in Orange Bowl at Miami.

Jan. 13: K. S. (Bud) Adams elected AFL president for 1961.

Jan. 17: Three members of eight-man Oakland syndicate—Ed McGah, Wayne Valley, Robert Osborne—purchased shares of other five owners, named McGah team president.

Feb. 10: Owner Barron Hilton transferred the Los Angeles Chargers' franchise to San Diego.

March 22: Arthur B. Modell headed a group that bought the Cleveland Browns of the NFL.

April 5: Commissioner Rozelle signed two-year contract awarding NBC radio and TV rights to the NFL championship game for $615,000 annually, $300,000 of which was to go directly into Bert Bell Player Benefit Plan.

April 27: Canton, Ohio, where the NFL was formed in 1920, was chosen as the site of the Professional Football Hall of Fame.

Sept. 30: A bill legalizing single network television contracts by professional sports leagues was introduced by Rep. Emanuel Celler, passed the House and Senate, and was signed into law by President Kennedy.

Dec. 24: Houston defeated San Diego, 10–3, for AFL championship before 29,556 at San Diego.

Dec. 31: Green Bay won its first NFL championship since 1944, defeating the New York Giants 37–0 at Green Bay in the first million-dollar gate in professional football.

1962—Jan. 7: West defeated East, 47–27, in first AFL All-Star game before 20,973 in San Diego.

Jan. 8: AFL voted to make scoreboard clock official timing device.

    : Pete Rozelle re-elected as NFL Commissioner for new five-year term.

Jan. 9: First NFL rule change in four years made it illegal to grab face mask of any player. Previously, grabbing of face mask of all players, except ball carrier, was illegal.

    : AFL Commissioner Foss given new five-year contract.

Jan. 10: NFL entered into a single network agreement with CBS for telecasting of all regular season games for $4,650,000 annually.

May 21: U.S. District Judge Roszel Thomsen, sitting in Baltimore's federal court, ruled against AFL in anti-trust suit against NFL. AFL had charged monopoly and conspiracy in areas of expansion, television and player signings. Case lasted 2½ years, trial 2 months.

May 24: Ed McGah and Wayne Valley acquired controlling interest in the Oakland Raiders of the AFL.

Nov. 8: AFL headquarters assumed financial responsibility for the New York Titans, owned by Harry Wismer.

Dec. 23: The Dallas Texans defeated Houston 20–17 in the AFL Championship game at Houston after 17 minutes, 54 seconds of sudden death overtime on a 25-yard field goal by rookie Tommy Brooker. The 77 minutes, 54 seconds made it the longest professional football game ever played.

Dec. 27: Dan Reeves purchased his partners' stock in the Los Angeles Rams and became majority owner.

Dec. 28: A federal judge in New York City upheld the legality of the NFL's TV blackout within a 75-mile radius of home games and denied an injunction sought by persons who requested the world championship game be televised in the New York City area.

1963—Jan. 6: Boston announced shift of home playing site from Boston University Field (capacity 23,681) to Fenway Park (37,216).

Jan. 10: AFL's guarantee for visiting teams during the season was increased from $20,000 to $30,000.

Feb. 8: AFL founder Lamar Hunt moved the Dallas Texans to Kansas City.

March 28: Five-member syndicate, headed by David (Sonny) Werblin bought the New York AFL franchise and changed the name from Titans to Jets.

April 17: Commissioner Rozelle suspended indefinitely Paul Hornung, Green Bay halfback, and Alex Karras, Detroit tackle, for placing bets on their own teams and on other NFL games; also fined five other Detroit players $2,000 each for betting on one game in which they did not participate, and the Detroit Lions Football Co. $2,000 on each of two counts for failure to report promptly information and for lack of sideline supervision.

May 11: A formula for player assistance to the New York and Oakland teams was decided upon by the AFL's executive board in a special meeting in New York.

May 23: NFL Commissioner Rozelle awarded NBC exclusive network broadcasting rights to 1963 NFL Championship game for $926,000.

Nov. 21: The U.S. Fourth Circuit Court of Appeals reaffirmed a lower court's finding for the NFL in a $10 million suit brought by the AFL charging monopoly and conspiracy on the part of the NFL in the areas of expansion, television and player signings—ending 3½ years of litigation.

Dec. 28: The Boston Patriots defeated the Buffalo Bills, 26–8, in the first divisional playoff in AFL history. A crowd of 33,044 attended the Buffalo game.

1964—Jan. 10: William Clay Ford purchased NFL's Detroit franchise.

Jan. 17: The AFL's executive committee voted to recognize the AFL Players Association, formed three days earlier.

Jan. 21: Philadelphia Eagles purchased by a group headed by Jerry Wolman.

Jan. 23: Carroll Rosenbloom, majority owner since 1953, acquired complete ownership of the Baltimore Colts.

Jan. 24: CBS submitted the winning bid of $14.1 million per year for NFL regular season television rights for 1964 and 1965.

Jan. 29: The AFL and National Broadcasting Company signed a 5-year, $36 million television contract to begin with the 1965 season.

March 16: NFL Commissioner Rozelle reinstated Paul Hornung of Green Bay and Alex Karras of Detroit after a review of their cases.

April 17: CBS acquired the rights to the 1964 and 1965 NFL championship games for $1.8 million per game.

May 22: AFL Commissioner Foss was given new three-year contract commencing in 1965.

Sept. 12: New York Jets (AFL) played their first game in Shea Stadium before a league record crowd of 45,665.

1965—Feb. 15: The 14 teams of the National Football League pledged: "No player will be signed to a contract or any form of document of intent, directly or through an agent, until after completion of all his team's football games, including bowl contests, in which he is available to participate during his senior year. This will include collegiate football players who actually compete in seasons beyond the graduating date of their original class." This was the first time any such pledge had been made and it augmented the rule first adopted in 1926 that no player can perform in the NFL until after graduation of his original college class. The new pledge was further augmented on Feb. 16 when the club owners authorized the commissioner to discipline an offending club up to as much as the loss of an entire draft list for violation of the pledge.

Feb. 19: A sixth official, the line judge, was added to the crew for each NFL game. His primary duties were defined as timekeeping and responsibility for checking action at the line of scrimmage.

April 5: The color of NFL officials' penalty flags changed from white to bright gold.

June 7: The AFL voted to expand by two teams for the 1966 season.

June 30: Atlanta awarded NFL franchise, with Rankin Smith as owner.

Aug. 16: Miami joined AFL as league's 9th franchise, with Joe Robbie and Danny Thomas as partners.

Dec. 26: Green Bay won the NFL's Western Conference championship 13–10 in a playoff with Baltimore. Don Chandler's field goal at 13:39 of sudden-death overtime period.

Dec. 29: CBS acquired the rights to NFL regular season games in 1966 and 1967, plus an option for 1968 for $18.8 million per year.

1966—Feb. 14: Rights to NFL 1966 and 1967 championship games sold to CBS for $2 million per game.

April 7: Joe Foss resigned after six years as AFL Commissioner.

April 8: Al Davis, General-Manager and coach of the Oakland Raiders, named AFL Commissioner.

May 16: NFL goal posts standardized (off-set from goal line; colored bright gold; uprights extend 20 feet above crossbar and will be not less than 3 nor more than 4 inches in diameter).

June 8: NFL and AFL entered into an agreement to form combined league of 24 teams, expanding to 26 by 1968. Pete Rozelle named Commissioner. Leagues to play separate schedules until 1970, but will meet, starting in 1967, in a championship game, and will play each other in pre-season games.

July 25: Milt Woodard named president of AFL after Al Davis announced termination of his term as Commissioner.

Aug. 25: Eugene Klein and Samuel Schulman leading figures in group that purchased San Diego Chargers from Barron Hilton.

Sept. 18: Oakland-Alameda County Coliseum opened with 50,746 watching Kansas City defeat Oakland 32–10.

Oct. 21: Congress passed special legislation exempting the agreement between the NFL and AFL from anti-trust action.

Dec. 2: NFL re-aligned into 4 four-team divisions for the 1967–68–69 seasons with the Coastal (Atlanta, Baltimore, Los Angeles and San Francisco) and Central (Chicago, Detroit, Green Bay and Minnesota) Divisions making up the Western Conference and the Capitol (Dallas, New Orleans, Philadelphia, Washington) and Century (Cleveland, New York, Pittsburgh, St. Louis) Divisions in the Eastern Conference for 1967. At the end of the regular season, the division champions play off for the conference title and the right to meet in the championship game. New York and New Orleans switch divisions in 1968 but return to 1967 alignment in 1969.

Dec. 13: Four-year, $9.5 million contract negotiated with CBS and NBC for broadcast rights to championship NFL-AFL Super Bowl game.

Dec. 15: New Orleans became NFL's 16th franchise, with John Mecom, Jr., as owner.

1967—Jan. 15: Green Bay (NFL) defeated Kansas City (AFL), 35–10, at Los Angeles Coliseum, in the first Super Bowl game; each Packer received $15,000 and each Chief $7,500.

Feb. 22: Owners voted by resolution for single standard goal post, and to line the playing field with a six-foot wide white restraining strip.

March 14: Bubba Smith, Michigan State defensive lineman, was first player chosen (by Baltimore) in first combined player selection meeting of the NFL and AFL in New York City.

May 24: Cincinnati became AFL's 10th franchise, with Paul Brown as general-manager, head coach, and part-owner.

May 28: Arthur B. Modell, president of the Cleveland Browns, elected president of NFL until February, 1968.

Aug. 5: Denver (AFL) defeated Detroit (NFL) in first of 16 pre-season, inter-league games scheduled as part of the agreement between the leagues. NFL teams won 13 of the 16 games.

Aug. 20: Detroit (NFL) defeated the San Diego Chargers 38–17 in the first game played in the new 50,000-seat San Diego Stadium.

Dec. 31: Green Bay defeated Los Angeles 28–7 at Milwaukee (Dec. 23) and Dallas defeated Cleveland 52–14 at Dallas (Dec. 24) in the first regularly scheduled Western and Eastern Conference championship games matching the winners of the four NFL divisions. Green Bay subsequently won its third straight NFL championship and fifth in seven years, defeating Dallas 21–17 in 13 below temperatures at Lambeau Field.

1968—Jan. 14: The first three million dollar gate in the history of professional football was achieved when the Green Bay

Packers defeated Oakland, Champion of the AFL, 33–14, in the second AFL-NFL World Championship Game at Miami's Orange Bowl.

May 15: All 26 pro football owners voted to require that by 1970 all member clubs would play in a stadium with a capacity "in the vicinity of 50,000" and that there would be no reduction of seating capacities in existing stadia.

: NFL and AFL voted unanimously to experiment with substituting a run or pass from the 2-yard-line for two points for the conversion kick during the 23 inter-league pre-season games.

Dec. 29: Baltimore, beaten only by Cleveland in 14 regular season games, won the Western Conference of the NFL 24–14 over Minnesota and then defeated Cleveland 34–0 for the NFL championship.

: New York Jets won the AFL championship, defeating Oakland 27–23. Weeb Ewbank became first coach to win titles in both NFL and AFL.

1969—Jan. 11: AFL inter-division playoffs, with winner in one division playing runner-up in other, voted new post-season format for 1969 only.

Jan. 12: AFL scored its first Super Bowl victory when the New York Jets defeated Baltimore Colts 16–7 before 75,377 at Miami's Orange Bowl.

March 20: NFL and AFL owners voted unanimously to discontinue experiment with run or pass for 1-point after touchdown play during pre-season, inter-league games.

: Fourth Super Bowl game awarded to Tulane Stadium in New Orleans and scheduled for Jan. 11, 1970.

May 17: Following two previous meetings and a non-stop 35-hour, 45-minute session in New York City, Commissioner Rozelle announced that the Baltimore Colts, Cleveland Browns and Pittsburgh Steelers had agreed to join the present 10 AFL teams and form a 13-team American Conference in the National Football League in 1970. The remaining 13 NFL teams would form the National Conference. Each would be realigned into three divisions, with the conference champions meeting each year in the Super Bowl. The 13 American Conference teams voted unanimously to realign into the following 3 divisions: Central—Cincinnati, Cleveland, Houston, Pittsburgh; Eastern—Baltimore, Boston, Buffalo, Miami, New York Jets; Western—Denver, Kansas City, Oakland, San Diego.

June 7: AFL and NFL owners voted to conduct open inter-conference trading between the present 26 teams from January 19 to March 1, 1970.

June 26: The American Broadcasting Company acquired the rights to televise in color 13 National Football League regular season Monday night games in each of the 1970, 1971 and 1972 seasons.

Aug. 9: George Preston Marshall, President Emeritus of the Washington Redskins, died at the age of 72.

Sept. 15: AFL-NFL pre-season attendance reached an all-time high of 3,099,292 for 74 games on 73 dates. Included were 33 inter-league games that attracted 1,529,799.

Dec. 20–21: In the AFL Division Playoffs, Kansas City defeated New York, 13–6 and Oakland defeated Houston, 56–7. In the NFL Conference championship games, Minnesota defeated Los Angeles 23–20 and Cleveland defeated Dallas, 38–14.

1970—Jan. 4: Kansas City defeated Oakland, 17–7, to win the AFL championship before 54,444 at Oakland-Alameda County Coliseum, with each full winning share worth $7,815.70 and each losing share worth $6,252.62.

Jan. 4: Minnesota defeated Cleveland, 27–7, to win the NFL championship before 46,503 at Metropolitan Stadium, Minnesota, with each full winning share worth $7,929.77 and each full losing share worth $5,117.80.

Jan. 11: AFL Champion Kansas City defeated NFL Champion Minnesota, 23–7, in the fourth annual World Championship Super Bowl Game before 80,562 at Tulane Stadium, New Orleans. The gross receipts of approximately $3.8 million were the largest ever for a one-day team sports event. The television audience was the largest ever for a one-day sports event.

Jan. 12: Regular season paid attendance set records in both the AFL and NFL. The 70-game regular season AFL schedule attracted 2,843,373; the 112-game NFL schedule attracted 6,096,127. The overall regular season total was 8,939,500. The total attendance for the pre-season, regular season and post-season games was 12,567,501.

Jan. 16: The 13-team National Football Conference was realigned into three divisions when one of five plans submitted by Commissioner Rozelle was drawn in a lottery. The divisions: Eastern—Dallas, New York Giants, Philadelphia, St. Louis, Washington; Central—Chicago, Detroit, Green Bay, Minnesota; Western—Atlanta, Los Angeles, New Orleans, San Francisco.

Jan. 26: The Columbia Broadcasting System acquired the rights to televise all National Football Conference games, except Monday night games, in 1970–71–72–73, including the Divisional Playoffs and the NFC Championship Game. CBS also will televise the NFL Pro Bowl Game in 1971 and 1973, and the Super Bowl in 1972 and 1974.

Jan. 26: The National Broadcasting Company acquired the rights to televise all American Football Conference games, except Monday night games, in 1970–71–72–73, including the Divisional Playoffs and the AFC Championship Game. NBC also will televise the Super Bowl in 1971 and 1973, and the NFL Pro Bowl in 1972 and 1974.

March 12: Arthur B. Modell, owner of the Cleveland Browns, resigned as President of the NFL. Modell was elected to that office in 1967.

March 13: Milt Woodard resigned as President of the AFL. Woodard became AFL president in 1966 after serving in several capacities in the league office since the inception of the AFL in 1960.

March 16: NFL owners voted to re-open inter-conference trading for 1970 until May 1. Beginning in 1971, the inter-conference trading period will begin the day following the final post-season game and continue until 4 P.M., New York Time, April 15.

March 17: Commissioner Rozelle announced that the fifth annual World Championship Super Bowl Game would be played at the Orange Bowl in Miami on Sunday, January 17, 1971.

March 18: NFL owners adopted the following rule changes: 1, All teams must place the names of players on the back of the uniform jerseys, directly above the number; 2, The ball must be a Wilson brand, hand selected, bearing the signature of the Commissioner of the League (Pete Rozelle); 3, The point after touchdown will be worth one point; 4, Official time of the game shall be kept on the stadium scoreboard clock. If the stadium is not properly equipped or if the clock mechanism becomes faulty, the game's Line Judge is to become the official timer.

March 19: Lamar Hunt, owner of the Kansas City Chiefs, was elected President of the American Football Conference, and George S. Halas, Sr., owner of the Chicago Bears, was elected President of the National Football Conference for two-year terms.

April 13: Commissioner Rozelle announced that the Miami Dolphins' first round choice in the 1971 NFL draft had been awarded to the Baltimore Colts as a result of circumstances under which Don Shula left as head coach and vice president at Baltimore to become head coach and vice president of the Dolphins.

PAST STANDINGS

1969

NFL
EASTERN CONFERENCE

Capitol Division

	W	L	T	Pct.	Pts.	O.P.
Dallas	11	2	1	.846	369	223
Washington	7	5	2	.583	307	319
New Orleans	5	9	0	.357	311	393
Philadelphia	4	9	1	.308	279	377

Century Division

	W	L	T	Pct.	Pts.	O.P.
Cleveland	10	3	1	.769	351	300
New York	6	8	0	.429	264	298
St. Louis	4	9	1	.308	314	389
Pittsburgh	1	13	0	.071	218	404

Cleveland won Eastern Conference championship, 38–14 over Dallas

WESTERN CONFERENCE

Coastal Division

	W	L	T	Pct.	Pts.	O.P.
Los Angeles	11	3	0	.786	320	243
Baltimore	8	5	1	.615	279	268
Atlanta	6	8	0	.429	276	268
San Francisco	4	8	2	.333	277	319

Central Division

	W	L	T	Pct.	Pts.	O.P.
Minnesota	12	2	0	.857	379	133
Detroit	9	4	1	.692	259	188
Green Bay	8	6	0	.571	269	221
Chicago	1	13	0	.071	210	339

Minnesota won Western Conference championship, 23–20 over Los Angeles
Minnesota defeated Cleveland 27–7 for Championship

AFL

Eastern Division

	W	L	T	Pct.	Pts.	O.P.
New York	10	4	0	.714	353	269
Houston	6	6	2	.500	278	279
Boston	4	10	0	.286	266	316
Buffalo	4	10	0	.286	230	359
Miami	3	10	1	.231	233	332

Western Division

	W	L	T	Pct.	Pts.	O.P.
Oakland	12	1	1	.923	377	242
Kansas City	11	3	0	.786	359	177
San Diego	8	6	0	.571	288	276
Denver	5	8	1	.385	297	344
Cincinnati	4	9	1	.308	280	367

Kansas City defeated New York, 13–6
Oakland defeated Houston, 56–7
Kansas City defeated Oakland, 17–7 for Championship

1968

NFL
EASTERN CONFERENCE

Capitol Division

	W	L	T	Pct.	Pts.	O.P.
Dallas	12	2	0	.857	431	186
New York	7	7	0	.500	294	325
Washington	5	9	0	.357	249	358
Philadelphia	2	12	0	.143	202	351

Century Division

	W	L	T	Pct.	Pts.	O.P.
Cleveland	10	4	0	.714	394	278
St. Louis	9	4	1	.692	325	289
New Orleans	4	9	1	.308	246	327
Pittsburgh	2	11	1	.154	244	397

Cleveland won Eastern Conference championship, 31–20 over Dallas

WESTERN CONFERENCE

Coastal Division

	W	L	T	Pct.	Pts.	O.P.
Baltimore	13	1	0	.929	402	144
Los Angeles	10	3	1	.769	312	200
San Francisco	7	6	1	.538	303	310
Atlanta	2	12	0	.143	170	389

Central Division

	W	L	T	Pct.	Pts.	O.P.
Minnesota	8	6	0	.571	282	242
Chicago	7	7	0	.500	250	333
Green Bay	6	7	1	.462	281	227
Detroit	4	8	2	.333	207	241

Baltimore won Western Conference championship, 24–14 over Minnesota
Baltimore defeated Cleveland, 34–0 for Championship

	W	L	T	Pct.	Pts.	O.P.		W	L	T	Pct.	Pts.	O.P.
Eastern Division							**Western Division**						
New York	11	3	0	.786	419	280	Kansas City	12	2	0	.857	371	170
Houston	7	7	0	.500	303	248	*Oakland	12	2	0	.857	453	233
Miami	5	8	1	.385	276	355	San Diego	9	5	0	.643	382	310
Boston	4	10	0	.286	229	406	Denver	5	9	0	.357	255	404
Buffalo	1	12	1	.077	199	367	Cincinnati	3	11	0	.214	215	329

*—Oakland defeated Kansas City 41–6 for Western Division championship
New York defeated Oakland, 27–23 for Championship

1967

NFL
EASTERN CONFERENCE

	W	L	T	Pct.	Pts.	O.P.		W	L	T	Pct.	Pts.	O.P.
Capitol Division							**Century Division**						
Dallas	9	5	0	.643	342	268	Cleveland	9	5	0	.643	334	297
Philadelphia	6	7	1	.462	351	409	New York	7	7	0	.500	369	379
Washington	5	6	3	.455	347	353	St. Louis	6	7	1	.462	333	356
New Orleans	3	11	0	.214	233	379	Pittsburgh	4	9	1	.308	281	320

Dallas won Eastern Conference championship, 52–14 over Cleveland

WESTERN CONFERENCE

	W	L	T	Pct.	Pts.	O.P.		W	L	T	Pct.	Pts.	O.P.
Coastal Division							**Central Division**						
Los Angeles	11	1	2	.917	398	196	Green Bay	9	4	1	.692	332	209
Baltimore	11	1	2	.917	394	198	Chicago	7	6	1	.538	239	218
San Francisco	7	7	0	.500	273	337	Detroit	5	7	2	.417	260	259
Atlanta	1	12	1	.077	175	422	Minnesota	3	8	3	.273	233	294

Green Bay won Western Conference championship, 28–7 over Los Angeles
Green Bay defeated Dallas, 21–17 for Championship

AFL

	W	L	T	Pct.	Pts.	O.P.		W	L	T	Pct.	Pts.	O.P.
Eastern Division							**Western Division**						
Houston	9	4	1	.692	258	199	Oakland	13	1	0	.929	468	233
New York	8	5	1	.615	371	329	Kansas City	9	5	0	.643	408	254
Buffalo	4	10	0	.286	237	285	San Diego	8	5	1	.615	360	352
Miami	4	10	0	.286	219	407	Denver	3	11	0	.214	256	409
Boston	3	10	1	.231	280	389							

Oakland defeated Houston, 40–7 for Championship

1966

NFL

	W	L	T	Pct.	Pts.	O.P.		W	L	T	Pct.	Pts.	O.P.
Eastern Conference							**Western Conference**						
Dallas	10	3	1	.769	445	239	Green Bay	12	2	0	.857	335	163
Cleveland	9	5	0	.643	403	259	Baltimore	9	5	0	.643	314	226
Philadelphia	9	5	0	.643	326	340	Los Angeles	8	6	0	.571	289	212
St. Louis	8	5	1	.615	264	265	San Francisco	6	6	2	.500	320	325
Washington	7	7	0	.500	351	355	Chicago	5	7	2	.417	234	272
Pittsburgh	5	8	1	.385	316	347	Detroit	4	9	1	.308	206	317
Atlanta	3	11	0	.214	204	437	Minnesota	4	9	1	.308	292	304
New York	1	12	1	.077	263	501							

Green Bay defeated Dallas, 34–27 for Championship

1966 (Cont'd)

AFL

			Eastern Division								Western Division				
	W	L	T	Pct.	Pts.	O.P.			W	L	T	Pct.	Pts.	O.P.
Buffalo	9	4	1	.692	358	255	Kansas City		11	2	1	.846	448	276
Boston	8	4	2	.667	315	283	Oakland		8	5	1	.615	315	288
New York	6	6	2	.500	322	312	San Diego		7	6	1	.538	335	284
Houston	3	11	0	.214	335	396	Denver		4	10	0	.286	196	381
Miami	3	11	0	.214	213	362								

Kansas City defeated Buffalo, 31–7 for Championship

1965

NFL

			Eastern Conference								Western Conference				
	W	L	T	Pct.	Pts.	O.P.			W	L	T	Pct.	Pts.	O.P.
Cleveland	11	3	0	.786	363	325	*Green Bay		10	3	1	.769	316	224
Dallas	7	7	0	.500	325	280	Baltimore		10	3	1	.769	389	284
New York	7	7	0	.500	270	338	Chicago		9	5	0	.643	409	275
Washington	6	8	0	.429	257	301	San Francisco		7	6	1	.538	421	402
Philadelphia	5	9	0	.357	363	359	Minnesota		7	7	0	.500	383	403
St. Louis	5	9	0	.357	296	309	Detroit		6	7	1	.462	257	295
Pittsburgh	2	12	0	.143	202	397	Los Angeles		4	10	0	.286	269	328

*—Green Bay defeated Baltimore, 13–10 for Conference championship
(sudden death—13:39)
Green Bay defeated Cleveland, 23–12 for Championship

AFL

			Eastern Division								Western Division				
	W	L	T	Pct.	Pts.	O.P.			W	L	T	Pct.	Pts.	O.P.
Buffalo	10	3	1	.769	313	226	San Diego		9	2	3	.818	340	227
New York	5	8	1	.385	285	303	Oakland		8	5	1	.615	298	239
Boston	4	8	2	.333	244	302	Kansas City		7	5	2	.583	322	285
Houston	4	10	0	.286	298	429	Denver		4	10	0	.286	303	392

Buffalo defeated San Diego, 23–0 for Championship

1964

NFL

			Eastern Conference								Western Conference			
	W	L	T	Pct.	Pts.	O.P.			W	L	T	Pct.	Pts.	O.P.
Cleveland	10	3	1	.769	415	293	Baltimore		12	2	0	.857	428	225
St. Louis	9	3	2	.750	357	331	Green Bay		8	5	0	.615	342	245
Philadelphia	6	8	0	.429	312	313	Minnesota		8	5	1	.615	355	296
Washington	6	8	0	.429	307	305	Detroit		7	5	2	.583	280	260
Dallas	5	8	1	.385	250	289	Los Angeles		5	7	2	.417	283	339
Pittsburgh	5	9	0	.357	253	315	Chicago		5	9	0	.357	260	379
New York	2	10	2	.167	241	399	San Francisco		4	10	0	.286	236	330

Cleveland defeated Baltimore, 27–0 for Championship

AFL

			Eastern Division								Western Division				
	W	L	T	Pct.	Pts.	O.P.			W	L	T	Pct.	Pts.	O.P.
Buffalo	12	2	0	.875	400	242	San Diego		8	5	1	.615	341	300
Boston	10	3	1	.769	365	297	Kansas City		7	7	0	.500	366	306
New York	5	8	1	.385	278	315	Oakland		5	7	2	.417	303	350
Houston	4	10	0	.286	310	355	Denver		2	11	1	.154	240	438

Buffalo defeated San Diego, 20–7 for Championship

1963

Eastern Conference	W	L	T	Pct.	Pts.	O.P.		Western Conference	W	L	T	Pct.	Pts.	O.P.
New York	11	3	0	.786	448	280		Chicago	11	1	2	.917	301	144
Cleveland	10	4	0	.714	343	262		Green Bay	11	2	1	.846	369	206
St. Louis	9	5	0	.643	341	283		Baltimore	8	6	0	.571	316	285
Pittsburgh	7	4	3	.636	321	295		Detroit	5	8	1	.385	326	265
Dallas	4	10	0	.286	305	378		Minnesota	5	8	1	.385	309	390
Washington	3	11	0	.214	279	398		Los Angeles	5	9	0	.357	210	350
Philadelphia	2	10	2	.167	242	381		San Francisco	2	12	0	.143	198	391

Chicago defeated New York, 14–10 for Championship

AFL

Eastern Division	W	L	T	Pct.	Pts.	O.P.		Western Division	W	L	T	Pct.	Pts.	O.P.
*Boston	7	6	1	.538	317	257		San Diego	11	3	0	.786	399	256
Buffalo	7	6	1	.538	304	291		Oakland	10	4	0	.714	363	288
Houston	6	8	0	.429	302	372		Kansas City	5	7	2	.417	347	263
New York	5	8	1	.385	249	399		Denver	2	11	1	.154	301	473

*—Boston defeated Buffalo, 26–8 for Division championship
San Diego defeated Boston, 51–10 for Championship

1962

NFL

Eastern Conference	W	L	T	Pct.	Pts.	O.P.		Western Conference	W	L	T	Pct.	Pts.	O.P.
New York	12	2	0	.857	398	283		Green Bay	13	1	0	.929	415	148
Pittsburgh	9	5	0	.643	312	363		Detroit	11	3	0	.786	315	177
Cleveland	7	6	1	.538	291	257		Chicago	9	5	0	.643	321	287
Washington	5	7	2	.417	305	376		Baltimore	7	7	0	.500	293	288
Dallas	5	8	1	.385	398	402		San Francisco	6	8	0	.429	282	331
St. Louis	4	9	1	.308	287	361		Minnesota	2	11	1	.154	254	410
Philadelphia	3	10	1	.231	282	356		Los Angeles	1	12	1	.077	220	334

Green Bay defeated New York, 16–7 for Championship

AFL

Eastern Division	W	L	T	Pct.	Pts.	O.P.		Western Division	W	L	T	Pct.	Pts.	O.P.
Houston	11	3	0	.786	387	270		Dallas	11	3	0	.786	389	233
Boston	9	4	1	.692	346	295		Denver	7	7	0	.500	353	334
Buffalo	7	6	1	.538	309	272		San Diego	4	10	0	.286	314	392
New York	5	9	0	.357	278	423		Oakland	1	13	0	.071	213	370

Dallas defeated Houston, 20–17 for Championship (sudden death—17:54)

1961

NFL

Eastern Conference	W	L	T	Pct.	Pts.	O.P.		Western Conference	W	L	T	Pct.	Pts.	O.P.
New York	10	3	1	.769	368	220		Green Bay	11	3	0	.786	391	223
Philadelphia	10	4	0	.714	361	297		Detroit	8	5	1	.615	270	258
Cleveland	8	5	1	.615	319	270		Baltimore	8	6	0	.571	302	307
St. Louis	7	7	0	.500	279	267		Chicago	8	6	0	.571	326	302
Pittsburgh	6	8	0	.429	295	287		San Francisco	7	6	1	.538	346	272
Dallas	4	9	1	.308	236	380		Los Angeles	4	10	0	.286	263	333
Washington	1	12	1	.077	174	392		Minnesota	3	11	0	.214	285	407

Green Bay defeated New York, 37–0 for Championship

1961 (Cont'd)

AFL

			Eastern Division								Western Division			
	W	L	T	Pct.	Pts.	O.P.			W	L	T	Pct.	Pts.	O.P.
Houston	10	3	1	.769	513	242	San Diego		12	2	0	.857	396	219
Boston	9	4	1	.692	413	313	Dallas		6	8	0	.429	334	343
New York	7	7	0	.500	301	390	Denver		3	11	0	.214	251	432
Buffalo	6	8	0	.429	294	342	Oakland		2	12	0	.143	237	458

Houston defeated San Diego, 10–3 for Championship

1960

NFL

			Eastern Conference								Western Conference			
	W	L	T	Pct.	Pts.	O.P.			W	L	T	Pct.	Pts.	O.P.
Philadelphia	10	2	0	.833	321	246	Green Bay		8	4	0	.667	332	209
Cleveland	8	3	1	.727	362	217	Detroit		7	5	0	.583	239	212
New York	6	4	2	.600	271	261	San Francisco		7	5	0	.583	208	205
St. Louis	6	5	1	.545	288	230	Baltimore		6	6	0	.500	288	234
Pittsburgh	5	6	1	.455	240	275	Chicago		5	6	1	.455	194	299
Washington	1	9	2	.100	178	309	Los Angeles		4	7	1	.364	265	297
							Dallas		0	11	1	.000	177	369

Philadelphia defeated Green Bay, 17–13 for Championship

AFL

			Eastern Division								Western Division			
	W	L	T	Pct.	Pts.	O.P.			W	L	T	Pct.	Pts.	O.P.
Houston	10	4	0	.714	379	285	Los Angeles		10	4	0	.714	373	336
New York	7	7	0	.500	382	399	Dallas		8	6	0	.571	362	253
Buffalo	5	8	1	.385	296	303	Oakland		6	8	0	.429	319	388
Boston	5	9	0	.357	286	349	Denver		4	9	1	.308	309	393

Houston defeated Los Angeles, 24–16 for Championship

1959

			Eastern Conference								Western Conference			
	W	L	T	Pct.	Pts.	O.P.			W	L	T	Pct.	Pts.	O.P.
N.Y. Giants	10	2	0	.833	284	170	Baltimore		9	3	0	.750	374	251
Cleveland	7	5	0	.583	270	214	Chicago Bears		8	4	0	.667	252	196
Philadelphia	7	5	0	.583	268	278	Green Bay		7	5	0	.583	248	246
Pittsburgh	6	5	1	.545	257	216	San Francisco		7	5	0	.583	255	237
Washington	3	9	0	.250	185	350	Detroit		3	8	1	.214	203	275
Chicago Cards	2	10	0	.167	234	324	Los Angeles		2	10	0	.167	242	315

Baltimore defeated New York 31–16

1958

			Eastern Conference								Western Conference			
	W	L	T	Pct.	Pts.	O.P.			W	L	T	Pct.	Pts.	O.P.
*N.Y. Giants	9	3	0	.750	246	183	Baltimore		9	3	0	.750	381	203
Cleveland	9	3	0	.750	302	217	Chicago Bears		8	4	0	.667	298	230
Pittsburgh	7	4	1	.636	261	230	Los Angeles		8	4	0	.667	344	278
Washington	4	7	1	.364	214	268	San Francisco		6	6	0	.500	257	324
Chicago Cards	2	9	1	.182	261	356	Detroit		4	7	1	.364	261	276
Philadelphia	2	9	1	.182	235	306	Green Bay		1	10	1	.091	193	382

*—New York defeated Cleveland, 10–0, in conference playoff
Baltimore defeated New York, 23–17 (Sudden Death—8:15)

1957

Eastern Conference

	W	L	T	Pct.	Pts.	O.P.
Cleveland	9	2	1	.818	269	172
N.Y. Giants	7	5	0	.583	254	211
Pittsburgh	6	6	0	.500	161	178
Washington	5	6	1	.455	251	230
Philadelphia	4	8	0	.333	173	230
Chicago Cards	3	9	0	.250	200	299

Western Conference

	W	L	T	Pct.	Pts.	O.P.
*Detroit	8	4	0	.667	251	231
San Francisco	8	4	0	.667	260	264
Baltimore	7	5	0	.583	303	235
Los Angeles	6	6	0	.500	307	278
Chicago Bears	5	7	0	.417	203	211
Green Bay	3	9	0	.250	218	311

*—Detroit defeated San Francisco, 31–27, in conference playoff
Detroit defeated Cleveland, 59–14

1956

Eastern Conference

	W	L	T	Pct.	Pts.	O.P.
N.Y. Giants	8	3	1	.727	264	197
Chicago Cards	7	5	0	.583	240	182
Washington	6	6	0	.500	183	225
Cleveland	5	7	0	.417	167	177
Pittsburgh	5	7	0	.417	217	250
Philadelphia	3	8	1	.273	143	215

Western Conference

	W	L	T	Pct.	Pts.	O.P.
Chicago Bears	9	2	1	.818	363	246
Detroit	9	3	0	.750	300	188
San Francisco	5	6	1	.455	233	284
Baltimore	5	7	0	.417	270	322
Green Bay	4	8	0	.333	264	342
Los Angeles	4	8	0	.333	291	307

New York defeated Chicago Bears, 47–7

1955

Eastern Conference

	W	L	T	Pct.	Pts.	O.P.
Cleveland	9	2	1	.818	349	218
Washington	8	4	0	.667	246	222
N.Y. Giants	6	5	1	.545	267	223
Chicago Cards	4	7	1	.364	224	252
Philadelphia	4	7	1	.364	248	231
Pittsburgh	4	8	0	.333	195	285

Western Conference

	W	L	T	Pct.	Pts.	O.P.
Los Angeles	8	3	1	.727	260	231
Chicago Bears	8	4	0	.667	294	251
Green Bay	6	6	0	.500	258	276
Baltimore	5	6	1	.455	214	239
San Francisco	4	8	0	.333	216	298
Detroit	3	9	0	.250	230	275

Cleveland defeated Los Angeles, 38–14

1954

Eastern Conference

	W	L	T	Pct.	Pts.	O.P.
Cleveland	9	3	0	.750	336	162
Philadelphia	7	4	1	.636	284	230
N.Y. Giants	7	5	0	.583	293	184
Pittsburgh	5	7	0	.417	219	263
Washington	3	9	0	.250	207	432
Chicago Cards	2	10	0	.167	183	347

Western Conference

	W	L	T	Pct.	Pts.	O.P.
Detroit	9	2	1	.818	337	189
Chicago Bears	8	4	0	.667	301	279
San Francisco	7	4	1	.636	313	251
Los Angeles	6	5	1	.545	314	285
Green Bay	4	8	0	.333	234	251
Baltimore	3	9	0	.250	131	279

Cleveland defeated Detroit, 56–10

1953

Eastern Conference

	W	L	T	Pct.	Pts.	O.P.
Cleveland	11	1	0	.917	348	162
Philadelphia	7	4	1	.636	352	215
Washington	6	5	1	.545	208	215
Pittsburgh	6	6	0	.500	211	263
N.Y. Giants	3	9	0	.250	179	277
Chicago Cards	1	10	1	.091	190	337

Western Conference

	W	L	T	Pct.	Pts.	O.P.
Detroit	10	2	0	.833	271	205
San Francisco	9	3	0	.750	372	237
Los Angeles	9	3	0	.750	366	236
Chicago Bears	3	8	1	.273	218	262
Baltimore	3	9	0	.250	182	350
Green Bay	2	9	1	.182	200	338

Detroit defeated Cleveland, 17–16

1952

	American Conference						National Conference					
	W	L	T	Pct.	Pts.	O.P.		W	L	T	Pct.	Pts.	O.P.
Cleveland	8	4	0	.667	310	213	*Detroit	9	3	0	.750	344	192
N.Y. Giants	7	5	0	.583	234	231	Los Angeles	9	3	0	.750	349	234
Philadelphia	7	5	0	.583	252	271	San Francisco	7	5	0	.583	285	221
Pittsburgh	5	7	0	.417	300	273	Green Bay	6	6	0	.500	295	312
Chicago Cards	4	8	0	.333	172	221	Chicago Bears	5	7	0	.417	245	326
Washington	4	8	0	.333	240	287	†Dallas Texans	1	11	0	.083	182	427

*—Detroit defeated Los Angeles, 31–21, in conference playoff
†—Franchise transferred to Baltimore, Jan. 23, 1953.
Detroit defeated Cleveland, 17–7

1951

	American Conference						National Conference					
	W	L	T	Pct.	Pts.	O.P.		W	L	T	Pct.	Pts.	O.P.
Cleveland	11	1	0	.917	331	152	Los Angeles	8	4	0	.667	392	261
N.Y. Giants	9	2	1	.818	254	161	Detroit	7	4	1	.636	336	259
Washington	5	7	0	.417	183	296	San Francisco	7	4	1	.636	255	205
Pittsburgh	4	7	1	.364	183	235	Chicago Bears	7	5	0	.583	286	282
Philadelphia	4	8	0	.333	234	264	Green Bay	3	9	0	.250	254	375
Chicago Cards	3	9	0	.250	210	287	*N.Y. Yanks	1	9	2	.100	241	382

*—Franchise transferred to Dallas, Jan. 24, 1952.
Los Angeles defeated Cleveland, 24–17

1950

	American Conference						National Conference					
	W	L	T	Pct.	Pts.	O.P.		W	L	T	Pct.	Pts.	O.P.
*Cleveland	10	2	0	.833	310	144	†Los Angeles	9	3	0	.750	466	309
N.Y. Giants	10	2	0	.833	268	150	Chicago Bears	9	3	0	.750	279	207
Philadelphia	6	6	0	.500	254	141	N.Y. Yanks	7	5	0	.583	366	367
Pittsburgh	6	6	0	.500	180	195	Detroit	6	6	0	.500	321	285
Chicago Cards	5	7	0	.417	233	287	Green Bay	3	9	0	.250	244	406
Washington	3	9	0	.250	229	326	San Francisco	3	9	0	.250	213	297
							Baltimore	1	11	0	.083	213	462

*—Cleveland defeated New York Giants, 8–3, in conference playoff
†—Los Angeles defeated Chicago Bears, 24–14, in conference playoff
Cleveland defeated Los Angeles, 30–28

1949

	Eastern Division						Western Division					
	W	L	T	Pct.	Pts.	O.P.		W	L	T	Pct.	Pts.	O.P.
Philadelphia	11	1	0	.917	364	134	Los Angeles	8	2	2	.800	360	239
Pittsburgh	6	5	1	.545	224	214	Chicago Bears	9	3	0	.750	332	218
N.Y. Giants	6	6	0	.500	287	298	Chicago Cards	6	5	1	.545	360	301
Washington	4	7	1	.364	268	339	Detroit	4	8	0	.333	237	259
N.Y. Bulldogs	1	10	1	.091	153	368	Green Bay	2	10	0	.167	114	329

Philadelphia defeated Los Angeles, 14–0

1948

	Eastern Division						Western Division					
	W	L	T	Pct.	Pts.	O.P.		W	L	T	Pct.	Pts.	O.P.
Philadelphia	9	2	1	.818	376	156	Chicago Cards	11	1	0	.917	395	226
Washington	7	5	0	.583	291	287	Chicago Bears	10	2	0	.833	375	151
N.Y. Giants	4	8	0	.333	297	388	Los Angeles	6	5	1	.545	327	269
Pittsburgh	4	8	0	.333	200	243	Green Bay	3	9	0	.250	154	290
Boston Yanks	3	9	0	.250	174	372	Detroit	2	10	0	.167	200	407

Philadelphia defeated Chicago Cardinals, 7–0

1947

Eastern Division

	W	L	T	Pct.	Pts.	O.P.
*Philadelphia	8	4	0	.667	308	242
Pittsburgh	8	4	0	.667	240	259
Boston Yanks	4	7	1	.364	168	256
Washington	4	8	0	.333	295	367
N.Y. Giants	2	8	2	.200	190	309

Western Division

	W	L	T	Pct.	Pts.	O.P.
Chicago Cards	9	3	0	.750	306	231
Chicago Bears	8	4	0	.667	363	241
Green Bay	6	5	1	.545	274	210
Los Angeles	6	6	0	.500	259	214
Detroit	3	9	0	.250	231	305

*—Philadelphia defeated Pittsburgh, 21–0, in Divisional Playoff
Chicago Cardinals defeated Philadelphia, 28–21

1946

Eastern Division

	W	L	T	Pct.	Pts.	O.P.
N.Y. Giants	7	3	1	.700	236	162
Philadelphia	6	5	0	.545	231	220
Washington	5	5	1	.500	171	191
Pittsburgh	5	5	1	.500	136	117
Boston Yanks	2	8	1	.200	189	273

Western Division

	W	L	T	Pct.	Pts.	O.P.
Chicago Bears	8	2	1	.800	289	193
Los Angeles	6	4	1	.600	277	257
Green Bay	6	5	0	.545	148	158
Chicago Cards	6	5	0	.545	260	198
Detroit	1	10	0	.091	142	310

Chicago Bears defeated New York, 24–14

1945

Eastern Division

	W	L	T	Pct.	Pts.	O.P.
Washington	8	2	0	.800	209	121
Philadelphia	7	3	0	.700	272	133
N.Y. Giants	3	6	1	.333	179	198
Boston	3	6	1	.333	123	211
Pittsburgh	2	8	0	.200	79	220

Western Division

	W	L	T	Pct.	Pts.	O.P.
*Clev. Rams	9	1	0	.900	244	136
Detroit	7	3	0	.700	195	194
Green Bay	6	4	0	.600	258	173
Chicago Bears	3	7	0	.300	192	235
Chicago Cards	1	9	0	.100	98	228

*—Franchise transferred to Los Angeles, Jan. 12, 1946.
Cleveland defeated Washington, 15–14

1944

Eastern Division

	W	L	T	Pct.	Pts.	O.P.
N.Y. Giants	8	1	1	.889	206	75
Philadelphia	7	1	2	.875	267	131
Washington	6	3	1	.667	169	180
Boston Yanks	2	8	0	.200	82	233
Brooklyn	0	10	0	.000	69	166

Western Division

	W	L	T	Pct.	Pts.	O.P.
Green Bay	8	2	0	.800	238	141
Chicago Bears	6	3	1	.667	258	172
Detroit	6	3	1	.667	216	151
Clev. Rams	4	6	0	.400	188	224
Card-Pitt	0	10	0	.000	108	328

Green Bay defeated New York, 14–7

1943

Eastern Division

	W	L	T	Pct.	Pts.	O.P.
*Washington	6	3	1	.667	229	137
N.Y. Giants	6	3	1	.667	197	170
Phil-Pitt	5	4	1	.556	225	230
Brooklyn	2	8	0	.200	65	234

Western Division

	W	L	T	Pct.	Pts.	O.P.
Chicago Bears	8	1	1	.889	303	157
Green Bay	7	2	1	.778	264	172
Detroit	3	6	1	.333	178	218
Chicago Cards	0	10	0	.000	95	238

*—Washington defeated New York, 28–0, in Divisional Playoff
Chicago Bears defeated Washington, 41–21

1942

Eastern Division

	W	L	T	Pct.	Pts.	O.P.
Washington	10	1	0	.909	227	102
Pittsburgh	7	4	0	.636	167	119
New York	5	5	1	.500	155	139
Brooklyn	3	8	0	.273	100	168
Philadelphia	2	9	0	.182	134	239

Western Division

	W	L	T	Pct.	Pts.	O.P.
Chicago Bears	11	0	0	1.000	376	84
Green Bay	8	2	1	.800	300	215
Clev. Rams	5	6	0	.455	150	207
Chicago Cards	3	8	0	.273	98	209
Detroit	0	11	0	.000	38	263

Washington defeated Bears, 14–6

1941

Eastern Division

	W	L	T	Pct.	Pts.	O.P.
New York	8	3	0	.727	238	114
Brooklyn	7	4	0	.636	158	127
Washington	6	5	0	.545	176	174
Philadelphia	2	8	1	.200	119	218
Pittsburgh	1	9	1	.100	103	276

Western Division

	W	L	T	Pct.	Pts.	O.P.
*Chicago Bears	10	1	0	.909	396	147
Green Bay	10	1	0	.909	258	120
Detroit	4	6	1	.400	121	195
Chicago Cards	3	7	1	.300	127	197
Clev. Rams	2	9	0	.182	116	244

*—Bears defeated Green Bay, 33–14, in Divisional Playoff
Bears defeated New York, 37–9

1940

Eastern Division

	W	L	T	Pct.	Pts.	O.P.
Washington	9	2	0	.818	245	142
Brooklyn	8	3	0	.727	186	120
N.Y. Giants	6	4	1	.600	131	133
Pittsburgh	2	7	2	.222	60	178
Philadelphia	1	10	0	.091	111	211

Western Division

	W	L	T	Pct.	Pts.	O.P.
Chicago Bears	8	3	0	.727	238	152
Green Bay	6	4	1	.600	238	155
Detroit	5	5	1	.500	138	153
Clev. Rams	4	6	1	.400	171	191
Chicago Cards	2	7	2	.222	139	222

Bears defeated Washington, 73–0

1939

Eastern Division

	W	L	T	Pct.	Pts.	O.P.
N.Y. Giants	9	1	1	.900	168	85
Washington	8	2	1	.800	242	94
Brooklyn	4	6	1	.400	108	219
Philadelphia	1	9	1	.100	105	200
Pittsburgh	1	9	1	.100	114	216

Western Division

	W	L	T	Pct.	Pts.	O.P.
Green Bay	9	2	0	.818	233	153
Chicago Bears	8	3	0	.727	298	157
Detroit	6	5	0	.545	145	150
Clev. Rams	5	5	1	.500	195	164
Chicago Cards	1	10	0	.091	84	254

Green Bay defeated New York, 27–0

1938

Eastern Division

	W	L	T	Pct.	Pts.	O.P.
N.Y. Giants	8	2	1	.800	194	79
Washington	6	3	2	.667	148	154
Brooklyn	4	4	3	.500	131	161
Philadelphia	5	6	0	.455	154	164
Pittsburgh	2	9	0	.182	79	169

Western Division

	W	L	T	Pct.	Pts.	O.P.
Green Bay	8	3	0	.727	223	118
Detroit	7	4	0	.636	119	108
Chicago Bears	6	5	0	.545	194	148
Clev. Rams	4	7	0	.364	131	215
Chicago Cards	2	9	0	.182	111	168

New York defeated Green Bay, 23–17

1937

	W	L	T	Pct.	Pts.	O.P.
Eastern Division						
Washington	8	3	0	.727	195	120
N.Y. Giants	6	3	2	.667	128	109
Pittsburgh	4	7	0	.364	122	145
Brooklyn	3	7	1	.300	82	174
Philadelphia	2	8	1	.200	86	177

	W	L	T	Pct.	Pts.	O.P.
Western Division						
Chicago Bears	9	1	1	.900	201	100
Green Bay	7	4	0	.636	220	122
Detroit	7	4	0	.636	180	105
Chicago Cards	5	5	1	.500	135	165
Clev. Rams	1	10	0	.091	75	207

Washington defeated Bears, 28–21

1936

	W	L	T	Pct.	Pts.	O.P.
Eastern Division						
*Boston Red.	7	5	0	.583	149	110
Pittsburgh	6	6	0	.500	98	187
N.Y. Giants	5	6	1	.455	115	163
Brooklyn	3	8	1	.273	92	161
Philadelphia	1	11	0	.083	51	206

	W	L	T	Pct.	Pts.	O.P.
Western Division						
Green Bay	10	1	1	.909	248	118
Chicago Bears	9	3	0	.750	222	94
Detroit	8	4	0	.667	235	102
Chicago Cards	3	8	1	.273	74	143

*—Franchise transferred to Washington, Feb. 13, 1937
Green Bay defeated Boston, 21–6

1935

	W	L	T	Pct.	Pts.	O.P.
Eastern Division						
N.Y. Giants	9	3	0	.750	180	96
Brooklyn	5	6	1	.455	90	141
Pittsburgh	4	8	0	.333	100	209
*Boston	2	8	1	.200	65	123
*Philadelphia	2	9	0	.182	60	179

	W	L	T	Pct.	Pts.	O.P.
Western Division						
Detroit	7	3	2	.700	191	111
Green Bay	8	4	0	.667	181	96
Chicago Bears	6	4	2	.600	192	106
Chicago Cards	6	4	2	.600	99	97

Detroit defeated New York Giants, 26–7
*—One game canceled.

1934

	W	L	T	Pct.	Pts.	O.P.
Eastern Division						
N.Y. Giants	8	5	0	.615	147	107
Boston Red.	6	6	0	.500	101	100
Brooklyn	4	7	0	.364	61	153
Philadelphia	4	7	0	.364	75	79
Pittsburgh	2	10	0	.167	51	206

	W	L	T	Pct.	Pts.	O.P.
Western Division						
Chicago Bears	13	0	0	1.000	286	86
Detroit	10	3	0	.769	238	59
Green Bay	7	6	0	.538	156	112
Chicago Cards	5	6	0	.455	80	91
St. L. Gunners	1	2	0	.333	27	61
*Cincinnati	0	8	0	.000	17	185

*—Franchise transferred to St. Louis, Nov. 5, 1934.
New York Giants defeated Bears, 30–13

1933

	W	L	T	Pct.	Pts.	O.P.
Eastern Division						
N.Y. Giants	11	3	0	.786	244	101
Brooklyn	5	4	1	.556	93	54
Boston Red.	5	5	2	.500	103	97
Philadelphia	3	5	1	.375	77	158
Pittsburgh	3	6	2	.333	67	208

	W	L	T	Pct.	Pts.	O.P.
Western Division						
Chicago Bears	10	2	1	.833	133	82
Portsmouth	6	5	0	.545	128	87
Green Bay	5	7	1	.417	170	107
Cincinnati	3	6	1	.333	38	110
Chicago Cards	1	9	1	.100	52	101

Bears defeated New York, 23–21

1932

	W	L	T	Pct.		W	L	T	Pct.
Chicago Bears	7	1	6	.875	N.Y. Giants	4	6	2	.400
Green Bay	10	3	1	.769	Brooklyn	3	9	0	.250
Portsmouth	6	2	4	.750	Chicago Cards	2	6	2	.250
Boston	4	4	2	.500	Stapleton	2	7	3	.222

1931

	W	L	T	Pct.		W	L	T	Pct.
Green Bay	12	2	0	.857	Providence	4	4	3	.500
Portsmouth	11	3	0	.786	Stapleton (N.Y.)	4	6	1	.400
Chicago Bears	8	4	0	.667	Cleveland	2	8	0	.200
Chicago Cards	5	4	0	.556	Brooklyn	2	12	0	.143
N.Y. Giants	6	6	1	.500	Frankford	1	6	1	.143

1930

	W	L	T	Pct.		W	L	T	Pct.
Green Bay	10	3	1	.769	Chicago Cards	5	6	2	.455
N.Y. Giants	13	4	0	.765	Portsmouth	5	6	3	.455
Chicago Bears	9	4	1	.692	Frankford	4	14	1	.222
Brooklyn	7	4	1	.636	Minneapolis	1	7	1	.125
Providence	6	4	1	.600	Newark	1	10	1	.091
Stapleton (N.Y.)	5	5	2	.500					

1929

	W	L	T	Pct.		W	L	T	Pct.
Green Bay	12	0	1	1.000	Stapleton (N.Y.)	3	4	3	.429
N.Y. Giants	12	1	1	.923	Providence	4	6	2	.400
Frankford	9	4	5	.692	Chicago Bears	4	8	2	.333
Chicago Cards	6	6	1	.500	Buffalo	1	7	1	.125
Boston	4	4	0	.500	Minneapolis	1	9	0	.100
Orange	3	4	4	.429	Dayton	0	6	0	.000

1928

	W	L	T	Pct.		W	L	T	Pct.
Providence	8	1	2	.889	N.Y. Giants	4	7	2	.364
Frankford	11	3	2	.786	N.Y. Yankees	4	8	1	.333
Detroit	7	2	1	.778	Pottsville	2	8	0	.200
Green Bay	6	4	3	.600	Chicago Cards	1	5	0	.167
Chicago Bears	7	5	1	.583	Dayton	0	7	0	.000

1927

	W	L	T	Pct.		W	L	T	Pct.
N.Y. Giants	11	1	1	.917	Frankford	6	9	3	.400
Green Bay	7	2	1	.778	Pottsville	5	8	0	.385
Chicago Bears	9	3	2	.750	Chicago Cards	3	7	1	.300
Cleveland	8	4	1	.667	Dayton	1	6	1	.143
Providence	8	5	1	.615	Duluth	1	8	0	.111
N.Y. Yankees	7	8	1	.467	Buffalo	0	5	0	.000

1926

	W	L	T	Pct.		W	L	T	Pct.
Frankford	14	1	1	.933	Detroit	4	6	2	.400
Chicago Bears	12	1	3	.923	Hartford	3	7	0	.300
Pottsville	10	2	1	.833	Brooklyn	3	8	0	.273
Kansas City	8	3	1	.727	Milwaukee	2	7	0	.222
Green Bay	7	3	3	.700	Akron	1	4	3	.200
Los Angeles	6	3	1	.667	Dayton	1	4	1	.200
N.Y. Giants	8	4	0	.667	Racine	1	4	0	.200
Duluth	6	5	2	.545	Columbus	1	6	0	.143
Buffalo	4	4	2	.500	Canton	1	9	3	.100
Chicago Cards	5	6	1	.455	Hammond	0	4	0	.000
Providence	5	7	0	.417	Louisville	0	4	0	.000

1925

	W	L	T	Pct.		W	L	T	Pct.
Chicago Cards	11	2	1	.846	Canton	4	4	0	.500
Pottsville	10	2	0	.833	Cleveland	5	8	1	.385
Detroit	8	2	2	.800	Kansas City	2	5	1	.286
N.Y. Giants	8	4	0	.667	Hammond	1	3	0	.250
Akron	4	2	2	.667	Buffalo	1	6	2	.143
Frankford	13	7	0	.650	Duluth	0	3	0	.000
Chicago Bears	9	5	3	.643	Rochester	0	6	1	.000
Rock Island	5	3	3	.625	Milwaukee	0	6	0	.000
Green Bay	8	5	0	.615	Dayton	0	7	1	.000
Providence	6	5	1	.545	Columbus	0	9	0	.000

1924

	W	L	T	Pct.		W	L	T	Pct.
Cleveland	7	1	1	.875	Columbus	4	4	0	.500
Chicago Bears	6	1	4	.857	Hammond	2	2	1	.500
Frankford	11	2	1	.846	Milwaukee	5	8	0	.385
Duluth	5	1	0	.833	Dayton	2	7	0	.222
Rock Island	6	2	2	.750	Kansas City	2	7	0	.222
Green Bay	8	4	0	.667	Akron	1	6	0	.143
Buffalo	6	4	0	.600	Kenosha	0	5	1	.000
Racine	4	3	3	.571	Minneapolis	0	6	0	.000
Chicago Cards	5	4	1	.556	Rochester	0	7	0	.000

1923

	W	L	T	Pct.		W	L	T	Pct.
Canton	11	0	1	1.000	Toledo	2	3	2	.400
Chicago Bears	9	2	1	.818	Rock Island	2	3	3	.400
Green Bay	7	2	1	.778	Minneapolis	2	5	2	.286
Milwaukee	7	2	3	.778	St. Louis	1	4	2	.200
Cleveland	3	1	3	.750	Hammond	1	5	1	.167
Chicago Cards	8	4	0	.667	Dayton	1	6	1	.143
Duluth	4	3	0	.571	Akron	1	6	0	.143
Buffalo	5	4	3	.556	Marion	1	10	0	.091
Columbus	5	4	1	.556	Rochester	0	2	0	.000
Racine	4	4	2	.500	Louisville	0	3	0	.000

1922

	W	L	T	Pct.		W	L	T	Pct.
Canton	10	0	2	1.000	Buffalo	3	4	1	.429
Chicago Bears	9	3	0	.750	Milwaukee	2	4	3	.333
Chicago Cards	8	3	0	.727	Marion	2	6	0	.250
Toledo	5	2	2	.714	Minneapolis	1	3	0	.250
Rock Island	4	2	1	.667	Evansville	0	2	0	.000
Dayton	4	3	1	.571	Louisville	0	3	0	.000
Green Bay	4	3	3	.571	Rochester	0	3	1	.000
Racine	5	4	1	.556	Hammond	0	4	1	.000
Akron	3	4	2	.429	Columbus	0	7	0	.000

1921

	W	L	T	Pct.		W	L	T	Pct.
Chicago Bears*	10	1	1	.909	Rock Island	5	4	1	.556
Buffalo	9	1	2	.900	Chicago Cards	2	3	2	.400
Akron	7	2	1	.778	Cleveland	2	6	0	.250
Green Bay	6	2	2	.750	Rochester	2	6	0	.250
Canton	4	3	3	.571	Detroit	1	7	1	.125
Dayton	4	3	1	.571	Columbus	0	6	0	.000
					Cincinnati	0	8	0	.000

*Staleys.

1920

The National Football League was organized on September 17, 1920, in Canton, Ohio, under the name of the American Professional Football Association. The name was changed to NFL in 1922. At one stage or another during 1920, the first season, 13 clubs fielded teams. There was no planned schedule of games. The teams that season were the Akron Steels, Buffalo All Americans, Chicago Cardinals, Chicago Tigers, Canton Bulldogs, Cleveland Panthers, Columbus Panhandles, Dayton Triangles, Decatur Staleys, Detroit Heralds, Hammond Pros, Rochester Jeffersons, and Rock Island Independents. Formal standings were first compiled in 1921.

Dick Butkus of the Chicago Bears, oldest team in professional football.

ALL-TIME TEAM vs. TEAM RECORDS

(Key: All series listed alphabetically with cross reference. In 1943, Philadelphia and Pittsburgh were combined, and in 1944 Pittsburgh and the Chicago Cardinals were combined. Scores of those teams in those years are listed under both Philadelphia and Pittsburgh, and Pittsburgh and the Cardinals. Also, the St. Louis heading covers all games of the original Chicago Cardinals. The cities in which the games were played appear abbreviated after the scores.)

ATLANTA FALCONS vs. BALTIMORE COLTS

(Colts lead series, 7–0)

1966—Colts, 19–7 (A)	1969—Colts, 21–14 (A)
1967—Colts, 38–31 (B)	Colts, 13–6 (B)
Colts, 49–7 (A)	
1968—Colts, 28–20 (A)	
Colts, 44–0 (B)	

(Points—Colts 212, Falcons 85)

ATLANTA FALCONS vs. CHICAGO BEARS

(Series tied, 2–2)

1966—Bears, 23–6 (C)	1968—Falcons, 16–13 (C)
1967—Bears, 23–14 (A)	1969—Falcons, 48–31 (A)

(Points—Bears 90, Falcons 84)

ATLANTA FALCONS vs. CLEVELAND BROWNS

(Browns lead series, 2–0)

1966—Browns, 49–17 (A)	1968—Browns, 30–7 (C)

(Points—Browns 79, Falcons 24)

ATLANTA FALCONS vs. DALLAS·COWBOYS

(Cowboys lead series, 3–0)

1966—Cowboys, 47–14 (A)	1969—Cowboys, 24–17 (A)
1967—Cowboys, 37–7 (D)	

(Points—Cowboys 84, Falcons 21)

ATLANTA FALCONS vs. DETROIT LIONS

(Lions lead series, 4–0)

1966—Lions, 28–10 (D)	1968—Lions 24–7 (A)
1967—Lions, 24–3 (D)	1969—Lions, 27–21 (D)

(Points—Lions 103, Falcons 41)

ATLANTA FALCONS vs. GREEN BAY PACKERS

(Packers lead series, 4–0)

1966—Packers, 56–3 (Mil)	1968—Packers 38–7 (A)
1967—Packers, 23–0 (Mil)	1969—Packers, 28–10 (GB)

(Points—Packers 145, Falcons 20)

ATLANTA FALCONS vs. LOS ANGELES RAMS

(Rams lead series, 7–0)

1966—Rams, 19–14 (A)	1969—Rams, 17–7 (LA)
1967—Rams, 31–3 (A)	Rams, 38–6 (A)
Rams, 20–3 (LA)	
1968—Rams, 27–14 (LA)	
Rams, 17–10 (A)	

(Points—Rams 169, Falcons 57)

ATLANTA FALCONS vs. MINNESOTA VIKINGS

(Falcons lead series, 3–1)

1966—Falcons, 20–13 (M)	1968—Vikings, 47–7 (M)
1967—Falcons, 21–20 (A)	1969—Falcons, 10–3 (A)

(Points—Vikings 83, Falcons 58)

ATLANTA FALCONS vs. NEW ORLEANS SAINTS

(Series tied, 1–1)

1967—Saints, 27–24 (NO)   1969—Falcons, 45–17 (A)
(Points—Falcons 69, Saints 44)

ATLANTA FALCONS vs. NEW YORK GIANTS

(Falcons lead series, 2–0)

1966—Falcons, 27–16 (NY)   1968—Falcons, 24–21 (A)
(Points—Falcons 51, Giants 37)

ATLANTA FALCONS vs. PHILADELPHIA EAGLES

(Eagles lead series, 2–1)

1966—Eagles, 23–10 (P)   1969—Falcons, 27–3 (P)
1967—Eagles, 38–7 (A)
(Points—Eagles 64, Falcons 44)

ATLANTA FALCONS vs. PITTSBURGH STEELERS

(Steelers lead series, 2–0)

1966—Steelers, 57–33 (A)   1968—Steelers, 41–21 (A)
(Points—Steelers 98, Falcons 54)

ATLANTA FALCONS vs. ST. LOUIS CARDINALS

(Series tied, 1–1)

1966—Falcons, 16–10 (A)   1968—Cardinals, 17–12 (St L)
(Points—Falcons 28, Cardinals 27)

ATLANTA FALCONS vs. SAN FRANCISCO 49ERS

(49ERS lead series, 5–2)

1966—49ERS, 44–7 (A)   1969—Falcons, 24–12 (A)
1967—49ERS, 38–7 (SF)   Falcons, 21–7 (SF)
      49ERS, 34–28 (A)
1968—49ERS, 28–13 (SF)
      49ERS, 14–12 (A)
(Points—49ERS 177, Falcons 112)

ATLANTA FALCONS vs. WASHINGTON REDSKINS

(Redskins lead series, 2–0–1)

1966—Redskins, 33–20 (W)   1969—Redskins, 27–20 (W)
1967—Tie, 20–20 (A)
(Points—Redskins 80, Falcons 60)

BALTIMORE COLTS vs. ATLANTA FALCONS

(Colts lead series, 7–0; See Atlanta vs. Baltimore)

BALTIMORE COLTS vs. CHICAGO BEARS

(Colts lead series, 18–13)

1953—Colts, 13–9 (B)   1959—Bears, 26–21 (B)
      Colts, 16–14 (C)   Colts, 21–7 (C)
1954—Bears, 28–9 (C)   1960—Colts, 42–7 (B)
      Bears, 28–13 (B)   Colts, 24–20 (C)
1955—Colts, 23–17 (B)   1961—Bears, 24–10 (C)
      Bears, 38–10 (C)   Bears, 21–20 (B)
1956—Colts, 28–21 (B)   1962—Bears, 35–15 (C)
      Bears, 58–27 (C)   Bears, 57–0 (B)
1957—Colts, 21–10 (B)   1963—Bears, 10–3 (C)
      Colts, 29–14 (C)   Bears, 17–7 (B)
1958—Colts, 51–38 (B)   1964—Colts, 52–0 (B)
      Colts, 17–0 (C)   Colts, 40–24 (C)

Baltimore vs. Chicago Bears (Cont'd)

1965—Colts, 26–21 (C)   1967—Colts, 24–3 (C)
      Bears, 13–0 (B)   1968—Colts, 28–7 (B)
1966—Bears, 27–17 (C)   1969—Colts, 24–21 (B)
      Colts, 21–16 (B)
(Points—Colts 652, Bears 631)

BALTIMORE COLTS vs. CLEVELAND BROWNS

(Browns lead series, 4–3)

1950—Browns, 31–0 (B)   1964—*Browns, 27–0 (C)
1956—Colts, 21–7 (C)   1968—Browns, 30–20 (B)
1959—Browns, 38–31 (B)   *Colts, 34–0 (C)
1962—Colts, 36–14 (C)
(Points—Browns 147, Colts 142)
*NFL Championship

BALTIMORE COLTS vs. DALLAS COWBOYS

(Colts lead series, 3–1)

1960—Colts, 45–7 (D)   1967—Colts, 23–17 (B)
1966—*Colts, 35–3 (Miami)   1969—Cowboys, 27–10 (D)
(Points—Colts 115, Cowboys 54)
*Playoff Bowl

BALTIMORE COLTS vs. DETROIT LIONS

(Lions lead series, 16–14–2)

1950—Lions, 45–21 (B)   1961—Lions, 16–15 (B)
1953—Lions, 27–17 (B)   Colts, 17–14 (D)
      Lions, 17–7 (D)   1962—Lions, 29–20 (B)
1954—Lions, 35–0 (D)   Lions, 21–14 (D)
      Lions, 27–3 (B)   1963—Colts, 25–21 (D)
1955—Colts, 28–13 (B)   Colts, 24–21 (B)
      Lions, 24–14 (D)   1964—Colts, 34–0 (D)
1956—Lions, 31–14 (B)   Lions, 31–14 (B)
      Lions, 27–3 (D)   1965—Colts, 31–7 (B)
1957—Colts, 34–14 (B)   Tie, 24–24 (D)
      Lions, 31–27 (D)   1966—Colts, 45–14 (B)
1958—Colts, 28–15 (B)   Lions, 20–14 (D)
      Colts, 40–14 (D)   1967—Colts, 41–7 (B)
1959—Colts, 21–9 (B)   1968—Colts, 27–10 (D)
      Colts, 31–24 (D)   1969—Tie, 17–17 (B)
1960—Lions, 30–17 (D)
      Lions, 20–15 (B)
(Points—Colts 682, Lions 655)

BALTIMORE COLTS vs. GREEN BAY PACKERS

(Packers lead series, 17–16)

1950—Colts, 41–21 (B)   1959—Colts, 38–21 (B)
1953—Packers, 37–14 (GB)   Colts, 28–24 (Mil)
      Packers, 35–24 (B)   1960—Packers, 35–21 (GB)
1954—Packers, 7–6 (B)   Colts, 38–24 (B)
      Packers, 24–13 (Mil)   1961—Packers, 45–7 (GB)
1955—Colts, 24–20 (Mil)   Colts, 45–21 (B)
      Colts, 14–10 (B)   1962—Packers, 17–6 (B)
1956—Packers, 38–33 (Mil)   Packers, 17–13 (GB)
      Colts, 28–21 (B)   1963—Packers, 31–20 (GB)
1957—Colts, 45–17 (Mil)   Packers, 34–20 (B)
      Packers, 24–21 (B)   1964—Colts, 21–20 (GB)
1958—Colts, 24–17 (Mil)   Colts, 24–21 (B)
      Colts, 56–0 (B)

```
1965—Packers, 20–17 (Mil)          1967—Colts, 13–10 (B)
       Packers, 42–27 (B)          1968—Colts, 16–3 (GB)
      *Packers, 13–10 (GB)         1969—Colts, 14–6 (B)
1966—Packers, 24–3 (Mil)
       Packers, 14–10 (B)
                    (Points—Colts 734, Packers 713)
```

*Conference playoff.

BALTIMORE COLTS vs. LOS ANGELES RAMS

(Colts lead series, 19–14–2)

```
1950—Rams, 70–27 (LA)            1962—Colts, 30–27 (B)
1953—Rams, 21–13 (B)                   Colts, 14–2 (LA)
       Rams, 45–2 (LA)           1963—Rams, 17–16 (LA)
1954—Rams, 48–0 (B)                    Colts, 19–16 (B)
       Colts, 22–21 (LA)         1964—Colts, 35–20 (B)
1955—Tie, 17–17 (B)                    Colts, 24–7 (LA)
       Rams, 20–14 (LA)          1965—Colts, 35–20 (B)
1956—Colts, 56–21 (B)                  Colts, 20–17 (LA)
       Rams, 31–7 (LA)           1966—Colts, 17–3 (LA)
1957—Colts, 31–14 (B)                  Rams, 23–7 (B)
       Rams, 37–21 (LA)          1967—Tie, 24–24 (B)
1958—Colts, 34–7 (B)                   Rams, 34–10 (LA)
       Rams, 30–28 (LA)          1968—Colts, 27–10 (B)
1959—Colts, 35–21 (B)                  Colts, 28–24 (LA)
       Colts, 45–26 (LA)         1969—Rams, 27–20 (B)
1960—Colts, 31–17 (B)                  Colts, 13–7 (LA)
       Rams, 10–3 (LA)
1961—Colts, 27–24 (B)
       Rams, 34–17 (LA)
                    (Points—Rams 792, Colts 769)
```


BALTIMORE COLTS vs. MINNESOTA VIKINGS

(Colts lead series, 12–3–1)

```
1961—Colts, 34–33 (B)            1965—Colts, 35–16 (B)
       Vikings, 28–20 (M)               Colts, 41–21 (M)
1962—Colts, 34–7 (M)             1966—Colts, 38–23 (M)
       Colts, 42–17 (B)                 Colts, 20–17 (B)
1963—Colts, 37–34 (M)            1967—Tie, 20–20 (M)
       Colts, 41–10 (B)          1968—Colts, 21–9 (B)
1964—Vikings, 34–24 (M)                *Colts, 24–14 (B)
       Colts, 17–14 (B)          1969—Vikings, 52–14 (M)
                   (Points—Colts 462, Vikings 339)
```

*Conference Championship

BALTIMORE COLTS vs. NEW ORLEANS SAINTS

(Colts lead series, 2–0)

```
1967—Colts, 30–10 (B)         1969—Colts, 30–10 (NO)
             (Points—Colts 60, Saints 20)
```


BALTIMORE COLTS vs. NEW YORK GIANTS

(Series tied, 4–4)

```
1950—Giants, 55–20 (B)        1959—*Colts, 31–16 (B)
1954—Colts, 20–14 (B)         1963—Giants, 37–28 (B)
1955—Giants, 17–7 (NY)        1968—Colts, 26–0 (NY)
1958—Giants, 24–21 (NY)
      *Colts, 23–17 (NY)
             (Points—Giants 180, Colts 176)
```

*NFL Championship

BALTIMORE COLTS vs. NEW YORK JETS

(Jets lead series, 1–0)

1969—*Jets, 16–7 (Miami)
*Super Bowl

BALTIMORE COLTS vs. PHILADELPHIA EAGLES

(Colts lead series, 4–2)

1950—Eagles, 24–14 (B)
1953—Eagles, 45–14 (P)
1965—Colts, 34–24 (B)

1967—*Colts, 20–14 (Miami)
Colts, 38–6 (P)
1969—Colts, 24–20 (B)

(Points—Colts 144, Eagles 133)

*Playoff Bowl

BALTIMORE COLTS vs. PITTSBURGH STEELERS

(Steelers lead series, 2–1)

1950—Steelers, 17–7 (P)
1957—Steelers, 19–13 (B)

1968—Colts, 41–7 (P)

(Points—Colts 61, Steelers 43)

BALTIMORE COLTS vs. *ST. LOUIS CARDINALS

(Colts lead series, 3–1)

1950—Cardinals, 55–13 (C)
1961—Colts, 16–0 (B)

1964—Colts, 47–27 (B)
1968—Colts, 27–0 (B)

(Points—Colts 103, Cardinals 82)

*Franchise in Chicago prior to 1960

BALTIMORE COLTS vs. SAN FRANCISCO 49ERS

(Colts lead series, 21–14)

1950—49ERS, 17–14 (SF)
1953—49ERS, 38–21 (B)
      49ERS, 45–14 (SF)
1954—Colts, 17–13 (B)
      49ERS, 10–7 (SF)
1955—Colts, 26–14 (B)
      49ERS, 35–24 (SF)
1956—49ERS, 20–17 (B)
      49ERS, 30–17 (SF)
1957—Colts, 27–21 (B)
      49ERS, 17–13 (SF)
1958—Colts, 35–27 (B)
      49ERS, 21–12 (SF)
1959—Colts, 45–14 (B)
      Colts, 34–14 (SF)
1960—49ERS, 30–22 (B)
      49ERS, 34–10 (SF)
1961—Colts, 20–17 (B)
      Colts, 27–24 (SF)

1962—49ERS, 21–13 (B)
      Colts, 22–3 (SF)
1963—Colts, 20–14 (B)
      Colts, 20–3 (SF)
1964—Colts, 37–7 (B)
      Colts, 14–3 (SF)
1965—Colts, 27–24 (B)
      Colts, 34–28 (SF)
1966—Colts, 36–14 (B)
      Colts, 30–14 (SF)
1967—Colts, 41–7 (B)
      Colts, 26–9 (SF)
1968—Colts, 27–10 (B)
      Colts, 42–14 (SF)
1969—49ERS, 24–21 (B)
      49ERS, 20–17 (SF)

(Points—Colts 829, 49ERS 656)

BALTIMORE COLTS vs. WASHINGTON REDSKINS

(Colts lead series, 13–5)

1950—Redskins, 38–14 (B)
      Redskins, 38–28 (W)
1953—Colts, 27–17 (B)
1954—Redskins, 24–21 (W)
1955—Redskins, 14–13 (B)
1956—Colts, 19–17 (B)
1957—Colts, 21–17 (W)
1958—Colts, 35–10 (B)
1959—Redskins, 27–24 (W)

1960—Colts, 20–0 (B)
1961—Colts, 27–6 (W)
1962—Colts, 34–21 (B)
1963—Colts, 36–20 (W)
1964—Colts, 45–27 (B)
1965—Colts, 38–7 (B)
1966—Colts, 37–10 (B)
1967—Colts, 17–13 (W)
1969—Colts, 41–17 (B)

(Points—Colts 497, Redskins 323)

BOSTON PATRIOTS vs. BUFFALO BILLS

(Patriots lead series, 12–8–1)

1960—Bills, 13–0 (Bo)	1965—Bills, 24–7 (Bu)
Bills, 38–14 (Bu)	Bills, 23–7 (Bo)
1961—Patriots, 23–21 (Bu)	1966—Patriots, 20–10 (Bu)
Patriots, 52–21 (Bo)	Patriots, 14–3 (Bo)
1962—Tie, 28–28 (Bu)	1967—Patriots, 23–0 (Bu)
Patriots, 21–10 (Bo)	Bills, 44–16 (Bo)
1963—Bills, 28–21 (Bu)	1968—Patriots, 16–7 (Bu)
Patriots, 17–7 (Bo)	Patriots, 23–6 (Bo)
*Patriots, 26–8 (Bu)	1969—Bills, 23–16 (Bu)
1964—Patriots, 36–28 (Bu)	Patriots, 35–21 (Bo)
Bills, 24–14 (Bo)	

(Points—Patriots 429, Bills 387)

*Eastern Division Playoff

BOSTON PATRIOTS vs. CINCINNATI BENGALS

(Patriots lead series, 2–0)

1968—Patriots, 33–14 (B)   1969—Patriots, 25–14 (C)

(Points—Patriots 58, Bengals 28)

BOSTON PATRIOTS vs. DENVER BRONCOS

(Patriots lead series, 10–8)

1960—Broncos, 13–10 (B)	1965—Broncos, 27–10 (B)
Broncos, 31–24 (D)	Patriots, 28–20 (D)
1961—Patriots, 45–17 (B)	1966—Patriots, 24–10 (D)
Patriots, 28–24 (D)	Broncos, 17–10 (B)
1962—Patriots, 42–16 (B)	1967—Broncos, 26–21 (D)
Patriots, 33–29 (D)	1968—Patriots, 20–17 (D)
1963—Broncos, 14–10 (D)	Broncos, 35–14 (B)
Patriots, 40–21 (B)	1969—Broncos, 35–7 (D)
1964—Patriots, 39–10 (D)	
Patriots, 12–7 (B)	

(Points—Patriots 417, Broncos 369)

BOSTON PATRIOTS vs. HOUSTON OILERS

(Patriots lead series, 10–9–1)

1960—Oilers, 24–10 (B)	1965—Oilers, 31–10 (H)
Oilers, 37–21 (H)	Patriots, 42–14 (B)
1961—Tie, 31–31 (B)	1966—Patriots, 27–21 (B)
Oilers, 27–15 (H)	Patriots, 38–14 (H)
1962—Patriots, 34–21 (B)	1967—Patriots, 18–7 (B)
Oilers, 21–17 (H)	Oilers, 27–6 (H)
1963—Patriots, 45–3 (B)	1968—Oilers, 16–0 (B)
Patriots, 46–28 (H)	Oilers, 45–17 (H)
1964—Patriots, 25–24 (B)	1969—Patriots, 24–0 (B)
Patriots, 34–17 (H)	Oilers, 27–23 (H)

(Points—Patriots 483, Oilers 435)

BOSTON PATRIOTS vs. *KANSAS CITY CHIEFS

(Chiefs lead series, 9–5–3)

1960—Patriots, 42–14 (B)	1963—Tie, 24–24 (B)
Texans, 34–0 (D)	Chiefs, 35–3 (KC)
1961—Patriots, 18–17 (D)	1964—Patriots, 24–7 (B)
Patriots, 28–21 (B)	Patriots, 31–24 (KC)
1962—Texans, 42–28 (D)	1965—Chiefs, 27–17 (KC)
Texans, 27–7 (B)	Tie, 10–10 (B)

Boston Patriots vs. Kansas City Chiefs (Cont'd)

1966—Chiefs, 43–24 (B)
       Tie, 27–27 (KC)
1967—Chiefs, 33–10 (B)

1968—Chiefs, 31–17 (KC)
1969—Chiefs, 31–0 (B)

(Points—Chiefs 447, Patriots 310)
*Franchise located in Dallas (D) prior to 1963 and known as Texans

BOSTON PATRIOTS vs. MIAMI DOLPHINS

(Dolphins lead series, 4–3)

1966—Patriots, 20–14 (M)
1967—Patriots, 41–10 (B)
       Dolphins, 41–32 (M)
1968—Dolphins, 34–10 (B)
       Dolphins, 38–7 (M)

1969—Dolphins, 17–16 (B)
       Patriots, 38–23 (Tampa)

(Points—Dolphins 177, Patriots 164)

BOSTON PATRIOTS vs. *NEW YORK JETS

(Jets lead series, 12–7–1)

1960—Patriots, 28–24 (NY)
       Patriots, 38–21 (B)
1961—Titans, 21–20 (B)
       Titans, 37–30 (NY)
1962—Patriots, 43–14 (NY)
       Patriots, 24–17 (B)
1963—Patriots, 38–14 (B)
       Jets, 31–24 (NY)
1964—Patriots, 26–10 (B)
       Jets, 35–14 (NY)

1965—Jets, 30–20 (B)
       Patriots, 27–23 (NY)
1966—Tie, 24–24 (B)
       Jets, 38–28 (NY)
1967—Jets, 30–23 (NY)
       Jets, 29–24 (B)
1968—Jets, 47–31 (Birm'h'm)
       Jets, 48–14 (NY)
1969—Jets, 23–14 (B)
       Jets, 23–17 (NY)

(Points—Jets 539, Patriots 507)
*Known as Titans prior to 1963

BOSTON PATRIOTS vs. OAKLAND RAIDERS

(Series tied, 8–8–1)

1960—Raiders, 27–14 (O)
       Patriots, 34–28 (B)
1961—Patriots, 20–17 (B)
       Patriots, 35–21 (O)
1962—Patriots, 26–16 (B)
       Raiders, 20–0 (O)
1963—Patriots, 20–14 (O)
       Patriots, 20–14 (B)
1964—Patriots, 17–14 (O)
       Tie, 43–43 (B)

1965—Raiders, 24–10 (B)
       Raiders, 30–21 (O)
1966—Patriots, 24–21 (B)
1967—Raiders, 35–7 (O)
       Raiders, 48–14 (B)
1968—Raiders, 41–10 (O)
1969—Raiders, 38–23 (B)

(Points—Raiders 451, Patriots 338)

BOSTON PATRIOTS vs. *SAN DIEGO CHARGERS

(Chargers lead series, 11–7–2)

1960—Patriots, 35–0 (LA)
       Chargers, 45–16 (B)
1961—Chargers, 38–27 (B)
       Patriots, 41–0 (SD)
1962—Patriots, 24–20 (B)
       Patriots, 20–14 (SD)

1963—Chargers, 17–13 (SD)
       Chargers, 7–6 (B)
       **Chargers, 51–10 (SD)
1964—Patriots, 33–28 (SD)
       Chargers, 26–17 (B)

1965—Tie, 10-10 (B)   1968—Chargers, 27-17 (B)
      Patriots, 22-6 (SD)   1969—Chargers, 13-10 (B)
1966—Chargers, 24-0 (SD)   Chargers, 28-18 (SD)
      Patriots, 35-17 (B)
1967—Chargers, 28-14 (SD)
      Tie, 31-31 (SD)
                (Points—Chargers 430, Patriots 399)
*Franchise in Los Angeles prior to 1961
**Championship Game

BUFFALO BILLS vs. BOSTON PATRIOTS

(Patriots lead series, 12-8-1; See Boston vs. Buffalo)

BUFFALO BILLS vs. CINCINNATI BENGALS

(Series tied, 1-1)
1968—Bengals, 34-23 (C)   1969—Bills, 16-13 (B)
              (Points—Bengals 47, Bills 39)

BUFFALO BILLS vs. DENVER BRONCOS

(Bills lead series, 11-5-1)
1960—Broncos, 27-21 (B)   1965—Bills, 30-15 (D)
      Tie, 38-38 (D)   Bills, 31-13 (B)
1961—Broncos, 22-10 (B)   1966—Bills, 38-21 (B)
      Bills, 23-10 (D)   1967—Bills, 17-16 (D)
1962—Broncos, 23-20 (B)   Broncos 21-20 (B)
      Bills, 45-38 (D)   1968—Broncos 34-32 (D)
1963—Bills, 30-28 (D)   1969—Bills, 41-28 (B)
      Bills, 27-17 (B)
1964—Bills, 30-13 (B)
      Bills, 30-19 (D)
              (Points—Bills 483, Broncos 383)

BUFFALO BILLS vs. HOUSTON OILERS

(Oilers lead series, 13-7)
1960—Bills, 25-24 (B)   1965—Oilers, 19-17 (B)
      Oilers, 31-23 (H)   Bills, 29-18 (H)
1961—Bills, 22-12 (H)   1966—Bills, 27-20 (B)
      Oilers, 28-16 (B)   Bills, 42-20 (H)
1962—Oilers, 28-23 (B)   1967—Oilers, 20-3 (B)
      Oilers, 17-14 (H)   Oilers, 10-3 (H)
1963—Oilers, 31-20 (B)   1968—Oilers, 30-7 (B)
      Oilers, 28-14 (H)   Oilers, 35-6 (H)
1964—Bills, 48-17 (H)   1969—Oilers, 17-3 (B)
      Bills, 24-10 (B)   Oilers, 28-14 (H)
              (Points—Oilers 443, Bills 380)

BUFFALO BILLS vs. *KANSAS CITY CHIEFS

(Series tied, 9-9-1)
1960—Texans, 45-28 (B)   1963—Tie, 27-27 (B)
      Texans, 24-7 (D)   Bills, 35-26 (KC)
1961—Bills, 27-24 (B)   1964—Bills, 35-17 (B)
      Bills, 30-20 (D)   Bills, 35-22 (KC)
1962—Texans, 41-21 (D)   1965—Bills, 23-7 (KC)
      Bills, 23-14 (B)   Bills, 34-25 (B)

Buffalo Bills vs. Kansas City Chiefs (Cont'd)

1966—Chiefs, 42–20 (B)　　　　1968—Chiefs, 18–7 (B)
　　　Bills, 29–14 (KC)　　　　1969—Chiefs, 29–7 (B)
　　　**Chiefs, 31–7 (B)　　　　　　　Chiefs, 22–19 (KC)
1967—Chiefs, 23–13 (KC)

(Points—Chiefs 471, Bills 427)

*Franchise located in Dallas (D) prior to 1963 and known as Texans
**Championship Game

BUFFALO BILLS vs. MIAMI DOLPHINS

(Bills lead series, 4–3–1)

1966—Bills, 58–24 (B)　　　　1968—Tie, 14–14 (M)
　　　Bills, 29–0 (M)　　　　　　　　Dolphins, 21–17 (B)
1967—Bills, 35–13 (B)　　　　1969—Dolphins, 24–6 (M)
　　　Dolphins, 17–14 (M)　　　　　　Bills, 28–3 (B)

(Points—Bills 201, Dolphins 116)

BUFFALO BILLS vs. *NEW YORK JETS

(Bills lead series, 11–9)

1960—Titans, 27–3 (NY)　　　　1965—Jets, 14–12 (NY)
　　　Titans, 17–13 (B)　　　　　　　Bills, 33–21 (B)
1961—Bills, 41–31 (B)　　　　1966—Bills, 33–23 (NY)
　　　Titans, 21–14 (NY)　　　　　　Bills, 14–3 (B)
1962—Titans, 17–6 (B)　　　　1967—Bills, 20–17 (B)
　　　Bills, 20–3 (NY)　　　　　　　Jets, 20–10 (NY)
1963—Bills, 45–14 (B)　　　　1968—Bills, 37–35 (B)
　　　Bills, 19–10 (NY)　　　　　　Jets, 25–21 (NY)
1964—Bills, 34–24 (B)　　　　1969—Jets, 33–19 (B)
　　　Bills, 20–7 (NY)　　　　　　Jets, 16–6 (NY)

(Points—Bills 420, Jets 378)

*Jets known as Titans prior to 1963

BUFFALO BILLS vs. OAKLAND RAIDERS

(Series tied, 9–9)

1960—Bills, 38–9 (B)　　　　1965—Bills, 17–12 (B)
　　　Raiders, 20–7 (O)　　　　　　Bills, 17–14 (O)
1961—Raiders, 31–22 (B)　　　1966—Bills, 31–10 (O)
　　　Bills, 26–21 (O)　　　　1967—Raiders, 24–20 (B)
1962—Bills, 14–6 (B)　　　　　　　Raiders, 28–21 (O)
　　　Bills, 10–6 (O)　　　　1968—Raiders, 48–6 (B)
1963—Raiders, 35–17 (O)　　　　　Raiders, 13–10 (O)
　　　Bills, 12–0 (B)　　　　1969—Raiders, 50–21 (O)
1964—Bills, 23–20 (B)
　　　Raiders, 16–13 (O)

(Points—Raiders 363, Bills 325)

BUFFALO BILLS vs. *SAN DIEGO CHARGERS

(Chargers lead series, 10–7–2)

1960—Chargers, 24–10 (B)　　　1965—Chargers, 34–3 (B)
　　　Bills, 32–3 (LA)　　　　　　Tie, 20–20 (SD)
1961—Chargers, 19–11 (B)　　　　**Bills, 23–0 (SD)
　　　Chargers, 28–10 (SD)　　1966—Chargers, 27–7 (SD)
1962—Bills, 35–10 (B)　　　　　　Tie, 17–17 (B)
　　　Bills, 40–20 (SD)　　　1967—Chargers, 37–17 (B)
1963—Chargers, 14–10 (SD)　　1968—Chargers, 21–6 (B)
　　　Chargers, 23–13 (B)　　　1969—Chargers, 45–6 (SD)
1964—Bills, 30–3 (B)
　　　Bills, 27–24 (SD)
　　　**Bills, 20–7 (B)

(Points—Chargers 376, Bills 337)

*Franchise located in Los Angeles prior to 1961
**AFL Championship

CHICAGO BEARS vs. ATLANTA FALCONS

(Series tied, 2–2; See Atlanta vs. Chicago)

CHICAGO BEARS vs. BALTIMORE COLTS

(Colts lead series, 18–13; See Baltimore vs. Chicago)

CHICAGO BEARS vs. CLEVELAND BROWNS

(Browns lead series, 5–1)

1951—Browns, 42–21 (Cle)	1960—Browns, 42–0 (Cle)
1954—Browns, 39–10 (Chi)	1961—Bears, 17–14 (Chi)
	1967—Browns, 24–0 (Cle)
	1969—Browns, 28–24 (Chi)

(Points—Browns 189, Bears 72)

CHICAGO BEARS vs. DALLAS COWBOYS

(Series tied, 2–2)

1960—Bears, 17–7 (C)	1964—Cowboys, 24–10 (C)
1963—Bears, 34–33 (D)	1968—Cowboys, 34–3 (C)

(Points—Cowboys 98, Bears 64)

CHICAGO BEARS vs. DETROIT LIONS

(Bears lead series, 44–25–3)

1934—Bears, 19–16 (D)	1952—Bears, 24–23 (C)
Bears, 10–7 (C)	Lions, 45–21 (D)
1935—Tie, 20–20 (C)	1953—Lions, 20–16 (C)
Lions, 14–2 (D)	Lions, 13–7 (D)
1936—Bears, 12–10 (C)	1954—Lions, 48–23 (D)
Lions, 13–7 (D)	Bears, 28–24 (C)
1937—Bears, 28–20 (C)	1955—Bears, 24–14 (D)
Bears, 13–0 (D)	Bears, 21–20 (C)
1938—Lions, 13–7 (C)	1956—Lions, 42–10 (D)
Lions, 14–7 (D)	Bears, 38–21 (C)
1939—Lions, 10–0 (C)	1957—Bears, 27–7 (D)
Bears, 23–13 (D)	Lions, 21–13 (C)
1940—Bears, 7–0 (C)	1958—Bears, 20–7 (D)
Lions, 17–14 (D)	Bears, 21–16 (C)
1941—Bears, 49–0 (C)	1959—Bears, 24–14 (D)
Bears, 24–7 (D)	Bears, 25–14 (C)
1942—Bears, 16–0 (C)	1960—Bears, 28–7 (C)
Bears, 42–0 (D)	Lions, 36–0 (D)
1943—Bears, 27–21 (D)	1961—Bears, 31–17 (D)
Bears, 35–14 (C)	Lions, 16–15 (C)
1944—Tie, 21–21 (C)	1962—Lions, 11–3 (D)
Lions, 41–21 (D)	Bears, 3–0 (C)
1945—Lions, 16–10 (D)	1963—Bears, 37–21 (D)
Lions, 35–28 (C)	Bears, 24–14 (C)
1946—Bears, 42–6 (C)	1964—Lions, 10–0 (C)
Bears, 45–24 (D)	Bears, 27–24 (D)
1947—Bears, 33–24 (C)	1965—Bears, 38–10 (C)
Bears, 34–14 (D)	Bears, 17–10 (D)
1948—Bears, 28–0 (C)	1966—Bears, 14–3 (D)
Bears, 42–14 (D)	Tie, 10–10 (C)
1949—Bears, 27–24 (C)	1967—Bears, 14–3 (C)
Bears, 28–7 (D)	Bears, 27–13 (D)
1950—Bears, 35–21 (D)	1968—Lions, 42–0 (C)
Bears, 6–3 (C)	Lions, 28–10 (C)
1951—Bears, 28–23 (D)	1969—Lions, 13–7 (D)
Lions, 41–28 (C)	Lions, 20–3 (C)

(Points—Bears 1,457, Lions 1,191)

CHICAGO BEARS vs. GREEN BAY PACKERS

(Bears lead series, 54–42–6)

1921—Bears, 20–0 (C)
1923—Bears, 3–0 (GB)
1924—Packers, 5–0 (GB)
    Bears, 3–0 (C)
1925—Packers, 14–10 (GB)
    Bears, 21–0 (C)
1926—Tie, 6–6 (GB)
    Bears, 19–13 (C)
    Tie, 3–3 (C)
1927—Bears, 7–6 (GB)
    Bears, 14–6 (C)
1928—Tie, 12–12 (GB)
    Packers, 16–6 (C)
    Packers, 6–0 (C)
1929—Packers, 23–0 (GB)
    Packers, 14–0 (C)
    Packers, 25–0 (C)
1930—Packers, 7–0 (GB)
    Packers, 13–12 (C)
    Bears, 21–0 (C)
1931—Packers, 7–0 (GB)
    Packers, 6–2 (C)
    Bears, 7–6 (C)
1932—Tie, 0–0 (GB)
    Packers, 2–0 (C)
    Bears, 9–0 (C)
1933—Bears, 14–7 (GB)
    Bears, 10–7 (C)
    Bears, 7–6 (C)
1934—Bears, 24–10 (GB)
    Bears, 27–14 (C)
1935—Packers, 7–0 (GB)
    Packers, 17–14 (C)
1936—Bears, 30–3 (GB)
    Packers, 21–10 (C)
1937—Bears, 14–2 (GB)
    Packers, 24–14 (C)
1938—Bears, 2–0 (GB)
    Packers, 24–17 (C)
1939—Packers, 21–16 (GB)
    Bears, 30–27 (C)
1940—Bears, 41–10 (GB)
    Bears, 14–7 (C)
1941—Bears, 25–17 (GB)
    Packers, 16–14 (C)
    *Bears, 33–14 (C)
1942—Bears, 44–28 (GB)
    Bears, 38–7 (C)
1943—Tie, 21–21 (GB)
    Bears, 21–7 (C)
1944—Packers, 42–28 (GB)
    Bears, 21–0 (C)

1945—Packers, 31–21 (GB)
    Bears, 28–24 (C)
1946—Bears, 30–7 (GB)
    Bears, 10–7 (C)
1947—Packers, 29–20 (GB)
    Bears, 20–17 (C)
1948—Bears, 45–7 (GB)
    Bears, 7–6 (C)
1949—Bears, 17–0 (GB)
    Bears, 24–3 (C)
1950—Packers, 31–21 (GB)
    Bears, 28–14 (C)
1951—Bears, 31–20 (GB)
    Bears, 24–13 (C)
1952—Bears, 24–14 (GB)
    Packers, 41–28 (C)
1953—Bears, 17–13 (GB)
    Tie, 21–21 (C)
1954—Bears, 10–3 (GB)
    Bears, 28–23 (C)
1955—Packers, 24–3 (GB)
    Bears, 52–31 (C)
1956—Bears, 37–21 (GB)
    Bears, 38–14 (C)
1957—Packers, 21–17 (GB)
    Bears, 21–14 (C)
1958—Bears, 34–20 (GB)
    Bears, 24–10 (C)
1959—Packers, 9–6 (GB)
    Bears, 28–17 (C)
1960—Bears, 17–14 (GB)
    Packers, 41–13 (C)
1961—Packers, 24–0 (GB)
    Packers, 31–28 (C)
1962—Packers, 49–0 (GB)
    Packers, 38–7 (C)
1963—Bears, 10–3 (GB)
    Bears, 26–7 (C)
1964—Packers, 23–12 (GB)
    Packers, 17–3 (C)
1965—Packers, 23–14 (GB)
    Bears, 31–10 (C)
1966—Packers, 17–0 (C)
    Packers, 13–6 (GB)
1967—Packers, 13–10 (GB)
    Packers, 17–13 (C)
1968—Bears, 13–10 (GB)
    Packers, 28–27 (C)
1969—Packers, 17–0 (GB)
    Packers, 21–3 (C)

(Points—Bears 1,651, Packers 1,470)

*Conference Playoff

CHICAGO BEARS vs. LOS ANGELES RAMS

(Bears lead series, 28–15–2)

1946—Tie, 28–28 (C)
    Bears, 27–21 (LA)
1947—Bears, 41–21 (LA)
    Rams, 17–14 (C)

1948—Bears, 42–21 (C)
    Bears, 21–6 (LA)
1949—Rams, 31–16 (C)
    Rams, 27–24 (LA)

1950—Bears, 24–20 (LA)
       Bears, 24–14 (C)
       *Rams, 24–14 (LA)
1951—Rams, 42–17 (C)
1952—Rams, 31–7 (LA)
       Rams, 40–24 (C)
1953—Rams, 38–24 (LA)
       Bears, 24–21 (C)
1954—Rams, 42–38 (LA)
       Bears, 24–13 (C)
1955—Bears, 31–20 (LA)
       Bears, 24–3 (C)
1956—Bears, 35–24 (LA)
       Bears, 30–21 (C)
1957—Bears, 34–26 (C)
       Bears, 16–10 (LA)
1958—Bears, 31–10 (C)
       Rams, 41–35 (LA)
1959—Rams, 28–21 (C)
       Bears, 26–21 (LA)

1960—Bears, 34–27 (C)
       Tie, 24–24 (LA)
1961—Bears, 21–17 (LA)
       Bears, 28–24)C)
1962—Bears, 27–23 (LA)
       Bears, 30–14 (C)
1963—Bears, 52–14 (LA)
       Bears, 6–0 (C)
1964—Bears, 38–17 (C)
       Bears, 34–24 (LA)
1965—Rams, 30–28 (LA)
       Bears, 31–6 (C)
1966—Rams, 31–17 (LA)
       Bears, 17–10 (C)
1967—Rams, 28–17 (C)
1968—Bears, 17–16 (LA)
1969—Rams, 9–7 (C)

(Points—Bears 1,144, Rams 975)

*Conference Playoff

CHICAGO BEARS vs. MINNESOTA VIKINGS

(Bears lead series, 11–5–2)

1961—Vikings, 37–13 (M)
       Bears, 52–35 (C)
1962—Bears, 13–0 (M)
       Bears, 31–30 (C)
1963—Bears, 28–7 (M)
       Tie, 17–17 (C)
1964—Bears, 34–28 (M)
       Vikings, 41–14 (C)
1965—Bears, 45–37 (M)
       Vikings, 24–17 (C)

1966—Bears, 13–10 (M)
       Bears, 41–28 (C)
1967—Bears, 17–7 (M)
       Tie, 10–10 (C)
1968—Bears, 27–17 (M)
       Bears, 26–24 (C)
1969—Vikings, 31–0 (C)
       Vikings, 31–14 (M)

(Points—Bears, 412, Vikings 314)

CHICAGO BEARS vs. NEW ORLEANS SAINTS

(Bears lead series, 1–0)

1968—Bears, 23–17 (NO)

CHICAGO BEARS vs. NEW YORK GIANTS

(Bears lead series, 23–16–2)

1925—Bears, 19–7 (NY)
       Giants, 9–0 (C)
1926—Bears, 7–0 (C)
1927—Bears, 13–7 (NY)
1928—Bears, 13–0 (C)
1929—Giants, 26–14 (C)
       Giants, 14–9·(C)
       Giants, 34–0 (NY)
1930—Giants, 12–0 (C)
       Bears, 12–0 (C)
1931—Bears, 6–0 (C)
       Bears, 12–6 (NY)
       Giants, 25–6 (C)
1932—Bears, 28–8 (NY)
       Bears, 6–0 (C)
1933—Bears, 14–10 (C)
       Giants, 3–0 (NY)
       *Bears, 23–21 (C)

1934—Bears, 27–7 (C)
       Bears, 10–9 (NY)
       *Giants, 30–13 (NY)
1935—Bears, 20–3 (NY)
       Giants, 3–0 (C)
1936—Bears, 25–7 (NY)
1937—Tie, 3–3 (NY)
1939—Giants, 16–13 (NY)
1940—Bears, 37–21 (NY)
1941—*Bears, 37–9 (C)
1942—Bears, 26–7 (NY)
1943—Bears, 56–7 (NY)
1946—Giants, 14–0 (NY)
       *Bears, 24–14 (NY)
1948—Bears, 35–14 (C)
1949—Giants, 35–28 (NY)
1956—Tie, 17–17 (NY)
       *Giants, 47–7 (NY)

1962—Giants, 26–24 (C)   1967—Bears, 34–7 (C)
1963—*Bears, 14–10 (C)   1969—Giants, 28–24 (NY)
1965—Bears, 35–14 (NY)

(Points—Bears 685, Giants 536)

*NFL Championship

CHICAGO BEARS vs. PHILADELPHIA EAGLES

(Bears lead series, 15–2–1)

1933—Tie, 3–3 (P)   1944—Bears, 28–7 (P)
1935—Bears, 39–0 (P)   1946—Bears, 21–14 (C)
1936—Bears, 17–0 (P)   1947—Bears, 40–7 (C)
      Bears, 28–7 (P)   1948—Eagles, 12–7 (P)
1938—Bears, 28–6 (P)   1949—Bears, 38–21 (C)
1939—Bears, 27–14 (C)   1955—Bears, 17–10 (C)
1941—Bears, 49–14 (P)   1961—Eagles, 16–14 (P)
1942—Bears, 45–14 (C)   1963—Bears, 16–7 (C)
1943—Bears, 48–21 (C)   1968—Bears, 29–16 (P)

(Points—Bears 494, Eagles 189)

CHICAGO BEARS vs. PITTSBURGH STEELERS

(Bears lead series, 15–2–1)

1934—Bears, 28–0 (P)   1945—Bears, 28–7 (P)
1935—Bears, 23–7 (P)   1947—Bears, 49–7 (C)
1936—Bears, 27–9 (P)   1949—Bears, 30–21 (C)
      Bears, 26–6 (C)   1958—Steelers, 24–10 (C)
1937—Bears, 7–0 (P)   1959—Bears, 27–21 (C)
1939—Bears, 32–0 (P)   1963—Tie, 17–17 (P)
1941—Bears, 34–7 (C)   1967—Steelers, 41–13 (P)
1943—Bears, 48–21 (C)   1969—Bears, 38–7 (C)
1944—Bears, 34–7 (C)
      Bears, 49–7 (P)

(Points—Bears 520, Steelers 209)

CHICAGO BEARS vs. *ST. LOUIS CARDINALS

(Bears lead series, 49–21–6)
(Wr denotes Wrigley Field; Co denotes Comiskey Park;
So denotes Soldier Field, all Chicago)

1920—Cardinals, 7–6 (Decatur)   1932—Tie, 0–0 (Wr)
      Bears, 10–0 (Wr)   Bears, 34–0 (Wr)
1921—Tie, 0–0 (Co)   1933—Bears, 12–9 (Wr)
1922—Cardinals, 6–0 (Co)   Bears, 22–6 (Wr)
      Cardinals, 9–0 (Wr)   1934—Bears, 20–0 (Wr)
1923—Bears, 3–0 (Wr)   Bears, 17–6 (Wr)
1924—Bears, 6–0 (Wr)   1935—Tie, 7–7 (Wr)
      Bears, 21–0 (Co)   Bears, 13–0 (Wr)
1925—Cardinals, 9–0 (Co)   1936—Bears, 7–3 (Wr)
      Tie, 0–0 (Wr)   Cardinals, 14–7 (Wr)
1926—Bears, 16–0 (Co)   1937—Bears, 16–7 (Wr)
      Tie, 0–0 (Wr)   Bears, 42–28 (Wr)
1927—Bears, 10–0 (Co)   1938—Bears, 16–13 (So)
      Cardinals, 3–0 (Wr)   Bears, 34–28 (Wr)
1928—Bears, 13–0 (Co)   1939—Bears, 44–7 (Wr)
      Bears, 34–0 (Wr)   Bears, 48–7 (Co)
1929—Tie, 0–0 (Wr)   1940—Cardinals, 21–7 (Co)
      Cardinals, 40–6 (Co)   Bears, 31–23 (Wr)
1930—Bears, 32–6 (Co)   1941—Bears, 53–7 (Wr)
      Bears, 6–0 (Wr)   Bears, 34–24 (Co)
      Bears, 9–7 (Wr)   1942—Bears, 41–14 (Wr)
1931—Bears, 26–13 (Wr)   Bears, 21–7 (Co)
      Bears, 18–7 (Wr)

1943—Bears, 20–0 (Wr)
Bears, 35–24 (Co)
1944—Bears, 34–7 (Wr)
Bears, 49–7 (Pitt)
1945—Cardinals, 16–7 (Wr)
Bears, 28–20 (Co)
1946—Bears, 34–17 (Co)
Cardinals, 35–28 (Wr)
1947—Cardinals, 31–7 (Co)
Cardinals, 30–21 (Wr)
1948—Bears, 28–17 (Co)
Cardinals, 24–21 (Wr)
1949—Bears, 17–7 (Co)
Bears, 52–21 (Wr)
1950—Bears, 27–6 (Wr)
Cardinals, 20–10 (Co)

1951—Cardinals, 28–14 (Co)
Cardinals, 24–14 (Wr)
1952—Cardinals, 21–10 (Co)
Bears, 10–7 (Wr)
1953—Cardinals, 24–17 (Wr)
1954—Bears, 29–7 (Co)
1955—Cardinals, 53–14 (Co)
1956—Bears, 10–3 (Wr)
1957—Bears, 14–6 (Co)
1958—Bears, 30–14 (Wr)
1959—Bears, 31–7 (So)
1965—Bears, 34–13 (C)
1966—Cardinals, 24–17 (StL)
1967—Bears, 30–3 (C)
1969—Cardinals, 20–17 (St. L)

(Points—Bears 1,454, Cardinals 871)

*Franchise in Chicago prior to 1960

CHICAGO BEARS vs. SAN FRANCISCO 49ERS

(Bears lead series, 19–16–1)

1950—Bears, 32–20 (SF)
Bears, 17–0 (C)
1951—Bears, 13–7 (C)
1952—49ERS, 40–16 (C)
Bears, 20–17 (SF)
1953—49ERS, 35–28 (C)
49ERS, 24–14 (SF)
1954—49ERS, 31–24 (C)
Bears, 31–27 (SF)
1955—49ERS, 20–19 (C)
Bears, 34–23 (SF)
1956—Bears, 31–7 (C)
Bears, 38–21 (SF)
1957—49ERS, 21–17 (C)
49ERS, 21–17 (SF)
1958—Bears, 28–6 (C)
Bears, 27–14 (SF)
1959—49ERS, 20–17 (SF)
Bears, 14–3 (C)

1960—Bears, 27–10 (C)
49ERS, 25–7 (SF)
1961—Bears, 31–0 (C)
49ERS, 41–31 (SF)
1962—Bears, 30–14 (SF)
49ERS, 34–27 (C)
1963—49ERS, 20–14 (SF)
Bears, 27–7 (C)
1964—49ERS, 31–21 (SF)
Bears, 23–21 (C)
1965—49ERS, 52–24 (SF)
Bears, 61–20 (C)
1966—Tie, 30–30 (C)
49ERS, 41–14 (SF)
1967—Bears, 28–14 (SF)
1968—Bears, 27–19 (C)
1969—49ERS, 42–21 (SF)

(Points—Bears 880, 49ers 778)

CHICAGO BEARS vs. WASHINGTON REDSKINS

(Bears lead series, 10–8)

1937—*Redskins, 28–21 (C)
1938—Bears, 31–7 (C)
1940—Redskins, 7–3 (W)
*Bears, 73–0 (W)
1941—Bears, 35–21 (C)
1942—*Redskins, 14–6 (W)
1943—Redskins, 21–7 (W)
*Bears, 41–21 (C)
1945—Redskins, 28–21 (W)

1946—Bears, 24–20 (C)
1947—Bears, 56–20 (W)
1948—Bears, 48–13 (C)
1949—Bears, 31–21 (W)
1951—Bears, 27–0 (W)
1953—Bears, 27–24 (W)
1957—Redskins, 14–3 (C)
1964—Redskins, 27–20 (W)
1968—Redskins, 38–28 (C)

(Points—Bears 502, Redskins 324)

*NFL Championship

CINCINNATI BENGALS vs. BOSTON PATRIOTS

(Patriots lead series, 2–0; See Boston vs. Cincinnati)

CINCINNATI BENGALS vs. BUFFALO BILLS

(Series tied, 1–1; See Buffalo vs. Cincinnati)

CINCINNATI BENGALS vs. DENVER BRONCOS

(Broncos lead series, 3-1)

1968—Bengals, 24–10 (C)   1969—Broncos, 30–23 (C)
Broncos, 10–7 (D)   Broncos, 27–16 (D)
(Points—Broncos, 77, Bengals, 70)

CINCINNATI BENGALS vs. HOUSTON OILERS

(Oilers lead series, 1-0-1)

1968—Oilers, 27–17 (C)   1969—Tie, 31–31 (H)
(Points—Oilers 58, Bengals, 48)

CINCINNATI BENGALS vs. KANSAS CITY CHIEFS

(Chiefs lead series, 3-1)

1968—Chiefs, 13–3 (KC)   1969—Bengals, 24–19 (C)
Chiefs, 16–9 (C)   Chiefs, 42–22 (KC)
(Points—Chiefs 90, Bengals 58)

CINCINNATI BENGALS vs. MIAMI DOLPHINS

(Bengals lead series, 2-1)

1968—Dolphins, 24–22 (C)   1969—Bengals, 27–21 (C)
Bengals, 38–21 (M)
(Points—Bengals 87, Dolphins 66)

CINCINNATI BENGALS vs. NEW YORK JETS

(Jets lead series, 3-0)

1968—Jets, 27–14 (NY)   1969—Jets, 21–7 (C)
Jets, 40–7 (NY)
(Points—Jets 88, Bengals 28)

CINCINNATI BENGALS vs. OAKLAND RAIDERS

(Raiders lead series, 3-1)

1968—Raiders, 31–10 (O)   1969—Bengals, 31–17 (C)
Raiders, 34–0 (C)   Raiders, 37–17 (O)
(Points—Raiders 119, Bengals 58)

CINCINNATI BENGALS vs. SAN DIEGO CHARGERS

(Chargers lead series, 3-1)

1968—Chargers, 29–13 (SD)   1969—Bengals, 34–20 (C)
Chargers, 31–10 (C)   Chargers, 21–14 (SD)
(Points—Chargers 101, Bengals 71)

CLEVELAND BROWNS vs. ATLANTA FALCONS

(Browns lead series, 2-0; See Atlanta vs. Cleveland)

CLEVELAND BROWNS vs. BALTIMORE COLTS

(Browns lead series, 4-3; See Baltimore vs. Cleveland)

CLEVELAND BROWNS vs. CHICAGO BEARS

(Browns lead series, 5-1; See Chicago vs. Cleveland)

CLEVELAND BROWNS vs. DALLAS COWBOYS

(Browns lead series, 14-5)

1960—Browns, 48–7 (C)   1964—Browns, 27–6 (C)
1961—Browns, 25–7 (C)   Browns, 20–16 (D)
Browns, 38–17 (D)   1965—Browns, 23–17 (C)
1962—Browns, 19–10 (C)   Browns, 24–17 (D)
Cowboys, 45–21 (D)   1966—Browns, 30–21 (C)
1963—Browns, 41–24 (D)   Cowboys, 26–14 (D)
Browns, 27–17 (C)

1967—Cowboys, 21–14 (C)   1969—Browns, 42–10 (C)
        *Cowboys, 52–14 (D)   *Browns, 38–14 (D)
1968—Cowboys, 28–7 (D)
        *Browns, 31–20 (C)
                    (Points—Browns 503, Cowboys 375)
*Conference Championship

CLEVELAND BROWNS vs. DETROIT LIONS

(Lions lead series, 11–2)

1952—Lions, 17–6 (D)   1958—Lions, 30–10 (C)
        *Lions, 17–7 (C)   1961—**Lions, 17–16
1953—*Lions, 17–16 (D)   (Miami)
1954—Lions, 14–10 (C)   1963—Lions, 38–10 (D)
        *Browns, 56–10 (C)   1964—Browns, 37–21 (C)
1957—Lions, 20–7 (D)   1967—Lions, 31–14 (D)
        *Lions, 59–14 (D)   1969—Lions, 28–21 (C)
                    (Points—Lions 319, Browns 224)
 *NFL Championship
**Playoff Bowl

CLEVELAND BROWNS vs. GREEN BAY PACKERS

(Packers lead series, 6–4)

1953—Browns, 27–0 (Mil)   1965—**Packers, 23–12 (GB)
1955—Browns, 41–10 (C)   1966—Packers, 21–20 (C)
1956—Browns, 24–7 (Mil)   1967—Packers, 55–7 (Mil)
1961—Packers, 49–17 (C)   1969—Browns, 20–7 (C)
1964—*Packers, 40–23 (Miami)
        Packers, 28–21 (Mil)
                    (Points—Packers 240, Browns 212)
 *Playoff Bowl
**NFL Championship

CLEVELAND BROWNS vs. LOS ANGELES RAMS

(Browns lead series, 7–4)

1950—*Browns, 30–28 (C)   1958—Browns, 30–27 (LA)
1951—Browns, 38–23 (LA)   1963—Browns, 20–6 (C)
        *Rams, 24–17 (LA)   1965—Rams, 42–7 (LA)
1952—Browns, 37–7 (C)   1968—**Rams, 30–6 (Miami)
1955—*Browns, 38–14 (LA)   Rams, 24–6 (C)
1957—Browns, 45–31 (C)
                    (Points—Browns 274, Rams 256)
 *NFL Championship
**Playoff Bowl

CLEVELAND BROWNS vs. MINNESOTA VIKINGS

(Vikings lead series, 3–1)

1965—Vikings, 27–17 (C)   1969—Vikings, 51–3 (M)
1967—Browns, 14–10 (C)   *Vikings, 27–7 (M)
                    (Points—Vikings 115, Browns 41)
*NFL Championship

CLEVELAND BROWNS vs. NEW ORLEANS SAINTS

(Browns lead series, 4–0)

1967—Browns, 42–7 (NO)   1969—Browns, 27–17 (NO)
1968—Browns, 24–10 (NO)
        Browns, 35–17 (NO)
                    (Points—Browns 128, Saints 41)

CLEVELAND BROWNS vs. NEW YORK GIANTS

(Browns lead series, 23–16–2)

1950—Giants, 6–0 (C)
      Giants, 17–13 (NY)
      *Browns, 8–3 (C)
1951—Browns, 14–13 (C)
      Browns, 10–0 (NY)
1952—Giants, 17–9 (C)
      Giants, 37–34 (NY)
1953—Browns, 7–0 (NY)
      Browns, 62–14 (C)
1954—Browns, 24–14 (C)
      Browns, 16–7 (NY)
1955—Browns, 24–14 (C)
      Tie, 35–35 (NY)
1956—Giants, 21–9 (C)
      Browns, 24–7 (NY)
1957—Browns, 6–3 (C)
      Browns, 34–28 (NY)
1958—Giants, 21–17 (C)
      Giants, 13–10 (NY)
      *Giants, 10–0 (NY)
1959—Giants, 10–6 (C)
      Giants, 48–7 (NY)

1960—Giants, 17–13 (C)
      Browns, 48–34 (NY)
1961—Giants, 37–21 (C)
      Tie, 7–7 (NY)
1962—Browns, 17–7 (C)
      Giants, 17–13 (NY)
1963—Browns, 35–24 (NY)
      Giants, 33–6 (C)
1964—Browns, 42–20 (C)
      Browns, 52–20 (NY)
1965—Browns, 38–14 (NY)
      Browns, 34–21 (C)
1966—Browns, 28–7 (NY)
      Browns, 49–40 (C)
1967—Giants, 38–34 (NY)
      Browns, 24–14 (C)
1968—Browns, 45–10 (C)
1969—Browns, 28–17 (C)
      Giants, 27–14 (NY)

(Points—Browns 917, Giants 742)
*Conference Playoff

CLEVELAND BROWNS vs. PHILADELPHIA EAGLES

(Browns lead series, 26–10–1)

1950—Browns, 35–10 (P)
      Browns, 13–7 (C)
1951—Browns, 20–17 (C)
      Browns, 24–9 (P)
1952—Browns, 49–7 (P)
      Eagles, 28–20 (C)
1953—Browns, 37–13 (C)
      Eagles, 42–27 (P)
1954—Eagles, 28–10 (P)
      Browns, 6–0 (C)
1955—Browns, 21–17 (C)
      Eagles, 33–17 (P)
1956—Browns, 16–0 (P)
      Browns, 17–14 (C)
1957—Browns, 24–7 (C)
      Eagles, 17–7 (P)
1958—Browns, 28–14 (C)
      Browns, 21–14 (P)
1959—Browns, 28–7 (C)
      Browns, 28–21 (P)

1960—Browns, 41–24 (P)
      Eagles, 31–29 (C)
1961—Eagles, 27–20 (P)
      Browns, 45–24 (C)
1962—Eagles, 35–7 (P)
      Tie, 14–14 (C)
1963—Browns, 37–7 (C)
      Browns, 23–17 (P)
1964—Browns, 28–20 (P)
      Browns, 38–24 (C)
1965—Browns, 35–17 (P)
      Browns, 38–34 (C)
1966—Browns, 27–7 (C)
      Eagles, 33–21 (P)
1967—Eagles, 28–24 (P)
1968—Browns, 47–13 (C)
1969—Browns, 27–20 (P)

(Points—Browns 949, Eagles 680)

CLEVELAND BROWNS vs. PITTSBURGH STEELERS

(Browns lead series, 31–9)

1950—Browns, 30–17 (P)
      Browns, 45–7 (C)
1951—Browns, 17–0 (C)
      Browns, 28–0 (P)
1952—Browns, 21–20 (P)
      Browns, 29–28 (C)
1953—Browns, 34–16 (C)
      Browns, 20–16 (P)
1954—Steelers, 55–27 (P)
      Browns, 42–7 (C)

1955—Browns, 41–14 (C)
      Browns, 30–7 (P)
1956—Browns, 14–10 (P)
      Steelers, 24–16 (C)
1957—Browns, 23–12 (P)
      Browns, 24–0 (C)
1958—Browns, 45–12 (P)
      Browns, 27–10 (C)
1959—Steelers, 17–7 (P)
      Steelers, 21–20 (C)

1960—Browns, 28-20 (C)
     Steelers, 14-10 (P)
1961—Browns, 30-28 (P)
     Steelers, 17-13 (C)
1962—Browns, 41-14 (P)
     Browns, 35-14 (C)
1963—Browns, 35-23 (C)
     Steelers, 9-7 (P)
1964—Steelers, 23-7 (C)
     Browns, 30-17 (P)

1965—Browns, 24-19 (C)
     Browns, 42-21 (P)
1966—Browns, 41-10 (C)
     Steelers, 16-6 (P)
1967—Browns, 21-10 (C)
     Browns, 34-14 (P)
1968—Browns, 31-24 (C)
     Browns, 45-24 (P)
1969—Browns, 42-31 (C)
     Browns, 24-3 (P)

(Points—Browns 489, Steelers 385)

CLEVELAND BROWNS vs. *ST. LOUIS CARDINALS

(Browns lead series, 29-8-3)

1950—Browns, 34-24 (Cle)
     Browns, 10-7 (Chi)
1951—Browns, 34-17 (Chi)
     Browns, 49-28 (Cle)
1952—Browns, 28-13 (Cle)
     Browns, 10-0 (Chi)
1953—Browns, 27-7 (Chi)
     Browns, 27-16 (Cle)
1954—Browns, 31-7 (Cle)
     Browns, 35-3 (Chi)
1955—Browns, 26-20 (Chi)
     Browns, 35-24 (Cle)
1956—Cardinals, 9-7 (Chi)
     Cardinals, 24-7 (Cle)
1957—Browns, 17-7 (Chi)
     Browns, 31-0 (Cle)
1958—Browns, 35-28 (Cle)
     Browns, 38-24 (Chi)
1959—Browns, 34-7 (Chi)
     Browns, 17-7 (Cle)

1960—Browns, 28-27 (C)
     Tie, 17-17 (StL)
1961—Browns, 20-17 (C)
     Browns, 21-10 (StL)
1962—Browns, 34-7 (C)
     Browns, 38-14 (StL)
1963—Cardinals, 20-14 (C)
     Browns, 24-10 (StL)
1964—Tie, 33-33 (C)
     Cardinals, 28-19 (StL)
1965—Cardinals, 49-13 (C)
     Browns, 27-24 (StL)
1966—Cardinals, 34-28 (C)
     Browns, 38-10 (StL)
1967—Browns, 20-16 (C)
     Browns, 20-16 (StL)
1968—Cardinals, 27-21 (C)
     Cardinals, 27-16 (StL)
1969—Tie, 21-21 (C)
     Browns, 27-21 (StL)

(Points—Browns 1,011, Cardinals 700)

*Franchise in Chicago prior to 1960

CLEVELAND BROWNS vs. SAN FRANCISCO 49ERS

(Browns lead series, 5-2)

1950—Browns, 34-14 (C)
1951—49ERS, 24-10 (SF)
1953—Browns, 23-21 (C)
1955—Browns, 38-3 (SF)

1959—49ERS, 21-20 (C)
1962—Browns, 13-10 (SF)
1968—Browns, 33-21 (SF)

(Points—Browns 171, 49ERS 115)

CLEVELAND BROWNS vs. WASHINGTON REDSKINS

(Browns lead series, 30-5-1)

1950—Browns, 20-14 (C)
     Browns, 45-21 (W)
1951—Browns, 45-0 (C)
1952—Browns, 19-15 (C)
     Browns, 48-24 (W)
1953—Browns, 30-14 (W)
     Browns, 27-3 (C)
1954—Browns, 62-3 (C)
     Browns, 34-14 (W)
1955—Redskins, 27-17 (C)
     Browns, 24-14 (W)
1956—Redskins, 20-9 (W)
     Redskins, 20-17 (C)

1957—Browns, 21-17 (C)
     Tie, 30-30 (W)
1958—Browns, 20-10 (W)
     Browns, 21-14 (C)
1959—Browns, 34-7 (C)
     Browns, 31-17 (W)
1960—Browns, 31-10 (W)
     Browns, 27-16 (C)
1961—Browns, 31-7 (C)
     Browns, 17-6 (W)
1962—Redskins, 17-16 (C)
     Redskins, 17-9 (W)

Cleveland Browns vs. Washington Redskins (Cont'd)

1963—Browns, 37–14 (C)
    Browns, 27–20 (W)
1964—Browns, 27–13 (W)
    Browns, 34–24 (C)
1965—Browns, 17–7 (W)
    Browns, 24–16 (C)

1966—Browns, 38–14 (W)
    Browns, 14–3 (C)
1967—Browns, 42–37 (C)
1968—Browns, 24–21 (W)
1969—Browns, 27–23 (C)

(Points—Browns 996, Redskins 549)

DALLAS COWBOYS vs. ATLANTA FALCONS

(Cowboys lead series, 3–0; See Atlanta vs. Dallas)

DALLAS COWBOYS vs. BALTIMORE COLTS

(Colts lead series, 3–1; See Baltimore vs. Dallas)

DALLAS COWBOYS vs. CHICAGO BEARS

(Series tied, 2–2; See Chicago vs. Dallas)

DALLAS COWBOYS vs. CLEVELAND BROWNS

(Browns lead series, 14–5; See Cleveland vs. Dallas)

DALLAS COWBOYS vs. DETROIT LIONS

(Cowboys lead series, 2–1)

1960—Lions, 23–14 (Det)
1963—Cowboys, 17–14 (Dal)

1968—Dallas, 59–13 (Det)

(Points—Cowboys 90, Lions 50)

DALLAS COWBOYS vs. GREEN BAY PACKERS

(Packers lead series, 6–0)

1960—Packers, 41–7 (GB)
1964—Packers, 45–21 (D)
1965—Packers, 13–3 (Mil)

1966—*Packers, 34–27 (D)
1967—*Packers, 21–17 (GB)
1968—Packers, 28–17 (D)

(Points—Packers 182, Cowboys 92)

*NFL Championship

DALLAS COWBOYS vs. LOS ANGELES RAMS

(Rams lead series, 4–1)

1960—Rams, 38–13 (D)
1962—Cowboys, 27–17 (LA)
1967—Rams, 35–13 (D)

1969—Rams, 24–23 (LA)
1970—*Rams, 31–0 (Miami)

(Points—Rams 145, Cowboys 76)

*Playoff Bowl

DALLAS COWBOYS vs. MINNESOTA VIKINGS

(Cowboys lead series, 5–0)

1961—Cowboys, 21–7 (D)
    Cowboys, 28–0 (M)

1966—Cowboys, 28–17 (D)
1968—Cowboys, 20–7 (M)
1969—*Cowboys, 17–13 (Miami)

(Points—Cowboys 114, Vikings 44)

*Playoff Bowl

DALLAS COWBOYS vs. NEW ORLEANS SAINTS

(Cowboys lead series, 5–0)

1967—Cowboys, 14–10 (D)
    Cowboys, 27–10 (NO)

1968—Cowboys, 17–3 (NO)
1969—Cowboys, 21–17 (NO)
    Cowboys, 33–17 (D)

(Points—Cowboys 112, Saints 57)

DALLAS COWBOYS vs. NEW YORK GIANTS

(Cowboys lead series, 9–6–2)

1960—Tie, 31–31 (NY)	1965—Cowboys, 31–2 (D)
1961—Giants, 31–10 (D)	Cowboys, 38–20 (NY)
Cowboys, 17–16 (NY)	1966—Cowboys, 52–7 (D)
1962—Giants, 41–10 (D)	Cowboys, 17–7 (NY)
Giants, 41–31 (NY)	1967—Cowboys, 38–24 (D)
1963—Giants, 37–21 (NY)	1968—Giants, 27–21 (D)
Giants, 34–27 (D)	Cowboys, 28–10 (NY)
1964—Tie, 13–13 (D)	1969—Cowboys, 25–3 (D)
Cowboys, 31–21 (NY)	

(Points—Cowboys 441, Giants 365)

DALLAS COWBOYS vs. PHILADELPHIA EAGLES

(Eagles lead series, 11–7)

1960—Eagles, 27–25 (D)	1965—Eagles, 35–24 (D)
1961—Eagles, 43–7 (D)	Cowboys, 21–19 (P)
Eagles, 35–13 (P)	1966—Cowboys, 56–7 (D)
1962—Cowboys, 41–19 (D)	Eagles, 24–23 (P)
Eagles, 28–14 (P)	1967—Eagles, 21–14 (P)
1963—Eagles, 24–21 (P)	Cowboys, 38–17 (D)
Cowboys, 27–20 (D)	1968—Cowboys, 45–13 (P)
1964—Eagles, 17–14 (D)	Cowboys, 34–14 (D)
Eagles, 24–14 (P)	1969—Cowboys, 49–14 (D)

(Points—Cowboys 480, Eagles 401)

DALLAS COWBOYS vs. PITTSBURGH STEELERS

(Cowboys lead series, 9–7)

1960—Steelers, 35–28 (D)	1964—Steelers, 23–17 (P)
1961—Cowboys, 27–24 (D)	Cowboys, 17–14 (D)
Steelers, 37–7 (P)	1965—Steelers, 22–13 (P)
1962—Steelers, 30–28 (D)	Cowboys, 24–17 (D)
Cowboys, 42–27 (P)	1966—Cowboys, 52–21 (D)
1963—Steelers, 27–21 (P)	Cowboys, 20–7 (P)
Steelers, 24–19 (D)	1967—Cowboys, 24–21 (P)
	1968—Cowboys, 28–7 (D)
	1969—Cowboys, 10–7 (P)

(Points—Cowboys 377, Steelers 343)

DALLAS COWBOYS vs. ST. LOUIS CARDINALS

(Cardinals lead series, 8–7–1)

1960—Cardinals, 12–10 (StL)	1964—Cardinals, 16–6 (D)
1961—Cardinals, 31–17 (D)	Cowboys, 31–13 (StL)
Cardinals, 31–13 (StL)	1965—Cardinals, 20–13 (StL)
1962—Cardinals, 28–24 (D)	Cowboys, 27–13 (D)
Cardinals, 52–20 (StL)	1966—Tie, 10–10 (StL)
1963—Cardinals, 34–7 (D)	Cowboys, 31–17 (D)
Cowboys, 28–24 (StL)	1967—Cowboys, 46–21 (D)
	1968—Cowboys, 27–10 (StL)
	1969—Cowboys, 24–3 (D)

(Points—Cardinals 335, Cowboys 334)

DALLAS COWBOYS vs. SAN FRANCISCO 49ERS

(49ERS lead series, 3–1–1)

1960—49ERS, 26–14 (D)	1965—Cowboys, 39–31 (D)
1963—49ERS, 31–24 (SF)	1967—49ERS, 24–16 (SF)
	1969—Tie, 24–24 (D)

(Points—49ERS 136, Cowboys 117)

DALLAS COWBOYS vs. WASHINGTON REDSKINS

(Cowboys lead series, 10-7-2)

1960—Redskins, 26–14 (W)	1965—Cowboys, 27–7 (D)
1961—Tie, 28–28 (D)	Redskins, 34–31 (W)
Redskins, 34–24 (W)	1966—Cowboys, 31–30 (W)
1962—Tie, 35–35 (D)	Redskins, 34–31 (D)
Cowboys, 38–10 (W)	1967—Cowboys, 17–14 (W)
1963—Redskins, 21–17 (W)	Redskins, 27–20 (D)
Cowboys, 35–20 (D)	1968—Cowboys, 44–24 (W)
1964—Cowboys, 24–18 (D)	Cowboys, 29–20 (D)
Redskins, 28–16 (W)	1969—Cowboys, 41–28 (W)
	Cowboys, 20-10 (D)

(Points—Cowboys 522, Redskins 448)

DENVER BRONCOS vs. BOSTON PATRIOTS

(Patriots lead series, 10-8; See Boston vs. Denver)

DENVER BRONCOS vs. BUFFALO BILLS

(Bills lead series, 11-5-1; See Buffalo vs. Denver)

DENVER BRONCOS vs. CINCINNATI BENGALS

(Broncos lead series, 3-1; See Cincinnati vs. Denver)

DENVER BRONCOS vs. HOUSTON OILERS

(Oilers lead series, 14-4-1)

1960—Oilers, 45–25 (D)	1965—Broncos, 28–17 (D)
Oilers, 20–10 (H)	Broncos, 31–21 (H)
1961—Oilers, 55–14 (D)	1966—Oilers, 45–7 (H)
Oilers, 45–14 (H)	Broncos, 40–38 (H)
1962—Broncos, 20–10 (D)	1967—Oilers, 10–6 (H)
Oilers, 34–17 (H)	Oilers, 20–18 (D)
1963—Oilers, 20–14 (H)	1968—Oilers, 38–17 (H)
Oilers, 33–24 (D)	1969—Oilers, 24–21 (H)
1964—Oilers, 38–17 (D)	Tie, 20–20 (D)
Oilers, 34–15 (H)	

(Points—Oilers 567, Broncos 358)

DENVER BRONCOS vs. *KANSAS CITY CHIEFS

(Chiefs lead series, 19-1)

1960—Texans, 17–14 (D)	1965—Chiefs, 31–23 (D)
Texans, 34–7 (Da)	Chiefs, 45–35 (KC)
1961—Texans, 19–12 (D)	1966—Chiefs, 37–10 (KC)
Texans, 49–21 (Da)	Chiefs, 56–10 (D)
1962—Texans, 24–3 (D)	1967—Chiefs, 52–9 (KC)
Texans, 17–10 (Da)	Chiefs, 38–24 (D)
1963—Chiefs, 59–7 (D)	1968—Chiefs, 34–2 (KC)
Chiefs, 52–21 (KC)	Chiefs, 30–7 (D)
1964—Broncos, 33–27 (D)	1969—Chiefs, 26–13 (D)
Chiefs, 49–39 (KC)	Chiefs, 31–17 (KC)

(Points—Chiefs 727, Broncos 317)

*Prior to 1963 franchise located in Dallas (Da) and known as Texans

DENVER BRONCOS vs. MIAMI DOLPHINS

(Dolphins lead series, 3-2)

1966—Dolphins, 24–7 (M)	1968—Broncos, 21–14 (D)
Broncos, 17–7 (D)	1969—Dolphins, 27–24 (M)
1967—Dolphins, 35–21 (M)	

(Points—Dolphins 107, Broncos 90)

DENVER BRONCOS vs. *NEW YORK JETS

(Jets lead series, 9–7–1)

1960—Titans, 28–24 (NY)
    Titans, 30–27 (D)
1961—Titans, 35–28 (NY)
    Broncos, 27–10 (D)
1962—Broncos, 32–10 (NY)
    Titans, 46–45 (D)
1963—Tie, 35–35 (NY)
    Jets, 14–9 (D)
1964—Jets, 30–6 (NY)
    Broncos, 20–16 (D)

1965—Broncos, 16–13 (D)
    Jets, 45–10 (NY)
1966—Jets, 16–7 (D)
1967—Jets, 38–24 (D)
    Broncos, 33–24 (NY)
1968—Broncos, 21–13 (NY)
1969—Broncos, 21–19 (D)

(Points—Jets 422, Broncos 385)

*Jets known as Titans prior to 1963

DENVER BRONCOS vs. OAKLAND RAIDERS

(Raiders lead series, 15–4–1)

1960—Broncos, 31–14 (D)
    Raiders, 48–10 (O)
1961—Raiders, 33–19 (O)
    Broncos, 27–24 (D)
1962—Broncos, 44–7 (D)
    Broncos, 23–6 (O)
1963—Raiders, 26–10 (D)
    Raiders, 35–31 (O)
1964—Raiders, 40–7 (O)
    Tie, 20–20 (D)

1965—Raiders, 28–20 (D)
    Raiders, 24–13 (O)
1966—Raiders, 17–3 (D)
    Raiders, 28–10 (O)
1967—Raiders, 51–0 (O)
    Raiders, 21–17 (D)
1968—Raiders, 43–7 (D)
    Raiders, 33–27 (O)
1969—Raiders, 24–14 (D)
    Raiders, 41–10 (O)

(Points—Raiders 563, Broncos 343)

DENVER BRONCOS vs. *SAN DIEGO CHARGERS

(Chargers lead series, 15–5)

1960—Chargers, 23–19 (D)
    Chargers, 41–33 (LA)
1961—Chargers, 37–0 (SD)
    Chargers, 19–16 (D)
1962—Broncos, 30–21 (D)
    Broncos, 23–20 (SD)
1963—Broncos, 50–34 (D)
    Chargers, 58–20 (SD)
1964—Chargers, 42–14 (SD)
    Chargers, 31–20 (D)

1965—Chargers, 34–31 (SD)
    Chargers, 33–21 (D)
1966—Chargers, 24–17 (SD)
    Broncos, 20–17 (D)
1967—Chargers, 38–21 (D)
    Chargers, 24–20 (SD)
1968—Chargers, 55–24 (SD)
    Chargers, 47–23 (D)
1969—Broncos, 13–0 (D)
    Chargers, 45–24 (SD)

(Points—Chargers 643, Broncos 439)

*Prior to 1961 franchise located in Los Angeles.

DETROIT LIONS vs. ATLANTA FALCONS

(Lions lead series, 4–0; See Atlanta vs. Detroit)

DETROIT LIONS vs. BALTIMORE COLTS

(Lions lead series, 16–14–2; See Baltimore vs. Detroit)

DETROIT LIONS vs. CHICAGO BEARS

(Bears lead series, 44–25–3; See Chicago vs. Detroit)

DETROIT LIONS vs. CLEVELAND BROWNS

(Lions lead series, 11–2; See Cleveland vs. Detroit)

DETROIT LIONS vs. DALLAS COWBOYS

(Cowboys lead series, 2–1; See Dallas vs. Detroit)

DETROIT LIONS vs. GREEN BAY PACKERS

(Packers lead series, 41–28–4)

1934—Lions, 3–0 (GB)
Packers, 3–0 (D)
1935—Packers, 13–9 (GB)
Packers, 31–7 (GB)
Lions, 20–10 (D)
1936—Packers, 20–18 (GB)
Packers, 26–17 (D)
1937—Packers, 26–6 (GB)
Packers, 14–13 (D)
1938—Lions, 17–7 (GB)
Packers, 28–7 (D)
1939—Packers, 26–7 (GB)
Packers, 12–7 (D)
1940—Lions, 23–14 (GB)
Packers, 50–7 (D)
1941—Packers, 23–0 (GB)
Packers, 24–7 (D)
1942—Packers, 38–7 (Mil)
Packers, 28–7 (D)
1943—Packers, 35–14 (GB)
Packers, 27–6 (D)
1944—Packers, 27–6 (GB)
Packers, 14–0 (D)
1945—Packers, 57–21 (Mil)
Lions, 14–3 (D)
1946—Packers, 10–7 (Mil)
Packers, 9–0 (D)
1947—Packers, 34–17 (GB)
Packers, 35–14 (D)
1948—Packers, 33–21 (GB)
Lions, 24–20 (D)
1949—Packers, 16–14 (GB)
Lions, 21–7 (D)
1950—Lions, 45–7 (GB)
Lions, 24–21 (D)
1951—Lions, 24–17 (GB)
Lions, 52–35 (D)

1952—Lions, 52–17 (GB)
Lions, 48–24 (D)
1953—Lions, 14–7 (GB)
Lions, 34–15 (D)
1954—Lions, 21–17 (GB)
Lions, 28–24 (D)
1955—Packers, 20–17 (GB)
Lions, 24–10 (D)
1956—Lions, 20–16 (GB)
Packers, 24–20 (D)
1957—Lions, 24–14 (GB)
Lions, 18–6 (D)
1958—Tie, 13–13 (GB)
Lions, 24–14 (D)
1959—Packers, 28–10 (GB)
Packers, 24–17 (D)
1960—Packers, 28–9 (GB)
Lions, 23–10 (D)
1961—Lions, 17–13 (Mil)
Packers, 17–9 (D)
1962—Packers, 9–7 (GB)
Lions, 26–14 (D)
1963—Packers, 31–10 (Mil)
Tie, 13–13 (D)
1964—Packers, 14–10 (D)
Packers, 30–7 (GB)
1965—Packers, 31–21 (D)
Lions, 12–7 (GB)
1966—Packers, 23–14 (GB)
Packers, 31–7 (D)
1967—Tie, 17–17 (GB)
Packers, 27–17 (D)
1968—Lions, 23–17 (GB)
Tie, 14–14 (D)
1969—Packers, 28–17 (D)
Lions, 16–10 (GB)

(Points—Packers 1,457, Lions 1,179)

DETROIT LIONS vs. LOS ANGELES RAMS

(Rams lead series, 23–22–1)

1946—Rams, 35–14 (LA)
Rams, 41–20 (D)
1947—Rams, 27–13 (D)
Rams, 28–17 (LA)
1948—Rams, 44–7 (LA)
Rams, 34–27 (D)
1949—Rams, 27–24 (LA)
Rams, 21–10 (D)
1950—Rams, 30–28 (D)
Rams, 65–24 (LA)
1951—Rams, 27–21 (D)
Lions, 24–22 (LA)
1952—Lions, 17–14 (LA)
Lions, 24–16 (D)
*Lions, 31–21 (D)
1953—Rams, 31–19 (D)
Rams, 37–24 (LA)

1954—Lions, 21–3 (D)
Lions, 27–24 (LA)
1955—Rams, 17–10 (D)
Rams, 24–13 (LA)
1956—Lions, 24–21 (D)
Lions, 16–7 (LA)
1957—Lions, 10–7 (D)
Rams, 35–17 (LA)
1958—Rams, 42–28 (D)
Lions, 41–24 (LA)
1959—Lions, 17–7 (LA)
Lions, 23–17 (D)
1960—Rams, 48–35 (LA)
Lions, 12–10 (D)
1961—Lions, 14–13 (D)
Lions, 28–10 (LA)

1962—Lions, 13–10 (D)   1966—Rams, 14–7 (D)
Lions, 12–3 (LA)   Rams, 23–3 (LA)
1963—Lions, 23–2 (LA)   1967—Rams, 31–7 (D)
Rams, 28–21 (D)   1968—Rams, 10–7 (LA)
1964—Tied, 17–17 (LA)   1969—Lions, 28–0 (D)
Lions, 37–17 (D)
1965—Lions, 20–0 (D)
Lions, 31–7 (LA)

(Points—Rams 991, Lions 906)

*Conference Playoff

DETROIT LIONS vs. MINNESOTA VIKINGS

(Lions lead series, 9–7–2)

1961—Lions, 37–10 (M)   1966—Lions, 32–31 (M)
Lions, 13–7 (D)   Vikings, 28–16 (D)
1962—Lions, 17–6 (M)   1967—Tie, 10–10 (M)
Lions, 37–23 (D)   Lions, 14–3 (D)
1963—Lions, 28–10 (D)   1968—Vikings, 24–10 (M)
Vikings, 34–31 (M)   Vikings, 13–6 (D)
1964—Lions, 24–20 (M)   1969—Vikings, 24–10 (M)
Tied, 23–23 (D)   Vikings, 27–0 (D)
1965—Lions, 31–29 (M)
Vikings, 29–7 (D)

(Points—Vikings 351, Lions 346)

DETROIT LIONS vs. NEW ORLEANS SAINTS

(Lions and Saints tied in only meeting)
1968—Tie, 20–20 (D)

DETROIT LIONS vs. NEW YORK GIANTS

(Lions lead series, 11–6–1)

1934—Lions, 9–0 (D)   1947—Lions, 35–7 (D)
1935—*Lions, 26–7 (D)   1949—Lions, 45–21 (NY)
1936—Giants, 14–7 (NY)   1953—Lions, 27–16 (NY)
Lions, 38–0 (D)   1955—Giants, 24–19 (D)
1937—Lions, 17–0 (NY)   1958—Giants, 19–17 (D)
1939—Lions, 18–14 (D)   1962—Giants, 17–14 (NY)
1941—Giants, 20–13 (NY)   1964—Lions, 26–3 (D)
1943—Tie, 0–0 (D)   1967—Lions, 30–7 (NY)
1945—Giants, 35–14 (NY)   1969—Lions, 24–0 (D)

(Points—Lions 379, Giants 204)

*NFL Championship

DETROIT LIONS vs. PHILADELPHIA EAGLES

(Lions lead series, 10–7–1)

1934—Lions, 10–0 (P)   1949—Eagles, 22–14 (D)
1935—Lions, 35–0 (D)   1951—Lions, 28–10 (P)
1936—Lions, 23–0 (P)   1954—Tie, 13–13 (D)
1938—Eagles, 21–7 (D)   1957—Lions, 27–16 (P)
1940—Lions, 21–0 (P)   1960—Eagles, 28–10 (P)
1941—Lions, 21–17 (D)   1961—Eagles, 27–24 (D)
1943—Eagles, 35–34 (Pitt)   1962—*Lions, 38–10 (Miami)
1945—Lions, 28–24 (D)   1965—Lions, 35–28 (P)
1948—Eagles, 45–21 (P)   1968—Eagles, 12–0 (D)

(Points—Lions 389, Eagles 308)

*Playoff Bowl

DETROIT LIONS vs. PITTSBURGH STEELERS

(Lions lead series, 15-8-1)

1934—Lions, 40-7 (D)	1949—Steelers, 14-7 (P)
1936—Lions, 28-3 (D)	1950—Lions, 10-7 (D)
1937—Lions, 7-3 (D)	1952—Lions, 31-6 (P)
1938—Lions, 16-7 (D)	1953—Lions, 38-21 (D)
1940—Steelers, 10-7 (D)	1955—Lions, 31-28 (P)
1942—Steelers, 35-7 (D)	1956—Lions, 45-7 (D)
1943—Steelers, 35-34 (P)	1959—Tie, 10-10 (P)
1944—Lions, 27-6 (P)	1962—Lions, 45-7 (D)
Lions, 21-7 (D)	1963—*Lions, 17-10 (Miami)
1946—Lions, 17-7 (D)	1966—Steelers, 17-3 (P)
1947—Steelers, 17-10 (P)	1967—Steelers, 24-14 (D)
1948—Lions, 17-14 (D)	1969—Steelers, 16-13 (P)

(Points—Lions 495, Steelers 318)

*Playoff Bowl

DETROIT LIONS vs. *ST. LOUIS CARDINALS

(Lions lead series, 23-10-3)

1934—Lions, 6-0 (D)	1943—Lions, 35-17 (D)
Lions, 17-13 (C)	Lions, 7-0 (C)
1935—Tie, 10-10 (D)	1944—Lions, 27-6 (Pitt)
Lions, 7-6 (C)	Lions, 21-7 (D)
1936—Lions, 39-0 (D)	1945—Lions, 10-0 (C)
Lions, 14-7 (C)	Lions, 26-0 (D)
1937—Lions, 16-7 (C)	1946—Cardinals, 34-14 (C)
Lions, 16-7 (D)	Cardinals, 36-14 (D)
1938—Lions, 10-0 (D)	1947—Cardinals, 45-21 (C)
Lions, 7-3 (C)	Cardinals, 17-7 (D)
1939—Lions, 21-13 (D)	1948—Cardinals, 56-20 (C)
Lions, 17-3 (C)	Cardinals, 28-14 (D)
1940—Tie, 0-0 (Buffalo)	1949—Lions, 24-7 (C)
Lions, 43-14 (D)	Cardinals, 42-19 (D)
1941—Tie, 14-14 (C)	1959—Lions, 45-21 (D)
Lions, 21-3 (D)	1961—Lions, 45-14 (StL)
1942—Cardinals, 13-0 (C)	1967—Cardinals, 38-28 (StL)
Cardinals, 7-0 (D)	1969—Lions, 20-0 (D)

(Points—Lions 655, Cardinals 488)

*Franchise in Chicago prior to 1960

DETROIT LIONS vs. SAN FRANCISCO 49ERS

(49ERS lead series, 19-18-1)

1950—Lions, 24-7 (D)	1959—49ERS, 34-13 (D)
49ERS, 28-27 (SF)	49ERS, 33-7 (SF)
1951—49ERS, 20-10 (D)	1960—49ERS, 14-10 (D)
49ERS, 21-17 (SF)	Lions, 24-0 (SF)
1952—49ERS, 17-3 (SF)	1961—49ERS, 49-0 (D)
49ERS, 28-0 (SF)	Tie, 20-20 (SF)
1953—Lions, 24-21 (D)	1962—Lions, 45-24 (D)
Lions, 14-10 (SF)	Lions, 38-24 (SF)
1954—49ERS, 37-31 (SF)	1963—Lions, 26-3 (D)
Lions, 48-7 (D)	Lions, 45-7 (SF)
1955—49ERS, 27-24 (D)	1964—Lions, 26-17 (SF)
49ERS, 38-21 (SF)	Lions, 24-7 (D)
1956—Lions, 20-17 (D)	1965—49ERS, 27-21 (D)
Lions, 17-13 (SF)	49ERS, 17-14 (SF)
1957—49ERS, 35-31 (SF)	1966—49ERS, 27-24 (SF)
Lions, 31-10 (D)	49ERS, 41-14 (D)
*Lions, 31-27 (SF)	1967—Lions, 45-3 (SF)
1958—49ERS, 24-21 (SF)	1968—49ERS, 14-7 (D)
Lions, 35-21 (D)	1969—Lions, 26-14 (SF)

(Points—Lions 858, 49ERS 783)

*Conference Playoff

DETROIT LIONS vs. WASHINGTON REDSKINS

(Redskins lead series, 9–3)

1938—Redskins, 7–5 (D)	1947—Lions, 38–21 (D)
1939—Redskins, 31–7 (W)	1948—Redskins, 46–21 (W)
1940—Redskins, 20–14 (D)	1951—Lions, 35–17 (D)
1942—Redskins, 15–3 (D)	1956—Redskins, 18–17 (W)
1943—Redskins, 42–20 (W)	1965—Lions, 14–10 (D)
1946—Redskins, 17–16 (W)	1968—Redskins, 14–3 (W)

(Points—Redskins 258, Lions 193)

GREEN BAY PACKERS vs. ATLANTA FALCONS

(Packers lead series, 4–0; See Atlanta vs. Green Bay)

GREEN BAY PACKERS vs. BALTIMORE COLTS

(Packers lead series, 17–16; See Baltimore vs. Green Bay)

GREEN BAY PACKERS vs. CHICAGO BEARS

(Bears lead series, 54–42–6; See Chicago vs. Green Bay)

GREEN BAY PACKERS vs. CLEVELAND BROWNS

(Packers lead series, 6–4; See Cleveland vs. Green Bay)

GREEN BAY PACKERS vs. DALLAS COWBOYS

(Packers lead series, 6–0; See Dallas vs. Green Bay)

GREEN BAY PACKERS vs. DETROIT LIONS

(Packers lead series, 41–28–4; See Detroit vs. Green Bay)

GREEN BAY PACKERS vs. KANSAS CITY CHIEFS

(Packers lead series, 1–0)

1967—*Packers, 35–10 (Los Angeles)
*Super Bowl

GREEN BAY PACKERS vs. LOS ANGELES RAMS

(Rams lead series, 27–18–1)

1946—Rams, 21–17 (Mil)	1957—Rams, 31–27 (Mil)
Rams, 38–17 (LA)	Rams, 42–17 (LA)
1947—Packers, 17–14 (Mil)	1958—Rams, 20–7 (GB)
Packers, 30–10 (LA)	Rams, 34–20 (LA)
1948—Packers, 16–0 (GB)	1959—Rams, 45–6 (Mil)
Rams, 24–10 (LA)	Packers, 38–20 (LA)
1949—Rams, 48–7 (GB)	1960—Rams, 33–31 (Mil)
Rams, 35–7 (LA)	Packers, 35–21 (LA)
1950—Rams, 45–14 (Mil)	1961—Packers, 35–17 (GB)
Rams, 51–14 (LA)	Packers, 24–17 (LA)
1951—Rams, 28–0 (Mil)	1962—Packers, 41–10 (Mil)
Rams, 42–14 (LA)	Packers, 20–17 (LA)
1952—Rams, 30–28 (Mil)	1963—Packers, 42–10 (GB)
Rams, 45–27 (LA)	Packers, 31–14 (LA)
1953—Rams, 38–20 (Mil)	1964—Rams, 27–17 (Mil)
Rams, 33–17 (LA)	Tied, 24–24 (LA)
1954—Packers, 35–17 (Mil)	1965—Packers, 6–3 (Mil)
Rams, 35–27 (LA)	Rams, 21–10 (LA)
1955—Packers, 30–28 (Mil)	1966—Packers, 24–13 (GB)
Rams, 31–17 (LA)	Packers, 27–23 (LA)
1956—Packers, 42–17 (Mil)	1967—Rams, 27–24 (LA)
Rams, 49–21 (LA)	*Packers, 28–7 (Mil)
	1968—Rams, 16–14 (LA)
	1969—Rams, 34–21 (LA)

(Points—Rams 1,305, Packers 996)

*Conference Playoff.

GREEN BAY PACKERS vs. MINNESOTA VIKINGS

(Packers lead series, 11–7)

1961—Packers, 33–7 (Minn)
    Packers, 28–10 (Mil)
1962—Packers, 34–7 (GB)
    Packers, 48–21 (Minn)
1963—Packers, 37–28 (Minn)
    Packers, 28–7 (GB)
1964—Vikings, 24–23 (GB)
    Packers, 42–13 (Minn)

1965—Packers, 38–13 (Minn)
    Packers, 24–19 (GB)
1966—Vikings, 20–17 (GB)
    Packers, 28–16 (Minn)
1967—Vikings, 10–7 (Mil)
    Packers, 30–27 (Minn)
1968—Vikings, 26–13 (Mil)
    Vikings, 14–10 (Minn)
1969—Vikings, 19–7 (Minn)
    Vikings, 9–7 (Mil)

(Points—Packers 454, Vikings 290)

GREEN BAY PACKERS vs. NEW ORLEANS SAINTS

(Packers lead series, 1–0)

1968—Packers, 29–7 (Mil)

GREEN BAY PACKERS vs. NEW YORK GIANTS

(Packers lead series, 19–15–2)

1928—Giants, 6–0 (GB)
    Packers, 7–0 (NY)
1929—Packers, 20–6 (NY)
1930—Packers, 14–7 (GB)
    Giants, 13–6 (NY)
1931—Packers, 27–7 (GB)
    Packers, 14–10 (NY)
1932—Packers, 13–0 (GB)
    Ginats, 6–0 (NY)
1933—Giants, 10–7 (Mil)
    Giants, 17–6 (NY)
1934—Packers, 20–6 (Mil)
    Giants, 17–3 (NY)
1935—Packers, 16–7 (GB)
1936—Packers, 26–14 (NY)
1937—Giants, 10–0 (NY)
1938—Giants, 15–3 (NY)
    *Giants, 23–17 (NY)

1939—*Packers, 27–0 (Mil)
1940—Giants, 7–3 (NY)
1942—Tie, 21–21 (NY)
1943—Packers, 35–21 (NY)
1944—Giants, 24–0 (NY)
    *Packers, 14–7 (NY)
1945—Packers, 23–14 (NY)
1947—Tie, 24–24 (NY)
1948—Giants, 49–3 (Mil)
1949—Giants, 30–10 (GB)
1952—Packers, 17–3 (NY)
1957—Giants, 31–17 (GB)
1959—Giants, 20–3 (NY)
1961—Packers, 20–17 (Mil)
    *Packers, 37–0 (GB)
1962—*Packers, 16–7 (NY)
1967—Packers, 48–21 (NY)
1969—Packers, 20–10 (Mil)

(Points—Packers 537, Giants 480)

*NFL Championship

GREEN BAY PACKERS vs. OAKLAND RAIDERS

(Packers lead series, 1–0)

1968—*Packers, 33–14 (Miami)
*Super Bowl

GREEN BAY PACKERS vs. PHILADELPHIA EAGLES

(Packers lead series, 16–2)

1933—Packers, 35–9 (GB)
    Packers, 10–0 (P)
1934—Packers, 19–6 (GB)
1935—Packers, 13–6 (P)
1937—Packers, 37–7 (GB)
1939—Packers, 23–16 (P)
1940—Packers, 27–20 (GB)
1942—Packers, 7–0 (P)
1943—Packers, 38–28 (P)

1946—Packers, 19–7 (P)
1947—Eagles, 28–14 (P)
1951—Packers, 37–24 (GB)
1952—Packers, 12–10 (Mil)
1954—Packers, 37–14 (P)
1958—Packers, 38–35 (GB)
1960—*Eagles, 17–13 (P)
1962—Packers, 49–0 (P)
1963—Packers, 30–13 (GB)

(Points—Packers 458, Eagles 240)

*NFL Championship

GREEN BAY PACKERS vs. PITTSBURGH STEELERS

(Packers lead series, 18–7)

1933—Packers, 47–0 (GB)	1947—Steelers, 18–17 (Mil)
1935—Packers, 27–0 (GB)	1948—Steelers, 38–7 (P)
Packers, 34–14 (P)	1949—Steelers, 30–7 (Mil)
1936—Packers, 42–10 (Mil)	1951—Packers, 35–33 (Mil)
1938—Packers, 20–0 (GB)	Steelers, 28–7 (P)
1940—Packers, 24–3 (Mil)	1953—Steelers, 31–14 (P)
1941—Packers, 54–7 (P)	1954—Steelers, 21–20 (GB)
1942—Packers, 24–21 (Mil)	1957—Packers, 27–10 (P)
1943—Packers, 38–28 (Phila)	1960—Packers, 19–13 (P)
1944—Packers, 34–7 (GB)	1963—Packers, 33–14 (Mil)
Packers, 35–20 (Chi)	1965—Packers, 41–9 (P)
1946—Packers, 17–7 (GB)	1967—Steelers, 24–17 (GB)
	1969—Packers, 38–34 (P)

(Points—Packers 678, Steelers 420)

GREEN BAY PACKERS vs. *ST. LOUIS CARDINALS

(Packers lead series, 37–20–3)

1921—Tie, 3–3 (C)	1938—Packers, 28–7 (Mil)
1922—Cardinals, 16–3 (C)	Packers, 24–22 (Buffalo)
1924—Cardinals, 3–0 (C)	1939—Packers, 14–10 (GB)
1925—Packers, 9–6 (C)	Packers, 27–20 (Mil)
1926—Cardinals, 13–7 (GB)	1940—Packers, 31–6 (Mil)
Packers, 3–0 (C)	Packers, 28–7 (C)
1927—Packers, 13–0 (GB)	1941—Packers, 14–13 (Mil)
Tie, 6–6 (C)	Packers, 17–9 (GB)
1928—Packers, 20–0 (GB)	1942—Packers, 17–13 (C)
1929—Packers, 9–2 (GB)	Packers, 55–24 (GB)
Packers, 7–6 (C)	1943—Packers, 28–7 (C)
Packers, 13–0 (C)	Packers, 35–14 (Mil)
1930—Packers, 14–0 (GB)	1944—Packers, 34–7 (GB)
Cardinals, 13–6 (C)	Packers, 35–20 (C)
1931—Packers, 26–7 (GB)	1945—Packers, 33–14 (GB)
Cardinals, 21–13 (C)	1946—Packers, 19–7 (C)
1932—Packers, 15–7 (GB)	Cardinals, 24–6 (GB)
Packers, 19–9 (C)	1947—Cardinals, 14–10 (GB)
1933—Packers, 14–6 (C)	Cardinals, 21–20 (C)
1934—Packers, 15–0 (GB)	1948—Cardinals, 17–7 (Mil)
Cardinals, 9–0 (Mil)	Cardinals, 42–7 (C)
Cardinals, 6–0 (C)	1949—Cardinals, 39–17 (Mil)
1935—Cardinals, 7–6 (GB)	Cardinals, 41–21 (C)
Cardinals, 3–0 (Mil)	1955—Packers, 31–14 (GB)
Cardinals, 9–7 (C)	1956—Packers, 24–21 (C)
1936—Packers, 10–7 (GB)	1962—Packers, 17–0 (Mil)
Packers, 24–0 (Mil)	1963—Packers, 30–7 (StL)
Tie, 0–0 (C)	1965—**Cardinals, 24–17 (Miami)
1937—Cardinals, 14–7 (GB)	1967—Packers, 31–23 (StL)
Packers, 34–13 (Mil)	1969—Packers, 45–28 (GB)

(Points—Packers 1,022, Cardinals 704)

*Franchise in Chicago prior to 1960
**Playoff Bowl

GREEN BAY PACKERS vs. SAN FRANCISCO 49ERS

(Series tied, 17–17–1)

1950—Packers, 25–21 (GB)	1954—49ERS, 23–17 (Mil)
49ERS, 30–14 (SF)	49ERS, 35–0 (SF)
1951—49ERS, 31–19 (SF)	1955—Packers, 27–21 (Mil)
1952—49ERS, 24–14 (SF)	Packers, 28–7 (SF)
1953—49ERS, 37–7 (Mil)	1956—49ERS, 17–16 (GB)
49ERS, 48–14 (SF)	49ERS, 38–20 (SF)

Green Bay Packers vs. San Francisco 49ERS (Cont'd)

1957—49ERS, 24–14 (Mil)	1963—Packers, 28–10 (Mil)
49ERS, 27–20 (SF)	Packers, 21–17 (SF)
1958—49ERS, 33–12 (Mil)	1964—Packers, 24–14 (Mil)
49ERS, 48–21 (SF)	49ERS, 24–14 (SF)
1959—Packers, 21–20 (GB)	1965—Packers, 27–10 (GB)
Packers, 36–14 (SF)	Tie, 24–24 (SF)
1960—Packers, 41–14 (Mil)	1966—49ERS, 21–20 (SF)
Packers, 13–0 (SF)	Packers, 20–7 (Mil)
1961—Packers, 30–10 (GB)	1967—Packers, 13–0 (GB)
49ERS, 22–21 (SF)	1968—49ERS, 27–20 (SF)
1962—Packers, 31–13 (Mil)	1969—Packers, 14–7 (Mil)
Packers, 31–21 (SF)	

(Points—49ERS 739, Packers 717)

GREEN BAY PACKERS vs. WASHINGTON REDSKINS

(Packers lead series, 6–5)

1937—Redskins, 14–6 (W)	1948—Redskins, 23–7 (Mil)
1939—Packers, 24–14 (Mil)	1949—Redskins, 30–0 (W)
1941—Packers, 22–17 (W)	1950—Packers, 35–21 (Mil)
1943—Redskins, 33–7 (Mil)	1952—Packers, 35–20 (Mil)
1946—Packers, 20–7 (W)	1958—Redskins, 37–21 (W)
1947—Packers, 27–10 (Mil)	1959—Packers, 21–0 (GB)
	1968—Packers, 27–7 (W)

(Points—Packers 252, Redskins 233)

HOUSTON OILERS vs. BOSTON PATRIOTS

(Patriots lead series, 10–9–1; See Boston vs. Houston)

HOUSTON OILERS vs. BUFFALO BILLS

(Oilers lead series, 13–7; See Buffalo vs. Houston)

HOUSTON OILERS vs. CINCINNATI BENGALS

(Oilers lead series, 1–0–1; See Cincinnati vs. Houston)

HOUSTON OILERS vs. DENVER BRONCOS

(Oilers lead series, 14–4–1; See Denver vs. Houston)

HOUSTON OILERS vs. *KANSAS CITY CHIEFS

(Chiefs lead series, 12–6)

1960—Oilers, 20–10 (H)	1964—Chiefs, 28–7 (KC)
Texans, 24–0 (Da)	Chiefs, 28–19 (H)
1961—Texans, 26–21 (Da)	1965—Chiefs, 52–21 (KC)
Oilers, 38–7 (H)	Oilers, 38–36 (H)
1962—Texans, 31–7 (H)	1966—Chiefs, 48–23 (KC)
Oilers, 14–6 (Da)	1967—Chiefs, 25–20 (H)
**Texans, 20–17 (H)	Oilers, 24–19 (KC)
1963—Chiefs, 28–7 (KC)	1968—Chiefs, 26–21 (H)
Oilers, 28–7 (H)	1969—Chiefs, 24–0 (KC)

(Points—Chiefs 445, Oilers 325)

*Prior to 1963 franchise located in Dallas and known as Texans
**AFL Championship

HOUSTON OILERS vs. MIAMI DOLPHINS

(Oilers lead series, 5–3)

1966—Dolphins, 20–13 (H)	1968—Oilers, 24–10 (M)
Dolphins, 29–28 (M)	Dolphins, 24–7 (H)
1967—Oilers, 17–14 (H)	1969—Oilers, 22–10 (H)
Oilers, 41–10 (M)	Oilers, 32–7 (M)

(Points—Oilers 184, Dolphins 124)

HOUSTON OILERS vs. NEW YORK JETS

(Oilers lead series, 10–8–1)

1960—Oilers, 27–21 (H)	1965—Oilers, 27–21 (H)
Oilers, 42–28 (NY)	Jets, 41–14 (NY)
1961—Oilers, 49–13 (H)	1966—Jets, 52–13 (NY)
Oilers, 48–21 (NY)	Oilers, 24–0 (H)
1962—Oilers, 56–17 (H)	1967—Tie, 28–28 (NY)
Oilers, 44–10 (NY)	1968—Jets, 20–14 (H)
1963—Jets 24–17 (NY)	Jets, 26–7 (NY)
Oilers, 31–27 (H)	1969—Jets, 26–17 (NY)
1964—Jets, 24–21 (NY)	Jets, 34–26 (H)
Oilers, 33–17 (H)	

(Points—Oilers 538, Jets 450)

HOUSTON OILERS vs. OAKLAND RAIDERS

(Raiders lead series, 12–7)

1960—Oilers 37–22 (O)	1965—Raiders, 21–17 (O)
Raiders, 14–13 (H)	Raiders, 33–21 (H)
1961—Oilers, 55–0 (H)	1966—Oilers, 31–0 (H)
Oilers, 47–16 (O)	Raiders, 38–23 (O)
1962—Oilers, 28–20 (O)	1967—Raiders, 19–7 (O)
Oilers, 32–17 (H)	*Raiders, 40–7 (O)
1963—Raiders, 24–13 (H)	1968—Raiders, 24–15 (H)
Raiders, 52–19 (O)	1969—Raiders, 21–17 (O)
1964—Oilers, 42–28 (H)	**Raiders, 56–7 (O)
Raiders, 20–10 (O)	

(Points—Raiders 465, Oilers 441)

*AFL Championship Game
*Inter-Divisional Playoff

HOUSTON OILERS vs. *SAN DIEGO CHARGERS

(Chargers lead series, 12–7)

1960—Oilers, 38–28 (H)	1964—Chargers, 27–21 (SD)
Chargers, 24–21 (LA)	Chargers, 20–17 (H)
*Oilers, 24–16 (H)	1965—Chargers, 31–14 (SD)
1961—Chargers, 34–24 (SD)	Chargers, 37–26 (H)
Oilers, 33–13 (H)	1966—Chargers, 28–22 (H)
*Oilers, 10–3 (SD)	1967—Chargers, 13–3 (SD)
1962—Oilers, 42–17 (SD)	Oilers, 24–17 (H)
Oilers, 33–27 (H)	1968—Chargers, 30–14 (SD)
1963—Oilers, 27–0 (SD)	1969—Chargers, 21–17 (H)
Chargers, 20–14 (H)	

(Points—Chargers 433, Oilers 397)

AFL Championship Games

KANSAS CITY CHIEFS vs. BOSTON PATRIOTS

(Chiefs lead series, 9–5–3; See Boston vs. Kansas City)

KANSAS CITY CHIEFS vs. BUFFALO BILLS

(Series tied 9–9–1; See Buffalo vs. Kansas City)

KANSAS CITY CHIEFS vs. CINCINNATI BENGALS

(Chiefs lead series, 3–1; See Cincinnati vs. Kansas City)

KANSAS CITY CHIEFS vs. DENVER BRONCOS

(Chiefs lead series, 19–1; See Denver vs. Kansas City)

KANSAS CITY CHIEFS vs. GREEN BAY PACKERS

(Packers lead series, 1–0; See Green Bay vs. Kansas City)

KANSAS CITY CHIEFS vs. HOUSTON OILERS

(Chiefs lead series, 13–6; See Houston vs. Kansas City)

KANSAS CITY CHIEFS vs. MIAMI DOLPHINS

(Chiefs lead series, 6–0)

1966—Chiefs, 34–16 (KC)	1968—Chiefs, 48–3 (M)
Chiefs, 19–18 (M)	1969—Chiefs, 17–10 (KC)
1967—Chiefs, 24–0 (M)	
Chiefs, 41–0 (KC)	

(Points—Chiefs 183, Dolphins 47)

KANSAS CITY CHIEFS vs. MINNESOTA VIKINGS

(Chiefs lead series, 1–0)

1970—*Chiefs, 23–7 (New Orleans)
*Super Bowl

*KANSAS CITY CHIEFS vs. **NEW YORK JETS

(Chiefs lead series, 11–7)

1960—Titans, 37–35 (Da)	1965—Chiefs, 14–10 (NY)
Titans, 41–35 (NY)	Jets, 13–10 (KC)
1961—Titans, 28–7 (NY)	1966—Chiefs, 32–24 (NY)
Texans, 35–24 (Da)	1967—Chiefs, 42–18 (KC)
1962—Texans, 20–17 (Da)	Chiefs, 21–7 (NY)
Texans, 52–31 (NY)	1968—Jets, 20–19 (KC)
1963—Jets, 17–0 (NY)	1969—Chiefs, 34–16 (NY)
Chiefs, 48–0 (KC)	***Chiefs, 13–6 (NY)
1964—Jets, 27–14 (NY)	
Chiefs, 24–7 (KC)	

(Points—Chiefs 455, Jets 343)

*Prior to 1963 franchise located in Dallas (Da) and known as Texans
**Jets known as Titans prior to 1963
***Inter-Divisional Playoff

*KANSAS CITY CHIEFS vs. OAKLAND RAIDERS

(Series tied 11–11)

1960—Texans, 34–16 (O)	1965—Raiders, 37–10 (O)
Raiders, 20–10 (Da)	Chiefs, 14–7 (KC)
1961—Texans, 42–35 (O)	1966—Chiefs, 32–10 (O)
Texans, 43–11 (Da)	Raiders, 34–13 (KC)
1962—Texans, 26–16 (O)	1967—Raiders, 23–21 (O)
Texans, 35–7 (Da)	Raiders, 44–22 (KC)
1963—Raiders, 10–7 (O)	1968—Chiefs, 24–10 (KC)
Raiders, 22–7 (KC)	Raiders, 38–21 (O)
1964—Chiefs, 21–9 (O)	**Raiders, 41–6 (O)
Chiefs, 42–7 (KC)	1969—Raiders, 27–24 (KC)
	Raiders, 10–6 (O)
	***Chiefs, 17–7 (O)

(Points—Chiefs 477, Raiders 441)

*Prior to 1963 franchise located in Dallas (Da) and known as Texans
**Western Division Playoff
***AFL Championship

*KANSAS CITY CHIEFS vs. **SAN DIEGO CHARGERS

(Chiefs lead series, 10–9–1)

1960—Chargers, 21–20 (LA)	1963—Chargers, 24–10 (SD)
Texans, 17–0 (Da)	Chargers, 38–17 (KC)
1961—Chargers, 26–10 (Da)	1964—Chargers, 28–14 (SD)
Chargers, 24–14 (SD)	Chiefs, 49–6 (SD)
1962—Chargers, 32–28 (SD)	1965—Tie, 10–10 (SD)
Texans, 26–17 (Da)	Chiefs, 31–7 (KC)

1966—Chiefs, 24–14 (KC)   1968—Chiefs, 27–20 (KC)
    Chiefs, 27–17 (SD)   Chiefs, 40–3 (SD)
1967—Chargers, 45–31 (SD)   1969—Chiefs, 27–9 (SD)
    Chargers, 17–16 (KC)   Chiefs, 27–3 (KC)
            (Points—Chiefs 465, Chargers 361)
*Prior to 1963 franchise located in Dallas (Da) and known as Texans
**Prior to 1961 franchise located in Los Angeles

LOS ANGELES RAMS vs. ATLANTA FALCONS

(Rams lead series, 7–0; See Atlanta vs. Los Angeles)

LOS ANGELES RAMS vs. BALTIMORE COLTS

(Colts lead series, 19–14–2; See Baltimore vs. Los Angeles)

LOS ANGELES RAMS vs. CHICAGO BEARS

(Bears lead series, 28–15–2; See Chicago vs. Los Angeles)

LOS ANGELES RAMS vs. CLEVELAND BROWNS

(Browns lead series, 7–3; See Cleveland vs. Los Angeles)

LOS ANGELES RAMS vs. DALLAS COWBOYS

(Rams lead series, 4–1; See Dallas vs. Los Angeles)

LOS ANGELES RAMS vs. DETROIT LIONS

(Rams lead series, 23–22–1; See Detroit vs. Los Angeles)

LOS ANGELES RAMS vs. GREEN BAY PACKERS

(Rams lead series, 27–18–1; See Green Bay vs. Los Angeles)

LOS ANGELES RAMS vs. MINNESOTA VIKINGS

(Vikings lead series, 9–6–1)
1961—Rams, 31–17 (LA)   1965—Vikings, 38–35 (LA)
    Vikings, 42–21 (M)   Vikings, 24–13 (M)
1962—Vikings, 38–14 (LA)   1966—Vikings, 35–7 (M)
    Tie, 24–24 (M)   Rams, 21–6 (LA)
1963—Rams, 27–24 (LA)   1967—Rams, 39–3 (LA)
    Vikings, 21–13 (M)   1968—Rams, 31–3 (M)
1964—Rams, 22–13 (LA)   1969—Vikings, 20–13 (LA)
    Vikings, 34–13 (M)   *Vikings, 23–20 (M)
            (Points—Vikings 365, Rams 344)
*Conference Championship

LOS ANGELES RAMS vs. NEW ORLEANS SAINTS

(Rams lead series, 2–0)
1967—Rams 27–13 (NO)   1969—Rams, 36–17 (LA)
        (Points—Rams 63, Saints 30)

LOS ANGELES RAMS vs. NEW YORK GIANTS

(Rams lead series, 7–2)
1946—Rams, 31–21 (NY)   1954—Rams, 17–16 (NY)
1947—Rams, 34–10 (LA)   1959—Giants, 23–21 (LA)
1948—Rams, 52–37 (NY)   1961—Giants, 24–14 (NY)
1953—Rams, 21–7 (LA)   1966—Rams, 55–14 (LA)
                                1968—Rams, 24–21 (LA)
        (Points—Rams 269, Giants 173)

LOS ANGELES RAMS vs. PHILADELPHIA EAGLES

(Series tied, 6–6–1)

1946—Eagles, 25–14 (LA)	1955—Rams, 23–21 (P)
1947—Eagles, 14–7 (P)	1956—Rams, 27–7 (LA)
1948—Tie, 28–28 (LA)	1957—Rams, 17–13 (LA)
1949—Eagles, 38–14 (P)	1959—Eagles, 23–20 (P)
*Eagles, 14–0 (LA)	1964—Rams, 20–10 (LA)
1950—Eagles, 56–20 (P)	1967—Rams, 33–17 (LA)
	1969—Rams, 23–17 (P)

(Points—Eagles 283, Rams 246)

*NFL Championship Game

LOS ANGELES RAMS vs. PITTSBURGH STEELERS

(Rams lead series, 7–1–1)

1947—Rams, 48–7 (P)	1956—Steelers, 30–13 (P)
1948—Rams, 31–14 (LA)	1961—Rams, 24–14 (LA)
1949—Tie, 7–7 (P)	1964—Rams, 26–14 (P)
1952—Rams, 28–14 (LA)	1968—Rams, 45–10, (LA)
1955—Rams, 27–26 (LA)	

(Points—Rams 249, Steelers 136)

LOS ANGELES RAMS vs. *ST. LOUIS CARDINALS

(Rams lead series, 7–6–2)

1946—Cardinals, 34–10 (C)	1951—Rams, 45–21 (LA)
Rams, 17–14 (LA)	1953—Tie, 24–24 (C)
1947—Rams, 27–7 (LA)	1954—Rams, 28–17 (LA)
Cardinals, 17–10 (C)	1958—Rams, 20–14 (C)
1948—Cardinals, 27–22 (LA)	1960—Cardinals, 43–21 (LA)
Cardinals, 27–24 (C)	1965—Rams, 27–3 (St L)
1949—Tie, 28–28 (C)	1968—Rams, 24–13 (St L)
Cardinals, 31–27 (LA)	

(Points—Rams 354, Cardinals 320)

*Franchise in Chicago prior to 1960

LOS ANGELES RAMS vs. SAN FRANCISCO 49ERS

(Rams lead series, 22–16–2)

1950—Rams, 35–14 (SF)	1960—49ERS, 13–9 (SF)
Rams, 28–21 (LA)	49ERS, 23–7 (LA)
1951—49ERS, 44–17 (SF)	1961—49ERS, 35–0 (SF)
Rams, 23–16 (LA)	Rams, 17–7 (LA)
1952—Rams, 35–9 (LA)	1962—Rams, 28–14 (SF)
Rams, 34–21 (SF)	49ERS, 24–17 (LA)
1953—49ERS, 31–30 (SF)	1963—Rams, 28–21 (LA)
49ERS, 31–27 (LA)	Rams, 21–17 (SF)
1954—Tie, 24–24 (LA)	1964—Rams, 42–14 (LA)
Rams, 42–34 (SF)	49ERS, 28–7 (SF)
1955—Rams, 23–14 (SF)	1965—49ERS, 45–21 (LA)
Rams, 27–14 (LA)	49ERS, 30–27 (SF)
1956—49ERS, 33–30 (SF)	1966—Rams, 34–3 (LA)
Rams, 30–6 (LA)	49ERS, 21–13 (SF)
1957—49ERS, 23–20 (SF)	1967—49ERS, 27–24 (LA)
Rams, 37–24 (LA)	Rams, 17–7 (SF)
1958—Rams, 33–3 (SF)	1968—Rams, 24–10 (LA)
Rams, 56–7 (LA)	Tie, 20–20 (SF)
1959—49ERS, 34–0 (SF)	1969—Rams, 27–21 (SF)
49ERS, 24–16 (LA)	Rams, 41–30 (LA)

(Points—Rams 991, 49ERS 837)

LOS ANGELES RAMS vs. WASHINGTON REDSKINS

(Series tied, 3–3–1)

1948—Rams, 41–13 (W)	1962—Redskins, 20–14 (W)
1949—Rams, 53–27 (LA)	1963—Redskins, 37–14 (LA)
1951—Redskins, 31–21 (W)	1967—Tie, 28–28, (LA)
	1969—Rams, 24–23 (W)

(Points—Rams 195, Redskins 179)

MIAMI DOLPHINS vs. BOSTON PATRIOTS

(Dolphins lead series, 4–3; See Boston vs. Miami)

MIAMI DOLPHINS vs. BUFFALO BILLS

(Bills lead series, 4–3–1; See Buffalo vs. Miami)

MIAMI DOLPHINS vs. CINCINNATI BENGALS

(Bengals lead series, 2–1; See Cincinnati vs. Miami)

MIAMI DOLPHINS vs. DENVER BRONCOS

(Dolphins lead series, 3–2; See Denver vs. Miami)

MIAMI DOLPHINS vs. HOUSTON OILERS

(Oilers lead series, 5–3; See Houston vs. Miami)

MIAMI DOLPHINS vs. KANSAS CITY CHIEFS

(Chiefs lead series, 6–0; See Kansas City vs. Miami)

MIAMI DOLPHINS vs. NEW YORK JETS

(Jets lead series, 8–0)

1966—Jets, 19–14 (M)	1968—Jets, 35–17 (NY)
Jets, 30–13 (NY)	Jets, 31–7 (M)
1967—Jets, 29–7 (NY)	1969—Jets, 34–31 (NY)
Jets, 33–14 (M)	Jets, 27–9 (M)

(Points—Jets 238, Dolphins 112)

MIAMI DOLPHINS vs. OAKLAND RAIDERS

(Raiders lead series, 5–0–1)

1966—Raiders, 23–14 (M)	1968—Raiders, 47–21 (M)
Raiders, 21–10 (O)	1969—Raiders, 20–17 (O)
1967—Raiders, 31–17 (O)	Tie, 20–20 (M)

(Points—Raiders 162, Dolphins 99)

MIAMI DOLPHINS vs. SAN DIEGO CHARGERS

(Chargers lead series, 4–1)

1966—Chargers, 44–10 (SD)	1968—Chargers, 34–28 (SD)
1967—Chargers, 24–0 (SD)	1969—Chargers, 21–14 (M)
Dolphins, 41–24 (M)	

(Points—Chargers 147, Dolphins 93)

MINNESOTA VIKINGS vs. ATLANTA FALCONS

(Falcons lead series, 3–1; See Atlanta vs. Minnesota)

MINNESOTA VIKINGS vs. BALTIMORE COLTS

(Colts lead series, 12–3–1; See Baltimore vs. Minnesota)

MINNESOTA VIKINGS vs. CHICAGO BEARS

(Bears lead series, 11–5–2; See Chicago vs. Minnesota)

MINNESOTA VIKINGS vs. CLEVELAND BROWNS
(Vikings lead series, 3–1; See Cleveland vs. Minnesota)

MINNESOTA VIKINGS vs. DALLAS COWBOYS
(Cowboys lead series, 4–0; See Dallas vs. Minnesota)

MINNESOTA VIKINGS vs. DETROIT LIONS
(Lions lead series 11–5–2; See Detroit vs. Minnesota)

MINNESOTA VIKINGS vs. GREEN BAY PACKERS
(Packers lead series, 11–7; See Green Bay vs. Minnesota)

MINNESOTA VIKINGS vs. KANSAS CITY CHIEFS
(Chiefs lead series, 1–0; See Kansas City vs. Minnesota)

MINNESOTA VIKINGS vs. LOS ANGELES RAMS
(Vikings lead series, 9–6–1; See Los Angeles vs. Minnesota)

MINNESOTA VIKINGS vs. NEW ORLEANS SAINTS
(Saints lead series, 1–0)
1968—Saints, 20–17 (NO)

MINNESOTA VIKINGS vs. NEW YORK GIANTS
(Vikings lead series, 3–1)

1964—Vikings, 30–21 (NY)	1967—Vikings, 27–24 (M)
1965—Vikings, 40–14 (M)	1969—Giants, 24–23 (NY)

(Points—Vikings 120, Giants 83)

MINNESOTA VIKINGS vs. PHILADELPHIA EAGLES
(Vikings lead series, 3–0)

1962—Vikings, 31–21 (M)	1963—Vikings, 34–13 (P)
	1968—Vikings, 24–17 (P)

(Points—Vikings 89, Eagles 51)

MINNESOTA VIKINGS vs. PITTSBURGH STEELERS
(Vikings lead series, 3–1)

1962—Steelers, 39–31 (P)	1967—Vikings, 41–27 (P)
1964—Vikings, 30–10 (M)	1969—Vikings, 52–14 (M)

(Points—Vikings 154, Steelers 90)

MINNESOTA VIKINGS vs. ST. LOUIS CARDINALS
(Cardinals lead series, 2–1)

1963—Cardinals, 56–14 (M)	1967—Cardinals, 34–24 (M)
	1969—Vikings, 27–10 (St L)

(Points—Cardinals 100, Vikings 65)

MINNESOTA VIKINGS vs. SAN FRANCISCO 49ERS
(Vikings lead series, 8–6–1)

1961—49ERS, 38–24 (M)	1965—Vikings, 42–41 (SF)
49ERS, 38–28 (SF)	49ERS, 45–24 (M)
1962—49ERS, 21–7 (SF)	1966—Tie, 20–20 (SF)
49ERS, 35–12 (M)	Vikings, 28–3 (M)
1963—Vikings, 24–20 (SF)	1967—49ERS, 27–21 (M)
Vikings, 45–14 (M)	1968—Vikings, 30–20 (M)
1964—Vikings, 27–22 (SF)	1969—Vikings, 10–7 (M)
Vikings, 24–7 (M)	

(Points—Vikings 366, 49ERS 358)

MINNESOTA VIKINGS vs. WASHINGTON REDSKINS

(Vikings lead series, 1–0)

1968—Vikings, 27–14 (M)

NEW ORLEANS SAINTS vs. ATLANTA FALCONS

(Series tied, 1–1; See Atlanta vs. New Orleans)

NEW ORLEANS SAINTS vs. BALTIMORE COLTS

(Colts lead series, 2–0; See Baltimore vs. New Orleans)

NEW ORLEANS SAINTS vs. CHICAGO BEARS

(Bears lead series, 1–0; See Chicago vs. New Orleans)

NEW ORLEANS SAINTS vs. CLEVELAND BROWNS

(Browns lead series, 4–0; See Cleveland vs. New Orleans)

NEW ORLEANS SAINTS vs. DALLAS COWBOYS

(Cowboys lead series, 5–0; See Dallas vs. New Orleans)

NEW ORLEANS SAINTS vs. DETROIT LIONS

(Saints and Lions tied in only meeting; See Detroit vs. New Orleans)

NEW ORLEANS SAINTS vs. GREEN BAY PACKERS

(Packers lead series, 1–0; See Green Bay vs. New Orleans)

NEW ORLEANS SAINTS vs. LOS ANGELES RAMS

(Rams lead series, 2–0; See Los Angeles vs. New Orleans)

NEW ORLEANS SAINTS vs. MINNESOTA VIKINGS

(Saints lead series, 1–0; See Minnesota vs. New Orleans)

NEW ORLEANS SAINTS vs. NEW YORK GIANTS

(Giants lead series, 2–1)

1967—Giants, 27–21 (NY)	1968—Giants, 38–21 (NY)
	1969—Saints, 25–24 (NY)

(Points—Giants 93, Saints 67)

NEW ORLEANS SAINTS vs. PHILADELPHIA EAGLES

(Saints lead series, 3–2)

1967—Saints, 31–24 (NO)	1968—Eagles, 29–17 (P)
Eagles, 48–21 (P)	1969—Saints, 10–13 (P)
	Saints, 26–17 (NO)

(Points—Eagles 131, Saints 105)

NEW ORLEANS SAINTS vs. PITTSBURGH STEELERS

(Saints lead series, 3–1)

1967—Steelers, 14–10 (NO)	1968—Saints, 16–12 (P)
	Saints, 24–14 (NO)
	1969—Saints, 27–24 (NO)

(Points—Saints 77, Steelers 64)

NEW ORLEANS SAINTS vs. ST. LOUIS CARDINALS

(Cardinals lead series, 3–1)

1967—Cardinals, 31–20 (St L)	1968—Cardinals, 21–20 (NO)
	Cardinals, 31–17 (St L)
	1969—Saints, 51–42 (St L)

(Points—Cardinals 125, Saints 108)

NEW ORLEANS SAINTS vs. SAN FRANCISCO 49ERS

(Series tied, 1–1)

1967—49ERS, 27–13 (SF)   1969—Saints, 43–38 (NO)

(Points—49ERS 65, Saints 56)

NEW ORLEANS SAINTS vs. WASHINGTON REDSKINS

(Redskins lead series, 3–2)

1967—Redskins, 30–10 (NO)   1968—Saints, 37–17 (NO)
Saints, 30–14 (W)   1969—Redskins, 26–20 (NO)
Redskins, 17–14 (W)

(Points—Saints 111, Redskins 104)

NEW YORK GIANTS vs. ATLANTA FALCONS

(Falcons lead series, 2–0; See Atlanta vs. New York)

NEW YORK GIANTS vs. BALTIMORE COLTS

(Series tied, 4–4; See Baltimore vs. New York)

NEW YORK GIANTS vs. CHICAGO BEARS

(Bears lead series, 23–16–2; See Chicago vs. New York)

NEW YORK GIANTS vs. CLEVELAND BROWNS

(Browns lead series, 23–16–2; See Cleveland vs. New York)

NEW YORK GIANTS vs. DALLAS COWBOYS

(Cowboys lead series, 9–6–2; See Dallas vs. New York)

NEW YORK GIANTS vs. DETROIT LIONS

(Lions lead series, 11–6–1; See Detroit vs. New York)

NEW YORK GIANTS vs. GREEN BAY PACKERS

(Packers lead series, 19–15–2; see Green Bay vs. New York)

NEW YORK GIANTS vs. LOS ANGELES RAMS

(Rams lead series, 7–2; See Los Angeles vs. New York)

NEW YORK GIANTS vs. MINNESOTA VIKINGS

(Vikings lead series, 3–1; See Minnesota vs. New York)

NEW YORK GIANTS vs. NEW ORLEANS SAINTS

(Giants lead series, 2–1; See New Orleans vs. New York)

NEW YORK GIANTS vs. PHILADELPHIA EAGLES

(Giants lead series, 45–26–1)

1933—Giants, 56–0 (NY)   1941—Giants, 24–0 (P)
Giants, 20–14 (P)   Giants, 16–0 (NY)
1934—Giants, 17–0 (NY)   1942—Giants, 35–17 (NY)
Eagles, 6–0 (P)   Giants, 14–0 (P)
1935—Giants, 10–0 (NY)   1943—Eagles, 28–14 (P)
Giants, 21–14 (P)   Giants, 42–14 (NY)
1936—Eagles, 10–7 (P)   1944—Eagles, 24–17 (NY)
Giants, 21–17 (NY)   Tie, 21–21 (P)
1937—Giants, 16–7 (P)   1945—Eagles, 38–17 (P)
Giants, 21–0 (NY)   Giants, 28–21 (NY)
1938—Eagles, 14–10 (P)   1946—Eagles, 24–14 (P)
Giants, 17–7 (NY)   Giants, 45–17 (NY)
1939—Giants, 13–3 (P)   1947—Eagles, 23–0 (P)
Giants, 27–10 (NY)   Eagles, 41–24 (NY)
1940—Giants, 20–14 (P)   1948—Eagles, 45–0 (P)
Giants, 17–7 (NY)   Eagles, 35–14 (NY)

1949—Eagles, 24–3 (NY)
   Eagles, 17–3 (P)
1950—Giants, 7–3 (NY)
   Giants, 9–7 (P)
1951—Giants, 26–24 (NY)
   Giants, 23–7 (P)
1952—Giants, 31–7 (P)
   Eagles, 14–10 (NY)
1953—Eagles, 30–7 (P)
   Giants, 37–28 (NY)
1954—Giants, 27–14 (NY)
   Eagles, 29–14 (P)
1955—Eagles, 27–17 (P)
   Giants, 31–7 (NY)
1956—Giants, 20–3 (NY)
   Giants, 21–7 (P)
1957—Giants, 24–20 (P)
   Giants, 13–0 (NY)
1958—Eagles, 27–24 (P)
   Giants, 24–10 (NY)

1959—Eagles, 49–21 (P)
   Giants, 24–7 (NY)
1960—Eagles, 17–10 (NY)
   Eagles, 31–23 (P)
1961—Giants, 38–21 (NY)
   Giants, 28–24 (P)
1962—Giants, 29–13 (P)
   Giants, 19–14 (NY)
1963—Giants, 37–14 (P)
   Giants, 42–14 (NY)
1964—Eagles, 38–7 (P)
   Eagles, 23–17 (NY)
1965—Giants, 16–14 (P)
   Giants, 35–27 (NY)
1966—Eagles, 35–17 (P)
   Eagles, 31–3 (NY)
1967—Giants, 44–7 (NY)
1968—Giants, 34–25 (P)
   Giants, 7–6 (NY)
1969—Eagles, 23–20 (NY)

(Points—Giants 1,460, Eagles 1,209)

NEW YORK GIANTS vs. PITTSBURGH STEELERS

(Giants lead series, 42–25–3)

1933—Giants, 23–2 (P)
   Giants, 27–3 (NY)
1934—Giants, 14–12 (P)
   Giants, 17–7 (NY)
1935—Giants, 42–7 (P)
   Giants, 13–0 (NY)
1936—Steelers, 10–7 (P)
1937—Giants, 10–7 (P)
   Giants, 17–0 (NY)
1938—Giants, 27–14 (P)
   Steelers, 13–10 (NY)
1939—Giants, 14–7 (P)
   Giants, 23–7 (NY)
1940—Tie, 10–10 (P)
   Giants, 12–0 (NY)
1941—Giants, 37–10 (P)
   Giants, 28–7 (NY)
1942—Steelers, 13–10 (P)
   Steelers, 17–9 (NY)
1943—Steelers, 28–14 (Phil)
   Giants, 42–14 (NY)
1944—Giants, 23–0 (NY)
1945—Giants, 34–6 (P)
   Steelers, 21–7 (NY)
1946—Giants, 17–14 (P)
   Giants, 7–0 (NY)
1947—Steelers, 38–21 (NY)
   Steelers, 24–7 (P)
1948—Giants, 34–27 (NY)
   Steelers, 38–28 (P)
1949—Steelers, 28–7 (P)
   Steelers, 21–17 (NY)
1950—Giants, 18–7 (P)
   Steelers, 17–6 (NY)
1951—Tie, 13–13 (P)
   Giants, 14–0 (NY)

1952—Steelers, 63–7 (P)
1953—Steelers, 24–14 (P)
   Steelers, 14–10 (NY)
1954—Giants, 30–6 (P)
   Giants, 24–3 (NY)
1955—Steelers, 30–23 (P)
   Steelers, 19–17 (NY)
1956—Giants, 38–10 (NY)
   Giants, 17–14 (P)
1957—Giants, 35–0 (NY)
   Steelers, 21–10 (P)
1958—Giants, 17–6 (NY)
   Steelers, 31–10 (P)
1959—Giants, 21–16 (P)
   Steelers, 14–9 (NY)
1960—Giants, 19–17 (P)
   Giants, 27–24 (NY)
1961—Giants, 17–14 (P)
   Giants, 42–21 (NY)
1962—Giants, 31–27 (P)
   Steelers, 20–17 (NY)
1963—Steelers, 31–0 (P)
   Giants, 33–17 (NY)
1964—Steelers, 27–24 (P)
   Giants, 44–17 (NY)
1965—Giants, 23–13 (P)
   Giants, 35–10 (NY)
1966—Tie, 34–34 (P)
   Steelers, 47–28 (NY)
1967—Giants, 27–24 (P)
   Giants, 28–20 (NY)
1968—Giants, 34–20 (P)
1969—Giants, 10–7 (NY)
   Giants, 21–17 (P)

(Points—Giants 1,408, Steelers 1,147)

NEW YORK GIANTS vs. *ST. LOUIS CARDINALS

(Giants lead series, 40–15–1)

1926—Giants, 20–0 (NY)	1955—Cardinals, 28–17 (C)
1927—Giants, 28–7 (NY)	Giants, 10–0 (NY)
1929—Giants, 24–21 (NY)	1956—Cardinals, 35–27 (C)
1930—Giants, 25–12 (NY)	Giants, 23–10 (NY)
Giants, 13–7 (C)	1957—Giants, 27–14 (NY)
1935—Cardinals, 14–13 (NY)	Giants, 28–21 (C)
1936—Giants, 14–6 (NY)	1958—Giants, 37–7 (Buffalo)
1938—Giants, 6–0 (NY)	Cardinals, 23–6 (NY)
1939—Giants, 17–7 (NY)	1959—Giants, 9–3 (NY)
1941—Cardinals, 10–7 (NY)	Giants, 30–20 (Minn)
1942—Giants, 21–7 (NY)	1960—Giants, 35–14 (St L)
1943—Giants, 24–13 (NY)	Cardinals, 20–13 (NY)
1944—Giants, 23–0 (NY)	1961—Cardinals, 21–10 (NY)
1946—Giants, 28–24 (NY)	Giants, 24–9 (St L)
1947—Giants, 35–31 (NY)	1962—Giants, 31–14 (St L)
1948—Cardinals, 63–35 (NY)	Giants, 31–28 (NY)
1949—Giants, 41–38 (C)	1963—Giants, 38–21 (St L)
1950—Cardinals, 17–3 (C)	Cardinals, 24–17 (NY)
Giants, 51–21 (NY)	1964—Giants, 34–17 (NY)
1951—Giants, 28–17 (NY)	Tie, 10–10 (St L)
Giants, 10–0 (C)	1965—Giants, 14–10 (NY)
1952—Cardinals, 24–23 (NY)	Giants, 28–15 (St L)
Giants, 28–6 (C)	1966—Cardinals, 24–19 (St L)
1953—Giants, 21–7 (NY)	Cardinals, 20–17 (NY)
Giants, 23–20 (C)	1967—Giants, 37–20 (St L)
1954—Giants, 41–10 (C)	Giants, 39–14 (NY)
Giants, 31–17 (NY)	1968—Cardinals, 28–21 (NY)
	1969—Cardinals, 42–17 (St L)
	Giants, 49–6 (NY)

(Points—Giants 1,329, Cardinals 917)

*Franchise in Chicago prior to 1960

NEW YORK GIANTS vs. SAN FRANCISCO 49ERS

(Giants lead series, 4–2)

1952—Giants, 23–14 (NY)	1960—Giants, 21–19 (SF)
1956—Giants, 38–21 (SF)	1963—Giants, 48–14 (NY)
1957—49ERS, 27–17 (NY)	1968—49ERS, 26–10 (NY)

(Points—Giants 157, 49ERS, 121)

NEW YORK GIANTS vs. WASHINGTON REDSKINS

(Giants lead series, 42–21–2)

1937—Redskins, 13–3 (W)	1946—Redskins, 24–14 (W)
Redskins, 49–14 (NY)	Giants, 31–0 (NY)
1938—Giants, 10–7 (W)	1947—Redskins, 28–20 (W)
Giants, 36–0 (NY)	Giants, 35–10 (NY)
1939—Tie, 0–0 (W)	1948—Redskins, 41–10 (W)
Giants, 9–7 (NY)	Redskins, 28–21 (NY)
1940—Redskins, 21–7 (W)	1949—Giants, 45–35 (W)
Giants, 21–7 (NY)	Giants, 23–7 (NY)
1941—Giants, 17–10 (W)	1950—Giants, 21–17 (W)
Giants, 20–13 (NY)	Giants, 24–21 (NY)
1942—Giants, 14–7 (W)	1951—Giants, 35–14 (W)
Redskins, 14–7 (NY)	Giants, 28–14 (NY)
1943—Giants, 14–10 (W)	1952—Giants, 14–10 (W)
Giants, 31–7 (NY)	Redskins, 27–17 (NY)
*Redskins, 28–0 (NY)	1953—Redskins, 13–9 (W)
1944—Giants, 16–13 (NY)	Redskins, 24–21 (NY)
Giants, 31–0 (W)	1954—Giants, 51–21 (W)
1945—Redskins, 24–14 (NY)	Giants, 24–7 (NY)
Redskins, 17–0 (W)	

1955—Giants, 35–7 (NY)	1962—Giants, 49–34 (NY)
Giants, 27–20 (W)	Giants, 42–24 (W)
1956—Redskins, 33–7 (W)	1963—Giants, 24–14 (W)
Giants, 28–14 (NY)	Giants, 44–14 (NY)
1957—Giants, 24–20 (W)	1964—Giants, 13–10 (NY)
Redskins, 31–14 (NY)	Redskins, 36–21 (W)
1958—Giants, 21–14 (W)	1965—Redskins, 23–7 (NY)
Giants, 30–0 (NY)	Giants, 27–10 (W)
1959—Giants, 45–14 (NY)	1966—Giants, 13–10 (NY)
Giants, 24–10 (W)	Redskins, 72–41 (W)
1960—Tie, 24–24 (NY)	1967—Redskins, 38–34 (W)
Giants, 17–3 (W)	1968—Giants, 48–21 (NY)
1961—Giants, 24–21 (W)	Giants, 13–10 (W)
Giants, 53–0 (NY)	1969—Redskins, 20–14 (W)

(Points—Giants 1,470, Redskins 1,135)

*Conference Playoff

NEW YORK JETS vs. BALTIMORE COLTS

(Jets lead series, 1–0; See Baltimore vs. N.Y. Jets)

NEW YORK JETS vs. BOSTON PATRIOTS

(Jets lead series, 12–7–1; See Boston vs. New York)

NEW YORK JETS vs. BUFFALO BILLS

(Bills lead series, 11–9; See Buffalo vs. New York)

NEW YORK JETS vs. CINCINNATI BENGALS

(Jets lead series, 3–1; See Cincinnati vs. New York)

NEW YORK JETS vs. DENVER BRONCOS

(Jets lead series, 9–7–1; See Denver vs. New York)

NEW YORK JETS vs. HOUSTON OILERS

(Oilers lead series, 10–8–1; See Houston vs. New York)

NEW YORK JETS vs. KANSAS CITY CHIEFS

(Chiefs lead series, 11–7; See Kansas City vs. New York)

NEW YORK JETS vs. MIAMI DOLPHINS

(Jets lead series, 8–0; See Miami vs. New York)

*NEW YORK JETS vs. OAKLAND RAIDERS

(Jets lead series, 9–8–2)

1960—Raiders, 28–27 (NY)	1965—Tie, 24–24 (NY)
Titans, 31–28 (O)	Raiders, 24–14 (O)
1961—Titans, 14–6 (O)	1966—Raiders, 24–21 (NY)
Titans, 23–12 (NY)	Tie, 28–28 (O)
1962—Titans, 28–17 (O)	1967—Jets, 27–14 (NY)
Titans, 31–21 (NY)	Raiders, 38–29 (O)
1963—Jets, 10–7 (NY)	1968—Raiders, 43–32 (O)
Raiders, 49–26 (O)	**Jets, 27–23 (NY)
1964—Jets, 35–13 (NY)	1969—Raiders, 27–14 (NY)
Raiders, 35–26 (O)	

(Points—Jets 467, Raiders 461)

*Jets known as Titans prior to 1963
**AFL Championship

*NEW YORK JETS vs. **SAN DIEGO CHARGERS

(Chargers lead series, 12–5–1)

1960—Chargers, 21–7 (NY)
Chargers, 50–43 (LA)
1961—Chargers, 25–10 (NY)
Chargers, 48–13 (SD)
1962—Chargers, 40–14 (SD)
Titans, 23–3 (NY)
1963—Chargers, 24–20 (SD)
Chargers, 53–7 (NY)
1964—Tie, 17–17 (NY)
Chargers, 38–3 (SD)

1965—Chargers, 34–9 (NY)
Chargers, 38–7 (SD)
1966—Jets, 17–16 (NY)
Chargers, 42–27 (SD)
1967—Jets, 42–31 (SD)
1968—Jets, 23–20 (NY)
Jets, 37–15 (SD)
1969—Chargers, 34–27 (SD)

(Points—Chargers 549, Jets 346)

*Jets known as Titans prior to 1963
**Prior to 1961 franchise located in Los Angeles

OAKLAND RAIDERS vs. BOSTON PATRIOTS

(Series tied, 8–8–1; See Boston vs. Oakland)

OAKLAND RAIDERS vs. BUFFALO BILLS

(Series tied, 9–9; See Buffalo vs. Oakland)

OAKLAND RAIDERS vs. CINCINNATI BENGALS

(Raiders lead series, 3–1; See Cincinnati vs. Oakland)

OAKLAND RAIDERS vs. DENVER BRONCOS

(Raiders lead series, 15–4–1; See Denver vs. Oakland)

OAKLAND RAIDERS vs. GREEN BAY PACKERS

(Packers lead series, 1–0; see Green Bay vs. Oakland)

OAKLAND RAIDERS vs. HOUSTON OILERS

(Raiders lead series, 12–7; See Houston vs. Oakland)

OAKLAND RAIDERS vs. KANSAS CITY CHIEFS

(Series tied, 11–11; See Kansas City vs. Oakland)

OAKLAND RAIDERS vs. MIAMI DOLPHINS

(Raiders lead series, 5–0–1; See Miami vs. Oakland)

OAKLAND RAIDERS vs. NEW YORK JETS

(Jets lead series, 9–8–2; See New York vs. Oakland)

OAKLAND RAIDERS vs. *SAN DIEGO CHARGERS

(Chargers lead series, 11–9)

1960—Chargers, 52–28 (LA)
Chargers, 41–17 (O)
1961—Chargers, 44–0 (SD)
Chargers, 41–10 (O)
1962—Chargers, 42–33 (O)
Chargers, 31–21 (SD)
1963—Raiders, 34–33 (SD)
Raiders, 41–27 (O)
1964—Chargers, 31–17 (O)
Raiders, 21–20 (SD)

1965—Chargers, 17–6 (O)
Chargers, 24–14 (SD)
1966—Chargers, 29–20 (O)
Raiders, 41–19 (SD)
1967—Raiders, 51–10 (O)
Raiders, 41–21 (SD)
1968—Chargers, 23–14 (O)
Raiders, 34–27 (SD)
1969—Raiders, 24–12 (SD)
Raiders, 21–16 (O)

(Points—Chargers 560, Raiders 488)

*Prior to 1961 franchise in Los Angeles

PHILADELPHIA EAGLES vs. ATLANTA FALCONS

(Eagles lead series, 2–1; See Atlanta vs. Philadelphia)

PHILADELPHIA EAGLES vs. BALTIMORE COLTS

(Colts lead series 4–2; See Baltimore vs. Philadelphia)

PHILADELPHIA EAGLES vs. CHICAGO BEARS

(Bears lead series, 15–2–1; See Chicago vs. Philadelphia)

PHILADELPHIA EAGLES vs. CLEVELAND BROWNS

(Browns lead series, 26–10–1; See Cleveland vs. Philadelphia)

PHILADELPHIA EAGLES vs. DALLAS COWBOYS

(Eagles lead series, 11–7; See Dallas vs. Philadelphia)

PHILADELPHIA EAGLES vs. DETROIT LIONS

(Lions lead series, 10–7–1; See Detroit vs. Philadelphia)

PHILADELPHIA EAGLES vs. GREEN BAY PACKERS

(Packers lead series, 16–2; See Green Bay vs. Philadelphia)

PHILADELPHIA EAGLES vs. LOS ANGELES RAMS

(Series tied, 6–6–1; See Los Angeles vs. Philadelphia)

PHILADELPHIA EAGLES vs. MINNESOTA VIKINGS

(Vikings lead series, 3–0; See Minnesota vs. Philadelphia)

PHILADELPHIA EAGLES vs. NEW ORLEANS SAINTS

(Saints lead series, 3–2; See New Orleans vs. Philadelphia)

PHILADELPHIA EAGLES vs. NEW YORK GIANTS

(Giants lead series, 45–26–1; See New York vs. Philadelphia)

PHILADELPHIA EAGLES vs. PITTSBURGH STEELERS

(Eagles lead series, 40–24–3)

1933—Eagles, 25–6 (Phila)	1946—Steelers, 10–7 (Pitt)
1934—Eagles, 17–0 (Pitt)	Eagles, 10–7 (Phila)
Steelers, 9–7 (Phila)	1947—Steelers, 35–24 (Pitt)
1935—Steelers, 17–7 (Phila)	Eagles, 21–0 (Phila)
Eagles, 17–6 (Pitt)	*Eagles, 21–0 (Pitt)
1936—Steelers, 17–0 (Pitt)	1948—Eagles, 34–7 (Pitt)
Steelers, 6–0 (Phila)	Eagles, 17–0 (Phila)
1937—Steelers, 27–14 (Pitt)	1949—Eagles, 38–7 (Pitt)
Steelers, 16–7 (Phila)	Eagles, 34–17 (Phila)
1938—Eagles, 27–7 (Buffalo)	1950—Eagles, 17–10 (Pitt)
Eagles, 14–7 (Charleston, W. Va)	Steelers, 9–7 (Phila)
1939—Eagles, 17–14 (Phila)	1951—Eagles, 34–13 (Pitt)
Steelers, 24–12 (Pitt)	Steelers, 17–13 (Phila)
1940—Steelers, 7–3 (Pitt)	1952—Eagles, 31–25 (Pitt)
Eagles, 7–0 (Phila)	Eagles, 26–21 (Phila)
1941—Eagles, 10–7 (Pitt)	1953—Eagles, 23–7 (Phila)
Tie, 7–7 (Phila)	Eagles, 35–7 (Pitt)
1942—Eagles, 24–14 (Pitt)	1954—Eagles, 24–22 (Phila)
Steelers, 14–0 (Phila)	Steelers, 17–7 (Pitt)
1945—Eagles, 45–3 (Pitt)	1955—Steelers, 13–7 (Pitt)
Eagles, 30–6 (Phil)	Eagles, 24–0 (Phila)

Philadelphia Eagles vs. Pittsburgh Steelers (Cont'd)

1956—Eagles, 35–21 (Pitt)
      Eagles, 14–7 (Phila)
1957—Steelers, 6–0 (Pitt)
      Eagles, 7–6 (Phila)
1958—Steelers, 24–3 (Pitt)
      Steelers, 31–24 (Phila)
1959—Eagles, 28–24 (Phila)
      Steelers, 31–0 (Pitt)
1960—Eagles, 34–7 (Phila)
      Steelers, 27–21 (Pitt)
1961—Eagles, 21–16 (Phila)
      Eagles, 35–24 (Pitt)
1962—Steelers, 13–7 (Pitt)
      Steelers, 26–17 (Phila)

1963—Tie, 21–21 (Phila)
      Tie, 20–20 (Pitt)
1964—Eagles, 21–7 (Phila)
      Eagles, 34–10 (Pitt)
1965—Steelers, 20–14 (Phila)
      Eagles, 47–13 (Pitt)
1966—Eagles, 31–14 (Pitt)
      Eagles, 27–23 (Phila)
1967—Eagles, 34–24 (Phila)
1968—Steelers, 6–3 (Pitt)
1969—Eagles, 41–27 (Phila)

(Points—Eagles 1,283, Steelers 906)
*Conference Playoff

PHILADELPHIA EAGLES vs. *ST. LOUIS CARDINALS

(Eagles lead series, 24–21–3)

1935—Cardinals, 12–3 (C)
1936—Cardinals, 13–0 (C)
1937—Tie, 6–6 (P)
1938—Eagles, 7–0 (C)
1941—Eagles, 21–14 (P)
1943—Eagles, 34–13 (Pitt)
1945—Eagles, 21–6 (P)
1947—Cardinals, 45–21 (P)
    **Cardinals, 28–21 (C)
1948—Cardinals, 21–14 (C)
    **Eagles, 7–0 (P)
1949—Eagles, 28–3 (P)
1950—Eagles, 45–7 (C)
      Cardinals, 14–10 (P)
1951—Eagles, 17–14 (C)
1952—Eagles, 10–7 (P)
      Cardinals, 28–22 (C)
1953—Eagles, 56–17 (C)
      Eagles, 38–0 (P)
1954—Eagles, 35–16 (C)
      Eagles, 30–14 (P)
1955—Tie, 24–24 (C)
      Eagles, 27–3 (P)
1956—Cardinals, 20–6 (P)
      Cardinals, 28–17 (C)

1957—Eagles, 38–21 (C)
      Cardinals, 31–27 (P)
1958—Tie, 21–21 (C)
      Eagles, 49–21 (P)
1959—Eagles, 28–24 (Minn)
      Eagles, 27–17 (P)
1960—Eagles, 31–27 (P)
      Eagles, 20–6 (StL)
1961—Cardinals, 30–27 (P)
      Eagles, 20–7 (StL)
1962—Cardinals, 27–21 (P)
      Cardinals, 45–35 (StL)
1963—Cardinals, 28–24 (P)
      Cardinals, 38–14 (StL)
1964—Cardinals, 38–13 (P)
      Cardinals, 36–34 (StL)
1965—Eagles, 34–27 (P)
      Eagles, 28–24 (StL)
1966—Cardinals, 16–13 (StL)
      Cardinals, 41–10 (P)
1967—Cardinals, 48–14 (StL)
1968—Cardinals, 45–17 (P)
1969—Eagles, 34–30 (StL)

(Points—Eagles 1,098, Cardinals 1,001)
*Franchise in Chicago prior to 1960
**NFL Championship Game

PHILADELPHIA EAGLES vs. SAN FRANCISCO 49ERS

(49ERS lead series, 6–2–1)

1951—Eagles, 21–14 (P)
1953—49ERS, 31–21 (SF)
1956—Tie, 10–10 (P)
1958—49ERS, 30–24 (P)
1959—49ERS, 24–14 (SF)

1964—49ERS, 28–24 (P)
1966—Eagles, 35–34 (SF)
1967—49ERS, 28–27 (P)
1969—49ERS, 14–13 (SF)

(Points—49ERS 1,238, Eagles 906)

PHILADELPHIA EAGLES vs. WASHINGTON REDSKINS

(Redskins lead series, 31–30–5)

1937—Eagles, 14–0 (W)
Redskins, 10–7 (P)
1938—Redskins, 26–23 (P)
Redskins, 20–14 (W)
1939—Redskins, 7–0 (P)
Redskins, 7–6 (W)
1940—Redskins, 34–17 (P)
Redskins, 13–6 (W)
1941—Redskins, 21–17 (P)
Redskins, 20–14 (W)
1942—Redskins, 14–10 (P)
Redskins, 30–27 (W)
1943—Tie, 14–14 (P)
Eagles, 27–14 (W)
1944—Tie, 31–31 (P)
Eagles, 37–7 (W)
1945—Redskins, 24–14 (W)
Eagles, 16–0 (P)
1946—Eagles, 28–24 (W)
Redskins, 27–10 (P)
1947—Eagles, 45–42 (P)
Eagles, 38–14 (W)
1948—Eagles, 45–0 (W)
Eagles, 42–21 (P)
1949—Eagles, 49–14 (P)
Eagles, 44–21 (W)
1950—Eagles, 35–3 (P)
Eagles, 33–0 (W)
1951—Redskins, 27–23 (P)
Eagles, 35–21 (W)
1952—Eagles, 38–20 (P)
Redskins, 27–21 (W)
1953—Tie, 21–21 (P)
Redskins, 10–0 (W)

1954—Eagles, 49–21 (W)
Eagles, 41–33 (P)
1955—Redskins, 31–30 (P)
Redskins, 34–21 (W)
1956—Eagles, 13–9 (P)
Redskins, 19–17 (W)
1957—Eagles, 21–12 (P)
Redskins, 42–7 (W)
1958—Redskins, 24–14 (P)
Redskins, 20–0 (W)
1959—Eagles, 30–23 (P)
Eagles, 34–14 (W)
1960—Eagles, 19–13 (P)
Eagles, 38–28 (W)
1961—Eagles, 14–7 (P)
Eagles, 27–24 (W)
1962—Redskins, 27–21 (P)
Eagles, 37–14 (W)
1963—Eagles, 37–24 (W)
Redskins, 13–10 (P)
1964—Redskins, 35–20 (W)
Redskins, 21–10 (P)
1965—Redskins, 23–21 (W)
Eagles, 21–14 (P)
1966—Redskins, 27–13 (P)
Eagles, 37–28 (W)
1967—Eagles, 35–24 (P)
Tie, 35–35 (W)
1968—Redskins, 17–14 (W)
Redskins, 16–10 (P)
1969—Tie, 28–28 (W)
Redskins, 34–29 (P)

(Points—Eagles 1,554, Redskins 1,318)

PITTSBURGH STEELERS vs. ATLANTA FALCONS

(Steelers lead series, 2–0; See Atlanta vs. Pittsburgh)

PITTSBURGH STEELERS vs. BALTIMORE COLTS

(Steelers lead series, 2–1; See Baltimore vs. Pittsburgh)

PITTSBURGH STEELERS vs. CHICAGO BEARS

(Bears lead series, 15–2–1; See Chicago vs. Pittsburgh)

PITTSBURGH STEELERS vs. CLEVELAND BROWNS

(Browns lead series, 31–9; See Cleveland vs. Pittsburgh)

PITTSBURGH STEELERS vs. DALLAS COWBOYS

(Cowboys lead series, 9–7; See Dallas vs. Pittsburgh)

PITTSBURGH STEELERS vs. DETROIT LIONS

(Lions lead series, 15–8–1; See Detroit vs. Pittsburgh)

PITTSBURGH STEELERS vs. GREEN BAY PACKERS

(Packers lead series, 18–7; See Green Bay vs. Pittsburgh)

PITTSBURGH STEELERS vs. LOS ANGELES RAMS

(Rams lead series, 7–1–1; See Los Angeles vs. Pittsburgh)

PITTSBURGH STEELERS vs. MINNESOTA VIKINGS

(Vikings lead series, 3–1; See Minnesota vs. Pittsburgh)

PITTSBURGH STEELERS vs. NEW ORLEANS SAINTS

(Saints lead series, 3–1; See New Orleans vs. Pittsburgh)

PITTSBURGH STEELERS vs. NEW YORK GIANTS

(Giants lead series, 42–25–3; See New York vs. Pittsburgh)

PITTSBURGH STEELERS vs. PHILADELPHIA EAGLES

(Eagles lead series, 40–24–3; See Philadelphia vs. Pittsburgh)

PITTSBURGH STEELERS vs. *ST. LOUIS CARDINALS

(Steelers lead series, 27–20–3)

1933—Steelers, 14–13 (C)	1957—Steelers, 29–20 (P)
1935—Steelers, 17–13 (P)	Steelers, 27–2 (C)
1936—Cardinals, 14–6 (C)	1958—Steelers, 27–20 (C)
1937—Cardinals, 13–7 (P)	Steelers, 38–21 (P)
1939—Cardinals, 10–0 (P)	1959—Cardinals, 45–24 (C)
1940—Tie, 7–7 (P)	Steelers, 35–20 (P)
1942—Steelers, 19–3 (P)	1960—Steelers, 27–14 (P)
1943—Steelers, 34–13 (P)	Cardinals, 38–7 (StL)
1945—Steelers, 23–0 (P)	1961—Steelers, 30–27 (P)
1946—Steelers, 14–7 (P)	Cardinals, 20–0 (StL)
1948—Cardinals, 24–7 (P)	1962—Steelers, 26–17 (StL)
1950—Steelers, 28–17 (C)	Steelers, 19–7 (P)
Steelers, 28–7 (P)	1963—Steelers, 23–10 (P)
1951—Steelers, 28–14 (C)	Cardinals, 24–23 (StL)
1952—Steelers, 34–28 (C)	1964—Cardinals, 34–30 (StL)
Steelers, 17–14 (P)	Cardinals, 21–20 (P)
1953—Steelers, 31–28 (P)	1965—Cardinals, 20–7 (P)
Steelers, 21–17 (C)	Cardinals, 21–17 (StL)
1954—Cardinals, 17–14 (C)	1966—Steelers, 30–9 (P)
Steelers, 20–17 (P)	Cardinals, 6–3 (StL)
1955—Steelers, 14–7 (P)	1967—Cardinals, 28–14 (P)
Cardinals, 27–13 (C)	Tie, 14–14 (StL)
1956—Steelers, 14–7 (P)	1968—Tie, 28–28 (StL)
Cardinals, 38–27 (C)	Cardinals, 20–10 (P)
	1969—Cardinals, 27–14 (P)
	Cardinals, 47–10 (StL)

(Points—Steelers 919, Cardinals 915)

*Franchise in Chicago prior to 1960

PITTSBURGH STEELERS vs. SAN FRANCISCO 49ERS

(49ERS lead series, 5–2)

1951—49ERS, 28–24 (P)	1958—49ERS, 23–20 (SF)
1952—Steelers, 24–7 (SF)	1961—Steelers, 20–10 (P)
1954—49ERS, 31–3 (SF)	1965—49ERS, 27–17 (SF)
	1968—49ERS, 45–28 (P)

(Points—49ERS 181, Steelers 126)

PITTSBURGH STEELERS vs. WASHINGTON REDSKINS

(Redskins lead series, 35–23–4)

1937—Redskins, 34–20 (W)	1939—Redskins, 44–14 (W)
Steelers, 21–13 (P)	Redskins, 21–14 (P)
1938—Redskins, 7–0 (P)	1940—Redskins, 40–10 (P)
Redskins, 15–0 (W)	Redskins, 37–10 (W)

1941—Redskins, 24–20 (P)	1955—Redskins, 23–14 (P)
Redskins, 23–3 (W)	Redskins, 28–17 (W)
1942—Redskins, 28–14 (W)	1956—Steelers, 30–13 (P)
Redskins, 14–0 (P)	Steelers, 23–0 (W)
1943—Tie, 14–14 (P)	1957—Steelers, 28–7 (P)
Steelers, 27–14 (W)	Redskins, 10–3 (W)
1944—Redskins, 42–20 (W)	1958—Steelers, 24–16 (P)
1945—Redskins, 14–0 (P)	Tie, 14–14 (W)
Redskins, 24–0 (W)	1959—Redskins, 23–17 (P)
1946—Tie, 14–14 (W)	Steelers, 27–6 (W)
Steelers, 14–7 (P)	1960—Tie, 27–27 (W)
1947—Redskins, 27–26 (W)	Steelers, 22–10 (P)
Steelers, 21–14 (P)	1961—Steelers, 20–0 (P)
1948—Redskins, 17–14 (W)	Steelers, 30–14 (W)
Steelers, 10–7 (P)	1962—Steelers, 23–21 (P)
1949—Redskins, 27–14 (P)	Steelers, 27–24 (W)
Redskins, 27–14 (W)	1963—Steelers, 38–27 (P)
1950—Steelers, 26–7 (W)	Steelers, 34–28 (W)
Redskins, 24–7 (P)	1964—Redskins, 30–0 (P)
1951—Redskins, 22–7 (P)	Steelers, 14–7 (W)
Steelers, 20–10 (W)	1965—Redskins, 31–3 (P)
1952—Redskins, 28–24 (P)	Redskins, 35–14 (W)
Steelers, 24–23 (W)	1966—Redskins, 33–27 (P)
1953—Redskins, 17–9 (P)	Redskins, 24–10 (W)
Steelers, 14–13 (W)	1967—Redskins, 15–10 (P)
1954—Steelers, 37–7 (P)	1968—Redskins, 16–13 (W)
Redskins, 17–14 (W)	1969—Redskins, 14–7 (P)

(Points—Redskins 1,212, Steelers 1,012)

ST. LOUIS CARDINALS vs. ATLANTA FALCONS
(Series tied, 1–1; See Atlanta vs. St. Louis)

ST. LOUIS CARDINALS vs. BALTIMORE COLTS
(Colts lead series, 3–1; See Baltimore vs. St. Louis)

ST. LOUIS CARDINALS vs. CHICAGO BEARS
(Bears lead series, 49–21–6; See Chicago vs. St. Louis)

ST. LOUIS CARDINALS vs. CLEVELAND BROWNS
(Browns lead series, 29–8–3; See Cleveland vs. St. Louis)

ST. LOUIS CARDINALS vs. DALLAS COWBOYS
(Cardinals lead series, 8–7–1; See Dallas vs. St. Louis)

ST. LOUIS CARDINALS vs. DETROIT LIONS
(Lions lead series, 23–10–3; See Detroit vs. St. Louis)

ST. LOUIS CARDINALS vs. GREEN BAY PACKERS
(Packers lead series, 37–20–3; See Green Bay vs. St. Louis)

ST. LOUIS CARDINALS vs. LOS ANGELES RAMS
(Rams lead series, 7–6–2; See Los Angeles vs. St. Louis)

ST. LOUIS CARDINALS vs. MINNESOTA VIKINGS
(Cardinals lead series, 2–1; See Minnesota vs. St. Louis)

ST. LOUIS CARDINALS vs. NEW ORLEANS SAINTS
(Cardinals lead series, 3–1; See New Orleans vs. St. Louis)

ST. LOUIS CARDINALS vs. NEW YORK GIANTS

(Giants lead series, 40–15–1; See New York vs. St. Louis)

ST. LOUIS CARDINALS vs. PHILADELPHIA EAGLES

(Eagles lead series, 24–21–3; See Philadelphia vs. St. Louis)

ST. LOUIS CARDINALS vs. PITTSBURGH STEELERS

(Steelers lead series, 27–20–3; See Pittsburgh vs. St. Louis)

*ST. LOUIS CARDINALS vs. SAN FRANCISCO 49ERS

(Cardinals lead series, 3–2)

1951—Cardinals, 27–21 (SF)	1962—49ERS, 24–17 (StL)
1957—Cardinals, 20–10 (SF)	1964—Cardinals, 23–13 (SF)
	1968—49ERS, 35–17 (SF)

(Points—Cardinals 104, 49ERS 103)

*Franchise in Chicago prior to 1960

*ST. LOUIS CARDINALS vs. WASHINGTON REDSKINS

(Series tied, 22–22–1)

1937—Cardinals, 21–14 (W)	1957—Redskins, 37–14 (C)
1939—Redskins, 28–7 (W)	Cardinals, 44–14 (W)
1940—Redskins, 28–21 (W)	1958—Cardinals, 37–10 (C)
1942—Redskins, 28–0 (W)	Redskins, 45–31 (W)
1943—Redskins, 13–7 (W)	1959—Cardinals, 49–21 (C)
1944—Redskins, 42–20 (W)	Redskins, 23–14 (W)
1945—Redskins, 24–21 (W)	1960—Cardinals, 44–7 (StL)
1947—Redskins, 45–21 (W)	Cardinals, 26–14 (W)
1949—Cardinals, 38–7 (C)	1961—Cardinals, 24–0 (W)
1950—Cardinals, 38–28 (W)	Cardinals, 38–24 (StL)
1951—Redskins, 7–3 (C)	1962—Redskins, 24–14 (W)
Redskins, 20–17 (W)	Tie, 17–17 (StL)
1952—Redskins, 23–7 (C)	1963—Cardinals, 21–7 (W)
Cardinals, 17–6 (W)	Cardinals, 24–20 (StL)
1953—Redskins, 24–13 (C)	1964—Cardinals, 23–17 (W)
Redskins, 28–17 (W)	Cardinals, 38–24 (StL)
1954—Cardinals, 38–16 (C)	1965—Cardinals, 37–16 (W)
Redskins, 37–20 (W)	Redskins, 24–20 (StL)
1955—Cardinals, 24–10 (W)	1966—Cardinals, 23–7 (StL)
Redskins, 31–0 (C)	Redskins, 26–20 (W)
1956—Cardinals, 31–3 (W)	1967—Cardinals, 27–21 (W)
Redskins, 17–14 (C)	1968—Cardinals, 41–14 (StL)
	1969—Redskins, 33–17 (W)

(Points—Cardinals 1,038, Redskins 924)

*Franchise in Chicago prior to 1960

SAN DIEGO CHARGERS vs. BOSTON PATRIOTS

(Chargers lead series, 11–7–2; See Boston vs. San Diego)

SAN DIEGO CHARGERS vs. BUFFALO BILLS

(Chargers lead series, 10–7–2; See Buffalo vs. San Diego)

SAN DIEGO CHARGERS vs. CINCINNATI BENGALS

(Chargers lead series, 3–1; See Cincinnati vs. San Diego)

SAN DIEGO CHARGERS vs. DENVER BRONCOS

(Chargers lead series, 15–5; See Denver vs. San Diego)

SAN DIEGO CHARGERS vs. HOUSTON OILERS

(Chargers lead series, 12–7; See Houston vs. San Diego)

SAN DIEGO CHARGERS vs. KANSAS CITY CHIEFS
(Chiefs lead series, 10–9–1; See Kansas City vs. San Diego)

SAN DIEGO CHARGERS vs. MIAMI DOLPHINS
(Chargers lead series, 4–1; See Miami vs. San Diego)

SAN DIEGO CHARGERS vs. NEW YORK JETS
(Chargers lead series, 12–5–1; See New York vs. San Diego)

SAN DIEGO CHARGERS vs. OAKLAND RAIDERS
(Chargers lead series, 11–9; See Oakland vs. San Diego)

SAN FRANCISCO 49ERS vs. ATLANTA FALCONS
(49ERS lead series, 5–2; See Atlanta vs. San Francisco)

SAN FRANCISCO 49ERS vs. BALTIMORE COLTS
(Colts lead series, 21–14; See Baltimore vs. San Francisco)

SAN FRANCISCO 49ERS vs. CHICAGO BEARS
(Bears lead series, 19–16–1; See Chicago vs. San Francisco)

SAN FRANCISCO 49ERS vs. CLEVELAND BROWNS
(Browns lead series, 5–2; See Cleveland vs. San Francisco)

SAN FRANCISCO 49ERS vs. DALLAS COWBOYS
(49ERS lead series, 3–1–1; See Dallas vs. San Francisco)

SAN FRANCISCO 49ERS vs. DETROIT LIONS
(49ERS lead series, 19–18–1; See Detroit vs. San Francisco)

SAN FRANCISCO 49ERS vs. GREEN BAY PACKERS
(Series tied, 17–17–1; See Green Bay vs. San Francisco)

SAN FRANCISCO 49ERS vs. LOS ANGELES RAMS
(Rams lead series, 22–16–2; See Los Angeles vs. San Francisco)

SAN FRANCISCO 49ERS vs. MINNESOTA VIKINGS
(Vikings lead series, 8–6–1; See Minnesota vs. San Francisco)

SAN FRANCISCO 49ERS vs. NEW ORLEANS SAINTS
(Series tied, 1–1; See New Orleans vs. San Francisco)

SAN FRANCISCO 49ERS vs. NEW YORK GIANTS
(Giants lead series, 4–2; See New York vs. San Francisco)

SAN FRANCISCO 49ERS vs. PHILADELPHIA EAGLES
(49ERS lead series, 6–2–1; See Philadelphia vs. San Francisco)

SAN FRANCISCO 49ERS vs. PITTSBURGH STEELERS
(49ERS lead series, 5–2; See Pittsburgh vs. San Francisco)

SAN FRANCISCO 49ERS vs. ST. LOUIS CARDINALS
(Cardinals lead series, 3–2; See St. Louis vs. San Francisco)

SAN FRANCISCO 49ERS vs. WASHINGTON REDSKINS

(49ERS lead series 3–2–1)

1952—49ERS, 23–17 (W)	1961—49ERS, 35–3 (SF)
1954—49ERS, 41–7 (SF)	1967—Redskins, 31–28 (W)
1955—Redskins, 7–0 (W)	1969—Tie, 17–17 (SF)

(Points—49ERS 144, Redskins 82)

WASHINGTON REDSKINS vs. ATLANTA FALCONS

(Redskins lead series, 2–0–1; See Atlanta vs. Washington)

WASHINGTON REDSKINS vs. BALTIMORE COLTS

(Colts lead series, 13–5; See Baltimore vs. Washington)

WASHINGTON REDSKINS vs. CHICAGO BEARS

(Bears lead series, 10–8; See Chicago vs. Washington)

WASHINGTON REDSKINS vs. CLEVELAND BROWNS

(Browns lead series, 30–5–1; See Cleveland vs. Washington)

WASHINGTON REDSKINS vs. DALLAS COWBOYS

(Cowboys lead series, 10–7–2; See Dallas vs. Washington)

WASHINGTON REDSKINS vs. DETROIT LIONS

(Redskins lead series, 9–3; See Detroit vs. Washington)

WASHINGTON REDSKINS vs. GREEN BAY PACKERS

(Packers lead series, 8–5; See Green Bay vs. Washington)

WASHINGTON REDSKINS vs. LOS ANGELES RAMS

(Series tied, 3–3–1; See Los Angeles vs. Washington)

WASHINGTON REDSKINS vs. MINNESOTA VIKINGS

(Vikings lead series, 1–0; See Minnesota vs. Washington)

WASHINGTON REDSKINS vs. NEW ORLEANS SAINTS

(Redskins lead series, 3–2; See New Orleans vs. Washington)

WASHINGTON REDSKINS vs. NEW YORK GIANTS

(Giants lead series, 41–21–2; See New York vs. Washington)

WASHINGTON REDSKINS vs. PHILADELPHIA EAGLES

(Redskins lead series, 31–30–5, See Philadelphia vs. Washington)

WASHINGTON REDSKINS vs. PITTSBURGH STEELERS

(Redskins lead series, 35–23–4; See Pittsburgh vs. Washington)

WASHINGTON REDSKINS vs. ST. LOUIS CARDINALS

(Series tied, 22–22–1; See St. Louis vs. Washington)

WASHINGTON REDSKINS vs. SAN FRANCISCO 49ERS

(49ERS lead series, 3–2–1; See San Francisco vs. Washington)

Atlanta's Harmon Wages (5) runs against Bears.

NO. 1 DRAFT CHOICES

(From 1967 combined NFL-AFL draft)

SEASON	CLUB	PLAYER	POS.	SCHOOL
1970	Pittsburgh	Terry Bradshaw	QB	Louisiana Tech
1969	Buffalo (AFL)	O. J. Simpson	RB	So. California
1968	Minnesota	Ron Yary	T	So. California
1967	Baltimore	Bubba Smith	DT	Michigan State
1966	Atlanta	Tommy Nobis	LB	Texas
	Miami (AFL)	Jim Grabowski	RB	Illinois
1965	New York	Tucker Frederickson	RB	Auburn
	New York (AFL)	Joe Namath	QB	Alabama
1964	San Francisco	Dave Parks	E	Texas Tech
	Denver (AFL)	Bob Brown	T	Nebraska
1963	Los Angeles	Terry Baker	QB	Oregon State
	Kansas City (AFL)	Buck Buchanan	DT	Grambling
1962	Washington	Ernie Davis	RB	Syracuse
	Oakland (AFL)	Roman Gabriel	QB	No. Car. State
1961	Minnesota	Tommy Mason	RB	Tulane
	Denver (AFL)	Bob Gaiters	RB	New Mexico State
1960	Los Angeles	Billy Cannon	RB	LSU
	(AFL had no formal first pick)			
1959	Green Bay	Randy Duncan	QB	Iowa
1958	Chicago Cards	King Hill	QB	Rice
1957	Green Bay	Paul Hornung	B	Notre Dame
1956	Pittsburgh	Gary Glick	B	Colorado A&M
1955	Baltimore	George Shaw	QB	Oregon
1954	Cleveland	Bobby Garrett	QB	Stanford
1953	San Francisco	Harry Babcock	E	Georgia
1952	Los Angeles	Bill Wade	QB	Vanderbilt
1951	New York	Kyle Rote	B	SMU
1950	Detroit	Leon Hart	E	Notre Dame
1949	Philadelphia	Chuck Bednarik	C	Pennsylvania
1948	Washington	Harry Gilmer	QB	Alabama
1947	Chicago Bears	Bob Fenimore	B	Oklahoma A&M
1946	Boston Yanks	Frank Dancewicz	QB	Notre Dame
1945	Chicago Cards	Charley Trippi	B	Georgia
1944	Chicago Cards	Pat Harder	B	Wisconsin
1943	Detroit	Frank Sinkwich	B	Georgia
1942	Pittsburgh	Bill Dudley	B	Virginia
1941	Philadelphia	Tom Harmon	B	Michigan
1940	Chicago Cards	George Cafego	B	Tennessee
1939	Chicago Cards	Ki Aldrich	C	TCU
1938	Cleveland	Corbett Davis	B	Indiana
1937	Philadelphia	Sam Francis	B	Nebraska
1936	Philadelphia	Jay Berwanger	B	Chicago U.

NFL DRAFT LIST FOR 1970

Number Following Name Designates Order of Selection Among 442
Players Drafted

ATLANTA FALCONS
(Drafted Alternately 12–13)

1. Small, John—12 (LB) Citadel
2. Malone, Art—39 (RB) Arizona
   State
3. Maurer, Andy—64 (G) Oregon
   Snyder, Todd—65 (WR) Ohio U.
   (from New York Giants)
4. Reed, Paul—84 (T) Johnson C.
   Smith
   (from Philadelphia)
   Choice to St. Louis
5. Van Ness, Bruce—112 (RB)
   Rutgers
   (from Philadelphia thru N.Y.
   Giants)
   Mendenhall, Ken—116 (C)
   Oklahoma
6. Herron, Mack—143 (RB)
   Kansas State
   Butcher, Jade—147 (WR)
   Indiana
   (from Washington)
   Marshall, Randy—152 (DE)
   Linfield, Ore.
   (from Los Angeles)
7. Choice to Los Angeles
   Orcutt, Gary—169 (WR)
   So. California
   (from New York Giants)
8. Brewer, Larry—194 (TE)
   Louisiana Tech
   (from New York Giants)
   Miller, Seth—195 (DB) Arizona
   State
9. Robinson, Roy—220 (DB)
   Montana
10. Hatcher, Jim—246 (DB) Kansas
11. Brunson, Mike—272 (RB)
    Arizona State
12. Holton, Lonnie—298 (RB)
    No. Michigan
13. Stepanek, Rich—324 (DT)
    Iowa
14. Wald, Charles—351 (WR)
    No. Dakota State
15. Mauney, Keith—376 (DB)
    Princeton
16. Parnell, Steve—403 (WR)
    Massachusetts
17. Bell, Bill—428 (K) Kansas

BALTIMORE COLTS
(Drafted 18th)

1. Bulaich, Norm—18 (RB) Texas
   Christian
2. Bailey, James—44 (DT) Kansas

3. O'Brien, James—70 (WR)
   Cincinnati
   Person, Ara—74 (TE) Morgan
   State
   (from Los Angeles thru
   Philadelphia)
4. Smear, Steve—95 (LB) Penn
   State
   (from Washington)
   Choice to Green Bay
5. Newsome, Bill—122 (DE)
   Grambling
6. Gardin, Ron—148 (DB) Arizona
7. Slade, Gordon—174 (QB)
   Davidson
8. Bouley, Robert—199 (T) Boston College
9. Harris, Barney—226 (DB)
   Texas A&M
10. Palmer, Dick—252 (LB)
    Kentucky
11. Edwards, George—278 (RB)
    Fairmont State
12. Burrell, Don—304 (WR) Angelo
    State, Tex.
13. Polak, Dave—330 (LB) Bowling
    Green
14. Curtis, Thomas—356 (DB)
    Michigan
15. Gary, Phillip—382 (DE)
    Kentucky State
16. Maitland, John—408 (RB)
    Williams
17. Pearman, Alvin—434 (WR)
    Colgate

BOSTON PATRIOTS
(Drafted Alternately 4–5)

1. Olsen, Phil—4 (DT) Utah State
2. Choice to Houston
3. Ballou, Mike—56 (LB) UCLA
4. Ray, Eddie—83 (DB) LSU
5. Olson, Bob—107 (LB) Notre
   Dame
   (from Miami)
   Choice to New York Jets
6. Choice to Buffalo
7. Lawson, Odell—160 (RB)
   Langston, Okla.
8. Choice to New York Jets
9. Wirgowski, Dennis—212 (DE)
   Purdue
10. Brown, Henry—239 (K-WR)
    Missouri
11. Bramlett, Dennis—264 (T)
    Texas-El Paso
12. Roero, Greg—291 (DT) New
    Mex. Highlands

13. Shelley, Ronnie—316 (DB)
    Troy State
14. Craw, Garvie—343 (RB-TE)
    Michigan
15. Schoolfield, Kent—368 (WR)
    Florida A&M
16. McDaniel, Otis—395 (DE)
    Tuskegee
17. Killingsworth, Joe—420 (WR)
    Oklahoma

BUFFALO BILLS
(Drafted Alternately 5–4)

1. Cowlings, Al—5 (DE) So. California
2. Shaw, Dennis—30 (QB) San
   Diego State
3. Reilly, Jim—57 (G) Notre Dame
   Alexander, Glenn—67 (DB)
   Grambling
   (from San Diego)
4. Gantt, Jerome—82 (DE)
   No. Carolina Central
5. Starnes, Steve—109 (LB)
   Tampa
6. Edwards, Ken—134 (RB)
   Virginia Tech
   Guthrie, Grant—135 (K)
   Florida State
   (from Boston)
7. Fowler, Wayne—161 (T)
   Richmond
8. Cheek, Richard—186 (T)
   Auburn
9. Bridges, Bill—213 (G) Houston
10. Dixon, Willie—238 (DB) Albany
    State
11. Williams, Terry—265 (RB)
    Grambling
12. Simpson, Dave—290 (T) Drake
13. Schroeder, Stefan—317 (K)
    Pacific
14. Costen, William—342 (T) Morris
    Brown
15. Farris, Dave—369 (TE) Central
    Michigan
16. Davis, Larry—394 (WR) Rice
17. Bevan, George—421 (DB) LSU

CHICAGO BEARS
(Drafted Alternately 2–1)

1. Choice to Green Bay
2. Choice to Dallas
3. Farmer, George—54 (WR)
   UCLA
4. Larson, Lynn—79 (T) Kansas
   State
   Brupbacher, Ross—100 (LB)
   Texas A&M
   (from Los Angeles)
5. Choice to New Orleans

6. Cutburth, Bob—133 (QB)
   Oklahoma State
   Curchin, Jeff—139 (T) Florida
   State
   (from St. Louis)
7. Choice to Philadelphia
8. Stephenson, Dana—183 (DB)
   Nebraska
9. Cole, Linzy—210 (WR) Texas
   Christian
10. Holloway, Glen—235 (G)
    No. Texas State
11. *Rose, Ted—262 (TE)
    No. Michigan
12. Davis, Butch—287 (DB) Mis-
    souri
13. Gunn, Jim—314 (DB) So. Cali-
    fornia
14. Morgan, Jim—339 (WR)
    Henderson, Ark.
15. Abraira, Phil—366 (DB) Florida
    State
16. Helterbran, Robert—390 (G)
    No. Texas State
17. Brunson, Joe—416 (DT)
    Furman

CINCINNATI BENGALS
(Drafted Alternately 7–6–8)

1. Reid, Mike—7 (DT) Penn State
2. Carpenter, Ron—32 (DT)
   No. Carolina State
3. Bennett, Chip—60 (LB) Abilene
   Christian
4. Stephen, Joe—85 (G) Jackson
   State
   Hayes, Billie—104 (DB) San
   Diego State
   (from Kansas City)
5. Choice to Houston thru New
   York Jets
6. Durko, Sandy—137 (DB)
   So. California
7. Parrish, Lamar—163 (DB)
   Lincoln
8. Trout, Bill—188 (DT) Miami
9. Bolden, Bill—216 (RB) UCLA
10. Roman, Nick—241 (DE) Ohio
    State
11. Wallace, Sam—266 (LB)
    Grambling
12. Truesdell, Tom—294 (DT) Ohio
    Wesleyan
13. Dunn, Paul—319 (WR) Interna-
    tional-Cal.
14. *Johnson, Joe—344 (WR)
    Johnson C. Smith
15. Weeks, Marvin—372 (DB)
    Alcorn A&M

—————————
*Selection voided, ineligible

16. Ely, Lawrence—397 (LB) Iowa
17. Smith, Richard—422 (RB)
    Washington State

CLEVELAND BROWNS
(Drafted 21st)

1. Phipps, Mike—3 (QB) Purdue
   (from Miami)
   McKay, Bob—21 (T) Texas
2. Jones, Joe—36 (DE) Tennessee State
   (from New Orleans)
   Sherk, Jerry—47 (DT) Oklahoma State
3. Choice to Dallas
4. Stevenson, Ricky—99 (DB)
   Arizona
5. Engel, Steve—125 (RB)
   Colorado
6. Cilek, Mike—151 (QB) Iowa
7. Wycinsky, Craig—177 (G)
   Michigan State
8. Davidson, Honester—203 (DB)
   Bowling Green
9. Brown, Geoff—229 (LB)
   Pittsburgh
10. Yanchar, Bill—255 (DT) Purdue
11. Benner, Gene—281 (WR)
    Maine
12. Sanders, Jerry—307 (K) Texas
    Tech
13. Roberts, Larry—333 (RB)
    Central Missouri
14. Tharpe, Jim—359 (LB) Lincoln
15. Homoly, Guy—385 (DB)
    Illinois State
16. Redebough, John—410 (TE)
    Bemidji
17. Tabb, Charles—436 (RB)
    McMurry

DALLAS COWBOYS
(Drafted 23rd)

1. Thomas, Duane—23 (RB)
   W. Texas State
2. Asher, Bob—27 (T) Vanderbilt
   (from Chicago)
   Adkins, Margene—49 (WR)
   Henderson J.C.
3. Waters, Charlie—66 (DB)
   Clemson
   (from Houston thru Cleveland)
   Kiner, Steve—73 (LB) Tennessee
   (from Cleveland)
   Fox, Denton—75 (DB) Texas
   Tech
4. Fitzgerald, John—101 (T)
   Boston College

5. Choice to St. Louis
6. Toomay, Pat—153 (DE) Vanderbilt
7. Abbey, Don—179 (LB) Penn
   State
8. Dossey, Jerry—205 (G)
   Arkansas
9. Andrushyshyn, Zenon—231
   (K) UCLA
10. Athas, Pete—257 (DB) Ten-
    nessee
11. Southerland, Ivan—283 (T)
    Clemson
12. Williams, Joe—309 (RB)
    Wyoming
13. Washington, Mark—335 (DB)
    Morgan State
14. Martin, Julian—361 (WR)
    No. Carolina Central
15. DeLong, Ken—387 (TE) Ten-
    nessee
16. Hill, Seabern—411 (DB)
    Arizona State
17. Patterson Glenn—438 (C)
    Nebraska

DENVER BRONCOS
(Drafted 11th)

1. Anderson, Bob—11 (RB)
   Colorado
2. Roche, Alden—37 (DE)
   Southern U.
3. Kohler, John—63 (T) South
   Dakota
4. Hendren, Jerry—89 (WR)
   Idaho
5. McKoy, Bill—115 (LB) Purdue
6. Mosier, John—141 (TE) Kansas
7. Montgomery, Randy—167 (DB)
   Weber State
8. Choice to Kansas City
   Porter, Lewis—208 (RB)
   Southern U.
   (from Kansas City)
9. Washington, David—219 (LB)
   Alcorn A&M
10. Fullerton, Maurice—247 (DT)
    Tuskegee
11. Bryant, Cleve—271 (DB)
    Ohio U.
12. Jones, Greg—301 (RB) White-
    water, Wis.
13. McKoy, Jim—323 (DB) Parsons
14. Slipp, Jeff—349 (DE) Brigham
    Young
15. Barakat, Maher—375 (K)
    So. Dakota Tech
16. Stewart, Robert—401 (QB)
    No. Arizona
17. Kalfoss, Frank—427 (K) Mon-
    tana State

DETROIT LIONS
(Drafted 19th)

1. Owens, Steve—19 (RB) Oklahoma
2. Parsons, Ray—45 (DE) Minnesota
3. Mitchell, Jim—71 (DE) Virginia State
4. Choice to New York Giants
5. Parker, Bob—123 (G) Memphis State
6. Terry, Tony—149 (DT) So. California
7. Geddes, Ken—175 (LB) Nebraska
8. Choice to St. Louis
9. Weaver, Herman—227 (P) Tennessee
10. Maxwell, Bruce—253 (RB) Arkansas
11. Laird, Roger—279 (DB) Kentucky State
12. Murrell, Emanuel—305 (DB) Cal Poly-Obispo
13. Haverdick, Dave—331 (DT) Morehead State
14. Brown, Charlie—357 (WR) No. Arizona
15. Haney, Bob—383 (T) Idaho
16. Todd, Jerry—409 (DB) Memphis State
17. Marshall, Jesse—435 (DT) Centenary

GREEN BAY PACKERS
(Drafted Alternately 16–15)

1. McCoy, Mike—2 (DT) Notre Dame
   (from Chicago)
   McGeorge, Rich—16 (TE) Elon
2. Matthews, Al—41 (DB) Texas A&M
3. Carter, James—68 (LB) Minnesota
4. Ellis, Ken—93 (WR) Southern U.
   Butler, Skip—96 (K) Texas-Arlington
   (from Baltimore)
5. Pryor, Cecil—120 (DE) Michigan
6. Hunt, Ervin—145 (DB) Fresno State
7. Walker, Cleo—172 (C) Louisville
8. Mjos, Tim—197 (RB) No. Dakota State
9. Reinhard, Bob—224 (G) Stanford
10. Melby, Russ—248 (DT) Weber State
    Patrick, Frank—251 (TE) Nebraska
    (from Washington)

11. Hook, Dan—276 (LB) Humboldt State
12. Foreman, Frank—300 (WR) Michigan State
13. Smith, Dave—328 (RB) Utah
14. Lints, Robert—353 (G) E. Michigan
15. Carter, Mike—380 (WR) Sacramento State
16. Heacock, Jim—405 (DB) Muskingum
17. Krause, Lawrence—432 (RB) St. Norbert

HOUSTON OILERS
(Drafted 14th)

1. Wilkerson, Doug—14 (G) No. Carolina Central
2. Brooks, Leo—31 (DT) Texas
   (from Boston)
   Dusenbery, Bill—40 (RB) Johnson C. Smith
3. Choice to Dallas thru Cleveland
4. Jones, John—92 (P) Georgia
5. Saul, Ron—110 (G) Michigan State
   (from Cincinnati thru N.Y. Jets)
   Duley, Ed—118 (DT) No. Arizona
6. Johnson, Benny—144 (DB) Johnson C. Smith
7. Olson, Charles—170 (DB) Concordia, Minn.
8. McClish, Mike—196 (T) Wisconsin
9. Blossoms, Charles—222 (DE) Texas Southern
10. Dawkins, Joe—249 (RB) Wisconsin
11. Morris, Robert—274 (C) Duke
12. *Dawkins, Richard—299 (TE) Johnson C. Smith
13. Lewis, Jess—326 (LB) Oregon State
14. Rasmussen, Clair—352 (G) Oshkosh, Wis.
15. Sharp, David—378 (T) Stanford
16. *Myers, Chris—404 (WR) Kenyon
17. Fagan, Julian—430 (P) Mississippi

KANSAS CITY CHIEFS
(Drafted 26th)

1. Smith, Sid—26 (T) So. California
2. Werner, Clyde—52 (LB) Washington

---

*Selection voided, ineligible

3. Barnett, Billy Bob—61 (DE) Texas A&M (from San Francisco)
   Hadley, David—78 (DB) Alcorn A&M
4. Choice to Cincinnati
5. Oriard, Mike—130 (C) Notre Dame
6. Hews, Robert—156 (T) Princeton
7. Glosson, Clyde—182 (WR) Texas-El Paso
8. Barry, Fred—193 (DB) Boston U. (from Denver)
   Choice to Denver
9. Evans, Charley—234 (T) Texas Tech
10. Stankovich, Bob—259 (G) Arkansas
11. O'Neal, Bill—285 (RB) Grambling
12. Fedorchak, Rodney—312 (G) Pittsburgh
13. Patridge, Troy—338 (DE) Texas-Arlington
14. Dumont, Glen—364 (RB) American Intl.
15. Liggett, Bob—389 (DT) Nebraska
16. Ross, Randy—413 (LB) Kansas State
17. Jenkins, Rayford—442 (DB) Alcorn A&M

LOS ANGELES RAMS
(Drafted 22nd)

1. Reynolds, Jack—22 (LB) Tennessee
2. Williams, Charles—35 (WR) Prairie View A&M (from San Francisco)
   Choice to San Francisco thru Philadelphia
3. Choice to Baltimore thru Philadelphia
4. Choice to Chicago
5. Choice to New Orleans
6. Choice to Atlanta
7. Provost, Ted—162 (DB) Ohio State (from Philadelphia)
   Nelson, Bill—168 (DT) Oregon State (from Atlanta)
   Choice to Washington
8. Saul, Rich—204 (LB) Michigan State
9. Graham, David—230 (T) New Mex. Highlands
10. Opalsky, Vince—256 (RB) Miami

11. Bookert, David—282 (RB) New Mexico
12. Arnold, Larry—308 (QB) Hawaii
13. Jones, Melvin—334 (WR) Florida A&M
14. Geddes, Bob—360 (LB) UCLA
15. Azam, Dag—386 (G) W. Texas State
16. Reichardt, Roland—412 (K) W. Texas State
17. Crenshaw, Don—437 (DB) So. California

MIAMI DOLPHINS
(Drafted 3rd)

1. Choice to Cleveland
2. Mandich, Jim—29 (TE) Michigan
3. Foley, Tim—55 (DB) Purdue
4. Johnson, Curtis—81 (DB) Toledo
5. Choice to Boston
6. Campbell, Dave—132 (DE) Auburn
7. Scott, Jake—159 (DB) Georgia
8. Chavers, Narvel—185 (RB) Jackson State
9. Ginn, Hubert—211 (RB) Florida A&M
10. Nittenger, Dick—237 (G) Tampa
11. *Wheless, Brownie—263 (T) Rice
12. Kolen, Mike—289 (LB) Auburn
13. Buddington, Dave—315 (RB) Springfield, Mass.
14. Brackett, Gary—341 (G) Holy Cross
15. Hauser, Pat—367 (WR) E. Tennessee
16. Williams, Charles—393 (G) Tennessee State
17. Myles, George—419 (DT) Morris Brown

MINNESOTA VIKINGS
(Drafted 25th)

1. Ward, John—25 (T) Oklahoma State
2. Cappleman, Bill—51 (QB) Florida State
3. Burgoon, Chuck—77 (LB) North Park, Ill.
4. Choice to Washington thru L.A. thru N.O.
5. Jones, Greg—129 (RB) UCLA
6. Choice to Pittsburgh
7. Farber, Hap—181 (LB) Mississippi
8. Carroll, Mike—206 (G) Missouri

---

*Selection voided, ineligible

9. Morrow, George—233 (DE)
   Mississippi
10. Voight, Stu—260 (TE) Wisconsin
11. Zaunbrecher, Godfrey—286
    (C) LSU
12. Holland, James—311 (DB)
    Jackson State
13. Pearce, Robert—337 (DB)
    Stephen F. Austin
14. Spinks, Tom—363 (WR)
    Louisiana Tech
15. Francis, Bennie—388 (DE)
    Chadron, Neb.
16. Cerone, Bruce—417 (WR)
    Emporia State
17. Healy, Brian—441 (DB) Michigan

NEW ORLEANS SAINTS
(Drafted 10th)

1. Burroughs, Ken—10 (WR)
   Texas Southern
2. Choice to Cleveland
3. Swinney, Clovis—62 (DE)
   Arkansas State
4. Howell, Delles—88 (DB)
   Grambling
5. Cannon, Glenn—106 (DB)
   Mississippi
   (from Chicago)
   Choice to Washington
   Ramsey, Steve—126 (QB)
   No. Texas State
   (from Los Angeles)
6. Easley, Mel—140 (DB) Oregon
   State
7. Woodard, Lon—166 (DE) San
   Diego State
8. Estes, Lawrence—192 (DE)
   Alcorn A&M
9. Otis, Jim—218 (RB) Ohio State
10. Brumfield, Jim—244 (RB)
    Indiana State
11. Klahr, Gary—270 (LB) Arizona
12. Davenport, Willie—296 (DB)
    Southern U.
13. *Miller, Ralph—322 (TE) Alabama State
14. Sutherland, Doug—348 (DE)
    Superior, Wis.
15. Vest, Jim—374 (DE) Washington State
16. Gaspar, Cliff—400 (DT) Grambling
17. Wyatt, Doug—426 (DB) Tulsa

NEW YORK GIANTS
(Drafted Alternately 13-12)

1. Files, Jim—13 (LB) Oklahoma
2. Choice to St. Louis

*Selection voided, ineligible

3. Choice to Atlanta
4. Choice to Pittsburgh
   Grant, Wesley—97 (DE) UCLA
   (from Detroit)
5. Brumfield, Claude—117 (G)
   Tennessee State
6. Miller, Duane—142 (WR) Drake
7. Choice to Atlanta
8. Choice to Atlanta
9. Hughes, Pat—221 (C) Boston
   U.
10. Fortier, Matt—245 (DE) Fairmont State
11. Pitcaithley, Alan—273 (RB)
    Oregon
12. Nels, Larry—297 (LB) Wyoming
13. Inskeep, Gary—325 (T) Stout,
    Wis.
14. Brand, Rodney—350 (C)
    Arkansas
15. Muir, Warren—377 (RB) So.
    Carolina
16. Nolting, Victor—402 (DB)
    Xavier
17. Breaux, Walter—429 (DT)
    Grambling

NEW YORK JETS
(Drafted 20th)

1. Tannen, Steve—20 (DB)
   Florida
2. Caster, Richard—46 (WR)
   Jackson State
3. Onkotz, Dennis—72 (LB) Penn
   State
4. Ebersole, John—98 (DE) Penn
   State
5. McClain, Clifford—108 (RB)
   So. Carolina State
   (from Boston)
   Arthur, Gary—124 (TE) Miami,
   Ohio
6. Stewart, Terry—150 (DB)
   Arkansas
7. Williams, James—176 (DB)
   Virginia State
8. Porter, Jack—187 (G) Oklahoma
   (from Boston)
   Lomas, Mark—202 (DE) No.
   Arizona
9. Bell, Ed—228 (WR) Idaho State
10. Dickerson, Cleve—254 (RB)
    Miami, Ohio
11. Thomas, Earlie—280 (DB)
    Colorado State
12. Pierson, Bill—306 (C-G) San
    Diego State
13. Groth, Walter—332 (DT) Baylor
14. Little, John—358 (LB) Oklahoma State
15. Bayless, Tom—384 (DT) Purdue

16. Herard, Claude—418 (DT) Mississippi
17. Beard, Dick—440 (RB) Kentucky

OAKLAND RAIDERS
(Drafted 24th)

1. Chester, Raymond—24 (TE) Morgan State
2. Koy, Ted—50 (RB) Texas
3. Irons, Gerald—76 (DE-DT) Maryland State
4. Cline, Tony—102 (LB) Miami
5. Laster, Art—128 (T) Maryland State
6. Wyatt, Alvin—154 (DB) Bethune-Cookman
7. Svitak, Steve—180 (LB) Boise State
8. Wynn, Mike—207 (DE-DT) Nebraska
9. Hill, Ike—232 (DB) Catawba
10. Bosserman, Gordon—258 (T) UCLA
11. Hicks, Emery—284 (LB) Kansas
12. Deloach, Gerry—310 (G) California-Davis
13. Highsmith, Don—336 (RB) Michigan State
14. Riley, John—362 (K-P) Auburn
15. Moore, Fred—392 (WR) Washington State
16. Roth, Tim—414 (DB) So. Dakota State
17. Stolberg, Eric—439 (WR) Indiana

PHILADELPHIA EAGLES
(Drafted Alternately 6-8-7)

1. Zabel, Steve—6 (TE) Oklahoma
2. Jones, Raymond—34 (DB) Southern U.
3. Bouggess, Lee—59 (RB) Louisville
4. Choice to Atlanta
5. Choice to Atlanta thru N.Y. Giants
6. Choice to St. Louis
7. Brennan, Terry—158 (T) Notre Dame (from Chicago) Choice to Los Angeles
8. Gordon, Ira—190 (T) Kansas State
9. King, David—215 (LB) Stephen F. Austin
10. Jaggard, Steve—240 (DB) Memphis State
11. Walik, Bill—268 (DB) Villanova
12. Jones, Robert—293 (DT) Grambling

13. Stevens, Richard—318 (T) Baylor
14. Moseley, Mark—346 (K) Stephen F. Austin
15. Carlos, John—371 (WR) San Jose State
16. Uperesa, Tuufuli—396 (T) Montana
17. Sizelove, Mike—424 (TE) Idaho

PITTSBURGH STEELERS
(Drafted Alternately 1-2)

1. Bradshaw, Terry—1 (QB) Louisiana Tech
2. Shanklin, Ronnie—28 (WR) No. Texas State
3. Blount, Mel—53 (DB) Southern U.
4. George, Edward—80 (T) Wake Forest
   Evenson, Jim—90 (RB) Oregon (from New York Giants)
5. Staggers, Jon—105 (DB) Missouri
6. Barrera, Manuel—131 (LB) Kansas State
   Kegler, Clarence—155 (T) So. Carolina State (from Minnesota)
7. Griffin, Danny—157 (RB) Texas-Arlington
8. Smith, Dave—184 (WR) Indiana, Pa.
9. Crennel, Carl—209 (LB) West Virginia
10. Brown, Isaiah—236 (DB) Stanford
11. Hunt, Calvin—261 (C) Baylor
12. Sharp, Rick—288 (DT) Washington
13. Main, Billy—313 (RB) Oregon State
14. Askon, Bert—340 (LB) Texas Southern
15. Keppy, Glen—365 (DT) Platteville, Wis.
16. Yanossy, Frank—391 (DT) Tennessee
17. Key, Harry—415 (TE) Mississippi Valley

ST. LOUIS CARDINALS
(Drafted Alternately 8-7-6)

1. Stegent, Larry—8 (RB) Texas A&M
2. Corrigall, James—33 (LB) Kent State
   Hutchison, Charles—38 (G) Ohio State (from New York Giants)
3. Pittman, Charlie—58 (RB) Penn State

Harris, Eric—69 (DB) Colorado (from Washington)
4. Lens, Greg—86 (DT) Trinity, Tex.
Parish, Don—91 (LB) Stanford (from Atlanta)
5. Lloyd, Tom—111 (T) Bowling Green
Pierson, Barry—127 (DB) Michigan (from Dallas)
6. Manuel, James—136 (T) Toledo (from Philadelphia)
Choice to Chicago
7. McFarland, Jim—164 (TE) Nebraska
8. Banks, Thomas—189 (C) Auburn
Holmgren, Mike—201 (QB) So. California (from Detroit)
9. White, Paul—214 (RB) Texas-El Paso
10. Plummer, Tony—242 (DB) Pacific
11. Siwek, Michael—267 (DT) Western Michigan
12. Collins, Charles—292 (WR) Kansas State
13. Thomas, Jack—320 (G) Mississippi State
14. Groth, Ray—345 (WR) Utah
15. Wilson, Ron—370 (WR) W. Illinois
16. Fowler, Gary—398 (RB) California
17. Powell, Cliff—423 (LB) Arkansas

SAN DIEGO CHARGERS
(Drafted Alternately 15–16)

1. Gillette, Walker—15 (WR) Richmond
2. Williams, Tom—42 (DT) California-Davis
3. Choice to Buffalo
4. Maddox, Bill—94 (TE) Syracuse
5. Farrar, Pettus—119 (RB) Norfolk State
6. Parks, Bill—146 (WR) Long Beach State
7. Fabish, Jim—171 (DB) Texas-El Paso
8. Clark, Wayne—198 (QB) International-Cal.
9. Fletcher, Chris—213 (DB) Temple
10. Steen, Mac—250 (G) Florida
11. Protz, John—275 (LB) Syracuse
12. Gravelle, Howard—302 (TE) California-Davis

13. Bradley, Bernard—327 (DB) Utah State
14. Caldwell, Tyrone—354 (DT) So. Carolina State
15. Childs, Eugene—379 (RB) Texas-El Paso
16. Green, Mike—406 (RB) Nebraska
17. Sanks, David—431 (G) Louisville

SAN FRANCISCO 49ERS
(Drafted 9th)

1. Hardman, Cedrick—9 (DE) No. Texas State
Taylor, Bruce—17 (DB) Boston U. (from Washington)
2. Choice to Los Angeles
Isenbarger, John—48 (RB) Indiana (from Los Angeles thru Philadelphia)
3. Choice to Kansas City
4. Washington, Vic—87 (WR) Wyoming
5. McArthur, Gary—113 (T) So. California
6. Clark, Rusty—138 (QB) Houston
7. Strong, Jim—165 (RB) Houston
8. Campbell, Carter—191 (LB) Weber State
9. Riley, Preston—217 (DB-WR) Memphis State
10. Schreiber, Larry—243 (RB) Tennessee Tech
11. Crockett, Dan—269 (WR) Toledo
12. Tant, Bill—295 (T) Dayton
13. Vanderslice, Jim—321 (LB) Texas Christian
14. King, Jack—347 (G) Clemson
15. Delsignore, Dave—373 (WR) Youngstown
16. Perkins, Produs—399 (DB) Livingstone
17. Culton, Mike—425 (P) LaVerne

WASHINGTON REDSKINS
(Drafted 17th)

1. Choice to San Francisco
2. Brundige, Bill—43 (DE) Colorado
3. Choice to St. Louis
4. Choice to Baltimore
Laaveg, Paul—103 (T) Iowa (from Minnesota thru L.A. thru N.O.)
5. Sistrunk, Manuel—114 (DT) Arkansas AM&N (from New Orleans)

Cincinnati Bengals' Jesse Phillips runs into Chargers' Jeff Staggs (81).

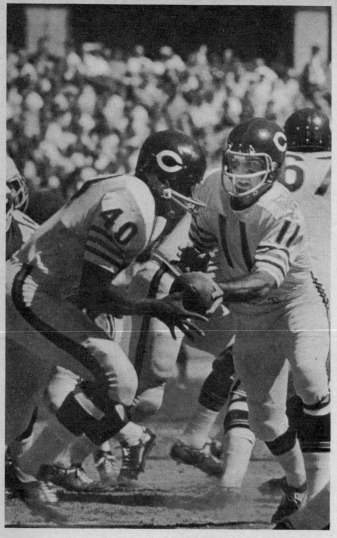

Gale Sayers (40), record holder, most touchdowns in a single season—22.

ALL-TIME INDIVIDUAL AND TEAM RECORDS

(Compiled by Elias Sports Bureau)

(Note: AFL or NFL footnoted at bottom of a record category shows record compiled in respective league that is not among top three performances overall. It is a point of information, and does not necessarily indicate the fourth best performance in that category overall. If no footnote follows category, AFL and NFL record is included in top three overall).

INDIVIDUAL RECORDS
SERVICE

Most Seasons, Active Player

20 George Blanda, Chi. Bears 1949–58; Balt. 1950; AFL: Hou. 1960–66; Oak. 1967–69
17 Lou Groza, Clev. 1950–59, 61–67
    Doug Atkins, Clev. 1953–54; Chi. Bears 1955–66; N.O. 1967–69
16 Sammy Baugh, Wash. 1937–52
AFL:
10 George Blanda, Hou. 1960–66; Oak. 1967–69
    Billy Cannon, Hou. 1960–63; Oak. 1964–69
    Gino Cappelletti, Bos. 1960–69
    Larry Grantham, N.Y. 1960–69
    Wayne Hawkins, Oak. 1960–69
    Jim Hunt, Bos. 1960–69
    Harry Jacobs, Bos. 1960–62; Buff. 1963–69
    Jack Lee, Hou. 1960–63, 66–67; Den. 1964–65; K.C. 1967–69
    Paul Maguire, L.A./S.D. 1960–63; Bugg. 1964–69
    Bill Mathis, N.Y. 1960–69
    Don Maynard, N.Y. 1960–69
    Ron Mix, L.A./S.D. 1960–69
    Jim Otto, Oak. 1960–69
    Vito (Babe) Parilli, Oak. 1960; Bos. 1961–67; N.Y. 1968–69
    Johnny Robinson, Dall./K.C. 1960–69
    Paul Rochester, Dall./K.C. 1960–63; N.Y. 1963–69
    Ernie Wright, L.A./S.D. 1960–67; Cin. 1968–69

Most Games Played, Lifetime

256 George Blanda, Chi. Bears 1949–58; Balt. 1950; AFL: Hou. 1960–66; Oak. 1967–69
216 Lou Groza, Clev. 1950–59, 61–67
205 Doug Atkins, Clev. 1953–54; Chi. Bears 1955–66; N.O. 1967–69
AFL:
140 George Blanda, Hou. 1960–66; Oak. 1967–69
    Gino Cappelletti, Bos. 1960–69
    Jim Otto, Oak. 1960–69

Most Consecutive Games Played, Lifetime

  182   Jim Ringo, G.B. (126) 1953–63; Phil. (56) 1964–67
  180   Dick Modzelewski, Wash. (24) 1953–54; Pitt. (12) 1955; N.Y. (102) 1956–63; Clev. (42) 1964–66
  174   Leo Nomellini, S.F. 1950–63
   AFL:
  140   *George Blanda, Hou. 1960–66; Oak. 1967–69*
         Gino Cappelletti, Bos. 1960–69
         Jim Otto, Oak. 1960–69

Most Seasons, Head Coach

   40   George Halas, Chi. Bears 1920–29, 33–42, 46–55, 58–67
   32   Earl (Curly) Lambeau, G.B. 1921–49; Chi. Cards 1950–51; Wash. 1952–53
   22   Steve Owen, N.Y. 1931–52
   AFL:
   10   *Sid Gillman, L.A./S.D. 1960–69*
         Hank Stram, Dall./K.C. 1960–69

SCORING

Most Seasons Leading League

    5   Don Hutson, G.B. 1940–44
         Gino Cappelletti, Bos. 1961, 63–66 (AFL)
    3   Earl (Dutch) Clark, Det. 1932, 35–36
         Marlin (Pat) Harder, Chi. Cards 1947–49
         Paul Hornung, G.B. 1959–61
    2   Jack Manders, Chi. Bears 1934, 37
         Gordy Soltau, S.F. 1952–53
         Doak Walker, Det. 1950, 55
         Gene Mingo, Den. 1960, 62 (AFL)
         Jim Turner, N.Y. 1968–69 (AFL)

TOTAL POINTS

Most Points, Lifetime

1,477   George Blanda, Chi. Bears 1949–58; Balt. 1950; AFL: Hou. 1960–66; Oak. 1967–69 (9-td, 703-pat, 240-fg)
1,349   Lou Groza, Clev. 1950–59, 61–67 (1-td, 641-pat, 234-fg)
1,100   Gino Cappelletti, Bos. 1960–69 (42-td, 338-pat, 170-fg) (AFL)

Most Points, Season

  176   Paul Hornung, G.B. 1960 (15-td, 41-pat, 15-fg)
  155   Gino Cappelletti, Bos. 1964 (7-td, 38-pat, 25-fg) (AFL)
  147   Gino Cappelletti, Bos. 1961 (8-td, 48-pat, 17-fg) (AFL)

Most Points, Rookie, Season

  132   Gale Sayers, Chi. 1965 (22-td)
  128   Doak Walker, Det. 1950 (11-td, 38-pat, 8-fg)
         Carlton (Cookie) Gilchrist, Buff. 1962 (15-td, 14-pat, 8-fg) (AFL)
  123   Gene Mingo, Den. 1960 (6-td, 33-pat, 18-fg) (AFL)

Most Points, Game

   40   Ernie Nevers, Chi. Cards vs Chi. Bears, Nov. 28, 1929 (6-td, 4-pat)
   36   William (Dub) Jones, Clev. vs Chi. Bears, Nov. 25, 1951 (6-td)
         Gale Sayers, Chi. vs S.F., Dec. 12, 1965 (6-td)
   33   Paul Hornung, G.B. vs Balt., Oct. 8, 1961 (4-td, 6-pat, 1-fg)
   AFL:
   30   *Abner Haynes, Dall. vs. Oak., Nov. 26, 1961 (5-td)*
         Billy Cannon, Hou. vs N.Y., Dec. 10, 1961 (5-td)
         Carlton (Cookie) Gilchrist, Buff. vs N.Y., Dec. 8, 1963 (5-td)

Most Consecutive Games Scoring

  110   Loris (Sam) Baker, Dall. 1962–63; Phil. 1964–69 (current)
  107   Lou Groza, Clev. 1950–59
   98   Fred Cox, Minn. 1963–69 (current)
  AFL:
   56   George Blanda, Hou. 1966; Oak. 1967–69 (current)

TOUCHDOWNS

Most Seasons Leading League

   8   Don Hutson, G.B. 1935–38, 41–44
   3   Jim Brown, Clev. 1958–59, 63
       Lance Alworth, S.D. 1964–66 (AFL)
   2   By many players

Most Touchdowns, Lifetime

  126   Jim Brown, Clev. 1957–65 (106-r, 20-p)
  113   Lenny Moore, Balt. 1956–67 (63-r, 48-p, 2-rb)
  105   Don Hutson, G.B. 1935–45 (3-r, 100-p, 2-rb)
  AFL:
   84   Don Maynard, N.Y. 1960–69 (84-p)

Most Touchdowns, Season

  22   Gale Sayers, Chi. 1965 (14-r, 6-p, 1-prb, 1-krb)
  21   Jim Brown, Clev. 1965 (17-r, 4-p)
  20   Lenny Moore, Balt. 1964 (16-r, 3-p, 1-f)
      Leroy Kelly, Clev. 1968 (16-r, 4-p)
  AFL:
  19   Abner Haynes, Dall. 1962 (13-r, 6-p)

Most Touchdowns, Rookie, Season

  22   Gale Sayers, Chi. 1965 (14-r, 6-p, 1-prb, 1 krb)
  15   Carlton (Cookie) Gilchrist, Buff. 1962 (13-r, 2-p) (AFL)
  13   Billy Howton, G.B. 1952 (13-p)
      Bob Hayes, Dall. 1965 (1-r, 12-p)

Most Touchdowns, Game

   6   Ernie Nevers, Chi. Cards vs Chi. Bears, Nov. 28, 1929 (6-r)
      William (Dub) Jones, Clev. vs Chi. Bears, Nov. 25, 1951 (4-r, 2-p)
      Gale Sayers, Chi. vs S.F., Dec. 12, 1965 (4-r, 1-p, 1-prb)
   5   Bob Shaw, Chi. Cards vs Balt., Oct. 2, 1950 (5-p)
      Jim Brown, Clev. vs Balt., Nov. 1, 1959 (5-r)
      Paul Hornung, G.B. vs Balt., Dec. 12, 1965 (3-r, 2-p)
      Abner Haynes, Dall. vs Oak., Nov. 26, 1951 (4-r, 1-p) (AFL)
      Billy Cannon, Hou. vs N.Y., Dec. 10, 1961 (3-r, 2-p) (AFL)
      Carlton (Cookie) Gilchrist, Buff. vs N.Y., Dec. 8, 1963 (5-r) (AFL)
   4   By many

Most Consecutive Games Scoring Touchdowns

  18   Lenny Moore, Balt. 1963–65
  11   Elroy Hirsch, L.A. 1950–51
      Gilbert (Buddy) Dial, Pitt. 1959–60
  10   Frank Gifford, N.Y. 1957–58
      Jim Brown, Clev. 1965
  AFL:
   9   Lance Alworth, S.D. 1963–64

POINTS AFTER TOUCHDOWN

Most Seasons Leading League

   6 George Blanda, Chi. Bears 1956; AFL: Hou. 1961–62; Oak. 1967–69
   5 George Blanda, Hou. 1961–62; Oak. 1967–69 (AFL)
   4 Bob Waterfield, Clev. 1945; L.A. 1946, 50, 52

Most Points After Touchdown Attempted, Lifetime

 712 George Blanda, Chi. Bears 1949–58; Balt. 1950; AFL: Hou. 1960–66; Oak. 1967–69
 657 Lou Groza, Clev. 1950–59, 61–67
 462 George Blanda, Hou. 1960–66; Oak. 1967–69 (AFL)

Most Points After Touchdown Attempted, Season

  65 George Blanda, Hou. 1961 (AFL)
  58 Bob Waterfield, L.A. 1950
  57 George Blanda, Oak. 1967 (AFL)

Most Points After Touchdown Attempted, Game

  10 Charlie Gogolak, Wash. vs N.Y., Nov. 27, 1966
   9 Marlin (Pat) Harder, Chi. Cards vs. N.Y., Oct. 17, 1948
      Bob Waterfield, L.A. vs Balt., Oct. 22, 1950
   8 By many players (NFL—AFL)

Most Points After Touchdown, Lifetime

 703 George Blanda, Chi. Bears 1948–58; Balt. 1950; AFL: Hou. 1960–66; Oak. 1967–69
 641 Lou Groza, Clev. 1950–59, 61–67
 456 George Blanda, Hou. 1960–66; Oak. 1967–69 (AFL)

Most Points After Touchdown, Season

  64 George Blanda, Hou. 1961 (AFL)
  56 Danny Villanueva, Dall. 1956
      George Blanda, Oak. 1967 (AFL)
  54 Bob Waterfield, L.A. 1950
      Mike Clark, Dall. 1968
      George Blanda, Oak. 1968 (AFL)

Most Points After Touchdown, Game

   9 Marlin (Pat) Harder, Chi. Cards vs N.Y., Oct., 17, 1948
      Bob Waterfield, L.A. vs Balt., Oct. 22, 1950
      Charlie Gogolak, Wash. vs N.Y., Nov. 27, 1966
   8 By many players (NFL—AFL)

Most Consecutive Points After Touchdown

 234 Tommy Davis, S.F. 1959–65
 156 George Blanda, Chi. Bears, 1949–56
 154 George Blanda, Oak. 1967–69 (AFL) (current)

Most Points After Touchdown (no misses), Season

  56 Danny Villanueva, Dall. 1966
  54 Mike Clark, Dall. 1968
      George Blanda, Oak. 1968 (AFL)
  53 Marlin (Pat) Harder, Chi. Cards, 1948

Most Points After Touchdown (no Misses), Game

   9 Marlin (Pat) Harder, Chi. Cards vs N.Y., Oct. 17, 1948
      Bob Waterfield, L.A. vs Balt., Oct. 22, 1950
   8 By many (NFL–AFL)

Larry Wilson shares the NFL record for consecutive-game interceptions.

FIELD GOALS

Most Seasons Leading League

- 5 Lou Groza, Clev., 1950, 52–54, 57
- 4 Jack Manders, Chi. Bears, 1933–34, 36–37
  Ward Cuff, N.Y. 1938–39, 43; G.B. 1947
- 3 Bob Waterfield, L.A. 1947–49, 51
  Gino Cappelletti, Bos. 1961, 63–64 (AFL)

Most Field Goals Attempted, Lifetime

- 490 George Blanda, Chi. Bears 1949–58; Balt. 1950; AFL: Hou. 1960–66; Oak. 1967–69
- 405 Lou Groza, Clev. 1950–59, 61–67
- 327 Lou Michaels, L.A. 1958–60; Pitt. 1961–63; Balt. 1964–69
- **AFL:**
- *318 Gino Cappelletti, Bos. 1960–69*

Most Field Goals Attempted, Season

- 49 Bruce Gossett, L.A. 1966
- 47 Jim Turner, N.Y. 1969 (AFL)
- 46 Pete Gogolak, Buff. 1965 (AFL)
  Jim Turner, N.Y. 1968 (AFL)

Most Field Goals Attempted, Game

- 9 Jim Bakken, St. L. vs Pitt., Sept. 24, 1967
- 8 Lou Michaels, Pitt. vs St. L., Dec. 2, 1962
  Garo Yepremian, Det. vs Minn., Nov. 13, 1966
  Jim Turner, N.Y. vs Buff., Nov. 3, 1968 (AFL)
- 7 By many players (NFL-AFL)

Most Field Goals, Lifetime

- 240 George Blanda, Chi. Bears 1949–58; Balt. 1950; AFL: Hou. 1960–66; Oak. 1967–69
- 234 Lou Groza, Clev. 1950–59, 61–67
- 179 Lou Michaels, L.A. 1958–60; Pitt. 1961–63; Balt. 1964–69
  Loris (Sam) Baker, Wash. 1953, 56–59; Clev. 1960–61; Dall. 1962–63; Phil. 1964–69
- **AFL:**
- *170 Gino Cappelletti, Bos. 1960–69*

Most Field Goals, Season

- 34 Jim Turner, N.Y. 1968 (AFL)
- 32 Jim Turner, N.Y. 1969 (AFL)
- 30 Jan Stenerud, K.C. 1968 (AFL)
- **NFL:**
- *28 Bruce Gossett, L.A. 1966*

Most Field Goals, Game

- 7 Jim Bakken, St. L. vs Pitt., Sept. 24, 1967
- 6 Gino Cappelletti, Bos. vs Den., Oct. 4, 1964 (AFL)
  Garo Yepremian, Det. vs Minn., Nov. 13, 1966
  Jim Turner, N.Y. vs Buff., Nov. 3, 1968 (AFL)
- 5 By many players (NFL-AFL)

Most Consecutive Games, Field Goals

19   Jim Bakken, St. L. 1966–67
      Bruce Gossett, L. A. 1967–68
      Fred Cox, Minn. 1968–69 (current)
18   Jim Turner, N.Y. 1966–67 (AFL)
16   Fred Cox, Minn. 1967–68

Most Consecutive Field Goals

16   Jan Stenerud, K.C. 1969 (AFL)
12   Lou Groza, Clev. 1953
      Bobby Layne, Det. 1956–57
11   Don Cockroft, Clev. 1968–69

Longest Field Goal

56   Bert Rechichar, Balt. vs Chi. Bears, Sept. 27, 1953
55   George Blanda, Hou. vs S.D., Dec. 3, 1961 (AFL)
      Tom Dempsey, N.O. vs L.A., Oct. 5, 1969
54   Glenn Presnell, Det. vs G.B., Oct. 7, 1934
      George Fleming, Oak. vs Den., Oct. 1, 1961 (AFL)
      George Blanda, Hou. vs Oak., Dec. 9, 1962 (AFL)
      Jan Stenerud, K.C. vs Hou., Sept. 9, 1967; vs Den., Oct. 5, 1969
      (AFL)

Highest Completion Percentage, Season (14 attempts)

88.5   Lou Groza, Clev., 1953 (26-23)
85.0   George Blair, S.D., 1962 (20-17) (AFL)
80.0   Bobby Layne, Det., 1956 (15-12)

Highest Completion Percentage, Game (5 attempts)

100.0   Gino Cappelletti, Bos. vs Den., Oct. 4, 1964 (6-6) (AFL)
        Roger Leclerc, Chi. vs Det., Dec. 3, 1961 (5-5)
        Lou Michaels, Balt. vs S.F., Sept. 25, 1966 (5–5)
        Mac Percival, Chi. vs Phil., Oct. 20, 1968 (5–5)
        Roy Gerela, Hou. vs Mia., Sept. 28, 1969 (5-5) (AFL)
        Jan Stenerud, K.C. vs Buff., Nov. 2 & Dec. 7, 1969 (5-5) (AFL)

SAFETIES

Most Safeties, Lifetime

3   Bill McPeak, Pitt., 1954, 56, 57
     Charlie Krueger, S.F., 1959, 60, 61
     Ernie Stautner, Pitt., 1950, 58, 62
     Jim Katcavage, N.Y., 1958, 61, 65
     Roger Brown, Det., 1962 (2), 65
     Bruce Maher, Det., 1960, 63, 67
2   Dick Modzelewski, Wash., 1954; N.Y. 61
     Leo Nomellini, S.F., 1957, 60
     Roosevelt Grier, N.Y. 1960; L.A. 66
     Ron McDole, Buff. 1964 (AFL)

Most Safeties, Season

2   Roger Brown, Det. 1962
     Ron McDole, Buff. 1964 (AFL)

Most Safeties, Game

1   By many

RUSHING

Most Seasons Leading League

  8 Jim Brown, Clev., 1957–61, 63–65
  4 Steve Van Buren, Phil., 1945, 47–49
  2 By many players (NFL-AFL)

Most Consecutive Seasons Leading League

  5 Jim Brown, Clev., 1957–61
  3 Steve Van Buren, Phil, 1947–49
     Jim Brown, Clev., 1963–65
  2 Bill Paschal, N.Y., 1943–44
     Fletcher (Joe) Perry, S.F., 1953–54
     Jim Nance, Bos. 1966–67 (AFL)
     Leroy Kelly, Clev., 1967–68

RUSHING ATTEMPTS

Most Attempts, Lifetime

2,359 Jim Brown, Clev., 1957–65
1,941 Jim Taylor, G.B. 1958–66; N.O. 1967
1,737 Fletcher (Joe) Perry, S.F., 1950–60, 63; Balt., 1961–62
  AFL:
1,134 Clem Daniels, Dall. 1960; Oak. 1961–67

Most Attempts, Season

  305 Jim Brown, Clev., 1961
  299 Jim Nance, Bos. 1966 (AFL)
  291 Jim Brown, Clev., 1963

Most Attempts, Game

  38 Harry Newman, N.Y. vs G.B., Nov. 11, 1934
     Jim Nance, Bos. vs Oak., Oct. 30, 1966 (AFL)
  37 Jim Brown, Clev. vs Chi. Cards, Oct. 4, 1959
  36 Carlton (Cookie) Gilchrist, Buff. vs N.Y., Dec. 8, 1963 (AFL)

RUSHING YARDAGE

Most Yards Gained, Lifetime

12,312 Jim Brown, Clev., 1957–65
 8,597 Jim Taylor, G.B. 1958–66; N.O. 1967
 8,378 Fletcher (Joe) Perry, S.F., 1950–60, 63; Balt., 1961–62
  AFL:
5,101 Clem Daniels, Dall. 1960; Oak. 1961–67

Most Yards Gained, Season

1,863 Jim Brown, Clev., 1963
1,544 Jim Brown, Clev., 1965
1,527 Jim Brown, Clev., 1958
  AFL:
1,458 Jim Nance, Bos. 1966

Most Yards Gained, Game

  243 Carlton (Cookie) Gilchrist, Buff. vs N.Y., Dec. 8, 1963 (AFL)
  237 Jim Brown, Clev. vs L.A., Nov. 24, 1957
     Jim Brown, Clev. vs Phil., Nov. 19, 1961
  232 Bobby Mitchell, Clev. vs Wash., Nov. 15, 1959
     Jim Brown, Clev. vs Dall., Sept. 22, 1963

Most Games, 100 Yds. or More, Rushing, Lifetime

    58 Jim Brown, Clev., 1957–65
    26 Jim Taylor, G.B., 1958–66
    22 Fletcher (Joe) Perry, S.F. (19), 1950–60, 63; Balt. (3), 1961–62
    AFL:
    17 Jim Nance, Bos., 1966–69

Longest Run from Scrimmage

    97 Andy Uram, G.B. vs Chi. Cards, Oct. 8, 1939 (td)
          Bob Gage, Pitt. vs Chi. Bears, Dec. 4, 1949 (td)
    96 Bob Hoernschemeyer, Det. vs N.Y. Yanks, Nov. 23, 1950 (td)
          Jim Spivital, Balt. vs G.B., Nov. 5, 1950 (td)
    92 Kenny Washington, L.A. vs Chi. Cards, Nov. 2, 1947 (td)
    AFL:
    91 Sid Blanks, Hou. vs N.Y., Dec. 13, 1964 (td)

AVERAGE GAIN RUSHING

Highest Average Gain, Lifetime (700 att)

    5.22 Jim Brown, Clev. 1957–65 (2359-12, 312)
    5.10 Gale Sayers, Chi. 1965–69 (955-4866)
    4.89 Leroy Kelly, Clev. 1964–69 (931-4553)
    AFL:
    4.87 Paul Lowe, L.A./S.D. 1960–68; K.C. 1968–69 (1026-4995)

Highest Average Gain, Season (Qualifiers)

    9.94 Beattie Feathers, Chi. Bears 1934 (101-1004)
    6.78 Dan Towler, L.A. 1951 (126-854)
    6.45 Keith Lincoln, S.D. 1963 (128-826) (AFL)

Highest Average Gain, Game (10 att.)

    17.09 Marion Motley, Clev. vs Pitt., Oct. 29, 1950 (11-188)
    16.70 Bill Grimes, G.B. vs N.Y. Yanks, Oct. 8, 1950 (10-167)
    16.57 Bobby Mitchell, Clev. vs Wash., Nov. 15, 1959 (14-232)
    AFL:
    13.83 Keith Lincoln, S.D. vs Oak., Sept. 30, 1962 (12-166)

TOUCHDOWNS RUSHING

Most Touchdowns Rushing, Lifetime

    106 Jim Brown, Clev., 1957–65
    83 Jim Taylor, G.B. 1958–66; N.O. 1967
    69 Steve Van Buren, Phil., 1944–51
    AFL:
    46 Abner Haynes, Dall./K.C. 1960–64; Den. 1965–66; Mia. 1967;
          N.Y. 1967

Most Touchdowns Rushing, Season

    19 Jim Taylor, G.B., 1962
    17 Jim Brown, Clev., 1958, 65
    16 Lenny Moore, Balt., 1964
          Leroy Kelly, Clev., 1968
    AFL:
    13 Carlton (Cookie) Gilchrist, Buff. 1962
          Abner Haynes, Dall. 1962

Most Touchdowns Rushing, Game

  6 Ernie Nevers, Chi. Cards vs Chi. Bears, Nov. 28, 1929
  5 Jim Brown, Clev. vs Balt., Nov. 1, 1959
     Carlton (Cookie) Gilchrist, Buff. vs N.Y., Dec. 8, 1963 (AFL)
  4 By many players (NFL-AFL)

Most Consecutive Games Rushing Touchdowns

 11 Lenny Moore, Balt., 1963–64
  9 Leroy Kelly, Clev. 1968
  8 Steve Van Buren, Phil., 1947
AFL:
  7 *Carlton (Cookie) Gilchrist, Buff. 1962*

PASSING

Most Seasons Leading League

  6 Sammy Baugh, Wash., 1937, 40, 43, 45, 47, 49
  4 Len Dawson, Dall. 1962; K.C. 1964, 66, 68 (AFL)
  3 Arnie Herber, G.B., 1932, 34, 36
     Norm Van Brocklin, L.A., 1950, 52, 54
     Bryan (Bart) Starr, G.B., 1962, 64, 66

Most Consecutive Seasons Leading League

  2 Cecil Isbell, G.B., 1941–42
     Milt Plum, Clev., 1960–61
     AFL: Not accomplished

PASSING ATTEMPTS

Most Passes Attempted, Lifetime

4,456 John Unitas, Balt. 1956–69
3,872 George Blanda, Chi. Bears 1949–58; Balt. 1950; AFL: Hou. 1960–66; Oak. 1967–69
3,817 Y. A. Tittle, Balt. 1950; S.F. 1951–60; N.Y. 1961–64
  AFL:
3.055 *Jack Kemp, L.A./S.D. 1960–62; Buff. 1962–67, 69*

Most Passes Attempted, Season

508 C.A. (Sonny) Jurgensen, Wash. 1967
505 George Blanda, Hou. 1964 (AFL)
491 Joe Namath, N.Y. 1967 (AFL)

Most Passes Attempted, Game

 68 George Blanda, Hou. vs Buff., Nov. 1, 1964 (AFL)
 60 Robert (Davey) O'Brien, Phil. vs Wash., Dec. 1, 1940
     George Blanda, Hou. vs Oak., Nov. 7, 1965 (AFL)
     Joe Namath, N.Y. vs Den., Dec. 3, 1967 (AFL)
 57 C. A. (Sonny) Jurgensen, Phil. vs N.Y., Sept. 23, 1962
     Bill Wade, Chi. vs Wash., Oct. 25, 1964

COMPLETIONS

Most Passes Completed, Lifetime

2,450   John Unitas, Balt. 1956–69
2,118   Y. A. Tittle, Balt. 1950; S.F. 1951–60; N.Y. 1961–64
1,982   C. A. (Sonny) Jurgensen, Phil. 1957–63; Wash. 1964–69
   AFL:
1,428   Jack Kemp, L.A./S.D. 1960–62; Buff. 1962–67, 69

Most Passes Completed, Season

288   C. A. (Sonny) Jurgensen, Wash. 1967
262   George Blanda, Hou. 1964 (AFL)
258   Joe Namath, N.Y. 1967 (AFL)

Most Passes Completed, Game

37   George Blanda, Hou. vs Buff., Nov. 1, 1964 (AFL)
36   Charley Conerly, N.Y. vs Pitt., Dec. 5, 1948
34   Mickey Slaughter, Den. vs Hou., Dec. 20, 1964 (AFL)

Most Consecutive Passes Completed

15   Len Dawson, K.C. vs Hou., Sept. 9, 1967 (AFL)
13   Fran Tarkenton, Minn. vs L.A., Dec. 3, 1961
      Rudy Bukich, Chi. vs S.F. (6), Nov. 22—vs Det. (7), Nov. 26, 1964
      Bill Nelsen, Pitt. vs Atl. (11), Dec. 18, 1966—vs Chi. (2), Sept. 17, 1967
12   Y. A. Tittle, N.Y. vs Wash., Oct. 28, 1962
      John Unitas, Balt. vs Atl., Nov. 27, 1967

EFFICIENCY

Highest Passing Efficiency, Lifetime (1,500 atts)

57.70   Bryan (Bart) Starr, G.B. 1956–69
56.57   Len Dawson, Pitt. 1957–59; Clev. 1960–61; AFL: Dall./K.C. 1962–69
56.53   Sammy Baugh, Wash. 1937–52
   AFL:
* 56.8   Len Dawson, Dal. 1962; K.C. 1963–69*

Highest Passing Efficiency, Season (Qualifiers)

70.32   Sammy Baugh, Wash. 1945
64.72   Otto Graham, Clev. 1953
63.74   Bryan (Bart) Starr, G.B. 1968
   AFL:
60.96   Len Dawson, Dall. 1962

Highest Passing Efficiency, Game (20 atts)

85.71   Sammy Baugh, Wash. vs Pitt., Oct. 14, 1945
85.00   John Unitas, Balt. vs Atl., Nov. 12, 1967
         John Brodie, S.F. vs Balt., Sept. 29, 1968
83.33   Sammy Baugh, Wash. vs N.Y., Oct. 28, 1945
  AFL:
80.95   Bob Griese, Mia. vs N.Y., Oct. 22, 1967

PASSING YARDAGE

Most Yards Gained, Lifetime

35,502   John Unitas, Balt. 1956–69
28,339   Y. A. Tittle, Balt. 1950; S.F. 1951–60; N.Y. 1961–64
26,978   C. A. (Sonny) Jurgensen, Phil. 1957–63; Wash. 1964–69
  AFL:
21,130   Jack Kemp, L.A./S.D. 1960–62; Buff. 1962–67, 69

Most Yards Gained, Season

4,007   Joe Namath, N.Y. 1967 (AFL)
3,747   C. A. (Sonny) Jurgensen, Wash. 1967
3,723   C. A. (Sonny) Jurgensen, Phil. 1961

Most Yards Gained, Game

554   Norm Van Brocklin, L.A. vs N.Y. Yanks, Sept. 28, 1951
505   Y. A. Tittle, N.Y. vs Wash., Oct. 28, 1962
468   John Lujack, Chi. Bears vs Chi. Cards, Dec. 11, 1949
  AFL:
464   George Blanda, Hou. vs Buff., Oct. 29, 1961

Most Games, 300 Yds. or More, Passing, Lifetime

25   John Unitas, Balt. 1956–69
23   C. A. (Sonny) Jurgensen, Phil. 1957–63; Wash. 1964–69
19   George Blanda, Chi. Bears 1949–58; Balt. 1950; AFL: Hou. 1960–66; Oak. 1967–69
  AFL:
16   Joe Namath, N.Y. 1965–69

Longest Pass Completion (all TDs)

99   Frank Filchock (to Farkas), Wash. vs Pitt., Oct. 15, 1939
     George Izo (to Mitchell), Wash. vs Clev., Sept. 15, 1963
     Karl Sweetan (to Studstill), Det. vs Balt., Oct. 16, 1966
     C. A. Jurgensen (to Allen), Wash. vs Chi., Sept. 15, 1968
98   Doug Russell (to Tinsley), Chi. Cards vs Clev., Nov. 27, 1938
     Ogden Compton (to Lane), Chi. Cards vs G.B., Nov. 13, 1955
     Bill Wade (to Farrington), Chi. Bears vs Det., Oct. 8, 1961
     Jack Lee (to Dewveall), Hou. vs S.D., Nov. 25, 1962 (AFL)
     Earl Morrall (to Jones), N.Y. vs Pitt., Sept. 11, 1966
97   James (Pat) Coffee (to Tinsley), Chi. Cards vs Chi. Bears, Dec. 5, 1937
     Bobby Layne (to Box), Det. vs G.B., Nov. 26, 1953
     George Shaw (to Tarr), Den. vs Bos., Sept. 21, 1962 (AFL)

Shortest Pass Completion for Touchdown

2"   Eddie LeBaron (to Bielski), Dall. vs Wash., Oct. 9, 1960
4"   Cecil Isbell (to Hutson), G.B. vs Clev., Oct. 18, 1942

TOUCHDOWN PASSES

Most Touchdown Passes, Lifetime

266 John Unitas, Balt. 1956–69
224 George Blanda, Chi. Bears 1949–58; Balt. 1950; AFL: Hou. 1960–66; Oak. 1967–69
213 C. A. (Sonny) Jurgensen, Phil. 1957–63; Wash. 1964–69
AFL:
182 Len Dawson, Dall./K.C. 1962–69

Most Touchdown Passes, Season

36 George Blanda, Hou. 1961 (AFL)
  Y. A. Tittle, N.Y. 1963
34 Daryle Lamonica, Oak. 1969 (AFL)
33 Y. A. Tittle, N.Y. 1962

Most Touchdown Passes, Game

7 Sid Luckman, Chi. Bears vs N.Y., Nov. 14, 1943
  Adrian Burk, Phil. vs Wash., Oct. 17, 1954
  George Blanda, Hou. vs N.Y., Nov. 19, 1961 (AFL)
  Y. A. Tittle, N.Y. vs Wash., Oct. 28, 1962
  Joe Kapp, Minn. vs Balt. Sept. 28, 1969
6 By many players (NFL-AFL)

Most Consecutive Games, Touchdown Passes

47 John Unitas, Balt. 1956–60
23 Frank Ryan, Clev. 1965–67
  C. A. (Sonny) Jurgensen, Wash. 1966–68
22 Cecil Isbell, G.B. 1941–42
AFL:
19 Al Dorow, N.Y. 1960–61
  John Hadl, S.D. 1966–67

PASSES HAD INTERCEPTED

Fewest Passes Had Intercepted, Lifetime (1,500 atts)

75 Roman Gabriel, L.A. 1962–69
83 Daryle Lamonica, Buff. 1963–66; Oak. 1967–69 (AFL)
92 Tom Flores, Oak. 1960–61, 63–66; Buff. 1967–69; K.C. 1969 (AFL)

Fewest Passes Had Intercepted, Season (Qualifiers)

3 Gary Wood, N.Y. 1964
  Bryan (Bart) Starr, G.B. 1966
4 Sammy Baugh, Wash. 1945
  Harry Gilmer, Det. 1955
  Charley Conerly, N.Y. 1959
  Bryan (Bart) Starr, G.B. 1964
5 Fred Enke, Det. 1949
  Milt Plum, Clev. 1960
  Roman Gabriel, L.A. 1964–65
  Don Trull, Hou. 1966 (AFL)
  John Stofa, Cin. 1968 (AFL)

Most Consecutive Passes Attempted, None Intercepted

    294   Bryan (Bart) Starr, G.B., 1964–65
    208   Milt Plum, Clev., 1959–60
    152   Bryan (Bart) Starr, G.B., 1963–64
    AFL:
    128   Edward (Butch) Songin, Bos. 1960–61

Most Passes Had Intercepted, Lifetime

    265   George Blanda, Chi. Bears 1949–58; Balt. 1950; AFL: Hou.
          1960–66; Oak. 1967–69
    243   Bobby Layne, Chi. Bears 1948; N.Y. Bulldogs 1949; Det.
          1950–58; Pitt. 1958–62
    221   Y. A. Tittle, Balt. 1950; S.F. 1951–60; N.Y. 1961–64
    AFL:
    195   George Blanda, Hou. 1960–66; Oak. 1967–69

Most Passes Had Intercepted, Season

    42   George Blanda, Hou. 1962 (AFL)
    34   Frank Tripucka, Den. 1960 (AFL)
    32   John Hadl, S.D. 1968 (AFL)
    NFL:
    31   Sid Luckman, Chi. Bears 1947

Most Passes Had Intercepted, Game

    8   Jim Hardy, Chi. Cards vs Phil., Sept. 24, 1950
    7   Parker Hall, Clev. Rams vs G.B., Nov. 8, 1942
        Frank Sinkwich, Det. vs G.B., Oct. 24, 1943
        Bob Waterfield, L.A. vs G.B., Oct. 17, 1948
        Edmund (Zeke) Bratkowski, Chi. vs Balt., Oct. 2, 1960
        Tommy Wade, Pitt. vs Phil., Dec. 12, 1965
    6   By many players (NFL-AFL)

Lowest Percentage Passes Had Intercepted, Lifetime (1,500 atts)

    3.36   Roman Gabriel, L.A. 1962–69
    4.28   Bryan (Bart) Starr, G.B. 1956–69
    4.43   Fran Tarkenton, Minn. 1961–66; N.Y. 1967–69
    AFL:
    4.97   Len Dawson, Dall./K.C. 1962–69

Lowest Percentage Passes Had Intercepted, Season (Qualifiers)

    1.19   Bryan (Bart) Starr, G.B. 1966
    1.47   Bryan (Bart) Starr, G.B. 1964
    1.75   Roman Gabriel, L.A. 1969
    AFL:
    2.82   John Stofa, Cin. 1968

PASS RECEPTIONS

Most Seasons Leading League

    8   Don Hutson, G.B., 1936–37, 39, 41–45
    5   Lionel Taylor, Den. 1960–63, 65 (AFL)
    3   Tom Fears, L.A., 1948–50
        Pete Pihos, Phil., 1953–55
        Billy Wilson, S.F., 1954, 56–57
        Raymond Berry, Balt., 1958–60
        Lance Alworth, S.D. 1966, 68–69 (AFL)

Most Consecutive Seasons Leading League

    5   Don Hutson, G.B., 1941–45

    4   Lionel Taylor, Den. 1960–63 (AFL)
    3   Tom Fears, L.A., 1948–50
        Pete Pihos, Phil., 1953–55
        Raymond Berry, Balt., 1958–60

Most Pass Receptions, Lifetime

   631 Raymond Berry, Balt., 1955–67
   567 Lionel Taylor, Den. 1960–66; Hou. 1967–68 (AFL)
   551 Don Maynard, N.Y. Giants 1958; AFL: N.Y. 1960–69

Most Pass Receptions, Season

   101 Charley Hennigan, Hou. 1964 (AFL)
   100 Lionel Taylor, Den. 1961 (AFL)
    93 Johnny Morris, Chi. 1964

Most Pass Receptions, Game

    18 Tom Fears, L.A. vs G.B., Dec. 3, 1950
    16 Ulmo (Sonny) Randle, St. L. vs N.Y., Nov. 4, 1962
    14 By many players
AFL:
   13 Charley Hennigan, Hou. vs Bos., Oct. 13, 1961
        Lance Alworth, S.D. vs Bos., Nov. 10, 1963
        Sid Blanks, Hou. vs S.D., Sept. 12, 1964
        Lionel Taylor, Den. vs Oak., Nov. 29, 1964

Most Consecutive Games, Pass Receptions

    96 Lance Alworth, S.D., 1962–69 (current) (AFL)
    95 Don Hutson, G.B., 1937–45
    94 Bobby Joe Conrad, St. L., 1961–68

YARDAGE RECEIVING

Most Yards Gained, Lifetime

10,373 Don Maynard, N.Y. Giants 1958; AFL: N.Y. 1960–69
10,289 Don Maynard, N.Y. 1960–69 (AFL)
 9,275 Raymond Berry, Balt. 1955–67

Most Yards Gained, Season

 1,746 Charley Hennigan, Hou. 1961 (AFL)
 1,602 Lance Alworth, S.D. 1965 (AFL)
 1,546 Charley Hennigan, Hou. 1964 (AFL)
 NFL:
 1,495 Elroy Hirsch, L.A. 1951

Most Yards Gained, Game

   303 Jim Benton, Clev. Rams vs Det., Nov. 22, 1945
   302 Cloyce Box, Det. vs Balt., Dec. 3, 1950
   272 Charley Hennigan, Hou. vs Bos., Oct. 13, 1961 (AFL)

Longest Pass Reception (all TDs)

    99 Andy Farkas (Filchock), Wash. vs Pitt., Oct. 15, 1939
        Bobby Mitchell (Izo), Wash. vs Clev., Sept. 15, 1963
        Pat Studstill (Sweetan), Det. vs Balt., Oct. 16, 1966
        Gerry Allen (Jurgensen), Wash. vs Chi., Sept. 15, 1968
    98 Gaynell Tinsley (Russell), Chi. Cards vs Clev., Nov. 17, 1938
        Richard (Night Train) Lane (Compton), Chi. Cards vs G.B.,
        Nov. 13, 1955
        John Farrington (Wade), Chi. Bears vs Det., Oct. 8, 1961
        Willard Dewveall (Lee), Hou. vs S.D., Nov. 25, 1962 (AFL)
        Homer Jones (Morrall), N.Y. vs Pitt., Sept. 11, 1966

Longest Pass Reception (all TDs) (Cont'd)

  97 Gaynell Tinsley (Coffee), Chi. Cards vs Chi. Bears, Dec. 5, 1937
       Cloyce Box (Layne), Det. vs G.B., Nov. 26, 1953
       Jerry Tarr (Shaw), Den. vs Bos., Sept. 21, 1962 (AFL)

Shortest Pass Reception for Touchdown

  2" Dick Bielski (LeBaron), Dall. vs Wash., Oct. 9, 1960
  4" Don Hutson (Isbell), G.B. vs Clev., Oct. 18, 1942

TOUCHDOWNS RECEIVING

Most Touchdown Passes, Lifetime

 100 Don Hutson, G.B., 1935–45
  84 Tommy McDonald, Phil. (66) 1957–63; Dall. (2) 1964; L.A. (11)
       1965–66; Atl. (4) 1967; Clev. (1) 1968
       Don Maynard, N.Y. Giants (0) 1958; AFL: N.Y. (84) 1960–69
  81 Art Powell, Phil. (0) 1959; Minn. (0) 1968; AFL: N.Y. (27)
       1960–62; Oak. (50) 1963–66; Buff. (4) 1967

Most Touchdown Passes, Season

  17 Don Hutson, G.B. 1942
       Elroy Hirsch, L.A. 1951
       Bill Groman, Hou. 1961 (AFL)
  16 Art Powell, Oak. 1963 (AFL)
  15 Cloyce Box, Det. 1952
       Ulmo (Sonny) Randle, St. L. 1960

Most Touchdown Passes, Game

  5 Bob Shaw, Chi. Cards vs Balt., Oct. 2, 1950
  4 Joe Carter, Phil. vs Cin., Nov. 6, 1934
      Don Hutson, G.B. vs Det., Oct. 7, 1945
      Bob Shaw, L.A. vs Wash., Dec. 11, 1949
      Cloyce Box, Det. vs Balt., Dec. 3, 1950
      Elroy Hirsch, L.A. vs N.Y. Yanks, Sept. 28, 1951
      Harlon Hill, Chi. Bears vs S.F., Oct. 31, 1954
      Mike Ditka, Chi. vs L.A., Oct. 13, 1963
      Art Powell, Oak. vs Hou., Dec. 22, 1963 (AFL)
      Frank Jackson, K.C. vs S.D., Dec. 13, 1964 (AFL)
      Roy Jefferson, Pitt. vs Atl., Nov. 3, 1968
      Lance Alworth, S.D. vs Den., Dec. 1, 1968 (AFL)

Most Consecutive Games, Touchdown Passes

  11 Elroy Hirsch, L.A., 1950–51
       Gilbert (Buddy) Dial, Pitt., 1959–60
   9 Lance Alworth, S.D. 1963 (AFL)
   8 Bill Groman, Hou. 1961 (AFL)
       Dave Parks, S.F. 1965

INTERCEPTIONS BY

Most Seasons Leading League

  2 Richard (Night Train) Lane, L.A. 1952; Chi. Cards 1954
     Jack Christiansen, Det. 1953, 57
     Milt Davis, Balt. 1957, 59
     Dick Lynch, N.Y., 1961, 63
  AFL:
  1 *By many players*

Most Interceptions by, Lifetime

  79 Emlen Tunnell, N.Y. (74), 1948–58; G.B. (5) 1959–61
  68 Richard (Night Train) Lane, L.A. (17), 1952–53; Chi. Cards (30),
       1954–59; Det. (21), 1960–65

57 Bob Boyd, Balt., 1960–68
AFL:
47 *Dave Grayson, Dall./K.C. (19) 1961–64; Oak. (28) 1965–69*

Most Interceptions by, Season

14 Richard (Night Train) Lane, L.A. 1952
13 Dan Sandifer, Wash. 1948
    Orban (Spec) Sanders, N.Y. Yanks 1950
12 By five NFL players
    Fred Glick, Hou. 1963 (AFL)
    Dainard Paulson, N.Y. 1964 (AFL)

Most Interceptions by, Game

4 Sammy Baugh, Wash. vs Det., Nov. 14, 1943
   Dan Sandifer, Wash. vs Bos., Oct. 31, 1948
   Don Doll, Det. vs Chi. Cards, Oct. 23, 1949
   Bob Nussbaumer, Chi. Cards vs N.Y. Bulldogs, Nov. 13, 1949
   Russ Craft, Phil. vs Chi. Cards, Sept. 24, 1950
   Bob Dillon, G.B. vs Det., Nov. 26, 1953
   Jack Butler, Pitt. vs Wash., Dec. 13, 1953
   Austin Gonsoulin, Den. vs Buff., Sept. 18, 1960 (AFL)
   Jerry Norton, St. L. vs Wash., Nov. 20, 1960; vs Pitt., Nov. 20, 1961
   Dave Baker, S.F. vs L.A., Dec. 4, 1960
   Bobby Ply, Dall. vs S.D., Dec. 16, 1962 (AFL)
   Bobby Hunt, K.C. vs Hou., Oct. 4, 1964 (AFL)
   Willie Brown, Den. vs N.Y., Nov. 15, 1964 (AFL)

Most Consecutive Games, Passes Intercepted by

8 Tom Morrow, Oak. 1962–63 (AFL)
7 Paul Krause, Wash., 1964
   Larry Wilson, St. L., 1966
   Ben Davis, Clev. 1968
6 Richard (Night Train) Lane, Chi. Cards 1954–55
   Will Sherman, L.A. 1954–55
   Jim Shofner, Clev. 1960
   Paul Krause, Minn. 1968
   Willie Williams, N.Y. 1968
   Kermit Alexander, S.F. 1968–69

INTERCEPTION YARDAGE

Most Yards Gained, Lifetime

1,282 Emlen Tunnell, N.Y. 1948–58; G.B. 1959–61
1,207 Richard (Night Train) Lane, L.A., 1952–53; Chi. Cards, 1954–59; Det., 1960–65
  994 Bob Boyd, Balt. 1960–68
  AFL:
  908 *Dave Grayson, Dall./K.C. 1961–64; Oak. 1965–69*

Most Yards Gained, Season

349 Charley McNeil, S.D. 1961 (AFL)
301 Don Doll, Det. 1949
298 Richard (Night Train) Lane, L.A. 1952

Most Yards Gained, Game

177 Charley McNeil, S.D. vs Hou., Sept. 24, 1961 (AFL)
137 Tom Janik, Buff. vs N.Y., Sept. 29, 1968 (AFL)
128 Miller Farr, Hou. vs N.Y., Oct. 15, 1967 (AFL)
NFL:
121 *Milt Davis, Balt. vs Chi. Bears, Nov. 17, 1957*
     Mike Gaechter, Dall. vs Wash., Nov. 3, 1963

Longest Gain (all Tds)

102   Bob Smith, Det. vs Chi. Bears, Nov. 24, 1949
      Erich Barnes, N.Y. vs Dall., Oct. 22, 1961
101   Richie Petitbon, Chi. Bears vs L.A., Dec. 9, 1962
      Henry Carr, N.Y. vs L.A., Nov. 13, 1966
100   Vern Huffman, Det. vs Brk., Oct. 17, 1937
      Mike Gaechter, Dall. vs Phil., Oct. 14, 1962
      Les Duncan, S.D. vs K.C., Oct. 15, 1967 (AFL)
      Tom Janik, Buff. vs N.Y., Sept. 29, 1968 (AFL)

TOUCHDOWNS ON INTERCEPTIONS

Most Touchdowns, Lifetime

7   Herb Adderley, G.B. 1961–69
6   Erich Barnes, Chi. Bears 1958–60; N.Y. 1961–64; Clev. 1965–69
   Tom Janik, Den. 1963–64; Buff. 1965–68; Bos. 1969 (AFL)
5   By many players (NFL-AFL)

Most Touchdowns, Season

3   Dick Harris, S.D. 1961 (AFL)
   Dick Lynch, N.Y. 1963
   Herb Adderley, G.B. 1965
   Lem Barney, Det. 1967
   Miller Farr, Hou. 1967 (AFL)
2   By many players (NFL-AFL)

Most Touchdowns, Game

2   William Blackburn, Chi. Cards vs Bos., Oct. 24, 1948
   Dan Sandifer, Wash. vs Bos., Oct. 31, 1948
   Bob Franklin, Clev. vs Chi., Dec. 11, 1960
   Bill Stacy, St. L., vs Dall., Nov. 5, 1961
   Jerry Norton, St. L. vs Pitt., Nov. 26, 1961
   Miller Farr, Hou. vs Buff., Dec. 7, 1968 (AFL)

PUNTING

Most Seasons Leading League

4   Sammy Baugh, Wash., 1940–43
3   R. Yale Lary, Det., 1959, 61, 63
   Jim Fraser, Den., 1962–64 (AFL)
2   By many players (NFL–AFL)

Most Punts, Lifetime

712   Paul Maguire, L.A./S.D. 1960–63; Buff. 1964–69 (AFL)
703   Loris (Sam) Baker, Wash. 1953, 56–59; Clev. 1960–61; Dall. 1962–63; Phil. 1964–69
661   Bobby Joe Green, Pitt. 1960–61; Chi. 1962–69

Most Punts, Season

105   Bob Scarpitto, Den. 1967 (AFL)
100   Paul Maguire, Buff. 1968 (AFL)
 92   Howard Maley, Bos. 1947

Most Punts, Game

14   Sammy Baugh, Wash. vs Phil., Nov. 5, 1939
   John Kinscherf, N.Y. vs Det., Nov. 7, 1943
   George Taliaferro, N.Y. Yanks vs L.A., Sept. 28, 1951
12   Parker Hall, Clev. vs G.B., Nov. 26, 1939
   Beryl Clark, Chi. Cards vs Det., Sept. 15, 1940

Horace Gillom, Clev. vs Phil., Dec. 3, 1950
Bob Scarpitto, Den. vs Oak., Sept. 10, 1967 (AFL)
Bill Van Heusen, Den. vs Cin., Oct. 6, 1968 (AFL)

Longest Punt

98 Steve O'Neal, N.Y. vs Den., Sept. 21, 1969 (AFL)
94 Wilbur Henry, Canton vs Akron, Oct. 28, 1923
90 Don Chandler, G.B. vs S.F., Oct. 10, 1965

AVERAGE YARDAGE PUNTING

Highest Punting Average, Lifetime (300 punts)

44.93 Sammy Baugh, Wash. 1937-52
44.68 Tommy Davis, S.F. 1959-69
44.30 R. Yale Lary, Det. 1952-53, 56-64
AFL:
43.90 Jerrel Wilson, K.C. 1963-69

Highest Punting Average, Season (Qualifiers)

51.3 Sammy Baugh, Wash., 1940
48.9 R. Yale Lary, Det. 1963
48.7 Sammy Baugh, Wash. 1941
AFL:
45.4 Jerrel Wilson, K.C. 1965

Highest Punting Average, Game (4 punts)

59.4 Sammy Baugh, Wash. vs Det., Oct. 27, 1940
56.8 Sammy Baugh, Wash. vs Clev., Oct. 26, 1941
55.8 Sammy Baugh, Wash. vs Chi. Bears, Nov. 17, 1940
AFL:
55.3 Mike Mercer, Oak. vs S.D., Sept. 19, 1965

PUNT RETURNS

Most Seasons Leading League

2 Dick Christy, N.Y. 1961-62 (AFL)
Claude Gibson, Oak. 1963-64 (AFL)
Les Duncan, S.D. 1965-66 (AFL)
NFL:
1 By many players

Most Punt Returns, Lifetime

258 Emlen Tunnell, N.Y. 1948-58; G.B. 1959-61
172 Willie Wood, G.B. 1960-69
156 Alvin Haymond, Balt. 1964-67; Phil. 1968; L.A. 1969
AFL:
133 Les Duncan, S.D. 1964-69

Most Punt Returns, Season

46 Rodger Bird, Oak. 1967 (AFL)
41 Alvin Haymond, Balt. 1965
40 Alvin Haymond, Balt. 1966

Most Punt Returns, Game

9 Rodger Bird, Oak. vs Den., Sept. 10, 1967 (AFL)
8 Emlen Tunnell, N.Y. Giants vs N.Y. Yanks, Dec. 3, 1950
Joe Arenas, S.F. vs Det., Oct. 16, 1955
Hugh McElhenny, S.F. vs Det., Nov. 2, 1958
7 By many players (NFL-AFL)

FAIR CATCHES

Most Fair Catches, Season

24 Ken Graham, S.D. 1969 (AFL)
19 Charlie West, Minn. 1969
18 Abe Woodson, St. L. 1965
     Johnny Roland, St. L. 1966

Most Fair Catches, Game

5 Bill Butler, Minn. vs Balt., Nov. 17, 1963
  Tom Watkins, Det. vs L.A., Sept. 19, 1965
  Johnny Roland, St. L. vs G.B., Oct. 30, 1967
  Ken Graham, S.D. vs Cin., Oct. 4, 1969 (AFL)

YARDAGE RETURNING PUNTS

Most Yards Gained, Lifetime

2,209 Emlen Tunnell, N.Y. 1948–58; G.B. 1959–61
1,641 Les Duncan, S.D. 1964–69 (AFL)
1,547 Alvin Haymond, Balt. 1964–67; Phil. 1968; L.A. 1969

Most Yards Gained, Season

612 Rodger Bird, Oak. 1967 (AFL)
555 Bill Grimes, G.B. 1950
490 George Atkinson, Oak. 1968 (AFL)

Most Yards Gained, Game

205 George Atkinson, Oak. vs. Buff., Sept. 15, 1968 (AFL)
184 Tom Watkins, Det. vs S.F., Oct. 6, 1963
175 Jack Christiansen, Det. vs G.B., Nov. 22, 1951

Longest Punt Return (all TDs)

98 Gil LeFebvre, Cin. vs Brk., Dec. 3, 1933
    Charlie West, Minn. vs Wash., Nov. 3, 1968
96 Bill Dudley, Wash. vs Pitt., Dec. 3, 1950
95 Frank Bernardi, Chi. Cards vs Wash., Oct. 14, 1956
    Les Duncan, S.D. vs N.Y., Nov. 24, 1968 (AFL)

AVERAGE YARDAGE RETURNING PUNTS

Highest Average, Lifetime (75 returns)

12.78 George McAfee, Chi. Bears 1940–41, 45-50
12.75 Jack Christiansen, Det. 1951–58
12.55 Claude Gibson, S.D. 1961–62; Oak. 1963–65 (AFL)

Highest Average, Season (Qualifiers)

21.47 Jack Christiansen, Det. 1952
21.28 Dick Christy, N.Y. 1961 (AFL)
20.93 John Cochran, Chi. Cards 1949

Highest Average, Game (3 returns)

47.67 Charles Latourette, St. L. vs N.O., Sept. 29, 1968
47.33 Johnny Roland, St. L. vs Phil., Oct. 2, 1966
45.67 Dick Christy, N.Y. vs Den., Sept. 24, 1961 (AFL)

TOUCHDOWNS RETURNING PUNTS

Most Touchdowns, Lifetime

8 Jack Christiansen, Det. 1951 (4), 52 (2), 54, 56
5 Emlen Tunnell, N.Y. Giants 1949, 51 (3), 55

    4   Dick Christy, N.Y. 1961 (2), 62 (2) (AFL)
        Les Duncan, S.D. 1965 (2), 66, 68 (AFL)

Most Touchdowns, Season

    4   Jack Christiansen, Det. 1951
    3   Emlen Tunnell, N.Y. Giants 1951
    2   By many players (NFL–AFL)

Most Touchdowns, Game

    2   Jack Christiansen, Det. 1951: vs L.A. Oct. 14; vs G.B. Nov. 22
        Dick Christy, N.Y. vs Den., Sept. 24, 1961 (AFL)

KICKOFF RETURNS

Most Seasons Leading League

    3   Abe Woodson, S.F., 1959, 62–63
    2   Lynn Chandnois, Pitt., 1951–52
        Bobby Jancik, Hou. 1962–63 (AFL)

Most Kickoff Returns, Lifetime

    193   Abe Woodson, S.F. 1958–64; St. L. 1965–66
    191   Al Carmichael, G.B. 1953–58; AFL; Den. 1960–61
    189   Dick James, Wash. 1956–63; N.Y. 1964; Minn. 1965
    AFL:
    158   Bobby Jancik, Hou. 1962–67

Most Kickoff Returns, Season

    47   Odell Barry, Den. 1964 (AFL)
    46   Chuck Latourette, St. L. 1968
    45   Bobby Jancik, Hou. 1963 (AFL)

Most Kickoff Returns, Game

    9   Noland Smith, K.C. vs Oak., Nov. 23, 1967 (AFL)
    8   George Taliaferro, N.Y. Yanks vs N.Y. Giants, Dec. 3, 1950
        Bobby Jancik, Hou. vs Bos., Dec. 8; vs Oak., Dec. 22, 1963
        (AFL)
        Mel Renfro, Dall. vs G.B., Nov. 29, 1964
        Willie Porter, Bos. vs N.Y., Sept. 22, 1968 (AFL)
    7   By many players (NFL–AFL)

YARDAGE RETURNING KICKOFFS

Most Yards Gained, Lifetime

    5,538   Abe Woodson, S.F. 1958–64; St. L. 1965–66
    4,798   Al Carmichael, G.B. 1953–58; AFL: Den. 1960–61
    4,781   Thomas (Tim) Brown, G.B. 1959; Phil. 1960–67; Balt. 1968
    AFL:
    4,185   Bobby Jancik, Hou. 1962–67

Most Yards Gained, Season

    1,317   Bobby Jancik, Hou. 1963 (AFL)
    1,245   Odell Barry, Den. 1964 (AFL)
    1,237   Chuck Latourette, St. L. 1968

Most Yards Gained, Game

    294   Wally Triplett, Det. vs L.A., Oct. 29, 1950
    247   Thomas (Tim) Brown, Phil. vs Dall., Nov. 6, 1966
    244   Noland Smith, K.C. vs S.D., Oct. 15, 1967 (AFL)

Longest Kickoff Return (all TDs)

- 106   Al Carmichael, G.B. vs Chi. Bears, Oct. 7, 1956
  - Noland Smith, K.C. vs Den., Dec. 17, 1967 (AFL)
- 105   Frank Seno, Chi. Cards vs N.Y., Oct. 20, 1946
  - Ollie Matson, Chi. Cards vs Wash., Oct. 14, 1956
  - Abe Woodson, S.F. vs L.A., Nov. 8, 1959
  - Thomas (Tim) Brown, Phil. vs Clev., Sept. 17, 1961
  - Jon Arnett, L.A. vs Det., Oct. 29, 1961
  - Eugene Morris, Mia. vs Cin., Sept. 14, 1969 (AFL)
- 104   By many players (NFL–AFL)

AVERAGE YARDAGE RETURNING KICKOFFS

Highest Average, Lifetime (75 returns)

- 30.56   Gale Sayers, Chi. 1965–69
- 29.57   Lynn Chandnois, Pitt. 1950–56
- 28.69   Abe Woodson, S.F. 1958–64; St. L. 1965–66
- **AFL:**
- *26.49   Bobby Jancik, Hou. 1962–67*

Highest Average, Season (Qualifiers)

- 41.06   Travis Williams, G.B. 1967
- 37.69   Gale Sayers, Chi. 1967
- 35.50   Ollie Matson, Chi. Cards 1957
- **AFL:**
- *31.26   Ken Hall, Hou. 1960*

Highest Average, Game (3 returns)

- 73.50   Wally Triplett, Det. vs L.A., Oct. 29, 1950
- 67.33   Lenny Lyles, S.F. vs Balt., Dec. 18, 1960
- 65.33   Ken Hall, Hou. vs N.Y., Oct. 23, 1960 (AFL)

TOUCHDOWNS RETURNING KICKOFFS

Most Touchdowns, Lifetime

- 6   Ollie Matson, Chi. Cards 1952 (2), 54, 56, 58 (2)
  - Gale Sayers, Chi. 1965, 66 (2), 67 (3)
- 5   Bobby Mitchell, Clev. 1958, 60, 61; Wash. 1962, 63
  - Abe Woodson, S.F. 1959, 61, 63 (3)
  - Thomas (Tim) Brown, Phil. 1961, 62, 63, 66 (2)
  - Travis Williams, G.B. 1967 (4), 69
- **AFL:**
- *3   Charley Warner, Buff. 1965 (2), 66*

Most Touchdowns, Season

- 4   Travis Williams, G.B. 1967
- 3   Verda (Vitamin) Smith, L.A. 1950
  - Abe Woodson, S.F. 1963
  - Gale Sayers, Chi. 1967
- 2   By 8 NFL players
  - Leon Burton, N.Y. 1960 (AFL)
  - Charley Warner, Buff. 1965 (AFL)
  - Goldie Sellers, Den. 1966 (AFL)

Most Touchdowns, Game

- 2   Thomas (Tim) Brown, Phil. vs Dall., Nov. 6, 1966
  - Travis Williams, G.B. vs Clev., Nov. 12, 1967
- 1   By many players (NFL–AFL)

COMBINED KICK RETURNS

Most Combined Kick Returns, Lifetime

315 Abe Woodson, S.F.–St. L. 1958–66 (p-122, ko-193)
313 Al Carmichael, G.B. 1953–58; AFL: Den. 1960–61 (p-122, ko-191)
309 Dick James, Wash.–N.Y.–Minn. 1956–65 (p-120, ko-189)
AFL:
248 Les Duncan, S.D. 1964–69 (p-133, ko-115)

Most Combined Kick Returns, Season

74 Chuck Latourette, St. L. 1968 (p-28, ko-46)
73 Jerry Levias, Hou. 1969 (p-35, ko-38) (AFL)
72 Mel Renfro, Dall. 1964 (p-32, ko-40)

YARDAGE

Most Yards Gained, Lifetime

6,494 Abe Woodson, S.F.–St. L. 1958–66
5,710 Al Carmichael, G.B. 1953–58; AFL: Den. 1960–61
5,628 Dick James, Wash.–N.Y.–Minn. 1956–65
AFL:
4,832 Bobby Jancik, Hou. 1962–67

Most Yards Gained, Season

1,582 Chuck Latourette, St. L. 1968
1,462 Bobby Jancik, Hou. 1963 (AFL)
1,435 Mel Renfro, Dall. 1964

TOUCHDOWNS

Most Touchdowns, Lifetime

9 Ollie Matson, Chi. Cards–L.A.–Det.–Phil. 1952, 54–66
8 Bobby Mitchell, Clev–Wash. 1958–68
   Gale Sayers, Chi. 1965–68
7 Abe Woodson, S.F.–St. L. 1958–66
AFL:
3 Goldie Sellers, Den. 1966–67; 1968–69 K.C.

Most Touchdowns, Season

4 Emlen Tunnell, N.Y. Giants 1951
   Gale Sayers, Chi. 1967
2 By many players

Most Touchdowns, Game

2 Jim Patton, N.Y. vs Wash., Oct. 30, 1955
   Bobby Mitchell, Clev. vs Phil., Nov. 23, 1958
   Al Frazier, Den. vs Bos., Dec. 3, 1961 (AFL)
   Gale Sayers, Chi. vs S.F., Dec. 3, 1967
   Travis Williams, G.B. vs Pitt., Nov. 2, 1969

FUMBLES

Most Fumbles, Lifetime

84 John Unitas, Balt. 1956–69
80 Bobby Layne, Chi. Bears 1948; N.Y. Bulldogs 1949; Det. 1950–58; Pitt. 1958–62
78 Jack Kemp, Pitt. 1957; AFL: L.A./S.D. 1960–62; Buff. 1962–67, 69
AFL:
77 Jack Kemp, L.A./S.D. 1960–62; Buff. 1962–67, 69

Most Fumbles, Season

16   Don Meredith, Dall., 1964
15   Paul Christman, Chi. Cards 1946
     Sammy Baugh, Wash. 1947
     Sam Etcheverry, St. L. 1961
     Len Dawson, K.C. 1964 (AFL)
14   Bill Wade, L.A. 1958
     John Crow, St. L. 1962
     Tommy Mason, Minn. 1963
     Jack Kemp, Buff. 1967 (AFL)

Most Fumbles, Game

7   Len Dawson, K.C. vs S.D., Nov. 15, 1964 (AFL)
6   Sam Etcheverry, St. L. vs N.Y., Sept. 17, 1961
5   Paul Christman, Chi. Cards vs G.B., Nov. 10, 1946
    Charley Conerly, N.Y. vs S.F., Dec. 1, 1957
    Jack Kemp, Buff. vs Hou., Oct. 29, 1967 (AFL)

OWN RECOVERIES

Most Own Fumbles Recovered, Lifetime

38   Jack Kemp, Pitt. (0) 1957; AFL: L.A./S.D. 1960–62; Buff. 1962–67, 69
28   Vito (Babe) Parilli, G.B. 1952–53, 57–58; Clev. 1956; AFL: Oak. 1960; Bos. 1961–67; N.Y. 1968–69
27   Bobby Layne, Chi. Bears 1948; N.Y. Bulldogs 1949; Det. 1950–58; Pitt. 1958–62
     John Unitas, Balt. 1956–69

Most Own Fumbles Recovered, Season

8   Paul Christman, Chi. Cards 1945
   Bill Butler, Minn. 1963
7   Sammy Baugh, Wash. 1947
   Tommy Thompson, Phil. 1947
   John Roach, St. L. 1960
   Jack Larschied, Oak. 1960 (AFL)
6   By many players (NFL–AFL)

Most Own Fumbles Recovered, Game

4   Otto Graham, Clev. vs N.Y., Oct. 25, 1953
   Sam Etcheverry, St. L. vs N.Y., Sept. 17, 1961
   Roman Gabriel, L.A. vs S.F., Oct. 12, 1969
3   By many players (NFL–AFL)

OPPONENT'S RECOVERIES

Most Opponents' Fumbles Recovered, Lifetime

22   Andy Robustelli, L.A. (13), 1951–55; N.Y. (9), 1956–64
     Joe Fortunato, Chi. 1955–66
21   Ernie Stautner, Pitt., 1950–63
     Willie Davis, Clev. 1958–59; G.B. (21) 1960–69
20   Len Ford, Clev. (19), 1950–57; G.B. (1) 1958
     John Reger, Pitt. (17) 1955–63; Wash. (3) 1964–66
     Bill Koman, Balt. (2) 1956; Phil. (2) 1957–58; Chi. Cards (2) 1959; St. L. (14) 1960–67

AFL:

14   *Jim Hunt, Bos. 1960–69*

Most Opponents' Fumbles Recovered, Season

    9 Don Hultz, Minn. 1963
    8 Joe Schmidt, Det. 1955
    6 G. Barney Poole, Balt. 1953
       Gene Brito, Wash. 1955
       Dick Butkus, Chi. 1965
  AFL:
    5 *Bob Dee, Bos. 1961*
       Ron McDole, Buff. 1965

Most Opponents' Fumbles Recovered, Game

    3 Corwin Clatt, Chi. Cards vs Det., Nov. 6, 1949
       Vic Sears, Phil. vs G.B., Nov. 2, 1952
       Ed Beatty, S.F., vs L.A., Oct. 7, 1956
    2 By many players (NFL–AFL)

YARDAGE RETURNING FUMBLES

Longest Fumble Run (all TDs)

    98 George Halas, Chi. Bears vs Marion, Nov. 4, 1923
    97 Chuck Howley, Dall. vs Atl., Oct. 2, 1966
    92 Joe Carter, Phil. vs N.Y., Sept. 25, 1938
  AFL:
    75 *Fred Williamson, Oak. vs Buff., Nov. 5, 1961 (not TD)*

TOUCHDOWNS ON FUMBLES

Most Touchdowns, Lifetime

    3 Ralph Heywood, Bos. 1948 (2); N.Y. Bulldogs 1949 (2-opp,
       1-own)
       Leo Sugar, Chi. Cards 1954, 57 (2) (3-opp)
       Lewis (Bud) McFadin, L.A. 1956; AFL: Den. 1962, 63 (3-opp)
       Charles Cline, Hou. 1961 (2), 66 (3-opp) (AFL)

Most Touchdowns, Season

    2 By many players (NFL–AFL)

Most Touchdowns (Own Team's Fumbles), Lifetime

    2 Ken Kavanaugh, Chi. Bears, 1948, 50
       Mike Ditka, Chi., 1962, 64
       Gail Cogdill, Det., 1962, 64
    1 By many players (NFL–AFL)

Most Touchdowns (Own Team's Fumbles), Season

    1 By many players (NFL–AFL)

Most Touchdowns (Own Team's Fumbles), Game

    1 By many players (NFL–AFL)

Most Touchdowns (Opponents' Fumbles), Lifetime

    3 Leo Sugar, Chi. Cards 1954, 57 (2)
       Lewis (Bud) McFadin, L.A. 1956; AFL: Den. 1962, 63
       Charles Cline, Hou. 1961 (2) 66 (AFL)
    2 By many players (NFL–AFL)

Most Touchdowns (Opponents' Fumbles), Season

2   Frank Maznicki, Bos. 1947
     Fred Evans, Chi. Bears 1948
     Ralph Heywood, Bos. 1948
     Arthur Tait, N.Y. Yanks 1951
     John Dwyer, L.A. 1952
     Leo Sugar, Chi. Cards 1957
     Charles Cline Hou. 1961 (AFL)
     Jim Bradshaw, Pitt., 1964

Most Touchdowns, (Opponents' Fumbles), Game

2   Fred Evans, Chi. Bears vs Wash., Nov. 28, 1948
1   By many players (NFL–AFL)

COMBINED NET YARDS GAINED

(Includes Rushes, Pass Receptions and Runback of Pass Interceptions, Punts, Kickoffs and Fumbles)

ATTEMPTS—COMBINED

Most Attempts, Lifetime

2,658   Jim Brown, Clev., 1957–65
2,180   Jim Taylor, G.B., 1958–66; N.O. 1967
2,008   Fletcher (Joe) Perry, S.F., 1950–60; 63; Balt., 1961–62
    AFL:
1,532   Abner Haynes, Dall./K.C. 1960–64; Den. 1965–66; Mia. 1967; N.Y. 1967

Most Attempts, Season

354   Jim Brown, Clev. 1961
323   Jim Brown, Clev. 1965
319   Jim Brown, Clev. 1959
   AFL:
307   Jim Nance, Bos. 1966

Most Attempts, Game

39   Jim Brown, Clev. vs Chi. Cards, Oct. 4, 1959
38   Harry Newman, N.Y. vs G.B., Nov. 11, 1934
    Jim Brown, Clev. vs. Phil., Nov. 19, 1961
    Floyd Little, Den. vs Bos., Nov. 3, 1968 (AFL)
37   Jim Brown, Clev. vs Chi. Cards, Oct. 12, 1958

YARDAGE—COMBINED ATTEMPTS

Most Yards Gained, Lifetime

15,459   Jim Brown, Clev. 1957–65
14,078   Bobby Mitchell, Clev. 1958–61; Wash. 1962–68
12,844   Ollie Matson, Chi. Cards 1952, 54–58; L.A. 1959–62; Det. 1963; Phil. 1964–66
    AFL:
12,065   Abner Haynes, Dall./K.C. 1960–64; Den. 1965–66; Mia. 1967; N.Y. 1967

Most Yards Gained, Season

2,440   Gale Sayers, Chi., 1966
2,428   Thomas (Tim) Brown, Phil., 1963
2,306   Thomas (Tim) Brown, Phil., 1962
    AFL:
2,147   Dick Christy, N.Y. 1962

Most Yards Gained, Game (two or more categories)

373 Billy Cannon, Hou. vs N.Y., Dec. 10, 1961 (AFL)
341 Thomas (Tim) Brown, Phil. vs St. L., Dec. 16, 1962
339 Gale Sayers, Chi. vs Minn., Dec. 18, 1966

AVERAGE GAIN—COMBINED ATTEMPTS

Highest Average Gain, Lifetime

11.62 Bobby Mitchell, Clev. 1958–61; Wash. 1962–68 (1,212–14,078)
9.98 Dick James, Wash. 1956–63; N.Y. 1964; Minn. 1965 (939–9,369)
9.08 Thomas (Tim) Brown, G.B. 1959; Phil. 1960–67; Balt. 1968 (1,397–12,684)
  AFL:
8,62 *Billy Cannon, Hou. 1960–63; Oak. 1964–69 (912–7, 862)*

Highest Average Gain, Season (150 att.)

11.92 Bill Grimes, G.B., 1950 (159–1,896)
10.69 Hugh McElhenny, S.F., 1952 (162–1,731)
10.30 Dick James, Wash., 1963 (170–1,751)
  AFL:
9.80 *Paul Lowe, S.D. 1960 (188–1,843)*

Highest Average Gain, Game (two or more categories—15 attempts)

19.76 Gale Sayers, Chi. vs S.F., Dec. 12, 1965 (17–336)
18.28 Jerry Levias, Hou. vs N.Y., Dec. 6, 1969 (18–329) (AFL)
17.95 Thomas (Tim) Brown, Phil. vs St. L., Dec. 16, 1962 (19–341)

MISCELLANEOUS

SCORING

Most Drop Kick Field Goals, Game

4 John (Paddy) Driscoll, Chi. Cards vs Columbus, Oct. 11, 1925 (23, 18, 50, 35 yds)
  Elbert Bloodgood, Kansas City vs Duluth, Dec. 12, 1926 (35, 32, 20, 25 yds)

Longest Drop Kick Field Goal

50 Wilbur (Fats) Henry, Canton vs Toledo, Nov. 13, 1922
  John (Paddy) Driscoll, Chi. Cards vs Milwaukee, Sept. 28, 1924; vs Columbus, Oct. 11, 1925

RUNNING

Most Yards Returned Missed Field Goal

100 Al Nelson, Phil. vs Clev., Dec. 11, 1966 (td)
99 Jerry Williams, L.A. vs G.B., Dec. 16, 1951 (td)
  Carl Taseff, Balt. vs L.A., Dec. 12, 1959 (td)
  Thomas (Tim) Brown, Phil. vs St. L., Sept. 16, 1962 (td)

TEAM RECORDS—OFFENSE
CHAMPIONSHIPS

Most Seasons League Champion

11 Green Bay 1929–31, 36, 39, 44, 61–62, 65–67
 8 Chicago Bears 1921, 32–33, 40–41, 43, 46, 63
 4 New York 1927, 34, 38, 56
  Detroit 1935, 52–53, 57
  Cleveland 1950, 54–55, 64
  AFL:
 3 *Dall./K.C. 1962, 66, 69*

Most Consecutive Seasons League Champion

    3   Green Bay 1929–31; 1965–67
    2   Canton 1922–23
        Chicago Bears 1932–33; 1940–41
        Philadelphia 1948–49
        Detroit 1952–53
        Cleveland 1954–55
        Baltimore 1958–59
        Houston 1960–61 (AFL)
        Green Bay 1961–62
        Buffalo 1964–65 (AFL)

Most Seasons Leading Conference (Since 1933)

    14 New York 1933–35, 38–39, 41, 44, 46, 56, 58–59, 61–63
    11 Cleveland 1950–55, 57, 64–65, 68–69
    10 Chicago Bears 1933–34, 37, 40–43, 46, 56, 63
        Green Bay 1936, 38–39, 44, 60–62, 65–67
AFL:
    5   L.A./S.D. 1960–61, 63–65

Most Consecutive Seasons Leading Conference

    6   Cleveland 1950–55
    4   Chicago Bears 1940–43
    3   New York 1933–35; 61–63
        Philadelphia 1947–49
        Los Angeles 1949–51
        Detroit 1952–54
        Green Bay 1960–62; 65–67
        Houston 1960–62 (AFL)
        San Diego 1963–65 (AFL)
        Buffalo 1964–66 (AFL)
        Oakland 1967–69 (AFL)

GAMES

Most Consecutive Games Without Defeat (Regular Season)

    24 Canton 1922–23 (Won-21 Tied-3)
        Chicago Bears 1941–43 (Won-23 Tied-1)
    23 Green Bay 1928–30 (Won-21 Tied-2)
AFL:
    15 L.A./S.D. 1960–61
        Oakland 1968–69

Most Consecutive Victories (All Games)

    18 Chicago Bears (1933–34; 1941–42)

Most Consecutive Victories (Regular Season)

    17 Chicago Bears 1933–34
    16 Chicago Bears 1941–42
    15 L.A./S.D. 1960–61 (AFL)

Most Consecutive Shutout Games Won
    7   Detroit 1934

SCORING

Most Seasons Leading League

    9   Chicago Bears 1934–35, 39, 41–43, 46–47, 56
    6   Green Bay 1932, 36–38, 61–62
    5   Los Angeles 1950–52, 57, 67
AFL:
    3   Oakland 1967–69

Most Points, Season

513   Houston 1961 (AFL)
468   Oakland 1967 (AFL)
466   Los Angeles 1950

Most Points, Game

72   Washington vs. N.Y., Nov. 27, 1966
70   Los Angeles vs. Balt., Oct. 22, 1950
65   Chicago Cards vs. N.Y. Bulldogs, Nov. 13, 1949
     Los Angeles vs. Det., Oct. 29, 1950
AFL:
59   Kansas City vs Den., Sept. 7, 1963

Most Points, Both Teams, Game

113   Washington (72) vs N.Y. (41), Nov. 27, 1966
101   Oakland (52) vs Hou. (49), Dec. 22, 1963 (AFL)
98   Chicago Cards (63) vs N.Y. (35), Oct. 17, 1948

Most Points, One Quarter

41   Green Bay vs Det. (2d Q), Oct. 7, 1945
     Los Angeles vs Det. (3d Q), Oct. 29, 1950
35   Chicago Cards vs Bos. (3d Q), Oct. 24, 1948
     Green Bay vs Clev. (1st Q), Nov. 12, 1967
31   Chicago Cards vs N.Y. Bulldogs (2d Q), Nov. 13, 1949
     Oakland vs Den. (4th Q), Dec. 17, 1960 (AFL)
     Oakland vs S.D. (4th Q), Dec. 8, 1963 (AFL)
     Buffalo vs K.C. (1st Q), Sept. 13, 1964 (AFL)

Most Points, Both Teams, One Quarter

49   Oakland (28) vs Hou. (21), Dec. 22, 1963 (2Q) (AFL)
48   Green Bay (41) vs Det. (7), Oct. 7, 1945 (2Q)
     Los Angeles (41) vs Det. (7), Oct. 29, 1950 (3Q)
47   St. Louis (27) vs Phil. (20), Dec. 13, 1964 (2Q)

Most Points, Each Quarter

1st: 35   Green Bay vs Clev., Nov. 12, 1967
     31   Buffalo vs K.C., Sept. 13, 1964 (AFL)
2nd: 41   Green Bay vs Det., Oct. 7, 1945
     28   By 8 AFL teams. Last:
          Oakland vs Buffalo, Oct. 19, 1969
3rd: 41   Los Angeles vs Det., Oct. 29, 1950
     28   San Diego vs N.Y., Nov. 5, 1961 (AFL)
          Houston vs K.C., Oct. 24, 1965 (AFL)
4th: 31   Oakland vs Den., Dec. 17, 1960; vs S.D., Dec. 8, 1963 (AFL)
     28   By 11 NFL teams. Last:
          St. Louis vs Pitt., Nov. 30, 1969

Most Points, Both Teams, Each Quarter

1st: 42   Green Bay (35) vs Clev. (7), Nov. 12, 1967
     35   Dallas (21) vs N.Y. (14), Nov. 11, 1962 (AFL)
2nd: 49   Oakland (28) vs Hou. (21), Dec. 22, 1963 (AFL)
     48   Green Bay (41) vs Det. (7), Oct. 7, 1945
3rd: 48   Los Angeles (41) vs Det. (7), Oct. 29, 1950
     32   Los Angeles (17) vs N.Y. (15), Dec. 18, 1960 (AFL)
4th: 42   Chicago Cards (28) vs Phil. (14), Dec. 7, 1947
          Green Bay (28) vs Chicago Bears (14), Nov. 6, 1955
          New York (28) vs Bos. (14), Oct. 27, 1968 (AFL)
          Pittsburgh (21) vs Clev. (21), Oct. 18, 1969

Most Consecutive Games Scoring

255   Cleveland 1950–69 (current)
156   Green Bay 1958–69 (current)
145   Chicago Bears 1946–58
AFL:
105   San Diego 1962–69 (current)

Most Touchdowns, Season

66   Houston 1961 (AFL)
64   Los Angeles 1950
58   Oakland 1967 (AFL)

Most Touchdowns, Game

10   Philadelphia vs Cin., Nov. 6, 1934
     Los Angeles vs Balt., Oct. 22, 1950
     Washington vs N.Y., Nov. 27, 1966
 9   Chicago Cards vs Roch., Oct. 7, 1923
     Chicago Cards vs N.Y., Oct. 17, 1948
     Chicago Cards vs N.Y. Bulldogs, Nov. 13, 1949
     Los Angeles vs Det., Oct. 29, 1950
     Pittsburgh vs N.Y., Nov. 30, 1952
     Chicago vs S.F., Dec. 12, 1965
AFL:
*8   Houston vs N.Y., Oct. 14, 1962
     Kansas City vs Den., Sept. 7, 1963 & Oct. 23, 1966
     Buffalo vs Mia., Sept. 18, 1966*

Most Touchdowns, Both Teams, Game

16   Washington (10) vs N.Y. (6), Nov. 27, 1966
14   Chicago Cards (9) vs N.Y. (5), Oct. 17, 1948
     Los Angeles (10) vs Balt. (4), Oct. 22, 1950
     Houston (7) vs Oakland (7), Dec. 22, 1963 (AFL)
13   New Orleans (7) vs St. L. (6), Nov. 2, 1969

Most Points After Touchdown, Season (Kicking)

65   Houston 1961 (AFL)
59   Los Angeles 1950
56   Dallas 1966
     Oakland 1967 (AFL)

Most Points After Touchdown, Game

10   Los Angeles vs Balt., Oct. 22, 1950
 9   Chicago Cards vs N.Y., Oct. 17, 1948
     Pittsburgh vs N.Y., Nov. 30, 1952
     Washington vs N.Y., Nov. 27, 1966
AFL:
*8   Houston vs N.Y., Oct. 14, 1962
     Kansas City vs Den., Sept. 7, 1963 & Oct. 23, 1966*

Most Points After Touchdown, Both Teams, Game

14   Chicago Cards (9) vs N.Y. (5), Oct. 17, 1948
     Houston (7) vs Oak. (7), Dec. 22, 1963 (AFL)
     Washington (9) vs N.Y. (5), Nov. 27, 1966
13   Los Angeles (10) vs Balt. (3), Oct. 22, 1950
12   Many NFL games

Most Field Goals Attempted, Season

49   Los Angeles 1966
47   New York 1969 (AFL)
46   Buffalo 1965 (AFL)
     New York 1968 (AFL)

Most Field Goals Attempted, Game

  9 St. Louis vs Pitt., Sept. 24, 1967
  8 Pittsburgh vs St. L., Dec. 2, 1962
     Detroit vs Minn., Nov. 13, 1966
     New York vs Buff., Nov. 3, 1968 (AFL)
  7 By many teams (NFL-AFL)

Most Field Goals Attempted, Both Teams, Game

  11 St. Louis (6) vs Pitt. (5), Nov. 13, 1966
  10 Denver (5) vs Bos. (5), Nov. 11, 1962 (AFL)
      Boston (7) vs S.D. (3), Sept. 20, 1964 (AFL)
      Buffalo (7) vs Hou. (3), Dec. 5, 1965 (AFL)
      St. Louis (7) vs Atl. (3), Dec. 11, 1966
      Boston (7) vs Buff. (3), Sept. 24, 1967 (AFL)
   9 Many games (NFL-AFL)

Most Field Goals, Season

  34 New York 1968 (AFL)
  32 New York 1969 (AFL)
  30 Kansas City 1968 (AFL)
  NFL:
  28 Los Angeles 1966

Most Field Goals, Game

  7 St. Louis vs Pitt., Sept. 24, 1967
  6 Boston vs Den., Oct. 4, 1964 (AFL)
     Detroit vs Minn., Nov. 13, 1966
     New York vs Buff., Nov. 3, 1968 (AFL)
  5 By many teams (NFL-AFL)

Most Field Goals, Both Teams, Game

  8 Cleveland (4) vs St. L. (4), Sept. 20, 1964
     Chicago (5) vs Phil. (3), Oct. 20, 1968
  7 Denver (4) vs L.A. (3), Oct. 16, 1960 (AFL)
     Boston (4) vs Den. (3), Nov. 11, 1962 (AFL)
     Boston (6) vs Den. (1), Oct. 4, 1964 (AFL)
     Detroit (6) vs Minn. (1), Nov. 13, 1966
     Baltimore (4) vs S.F. (3), Nov. 26, 1967
     Kansas City (5) vs Buff. (2), Dec. 7, 1969 (AFL)
  6 Many games (NFL-AFL)

Most Consecutive Games Scoring Field Goals

  19 St. Louis 1966–67
      Los Angeles 1967–68
      Minnesota 1968–69 (current)
  18 New York 1966–67 (AFL)
  16 Minnesota 1967–68
      New Orleans 1968–69

FIRST DOWNS

Most Seasons Leading League

  7 Chicago Bears 1935, 41, 43, 45, 48–49, 55
  6 Green Bay 1939–40, 42, 44, 60, 62
  5 Los Angeles 1946, 50–51, 54, 57
  AFL:
  2 New York 1960, 67
  *   Houston 1961, 64*
  *   San Diego 1965, 69*

Most First Downs, Season

297 Dallas 1968
293 Houston 1961 (AFL)
292 San Francisco 1965

Fewest First Downs, Season

64 Pittsburgh 1935
68 Philadelphia 1937
75 Pittsburgh 1941
AFL:
159 Buffalo 1968

Most First Downs, Game

38 Los Angeles vs N.Y., Nov. 13, 1966
37 Green Bay vs Phil., Nov. 11, 1962
35 Pittsburgh vs Chi. Cards, Dec. 13, 1958
AFL:
33 Oakland vs Cin., Nov. 24, 1968

Fewest First Downs, Game

0 Hammond vs Canton, Sept. 30, 1923
Racine vs Chi. Cards, Oct. 3, 1926
New York vs G.B., Oct. 1, 1933
Pittsburgh vs Bos., Oct. 29, 1933
Philadelphia vs Det., Sept. 20, 1935
New York vs Wash., Sept. 27, 1942
Denver vs Hou., Sept. 3, 1966 (AFL)

Most First Downs, Both Teams, Game

58 Los Angeles (30) vs Chi. Bears (28), Oct. 24, 1954
57 Los Angeles (32) vs N.Y. Yanks (25), Nov. 19, 1950
54 New York (31) vs Pitt. (23), Dec. 5, 1948
Dallas (31) vs S.F. (23), Nov. 10, 1963
Washington (30) vs S.F. (24), Nov. 12, 1967
AFL:
53 Los Angeles (31) vs Oak. (22), Nov. 27, 1960
Kansas City (32) vs Buff. (21), Oct. 24, 1965

Fewest First Downs, Both Teams, Game

5 New York (0) vs G.B. (5), Oct. 1, 1933
AFL:
15 Boston (7) vs Mia. (8), Nov. 9, 1969

Most First Downs, Rushing, Season

145 Green Bay 1962
143 Philadelphia 1949
142 Philadelphia 1950
Green Bay 1961
AFL:
129 Kansas City 1969

Fewest First Downs, Rushing, Season

36 Cleveland Rams 1942
Boston 1944
39 Brooklyn 1943
40 Detroit 1945
AFL:
52 New York 1963

Most First Downs, Rushing, Game

    25   Philadelphia vs Wash., Dec. 2, 1951
    21   Cleveland vs Phil., Dec. 13, 1959
    AFL:
    20   Dallas vs Hou., Oct. 1, 1961

Fewest First Downs, Rushing, Game

    0   By many teams (NFL–AFL)

Most First Downs, Passing, Season

   186   Houston 1964 (AFL)
          Oakland 1964 (AFL)
   182   Houston 1961 (AFL)
   180   New York 1967 (AFL)
   NFL:
   177   Washington 1967

Fewest First Downs, Passing, Season

    18   Pittsburgh 1941
   – 23   Brooklyn 1942
         New York 1944
    24   New York 1943
   AFL:
   72   Buffalo 1968

Most First Downs, Passing, Game

    24   Houston vs Buff., Nov. 1, 1964 (AFL)
         Minnesota vs Balt., Sept. 28, 1969
    23   Dallas vs S.F., Nov. 10, 1963
         Denver vs Hou., Dec. 20, 1964 (AFL)
    22   New York vs Pitt., Dec. 5, 1948; vs St. L., Dec. 7, 1969
         St. Louis vs Phil., Dec. 13, 1964
         Washington vs Clev., Nov. 26, 1967

Fewest First Downs, Passing, Game

    0   By many teams (NFL–AFL)

Most First Downs, Penalty, Season

    32   Chicago 1963
    31   New Orleans 1969
    30   Chicago Cards 1947
   AFL:
   29   Boston 1965

Fewest First Downs, Penalty, Season

    4   New York 1942, 44
        Washington 1944
        Cleveland 1952
        Kansas City 1969 (AFL)
    5   Detroit 1953
        Los Angeles 1953
    6   By many teams (NFL)

Most First Downs, Penalty, Game

    9   Chicago Bears vs Clev., Nov. 25, 1951
    7   Boston vs Hou., Sept. 19, 1965 (AFL)
        Baltimore vs Det., Nov. 19, 1967
        Oakland vs Bos., Oct. 6, 1968 (AFL)
    6   By many teams (NFL-AFL)

Fewest First Downs, Penalty, Game

    0   By many teams (NFL–AFL)

NET YARDS GAINED

(RUSHES AND PASSES)

Most Seasons Leading League

12	Chicago Bears 1932, 34–35, 39, 41–44, 47, 49, 55–56
5	Los Angeles 1946, 50–51, 54, 57
	Baltimore 1958–60, 64, 67
3	Green Bay 1937–38, 40
	Houston 1960–62 (AFL)
	Dallas 1966, 68–69

Most Yards Gained, Season

6,288	Houston 1961 (AFL)
5,696	Oakland 1968 (AFL)
5,506	Los Angeles 1951

Fewest Yards Gained, Season

1,113	Cincinnati 1933
1,337	Chicago Cards 1933
1,481	Brooklyn 1934
AFL:	
2,870	*Buffalo 1968*

Most Yards Gained, Game

735	Los Angeles vs N.Y. Yanks, Sept. 28, 1951
683	Pittsburgh vs Chi. Cards, Dec. 13, 1958
682	Chicago Bears vs N.Y., Nov. 14, 1943
AFL:	
626	*Oakland vs Den., Oct. 25, 1964*

Fewest Yards Gained, Game

−5	Denver vs Oak., Sept. 10, 1967 (AFL)
14	Chi. Cards vs. Det., Sept. 15, 1940
16	Detroit vs Chi. Cards, Sept. 15, 1940

Most Yards Gained, Both Teams, Game

1,133	Los Angeles (636) vs N.Y. Yanks (497), Nov. 19, 1950
1,087	Philadelphia (498) vs St. L. (589), Dec. 16, 1962
AFL:	
1,057	*San Diego (581) vs Den. (476), Oct. 20, 1968*

Fewest Yards Gained, Both Teams, Game

30	Chi. Cards (14) vs Detroit (16), Sept. 15, 1940
AFL:	
262	*Denver (102) vs Oak. (160), Nov. 20, 1966*

RUSHING

Most Seasons Leading League

11	Chicago Bears 1932, 34–35, 39–42, 51, 55–56, 68
6	Cleveland 1958–59, 63, 65–67
4	Detroit 1934, 36–38
	Green Bay 1946, 61–62, 64
	Dall./K.C. 1961, 66, 68–69 (AFL)

Most Rushing Attempts, Season

632 Philadelphia 1949
581 Philadelphia 1950
578 Pittsburgh 1963
AFL:
537 Kansas City 1968

Fewest Rushing Attempts, Season

274 Detroit 1946
294 Detroit 1943
306 New York 1963 (AFL)

Most Rushing Attempts, Game

72 Chicago Bears vs Brk., Oct. 20,1935
70 Chicago Cards vs G.B., Dec. 5, 1948
69 Chicago Cards vs G.B., Dec. 6, 1936
AFL:
60 Kansas City vs Oak., Oct. 20, 1968

Fewest Rushing Attempts, Game

6 Chicago Cards vs Bos., Oct. 29, 1933
7 Oakland vs Buff., Oct. 15, 1963 (AFL)
8 Denver vs Oak., Dec. 17, 1960 (AFL)

Most Rushing Attempts, Both Teams, Game

108 Chicago Cards (70) vs G.B. (38), Dec. 5, 1948
102 Green Bay (51) vs Pitt. (51), Nov. 20, 1949
101 Chicago Cards (69) vs G.B. (32), Dec. 6, 1936
AFL:
83 Kansas City (48) vs Oak. (35), Dec. 13, 1969

Fewest Rushing Attempts, Both Teams, Game

34 Cincinnati (16) vs Chi. Bears (18), Sept. 30, 1934
38 New York (13) vs Buff. (25), Nov. 8, 1964 (AFL)
39 Denver (16) vs N.Y. (23), Sept. 24, 1961 (AFL)
 Denver (14) vs Bos. (25), Sept. 21, 1962 (AFL)
 Denver (14) vs Hou. (25), Dec. 2, 1962 (AFL)

Most Yards Gained Rushing, Season

2,885 Detroit 1936
2,835 Chicago Bears 1934
2,763 Detroit 1934
AFL:
2,480 Buffalo 1962

Fewest Yards Gained Rushing, Season

298 Philadelphia 1940
471 Boston 1944
472 Detroit 1946
AFL:
978 New York 1963

Most Yards Gained Rushing, Game

426 Detroit vs Pitt., Nov. 4, 1934
423 New York Giants vs Balt., Nov. 19, 1950
408 Chicago Bears vs Brk., Oct. 20, 1935
AFL:
398 Dallas vs Hou., Oct. 1, 1961

Fewest Yards Gained Rushing, Game

- —36 Philadelphia vs Chi. Bears, Nov. 19, 1939
- —33 Phil/Pitt vs Brk., Oct. 2, 1943
- —29 Cleveland Rams vs Wash., Oct. 11, 1942
  AFL:
- 0 *Kansas City vs Den., Dec. 19, 1965*

Most Yards Gained Rushing, Both Teams, Game

- 595 L.A. (371) vs N.Y. Yanks (224), Nov. 18, 1951
- 574 Pitt. (178) vs Chi. Bears (396), Oct. 10, 1934
- 557 Chi. Bears (406) vs G.B. (151), Nov. 6, 1955
  AFL:
- 502 *Dallas (398) vs Hou. (104), Oct. 1, 1961*

Fewest Yards Gained Rushing, Both Teams, Game

- 4 Detroit (—10) vs Chi. Cards (14), Sept. 15, 1940
- 16 Detroit (—22) vs Phil. (38), Oct. 17, 1943
- 63 Chicago Cards (–1) vs N.Y. (64), Oct. 18, 1953
  AFL:
- 90 *Boston (28) vs Buff. (62), Nov. 7, 1965*

Highest Average Gain Rushing, Season

- 5.7 Cleveland 1963
- 5.6 San Diego 1963 (AFL)
- 5.3 Cleveland 1958

Most Touchdowns Rushing, Season

- 36 Green Bay 1962
- 31 Chicago Bears 1941
- 29 Green Bay 1960
  Baltimore 1964
  AFL:
- 25 *Buffalo 1964*

Most Touchdowns Rushing, Game

- 6 By many teams. Last:
  Green Bay vs Phil., Nov. 11, 1962
  New York vs Bos., Oct. 27, 1968 (AFL)

Most Touchdowns Rushing, Both Teams, Game

- 8 Los Angeles (6) vs N.Y. Yanks (2), Nov. 18, 1951
  Cleveland (6) vs L.A. (2), Nov. 24, 1957
  AFL:
- 7 *Dallas (4) vs Bos. (3), Sept. 8, 1962*
  Kansas City (4) vs Den. (3), Oct. 10, 1965

PASSING

Most Seasons Leading League

- 9 Washington 1937, 39–40, 42–45, 47, 67
- 8 New York 1932, 34–35, 38, 48, 59, 62–63
- 5 Los Angeles 1946, 49–51, 54
  Green Bay 1931, 36, 41, 52, 66
  AFL:
- 4 *Houston 1960–61, 63–64*

Most Passes Attempted, Season

- 592 Houston 1964 (AFL)
- 568 Denver 1961 (AFL)

559   Denver 1962 (AFL)
  NFL:
527   Washington 1967

Fewest Passes Attempted, Season

120   Detroit 1937
125   New York 1944
127   Chicago Cards 1935
  AFL:
270   Kansas City 1968

Most Passes Attempted, Game

68   Houston vs Buff., Nov. 1, 1964 (AFL)
62   New York vs Den., Dec. 3, 1967 (AFL)
61   Houston vs Oak., Nov. 7, 1965 (AFL)
  NFL:
60   Philadelphia vs Wash., Dec. 1, 1940

Fewest Passes Attempted, Game

  0   Green Bay vs Port., Oct. 8, 1933
        Detroit vs Clev. Rams, Sept. 10, 1937
        Pittsburgh vs Brk., Nov. 16, 1941
        Green Bay vs Chi. Bears, Sept. 25, 1949
        Pittsburgh vs L.A., Nov. 13, 1949
        Cleveland vs Phil., Dec. 3, 1950

  AFL:
3   Kansas City vs Oak., Oct. 20, 1968

Most Passes Attempted, Both Teams, Game

98   Minnesota (56) vs Balt. (42), Sept. 28, 1969
97   Denver (53) vs Hou. (44), Dec. 2, 1962 (AFL)
95   Los Angeles (48) vs Chi. (47), Oct. 11, 1964

Fewest Passes Attempted, Both Teams, Game

  4   Chicago Cards (1) vs Det. (3), Nov. 3, 1935
  6   Chicago Cards (2) vs Det. (4), Sept. 15, 1940
  8   Brooklyn (2) vs Phil. (6), Oct. 1, 1939
  AFL:
19   Boston (9) vs Mia. (10), Nov. 9, 1969

Most Passes Completed, Season

301   Washington 1967
299   Houston 1964 (AFL)
292   Denver 1962 (AFL)

Fewest Passes Completed, Season

34   Chicago Cards 1934
        Detroit 1934
39   Boston 1934
        Philadelphia 1936
  AFL:
143   Houston 1967

Most Passes Completed, Game

37   Houston vs Buff., Nov. 1, 1964 (AFL)
36   New York vs Pitt., Dec. 5, 1948
        Minnesota vs Balt., Sept. 28, 1969
35   Denver vs Hou., Dec. 20, 1964 (AFL)

Most Passes Completed, Both Teams, Game

56   Minnesota (36) vs Balt. (20), Sept. 28, 1969
55   Chicago Bears (30) vs S.F. (25), Nov. 1, 1953
53   Denver (35) vs Hou. (18), Dec. 20, 1964 (AFL)

Fewest Passes Completed, Both Teams, Game

1   Detroit vs Clev. Rams (1), Sept. 10, 1937
    Chicago Cards vs Det. (1), Sept. 15, 1940
2   Chi. Cards vs Det. (2), Nov. 3, 1935
AFL:
9   *Boston (2) vs Mia. (7), Nov. 9, 1969*

Most Seasons Leading League, Passing Yardage

8   Chicago Bears 1932, 39, 41, 43, 45, 49, 54, 64
6   Washington 1938, 40, 44, 47–48, 67
5   Green Bay 1934–37, 42
AFL:
4   *Houston 1960–61, 63–64*

Most Yards Gained Passing, Season

4,392   Houston 1961 (AFL)
3,845   New York 1967 (AFL)
3,730   Washington 1967

Fewest Yards Gained Passing, Season

577   Brooklyn 1934
652   Pittsburgh 1945
654   Pittsburgh 1941
   AFL:
1,343   *Buffalo 1968*

Most Yards Gained Passing, Game

554   Los Angeles vs N.Y. Yanks, Sept. 28, 1951
530   Minnesota vs Balt., Sept. 28, 1969
505   New York vs Wash., Oct. 28, 1962
  AFL:
469   *Oakland vs K.C., Nov. 3, 1968*

Fewest Yards Gained Passing, Game

−53   Denver vs Oak., Sept. 10, 1967 (AFL)
−32   Washington vs Pitt., Nov. 27, 1955
−28   Washington vs Pitt., Dec. 7, 1958

Most Yards Gained Passing, Both Teams, Game

851   New York (505) vs Wash. (346), Oct. 28, 1962
834   Philadelphia (419) vs St. L. (415), Dec. 16, 1962
753   Dallas (406) vs Wash. (347), Nov. 13, 1966
  AFL:
733   *Oakland (378) vs Buff. (355), Sept. 15, 1963*

Fewest Yards Gained Passing, Both Teams, Game

−11   Green Bay (−10) vs Dall. (−1), Oct. 24, 1965
1   Chicago Cards vs Phil. (1), Nov. 8, 1936
7   Brooklyn vs Pitt. (7), Nov. 29, 1942
AFL:
91   *Boston (28) vs Mia. (63), Nov. 9, 1969*

Most Times Tackled Attempting Passes, Season

    70 Atlanta 1968
    68 Dallas 1964
    66 Pittsburgh 1966
AFL:
    63 *Buffalo 1961*

Fewest Times Tackled Attempting Passes, Season

     9 New York 1966 (AFL)
    11 Houston 1962 (AFL)
        San Diego 1967 (AFL)
    12 Oakland 1969 (AFL)
NFL:
    17 *Los Angeles 1969*

Most Times Tackled Attempting Passes, Game

    12 Pittsburgh vs Dall., Nov. 20, 1966
    11 St. Louis vs N.Y., Nov. 1, 1964
        Los Angeles vs Balt., Nov. 22, 1964
        Denver vs Buff., Dec. 13, 1964 (AFL)
        Green Bay vs Det., Nov. 7, 1965
        Buffalo vs Oak., Oct. 15, 1967 (AFL)
        Denver vs Oak., Nov. 5, 1967 (AFL)
        Atlanta vs St. L., Nov. 24, 1968
    10 By many teams (NFL-AFL)

Most Times Tackled Attempting Passes, Both Teams, Game

    17 Buffalo (10) vs N.Y. (7), Nov. 23, 1961 (AFL)
        Pittsburgh (12) vs Dall. (5), Nov. 20, 1966
    16 Los Angeles (11) vs Balt. (5), Nov. 22, 1964
        Buffalo (11) vs Oak. (5), Oct. 15, 1967 (AFL)
    15 Denver (11) vs Buff. (4), Dec. 13, 1964 (AFL)

Most Seasons Leading League (Completion Pct.)

    10 Washington 1937, 39–40, 42–45, 47–48, 69
     8 Green Bay 1931, 36, 41, 61–62, 64, 66, 68
     6 Cleveland 1951, 53–55, 59–60
        Dall./K.C. 1962, 64, 66, 69 (AFL)

Most Touchdowns Passing, Season

    48 Houston 1961 (AFL)
    39 New York 1963
    36 Oakland 1969 (AFL)

Fewest Touchdowns Passing, Season

     0 Pittsburgh 1945
     1 Detroit 1942
     2 Chicago Cards 1935
        Brooklyn 1936
        Pittsburgh 1942
AFL:
     7 *Buffalo 1968*

Most Touchdowns Passing, Game

- 7   Chicago Bears vs N.Y., Nov. 14, 1943
  Philadelphia vs Wash., Oct. 17, 1954
  Houston vs N.Y., Nov. 19, 1961 & Oct. 14, 1962 (AFL)
  New York vs Wash., Oct. 28, 1962
  Minnesota vs Balt., Sept. 28, 1969
- 6   By many teams (NFL-AFL)

Most Touchdowns Passing, Both Teams, Game

- 12   New Orleans (6) vs St. L. (6), Nov. 2, 1969
- 11   New York (7) vs Wash. (4), Oct. 28, 1962
  Oakland (6) vs Hou. (5), Dec. 22, 1963 (AFL)
- 10   Chicago Bears (6) vs Chi. Cards (4), Dec. 5, 1937

Most Passes Had Intercepted, Season

- 48   Houston 1962 (AFL)
- 45   Denver 1961 (AFL)
- 41   Card/Pitt 1944

Fewest Passes Had Intercepted, Season

- 5   Cleveland 1960
  Green Bay 1966
- 6   Green Bay 1964
- 7   Los Angeles 1969

AFL:

- *11   Cincinnati 1968*
  Kansas City 1968

Most Passes Had Intercepted, Game

- 9   Detroit vs G.B., Oct. 24, 1943
  Pittsburgh vs Phil., Dec. 12, 1965
- 8   Green Bay vs N.Y., Nov. 21, 1948
  Chicago Cards vs Phil., Sept. 24, 1950
  New York Yanks vs N.Y. Giants, Dec. 16, 1951
  Denver vs Hou., Dec. 2, 1962 (AFL)
  Chicago Bears vs Det., Sept. 22, 1968
- 7   By many teams (NFL-AFL)

Most Passes Had Intercepted, Both Teams, Game

- 13   Denver (8) vs Hou. (5), Dec. 2, 1962 (AFL)
- 11   Philadelphia (7) vs Bos. (4), Nov. 3, 1935
  Boston (6) vs Pitt. (5), Dec. 1, 1935
  Cleveland (7) vs G.B. (4), Oct. 30, 1938
  Green Bay (7) vs Det. (4), Oct. 20, 1940
  Detroit (7) vs Chi. Bears (4), Nov. 22, 1942
  Detroit (7) vs Clev. (4), Nov. 26, 1944
  Chicago Cards (8) vs Phil. (3), Sept. 24, 1950
  Washington (7) vs N.Y. (4), Dec. 8, 1963
  Pittsburgh (9) vs Phil. (2), Dec. 12, 1965

PUNTING

Most Seasons Leading League (Avg. Distance)

- 6   Washington 1940–43, 45, 58
- 5   Denver 1962–64, 66–67 (AFL)
- 4   Brooklyn 1935–38
  Los Angeles 1946, 49, 55–56

Most Punts, Season

- 113   Boston 1934
  Brooklyn 1934

112　Boston 1935
AFL:
105　Denver 1967

Fewest Punts, Season

32　Chicago Bears 1941
33　Washington 1945
38　Chicago Bears 1947
AFL:
54　Dallas 1962

Most Punts, Game

17　Chicago Bears vs G.B., Oct. 22, 1933
　　Cincinnati vs Pitt., Oct. 22, 1933
16　Cincinnati vs Port., Sept. 17, 1933
　　Chicago Cards vs Chi. Bears, Nov. 30, 1933
　　Chicago Cards vs Det., Sept. 15, 1940
AFL:
12　Denver vs Oak., Sept. 10, 1967
*　　Denver vs Cin., Oct. 6, 1968*

Fewest Punts, Game

0　By many teams. Last:
　　NFL: Dallas vs Det., Sept. 15, 1968
　　AFL: Boston vs Mia., Dec. 17, 1967

Most Punts, Both Teams, Game

31　Chicago Bears (17) vs G.B. (14), Oct. 22, 1933
　　Cincinnati (17) vs Pitt. (14), Oct. 22, 1933
29　Chicago Cards (15) vs Cin. (14), Nov. 12, 1933
　　Chicago Cards (16) vs Chi. Bears (13), Nov. 30, 1933
　　Chicago Cards (16) vs Det. (13), Sept. 15, 1940
AFL:
22　Denver (12) vs Cin. (10), Oct. 6, 1968

Highest Punting Average, Season

47.6　Detroit 1961
47.0　Pittsburgh 1961
46.9　Pittsburgh 1953
AFL:
45.3　New York 1965

PUNT RETURNS

Most Seasons Leading League

8　Detroit 1943–45, 51–52, 62, 66, 69
5　Chicago Cards 1948–49, 55–56, 59
　　Cleveland 1958, 60, 64–65, 67
4　Green Bay 1950, 53–54, 61
AFL:
3　Denver 1963, 67, 69

Most Punt Returns, Season

61　Cleveland 1954
60　Chicago Bears 1950
58　Los Angeles 1969
AFL:
55　Oakland 1968

Most Punt Returns, Game

  12 Philadelphia vs Clev., Dec. 3, 1950
  11 Chicago Bears vs Chi. Cards, Oct. 8, 1950
  10 Philadelphia vs N.Y. Giants, Nov. 26, 1950
AFL:
   9 *Buffalo vs Hou., Oct. 11, 1964*
     Oakland vs Den., Sept. 10, 1967

Most Punt Returns, Both Teams, Game

  17 Philadelphia (12) vs Clev. (5), Dec., 3, 1950
  16 New York (9) vs Phil. (7), Dec. 12, 1954
  15 Detroit (8) vs Clev. Rams (7), Sept. 27, 1942
     Los Angeles (8) vs Balt. (7), Nov. 27, 1966
AFL:
  12 *Oakland (6) vs K.C. (6), Nov. 8, 1963*
     Kansas City (6) vs Bos. (6), Nov. 17, 1968

Most Fair Catches, Season

  32 San Diego 1969 (AFL)
  30 St. Louis 1967
  28 Pittsburgh 1965
     Chicago 1967
     Detroit 1968
     Oakland 1969 (AFL)

Fewest Fair Catches, Season

   3 Dallas 1961
     New York 1967 (AFL)
   4 Atlanta 1966
     Washington 1968
     Miami 1968 (AFL)
   5 Minnesota 1962
     Chicago 1964

Most Fair Catches, Game

   7 Minnesota vs Dall., Sept. 25, 1966
   6 Minnesota vs Balt., Nov. 17, 1963
     Chicago vs St. L., Oct. 31, 1966; vs Minn., Dec. 10, 1967
     Cleveland vs St. L., Dec. 17, 1966
     San Francisco vs Balt., Oct. 13, 1968
AFL:
   5 *Houston vs Mia., Sept. 28, 1969*
     San Diego vs Cin., Oct. 4, 1969

Most Yards Gained Punt Returns, Season

 781 Chicago Bears 1948
 729 Green Bay 1950
 717 New York 1941
AFL:
 666 *Oakland 1968*

Most Yards Gained Punt Returns, Game

 231 Detroit vs S.F., Oct. 6, 1963
 225 Oakland vs Buff., Sept. 15, 1968 (AFL)
 178 Brooklyn vs Pitt., Nov. 29, 1942

Most Yards Gained Punt Returns, Both Teams, Game

 245 Detroit (231) vs S.F. (14), Oct. 6, 1963
 244 Oakland (225) vs Buff. (19), Sept. 15, 1968 (AFL)
 226 Pittsburgh (178) vs Brk. (48), Nov. 29, 1942

Highest Average Punt Returns, Season

20.2   Chicago Bears 1941
19.1   Chicago Cards 1948
18.2   Chicago Cards 1949
  AFL:
17.8   New York 1961

Most Touchdowns Punt Returns, Season

5   Chicago Cards 1959
4   Chicago Cards 1948
   Detroit 1951
   New York Giants 1951
  AFL:
2   New York 1961–62
  Oakland 1963, 68
  San Diego 1965
  Buffalo 1966

Most Touchdowns Punt Returns, Game

2   Detroit vs L.A., Oct. 14; vs G.B., Nov. 22, 1951
   Chicago Cards vs Pitt., Nov. 1; vs N.Y., Nov. 22, 1959
   New York vs Den., Sept. 24, 1961 (AFL)

Most Touchdowns Punt Returns, Both Teams, Game

2   Philadelphia (1) vs Wash. (1), Nov. 9, 1952
   Kansas City (1) vs Buff. (1), Sept. 11, 1966 (AFL)

KICKOFF RETURNS

Most Seasons Leading League

5   New York 1944, 46, 49, 51, 53
4   Washington 1942, 47, 62–63
   Chicago 1943, 48, 58, 66
3   Pittsburgh 1952, 55–56
   San Francisco 1957, 60–61
   Detroit 1941, 50, 65
   Denver 1965–67 (AFL)
   Houston 1962–63, 68 (AFL)

Most Kickoff Returns, Season

82   Atlanta 1966
80   New York 1966
78   Denver 1963 (AFL)

Most Kickoff Returns, Game

12   New York vs Wash., Nov. 27, 1966
10   New York vs Chi. Cards, Oct. 17, 1948
   New York Yanks vs N.Y. Giants, Dec. 3, 1950
   Chicago Bears vs Chi. Cards, Nov. 27, 1955
   New York vs L.A., Dec. 18, 1960 (AFL)
   Houston vs Oak., Dec. 22, 1963 (AFL)
   Denver vs S.D., Dec. 22, 1963; vs Bos., Oct. 4, 1964 (AFL)
   Atlanta vs Pitt., Dec. 18, 1966
   Kansas City vs Oak., Nov. 23, 1967 (AFL)
   Boston vs Buff., Dec. 9, 1967 (AFL)
   Detroit vs Dall., Sept. 15, 1968
9   By many teams (NFL-AFL)

Most Kickoff Returns, Both Teams, Game

19 New York (12) vs Wash. (7), Nov. 27, 1966
18 Houston (10) vs Oak. (8), Dec. 22, 1963 (AFL)
16 New York (10) vs Chi. Cards (6), Oct. 17, 1948
   New York (10) vs L.A. (6), Dec. 18, 1960 (AFL)
   Cleveland (8) vs St. L. (8), Sept. 20, 1964
   Cleveland (8) vs N.Y. (8), Dec. 4, 1966

Most Yards Gained Kickoff Returns, Season

1,824 Houston 1963 (AFL)
1,801 Denver 1963 (AFL)
1,758 Denver 1964 (AFL)
   NFL:
1,739 *San Francisco 1962*
   New Orleans 1967

Most Yards Gained Kickoff Returns, Game

362 Detroit vs L.A., Oct. 29, 1950
304 Chicago Bears vs G.B., Nov. 9, 1952
295 Denver vs Bos., Oct. 4, 1964 (AFL)

Most Yards Gained Kickoff Returns, Both Teams, Game

560 Detroit (362) vs L.A. (198), Oct. 29, 1950
453 Washington (236) vs Phil. (217), Sept. 28, 1947
447 New York (236) vs Clev. (211), Dec. 4, 1966
   AFL:
421 *Boston (226) vs Hou. (195), Dec. 18, 1960*

Highest Average Kickoff Returns, Season

28.9 Pittsburgh 1952
28.2 Washington 1962
28.0 San Francisco 1962
   AFL:
27.6 *Dallas 1961*

Most Touchdowns Kickoff Returns, Season

4 Green Bay 1967
3 Los Angeles 1950
   Chicago Cards 1954
   San Francisco 1963
   Denver 1966 (AFL)
   Chicago 1967
2 By many teams (NFL-AFL)

Most Touchdowns Kickoff Returns, Game

2 Chicago Bears vs G.B., Nov. 9, 1952
   Philadelphia vs Dall., Nov. 6, 1966
   Green Bay vs Clev., Nov. 12, 1967
1 By many teams (NFL–AFL)

Most Touchdowns Kickoff Returns, Both Teams, Game

2 Washington (1) vs Phil. (1), Nov. 1, 1942
   Washington (1) vs Phil. (1), Sept. 28, 1947
   Los Angeles (1) vs Det. (1), Oct. 29, 1950
   New York Yanks (1) vs N.Y. Giants (1), Nov. 4, 1951
   Baltimore (1) vs Chi. Bears (1), Oct. 4, 1958
   Buffalo (1) vs Bos. (1), Nov. 3, 1962 (AFL)
   Pittsburgh (1) vs Dall. (1), Oct. 30, 1966

FUMBLES

Most Fumbles, Season

56 Chicago Bears 1938
54 Philadelphia 1946
49 New York 1961
AFL:
41 Oakland 1960

Fewest Fumbles, Season

8 Cleveland 1959
11 Green Bay 1944
12 Brooklyn 1934
   Detroit 1943
AFL:
15 New York 1964, 67
   Boston 1969
   Denver 1969

Most Fumbles, Game

10 Phil./Pitt. vs N.Y., Oct. 9, 1943
   Detroit vs Minn., Nov. 12, 1967
   Kansas City vs Hou., Oct. 12, 1969 (AFL)
 9 Philadelphia vs G.B., Oct. 13, 1946
   Kansas City vs S.D., Nov. 15, 1964 (AFL)
 8 By many teams (NFL)

Most Fumbles, Both Teams, Game

14 Chicago Bears (7) vs Clev. (7), Nov. 24, 1940
   St. Louis (8) vs N.Y. (6), Sept. 17, 1961
   Kansas City (10) vs Hou. (4), Oct. 12, 1969 (AFL)
13 Washington (8) vs Pitt. (5), Nov. 14, 1937
   Philadelphia (7) vs Bos. (6), Dec. 8, 1946
   New York Giants (7) vs Wash. (6), Nov. 5, 1950
   New York (7) vs Hou. (6), Sept. 12, 1965 (AFL)
   Kansas City (9) vs S.D. (4), Nov. 15, 1964 (AFL)
   Buffalo (7) vs Den. (6), Dec. 13, 1964 (AFL)
12 Denver (6) vs Bos. (6), Nov. 6, 1966 (AFL)

Most Own Fumbles Recovered, Season

27 Philadelphia 1946
   Minnesota 1963
26 Pittsburgh 1948
25 Dallas 1961
AFL:
23 Oakland 1960

Fewest Own Fumbles Recovered, Season

2 Washington 1958
3 Detroit 1956
   Cleveland 1959
4 Chicago Cards 1949
   Detroit 1960
   Oakland 1963 (AFL)
   San Diego 1963 (AFL)
   Green Bay 1966
   New York 1968
   New York 1969 (AFL)

Most Opponents' Fumbles Recovered, Season

- 31 Minnesota 1963
- 29 Cleveland 1951
- 28 Green Bay 1946

AFL:
- *26 Houston 1960*

Fewest Opponents' Fumbles Recovered, Season

- 4 Philadelphia 1944
- 6 Brooklyn 1939
  Chicago Bears 1943, 45
  Washington 1945
  New York 1967 (AFL)
  San Diego 1969 (AFL)
- 7 New York 1966
  Philadelphia 1968
  Green Bay 1969

Most Opponents' Fumbles Recovered, Game

- 7 Buffalo vs Cin., Nov. 30, 1969 (AFL)
- 6 By many teams (NFL-AFL). Last:
  NFL: Detroit vs L.A., Oct. 31, 1965
  AFL: Houston vs K.C., Oct. 12, 1969

Most Fumbles (Opponents' and Own) Recovered, Season

- 58 Minnesota 1963
- 46 New York 1946
- 45 Philadelphia 1946
  Houston 1960 (AFL)

Most Fumbles (Opponents' and Own) Recovered, Game

- 10 Denver vs Buff., Dec. 13, 1964 (AFL)
- 9 St. Louis vs N.Y., Sept. 17, 1961
- 8 By many teams (NFL-AFL)

Fewest Fumbles (Opponents' and Own) Recovered, Season

- 13 Kansas City 1966 (AFL)
  Baltimore 1967
  New York 1967 (AFL)
  Philadelphia 1968
- 14 Cleveland 1956
- 15 Chicago Bears 1943
  San Francisco 1951
  Cleveland 1959

PENALTIES

Most Seasons Leading League, Fewest Penalties

- 9 Pittsburgh 1946–47, 50–52, 54, 63, 65, 68
- 4 Green Bay 1955–56, 66–67
- 3 Washington 1954, 57–58
  Boston 1962, 64–65 (AFL)

Most Seasons Leading League, Most Penalties

- 15 Chicago Bears, 1941–44, 46–49, 51, 59–61, 63, 65, 68
- 4 Los Angeles 1950, 52, 62, 69
  Oakland 1963, 66, 68–69 (AFL)
- 3 Chicago Cards 1954–56
  San Diego 1962, 64–65 (AFL)

Most Penalties, Season

    122   Washington 1948
          Chicago Bears 1948
    121   Chicago Bears 1944
    118   Chicago Bears 1951
     AFL:
    100   Oakland 1969

Fewest Penalties, Season

     19   Detroit 1937
     21   Boston 1935
     24   Philadelphia 1936
     AFL:
     48   Denver 1967
          Miami 1968

Most Penalties, Game

     22   Brooklyn vs G.B., Sept. 17, 1944
          Chicago Bears vs Phil., Nov. 26, 1944
     21   Cleveland vs Chi. Bears, Nov. 25, 1951
     18   Chicago Bears vs L.A., Nov. 10, 1946
          Cleveland vs L.A., Oct. 7, 1951
     AFL:
     17   Oakland vs Hou., Sept. 7, 1963

Fewest Penalties, Game

      0   By many teams (NFL-AFL)

Most Penalties, Both Teams, Game

     37   Cleveland (21) vs Chi. Bears (16), Nov. 25, 1951
     33   Brooklyn (22) vs G.B. (11), Sept. 17, 1944
     27   Green Bay (17) vs Bos. Yanks (10), Oct. 21, 1945
          Chicago Bears (18) vs L.A. (9), Nov. 10, 1946
          Chicago Cards (12) vs Phil. (15), Nov. 30, 1952
     AFL:
     23   Oakland (17) vs Hou. (6), Sept. 7, 1963

Fewest Penalties, Both Teams, Game

      0   Brooklyn vs Pitt., Oct. 28, 1934; vs Bos., Sept. 28, 1936
          Cleveland Rams vs Chi. Bears, Oct. 9, 1938
          Pittsburgh vs Phil., Nov. 10, 1940
     AFL:
      1   Kansas City vs Buff. (1), Oct. 2, 1966
          Boston vs N.Y. (1), Nov. 19, 1967

Most Yards Penalized, Season

  1,274   Oakland 1969 (AFL)
  1,194   Chicago Bears 1968
  1,107   Chicago Bears 1951

Fewest Yards Penalized, Season

    139   Detroit 1937
    146   Philadelphia 1937
    159   Philadelphia 1936
     AFL:
    456   Oakland 1961
          Boston 1962

Most Yards Penalized, Game

    209   Cleveland vs Chi. Bears, Nov. 25, 1951
    189   Houston vs Buff., Oct. 31, 1965 (AFL)
    184   Green Bay vs Bos., Oct. 21, 1945

Most Yards Penalized, Both Teams, Game

374   Cleveland (209) vs Chi. Bears (165), Nov. 25, 1951
309   Green Bay (184) vs Bos. (125), Oct. 21, 1945
AFL:
281   Oakland (176) vs Bos. (105), Sept. 28, 1969

TEAM RECORDS—DEFENSE
SCORING

Fewest Points Allowed, Season

20   New York 1927
59   Detroit 1934
75   New York 1944
AFL:
170   Kansas City 1968

Most Points Allowed, Season

501   New York 1966
473   Denver 1963 (AFL)
462   Baltimore 1950

Fewest Touchdowns Allowed, Season

3   New York Giants 1927
7   Detroit 1934
9   New York 1944
AFL:
18   Houston 1967
Kansas City 1968

Most Touchdowns Allowed, Season

66   New York 1966
63   Baltimore 1950
61   Denver 1963 (AFL)

FIRST DOWNS

Fewest First Downs Allowed, Season

86   Philadelphia 1944
95   Brooklyn 1944
96   Phil/Pitt 1943
AFL:
178   New York 1968

Most First Downs Allowed, Season

304   San Francisco 1963
302   Atlanta 1968
295   Atlanta 1966
AFL:
282   Houston 1960

Fewest First Downs Allowed, Rushing, Season

35   Chicago Bears 1942
41   Brooklyn 1944
42   Phil/Pitt 1943
AFL:
48   Buffalo 1964

Most First Downs Allowed, Rushing, Season

- 150 Baltimore 1950
- 149 Washington 1969
- 147 Minnesota 1961
- **AFL:**
- *142 Boston 1969*

Fewest First Downs Allowed, Passing, Season

- 33 Chicago Bears 1943
- 34 Pittsburgh 1941
  Washington 1943
- 35 Philadelphia 1944
- **AFL:**
- *93 Houston 1969*

Most First Downs Allowed, Passing, Season

- 185 St. Louis 1969
- 168 San Francisco 1963
- 165 Boston 1964 (AFL)

Fewest First Downs Allowed, Penalty, Season

- 1 Boston 1944
- 3 Pittsburgh 1945
  Washington 1957
- 4 Green Bay 1943
  New York 1943
- **AFL:**
- *10 Kansas City 1964*

Most First Downs Allowed, Penalty, Season

- 36 Washington 1965
  Chicago 1968
- 35 Oakland 1969 (AFL)
- 33 Chicago Bears 1948
  Los Angeles 1969

NET YARDS ALLOWED

(Rushing and Passing)

Fewest Yards Allowed, Season

- 1,578 Chicago Cards 1934
- 1,703 Chicago Bears 1942
- **AFL:**
- *3,163 Kansas City 1969*

Most Yards Allowed, Season

- 5,593 Minnesota 1961
- 5,531 Atlanta 1967
- 5,447 San Francisco 1963
- **AFL:**
- *5,337 Cincinnati 1969*

RUSHING

Fewest Yards Allowed, Rushing, Season

- 519 Chicago Bears 1942
- 558 Philadelphia 1944
- 793 Phil./Pitt. 1943
- **AFL:**
- *913 Buffalo 1964*

Most Yards Allowed Rushing, Season

2,857   Baltimore 1950
2,699   Houston 1965 (AFL)
2,667   Minnesota 1961

Fewest Touchdowns Allowed, Rushing, Season

1   New York Giants 1927
2   Dallas 1968
3   Detroit 1934
    Chicago Bears 1942
    Dallas 1969
AFL:
4   *Buffalo 1964*
    Kansas City 1968

Most Touchdowns Allowed, Rushing, Season

36   Oakland 1961 (AFL)
29   Baltimore 1950
     New York Yanks 1950
     Minnesota 1961
27   Detroit 1948

PASSING

Fewest Yards Allowed Passing, Season

625   Chicago Cards 1934
928   Boston 1934
939   Pittsburgh 1946
AFL:
1,671   *Houston 1968*

Most Yards Allowed Passing, Season

3,674   Dallas 1962
3,602   Washington 1962
3,532   St. Louis 1969
AFL:
3,525   *Houston 1960*

Most Opponents Tackled Attempting Passes, Season

67   Oakland 1967 (AFL)
60   Dallas 1966
57   New York 1963
     Baltimore 1964

Fewest Touchdowns Allowed, Passing, Season

2   New York Giants 1927
3   New York 1944
4   Detroit 1934
    New York 1942
AFL:
10   *Houston 1967*
     Kansas City 1969

Most Touchdowns Allowed, Passing, Season

40   Denver 1963 (AFL)
38   St. Louis 1969
37   Washington 1961

INTERCEPTIONS BY

Most Seasons Leading League, Intercepted by

- 8 New York 1937–39, 44, 48, 51, 54, 61
    Green Bay 1940, 42–43, 47, 55, 57, 62, 65
- 6 Chicago Bears 1935–36, 41–42, 46, 63
- 4 Kansas City 1966–69 (AFL)

Most Passes Intercepted by, Season

- 49 San Diego 1961 (AFL)
- 42 Green Bay 1943
- 41 New York Giants 1951

Fewest Passes Intercepted by, Season

- 7 Los Angeles 1959
- 8 Pittsburgh 1940
- 10 Brooklyn 1944
    Pittsburgh 1955
    Chicago Bears 1960, 64
    Cincinnati 1968 (AFL)

Most Consecutive Games, 1 or more Interceptions by

- 46 L.A./S.D. 1960–63 (AFL)
- 37 Detroit 1960–63
- 36 Washington 1962–65

Most Yards Gained, Interceptions, Season

- 929 San Diego 1961 (AFL)
- 712 Los Angeles 1952
- 676 Houston 1967 (AFL)

Most Yards Gained, Interceptions, Game

- 314 Los Angeles vs S.F., Oct. 18, 1964
- 245 Houston vs N.Y., Oct. 15, 1967 (AFL)
- 235 Buffalo vs N.Y., Sept. 29, 1968 (AFL)

Most Touchdowns, Interception Returns, Season

- 9 San Diego 1961 (AFL)
- 6 Cleveland 1960
    Green Bay 1966
    Detroit 1967
    Houston 1967 (AFL)
- 5 Green Bay 1945
    Los Angeles 1958
    St. Louis 1961, 64
    New York 1963
    Houston 1968 (AFL)

Most Touchdowns, Interception Returns, Game

- 3 Baltimore vs G.B., Nov. 5, 1950
    Cleveland vs Chi., Dec. 11, 1960
    Philadelphia vs Pitt., Dec. 12, 1965
    Baltimore vs Pitt., Sept. 29, 1968
    Buffalo vs N.Y., Sept. 29, 1968 (AFL)
- 2 By many teams (NFL-AFL)

Most Touchdowns, Interception Returns, Both Teams, Game

    4   Philadelphia (3) vs Pitt. (1), Dec. 12, 1965
    3   Los Angeles (2) vs Det. (1), Nov. 1, 1953
        Cleveland (2) vs N.Y. (1), Dec. 18, 1960
AFL:
    2   New York (1) vs Bos. (1), Sept. 22, 1968

PUNT RETURNS

Fewest Opponents' Punt Returns, Season

    7   Washington 1962
  11   Boston 1962 (AFL)
  13   Boston 1961 (AFL)
       Green Bay 1967

Most Opponents' Punt Returns, Season

  69   New York 1953
  63   Boston 1947
  61   Denver 1967 (AFL)

Fewest Yards Allowed Punt Returns, Season

  22   Green Bay 1967
  34   Washington 1962
  39   Cleveland 1959
AFL:
  54   Boston 1962

Most Yards Allowed Punt Returns, Season

 932   Green Bay 1949
 913   Boston 1947
 812   New York 1948
   AFL:
 718   Denver 1967

Most Touchdowns Allowed Punt Returns, Season

  4   New York 1959
  3   Green Bay 1949
      Chicago Cards 1951
      Los Angeles 1951
      Washington 1952
      Dallas 1952
      Pittsburgh 1959
      New York 1968 (AFL)

KICKOFF RETURNS

Fewest Opponents' Kickoff Returns, Season

  10   Brooklyn 1943
  15   Detroit 1942
       Brooklyn 1944
  18   Cleveland 1941
       Boston 1944
AFL:
 21   Denver 1969

Most Opponents' Kickoff Returns, Season

- 84 Kansas City 1966 (AFL)
- 82 Oakland 1967 (AFL)
  New York 1968 (AFL)
- 78 Dallas 1966

Fewest Yards Allowed Kickoff Returns, Season

- 293 Brooklyn 1944
- 368 Chicago Cards 1945
- 389 Detroit 1942

AFL:
- *471 Denver 1969*

Most Yards Allowed Kickoff Returns, Season

- 2,045 Kansas City 1966 (AFL)
- 1,816 New York 1963
- 1,785 New York 1960 (AFL)

Most Touchdowns Allowed Kickoff Returns, Season

- 3 Minnesota 1963
  Dallas 1966
- 2 By 19 teams (NFL)
  Houston 1966 (AFL)

OUTSTANDING RUSHERS

1,000 Yards or More in a Season

Year	Player	Team	Yards
1934	Beattie Feathers	Chicago Bears	1,004
1947	Steve Van Buren	Philadelphia	1,008
1949	Steve Van Buren	Philadelphia	1,146
	Tony Canadeo	Green Bay	1,052
1953	Joe Perry	San Francisco	1,018
1954	Joe Perry	San Francisco	1,049
1956	Rick Casares	Chicago Bears	1,126
1958	Jim Brown	Cleveland	1,527
1959	Jim Brown	Cleveland	1,329
	J. D. Smith	San Francisco	1,036
1960	Jim Brown	Cleveland	1,257
	Jim Taylor	Green Bay	1,101
	John David Crow	St. Louis	1,011
1961	Jim Brown	Cleveland	1,408
	Jim Taylor	Green Bay	1,307
1962	Jim Taylor	Green Bay	1,474
	John Henry Johnson	Pittsburgh	1,141
	Cookie Gilchrist	Buffalo (AFL)	1,096
	Abner Haynes	Dallas Texans (AFL)	1,049
	Dick Bass	Los Angeles	1,033
	Charlie Tolar	Houston (AFL)	1,012
1963	Jim Brown	Cleveland	1,863
	Clem Daniels	Oakland (AFL)	1,099
	Jim Taylor	Green Bay	1,018
	Paul Lowe	San Diego (AFL)	1,010

OUTSTANDING RUSHERS (Cont'd)

Year	Player	Team	Yard
1964	Jim Brown	Cleveland	1,44
	Jim Taylor	Green Bay	1,16
	John Henry Johnson	Pittsburgh	1,04
1965	Jim Brown	Cleveland	1,54
	Paul Lowe	San Diego (AFL)	1,12
1966	Jim Nance	Boston (AFL)	1,45
	Gale Sayers	Chicago	1,23
	Leroy Kelly	Cleveland	1,14
	Dick Bass	Los Angeles	1,09
1967	Jim Nance	Boston (AFL)	1,21
	Leroy Kelly	Cleveland	1,20
	Hoyle Granger	Houston (AFL)	1,19
	Mike Garrett	Kansas City (AFL)	1,08
1968	Leroy Kelly	Cleveland	1,23
	Paul Robinson	Cincinnati (AFL)	1,02
1969	Gale Sayers	Chicago	1,03

200 Yards or More in a Game

Year	Date	Player and Opponent	Yards	Atts
1933	Oct. 18	Cliff Battles, Bos. vs N.Y.	215	(16
1949	Nov. 27	Steve Van Buren, Phil. vs Pitt.	205	(27
1950	Nov. 12	Gene Roberts, N.Y. Giants vs Chi. Cards	218	(26
1953	Nov. 22	Dan Towler, L.A. vs Balt.	205	(14
1956	Dec. 16	Tom Wilson, L.A. vs G.B.	223	(23
1957	Nov. 24	Jim Brown, Clev. vs L.A.	237	(31
1959	Nov. 15	Bobby Mitchell, Clev. vs Wash.	232	(14
1960	Dec. 18	John David Crow, St. L. vs Pitt.	203	(24
1961	Nov. 19	Jim Brown, Clev. vs Phil.	237	(34
	Dec. 10	Billy Cannon, Hou. vs N.Y. (AFL)	216	(25
1963	Dec. 8	Cookie Gilchrist, Buff. vs N.Y. (AFL)	243	(36
	Sept. 22	Jim Brown, Clev. vs Dall.	232	(20
	Nov. 3	Jim Brown, Clev. vs Phil.	223	(28
	Oct. 20	Clem Daniels, Oak. vs N.Y. (AFL)	200	(27
1964	Oct. 10	John Henry Johnson, Pitt. vs Clev.	200	(30
1966	Oct. 30	Jim Nance, Bos. vs Oak. (AFL)	208	(38
1968	Nov. 3	Gale Sayers, Chi. vs G.B.	205	(24

TOP TEN RUSHERS—LIFETIME NFL & AFL

Player	Seasons	Yards	Attempts
Jim Brown	9	12,312	2,359
Jim Taylor	10	8,597	1,941
Joe Perry	14	8,378	1,737
John Henry Johnson	13	6.803	1,571
Don Perkins	8	6,217	1,500
Steve Van Buren	8	5,860	1,320
Rick Casares	12	5,797	1,431
Dick Bass	10	5,417	1,218
Hugh McElhenny	13	5,281	1,124
Lenny Moore	12	5,174	1,069

TOP TEN PASS RECEIVERS—LIFETIME
NFL & AFL

Player	Seasons	No.	Yards
ymond Berry	13	631	9,275
onel Taylor	9	567	7,195
on Maynard	11	551	10,373
bby Mitchell	11	521	7,954
lly Howton	12	503	8,459
mmy McDonald	12	495	8,410
on Hutson	11	488	7,991
t Powell	10	479	8,046
nce Alworth	8	458	8,976
te Retzlaff	11	452	7,412

TOP TEN INTERCEPTORS—LIFETIME
NFL & AFL

Player	Seasons	No.	Yards
nlen Tunnell	14	79	1,282
ck (Night Train) Lane	14	68	1,207
ob Boyd	9	57	994
ob Dillon	8	52	976
ck Butler	9	52	826
m Patton	12	52	712
le Lary	11	50	787
on Burroughs	10	50	564
ave Grayson	9	47	908
ck LeBeau	11	47	590

TOP TEN SCORERS—LIFETIME NFL & AFL

Player	Seasons	TDs	XP	FG	Points
eorge Blanda	20	9	703	240	1,477
ou Groza	17	1	641	234	1,349
ino Cappelletti	10	42	338	170	1,100
am Baker	15	2	428	179	977
ou Michaels	12	1	367	179	912*
obby Walston	12	46	365	80	881
on Hutson	11	105	172	7	823
aul Hornung	9	62	190	66	760
m Brown	9	126	0	0	756
ommy Davis	11	0	348	130	738

ncludes Safety.

TOP TEN LEADING PASSERS—LIFETIME
NFL & AFL

(1,500 or more attempts)

Player	Yrs.	Atts.	Comp.	Pct.	Yards	TDs	Had Int.	Pct. Int.	Avg. Gain per Att.
1. John Unitas	14	4,456	2,450	55.0	35,502	266	213	4.8	7.97
2. Sonny Jurgensen	13	3,526	1,982	56.2	26,978	213	163	4.6	7.65
3. Bart Starr	14	2,849	1,644	57.7	22,787	144	122	4.3	8.00
4. Len Dawson	13	2,397	1,356	56.6	19,103	184	122	5.1	7.97
5. Fran Tarkenton	9	3,022	1,630	53.9	23,140	186	134	4.4	7.66
6. Y. A. Tittle	15	3,817	2,118	55.5	28,339	212	221	5.8	7.42
7. Norm Van Brocklin	12	2,895	1,553	53.6	23,611	173	178	6.1	8.16
8. John Brodie	13	3,422	1,870	54.6	23,934	160	170	5.0	6.99
9. Frank Ryan	12	2,129	1,089	51.2	16,039	149	111	5.2	7.53
10. Sammy Baugh	16	2,995	1,693	56.5	21,886	186	203	6.8	7.31

PASSING 400 YARDS OR MORE—GAME

Year	Date	Player and Opponent	Yards
1943	Nov. 14	Sid Luckman, Chi. Bears vs N.Y.	433
1948	Oct. 31	Sammy Baugh, Wash. vs Bos.	446
	Oct. 31	Jim Hardy, L.A. vs Chi. Cards	406
1949	Dec. 11	Johnny Lujack, Chi. Bears vs Chi. Cards	468
1951	Sept. 28	Norm Van Brocklin, L.A. vs N.Y. Yanks	554
1952	Oct. 4	Otto Graham, Clev. vs Pitt.	401
1953	Nov. 8	Bobby Thomason, Phil. vs N.Y.	437
1958	Dec. 13	Bobby Layne, Pitt. vs Chi. Cards	409
1961	Oct. 29	George Blanda, Hou. vs Buff. (AFL)	464
	Oct. 13	Jack Lee, Hou. vs Bos. (AFL)	457
	Oct. 29	Sonny Jurgensen, Phil. vs Wash.	436
	Nov. 19	George Blanda, Hou. vs N.Y. (AFL)	418
	Dec. 17	Sonny Jurgensen, Phil. vs Det.	403
1962	Oct. 28	Y. A. Tittle, N.Y. vs Wash.	505
	Nov. 18	Billy Wade, Chi. vs Dall.	466
	Sept. 15	Frank Tripucka, Den. vs Buff. (AFL)	447
	Dec. 16	Sonny Jurgensen, Phil. vs St. L.	419
1963	Nov. 10	Don Meredith, Dall. vs S.F.	460
	Oct. 13	Charley Johnson, St. L. vs Pitt.	428
	Nov. 17	Norm Snead, Wash. vs Pitt.	424
	Dec. 22	Tom Flores, Oak. vs Hou. (AFL)	407
1964	Nov. 1	Len Dawson, K.C. vs Den. (AFL)	435
	Oct. 25	Cotton Davidson, Oak. vs Den. (AFL)	427
	Oct. 16	Babe Parilli, Bos. vs Oak. (AFL)	422
1965	Nov. 28	Sonny Jurgensen, Wash. vs Dall.	411
	Oct. 24	Fran Tarkenton, Minn. vs S.F.	407
1966	Nov. 13	Don Meredith, Dall. vs Wash.	406
1967	Nov. 26	Sonny Jurgensen, Wash. vs Clev.	418
	Oct. 1	Joe Namath, N.Y. vs Mia. (AFL)	415
	Sept. 17	John Unitas, Balt. vs Atl.	401
1968	Sept. 9	Pete Beathard, Hou. vs K.C. (AFL)	413
1969	Sept. 28	Joe Kapp, Minn. vs Balt.	449
	Dec. 21	Don Horn, G.B. vs St. L.	410

OUTSTANDING PASS RECEIVERS

(1,200 Yards or More in a Season)

Year	Player	Team	Yards
1942	Don Hutson	Green Bay	1,211
1951	Elroy Hirsch	Los Angeles	1,495
1952	Billy Howton	Green Bay	1,231
1954	Bob Boyd	Los Angeles	1,212
1960	Bill Groman	Houston (AFL)	1,473
	Raymond Berry	Baltimore	1,298
	Don Maynard	New York (AFL)	1,265
	Lionel Taylor	Denver (AFL)	1,235
1961	Charlie Hennigan	Houston (AFL)	1,746
1962	Bobby Mitchell	Washington	1,384
1963	Bobby Mitchell	Washington	1,436
	Art Powell	Oakland (AFL)	1,304
	Buddy Dial	Pittsburgh	1,295
1964	Charlie Hennigan	Houston (AFL)	1,546
	Art Powell	Oakland (AFL)	1,361
	Lance Alworth	San Diego (AFL)	1,235
	Johnny Morris	Chicago	1,200

OUTSTANDING PASS RECEIVERS (Cont'd)

Year	Player	Team	Yards
1965	Lance Alworth	San Diego (AFL)	1,602
	Dave Parks	San Francisco	1,344
	Don Maynard	New York (AFL)	1,218
1966	Lance Alworth	San Diego (AFL)	1,383
	Otis Taylor	Kansas City (AFL)	1,297
	Pat Studstill	Detroit	1,266
	Bob Hayes	Dallas	1,232
1967	Don Maynard	New York (AFL)	1,434
	Ben Hawkins	Philadelphia	1,265
	Homer Jones	New York	1,209
	Jackie Smith	St. Louis	1,205
1968	Lance Alworth	San Diego (AFL)	1,312
	Don Maynard	New York (AFL)	1,297
1969	Warren Wells	Oakland (AFL)	1,260

(250 Yards or More in a Game)

Year	Date	Player and Opponent	Yards	No.
1945	Nov. 22	Jim Benton, Clev. vs Det.	303	(10)
1950	Dec. 3	Cloyce Box, Det. vs Balt.	302	(12)
1956	Oct. 21	Billy Howton, G.B. vs L.A.	257	(7)
1961	Oct. 13	Charlie Hennigan, Hou. vs Bos. (AFL)	272	(13)
1962	Oct. 28	Del Shofner, N.Y. vs Wash.	269	(11)
	Nov. 4	Sonny Randle, St. L. vs N.Y.	256	(16)

COMBINED NET YARDAGE

(Includes Rushes, Pass Receptions and Runback of Interceptions, Punts, Kickoffs and Fumbles)

(2,000 Yards or More in a Season)

Year	Player	Team	Yards
1960	Abner Haynes	Dallas (AFL)	2,100
1961	Billy Cannon	Houston (AFL)	2,043
1962	Tim Brown	Philadelphia	2,306
	Dick Christy	New York (AFL)	2,147
1963	Tim Brown	Philadelphia	2,428
	Jim Brown	Cleveland	2,131
1965	Gale Sayers	Chicago	2,272
1966	Gale Sayers	Chicago	2,440
	Leroy Kelly	Cleveland	2,014

(300 Yards or More in a Game)

Year	Date	Player and Opponent	Yards	No.
1950	Oct. 29	Wally Triplett, Det. vs L.A.	331	(11)
1961	Dec. 10	Billy Cannon, Hou. vs N.Y. (AFL)	373	(32)
	Nov. 19	Jim Brown, Clev. vs Phil.	313	(38)
1962	Dec. 16	Tim Brown, Phil. vs St. L.	341	(19)
1963	Nov. 17	Gary Ballman, Pitt. vs Wash	320	(12)
1965	Dec. 12	Gale Sayers, Chi. vs S.F.	336	(17)
1966	Dec. 18	Gale Sayers, Chi. vs Minn.	339	(20)
1969	Dec. 6	Jerry Levias, Hou. vs N.Y. (AFL)	329	(18)
	Nov. 2	Travis Williams, G.B. vs Pitt.	314	(11)

DEPARTMENTAL CHAMPIONS

TEAM
TOTAL YARDS GAINED

1969	Dallas	5,122	1955	Chicago Bears	4,316
	Oakland (AFL)	5,036	1954	Los Angeles	5,187
1968	Dallas	5,117	1953	Philadelphia	4,811
	Oakland (AFL)	5,696	1952	Cleveland	4,352
1967	Baltimore	5,008	1951	Los Angeles	5,506
	New York (AFL)	5,152	1950	Los Angeles	5,420
1966	Dallas	5,145	1949	Chicago Bears	4,873
	Kansas City (AFL)	5,114	1948	Chicago Cards	4,705
1965	San Francisco	5,270	1947	Chicago Bears	5,053
	San Diego (AFL)	5,188	1946	Los Angeles	3,793
1964	Baltimore	4,779	1945	Washington	3,549
	Buffalo (AFL)	5,206	1944	Chicago Bears	3,239
1963	New York	5,024	1943	Chicago Bears	4,045
	San Diego (AFL)	5,153	1942	Chicago Bears	3,900
1962	New York	5,005	1941	Chicago Bears	4,265
	Houston (AFL)	4,971	1940	Green Bay	3,400
1961	Philadelphia	5,112	1939	Chicago Bears	3,988
	Houston (AFL)	6,288	1938	Green Bay	3,037
1960	Baltimore	4,245	1937	Green Bay	3,201
	Houston (AFL)	4,936	1936	Detroit	3,703
1959	Baltimore	4,458	1935	Chicago Bears	3,454
1958	Baltimore	4,539	1934	Chicago Bears	3,750
1957	Los Angeles	4,143	1933	New York Giants	2,970
1956	Chicago Bears	4,537	1932	Chicago Bears	2,755

YARDS RUSHING

1969	Dallas	2,276	1955	Chicago Bears	2,388
	Kansas City (AFL)	2,220	1954	San Francisco	2,498
1968	Chicago	2,377	1953	San Francisco	2,230
	Kansas City (AFL)	2,227	1952	San Francisco	1,905
1967	Cleveland	2,139	1951	Chicago Bears	2,408
	Houston (AFL)	2,122	1950	New York Giants	2,336
1966	Cleveland	2,166	1949	Philadelphia	2,607
	Kansas City (AFL)	2,274	1948	Chicago Cards	2,560
1965	Cleveland	2,331	1947	Los Angeles	2,171
	San Diego (AFL)	2,085	1946	Green Bay	1,765
1964	Green Bay	2,276	1945	Cleveland Rams	1,714
	Buffalo (AFL)	2,040	1944	Philadelphia	1,663
1963	Cleveland	2,639	1943	Phil-Pitt	1,730
	San Diego (AFL)	2,203	1942	Chicago Bears	1,881
1962	Green Bay	2,460	1941	Chicago Bears	2,156
	Buffalo (AFL)	2,480	1940	Chicago Bears	1,818
1961	Green Bay	2,350	1939	Chicago Bears	2,043
	Dallas (AFL)	2,189	1938	Detroit	1,893
1960	St. Louis	2,356	1937	Detroit	2,074
	Oakland (AFL)	2,056	1936	Detroit	2,885
1959	Cleveland	2,149	1935	Chicago Bears	2,096
1958	Cleveland	2,526	1934	Chicago Bears	2,835
1957	Los Angeles	2,142	1933	Boston Redskins	2,367
1956	Chicago Bears	2,468	1932	Chicago Bears	1,770

TEAM PASSING LEADER

1969—Dallas Cowboys	1954—Los Angeles Rams
—Cincinnati Bengals (AFL)	1953—Cleveland Browns
1968—Cleveland Browns	1952—Green Bay Packers
—Kansas City Chiefs (AFL)	1951—Los Angeles Rams
1967—Washington Redskins	1950—Los Angeles Rams
—Oakland Raiders (AFL)	1949—Los Angeles Rams
1966—Green Bay Packers	1948—New York Giants
—New York Jets (AFL)	1947—Washington Redskins
1965—San Francisco 49ers	1946—Los Angeles Rams
—San Diego Chargers (AFL)	1945—Washington Redskins
1964—Minnesota Vikings	1944—Washington Redskins
—Houston Oilers (AFL)	1943—Washington Redskins
1963—New York Giants	1942—Washington Redskins
—Houston Oilers (AFL)	1941—Green Bay Packers
1962—New York Giants	1940—Washington Redskins
—Denver Broncos (AFL)	1939—Washington Redskins
1961—Philadelphia Eagles	1938—New York Giants
—Houston Oilers (AFL)	1937—Washington Redskins
1960—Philadelphia Eagles	1936—Green Bay Packers
—Houston Oilers (AFL)	1935—New York Giants
1959—New York Giants	1934—New York Giants
1958—Pittsburgh Steelers	1933—Brooklyn Dodgers
1957—Cleveland Browns	1932—New York Giants
1956—Chicago Bears	1931—Green Bay Packers
1955—Cleveland Browns	

NOTE: Leadership 1931–1945 based on completion %; 1946–1949 based on completion %, yardage, and interception %; 1950–1959 based on net gain per attempt. Since 1960 based on completion %, TDs, interception % and net gain per attempt.

YARDS PASSING

1969—San Francisco	3,158	1955—Philadelphia	2,472
—Oakland (AFL)	3,271	1954—Chicago Bears	3,104
1968—Dallas	3,026	1953—Philadelphia	3,089
—San Diego (AFL)	3,623	1952—Cleveland	2,566
1967—Washington	3,730	1951—Los Angeles	3,199
—New York (AFL)	3,845	1950—Los Angeles	3,529
1966—Dallas	3,023	1949—Chicago Bears	2,930
—New York (AFL)	3,464	1948—Washington	2,861
1965—San Francisco	3,487	1947—Washington	3,336
—San Diego (AFL)	3,103	1946—Los Angeles	2,080
1964—Chicago	2,841	1945—Chicago Bears	1,857
—Houston (AFL)	3,527	1944—Washington	2,021
1963—Baltimore	3,296	1943—Chicago Bears	2,310
—Houston (AFL)	3,222	1942—Green Bay	2,407
1962—Philadelphia	3,385	1941—Chicago Bears	2,002
—Denver (AFL)	3,404	1940—Washington	1,887
1961—Philadelphia	3,605	1939—Chicago Bears	1,965
—Houston (AFL)	4,392	1938—Washington	1,536
1960—Baltimore	2,956	1937—Green Bay	1,398
—Houston (AFL)	3,203	1936—Green Bay	1,629
1959—Baltimore	2,753	1935—Green Bay	1,416
1958—Pittsburgh	2,752	1934—Green Bay	1,165
1957—Baltimore	2,388	1933—New York	1,335
1956—Los Angeles	2,419	1932—Chicago Bears	1,013

Since 1949 based on net yards.

POINTS SCORED

1969—Minnesota	379	1955—Cleveland	349
—Oakland (AFL)	377	1954—Detroit	337
1968—Dallas	431	1953—San Francisco	372
—Oakland (AFL)	453	1952—Los Angeles	349
1967—Los Angeles	398	1951—Los Angeles	392
—Oakland (AFL)	468	1950—Los Angeles	466
1966—Dallas	445	1949—Philadelphia	364
—Kansas City (AFL)	448	1948—Chicago Cards	395
1965—San Francisco	421	1947—Chicago Bears	363
—San Diego (AFL)	340	1946—Chicago Bears	289
1964—Baltimore	428	1945—Philadelphia	272
—Buffalo (AFL)	400	1944—Philadelphia	267
1963—New York	448	1943—Chicago Bears	303
—San Diego (AFL)	399	1942—Chicago Bears	376
1962—Green Bay	415	1941—Chicago Bears	396
—Dallas (AFL)	389	1940—Washington	245
1961—Green Bay	391	1939—Chicago Bears	298
—Houston (AFL)	513	1938—Green Bay	223
1960—Cleveland	362	1937—Green Bay	220
—New York (AFL)	382	1936—Green Bay	248
1959—Baltimore	374	1935—Chicago Bears	192
1958—Baltimore	381	1934—Chicago Bears	286
1957—Los Angeles	307	1933—New York Giants	244
1956—Chicago Bears	363	1932—Green Bay	152

INDIVIDUAL
SCORING

	TDs	XP	FG	Points
1969—Fred Cox, Minnesota	0	43	26	121
—Jim Turner, New York (AFL)	0	33	32	129
1968—Leroy Kelly, Cleveland	20	0	0	120
—Jim Turner, New York (AFL)	0	43	34	145
1967—Jim Bakken, St. Louis	0	36	27	117
—George Blanda, Oakland (AFL)	0	56	20	116
1966—Bruce Gossett, Los Angeles	0	29	28	113
—Gino Cappelletti, Boston (AFL)	6	35	16	119
1965—Gale Sayers, Chicago*	22	0	0	132
—Gino Cappelletti, Boston (AFL)	9	27	17	132
1964—Lenny Moore, Baltimore	20	0	0	120
—Gino Cappelletti, Boston (AFL)	7	36	25	155
1963—Don Chandler, New York	0	52	18	106
—Gino Cappelletti, Boston (AFL)	2	35	22	113
1962—Jim Taylor, Green Bay	19	0	0	114
—Gene Mingo, Denver (AFL)	4	32	27	137
1961—Paul Hornung, Green Bay	10	41	15	146
—Gino Cappelletti, Boston (AFL)	8	48	17	147
1960—Paul Hornung, Green Bay	15	41	15	176
—Gene Mingo, Denver (AFL)	6	33	18	123
1959—Paul Hornung, Green Bay	7	31	7	94
1958—Jim Brown, Cleveland Browns	18	0	0	108
1957 { Sam Baker, Washington	1	29	14	77
Lou Groza, Cleveland Browns	0	32	15	77
1956—Bobby Layne, Detroit	5	33	12	99
1955—Doak Walker, Detroit	7	27	9	96
1954—Robert Walston, Philadelphia	11	36	4	114
1953—Gordon Soltau, San Francisco	6	48	10	114
1952—Gordon Soltau, San Francisco	7	34	6	94

INDIVIDUAL SCORING (Cont'd)

	TDs	XP	FG	Points
1951—Elroy Hirsch, Los Angeles	17	0	0	102
1950—Doak Walker, Detroit*	11	38	8	128
1949 { Pat Harder, Chicago Cardinals	8	45	3	102
{ Gene Roberts, New York Giants	17	0	0	102
1948—Pat Harder, Chicago Cardinals	6	53	7	110
1947—Pat Harder, Chicago Cardinals	7	39	7	102
1946—Ted Fritsch, Green Bay	10	13	9	100
1945—Steve Van Buren, Philadelphia	18	2	0	110
1944—Don Hutson, Green Bay	9	31	0	85
1943—Don Hutson, Green Bay	12	36	3	117
1942—Don Hutson, Green Bay	17	33	1	138
1941—Don Hutson, Green Bay	12	20	1	95
1940—Don Hutson, Green Bay	7	15	0	57
1939—Andy Farkas, Washington	11	2	0	68
1938—Clarke Hinkle, Green Bay	7	7	3	58
1937—Jack Manders, Chicago Bears	5	15	8	69
1936—Earl (Dutch) Clark, Detroit	7	19	4	73
1935—Earl (Dutch) Clark, Detroit	6	16	1	55
1934—Jack Manders, Chicago Bears	3	31	10	79
1933 { Ken Strong, New York Giants	6	13	5	64
{ Glenn Presnell, Portsmouth	6	10	6	64
1932—Earl (Dutch) Clark, Portsmouth	4	6	3	39

*First year in League

RUSHING

	Yards	Atts.	TDs
1969—Gale Sayers, Chicago	1,032	236	8
—Dick Post, San Diego (AFL)	873	182	6
1968—Leroy Kelly, Cleveland	1,239	248	16
—Paul Robinson, Cincinnati* (AFL)	1,023	238	8
1967—Leroy Kelly, Cleveland	1,205	235	11
—Jim Nance, Boston (AFL)	1,216	269	7
1966—Gale Sayers, Chicago	1,231	229	8
—Jim Nance, Boston (AFL)	1,458	299	11
1965—Jim Brown, Cleveland	1,544	289	17
—Paul Lowe, San Diego (AFL)	1,121	222	7
1964—Jim Brown, Cleveland	1,446	280	7
—Cookie Gilchrist, Buffalo (AFL)	981	230	6
1963—Jim Brown, Cleveland	1,863	291	12
—Clem Daniels, Oakland (AFL)	1,099	215	3
1962—Jim Taylor, Green Bay	1,474	272	19
—Cookie Gilchrist, Buffalo (AFL)	1,096	214	13
1961—Jim Brown, Cleveland	1,408	305	8
—Billy Cannon, Houston (AFL)	948	200	6
1960—Jim Brown, Cleveland	1,257	215	9
—Abner Haynes, Dallas (AFL)	875	156	9
1959—Jim Brown, Cleveland	1,329	290	14
1958—Jim Brown, Cleveland	1,527	257	17
1957—Jim Brown, Cleveland*	942	202	9
1956—Rick Casares, Chicago Bears	1,126	234	12
1955—Alan Ameche, Baltimore*	961	213	9
1954—Joe Perry, San Francisco	1,049	173	8
1953—Joe Perry, San Francisco	1,018	192	10
1952—Dan Towler, Los Angeles	894	156	10
1951—Eddie Price, New York Giants	971	271	7
1950—Marion Motley, Cleveland*	810	140	3
1949—Steve Van Buren, Philadelphia	1,146	263	11

RUSHING (Cont'd)

	Yards	Atts.	TDs
1948—Steve Van Buren, Philadelphia	945	201	10
1947—Steve Van Buren, Philadelphia	1,008	217	13
1946—Bill Dudley, Pittsburgh	604	146	3
1945—Steve Van Buren, Philadelphia	832	143	15
1944—Bill Paschal, New York	737	196	9
1943—Bill Paschal, New York*	572	147	10
1942—Bill Dudley, Pittsburgh*	696	162	6
1941—Clarence Manders, Brooklyn	486	111	7
1940—Byron White, Detroit	514	146	5
1939—Bill Osmanski, Chicago Bears*	699	121	7
1938—Byron White, Pittsburgh*	567	152	4
1937—Cliff Battles, Washington	874	216	6
1936—Alphonse Leemans, New York*	830	206	2
1935—Doug Russell, Chicago Cardinals	499	140	0
1934—Beattie Feathers, Chicago Bears*	1,004	101	9
1933—Cliff Battles, Boston	737	146	4
1932—Bob Campiglio, Stapleton*	504	104	2

*First year in League

PASS RECEIVING

	No.	Yards	TDs
1969—Dan Abramowicz, New Orleans	73	1,015	7
—Lance Alworth, San Diego (AFL)	64	1,003	4
1968—Clifton McNeil, San Francisco	71	994	7
—Lance Alworth, San Diego (AFL)	68	1,312	10
1967—Charley Taylor, Washington	70	990	9
—George Sauer, New York (AFL)	75	1,189	6
1966—Charley Taylor, Washington	72	1,119	12
—Lance Alworth, San Diego (AFL)	73	1,383	13
1965—Dave Parks, San Francisco	80	1,344	12
—Lionel Taylor, Denver (AFL)	85	1,131	6
1964—Johnny Morris, Chicago	93	1,200	10
—Charley Hennigan, Houston (AFL)	101	1,546	8
1963—Bobby Joe Conrad, St. Louis	73	967	10
—Lionel Taylor, Denver (AFL)	78	1,101	10
1962—Bobby Mitchell, Washington	72	1,384	11
—Lionel Taylor, Denver (AFL)	77	908	4
1961—Jim Phillips, Los Angeles	78	1,092	5
—Lionel Taylor, Denver (AFL)	100	1,176	4
1960—Raymond Berry, Baltimore	74	1,298	10
—Lionel Taylor, Denver (AFL)	92	1,235	12
1959—Raymond Berry, Baltimore	66	959	14
1958—Raymond Berry, Baltimore &	56	794	9
Pete Retzlaff, Philadelphia	56	766	2
1957—Billy Wilson, San Francisco	52	757	6
1956—Billy Wilson, San Francisco	60	889	5
1955—Pete Pihos. Philadelphia	62	864	7
1954—Pete Pihos. Philadelphia &	60	872	10
Billy Wilson, San Francisco	60	830	5
1953—Pete Pihos. Philadelphia	63	1,049	10
1952—Mac Speedie, Cleveland	62	911	5
1951—Elroy Hirsch, Los Angeles	66	1,495	17
1950—Tom Fears, Los Angeles	84	1,116	7
1949—Tom Fears, Los Angeles	77	1,013	9
1948—Tom Fears, Los Angeles*	51	698	4

PASS RECEIVING (Cont'd)

	No.	Yards	TDs
1947—Jim Keane, Chicago Bears	64	910	10
1946—Jim Benton, Los Angeles	63	981	6
1945—Don Hutson, Green Bay	47	834	9
1944—Don Hutson, Green Bay	58	866	9
1943—Don Hutson, Green Bay	47	776	11
1942—Don Hutson, Green Bay	74	1,211	17
1941—Don Hutson, Green Bay	58	738	10
1940—Don Looney, Philadelphia*	58	707	4
1939—Don Hutson, Green Bay	34	846	6
1938—Gaynell Tinsley, Chi. Cards	41	516	1
1937—Don Hutson, Green Bay	41	552	7
1936—Don Hutson, Green Bay	34	526	9
1935—Tod Goodwin, New York*	26	432	4
1934—Joe Carter, Philadelphia	16	237	4
1933—John Kelly, Brooklyn	21	219	3
1932—Luke Johnsos, Chi. Bears	24	321	2

*First year in League

PASSING

	Passes	Completed	Yards	Tds	Inter.
1969—C.A. (Sonny) Jurgensen, Wash.	442	274	3,102	22	15
—Greg Cook, Cincinnati* (AFL)	197	106	1,854	15	11
1968—Earl Morrall, Baltimore	317	182	2,909	26	17
—Len Dawson, Kansas City (AFL)	224	131	2,109	17	9
1967—C.A. (Sonny) Jurgensen, Wash.	508	288	3,747	31	16
—Daryle Lamonica, Oakland (AFL)	425	220	3,228	30	20
1966—Bart Starr, Green Bay	251	156	2,257	14	3
—Len Dawson, Kansas City (AFL)	284	159	2,527	26	10
1965—Rudy Bukich, Chicago	312	176	2,641	20	9
—John Hadl, San Diego (AFL)	348	174	2,798	20	21
1964—Bart Starr, Green Bay	272	163	2,144	15	4
—Len Dawson, Kansas City (AFL)	354	199	2,879	30	18
1963—Y.A. Tittle, New York	367	221	3,145	36	14
—Tobin Rote, San Diego (AFL)	286	170	2,510	20	17
1962—Bart Starr, Green Bay	285	178	2,438	12	9
—Len Dawson, Dallas (AFL)	310	189	2,759	29	17
1961—Milt Plum, Cleveland	302	177	2,416	18	10
—George Blanda, Houston (AFL)	362	187	3,330	36	22
1960—Milt Plum, Cleveland	250	151	2,297	21	5
—Jack Kemp, Los Angeles (AFL)	406	211	3,018	20	25
1959—Charles Conerly, New York	194	113	1,706	14	4
1958—Eddie LeBaron, Washington	145	79	1,365	11	10
1957—Tommy O'Connell, Cleveland	110	63	1,229	9	8
1956—Eddie Brown, Chicago Bears	168	96	1,667	11	12
1955—Otto Graham, Cleveland	185	98	1,721	15	8
1954—Norman Van Brocklin, L.A.	260	139	2,637	13	21
1953—Otto Graham, Cleveland	258	167	2,722	11	9
1952—Norman Van Brocklin, L.A.	205	113	1,736	14	17
1951—Bob Waterfield, L.A.	176	88	1,566	13	10
1950—Norman Van Brocklin, L.A.	233	127	2,061	18	14
1949—Sammy Baugh, Washington	255	145	1,903	18	14
1948—Tommy Thompson, Phila.	246	141	1,965	25	11
1947—Sammy Baugh, Washington	354	210	2,938	25	15
1946—Bob Waterfield, L.A.	251	127	1,747	18	17
1945—Sammy Baugh, Washington	182	128	1,669	11	9

PASSING (Cont'd)

	Passes	Completed	Yards	Tds	Inter.
1944—Frank Filchock, Washington	147	84	1,139	13	9
1943—Sammy Baugh, Washington	239	133	1,754	23	19
1942—Cecil Isbell, Green Bay	268	146	2,021	24	14
1941—Cecil Isbell, Green Bay	206	117	1,479	15	11
1940—Sammy Baugh, Washington	177	111	1,367	12	10
1939—Parker Hall, Cleveland Rams*	208	106	1,227	9	13
1938—Ed Danowski, N.Y. Giants	129	70	848	8	8
1937—Sammy Baugh, Washington*	171	81	1,127	7	14
1936—Arnie Herber, Green Bay	173	77	1,239	9	13
1935—Ed Danowski, N.Y. Giants	113	57	795	9	9
1934—Arnie Herber, Green Bay	115	42	799	8	12
1933—Harry Newman, New York*	132	53	963	8	17
1932—Arnie Herber, Green Bay	101	37	639	9	9

*First year in League

MOST FIELD GOALS

1969—Fred Cox, Minn.	26	1954—Lou Groza, Clev.	16
—J. Turner, N.Y. (AFL)	32	1953—Lou Groza, Clev.	23
1968—Mac Percival, Chi.	25	1952—Lou Groza, Clev.	19
—J. Turner, N.Y. (AFL)	34	1951—Bob Waterfield, L.A.	13
1967—Jim Bakken. St. L.	27	1950—Lou Groza, Clev.*	13
—Jan Stenerud, K.C.		1949—Cliff Patton, Phil. &	
(AFL)	21	Bob Waterfield, L.A.	9
1966—Bruce Gossett, L.A.	28	1948—Cliff Patton, Phil.	8
—Mike Mercer, Oak.-K.C.		1947—Ward Cuff, G.B.,	
(AFL)	21	Pat Harder, Chi. Cards &	
1965—Fred Cox, Minn.	23	Bob Waterfield, L.A.	7
—Pete Gogolak, Buff.		1946—Ted Fritsch, G.B.	9
(AFL)	28	1945—Joe Aguirre, Wash.	7
1964—Jim Bakken, St. L.	25	1944—Ken Strong, N.Y.	6
—Gino Cappelletti, Bos.		1943—Ward Cuff, N.Y. &	
(AFL)	25	Don Hutson, G.B.	3
1963—Jim Martin, Balt.	24	1942—Bill Daddio, Chi. Cards	5
—Gino Cappelletti, Bos.		1941—Clarke Hinkle, G.B.	6
(AFL)	22	1940—Clarke Hinkle, G.B.	9
1962—Lou Michaels, Pitt.	26	1939—Ward Cuff, N.Y.	7
—Gene Mingo, Den.		1938—Ward Cuff, N.Y. &	
(AFL)	27	Ralph Kercheval, Brk.	5
1961—Steve Myhra, Balt.	21	1937—Jack Manders, Chi.	
—Gino Cappelletti, Bos.		Bears	8
(AFL)	17	1936—Jack Manders, Chi. Bears	
1960—Tom Davis, S.F.	19	& Armand Niccolai, Pitt.	7
—Gene Mingo, Den.		1935—Armand Niccolai. Pitt. &	
(AFL)	18	Bill Smith, Chi. Cards	6
1959—Pat Summerall, N.Y.	20	1934—Jack Manders, Chi.	
1958—Paige Cothren. L.A. &		Bears	10
Tom Miner, Pitt.*	14	1933—Jack Manders, Chi.	
1957—Lou Groza, Clev.	15	Bears* & Glenn Presnell,	
1956—Sam Baker, Wash.	17	Ports.	6
1955—Fred Cone, G.B.	16	1932—Earl Clark, Ports.	3

*First year in League

INTERCEPTIONS

	No.	Yards
1969—Mel Renfro, Dallas	10	118
—Emmitt Thomas, Kansas City (AFL)	9	146
1968—Willie Williams, New York	10	103
—Dave Grayson, Oakland (AFL)	10	195
1967—Lem Barney, Detroit* and	10	232
Dave Whitsell, New Orleans	10	178
—Miller Farr, Houston (AFL) and	10	264
Tom Janik, Buffalo (AFL) and	10	222
Dick Westmoreland, Miami (AFL)	10	127
1966—Larry Wilson, St. Louis	10	180
—Johnny Robinson, Kansas City (AFL) and	10	136
Bobby Hunt, Kansas City (AFL)	10	113
1965—Bobby Boyd, Baltimore	9	78
—W.K. Hicks, Houston (AFL)	9	156
1964—Paul Krause, Washington*	12	140
—Dainard Paulson, New York (AFL)	12	157
1963—Dick Lynch, New York and	9	251
Rosie Taylor, Chicago	9	172
—Fred Glick, Houston (AFL)	12	180
1962—Willie Wood, Green Bay	9	132
—Lee Riley, New York (AFL)	11	122
1961—Dick Lynch, New York	9	60
—Billy Atkins, Buffalo (AFL)	10	158
1960—Dave Baker, San Francisco and	10	96
Jerry Norton, St. Louis	10	96
—Austin Gonsoulin, Denver* (AFL)	11	98
1959—Dean Derby, Pittsburgh and	7	127
Milt Davis, Baltimore and	7	119
Don Shinnick, Baltimore	7	70
1958—Jim Patton, New York	11	183
1957—Milt Davis, Baltimore* and	10	219
Jack Christiansen, Detroit and	10	137
Jack Butler, Pittsburgh	10	85
1956—Lindon Crow, Chicago Cardinals	11	170
1955—Will Sherman, Los Angeles	11	101
1954—Dick (Night Train) Lane, Chicago Cardinals	10	181
1953—Jack Christiansen, Detroit	12	238
1952—Dick (Night Train) Lane, Los Angeles*	14	298
1951—Otto Schnellbacher, N.Y. Giants	11	194
1950—Orban (Spec) Sanders, N.Y. Yanks*	13	199
1949—Bob Nussbaumer, Chicago Cardinals	12	157
1948—Dan Sandifer, Washington*	13	258
1947—Frank Reagan, N.Y. Giants and	10	203
Frank Seno, Boston Yanks	10	100
1946—Bill Dudley, Pittsburgh	10	242
1945—Roy Zimmerman, Philadelphia	7	90
1944—Howard Livingston, N.Y. Giants*	9	172
1943—Sammy Baugh, Washington	11	112
1942—Clyde (Bulldog) Turner, Chicago Bears	8	96
1941—Marshall Goldberg, Chicago Cardinals and	7	54
Arthur Jones, Pittsburgh*	7	35

*First year in League

PUNTING

	Atts.	Avg.
1969—David Lee, Baltimore	57	45.3
—Dennis Partee, San Diego (AFL)	71	44.6
1968—Billy Lothridge, Atlanta	75	44.3
—Jerrel Wilson, Kansas City (AFL)	63	45.1
1967—Billy Lothridge, Atlanta	87	43.7
—Bob Scarpitto, Denver (AFL)	105	44.9
1966—David Lee, Baltimore	49	45.6
—Bob Scarpitto, Denver (AFL)	76	45.8
1965—Gary Collins, Cleveland	65	46.7
—Jerrel Wilson, Kansas City (AFL)	69	45.4
1964—Bobby Walden, Minnesota	72	46.4
—Jim Fraser, Denver (AFL)	73	44.2
1963—Yale Lary, Detroit	35	48.9
—Jim Fraser, Denver (AFL)	81	44.4
1962—Tommy Davis, San Francisco	48	45.6
—Jim Fraser, Denver, (AFL)	55	43.6
1961—Yale Lary, Detroit,	52	48.4
—Billy Atkins, Buffalo (AFL)	85	44.5
1960—Jerry Norton, St. Louis	39	45.6
—Paul Maguire, Los Angeles* (AFL)	43	40.5
1959—Yale Lary, Detroit	45	47.1
1958—Sam Baker, Washington	48	45.4
1957—Don Chandler, New York	60	44.6
1956—Norm Van Brocklin, Los Angeles	48	43.1
1955—Norm Van Brocklin, Los Angeles	60	44.6
1954—Pat Brady, Pittsburgh	66	43.2
1953—Pat Brady, Pittsburgh	80	46.9
1952—Horace Gillom, Cleveland Browns	61	45.7
1951—Horace Gillom, Cleveland Browns	73	45.5
1950—Fred Morrison, Chicago Bears*	57	43.3
1949—Mike Boyda, N.Y. Bulldogs*	56	44.2
1948—Joe Muha, Philadelphia	57	47.2
1947—Jack Jacobs, Green Bay	57	43.5
1946—Roy McKay, Green Bay	64	42.7
1945—Roy McKay, Green Bay	44	41.2
1944—Frank Sinkwich, Detroit	45	41.0
1943—Sammy Baugh, Washington	50	45.9
1942—Sammy Baugh, Washington	37	46.6
1941—Sammy Baugh, Washington	30	48.7
1940—Sammy Baugh, Washington	35	51.0
1939—Parker Hall, Cleveland Rams*	58	41.0

*First year in league.

PUNT RETURNS

	No.	Yards	Avg.
1969—Alvin Haymond, Los Angeles	33	435	13.2
—Bill Thompson, Denver * (AFL)	25	288	11.5
1968—Bob Hayes, Dallas	15	312	20.8
—Noland Smith, Kansas City (AFL)	18	270	15.0
1967—Ben Davis, Cleveland	18	229	12.7
—Floyd Little, Denver * (AFL)	16	270	16.9
1966—Johnny Roland, St. Louis*	20	221	11.1
—Les (Speedie) Duncan, San Diego (AFL)	18	238	13.2
1965—Leroy Kelly, Cleveland	17	265	15.6
—Les (Speedie) Duncan, San Diego (AFL)	30	464	15.5
1964—Tommy Watkins, Detroit	16	238	14.9
—Bobby Jancik, Houston (AFL)	12	220	18.3
1963—Dick James, Washington	16	214	13.4
—Claude (Hoot) Gibson, Oakland (AFL)	26	307	11.8
1962—Pat Studstill, Detroit	29	457	15.8
—Dick Christy, New York (AFL)	15	250	16.7
1961—Willie Wood, Green Bay	14	225	16.1
—Dick Christy, New York (AFL)	18	383	21.3
1960—Abe Woodson, San Francisco	13	174	13.4
—Abner Haynes, Dallas (AFL)	14	215	15.4
1959—Johnny Morris, Chicago Bears	14	171	12.2
1958—Jon Arnett, Los Angeles	18	223	12.4
1957—Bert Zagers, Washington	14	217	15.5
1956—Ken Konz, Cleveland Browns	13	187	14.4
1955—Ollie Matson, Chicago Cardinals	13	245	18.8
1954—Veryl Switzer, Green Bay*	24	306	12.8
1953—Charlie Trippi, Chicago Cardinals	21	239	11.4
1952—Jack Christiansen, Detroit	15	322	21.5
1951—Buddy Young, N.Y. Yanks	12	231	19.3
1950—Herb Rich, Baltimore*	12	276	23.0
1949—Vitamin Smith, Los Angeles*	27	427	15.8
1948—George McAfee, Chicago Bears	30	417	13.9
1947—Walt Slater, Pittsburgh*	28	435	15.5
1946—Bill Dudley, Pittsburgh	27	385	14.2
1945—Dave Ryan, Detroit*	15	220	14.7
1944—Steve Van Buren, Philadelphia*	15	230	15.3
1943—Andy Farkas, Washington	15	168	11.2
1942—Merlyn Condit, Brooklyn	21	210	10.0
1941—Byron (Whizzer) White, Detroit	19	262	13.8

*First year in league.

KICKOFF RETURNS

	No.	Yards	Avg.
1969—Bobby Williams, Detroit	17	563	33.1
—Bill Thompson, Denver* (AFL)	18	513	28.5
1968—Preston Pearson, Baltimore	15	527	35.1
—George Atkinson, Oakland* (AFL)	32	802	25.1
1967—Travis Williams, Green Bay*	18	739	41.1
—Zeke Moore, Houston* (AFL)	14	405	28.9
1966—Gale Sayers, Chicago	23	718	31.2
—Goldie Sellers, Denver* (AFL)	19	541	28.5
1965—Tommy Watkins, Detroit	17	584	34.4
—Abner Haynes, Denver (AFL)	34	901	26.5
1964—Clarence Childs, New York*	34	987	29.0
—Bo Roberson, Oakland (AFL)	36	975	27.1
1963—Abe Woodson, San Francisco	29	935	32.3
—Bobby Jancik, Houston (AFL)	45	1317	29.3
1962—Abe Woodson, San Francisco	37	1157	31.3
—Bobby Jancik, Houston* (AFL)	24	726	30.3
1961—Dick Bass, Los Angeles	23	698	30.3
—Dave Grayson, Dallas* (AFL)	16	453	28.3
1960—Tom Moore, Green Bay	12	397	33.1
—Ken Hall, Houston (AFL)	19	594	31.3
1959—Abe Woodson, San Francisco	13	382	29.4
1958—Ollie Matson, Chicago Cardinals	14	497	35.5
1957—Jon Arnett, Los Angeles*	18	504	28.0
1956—Tom Wilson, Los Angeles*	15	477	31.8
1955—Al Carmichael, Green Bay	14	418	29.9
1954—Billy Reynolds, Cleveland Browns	14	413	29.5
1953—Joe Arenas, San Francisco	16	551	34.4
1952—Lynn Chandnois, Pittsburgh	17	599	35.2
1951—Lynn Chandnois, Pittsburgh	12	390	32.5
1950—Vitamin Smith, Los Angeles	22	724	33.7
1949—Don Doll, Detroit*	21	536	25.5
1948—Joe Scott, N.Y. Giants*	20	569	28.5
1947—Ed Saenz, Washington	29	797	27.4
1946—Abe Karnofsky, Boston Yanks	21	599	28.5
1945—Steve Van Buren, Philadelphia	13	373	28.7
1944—Bob Thurbon, Card/Pitt	12	291	24.2
1943—Ken Heineman, Brooklyn	16	442	27.6
1942—Marshall Goldberg, Chicago Cardinals	15	393	26.2

*First year in league.

NATIONAL FOOTBALL LEAGUE
PAID ATTENDANCE

Year	Regular Season	Average	* Post-season	World Championship
1969	6,096,127 (112 games) NFL	54,430	162,279 (3)	80,562
	2,843,373 (70 games) AFL	40,620	167,088 (3)	
1968	5,882,313 (112 games) NFL	52,521	215,902 (3)	75,377
	2,635,004 (70 games) AFL	37,643	114,438 (2)	
1967	5,938,924 (112 games) NFL	53,026	166,208 (3)	75,546
	2,295,697 (63 games) AFL	36,439	53,330 (1)	
1966	5,337,044 (105 games) NFL	50,829	74,152 (1)	61,946
	2,160,369 (63 games) AFL	34,291	42,080 (1)	
1965	4,634,021 (98 games) NFL	47,286	100,304 (2)	
	1,782,384 (56 games) AFL	31,828	30,361 (1)	
1964	4,563,049 (98 games) NFL	46,562	79,544 (1)	
	1,447,875 (56 games) AFL	25,855	40,242 (1)	
1963	4,163,643 (98 games) NFL	42,486	45,801 (1)	
	1,208,697 (56 games) AFL	21,584	63,171 (2)	
1962	4,003,421 (98 games) NFL	40,851	64,892 (1)	
	1,147,302 (56 games) AFL	20,487	37,981 (1)	
1961	3,986,159 (98 games) NFL	40,675	39,029 (1)	
	1,002,657 (56 games) AFL	17,904	29,556 (1)	
1960	3,128,296 (78 games) NFL	40,106	67,325 (1)	
	926,156 (56 games) AFL	16,538	32,183 (1)	
1959	3,140,409 (72 games)	43,617	57,545 (1)	
1958	3,006,124 (72 games)	41,752	123,659 (2)	
1957	2,836,318 (72 games)	39,393	119,579 (2)	
1956	2,551,263 (72 games)	35,434	56,836 (1)	
1955	2,521,836 (72 games)	35,026	85,693 (1)	
1954	2,190,571 (72 games)	30,425	43,827 (1)	
1953	2,164,585 (72 games)	30,064	54,577 (1)	
1952	2,052,126 (72 games)	28,502	97,507 (2)	
1951	1,913,019 (72 games)	26,570	57,522 (1)	
1950	1,977,753 (78 games)	25,356	136,647 (3)	
1949	1,391,735 (60 games)	23,196	27,980 (1)	
1948	1,525,243 (60 games)	25,421	36,309 (1)	
1947	1,837,437 (60 games)	30,624	66,268 (2)	
1946	1,732,135 (55 games)	31,493	58,346 (1)	
1945	1,270,401 (50 games)	25,408	32,178 (1)	
1944	1,019,649 (50 games)	20,393	46,016 (1)	
1943	969,128 (50 games)	19,383	71,315 (2)	
1942	887,920 (55 games)	16,144	36,006 (1)	
1941	1,108,615 (55 games)	20,157	55,870 (2)	
1940	1,063,025 (55 games)	19,328	36,034 (1)	
1939	1,071,200 (55 games)	19,476	32,279 (1)	
1938	937,197 (55 games)	17,040	48,120 (1)	
1937	963,039 (55 games)	17,510	15,878 (1)	
1936	816,007 (54 games)	15,111	29,545 (1)	
1935	638,178 (53 games)	12,041	15,000 (1)	
1934	492,684 (60 games)	8,211	35,059 (1)	

*—Includes division, conference and league championship from 1934–1969; number of post-season games in parentheses.

WORLD CHAMPIONSHIP GAME
RESULTS AT A GLANCE

Year	Date	Winner	Loser	Site	Attendance
1970	Jan. 11	Kansas City (AFL) 23	Minnesota (NFL) 7	New Orleans	80,562
1969	Jan. 12	New York (AFL) 16	Baltimore (NFL) 7	Miami	75,389
1968	Jan. 14	Green Bay (NFL) 33	Oakland (AFL) 14	Miami	75,546
1967	Jan. 15	Green Bay (NFL) 35	Kansas City (AFL) 10	Los Angeles	61,946

1970 WORLD CHAMPIONSHIP GAME

Tulane Stadium, New Orleans, La.   Sunday, January 11, 1970
Attendance: 80,562

The AFL squared the Super Bowl at 2 games apiece with the NFL, building a 16–0 halftime lead behind Len Dawson's superb quarterbacking and a powerful defense and then easily fighting back a Viking rally in the second half. Dawson, the fourth consecutive quarterback to be chosen the Super Bowl's top player, called an almost flawless game, completing 12 of 17 passes and hitting Otis Taylor on a 46-yard play for the final Chiefs' touchdown. The Kansas City defense limited Minnesota's strong rushing game to 67 yards gained and made three interceptions and two fumble recoveries. The crowd of 80, 562 set a Super Bowl record as did the gross receipts of $3,817,872.69.

MINNESOTA (7)	Offense	KANSAS CITY (23)
Gene Washington	WR	Frank Pitts
Grady Alderman	LT	Jim Tyrer
Jim Vellone	LG	Ed Budde
Mick Tingelhoff	C	E. J. Holub
Milt Sunde	RG	Mo Moorman
Ron Yary	RT	Dave Hill
John Beasley	TE	Fred Arbanas
John Henderson	WR	Otis Taylor
Joe Kapp	QB	Len Dawson
Dave Osborn	RB	Mike Garrett
Bill Brown	RB	Robert Holmes

	Defense	
Carl Eller	LE	Jerry Mays
Gary Larsen	LT	Curley Culp
Alan Page	RT	Buck Buchanan
Jim Marshall	RE	Aaron Brown
Roy Winston	LLB	Bobby Bell
Lonnie Warwick	MLB	Willie Lanier
Wally Hilgenberg	RLB	Jim Lynch
Earsell Mackbee	LCB	Jim Marsalis
Ed Sharockman	RCB	Emmitt Thomas
Karl Kassulke	LS	Jim Kearney
Paul Krause	RS	Johnny Robinson

SUBSTITUTIONS

MINNESOTA—Offense: Receivers—Bob Grim, Kent Kramer, Linemen—Steve Smith, Ed White. Backs—Gary Cuozzo, Bob Lee, Clint Jones, Bill Harris, Oscar Reed, Jim Lindsey. Kicker—Fred Cox. Defense: Linebackers—Dale Hackbart, Mike McGill, Jim Hargrove. Lineman—Paul Dickson. Back—Charlie West. DNP—Doug Davis, Mike Reilly.

KANSAS CITY—Offense: Receivers—Gloster Richardson, Curtis McClinton. Linemen—George Daney, Remi Prudhomme. Backs—Mike Livingston, Warren McVea, Wendell Hayes, Ed Podolak. Kickers—Jerrel Wilson, Jan Stenerud. Defense: Linebacker—Bob Stein. Linemen—Gene Trosch, Ed Lothamer, Chuck Hurston. Backs—Goldie Sellers, Willie Mitchell, Ceaser Belser. DNP—Tom Flores.

Referee, John McDonough (AFL). Umpire, Lou Palazzi (NFL). Headlinesman, Harry Kessel (AFL). Field Judge, Charlie Musser (AFL). Back Judge, Tom Kelleher (NFL). Line Judge, Bill Schleibaum (NFL).

SCORING

MINNESOTA VIKINGS (NFL)	0	0	7	0——	7
KANSAS CITY CHIEFS (AFL)	3	13	7	0——	23

KC-FG Stenerud 48. KC-FG Stenerud 32. KC-FG Stenerud 25. KC-Garrett 5 run (Stenerud kick). Minn-Osborn 4 run (Cox kick). KC-Taylor 46 pass from Dawson (Stenerud kick).

INDIVIDUAL STATISTICS

MINNESOTA   Rushing   **KANSAS CITY**

	Atts.	Yds.	LG		Atts.	Yds.	LG
Brown	6	26	10	Garrett	11	39	6
Reed	4	17	15	Pitts	3	37	19
Osborn	7	15	4	Hayes	8	31	13
Kapp	2	9	7	McVea	12	26	9
				Dawson	3	11	11
				Holmes	5	7	7

Passing

	Atts.	Comp.	Yds.	Int.	TD		Atts.	Comp.	Yds.	Int.	TD
Kapp	25	16	183	2	0	Dawson	17	12	142	1	1
Cuozzo	3	1	16	1	0						

Receiving

	No.	Yds.	TD		No.	Yds.	TD
Henderson	7	111	0	Taylor	6	81	1
Brown	3	11	0	Pitts	3	33	0
Beasley	2	41	0	Garrett	2	25	0
Reed	2	16	0	Hayes	1	3	0
Osborn	2	11	0				
Washington	1	9	0				

Interceptions

	No.	Yds.	TD		No.	Yds.	TD
Krause	1	0	0	Lanier	1	9	0
				Robinson	1	9	0
				Thomas	1	6	0

Punting

	No.	Avg.	LG		No.	Avg.	LG
Lee	3	37.0	50	Wilson	4	48.5	59

Punt Returns

	No.	FC	Yds.	LG		No.	FC	Yds.	LG
West	2	0	18	0	Garrett	1	0	0	0

Kickoff Returns

	No.	Yds.	LG		No.	Yds.	LG
West	3	46	0	Hayes	2	36	0
Jones	1	33	0				

Field Goals

	Att.	Made		Att.	Made
Cox	1	0	Stenerud	3	3

Fumbles

	No.	Own Rec.	Opp. Rec.	TD		No.	Own Rec.	Opp. Rec.	TD
Henderson	1	0	0	0	Robinson	0	0	1	0
West	1	0	0	0	Prudhomme	0	0	1	0
Kapp	1	0	0	0					
Vellone	0	1	0	0					

Scoring

	TD	PAT	FG	Pts.		TD	PAT	FG	Pts.
Osborn	1	0	0	6	Stenerud	0	2	3	11
Cox	0	1	0	1	Garrett	1	0	0	6
					Taylor	1	0	0	6

TEAM STATISTICS

	MINNESOTA	KANSAS CITY
Total First Downs	13	18
First Downs Rushing	2	8
First Downs Passing	10	7
First Downs by Penalty	1	3
Rushes	19	42
Yards Gained Rushing (net)	67	151
Average Yards per Rush	3.5	3.6
Passes Attempted	28	17
Passes Completed	17	12
Had Intercepted	3	1
Times Tackled Attempting to Pass	3	3
Yards Lost Attempting to Pass	27	20
Yards Gained Passing (net)	172	122
Total Net Yardage	239	273
Punts	3	4
Average Distance Punts	37.0	48.5
Punt Returns	2	1
Punt Return Yardage	18	0
Kickoff Returns	4	2
Kickoff Return Yardage	79	36
Yards Interceptions Returned	0	24
Fumbles	3	0
Opponents' Fumbles Recovered	0	2
Total Return Yardage	97	79
Penalties	6	4
Yards Penalized	67	47
Total Points Scored	7	23
Touchdowns	1	2
Touchdowns Running	1	1
Touchdowns Passing	0	1
Extra Points	1	2
Field Goals Attempted	1	3
Field Goals Made	0	3
Total Offensive Plays	50	62
Avg. Gain per Offensive Play	4.8	4.4

FINANCIAL FIGURES

Paid Attendance	80,562
Gross Receipts (including TV, radio, films)	$3,817,872.69
Players' Shares (total)	$1,233,750.00
Winning Player's Share (each)	$15,000.00
Losing Player's Share (each)	$7,500.00

1969 WORLD CHAMPIONSHIP GAME

NEW YORK JETS 16, BALTIMORE 7—At Miami Orange Bowl Stadium, Sunday, January 11, 1969, attendance 75,337. Jets' quarterback Joe Namath "guaranteed" victory on the Thursday before the game, then went out and led the AFL to its first Super Bowl victory over a Baltimore team that had lost only once in 16 games all season. Namath, chosen the outstanding player, completed 17 of 28 passes for 206 yards and directed a steady attack that dominated the NFL champions after the Jet defense had intercepted Colt quarterback Earl Morrall three times in the first half. The Jets had 337 total yards, including 121 yards rushing by Matt Snell. John Unitas, who had missed most of the season with a sore elbow, came off the bench and led Baltimore to its only touchdown late in the fourth quarter after New York led 16–0.

New York (AFL)	0	7	6	3——16
Baltimore (NFL)	0	0	0	7—— 7

NY—Snell 4 run (Turner kick)
NY—FG Turner 32
NY—FG Turner 30
NY—FG Turner 9
Balt—Hill 1 run (Michaels kick)

1968 WORLD CHAMPIONSHIP GAME

GREEN BAY 33, OAKLAND 14—At Miami Orange Bowl Stadium, Sunday, January 14, 1968, attendance 75,546. Green Bay, after winning its third consecutive NFL championship, won the Super Bowl World title for the second straight year 33–14 over the AFL champion Raiders in a game that drew the first $3 million dollar gate in football history. Bart Starr again was chosen the game's most valuable player as he completed 13 of 24 passes for 202 yards and one touchdown and directed a Packer attack that was in control all the way after building a 16–7 halftime lead. Don Chandler kicked four field goals and Herb Adderley, All-Pro cornerback, capped the Green Bay scoring with a 60-yard run with an interception against Daryle Lamonica. The game marked the last for Vince Lombardi as Packer coach, ending nine years at Green Bay in which he won six Western Conference championships, five NFL championships and two Super Bowls.

Green Bay (NFL)	3	13	10	7——33
Oakland (AFL)	0	7	0	7——14

GB—FG Chandler 39
GB—FG Chandler 20
GB—Dowler 62 pass from Starr (Chandler kick)
Oak—Miller 23 pass from Lamonica (Blanda kick)
GB—FG Chandler 43
GB—Anderson 2 run (Chandler kick)
GB—FG Chandler 31
GB—Adderley 60 interception (Chandler kick)
Oak—Miller 23 pass from Lamonica (Blanda kick)

1967 WORLD CHAMPIONSHIP GAME

GREEN BAY 35, KANSAS CITY 10—At Los Angeles Memorial Coliseum, Sunday, January 15, 1967, attendance 61,946. The Green Bay Packers opened the Super Bowl series by defeating Kansas City's American Football League champions 35–10 behind the passing of Bart Starr, the receiving of Max McGee and a key interception by All-Pro safety Willie Wood. Green Bay broke open the game with three second-half touchdowns, the first of which was set up by Wood's 40-yard return of an interception to the Chiefs' five-yard-line with the Packers leading by only 14–10. McGee, filling in for ailing Boyd Dowler after having caught only three passes all season, caught seven from Starr for 138 yards and two touchdowns. Elijah Pitts ran for two other scores. The Chiefs' 10 points came in the second quarter; the only TD on a seven-yard pass from Len Dawson to Curtis McClinton. Starr completed 16 of 23 passes for 250 yards and 2 TDs and was chosen the Most Valuable Player. The Packers collected $15,000 per man and the Chiefs $7,500—the largest single-game shares in the history of team sports.

```
Kansas City (AFL)    0   10    0    0——10
Green Bay (NFL)      7    7   14    7——35
```

GB—McGee 37 pass from Starr (Chandler kick)
KC—McClinton 7 pass from Dawson (Mercer kick)
GB—Taylor 14 run (Chandler kick)
KC—FG Mercer 31
GB—Pitts 5 run (Chandler kick)
GB—McGee 13 pass from Starr (Chandler kick)
GB—Pitts 1 run (Chandler kick)

WORLD CHAMPIONSHIP GAME RECORDS
(Compiled by Elias Sports Bureau)

INDIVIDUAL RECORDS
SCORING

Most Points, Game

15   Don Chandler, GB. 1968 (3-pat, 4-fg)

Most Touchdowns, Game

2   Max McGee, G.B. 1967 (2-p)
Elijah Pitts, G.B. 1967 (2-r)
Bill Miller, Oak. 1968 (2-p)

Most Points After Touchdown, Game

5   Don Chandler, G.B. 1967 (5-att)

Most Fields Goals Attempted, Game

5   Jim Turner, N.Y. 1969

Most Field Goals, Game

4   Don Chandler, G.B. 1968

Longest Field Goal

48   Jan Stenerud, K.C. 1970

RUSHING

Most Attempts, Game

30   Matt Snell, N.Y. 1969

Most Yards Gained, Game

121   Matt Snell, N.Y. 1969

Longest Gain

58   Tom Matte, Balt. 1969

Most Touchdowns, Game

2   Elijah Pitts, G.B. 1967

PASSING

Most Attempts, Game

    34   Daryle Lamonica, Oak. 1968 (15-comp)

Most Completions, Game

    17   Joe Namath, N.Y. 1969 (28-att)

Highest Efficiency, Game

    70.6   Len Dawson, K.C. 1970 (17–12)

Most Yards Gained, Game

    250   Bart Starr, G.B. 1967

Longest Completion

    62   Bart Starr (to Dowler), G.B. 1968 (TD)

Most Touchdowns, Game

    2   Bart Starr, G.B. 1967
       Daryle Lamonica, Oak. 1968

Fewest Had Intercepted, Most Attempts, Game

    0   Joe Namath, N.Y. 1969 (28-att)

PASS RECEPTIONS

Most Receptions, Game

    8   George Sauer, N.Y. 1969 (133 yds)

Most Yards Gained, Game

    138   Max McGee, G.B. 1967 (7 rec)

Longest Reception

    62   Boyd Dowler (from Starr), G.B. 1968 (TD)

Most Touchdowns, Game

    2   Max McGee, G.B. 1967
       Bill Miller, Oak. 1968

INTERCEPTIONS BY

Most Interceptions By, Game

    2   Randy Beverly, N.Y. 1969

Most Yards Gained, Game

    60   Herb Adderley, G.B. 1968 (1)

Longest Gain

    60   Herb Adderley, G.B. 1968 (TD)

Most Touchdowns, Game

    1   Herb Adderley, G.B. 1968

PUNTING

Most Punts, Game

    7   Jerrel Wilson, K.C. 1967

Longest Punt

   61   Jerrel Wilson, K.C. 1967

Highest Punting Average, Game (3 Min.)

  48.5   Jerrel Wilson, K.C. 1970 (4)

PUNT RETURNS

Most Punt Returns, Game

    5   Willie Wood, G.B. 1968 (35 yds)

Most Fair Catches, Game

    1   Willie Wood, G.B. 1967
          Rodger Bird, Oak. 1968
          Bill Baird, N.Y. 1969

Most Yards Gained, Game

  35   Willie Wood, G.B. 1968 (5)

Longest Punt Return

  31   Willie Wood, G.B. 1968

Highest Average, Game (3 Min.)

  8.5   Tim Brown, Balt. 1969 (4)

Most Touchdowns, Game
    None

KICKOFF RETURNS

Most Kickoff Returns, Game

    4   Bert Coan, K.C. 1967 (87 yds)

Most Yards Gained, Game

  87   Bert Coan, K.C. 1967 (4)

Longest Kickoff Return

  33   Preston Pearson, Balt. 1969
          Clint Jones, Minn. 1970

Highest Average, Game (3 Min.)

  21.8   Bert Coan, K.C. 1967 (4)

Most Touchdowns, Game

    None

FUMBLES

Most Fumbles, Game

   1 By many players

Most Fumbles Recovered, Game

   1 By many players

TEAM RECORDS
SCORING

Most Points, Game

   35 Green Bay 1967

Fewest Points, Game

   7 Baltimore 1969
      Minnesota 1970

Most Points, Both Teams, Game

   47 Green Bay (33) vs Oak. (14) 1968

Fewest Points, Both Teams, Game

   23 Baltimore (7) vs N.Y. (16) 1969

Most Points, Each Quarter

1st:	7	Green Bay 1967
2nd:	13	Green Bay 1968
		Kansas City 1970
3rd:	14	Green Bay 1967
4th:	7	Green Bay 1967, 68
		Oakland 1968
		Baltimore 1969

Most Points, Both Teams, Each Quarter

1st:	7	Green Bay (7) vs K.C. (0) 1967
2nd:	20	Green Bay (13) vs Oak. (7) 1968
3rd:	14	Green Bay (14) vs K.C. (0) 1967
		Kansas City (7) vs Minn. (7) 1970
4th:	14	Green Bay (7) vs Oak. (7) 1968

Most Touchdowns, Game

   5 Green Bay 1967

Fewest Touchdowns, Game

   1 Kansas City 1967
      Baltimore 1969
      New York 1969
      Minnesota 1970

Most Touchdowns, Both Teams, Game

   6 Green Bay (5) vs K.C. (1) 1967

Fewest Touchdowns, Both Teams, Game

   2 Baltimore (1) vs N.Y. (1) 1969

Most Points After Touchdown, Game

     5   Green Bay 1967

Most Points After Touchdown, Both Teams, Game

     6   Green Bay (5) vs K.C. (1) 1967

Most Field Goals Attempted, Game

     5   New York 1969

Most Field Goals Attempted, Both Teams, Game

     7   New York (5) vs Balt. (2) 1969

Most Field Goals, Game

     4   Green Bay 1968

Most Field Goals, Both Teams, Game

     4   Green Bay (4) vs Oak. (0) 1968

FIRST DOWNS

Most First Downs, Game

    21   Green Bay 1967
           New York 1969

Most First Downs, Both Teams, Game

    39   New York (21) vs Balt. (18) 1969

Most First Downs, Rushing, Game

    11   Green Bay 1968

Most First Downs, Rushing, Both Teams, Game

    17   New York (10) vs Balt. (7) 1969

Most First Downs, Passing, Game

    12   Kansas City 1967

Most First Downs, Passing, Both Teams, Game

    23   Kansas City (12) vs G.B. (11) 1967

Most First Downs, Penalty, Game

     3   Kansas City 1970

NET YARDS GAINED

(Rushes & Passes)

Most Yards Gained, Game

   358   Green Bay 1967

Fewest Yards Gained, Game

   239   Kansas City 1967
           Minnesota 1970

Most Yards Gained, Both Teams, Game

661   New York (337) vs Balt. (324) 1969

Fewest Yards Gained, Both Teams, Game

512   Minnesota (239) vs K.C. (273) 1970

RUSHING

Most Attempts, Game

43   New York 1969

Fewest Attempts, Game

19   Kansas City 1967
Minnesota 1970

Most Attempts, Both Teams, Game

66   New York (43) vs Balt. (23) 1969

Fewest Attempts, Both Teams, Game

52   Kansas City (19) vs G.B. (33) 1967

Most Yards Gained, Game

160   Green Bay 1968

Fewest Yards Gained, Game

67   Minnesota 1970

Most Yards Gained, Both Teams, Game

285   Baltimore (143) vs N.Y. (142) 1969

Fewest Yards Gained, Both Teams, Game

202   Kansas City (72) vs G.B. (130) 1967

Most Touchdowns, Game

3   Green Bay 1967

Fewest Touchdowns, Game

0   Kansas City 1967
Oakland 1968

Most Touchdowns, Both Teams, Game

3   Green Bay (3) vs K.C. 1967

Fewest Touchdowns, Both Teams, Game

1   Oakland (0) vs G.B. (1) 1968

PASSING

Most Passes Attempted, Game

41   Baltimore 1969

Fewest Passes Attempted, Game

17   Kansas City 1970

Most Passes Attempted, Both Teams, Game

    70   Baltimore (41) vs N.Y. (29) 1969

Fewest Passes Attempted, Both Teams, Game

    45   Kansas City (17) vs Minn. (28) 1970

Most Passes Completed, Game

    17   Kansas City 1967
           Baltimore 1969
           New York 1969
           Minnesota 1970

Fewest Passes Completed, Game

    12   Kansas City 1970

Most Passes Completed, Both Teams, Game

    34   Baltimore (17) vs N.Y. (17) 1969

Fewest Passes Completed, Both Teams, Game

    28   Green Bay (13) vs Oak. (15) 1968

Most Yards Gained, Game

   228   Green Bay 1967

Fewest Yards Gained, Game

   122   Kansas City 1970

Most Yards Gained, Both Teams, Game

   395   Green Bay (228) vs K.C. (167) 1967

Fewest Yards Gained, Both Teams, Game

   294   Kansas City (122) vs Minn. (172) 1970

Most Times Tackled Attempting Passes, Game

    6   Kansas City 1967

Fewest Times Tackled Attempting Passes, Game

    0   Baltimore 1969

Most Times Tackled Attempting Passes, Both Teams, Game

    9   Kansas City (6) vs G.B. (3) 1967

Fewest Times Tackled Attempting Passes, Both Teams, Game

    2   Baltimore (0) vs N.Y. (2) 1969

Most Touchdowns, Game

    2   Green Bay 1967
           Oakland 1968

Fewest Touchdowns, Game

    0   Baltimore 1969
           New York 1969

Most Touchdowns, Both Teams, Game

    3   Green Bay (2) vs K.C. (1) 1967
           Oakland (2) vs G.B. (1) 1968

INTERCEPTIONS BY

Most Interceptions By, Game

    4 New York 1969

Most Yards Gained, Game

    60 Green Bay 1968

Most Interceptions By, Both Teams, Game

    4 New York (4) vs Balt. (0) 1969
       Kansas City (3) vs Minn. (1) 1970

Most Touchdowns, Game

    1 Green Bay 1968

PUNTING

Most Punts, Game

    7 Kansas City 1967

Fewest Punts, Game

    3 Baltimore 1969
       Minnesota 1970

Most Punts, Both Teams, Game

    12 Green Bay (6) vs Oak. (6) 1968

Fewest Punts, Both Teams, Game

    7 Baltimore (3) vs N.Y. (4) 1969
      Minnesota (3) vs K.C. (4) 1970

Highest Average, Game

    48.5 Kansas City 1970 (4)

Lowest Average, Game

    37.0 Minnesota 1970 (3)

PUNT RETURNS

Most Punt Returns, Game

    5 Green Bay 1968

Fewest Punt Returns, Games

    1 New York 1969
      Kansas City 1970

Most Punt Returns, Both Teams, Game

    8 Green Bay (5) vs Oak. (3) 1968

Fewest Punt Returns, Both Teams, Game

    3 Kansas City (1) vs Minn. (2) 1970

Most Yards Gained, Game

    35 Green Bay 1968

Fewest Yards Gained, Game

    0 New York 1969 (1)
        Kansas City 1970 (1)

Most Yards Gained, Both Teams, Game

    47 Green Bay (35) vs Oak. (12) 1968

Fewest Yards Gained, Both Teams, Game

    18 Kansas City (0) vs Minn. (18) 1970

Highest Average Gain, Game

    9.0 Minnesota 1970 (2)

Most Touchdowns, Game

    None

KICKOFF RETURNS

Most Kickoff Returns, Game

    7 Oakland 1968

Fewest Kickoff Returns, Game

    1 New York 1969

Most Kickoff Returns, Both Teams, Game

    10 Oakland (7) vs G.B. (3) 1968

Fewest Kickoff Returns, Both Teams, Game

    5 New York (1) vs Balt. (4) 1969

Most Yards Gained, Game

    130 Kansas City 1967

Fewest Yards Gained, Game

    25 New York 1969 (1)

Most Yards Gained, Both Teams, Game

    195 Kansas City (130) vs G.B. (65) 1967

Fewest Yards Gained, Both Teams, Game

    115 Kansas City (36) vs Minn. (79) 1970

Highest Average Gain, Game

    26.3 Baltimore 1969 (4)

Most Touchdowns, Game

    None

FUMBLES

Most Fumbles, Game

    3 Oakland 1968
        Minnesota 1970

Most Fumbles Recovered, Game

    2 Green Bay 1968 (2-opp)
        Kansas City 1970 (2-opp)

The Super Bowls—
A Pictorial Review

Kansas City Chiefs
vs.
Green Bay Packers
Jan. 15, 1967, Los Angeles
Green Bay 35, Kansas City 10

"In the AFL-NFL Joint Committee meetings, we had been referring to the game as the 'Big One' or the 'Final Game,'" Kansas City Chiefs owner Lamar Hunt recalled. Hunt was subconsciously thinking of the toy he had bought his daughter, something called Super Ball. So he called the game the Super Bowl, and from then on the final game had a name. The original Super Sunday took place January 15, 1967, as the AFL and NFL met for the first time.

At the start of the game, offense dominated. Green Bay was led by the experienced Bart Starr (15, left), the master of coach Vince Lombardi's "perfection football." Jerry Mays tried unsuccessfully to bring down the quarterback. Willie Mitchell did bring down Max McGee (above), but McGee later beat Mitchell to the ball and raced 27 yards to a touchdown, giving Green Bay an early lead.

278

Kansas City's game plan was predicated on the short pass, which, when Green Bay took a sizable lead, became "bomb"-oriented. Len Dawson (16, left) was capable of throwing the long pass, but was left open to the hard rush of end Willie Davis (87). Green Bay maintained its lead, as Hank Stram explained, by "Bart Starr's uncanny ability to come up with the big third down play." Starr (15, center) made good use of hard-running fullback Jim Taylor who followed the crunching blocks of Fuzzy Thurston (63), Jerry Kramer (64, below) or Bob Skoronski (76). Taylor ran 14 yards for the Packers' second touchdown in just such a way.

Green Bay Packers
vs.
Oakland Raiders
Jan. 14, 1968, Miami
Green Bay 33, Oakland 14

Daryle Lamonica, Raider quarterback: "We felt we could run on them but . . . they shut off the outside on us." And: "That Nitschke was great. We had everybody cut down on our sweeps except him." Or: "They did a great job taking away my passing lanes." For Oakland it was a case of ifs, ands or buts, a day of frustration and finally, defeat. The Green Bay Packers defended their title in a farewell to Vince Lombardi, who would resign shortly after.

As in the first Super Bowl game, Bart Starr (15, above left) was the key to the Packer offense. His first touchdown was a pass to Boyd Dowler that covered 62 yards. And, in the third quarter when ball control was vital, the Packers ran 25 plays to Oakland's 9. Donny Anderson (44) pushed for yards behind the blocking of Jerry Kramer and scored Green Bay's second touchdown. Ben Wilson (36, left) was a big factor in keeping control of the game as the Packer offensive lineman opened big holes. Finally, in the locker room (above), coach Vince Lombardi hugged his game stars, Don Chandler (four field goals) and quarterback Starr. Tackle Henry Jordan philosophized that perhaps the Raiders weren't really ready. "You can say you know how much it means and you think you are ready to play your best, but until you've once been there, maybe you're not. Next year, I dare say, it'll go right down to the wire."

Baltimore Colts
vs.
New York Jets
Jan. 12, 1969, Miami
New York 16, Baltimore 7

"And we're going to win Sunday—I'll guarantee you." The headlines in the *New York Post* the next day elaborated little: "Joe Guarantees It." Speaking in Miami, Jet quarterback Namath guaranteed that his team would defeat the Colts in the third Super Bowl, thus making what had previously seemed a routine NFL victory into something special—a chance to see Namath crushed. But the Jets did the crushing in sports' biggest upset—guaranteed.

Occasionally the Colts would rip for big yardage, sometimes by pass, sometimes by way of Tom Matte (41, above). But their gains were sporadic, while the Jets' were consistent. Fullback Matt Snell (41, above, right) pounded for 121 yards against the NFL's best defense and Jim Turner (11, right) added enough field goals to secure the Jets' final winning margin.

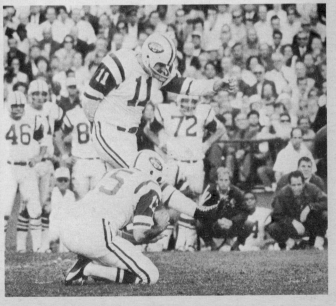

The Jets controlled the game as Namath (above) used up valuable time with his precision passing. Baltimore's vaunted rush did little. Dave Herman (above, blocking) was easily the equal of Bubba Smith (78). Baltimore's offensive line had a little more trouble protecting their passer. Earl Morrall (15, far left) felt the weight of the Jets' pass rush as he was sandwiched between Jim Hudson and Carl McAdams (50). After the game, Joe Namath (left) seemed to be thumb-signaling the rating he felt his team deserved.

Kansas City Chiefs
vs.
Minnesota Vikings
Jan. 11, 1970, New Orleans
Kansas City 23, Minnesota 7

The fourth Super Bowl—and the last between the AFL and the NFL—belonged to the Kansas City Chiefs and quarterback Len Dawson. Perhaps not so much a victory for the AFL, which it certainly was, the game established the fact that execution, strength and basic football were no longer enough. New, highly complex offensive and defensive formations proved to be the coming thing. The Vikings never were in the game. A new era of football began.

Len Dawson (16, above) overcame a season of injury to engineer the Chiefs' attack, an attack which employed a very successful reverse by Frank Pitts (25). Minnesota could do little rushing against Buck Buchanan as evidenced by Bill Brown's frustrated run.

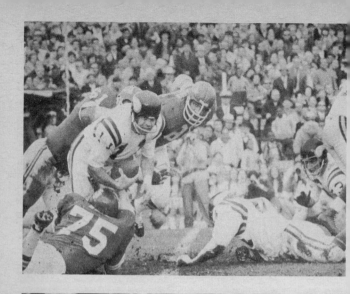

Clockwise from left: Minnesota fullback Dave Osborn was crushed by Willie Lanier who played a superb game; Jerry Mays (75), Curley Culp (61) and Buck Buchanan (86) dropped quarterback Kapp three times, allowed him only 9 yards on runs and eventually sent him to the sidelines with a shoulder injury; Jan Stenerud's marvelous toe sent the Chiefs to a 9–0 lead which they never relinquished; late in the third quarter the Chiefs broke open the game just as the Vikings gained momentum. Dawson threw to Otis Taylor (88) who, after cornerback Mackbee mistakenly thought a low shoulder would send the end out of bounds, sprinted down the sidelines for a touchdown.

1969 NFL CHAMPIONSHIP GAME

Metropolitan Stadium, Bloomington, Minn.　　　　　January 4, 1970
Attendance: 46,503

The Minnesota Vikings scored the first two times they had the ball and went on to defeat Cleveland 27–7, becoming the first expansion team to win the championship. On a snow-ringed field, chilled by a temperature of eight degrees, quarterback Joe Kapp scored the first touchdown on a seven-yard run four plays after a 33 yard pass to Gene Washington. On the next series, Kapp threw a 75-yard scoring pass to Washington.

CLEVELAND (7)	Offense	MINNESOTA (27)
Paul Warfield	WR	Gene Washington
Dick Schafrath	LT	Grady Alderman
John Demarie	LG	Jim Vellone
Fred Hoaglin	C	Mick Tingelhoff
Gene Hickerson	RG	Milt Sunde
Monte Clark	RT	Ron Yary
Milt Morin	TE	John Beasley
Gary Collins	WR	John Henderson
Bill Nelsen	QB	Joe Kapp
Leroy Kelly	RB	Dave Osborn
Bo Scott	RB	Bill Brown

Defense

Ron Snidow	LE	Carl Eller
Walter Johnson	LT	Gary Larsen
Jim Kanicki	RT	Alan Page
Jack Gregory	RE	Jim Marshall
Jim Houston	LLB	Roy Winston
Dale Lindsey	MLB	Lonnie Warwick
John Garlington	RLB	Wally Hilgenberg
Erich Barnes	LCB	Earsell Mackbee
Walt Sumner	RCB	Ed Sharockman
Ernie Kellermann	LS	Karl Kassulke
Mike Howell	RS	Paul Krause

SUBSTITUTIONS

CLEVELAND—Offense: Receivers—Dave Jones, Charles Glass. Linemen—Jim Copeland, Charles Reynolds, Joe Taffoni. Backs—Jerry Rhome, Charley Leigh, Reece Morrison, Ron Johnson. Kicker—Don Cockroft. Defense: Linebackers—Wayne Meylan, Bill Andrews, Bob Matheson. Linemen—Joe Righetti, Marvin Upshaw. Backs—Dean Brown, Alvin Mitchell. DNP—Fair Hooker.

MINNESOTA—Offense: Receivers—Bob Grim, Kent Kramer. Lineman—Ed White. Backs—Jim Lindsey, Clint Jones, Oscar Reed, Bill Harris. Kickers—Fred Cox, Bob Lee. Defense: Linebackers—Dale Hackbart, Jim Hargrove, Mike McGill. Linemen—Steve Smith, Paul Dickson. Back—Charlie West. DNP—Gary Cuozzo, Doug Davis, Mike Reilly.

OFFICIALS

Referee, Tom Bell. Umpire, Joe Connell. Headlinesman, George Murphy. Field Judge, Fritz Graf. Back Judge, Ralph Vandenberg. Line Judge, Jack Fette.

SCORING

CLEVELAND BROWNS	0	0	0	7——	7
MINNESOTA VIKINGS	14	10	3	0——	27

Minn—Kapp 7 run (Cox kick). Minn—Washington 75 pass from Kapp (Cox kick). Minn—FG Cox 30. Minn—Osborn 20 run (Cox kick). Minn—FG Cox 32. Clev—Collins 3 pass from Nelsen (Cockroft kick).

INDIVIDUAL STATISTICS

Rushing

CLEVELAND	Atts.	Yds.	LG		MINNESOTA	Atts.	Yds.	LG
Kelly	15	80	22	Osborn		18	108	20
Scott	6	17	5	Kapp		8	57	19
				Brown		12	43	9
				Jones		2	7	6
				Reed		5	7	5

Passing

	Atts.	Comp.	Yds.	Int.	TD		Atts.	Comp.	Yds.	Int.	TD
Nelsen	33	17	181	2	1	Kapp	13	7	169	0	1

Receiving

	No.	Yds.	TD		No.	Yds.	TD
Scott	5	56	0	Washington	3	120	1
Collins	5	43	1	Henderson	2	17	0
Warfield	4	47	0	Brown	1	20	0
Kelly	2	17	0	Beasley	1	12	0
Morin	1	18	0				

TEAM STATISTICS

	CLEVELAND	MINNESOTA
Total First Downs	14	18
First Downs Rushing	4	13
First Downs Passing	10	5
First Downs by Penalty	0	0
Total Offensive Yardage	268	383
Total No. Offensive Plays	56	59
Avg. Gain per Offensive Play	4.8	6.5
Net Rushing Yardage	97	222
Total Rushing Plays	21	45
Avg. Gain per Rushing Play	4.6	4.9
Net Passing Yardage	171	161
Gross Yards Gained Passing	181	169
Times Thrown and Yards Lost Attempting to Pass	2–10	1–8
Passes Att.–Comp.–Int.	33–17–2	13–7–0
Avg. Gain per Pass Play	4.9	11.5
Punts—Number and Average	3–33.0	3–41.0
Had Blocked	0	0
Fumbles–Number and Lost	2–1	0–0
Penalties–Number and Yards	1–5	3–33
Total Return Yardage	104	43
No. & Yards Punt Returns	3–21	1–1
No. & Yards Kickoff Returns	5–83	2–42
No. & Yards Interception Returns	0–0	2–0
No. & Yards Miscellaneous Returns	0–0	0–0

FINANCIAL SUMMARY

Paid Attendance	46,503
Net Receipts	$1,231,781.38
Total Players' Pool (70% of net receipts)	862,246.97
Second Place Clubs' Pool	100,000.00
Third Place Clubs' Pool	75,000.00
Winning Player's Share	7,929.77
Losing Player's Share	5,117.80
Minnesota Club Share (7½% of net)	92,383.60
Cleveland Club Share (7½% of net)	92,383.60
League Share (15% of net)	184,767.21

NATIONAL FOOTBALL CONFERENCE CHAMPIONSHIP GAMES AT A GLANCE

Year	Date	Winner—Share	Loser—Share	Score	Site	Attendance
1969	Jan. 4	Vikings ($7,930)	Browns ($5,118)	27–7	Minnesota	46,503
1968	Dec. 29	Colts ($9,306)	Browns ($5,963)	34–0	Cleveland	78,410
1967	Dec. 31	Packers ($7,950)	Cowboys ($5,299)	21–17	Green Bay	50,861
1966	Jan. 1	Packers ($9,813)	Cowboys ($6,527)	34–27	Dallas	74,152
1965	Jan. 2	Packers ($7,819)	Browns ($5,288)	23–12	Green Bay	50,777
1964	Dec. 27	Browns ($8,052)	Colts ($5,571)	27–0	Cleveland	79,544
1963	Dec. 29	Bears ($5,899)	Giants ($4,218)	14–10	Chicago	45,801
1962	Dec. 30	Packers ($5,888)	Giants ($4,166)	16–7	New York	64,892
1961	Dec. 31	Packers ($5,195)	Giants ($3,339)	37–0	Green Bay	39,029
1960	Dec. 26	Eagles ($5,116)	Packers ($3,105)	17–13	Philadelphia	67,325
1959	Dec. 27	Colts ($4,674)	Giants ($3,083)	31–16	Baltimore	57,545
1958	Dec. 28	Colts ($4,718)	Giants ($3,111)	23–17*	New York	64,185
1957	Dec. 29	Lions ($4,295)	Browns ($2,750)	59–14	Detroit	55,263
1956	Dec. 30	Giants ($3,779)	Bears ($2,485)	47–7	New York	56,836
1955	Dec. 26	Browns ($3,508)	Rams ($2,316)	38–14	Los Angeles	85,693
1954	Dec. 26	Browns ($2,478)	Lions ($1,585)	56–10	Cleveland	43,827
1953	Dec. 27	Lions ($2,424)	Browns ($1,654)	17–16	Detroit	54,577
1952	Dec. 28	Lions ($2,274)	Browns ($1,712)	17–7	Cleveland	50,934
1951	Dec. 23	Rams ($2,108)	Browns ($1,483)	24–17	Los Angeles	57,522
1950	Dec. 24	Browns ($1,113)	Rams ($686)	30–28	Cleveland	29,751
1949	Dec. 18	Eagles ($1,094)	Rams ($739)	14–0	Los Angeles	27,980
1948	Dec. 19	Eagles ($1,540)	Cardinals ($874)	7–0	Philadelphia	36,309
1947	Dec. 28	Cardinals ($1,132)	Eagles ($754)	28–21	Chicago	30,759
1946	Dec. 15	Bears ($1,975)	Giants ($1,295)	24–14	New York	58,346
1945	Dec. 16	Rams ($1,469)	Redskins ($902)	15–14	Cleveland	32,178
1944	Dec. 17	Packers ($1,449)	Giants ($814)	14–7	New York	46,016
1943	Dec. 26	Bears ($1,146)	Redskins ($765)	41–21	Chicago	34,320
1942	Dec. 13	Redskins ($965)	Bears ($637)	14–6	Washington	36,006
1941	Dec. 21	Bears ($430)	Giants ($288)	37–9	Chicago	13,341
1940	Dec. 8	Bears ($873)	Redskins ($606)	73–0	Washington	36,034
1939	Dec. 10	Packers ($850)	Giants ($650)	27–0	Milwaukee	32,279
1938	Dec. 11	Giants ($900)	Packers ($700)	23–17	New York	48,120
1937	Dec. 12	Redskins ($300)	Bears ($250)	28–21	Chicago	15,870
1936	Dec. 13	Packers ($540)	Redskins ($400)	21–6	New York	29,545
1935	Dec. 15	Lions ($300)	Giants ($200)	26–7	Detroit	15,000
1934	Dec. 9	Giants ($621)	Bears ($414.02)	30–13	New York	35,059
1933	Dec. 17	Bears ($210.34)	Giants ($140.22)	23–21	Chicago	26,000

(Shares 1935 through 1939 are estimated.)
*(Sudden death)

Hickerson (66) and Hoaglin (54) clear a path for fullback Johnson.

NFC CHAMPIONSHIP GAME
COMPOSITE STANDINGS

	W	L	Pct.	Pts.	O.P.
Vikings	1	0	1.000	27	7
Packers	8	2	.800	223	116
Lions	4	1	.800	129	100
Colts	3	1	.750	88	60
Eagles	3	1	.750	59	41
Bears	6	4	.600	259	194
*Cardinals	1	1	.500	28	28
**Rams	2	3	.400	81	113
Browns	4	7	.364	224	253
†Redskins	2	4	.333	83	177
Giants	3	11	.214	208	309
Cowboys	0	2	.000	44	55
Falcons	0	0	.000	—	—
Forty-Niners	0	0	.000	—	—
Saints	0	0	.000	—	—
Steelers	0	0	.000	—	—

*Both games played when franchise was in Chicago.
**One game played when franchise was in Cleveland. (Won 15–14)
†One game played when franchise was in Boston. (Lost 21–6)

Bob Hayes takes one going away from Elijah Nevett (24) of the Saints.

NATIONAL FOOTBALL CONFERENCE
CHAMPIONSHIP GAME RECORDS

(Compiled by Elias Sports Bureau)
INDIVIDUAL SERVICE

GAMES—PLAYER

Most Games Played

    9 Lou Groza (T-K), Clev. Browns 1950–55, 57, 64–65
       Don Chandler (K), N.Y. 1956, 58–59, 61–63; G.B. 1965–67
    8 Andy Robustelli (E), L.A. 1951, 55; N.Y. 1956, 58–59, 61–63
       Dick Modzelewski (T), N.Y. 1956, 58–59, 61–63; Clev. 1964–65

Most Games on Winning Team

    6 Fred Thurston (G), Balt. 1958; G.B. 1961–62, 65–67
    5 By 12 players

Most Different Teams Played On

    3 Lew Carpenter (HB), Det. 1953–54; Clev. 1957; G.B. 1960–62

GAMES—COACH

Most Games, Head Coach
    8 Steve Owen, N.Y. 1933–35, 38–39, 41, 44, 46
    7 Paul Brown, Clev. 1950–55, 57
       George Halas, Chi. Bears 1933–34, 37, 40–41, 46, 63

Most Games Won

    5 George Halas, Chi. Bears 1933, 40–41, 46, 63
       Vince Lombardi, G.B. 1961–62, 65–67

SCORING

TOTAL POINTS

Most Total Points, Lifetime

    55 Lou Groza, Clev. 9gs (25-xp, 10-fg)
    36 Ken Strong, N.Y. 5gs (4-td, 9-xp, 1-fg)

Most Total Points, Game

    19 Paul Hornung, G.B. vs N.Y. 1961 (1-td, 4-xp, 3-fg)
    18 Otto Graham, Clev. vs Det. 1954 (3-td)
        Gary Collins, Clev. vs. Balt. 1964 (3-td)
        Tom Matte, Balt. vs Clev. 1968 (3-td)

TOUCHDOWNS

Most Touchdowns, Lifetime

    5 Otto Graham, Clev. 6gs (5-r)
       Gary Collins, Clev. 4gs (5-p)
    4 Ken Strong, N.Y. 5gs (2-r, 2-p)
       Harry Clark, Chi. Bears 4gs (2-r, 2-p)
       Boyd Dowler, G.B. 6 gs (4-p)

Most Touchdowns, Game

    3 Otto Graham, Clev. vs Det. 1954 (3-r)
       Gary Collins, Clev. vs Balt. 1964 (3-p)
       Tom Matte, Balt. vs Clev. 1968 (3-r)
    2 By 22 players

POINTS AFTER TOUCHDOWN

Most Points After Touchdown, Lifetime

    25   Lou Groza, Clev. 9gs (25 atts)
    11   Don Chandler, N.Y.–G.B. 9 gs (12 atts)

Most Points After Touchdown, Game

    8   Lou Groza, Clev. vs Det. 1954 (8atts)
       Jim Martin, Det. vs Clev. 1957 (8 atts)
    5   By 3 players

FIELD GOALS

Most Field Goals Attempted, Lifetime

    17   Lou Groza, Clev. 9gs
    10   Jack Manders, Chi. Bears 4gs

Most Field Goals Attempted, Game

    5   Jerry Kramer, G.B. vs N.Y. 1962
    4   Jack Manders, Chi. Bears vs N.Y. 1933; 1934
       Lou Groza, Clev. vs Det. 1953

Most Field Goals, Lifetime

    10   Lou Groza, Clev. 9gs (17 atts)
    5   Jack Manders, Chi. Bears 4gs (10 atts)
       Paul Hornung, G.B. 4gs (6 atts)

Most Field Goals, Game

    3   Jack Manders, Chi. Bears vs N.Y. 1933 (4 atts)
       Bob Snyder, Chi. Bears vs N.Y. 1941 (3 atts)
       Lou Groza, Clev. vs Det. 1953 (4 atts)
       George (Pat) Summerall, N.Y. vs Balt. 1959 (3 atts)
       Paul Hornung, G.B. vs N.Y. 1961 (3 atts)
       Jerry Kramer, G.B. vs N.Y. 1962 (5 atts)
       Don Chandler, G.B. vs Clev. 1965 (3 atts)

Longest Field Goal

    52   Lou Groza, Clev. vs L.A. 1951
    43   Lou Groza, Clev. vs Det. 1953; vs Balt. 1964
       Ben Agajanian, N.Y. vs Chi. Bears 1956

RUSHING

ATTEMPTS

Most Attempts, Lifetime

   106   Jim Taylor, G.B. 5gs
    75   Steve Van Buren, Phil. 3gs

Most Attempts, Game

    31   Steve Van Buren, Phil. vs L.A. 1949
       Jim Taylor, G.B. vs N.Y. 1962
    27   Jim Brown, Clev. vs Balt. 1964
       Jim Taylor, G.B. vs Clev. 1965

YARDAGE

Most Yards Gained, Lifetime

   392   Jim Taylor, G.B. 5gs
   320   Steve Van Buren, Phil. 3gs

Most Yards Gained, Game

  196 Steve Van Buren, Phil. vs L.A. 1949
  159 Elmer Angsman, Chi. Cards vs Phil. 1947

Longest Run From Scrimmage

  70 Elmer Angsman, Chi. Cards vs Phil. 1947 (twice, 2tds)
  68 Bill Osmanski, Chi. Bears vs Wash. 1940 (td)

AVERAGE YARDAGE

Highest Average Gain, Lifetime

  9.6 Elmer Angsman, Chi. Cards 2gs (20–192)
  6.9 Harry Jagade, Clev. 3gs (30–206)

Highest Average Gain, Game

  15.9 Elmer Angsman, Chi. Cards vs Phil. 1947 (10–159)
  10.9 Bill Osmanski, Chi. Bears vs Wash. 1940 (10–109)

TOUCHDOWNS

Most Touchdowns, Lifetime

  5 Otto Graham, Clev. 6gs
  3 Dick Hoerner, L.A. 3gs
      Tom Matte, Balt. 2gs

Most Touchdowns, Game

  3 Otto Graham, Clev. vs Det. 1954
      Tom Matte, Balt. vs Clev. 1968
  2 By 10 Players

PASSING

ATTEMPTS

Most Passes Attempted, Lifetime

  159 Otto Graham, Clev. 6gs (86 comp)
  142 Bryan (Bart) Starr, G.B. 6gs (83 comp)

Most Passes Attempted, Game

  44 Tommy Thompson, Phil. vs Chi. Cards 1947 (27 comp)
  42 Bobby Layne, Det. vs Clev. 1954 (18 comp)

COMPLETIONS

Most Passes Completed, Lifetime

  86 Otto Graham, Clev. 6gs (159 att)
  83 Bryan (Bart) Starr, G.B. 6gs (142 att)

Most Passes Completed, Game

  27 Tommy Thompson, Phil. vs Chi. Cards 1947 (44 att)
  26 John Unitas, Balt. vs N.Y. 1958 (40 att)

EFFICIENCY

Passing Efficiency, Lifetime (40 atts)

  62.9 John Unitas, Balt. 3gs (89–56)
  58.5 Bryan (Bart) Starr, G.B. 6 gs (142–83)

Passing Efficiency, Game (20 atts)

  68.8 Otto Graham, Clev. vs L.A. 1950 (32–22)
  67.9 Bryan (Bart) Starr, G.B. vs Dall. 1966 (28–19)

YARDAGE

Most Yards Gained, Lifetime

1,161 Otto Graham, Clev. 6gs
1,069 Bryan (Bart) Starr, G.B. 6 gs

Most Yards Gained, Game

349 John Unitas, Balt. vs N.Y. 1958 (40–26)
335 Sammy Baugh, Wash. vs Chi. Bears 1937 (33–18)

Longest Pass Completion

82 Bob Waterfield (to Davis), L.A. vs Clev. 1950 (TD)
78 Tobin Rote (to Doran), Det. vs Clev. 1957 (TD)

TOUCHDOWNS

Most Touchdown Passes, Lifetime

11 Bryan (Bart) Starr, G.B. 6gs
10 Otto Graham, Clev. 6gs

Most Touchdown Passes, Game

5 Sid Luckman, Chi. Bears vs Wash. 1943
4 Otto Graham, Clev. vs L.A. 1950
Tobin Rote, Det. vs Clev. 1957
Bryan (Bart) Starr, G.B. vs Dall. 1966

HAD INTERCEPTED

Fewest Passes Had Intercepted, Lifetime (30 atts)

1 Bryan (Bart) Starr, G.B. 6 gs (142 atts)
Bill Wade, L.A.-Chi. Bears 2gs (31 atts)
2 Charley Conerly, N.Y. 4gs (69 atts)
Don Meredith, Dall. 2 gs (56 atts)

Most Attempts Game Without Interception

34 Bryan (Bart) Starr, G.B. vs Phil. 1960

Most Consecutive Attempts Without Interception

84 Bryan (Bart) Starr, G.B. 1960–62, 65 4gs

Most Passes Had Intercepted, Lifetime

13 Frank Filchock, Wash.-N.Y. 3gs (63 atts)
12 Otto Graham, Clev. 6gs (159 atts)

Most Passes Had Intercepted, Game

6 Frank Filchock, N.Y. vs Chi. Bears 1946 (26 atts)
Bobby Layne, Det. vs Clev. 1954 (42 atts)
Norm Van Brocklin, L.A. vs Clev. 1955 (25 atts)
5 Frank Filchock, Wash. vs Chi. Bears 1940 (23 atts)
Y. A. Tittle, N.Y. vs Chi. Bears 1963 (29 atts)

PASS RECEIVING

RECEPTIONS

Most Receptions, Lifetime

24 Dante Lavelli, Clev. 6gs
20 Raymond Berry, Balt. 3gs
Boyd Dowler, G.B. 6 gs

Most Receptions, Game

   12   Raymond Berry, Balt. vs N.Y. 1958
   11   Dante Lavelli, Clev. vs L.A. 1950

YARDAGE

Most Yards Gained, Lifetime

  340   Dante Lavelli, Clev. 6gs (24)
  313   Tom Fears, L.A. 4gs (16)

Most Yards Gained, Game

  178   Raymond Berry, Balt. vs N.Y. 1958 (12)
  175   Bob Schnelker, N.Y. vs Balt. 1959 (9)

Longest Reception

   82   Glenn Davis (Waterfield), L.A. vs Clev. 1950 (TD)
   78   Jim Doran (Rote), Det. vs Clev. 1957 (TD)

TOUCHDOWNS

Most Touchdown Passes, Lifetime

   5   Gary Collins, Clev. 4gs
   4   Boyd Dowler, G.B. 6gs

Most Touchdown Passes, Game

   3   Gary Collins, Clev. vs Balt. 1964
   2   Bill Karr, Chi. Bears vs N.Y. 1933
        Wayne Millner, Wash. vs Chi. Bears 1937
        Dante Magnani, Chi. Bears vs Wash. 1943
        Harry Clark, Chi. Bears vs Wash. 1943
        Dante Lavelli, Clev. vs L.A. 1950
        Ray Renfro, Clev. vs Det. 1954
        Steve Junker, Det. vs Clev. 1957
        Ron Kramer, G.B. vs N.Y. 1961
        Boyd Dowler, G.B. vs Dall. 1967

INTERCEPTIONS BY

Most Interceptions By, Lifetime

   4   Ken Konz, Clev. 4gs
        Joe Laws, G.B. 4gs
        Clyde (Bulldog) Turner, Chi. Bears 5gs
   3   By 8 players

Most Interceptions By, Game

   3   Joe Laws, G.B. vs N.Y. 1944
   2   By 15 players

YARDAGE

Most Yards Gained, Lifetime

   97   Don Paul, Clev. 3gs (2)
   83   Larry Morris, L.A.-Chi. Bears 2gs (2)

Most Yards Gained, Game

   66   John Sample, Balt. vs N.Y. 1959 (2)
   65   Don Paul, Clev. vs L.A. 1955 (1)

Longest Return

    65   Don Paul, Clev. vs L.A. 1955 (TD)
    61   Larry Morris, Chi. Bears vs N.Y. 1963

TOUCHDOWNS

Most Touchdowns, Lifetime

        See following category

Most Touchdowns, Game

     1   Hampton Pool, Chi. Bears vs Wash. 1940
         George McAfee, Chi. Bears vs Wash. 1940
         Clyde (Bulldog) Turner, Chi. Bears vs Wash. 1940
         Dante Magnani, Chi. Bears vs N.Y. 1946
         Don Paul, Clev. vs L.A. 1955
         Terry Barr, Det. vs Clev. 1957
         John Sample, Balt. vs N.Y. 1959

PUNTING

Most Punts, Lifetime

    38   Don Chandler, N.Y.-G.B. 9 gs
    26   Bob Waterfield, Clev. Rams-L.A. 4gs

Most Punts, Game

    11   Ken Strong, N.Y. vs Chi. Bears 1933
    10   By 3 players

Longest Punt

    72   R. Yale Lary, Det. vs Clev. 1953
    69   Joe Muha, Phil. vs Chi. Cards 1947

AVERAGE YARDAGE

Highest Punting Average, Lifetime (10 punts)

    42.4   Don Chandler, N.Y.-G.B. 9 gs (38)
           42.2 Sammy Baugh, Wash. 5gs (14)

Highest Punting Average, Game (4 punts)

    52.5   Sammy Baugh, Wash. vs Chi. Bears 1942 (6)
    50.8   Bob Waterfield, L.A. vs Clev. 1950 (4)
           Ray Brown, Balt. vs N.Y. 1958 (4)

HAD BLOCKED

Most Punts Had Blocked, Lifetime

     2   Riley Smith, Bos.-Wash. 2gs (11)
         Clark Hinkle, G.B. 3gs (5)
     1   By 5 players

Most Punts Had Blocked, Game

     2   Riley Smith, Bos. vs G.B. 1936 (10)
     1   By 7 players

PUNT RETURNS

Most Punt Returns, Lifetime

     8   Keith Molesworth, Chi. Bears 3gs
         Willie Wood, G.B. 5gs
     7   Billy Reynolds, Clev. 3gs

Most Punt Returns, Game

4   Keith Molesworth, Chi. Bears vs N.Y. 1934
     Irv Comp, G.B. vs N.Y. 1944
     Steve Bagarus, Wash. vs Clev. Rams 1945
     Ray Renfro, Clev. vs Det. 1952
     Carl Taseff, Balt. vs N.Y. 1958
     Willie Wood, G.B. vs Dall. 1967
3   By eleven players

YARDAGE

Most Yards Gained, Lifetime

113   Charley Trippi, Chi. Cards 2gs (4)
101   Keith Molesworth, Chi. Bears 3gs (8)

Most Yards Gained, Game

102   Charley Trippi, Chi. Cards vs Phil. 1947 (2)
 67   Keith Molesworth, Chi. Bears vs N.Y. 1934 (4)

Longest Return

75   Charley Trippi, Chi. Cards vs Phil. 1947 (TD)
42   Ken Strong, N.Y. vs Chi. Bears 1934
     Billy Reynolds, Clev. vs Det. 1954

AVERAGE YARDAGE

Highest Average Gain, Lifetime (4 returns)

28.3   Charley Trippi, Chi. Cards 2gs (4)
13.9   Billy Reynolds, Clev. 3gs (7)

Highest Average Gain, Game (3 returns)

22.0   Ken Strong, N.Y. vs Chi. Bears 1934 (3)
18.0   Billy Reynolds, Clev. vs Det. 1953 (3)

TOUCHDOWNS

Most Touchdowns, Lifetime

See following category

Most Touchdowns, Game

1   Charley Trippi, Chi. Cards vs Phil. 1947

KICKOFF RETURNS

Most Kickoff Returns, Lifetime

9   Ken Carpenter, Clev. 4gs
7   Don Bingham, Chi. Bears 1g

Most Kickoff Returns, Game

7   Don Bingham, Chi. Bears vs N.Y. 1956
5   Ken Carpenter, Clev. vs L.A. 1951
     Joel Wells, N.Y. vs G.B. 1961
     Mel Renfro, Dall. vs G.B. 1966

YARDAGE

Most Yards Gained, Lifetime

208   Ken Carpenter, Clev. 4gs (9)
143   Billy Reynolds, Clev. 3gs (6)

Most Yards Gained, Game

   132 Ken Carpenter, Clev. vs L.A. 1951 (5)
   127 Woodley Lewis, L.A. vs Clev. 1955 (4)

Longest Return

   62 Max Krause, Wash. vs Chi. Bears 1940
   58 Ted Dean, Phil. vs G.B. 1960

AVERAGE YARDAGE

Highest Average Gain, Lifetime (4 returns)

  31.8 Woodley Lewis, L.A. 1g (4)
  27.8 Frank Filchock, Wash.-N.Y. 3gs (4)

Highest Average Gain, Game (3 returns)

  31.8 Woodley Lewis, L.A. vs Clev. 1955 (4)
  31.7 Walter Roberts, Clev. vs G.B. 1965 (3)

TOUCHDOWNS

Most Touchdowns, Lifetime

      None

Most Touchdowns, Game

      None

FUMBLES

Most Fumbles, Lifetime

   3 Ken Carpenter, Clev. 4gs
      Otto Graham, Clev. 6gs
      William (Dub) Jones, Clev. 4gs
   2 By many players

Most Fumbles, Game

   2 By many players

RECOVERIES

Most Opponents Fumbles Recovered, Lifetime

   2 Andy Robustelli, L.A.-N.Y. 8gs
      Gerry Perry, Det. 2gs
      Ray Krouse, Det.-Balt. 3gs
      Ray Nitschke, G.B. 5gs
      Erich Barnes, N.Y.-Clev. 2gs

Most Fumbles Recovered, Game

   2 Ray Krouse, Balt. vs N.Y. 1958 (2-opp)
      Ray Nitschke, G.B. vs N.Y. 1962 (2-opp)

YARDAGE

Longest Gain, Fumble Recovery

   50 Lee Artoe, Chi. Bears vs Wash. 1942 (TD)
   42 Ken Kavanaugh, Chi. Bears vs N.Y. 1941 (TD)

TOUCHDOWNS

Most Touchdowns, Lifetime

See following category

Most Touchdowns, Game

1 Ken Kavanaugh, Chi. Bears vs N.Y. 1941
Lee Artoe, Chi. Bears vs Wash. 1942
Larry Brink, L.A. vs Clev. 1950
Jim Grabowski, G.B. vs Dall. 1966
George Andrie, Dall. vs G.B. 1967

MISCELLANEOUS

SCORING

Blocked Punt

Leo Skladany, Phil. vs L.A. 1949 (recovered in end zone)
Henry Moore, N.Y. vs Chi. Bears 1956 (recovered in end zone)
Jim Collier, N.Y. vs G.B. 1962 (recovered in end zone)

PASSING

Catching Own Pass

Tommy Thompson, Phila. vs L.A. 1949 (caught own deflected pass, lost 7 yds)

COMBINED NET YARDS GAINED

(Includes Rushes, Pass Receptions and Runbacks of Interceptions, Punts, Kickoffs and Fumbles)

ATTEMPTS

Most Attempts, Lifetime

122 Jim Taylor, G.B. 5gs
79 Steve Van Buren, Phil. 3gs

Most Attempts, Game

34 Jim Taylor, G.B. vs N.Y. 1962
30 Jim Taylor, G.B. vs Phil. 1960
Jim Brown, Clev. vs Balt. 1964

YARDAGE

Most Yards Gained, Lifetime

501 Jim Taylor, G.B. 5gs
420 Jim Brown, Clev. 3gs

Most Yards Gained, Game

241 Ken Strong, N.Y. vs Chi. Bears 1934
206 Charley Trippi, Chi. Cards vs Phil. 1947

AVERAGE YARDAGE

Highest Average Gain, Lifetime

13.0 Ken Strong, N.Y. 5gs (29–378)
11.4 Ken Carpenter, Clev. 4gs (27–309)

Highest Average Gain, Game

16.3 Ken Carpenter, Clev. vs L.A. 1951 (12–195)
14.7 Charley Trippi, Chi. Cards vs Phil. 1947 (14–206)

NATIONAL FOOTBALL CONFERENCE
CHAMPIONSHIP GAME RECORDS
TEAM
GAMES

Most Games

14 New York Giants 1933–35, 38–39, 41, 44, 46, 56, 58–59, 61–63
11 Cleveland Browns 1950–55, 57, 64–65, 68–69

Most Consecutive Games

6 Cleveland Browns 1950–55
4 Chicago Bears 1940–43

Most Games Won

8 Green Bay 1936, 39, 44, 61–62, 65–67
6 Chicago Bears 1933, 40–41, 43, 46, 63

Most Consecutive Games Won

3 Green Bay 1965–67
2 Chicago Bears 1940–41
   Philadelphia 1948–49
   Detroit 1952–53
   Cleveland Browns 1954–55
   Baltimore 1958–59

Most Games Lost

11 New York Giants 1933, 35, 39, 41, 44, 46, 58–59, 61–63
7 Cleveland Browns 1951–53, 57, 65, 68–69

Most Consecutive Games Lost

3 Cleveland Browns 1951–53
   New York Giants 1961–63
2 Los Angeles 1949–50
   New York Giants 1958–59
   Dallas 1966–67
   Cleveland Browns 1968–69

SCORING

TOTAL POINTS

Most Total Points

259 Chi. Bears 10gs
224 Cleveland Browns 11gs

Most Points, Game

73 Chi. Bears vs Wash. 1940
59 Detroit vs Clev. Browns 1957

Most Points, Both Teams, Game

73 Chi. Bears (73) vs Wash. (0) 1940
    Detroit (59) vs Clev. Browns (14) 1957
66 Clev. Browns (56) vs Det. (10) 1954

Fewest Points, Both Teams, Game

    7   Philadelphia (7) vs Chi. Cards (0) 1948

Most Shutouts By

    2   Green Bay vs N.Y. 1939; vs N.Y. 1961
         Philadelphia vs Chi. Cards 1948; vs L.A. 1949
    1   Chi. Bears vs Wash. 1940
         Cleveland vs Balt. 1964
         Baltimore vs Clev. 1968

Most Points, By Quarters

    1st: 21   Chi. Bears vs Wash. 1940
    2nd: 24   Green Bay vs N.Y. 1961
    3rd: 26   Chi. Bears vs Wash. 1940
    4th: 27   New York vs Chi. Bears 1934

TOUCHDOWNS

Most Touchdowns

    34   Chi. Bears 10gs (17-r, 11-p, 4-int, 2-f)
    28   Clev. Browns 11gs (12-r, 15-p, 1-int)

Most Touchdowns, Game

    11   Chi. Bears vs Wash. 1940 (7-r, 1-p, 3-int)
     8   Clev. Browns vs Det. 1954 (5-r, 3-p)
         Detroit vs Clev. Browns 1957 (2-r, 5-p, 1-int)

Most Touchdowns, Both Teams, Game

    11   Chi. Bears (11) vs Wash. (0) 1940
    10   Detroit (8) vs Clev. Browns (2) 1957

Fewest Touchdowns, Both Teams, Game

    1   Philadelphia (1) vs Chi. Cards (0) 1948

POINTS AFTER TOUCHDOWNS

Most Points After Touchdown

    28   Chi. Bears 10gs
    26   Clev. Browns 11gs

Most Points After Touchdown, Game

    8   Clev. Browns vs Det. 1954
       Detroit vs Clev. Browns 1957
    7   Chi. Bears vs Wash. 1940

Most Points After Touchdown, Both Teams, Game

    10   Detroit (8) vs Clev. Browns (2) 1957
     9   Clev. Browns (8) vs Det. (1) 1954

Fewest Points After Touchdowns, Both Teams, Game

    1   Philadelphia (1) vs Chi. Cards (0) 1948

FIELD GOALS

Most Field Goals

    14   Green Bay 10 gs (19 atts)
    10   New York 14gs (19 atts)
         Clev. Browns 11gs (19 atts)

Most Field Goals, Game

3   Chi. Bears vs N.Y. 1933 (4 atts)
Chi. Bears vs N.Y. 1941 (4 atts)
Clev. Browns vs Det. 1953 (4 atts)
New York vs Balt. 1959 (3 atts)
Green Bay vs N.Y. 1961 (3 atts)
Green Bay vs N.Y. 1962 (5 atts)
Green Bay vs Clev. 1965 (3 atts)

Most Field Goals, Both Teams, Game

5   Green Bay (3) vs Clev. (2) 1965
4   Chi. Bears (3) vs N.Y. (1) 1941
Clev. Browns (3) vs Det. (1) 1953
New York (3) vs Balt. (1) 1959

Most Field Goals Attempted

19   Chi. Bears 10gs (9 made)
New York 14gs (10 made)
Clev. Browns 11gs (10 made)

Most Field Goals Attempted, Game

5   Green Bay vs N.Y. 1962 (3 made)
4   By 4 teams

Most Field Goals Attempted, Both Teams, Game

7   Clev. Browns (4) vs Det. (3) 1953
6   Green Bay (5) vs N.Y. (1) 1962
Green Bay (3) vs Clev. (3) 1965

Longest Field Goal

52   Clev. Browns vs L.A. 1951
43   Clev. Browns vs Det. 1953; vs Balt. 1964
New York vs Chi. Bears 1956

SAFETIES

Most Safeties

1   Clev. Rams vs Wash. 1945 (automatic)

FIRST DOWNS

Most First Downs

182   Clev. Browns 11gs (80-r, 90-p, 12-pen)
166   New York 14gs (72-r, 80-p, 14-pen)

Most First Downs, Game

27   Baltimore vs N.Y. 1958 (9-r, 17-p, 1-pen)
23   Dallas vs G.B. 1966 (12-r, 10-p, 1-pen)

Fewest First Downs, Game

6   New York vs G.B. 1961 (1-r, 4-p, 1-pen)
7   By 3 teams

Most First Downs, Both Teams, Game

44   Clev. Browns (22) vs L.A. (22) 1950
42   Clev. Browns (22) vs L.A. (20) 1951
Dallas (23) vs G.B. (19) 1966

Fewest First Downs, Both Teams, Game

    15   Green Bay (7) vs Bos. (8) 1936

YARDS GAINED

(RUSHES AND PASSES)

Most Net Yards Gained

    3,378   New York 14gs (1428-r, 1950-p)
    3,201   Clev. Browns 11gs (1503-r, 1698-p)

Fewest Net Yards Gained

    407   Chi. Cards 2gs (378-r, 29-p)
    610   Dallas 2 gs (279-r, 331-p)

Most Net Yards Gained, Game

    501   Chi. Bears vs Wash. 1940 (382-r, 119-p)
    460   Baltimore vs N.Y. 1958 (138-r, 322-p)

Fewest Net Yards Gained, Game

    99   Chi. Cards vs Phil. 1948 (96-r, 3-p)
    109   Los Angeles vs Phil. 1949 (21-r, 88-p)

Most Net Yards Gained, Both Teams, Game

    785   Dallas (418) vs G.B. (367) 1966
    780   Los Angeles (407) vs Clev. Browns (373) 1950

Fewest Net Yards Gained, Both Teams, Game

    331   Chi. Cards (99) vs Phil. (232) 1948
    350   Boston (130) vs G.B. (220) 1936

RUSHING

ATTEMPTS

Most Attempts

    434   Chi. Bears 10gs
    417   Green Bay 10gs

Most Attempts, Game

    61   Philadelphia vs L.A. 1949
    57   Chi. Bears vs Wash. 1940
           Philadelphia vs Chi. Cards 1948

Fewest Attempts, Game

    14   Washington vs Chi. Bears 1940
           New York vs G.B. 1961
    18   Cleveland vs G.B. 1965

Most Attempts, Both Teams, Game

    91   Philadelphia (57) vs Chi. Cards (34) 1948
    88   Green Bay (46) vs N.Y. (42) 1938

Fewest Attempts, Both Teams, Game

    49   New York (24) vs Balt. (25) 1959
    58   New York (14) vs G.B. (44) 1961

YARDAGE

Most Yards Gained

1,503 Clev. Browns 11gs
1,462 Green Bay 10gs

Most Yards Gained, Game

382 Chi. Bears vs Wash. 1940
282 Chi. Cards vs Phil. 1947

Fewest Yards Gained, Game

21 Los Angeles vs Phil. 1949
22 Washington vs Chi. Bears 1940

Most Yards Gained, Both Teams, Game

426 Clev. Browns (227) vs Det. (199) 1952
404 Chi. Bears (382) vs Wash. (22) 1940

Fewest Yards Gained, Both Teams, Game

106 Boston (39) vs G.B. (67) 1936
170 Chi. Bears (69) vs Wash. (101) 1942

Longest Gain

70 Chi. Cards vs Phil. 1947 (twice, TDs)
68 Chi. Bears vs Wash. 1940 (TD)

AVERAGE YARDAGE

Highest Average Gain

5.18 Chi. Cards 2gs (73–378)
4.28 Clev. Browns 11gs (351–1503)

Highest Average Gain, Game

7.23 Chi. Cards vs Phil. 1947 (39–282)
6.70 Chi. Bears vs Wash. 1940 (57–382)

Lowest Average Gain, Game

0.88 Los Angeles vs Phil. 1949 (24–21)
1.03 Washington vs Clev. Rams 1945 (34–35)

Highest Average Gain, Both Teams, Game

6.26 Clev. Browns (6.68) vs Det. (5.85) 1952
5.69 Chi. Bears (6.70) vs Wash. (1.57) 1940

Lowest Average Gain, Both Teams, Game

1.54 Boston (1.22) vs G.B. (1.81) 1936
2.21 Chi. Bears (1.68) vs Wash. (2.81) 1942

TOUCHDOWNS

Most Touchdowns

17 Chi. Bears 10gs
12 Clev. Browns 11gs

Fewest Touchdowns

2 Dallas 2gs
3 Chi. Cards 2gs
  Baltimore 3gs

Most Touchdowns, Game

  7 Chi. Bears vs Wash. 1940
  5 Clev. Browns vs Det. 1954

Most Touchdowns, Both Teams, Game

  7 Chi. Bears (7) vs Wash. (0) 1940
  6 Chi. Cards (4) vs Phil. (2) 1947
     Clev. Browns (5) vs Det. (1) 1954

PASSING

ATTEMPTS

Most Attempts

  327 New York 14gs
  284 Clev. Browns 11gs

Most Attempts, Game

  51 Washington vs Chi. Bears 1940
  47 Chi. Bears vs N.Y. 1956

Fewest Attempts, Game

  5 Detroit vs N.Y. 1935
  9 Philadelphia vs L.A. 1949

Most Attempts, Both Teams, Game

  71 Washington (40) vs Chi. Bears (31) 1937
      Clev. Browns (41) vs L.A. (30) 1951
  69 New York (40) vs Balt. (29) 1959

Fewest Attempts, Both Teams, Game

  18 Detroit (5) vs N.Y. (13) 1935
  23 Chi. Cards (11) vs Phil. (12) 1948

COMPLETIONS

Most Passes Completed

  145 Clev. Browns 11gs
  142 New York 14gs

Most Passes Completed, Game

  27 Philadelphia vs Chi. Cards 1947
  26 Baltimore vs N.Y. 1958

Fewest Passes Completed, Game

  2 Detroit vs N.Y. 1935
     Philadelphia vs Chi. Cards 1948
  3 By 4 teams

Most Passes Completed, Both Teams, Game

  40 Clev. Browns (22) vs L.A. (18) 1950
  38 Baltimore (26) vs N.Y. (12) 1958

Fewest Passes Completed, Both Teams, Game

  5 Philadelphia (2) vs Chi. Cards (3) 1948
  6 Detroit (2) vs N.Y. (4) 1935

EFFICIENCY

Highest Passing Efficiency

58.8   Baltimore 4gs (114–67)
52.9   Green Bay 10gs (210-111)

Highest Passing Efficiency, Game

75.0   Clev. Browns vs Det. 1954 (12–9)
70.0   New York vs Chi. Bears 1933 (20–14)
        Also 3 other teams (10–7)

Lowest Passing Efficiency, Game

16.7   Philadelphia vs Chi. Cards 1948 (12–2)
18.8   Clev. Browns vs Det. 1953 (16–3)

Highest Passing Efficiency, Both Teams, Game

65.5   New York (66.7) vs Balt. (65.0) 1958 (58–38)
62.5   Clev. Browns (68.8) vs L.A. (56.3) 1950 (64–40)

Lowest Passing Efficiency, Both Teams, Game

21.7   Philadelphia (16.7) vs Chi. Cards (27.3) 1948 (23–5)
32.7   Boston (26.9) vs G.B. (39.1) 1936 (49–16)

YARDAGE

Most Yards Gained (net)

1,950   New York 14gs
1,698   Clev. Browns 11gs

Most Yards Gained, Game

371   Washington vs Chi. Bears 1937
322   Baltimore vs N.Y. 1958

Fewest Yards Gained, Game

3   Chi. Cards vs Phil. 1948
7   Philadelphia vs Chi. Cards 1948

Most Yards Gained, Both Teams, Game

578   Washington (371) vs Chi. Bears (207) 1937
558   Los Angeles (301) vs Clev. Browns (257) 1950

Fewest Yards Gained, Both Teams, Game

10   Chi. Cards (3) vs Phil. (7) 1948
140   Detroit (52) vs N.Y. (88) 1935

Longest Gain

82   Los Angeles vs Clev. Browns 1950 (TD)
78   Detroit vs Clev. Browns 1957 (TD)

TOUCHDOWNS

Most Touchdowns

17   Green Bay 10gs
15   Clev. Browns 11gs

Most Touchdowns, Game

    5 Chi. Bears vs Wash. 1943
       Detroit vs Clev. Browns 1957
    4 Clev. Browns vs L.A. 1950
       Green Bay vs Dall. 1966

Most Touchdowns, Both Teams, Game

    7 Chi. Bears (5) vs Wash. (2) 1943
    5 In four games

INTERCEPTIONS

Most Interceptions By

    34 Chi. Bears 10gs
    26 Clev. Browns 11gs

Most Passes Had Intercepted

    38 New York 14gs (327 atts)
    24 Clev. Browns 11gs (284 atts)

Most Passes Intercepted By, Game

    8 Chi. Bears vs Wash. 1940 (51 atts)
    7 Clev. Browns vs L.A. 1955 (28 atts)

Most Passes Intercepted By, Both Teams, Game

    10 Clev. Browns (7) vs L.A. (3) 1955 (53 atts)
    9 Green Bay (6) vs N.Y. (3) 1939 (36 atts)

Fewest Passes Intercepted By, Both Teams, Game

    1 Clev. Browns (0) vs Det. (1) 1952 (46 atts)
       Baltimore (0) vs N.Y. (1) 1958 (58 atts)
       Philadelphia (0) vs G.B. (1) 1960 (55 atts)
       New York (0) vs G.B. (1) 1962 (63 atts)
       Dallas (0) vs G.B. (1) 1966 (59 atts)
       Dallas (0) vs G.B. (1) 1967 (50 atts)

YARDAGE

Most Yards Gained

    426 Chi. Bears 10gs (34)
    298 Clev. Browns 11gs (26)

Most Yards Gained, Game

    123 Green Bay vs N.Y. 1939 (6)
    122 Clev. Browns vs Det. 1954 (6)

Most Yards Gained, Both Teams, Game

    156 Green Bay (123) vs N.Y. (33) 1939 (9)
    149 Clev. Browns (103) vs L.A. (46) 1955 (10)

Longest Return

    65 Clev. Browns vs L.A. 1955 (TD)
    61 Chi. Bears vs N.Y. 1963

Most Touchdowns

    4   Chi. Bears 10gs
    1   By 3 teams

Most Touchdowns, Game

    3   Chi. Bears vs Wash. 1940
    1   Chi. Bears vs N.Y. 1946
        Clev. Browns vs L.A. 1955
        Detroit vs Clev. Browns 1957
        Baltimore vs N.Y. 1959

PUNTING

Most Punts

    88 New York 14gs
    62 Green Bay 10gs

Most Punts, Game

    13 New York vs Chi. Bears 1933
    10 By 4 teams

Fewest Punts, Game

    2   Chi. Bears vs Wash. 1940; vs N.Y. 1941
        Baltimore vs Clev. 1968
    3   By eight teams

Most Punts, Both Teams, Game

    23 New York (13) vs Chi. Bears (10) 1933
    20 Green Bay (10) vs N.Y. (10) 1944

Fewest Punts, Both Teams, Game

    5   Chi. Bears (2) vs Wash. (3) 1940
    6   Clev. Browns (3) vs Minn. (3) 1969

AVERAGE YARDAGE

Highest Punting Average

    41.5 Clev. Rams-L.A. 5gs (30)
    39.7 Clev. Browns 11gs (43)

Highest Punting Average, Game

    52.5 Washington vs Chi. Bears 1942 (6)
    50.8 By 2 teams (4)

Lowest Punting Average, Game

    22.5 Detroit vs N.Y. 1935 (4)
    24.9 Washington vs Chi. Bears 1937 (7)

Highest Punting Average, Both Teams, Game

    47.7 Baltimore (50.8) vs N.Y. (45.7) 1958 (10)
    47.3 Washington (52.5) vs Chi. Bears (42.2) 1942 (12)

Lowest Punting Average, Both Teams, Game

    33.3 Chi. Cards (32.0) vs Phil. (34.5) 1947 (16)
    33.9 New York (29.4) vs Chi. Bears (39.8) 1933 (23)

PUNT RETURNS

Most Punt Returns

    35   New York 14gs
    31   Clev. Browns 11gs

Most Punt Returns, Game

    8   Green Bay vs N.Y. 1944
    6   By 2 teams

Fewest Punt Returns, Game

    0   Chi. Bears vs Wash. 1937; vs N.Y. 1941
        New York vs Chi. Bears 1941
        Green Bay vs Dall. 1966
        Dallas vs G.B. 1967

Most Punt Returns, Both Teams, Game

    11   Green Bay (8) vs N.Y. (3) 1944
    10   Washington (5) vs Clev. Rams (5) 1945

Fewest Punt Returns, Both Teams, Game

    0   Chi. Bears vs N.Y. 1941 (7)
    2   Baltimore (1) vs Clev. (1) 1968 (7)

YARDAGE

Most Yards Gained

    322   New York 14gs (35)
    234   Chi. Bears 10gs (23)

Most Yards Gained, Game

    150   Chi. Cards vs Phil. 1947 (4)
    98   Green Bay vs N.Y. 1944 (8)

Most Yards Gained, Both Teams, Game

    160   Chi. Cards (150) vs Phil. (10) 1947 (7)
    133   Chi. Bears (67) vs N.Y. (66) 1934 (8)

Longest Gain

    75   Chi. Cards vs Phil. 1947 (TD)
    42   New York vs Chi. Bears 1934
        Clev. Browns vs Det. 1954

AVERAGE YARDAGE

Highest Average Gain

    26.8   Chi. Cards 2gs (6)
    10.2   Chi. Bears 10gs (23)

Highest Average Gain, Game (Minimum 3)

    37.5   Chi. Cards vs Phil. 1947 (4)
    16.8   Chi. Bears vs N.Y. 1934 (4)

Highest Average Gain, Both Teams, Game

    22.9   Chi. Cards (37.5) vs Phil. (3.3) 1947 (7)
    16.6   Chi. Bears (16.8) vs N.Y. (16.5) 1934 (8)

TOUCHDOWNS

Most Touchdowns

    1   Chi. Cards vs Phil. 1947

KICKOFF RETURNS

Most Kickoff Returns

    57   New York 14gs
    46   Clev. Browns 11gs

Most Kickoff Returns, Game

    9   Chi. Bears vs N.Y. 1956
    8   By 2 teams

Fewest Kickoff Returns, Game

    0   Green Bay vs Bos. 1936; vs N.Y. 1939
    1   By many teams

Most Kickoff Returns, Both Teams, Game

    12   Dallas (6) vs G.B. (6) 1966
    11   Chi. Bears (9) vs N.Y. (2) 1956
          Clev. Browns (8) vs Det. (3) 1957

Fewest Kickoff Returns, Both Teams, Game

    1   Green Bay (0) vs Bos. (1) 1936

YARDAGE

Most Yards Gained

 1,266   New York 14gs
   982   Clev. Browns 11gs

Most Yards Gained, Game

   225   Washington vs Chi. Bears 1940 (8)
   215   Los Angeles vs Clev. Browns 1955 (7)

Most Yards Gained, Both Teams, Game

   263   New York (157) vs Chi. Bears (106) 1933 (10)
          Dallas (153) vs G.B. (110) 1966 (12)
   258   Clev. Browns (183) vs Det. (75) 1957 (11)

Longest Gain

   62   Washington vs Chi. Bears 1940
   58   Philadelphia vs G.B. 1960

AVERAGE YARDAGE

Highest Average Gain

  28.2   Chi. Cards 2gs (5)
  25.1   Clev.-L.A. 5gs (18)

Highest Average Gain, Game (3 min.)

  39.7   Chi. Bears vs N.Y. 1934 (3)
  32.3   New York vs Chi. Bears 1963 (3)

Highest Average Gain, Both Teams, Game

   31.2   Chi. Bears (39.7) vs N.Y. (22.7) 1934 (6)
   27.6   Clev. Browns (31.6) vs G.B. (22.0) 1965 (8)

TOUCHDOWNS

Most Touchdowns

     None

PENALTIES

Most Penalties

   59   Chi. Bears 10gs
   53   New York 14gs

Most Penalties, Game

   11   New York vs G.B. 1944
   10   By 2 teams

Fewest Penalties, Game

    0   Philadelphia vs G.B. 1960

Most Penalties, Both Teams, Game

   16   Chi. Cards (10) vs Phil. (6) 1947

Fewest Penalties, Both Teams, Game

    2   Washington (1) vs Chi. Bears (1) 1937

YARDAGE

Most Yards Penalized

   505   Chi. Bears 10gs (59)
   488   Clev. Browns 11gs (51)

Most Yards Penalized, Game

   102   Chi. Bears vs N.Y. 1946 (9)
    98   Chi. Cards vs Phil. 1947 (10)

Fewest Yards Penalized, Game

    0   Philadelphia vs G.B. 1960 (0)

Most Yards Penalized, Both Teams, Game

   172   Chi. Bears (102) vs N.Y. (70) 1946 (15)
   138   In 2 games

Fewest Yards Penalized, Both Teams, Game

   20   Washington (5) vs Chi. Bears (15) 1937 (2)
   27   Philadelphia (0) vs G.B. (27) 1960 (4)

FUMBLES

Most Fumbles

   36   New York 14gs
   22   Chi. Bears 10gs

Most Fumbles, Game

   6 New York vs Balt. 1958
   5 By 4 teams

Most Fumbles, Both Teams, Game

  10 Chi. Bears (5) vs N.Y. (5) 1934
   8 New York (6) Balt. (2) 1958

Fewest Fumbles, Both Teams, Game

   0 Green Bay vs Clev. Browns 1965
   1 New York (0) vs Chi. Bears (1) 1933
       Detroit (0) vs Clev. Browns (1) 1952
       Clev. Browns (0) vs L.A. (1) 1955

RECOVERIES

Most Opponents Fumbles Recovered

  14 Chi. Bears 10gs
  12 New York 14gs

Most Opponents Fumbles Recovered, Game

   4 Baltimore vs N.Y. 1958
   3 New York vs Det. 1935
       Chi. Bears vs Wash. 1937
       Los Angeles vs Clev. 1950
       Cleveland vs Det. 1954
       Detroit vs Clev. 1957

YARDAGE

Most Yards Gained, Recoveries

  98 Chi. Bears 10gs
  32 New York 14gs

Most Yards Gained, Recoveries, Game

  50 Chi. Bears vs Wash. 1942
  42 Chi. Bears vs N.Y. 1941

TOUCHDOWNS

Most Touchdowns, Recoveries, Game

   1 Chi. Bears vs N.Y. 1941 (50 yds)
       Chi. Bears vs Wash. 1942 (42 yds)
       Los Angeles vs Clev. Browns 1950 (6 yds)
       Green Bay vs Dall. 1966 (18 yds)
       Dallas vs G.B. 1967 (7 yds)

1969 AFL CHAMPIONSHIP GAME

Oakland—Alameda County Stadium, Oakland, Calif.　　　January 4, 1970
Attendance: 53,564

Kansas City's determined defense, highlighted by four interceptions, three in the final quarter, carried the Chiefs to a 17—7 victory over Oakland in the final AFL title game. It was Kansas City's third championship victory in ten seasons and it came after the Raiders had twice beaten the Chiefs in regular season play.

Oakland's Daryle Lamonica, who had thrown 34 TD passes during the season, suffered an injury to his throwing hand when he smashed it against Aaron Brown's helmet early in the third period.

KANSAS CITY (17)	Offense	OAKLAND (7)
Frank Pitts	WR	Rod Sherman
Jim Tyrer	LT	Bob Svihus
Ed Budde	LG	Gene Upshaw
E. J. Holub	C	Jim Otto
Mo Moorman	RG	Jim Harvey
Dave Hill	RT	Harry Schuh
Fred Arbanas	TE	Billy Cannon
Otis Taylor	WR	Fred Biletnikoff
Len Dawson	QB	Daryle Lamonica
Mike Garrett	RB	Charlie Smith
Robert Holmes	RB	Hewritt Dixon
	Defense	
Jerry Mays	LE	Ike Lassiter
Curley Culp	LT	Carleton Oats
Buck Buchanan	RT	Tom Keating
Aaron Brown	RE	Ben Davidson
Bobby Bell	LLB	Ralph Oliver
Willie Lanier	MLB	Dan Conners
Jim Lynch	RLB	Gus Otto
Jim Marsalis	LCB	Nemiah Wilson
Emmitt Thomas	RCB	Willie Brown
Jim Kearney	LS	George Atkinson
Johnny Robinson	RS	Dave Grayson

SUBSTITUTIONS

KANSAS CITY—Offense: Receivers—Morris Stroud, Curtis McClinton, Gloster Richardson. Linemen—George Daney, Remi Prodhomme. Backs—Warren McVea, Wendell Hayes, Ed Podolak. Kickers—Jerrel Wilson, Jan Stenerud. Defense: Linebackers—Bob Stein, Chuck Hurston. Linemen—Gene Trosch, Ed Lothamer. Backs—Goldie Sellers, Willie Mitchell. DNP—Mike Livingston, Tom Flores.

OAKLAND—Offense: Receivers—Roger Hagberg, Lloyd Edwards, Warren Wells, Drew Buie. Linemen—Art Shell, Wayne Hawkins. Backs—George Blanda, Larry Todd, Marv Hubbard, Pete Banaszak. Kicker—Mike Eischeid. Defense: Linebackers—Bill Budness, Duane Benson. Linemen—Al Dotson, Art Thoms. Back—Howie Williams. DNP—Kent McCloughan, Bill Laskey.

OFFICIALS

Referee, Jack Vest. Umpire, Paul Trepinski. Headlinesman, Cal LePore. Field Judge, Bob Bauer. Back Judge, Hugh Gamber. Line Judge, Aaron Wade.

SCORING

KANSAS CITY CHIEFS	0	7	7	3——17
OAKLAND RAIDERS	7	0	0	0——7

Oak-Smith 3 run (Blanda kick). KC-Hayes 1 run (Stenerud kick). KC-Holmes 5 run (Stenerud kick). KC-FG Stenerud 22.

INDIVIDUAL STATISTICS

KANSAS CITY   OAKLAND

Rushing

	Atts.	Yds.	LG		Atts.	Yds.	LG
Holmes	18	14	8	Dixon	12	36	9
Garrett	7	19	12	Smith	12	31	9
Hayes	8	35	12	Banaszak	2	8	4
McVea	3	13	10	Todd	2	4	3
Dawson	3	5	3				

Passing

	Atts.	Comp.	Yds.	Int.	TD		Atts.	Comp.	Yds.	Int.	TD
Dawson	17	7	129	0	0	Lamonica	39	15	167	3	0
						Blanda	6	2	24	1	0

Receiving

	No.	Yds.	TD		No.	Yds.	TD
Taylor	3	62	0	Smith	8	86	0
Holmes	2	16	0	Sherman	3	45	0
Pitts	1	41	0	Cannon	2	22	0
Arbanas	1	10	0	Wells	1	24	0
				Banaszak	2	13	0
				Dixon	1	1	0

TEAM STATISTICS

	KANSAS CITY	OAKLAND
Total First Downs	13	18
First Downs Rushing	5	6
First Downs Passing	6	10
First Downs by Penalty	2	2
Total Offensive Yardage	207	233
Total No. Offensive Plays	57	77
Avg. Gain per Offensive Play	3.6	3.0
Net Rushing Yardage	86	79
Total Rushing Plays	39	28
Avg. Gain per Rushing Play	2.2	2.8
Net Passing Yardage	121	154
Gross Yards Gained Passing	129	191
Times Thrown and Yards Lost Attempting to Pass	1–8	4–37
Passes Att.-Comp.-Int.	17–7–0	45–17–4
Average Gain per Pass Play	6.7	3.1
Punts—Number and Average	8–42.9	6–48.5
Had Blocked	0	0
Fumbles—Number and Lost	5–4	1–0
Penalties—Number and Yards	5–43	5–45
Total Return Yardage	159	117
No. & Yards Punt Returns	4–9	2–(—1)
No. & Yards Kickoff Returns	2–43	4–112
No. & Yards Interceptions Returns	4–109	0–0
No. & Yards Miscellaneous Returns	1–(—2)	1–6

FINANCIAL SUMMARY

Paid attendance	53,564
Gross receipts (includes TV and radio)	$1,285,929.00
Players' share (total)	721,181.32
Winning players' share (each)	7,815.70
Losing players' share (each)	6,252.62

Robert Holmes leads Kansas City to victory over Oakland in title game.

AMERICAN FOOTBALL CONFERENCE
CHAMPIONSHIP GAMES AT A GLANCE

Year	Date	Winner-Share	Loser-Share	Score	Site	Attend.
1969	1-4-70	K.C. $7,755.79	Oak. $6,252.62	17-7	Oakland	53,564
1968	12-29-68	N.Y. $7,007.91	Oak. $5,349.42	27-23	New York	62,627
1967	12-31-67	Oak. $6,321.77	Hou. $4,996.45	40-7	Oakland	53,330
1966	1-1-67	K.C. $5,309.39	Buff. $3,799.90	31-7	Buffalo	42,080
1965	12-26-65	Buff. $5,189.92	S.D. $3,447.85	23-0	San Diego	30,361
1964	12-26-64	Buff. $2,668.60	S.D. $1,738.63	20-7	Buffalo	40,242
1963	1-5-64	S.D. $2,498.89	Bos. $1,596.52	51-10	San Diego	30,127
1962	12-23-62	Dall. $2,206.64	Hou. $1,471.09	20-17*	Houston	37,981
1961	12-24-61	Hou. $1,792.79	S.D. $1,111.81	10-3	San Diego	29,556
1960	1-1-61	Hou. $1,025.73	L.A. $718.61	24-16	Houston	32,183

*Sudden death

AFC CHAMPIONSHIP GAME
COMPOSITE STANDINGS

	W	L	Pct.	Pts.	O.P.
Chiefs	3	0	1.000	68	31
Jets	1	0	1.000	27	23
Bills	2	1	.667	50	38
Oilers	2	2	.500	58	79
Raiders	1	2	.333	70	51
Chargers	1	4	.200	77	87
Patriots	0	1	.000	10	51
Broncos	0	0	.000	—	—
Dolphins	0	0	.000	—	—

Chiefs' Mike Garrett is enmeshed in the arms of Oakland's Dan Conners.

AMERICAN FOOTBALL CONFERENCE
CHAMPIONSHIP GAME RECORDS
(Compiled by Elias Sports Bureau)

INDIVIDUAL
SERVICE

GAMES—PLAYER

Most Games Played

    7 Dave Kocourek (E), L.A. 1960; S.D. 1961–63–65; Oak. 67–68.
    6 George Blanda (QB-K), Hou. 1960–62; Oak. 67–69.
       Billy Cannon (HB-E), Hou. 1960–62; Oak. 67–69.
       Daryle Lamonica (QB), Buff. 1964–66; Oak; 67–69.

Most Games on Winning Team

    3 Paul Maguire (LB-K), S.D. 1963; Buff. 1964–65.
       George Blanda (QB-K), Hou. 1960–61; Oak. 1967.
       Billy Cannon (HB-E), Hou. 1960–61; Oak. 1967.
       Daryle Lamonica (QB), Buff. 1964–65; Oak. 1967.
       Fred Arbanas (E), Dall./K.C. 1962, 66, 69.
       Len Dawson (QB), Dall./K.C. 1962, 66, 69.
       E. J. Holub (LB-C), Dall./K.C. 1962, 66, 69.
       Jerry Mays (DE), Dall./K.C. 1962, 66, 69.
       Curtis McClinton (FB-TE), Dall./K.C. 1962, 66, 69.
       Johnny Robinson (DB), Dall./K.C. 1962, 66, 69.
       Jim Tyrer (T), Dall./K.C. 1962, 66, 69.

GAMES—COACH

Most Games

    5 Sid Gillman, L.A. 1960; S.D. 1961, 63–65 (W-1, L-4).
    3 Hank Stram, Dall. 1962, K.C. 66, 69 (W-3).

SCORING

TOTAL POINTS

Most Total Points, Lifetime

   43 George Blanda, Hou.-Oak. 6gs (13-xp, 10-fg).
   19 Pete Gogolak, Buff. 2gs (4-xp, 5-fg).

Most Total Points, Game

   16 George Blanda, Oak. vs. Hou. 1967 (4-xp, 4-fg).
   12 Abner Haynes, Dall. vs. Hou. 1962 (2td).
       Keith Lincoln, S.D. vs. Bos. 1963 (2 td.).
       Mike Garrett, K.C. vs. Buff. 1966 (2 td.).

TOUCHDOWNS

Most Touchdowns, Lifetime

    2 Billy Cannon, Hou.-Oak. 4gs (2-p).
       Abner Haynes, Dall. 1g (1-r, 1-p).
       Keith Lincoln, S.D. 4gs (1-r, 1-p).
       Paul Lowe, L.A.-S.D. 5gs (2-r).
       Mike Garrett, K.C. 1g (2-r).
       Dave Kocourek, L.A.-S.D.-Oak. 6 gs (2-p).
       Don Maynard, N.Y. 1g (2-p).

Most Touchdowns, Game

2 Abner Haynes, Dall. vs. Hou. 1962 (1-r, 1-p).
Keith Lincoln, S.D. vs. Bos. 1963 (1-r, 1-p).
Mike Garrett, K.C. vs. Buff. 1966 (2-r).
Don Maynard, N.Y. (2-p).

POINTS AFTER TOUCHDOWN

Most Points After Touchdown, Lifetime

13 George Blanda, Hou.-Oak. 6gs (13 atts).
6 George Blair, S.D. 2gs (6 atts).

Most Points After Touchdown, Game

6 George Blair, S.D. vs. Bos. 1963 (6 atts).
4 Mike Mercer, K.C. vs. Buff. 1966 (4 atts).
George Blanda, Oak. vs. Hou. 1967 (4 atts).

FIELD GOALS

Most Field Goals Attempted, Lifetime

19 George Blanda, Hou.-Oak. 6gs.
7 Pete Gogolak, Buff. 2gs.

Most Field Goals Attempted, Game

6 George Blanda, Oak. vs. Hou. 1967.
5 Pete Gogolak, Buff. vs. S.D. 1965.

Most Field Goals, Lifetime

10 George Blanda, Hou.-Oak. 6gs.
5 Pete Gogolak, Buff. 2gs.

Most Field Goals, Game

4 George Blanda, Oak. vs. Hou. 1967.
3 Ben Agajanian, L.A. vs. Hou. 1960.
Pete Gogolak, Buff. vs. S.D. 1965.
George Blanda, Oak. vs. N.Y. 1968.

Longest Field Goal

46 George Blanda, Hou. vs. S.D. 1961.
42 George Blanda, Oak. vs. Hou. 1967.

RUSHING

ATTEMPTS

Most Attempts, Lifetime

57 Paul Lowe, L.A.-S.D. 5gs.
44 Billy Cannon, Hou.-Oak. 6gs.

Most Attempts, Game

24 Curt McClinton, Dall. vs. Hou. 1962.
21 Paul Lowe, L.A. vs. Hou. 1960.
Hewritt Dixon, Oak. vs. Hou. 1967.

YARDAGE

Most Yards Gained, Lifetime

380 Paul Lowe, L.A.-S.D. 5gs.
276 Keith Lincoln, S.D. 4gs.

Most Yards Gained, Game

   206   Keith Lincoln, S.D. vs. Bos. 1963.
   165   Paul Lowe, L.A. vs. Hou. 1960.

Longest Run from Scrimmage

   69   Hewritt Dixon, Oak. vs. Hou. 1967 (TD).
   67   Keith Lincoln, S.D. vs. Bos. 1963 (TD).

AVERAGE YARDAGE

Highest Average Gain, Lifetime

  12.00   Keith Lincoln, S.D. 4gs (23–276).
   6.67   Paul Lowe, L.A.-S.D. 5gs (57–380).

Highest Average Gain, Game

  15.85   Keith Lincoln S.D. vs. Bos. 1963 (13–206).
   7.86   Paul Lowe, L.A. vs. Hou. 1960 (21–165).

TOUCHDOWNS

Most Touchdowns, Lifetime

   2   Paul Lowe, L.A.-S.D. 5gs.
      Mike Garrett, K.C. 2gs.

Most Touchdowns, Game

   2   Mike Garrett, K.C. vs. Buff. 1966.

PASSING

ATTEMPTS

Most Passes Attempted, Lifetime

  139   Jack Kemp, L.A.-S.D.-Buff. 5gs (68 comp).
  125   George Blanda, Hou.-Oak. 6gs (59 comp).

Most Passes Attempted, Game

   49   Joe Namath, N.Y. vs. Oak. 1968 (19 comp).
   47   Daryle Lamonica, Oak. vs. N.Y. 1968 (20 comp).

COMPLETIONS

Most Passes Completed, Lifetime

   68   Jack Kemp, L.A.-S.D.-Buff. 5gs (139 att).
   59   George Blanda, Hou.-Oak. 6gs (125 atts).

Most Passes Completed, Game

   23   George Blanda, Hou. vs. Dall. 1962 (46 att).
   21   Jack Kemp, L.A. vs. Hou. 1960 (41 att).

EFFICIENCY

Passing Efficiency, Lifetime (35 atts)

  58.2   Len Dawson, Dall./K.C. 3gs (55–32).
  48.9   Jack Kemp, L.A.-S.D.-Buff. 5gs (139–68)

Passing Efficiency, Game (20 atts)

  66.7   Len Dawson, K.C. vs. Buff. 1966 (24–16).
  53.1   Jack Kemp, S.D. vs. Hou. 1961 (32–17).

Most Yards Gained, Lifetime

> 993 Jack Kemp, L.A.-S.D.-Buff. 5gs.
> 746 George Blanda, Hou.-Oak. 6gs.

Most Yards Gained, Game

> 401 Daryle Lamonica, Oak. vs. N.Y. 1968.
> 301 George Blanda, Hou. vs. L.A. 1960.

Longest Pass Completion

> 88 George Blanda (Cannon), Hou. vs. L.A. 1960 (TD).
> 69 Jack Kemp (Dubenion), Buff. vs. K.C. 1966 (TD)

TOUCHDOWNS

Most Touchdown Passes, Lifetime

> 5 George Blanda, Hou.-Oak. 6gs.
> 3 Tobin Rote, S.D. 2gs.
>   Len Dawson, Dall./K.C. 3gs.
>   Daryle Lamonica, Buff.-Oak. 6gs.
>   Joe Namath, N.Y. 1g.

Most Touchdown Passes, Game

> 3 George Blanda, Hou. vs. L.A. 1960.
>   Joe Namath, N.Y. vs. Oak. 1968.
> 2 Tobin Rote, S.D. vs. Bos. 1963.
>   Len Dawson, K.C. vs. Buff. 1966.
>   Daryle Lamonica, Oak. vs. Hou. 1967.

HAD INTERCEPTED

Fewest Passes Had Intercepted, Lifetime

> 0 Len Dawson, Dall./K.C. 3gs (55 atts).

Most Passes Had Intercepted, Lifetime

> 11 George Blanda, Hou.-Oak. 6gs (125 atts).
> 9 Jack Kemp, L.A.-S.D.-Buff. 5gs (139 atts).

Fewest Passes Had Intercepted, Game

> 0 Daryle Lamonica, Oak. vs. N.Y. 1968 (47 atts).
>   George Blanda, Hou. vs. L.A. 1960 (31 atts).

Most Passes Had Intercepted, Game

> 5 George Blanda, Hou. vs. S.D. 1961 (40 atts).
>   George Blanda, Hou. vs. Dall. 1962 (46 atts).
> 4 Jack Kemp, S.D. vs. Hou. 1961 (32 atts).

PASS RECEIVING

RECEPTIONS

Most Receptions, Lifetime

> 22 Billy Cannon, Hou.-Oak. 6gs.
> 15 Dave Kocourek, L.A.-S.D.-Oak. 6gs.

Most Receptions, Game

  8 Charles Smith, Oak. vs. K.C. 1969.
  7 Dave Kocourek, S.D. vs. Hou. 1961.
     Keith Lincoln, S.D. vs. Bos. 1963.
     Charlie Frazier, Hou. vs. Oak. 1967.
     Fred Biletnikoff, Oak. vs. N.Y. 1968.
     George Sauer, N.Y. vs. Oakland 1968.

YARDAGE

Most Yards Gained, Lifetime

 357 Billy Cannon, Hou.-Oak. 6gs.
 257 Dave Kocourek, L.A.-S.D.-Oak. 6gs.

Most Yards Gained, Game

 190 Fred Biletnikoff, Oak. vs. N.Y. 1968 (7).
 128 Billy Cannon, Hou. vs. L.A. 1960 (3).

Longest Reception

  88 Billy Cannon (Blanda), Hou. vs. L.A. 1960 (TD).
  69 Elbert Dubenion (Kemp), Buff. vs. K.C. 1966 (TD).

TOUCHDOWNS

Most Touchdown Passes, Lifetime

  2 Billy Cannon, Hou.-Oak. 6gs.
     Dave Kocourek, L.A.-S.D.-Oak. 6gs.
     Don Maynard, N.Y. 1g.

Most Touchdown Passes, Game

  2 Don Maynard, N.Y. vs. Oak. 1968.
  1 By nineteen players.

INTERCEPTIONS BY

Most Interceptions By, Lifetime

  3 Johnny Robinson, Dall./K.C. 3gs.
     Emmitt Thomas, K.C. 2gs.
  2 By five players.

Most Interceptions By, Game

  2 Charles McNeil, S.D. vs. Hou. 1961.
     Bud Whitehead, S.D. vs. Hou. 1961.
     Bob Zeman, S.D. vs. Hou. 1961.
     Johnny Robinson, Dall. vs. Hou. 1962.
     Emmitt Thomas, K.C. vs. Oak. 1969.

YARDAGE

Most Yards Gained, Lifetime

 122 Johnny Robinson, Dall./K.C. 3gs (3).
  95 Emmitt Thomas, K.C. 2gs (3).

Most Yards Gained, Game

  72 Johnny Robinson, K.C. vs. Buff. 1966 (1).
  69 Emmitt Thomas, K.C. vs. Oak. 1969 (2).

Longest Return

  72 Johnny Robinson, K.C. vs. Buff. 1966.
  62 Emmitt Thomas, K.C. vs. Oak. 1969.

Most Touchdowns, Lifetime

> None.

PUNTING

Most Punts, Lifetime

> 25 Paul Maguire, S.D.-Buff. 5gs.
> 18 Jim Norton, Hou. 4gs.

Most Punts, Game

> 11 Jim Norton, Hou. vs. Oak. 1967.
> 10 Curley Johnson, N.Y. vs. Oak. 1968.

Longest Punt

> 68 Tom Yewcic, Bos. vs. S.D. 1963.
> 64 Paul Maguire, Buff. vs. S.D. 1964.

AVERAGE YARDAGE

Highest Punting Average, Lifetime (10 punts)

> 45.1 Mike Eischeid, Oak. 3gs (17).
> 43.9 John Hadl, S.D. 3gs (10).

Highest Punting Average, Game (4 punts)

> 51.4 John Hadl, S.D. vs. Buff. 1965 (5).
> 48.5 Mike Eischeid, Oak. vs. K.C. 1969 (6).

HAD BLOCKED

Most Punts Had Blocked, Lifetime

> None.

PUNT RETURNS

Most Punt Returns, Lifetime

> 7 Rodger Bird, Oak. 2gs.
>   Mike Garrett, K.C. 2gs.
> 6 George Byrd, Buff. 3gs.

Most Punt Returns, Game

> 5 Rodger Bird, Oak. vs. Hou. 1967.
> 4 Mike Garrett, K.C. vs. Oak. 1969.

YARDAGE

Most Yards Gained, Lifetime

> 87 George Byrd, Buff. 3gs (6).
> 55 Rodger Bird, Oak. 2gs. (7).

Most Yards Gained, Game

> 87 George Byrd, Buff. vs. S.D. 1965 (3).
> 49 Rodger Bird, Oak. vs. Hou. 1967 (5).

Longest Return

> 74 George Byrd, Buff. vs. S.D. 1965 (TD).
> 30 Jerry Robinson, S.D. vs. Buff. 1964.

AVERAGE YARDAGE

Highest Average Gain, Lifetime (4 returns)

14.5 George Byrd, Buff. 3gs (6).
7.9 Rodger Bird, Oak. 2gs. (7).

Highest Average Gain, Game (3 returns)

29.0 George Byrd, Buff. vs. S.D. 1965 (3).
12.3 Mike Garrett, K.C. vs. Buff. 1966 (3).

TOUCHDOWNS

Most Touchdowns, Lifetime

See following category

Most Touchdowns, Game

1 George Byrd, Buff. vs. S.D. 1965.

KICKOFF RETURNS

Most Kickoff Returns, Lifetime

9 Bobby Jancik, Hou. 2gs.
7 Charley Warner, Buff. 3gs.
George Atkinson, Oak. 2gs.

Most Kickoff Returns, Game

5 Bobby Jancik, Hou. vs. Dall. 1962.
Charley Warner, Buff. vs. K.C. 1966.
4 Paul Lowe, L.A. vs. Hou. 1960.
Bobby Jancik, Hou. vs. Oak. 1967.
George Atkinson, Oak. vs. N.Y. 1968.

YARDAGE

Most Yards Gained, Lifetime

239 Bobby Jancik, Hou. 2gs.
209 Les Duncan, S.D. 2gs.

Most Yards Gained, Game

147 Les Duncan, S.D. vs. Buff. 1964 (3).
139 Bobby Jancik, Hou. vs. Dall. 1962 (5).

Longest Return

72 Les Duncan, S.D. vs. Buff. 1964.
52 George Atkinson, Oak. vs. K.C. 1969.

AVERAGE YARDAGE

Highest Average Gain, Lifetime (4 returns)

41.8 Les Duncan, S.D. 2gs (5).
29.6 George Atkinson, Oak. 2gs (7).

Highest Average Gain, Game (3 returns)

49.0 Les Duncan, S.D. vs. Buff. 1964 (3).
31.7 George Atkinson, Oak. vs. K.C. 1969 (3).

TOUCHDOWNS

Most Touchdowns, Lifetime

> None.

FUMBLES

Most Fumbles, Lifetime

> 2 Jack Kemp, L.A.-S.D.-Buff. 5gs.
>   Len Dawson, Dall./K.C. 3gs.
> 1 By many players.

Most Fumbles, Game

> 2 Jack Kemp, S.D. vs. Hou. 1961.
>   Mike Garrett, K.C. vs. Oak. 1969.
>   Robert Holmes, K.C. vs. Oak. 1969.
> 1 By many players.

RECOVERIES

Most Own Fumbles Recovered, Lifetime

> 1 By fifteen players.

Most Opponents' Fumbles Recovered, Lifetime

> 2 Dan Conners, Oak. 3gs.
> 1 By many players.

YARDAGE

Longest Gain

> 21 Bobby Hunt, K.C. vs. Buff. 1966 (opp).
> 6 Ken Herock, Oak. vs. Hou. 1967 (opp).

TOUCHDOWNS

Most Touchdowns, Lifetime

> None.

COMBINED NET YARDS

(INCLUDES RUSHES, RECEPTIONS AND RUNBACK OF INTERCEPTIONS, PUNTS, KICKOFFS AND FUMBLES)

ATTEMPTS

Most Attempts, Lifetime

> 72 Paul Lowe, L.A.-S.D. 5gs.
> 69 Billy Cannon, Hou.-Oak. 6gs.

Most Attempts, Game

> 28 Paul Lowe, L.A. vs. Hou. 1960.
> 25 Curt McClinton, Dall. vs. Hou. 1962.

YARDAGE

Most Yards Gained, Lifetime

> 573 Billy Cannon, Hou.-Oak. 6gs.
> 558 Paul Lowe, L.A.-S.D. 5gs.

Most Yards Gained, Game

   329   Keith Lincoln, S.D. vs. Bos. 1963.
   271   Paul Lowe, L.A. vs. Hou. 1960.

AVERAGE YARDAGE

Highest Average Gain, Lifetime

   12.8   Keith Lincoln, S.D. 4gs (34–436).
    8.3   Billy Cannon, Hou.-Oak. 6gs (69–573).

Highest Average Gain, Game

   16.5   Keith Lincoln, S.D. vs. Bos. 1963 (20–329).
   10.8   Billy Cannon, Hou. vs. L.A. 1960 (24–259).

AMERICAN FOOTBALL CONFERENCE
CHAMPIONSHIP GAME RECORDS
TEAM
GAMES

Most Games

   5   L.A./San Diego 1960; 61, 63–65.
   4   Houston 1960–62, 67.

Most Consecutive Games

   3   Houston 1960–62.
      San Diego 1963–65.
      Buffalo 1964–66.
      Oakland 1967–69.
   2   L.A./S.D. 1960–61.

Most Games Won

   3   Dallas./K.C. 1962, 66, 69.
   2   Houston 1960–61.
      Buffalo 1964–65.

Most Games Lost

   4   L.A./San Diego 1960; 61, 64–65.
   2   Houston 1962, 67.
      Oakland, 1968–69.

SCORING

Most Total Points

   77   L.A./San Diego 5gs.
   70   Oakland 3gs.

Most Points, Game

   51   San Diego vs. Bos. 1963.
   40   Oakland vs. Hou. 1967.

Most Points, Both Teams, Game

   61   San Diego (51) vs. Bos. (10) 1963.
   50   New York (27) vs. Oakland (23) 1968.

Fewest Points, Both Teams, Game

   13   San Diego (3) vs. Hou. (10) 1961.
   23   San Diego (0) vs. Buff. (23) 1965.

Shutout Games

    1   Buffalo (23) vs. S.D. 1965.

Most Points, By Quarters

1st: 21   San Diego vs. Bos. 1963.
2nd: 14   Dallas vs. Hou. 1962.
            Buffalo vs. S.D. 1965.
            Oakland vs. Hou. 1967.
3rd: 10   Oakland vs. Hou. 1967.
4th: 14   Kansas City vs. Buff. 1966.

TOUCHDOWNS

Most Touchdowns

    9   L.A./San Diego 5gs (5-r, 4-p).
    8   Dall./K.C. 3gs (5-r, 3-p).

Most Touchdowns, Game

    7   San Diego vs. Bos. 1963 (4-r, 3-p).
    4   Kansas City vs. Buff. 1966 (2-r, 2-p).
           Oakland vs. Hou. 1967 (2-r, 2-p).

Most Touchdowns, Both Teams, Game

    8   San Diego (7) vs. Bos. (1) 1963.
    5   Kansas City (4) vs. Buff. (1) 1966.
           Oakland (4) vs. Hou. (1) 1967.
           New York (3) vs. Oak. (2) 1968.

Fewest Touchdowns, Both Teams, Game

    1   San Diego (0) vs. Hou. (1) 1961.
    2   San Diego (0) vs. Buff. (2) 1965.

POINTS AFTER TOUCHDOWN

(Only 2-point play failed: Rote, S.D., 1963, threw incomplete pass following bad center snap on placement kick attempt.)

Most Points After Touchdown

    8   L.A./San Diego 5gs.
    8   Dall./K.C. 3gs.

Most Points After Touchdown, Game

    6   San Diego vs. Bos. 1963.
    4   Kansas City vs. Buff. 1966.
           Oakland vs. Hou. 1967.

Most Points After Touchdown, Both Teams, Game

    7   San Diego (6) vs. Bos. (1) 1963.
    5   Kansas City (4) vs. Buff. (1) 1966.
           Oakland (4) vs. Hou. (1) 1967.
           New York (3) vs. Oak. (2) 1968.

Fewest Points After Touchdown, Both Teams, Game

- 1 San Diego (0) vs. Hou. (1) 1961.
- 2 San Diego (0) vs. Buff. (2) 1965.

FIELD GOALS

Most Field Goals

- 7 Oakland 3gs (13 atts).
- 5 L.A./San Diego 5gs (9 atts).
  Buffalo 3gs (7 atts).

Most Field Goals, Game

- 4 Oakland vs. Hou. 1967 (6 atts).
- 3 Los Angeles vs. Hou. 1960 (3 atts).
  Buffalo vs. S.D. 1965 (5 atts).
  Oakland vs. N.Y. 1968 (4 atts).

Most Field Goals, Both Teams, Game

- 5 Oakland (3) vs. N.Y. (2) 1968 (7 atts).
- 4 Los Angeles (3) vs. Hou. (1) 1960 (5 atts).
  Oakland (4) vs. Hou. (0) 1967 (6 atts).

Most Field Goals Attempted

- 13 Oakland 3gs (7 made).
- 9 L.A./San Diego 5gs (5 made).

Most Field Goals Attempted, Game

- 6 Oakland vs. Hou. 1967 (4 made).
- 5 Buffalo vs. S.D. 1965 (3 made).

Most Field Goals Attempted, Both Teams, Game

- 7 Buffalo (5) vs. S.D. (2) 1965 (3 made).
  Oakland (4) vs. N.Y. (3) 1968 (5 made).
- 6 Dallas (3) vs. Hou. (3) 1962 (3 made).
  Oakland (6) vs. Hou. (0) 1967 (4 made).

Longest Field Goal

- 46 Houston vs. S.D. 1961.
- 42 Oakland vs Hou. 1967.

SAFETIES

Most Safeties

None.

FIRST DOWNS

Most First Downs

- 84 L.A./San Diego 5gs (40-r, 40-p, 4-pen).
- 67 Houston 4gs (20-r, 42-p, 5-pen).

Most First Downs, Game

- 25 New York vs. Oak. 1968 (9-r, 15-p, 1-pen).
- 23 Buffalo vs. S.D. 1965 (13-r, 9-p, 1-pen).

Fewest First Downs, Game

  9   Buffalo vs. K.C. 1966 (2-r, 7-p, 0-pen).
11   Houston vs. Oak. 1967 (4-r, 6-p, 1-pen).

Most First Downs, Both Teams, Game

43   New York (25) vs. Oak. (18) 1968.
40   Houston (21) vs. Dall. (19) 1962.

Fewest First Downs, Both Teams, Game

23   Buffalo (9) vs. K.C. (14) 1966.
29   Houston (11) vs. Oak. (18) 1967.

YARDS GAINED

(RUSHING AND PASSING)

Most Net Yards Gained

1,653   L.A./San Diego 5gs (787-r, 866-p).
1,162   Houston 4gs (332-r, 830-p).

Most Net Yards Gained, Game

610   San Diego vs. Bos. 1963 (318-r, 292-p).
443   Oakland vs. N.Y. 1968 (50-r, 393-p).

Fewest Net Yards Gained, Game

146   Houston vs. Oak. 1967 (38-r, 108-p).
207   Kansas City vs. Oak. 1969 (86-r, 121-p).

Most Net Yards Gained, Both Teams, Game

871   San Diego (610) vs. Buff. (261) 1963.
843   Oakland (443) vs. N.Y. (400) 1968.

Fewest Net Yards Gained, Both Teams, Game

440   Kansas City (207) vs. Oak. (233) 1969.
483   San Diego (223) vs. Buff. (260) 1965.

RUSHING

ATTEMPTS

Most Attempts

130   L.A./San Diego 5gs.
126   Dall./K.C. 3gs.

Most Attempts, Game

54   Dallas vs. Hou. 1962.
48   Oakland vs. Hou. 1967.

Fewest Attempts, Game

13   Buffalo vs. K.C. 1966.
16   Boston vs. S.D. 1963.

Most Attempts, Both Teams, Game

84   Dallas (54) vs. Hou. (30) 1962.
73   Houston (40) vs. L.A. (33) 1960.

Fewest Attempts, Both Teams, Game

    46   Buffalo (13) vs. K.C. (33) 1966.
    48   Boston (16) vs. S.D. (32) 1963.

YARDAGE

Most Yards Gained

   787   L.A./San Diego 5gs.
   398   Dall./K.C. 3gs.

Most Yards Gained, Game

   318   San Diego vs. Bos. 1963.
   263   Oakland vs. Hou. 1967.

Fewest Yards Gained, Game

    38   Houston vs. Oak. 1967.
    40   Buffalo vs. K.C. 1966.

Most Yards Gained, Both Teams, Game

   393   San Diego (318) vs. Bos. (75) 1963.
   343   Buffalo (219) vs. S.D. (124) 1964.

Fewest Yards Gained, Both Teams, Game

   153   Buffalo (40) vs. K.C. (113) 1966.
   165   Oakland (79) vs. K.C. (86) 1969.

Longest Gain

    69   Oakland vs. Hou. 1967 (TD).
    67   San Diego vs. Bos. 1963 (TD).

AVERAGE YARDAGE

Highest Average Gain

  6.05   L.A./SanDiego 5gs (130–787).
  4.13   Oakland 3gs (95–392).

Highest Average Gain, Game

  9.94   San Diego vs. Bos. 1963 (32–318).
  6.89   San Diego vs. Buff. 1964 (18–124).

Lowest Average Gain, Game

  1.73   Houston vs. Oak. 1967 (22–38).
  2.21   Kansas City vs. Oak. 1969 (39–86).

Highest Average Gain, Both Teams, Game

  8.19   San Diego (9.94) vs. Bos. (4.69) 1963.
  5.81   San Diego (6.89) vs. Buff. (5.34) 1964.

Lowest Average Gain, Both Teams, Game

  2.46   Kansas City (2.21) vs. Oak. (2.82) 1969.
  3.30   Houston (2.91) vs. S.D. (3.95) 1961.

TOUCHDOWNS

Most Touchdowns

     5   L.A./San Diego 5gs.
         Dall./K.C. 3gs.
     4   Oakland 3gs.

Most Touchdowns, Game

    4   San Diego vs. Bos. 1963.
    2   By four teams.

Fewest Touchdowns, Game

    0   By nine teams.
    1   By six teams.

Most Touchdowns, Both Teams, Game

    5   San Diego (4) vs. Bos. (1) 1963.
    3   Kansas City (2) vs. Oak. (1) 1969.

Fewest Touchdowns, Both Teams, Game

    0   Houston vs. S.D. 1961.
        Buffalo vs. S.D. 1965.
    1   Houston vs. L.A. (1) 1960.
        New York vs. Oak. (1) 1968.

PASSING

ATTEMPTS

Most Attempts

    160   L.A./San Diego 5gs.
    154   Houston 4gs.

Most Attempts, Game

    49   New York vs. Oak. 1968.
    47   Oakland vs. N.Y. 1968.

Fewest Attempts, Game

    14   Dallas vs. Hou. 1962.
    17   Kansas City vs. Oak. 1969.

Most Attempts, Both Teams, Game

    96   New York (49) vs. Oak. (47) 1968.
    73   Los Angeles (41) vs. Hou. (32) 1960.
        Houston (41) vs. S.D. (32) 1961.

Fewest Attempts, Both Teams, Game

    45   Buffalo (20) vs. S.D. (25) 1965.
    51   Kansas City (24) vs. Buff. (27) 1966.

COMPLETIONS

Most Passes Completed

    80   L.A./San Diego 5gs.
    72   Houston 4gs.

Most Passes Completed, Game

    23   Houston vs. Dall. 1962.
    21   Los Angeles vs. Hou. 1960.

Fewest Passes Completed, Game

    7   Kansas City vs. Oak. 1969.
    9   Dallas vs. Hou. 1962.
        Buffalo vs. S.D. 1965.

Most Passes Completed, Both Teams, Game

    39 Oakland (20) vs. N.Y. (19) 1968.
    37 Los Angeles (21) vs. Hou. (16) 1960.

Fewest Passes Completed, Both Teams, Game

    21 Buffalo (9) vs. S.D. (12) 1965.
    23 Buffalo (10) vs. S.D. (13) 1964.

EFFICIENCY

Highest Passing Efficiency

    58.2 Dall./K.C. 3gs (55–32).
    50.0 L.A./San Diego 5gs (160–80).

Highest Passing Efficiency, Game

    66.7 Kansas City vs. Buff. 1966 (24–16).
    65.4 San Diego vs. Bos. 1963 (26–17).

Lowest Passing Efficiency, Game

    36.1 San Diego vs. Buff. 1964 (36–13).
    37.8 Oakland vs. K.C. 1969 (45–17).

Highest Passing Efficiency, Both Teams, Game

    54.9 Kansas City (66.7) vs. Buff. (44.4) 1966.
    54.0 San Diego (65.4) vs. Bos. (45.9) 1963.

Lowest Passing Efficiency, Both Teams, Game

    38.7 Oakland (37.8) vs. K.C. (41.2) 1969.
    40.6 New York (38.8) vs. Oak. (42.6) 1968.

YARDAGE

Most Yards Gained

    866 L.A./San Diego 5gs.
    830 Houston 4gs.

Most Yards Gained, Game

    393 Oakland vs. N.Y. 1968.
    301 Houston vs. L.A. 1960.

Fewest Yards Gained, Game

    38 Dallas vs. Hou. 1962.
    101 Oakland vs. Hou. 1967.

Most Yards Gained, Both Teams, Game

    649 Oakland (393) vs. N.Y. (256) 1968.
    478 San Diego (292) vs. Bos. (186) 1963.

Fewest Yards Gained, Both Teams, Game

    209 Oakland (101) vs. Hou. (108) 1967.
    271 San Diego (119) vs. Buff. (152) 1965.

Longest Gain

    88 Houston vs. L.A. 1960 (TD).
    69 Buffalo vs. K.C. 1966 (TD).

TOUCHDOWNS

Most Touchdowns

    6 Houston 4gs.
    4 L.A./San Diego 5gs.

Most Touchdowns, Game

    3 Houston vs. L.A. 1960.
       San Diego vs. Bos. 1963.
       New York vs. Oak. 1968.
    2 Kansas City vs. Buff. 1966.
       Oakland vs. Hou. 1967.

Fewest Touchdowns, Game

    0 By seven teams.
    1 By eight teams.

Most Touchdowns, Both Teams, Game

    4 New York (3) vs. Oak. (1) 1968.
    3 Houston (3) vs. L.A. 1960.
       San Diego (3) vs. Bos. 1963.
       Kansas City (2) vs. Buff. (1) 1966.
       Oakland (2) vs. Hou. (1) 1967.

Fewest Touchdowns, Both Teams, Game

    0 Kansas City vs. Oak. 1969.
    1 San Diego vs. Hou. (1) 1961; vs. Buff. (1) 1965.
       Buffalo vs. S.D. (1) 1964.

INTERCEPTIONS

Most Interceptions By

   11 Dall./K.C. 3gs.
    9 L.A./San Diego 5gs.

Most Passes Had Intercepted

   12 Houston 4gs.
   11 L.A./San Diego 5gs.

Most Passes Had Intercepted, Game

    6 Houston vs. S.D. 1961 (41 atts).
    5 Houston vs. Dall. 1962 (46 atts).

Fewest Passes Had Intercepted, Game (Most Attempts)

    0 Oakland vs. N.Y. 1968 (47 atts).
       Houston vs. L.A. 1960 (32 atts).

Most Passes Intercepted By, Both Teams, Game

   10 San Diego (6) vs. Hou. (4) 1961.
    5 Dallas (5) vs. Hou. (0) 1962.

Fewest Passes Intercepted By, Both Teams, Game

    1 Houston vs. Oak. (1) 1967.
       New York vs. Oak. (1) 1968.
    2 In three games.

Most Yards Gained

343 Dall./K.C. 3gs (11).
75 L.A./San Diego 5gs (9).

Most Yards Gained, Game

136 Dallas vs. Hou. 1962 (5).
109 Kansas City vs. Oak. 1969 (4).

Most Yards Gained, Both Teams, Game

136 Dallas (136) vs. Hou. 1962.
109 Kansas City (109) vs. Oak. 1969.

Longest Return

72 Kansas City vs. Hou. 1966.
62 Kansas City vs. Oak. 1969.

TOUCHDOWNS

Most Touchdowns

None.

PUNTING

Most Punts

24 L.A./San Diego 5gs.
23 Houston 4gs.

Most Punts, Game

11 Houston vs. Oak. 1967.
10 New York vs. Oak. 1968.

Fewest Punts, Game

2 San Diego vs. Bos. 1963.
3 Houston vs. Dall. 1962.

Most Punts, Both Teams, Game

17 New York (10) vs. Oak. (7) 1968.
15 Houston (11) vs. Oak. (4) 1967.

Fewest Punts, Both Teams, Game

9 Los Angeles (4) vs. Hou. (5) 1960.
   San Diego (2) vs. Bos. (7) 1963.
10 Houston (4) vs. S.D. (6) 1961.
   Buffalo (5) vs. S.D. (5) 1964.

AVERAGE YARDAGE

Highest Punting Average

45.1 Oakland 3gs (17).
43.1 Buffalo 3gs (17).

Highest Punting Average, Game

48.5 Oakland vs. K.C. 1969 (6).
46.8 Buffalo vs. S.D. 1964 (5).

Lowest Punting Average, Game

   31.3 Dallas vs. Hou. 1962 (8).
   33.3 San Diego vs. Hou. 1961 (6).

Highest Punting Average, Both Teams, Game

   45.3 Oakland (48.5) vs. K.C. (42.9) 1969 (14).
   44.1 Boston (44.3) vs. S.D. (43.5) 1963 (9).

Lowest Punting Average, Both Teams, Game

   33.5 Dallas (31.3) vs. Hou. (39.3) 1962 (11).
   36.6 San Diego (33.3) vs. Hou. (41.5) 1961 (10).

PUNT RETURNS

Most Punt Returns

   12 Oakland 3gs.
    9 Buffalo 3gs.

Most Punt Returns, Game

   6 Oakland vs. Hou. 1967.
   5 Buffalo vs. K.C. 1966.

Fewest Punt Returns, Game

   0 Houston vs. L.A. 1960; vs. Oak. 1967.
      Boston vs. S.D. 1963.
      San Diego vs. Bos. 1963.
   1 By six teams.

Most Punt Returns, Both Teams, Game

   8 Buffalo (5) vs. K.C. (3) 1966.
   7 Oakland (4) vs. N.Y. (3) 1968.

Fewest Punt Returns, Both Teams, Game

   0 Boston vs. S.D. 1963.
   2 Houston vs. L.A. (2) 1960.
      Houston (1) vs. S.D. (1) 1961.
      Houston (1) vs. Dall. (1) 1962.

YARDAGE

Most Yards Gained

   128 L.A./San Diego 5gs (6).
   109 Buffalo 3gs (9).

Most Yards Gained, Game

   87 Buffalo vs. S.D. 1965 (3).
   58 San Diego vs. Buff. 1964 (2).

Fewest Yards Gained, Game

  −1 Oakland vs. K.C. 1969 (2).
   0 By seven teams.

Most Yards Gained, Both Teams, Game

   99 Buffalo (87) vs. S.D. (12) 1965 (4).
   64 San Diego (58) vs. Buff (6) 1964 (3).

Fewest Yards Gained, Both Teams, Game

    0 Dallas vs. Hou. 1962 (11).
        Boston vs. S.D. 1963 (9).
    8 Oakland (—1) vs. K.C. (9) 1969 (6).

Longest Gain

   74 Buffalo vs. S.D. 1965 (TD).
   28 San Diego vs. Buff. 1964.

AVERAGE YARDAGE

Highest Average Gain

  21.3 L.A./San Diego 5gs (6).
  12.1 Buffalo 3gs (9).

Highest Average Gain, Game (Minimum 3)

  29.0 Buffalo vs. S.D. 1965 (3).
  12.3 Kansas City vs. Buff. 1966 (3).

Highest Average Gain, Both Teams, Game

  24.8 Buffalo vs. S.D. 1965 (4).
  21.3 San Diego vs. Buff. 1964 (3).

TOUCHDOWNS

Most Touchdowns

      See following category.

Most Touchdowns, Game

    1 Buffalo vs. S.D. 1965.

KICKOFF RETURNS

Most Kickoff Returns

   19 Houston 4gs.
   17 L.A./San Diego 5gs.

Most Kickoff Returns, Game

    9 Boston vs. S.D. 1963.
      Houston vs. Oak. 1967.
    6 Buffalo vs. K.C. 1966.

Fewest Kickoff Returns, Game

    0 Houston vs. S.D. 1961.
    1 Buffalo vs. S.D. 1965.

Most Kickoff Returns, Both Teams, Game

   12 Boston (9) vs. S.D. (3) 1963.
   11 Houston (9) vs. Oak. (2) 1967.

Fewest Kickoff Returns, Both Teams, Game

    2 Houston vs. S.D. (2) 1961.
    4 Buffalo (1) vs. S.D. (3) 1965.

YARDAGE

Most Yards Gained

  515 L.A./San Diego 5gs (17).

482   Houston 4gs (19).

Most Yards Gained, Game

215   Houston vs. Oak. 1967 (9).
175   San Diego vs. Buff. 1964 (4).

Fewest Yards Gained, Game

0   Houston vs. S.D. 1961 (0).
17   Buffalo vs. S.D. 1965 (1).

Most Yards Gained, Both Teams, Game

294   Houston (215) vs. Oak. (79) 1967 (11).
251   Houston (128) vs. L.A. (123) 1960 (10).

Fewest Yards Gained, Both Teams, Game

50   Houston vs. S.D. (50) 1961 (2).
114   Buffalo (17) vs. S.D. (97) 1965 (4).

Longest Gain

72   San Diego vs. Buff. 1964.
52   Oakland vs. K.C. 1969.

AVERAGE YARDAGE

Highest Average Gain

30.3   L.A./San Diego 5gs (17).
29.1   Oakland 3gs (11).

Highest Average Gain, Game (Minimum 3)

43.8   San Diego vs. Buff. 1964 (4).
32.3   San Diego vs. Buff. 1965 (3).

Highest Average Gain, Both Teams, Game

36.5   San Diego vs. Buff. 1964 (6).
28.5   San Diego vs. Buff. 1965 (4).

TOUCHDOWNS

Most Touchdowns
None.

PENALTIES

Most Penalties

25   L.A./San Diego 5gs.
22   Houston 4gs.

Most Penalties, Game

10   San Diego vs. Hou. 1961.
7   Houston vs. Oak. 1967.

Fewest Penalties, Game

1   Boston vs. S.D. 1963.
2   Buffalo vs. S.D. 1965.
   Oakland vs. N.Y. 1968.

Most Penalties, Both Teams, Game

15   San Diego (10) vs. Hou. (5) 1961.
12   Dallas (6) vs. Hou. (6) 1962.

Fewest Penalties, Both Teams, Game

    5   Buffalo (2) vs. S.D. (3) 1965.
    6   San Diego (3) vs. Buff. (3) 1964.
         Oakland (2) vs. N.Y. (4) 1968.

YARDAGE

Most Yards Penalized

  217 Houston 4gs (22).
  212 L.A./San Diego 5gs (25).

Most Yards Penalized, Game

  106 San Diego vs. Hou. 1961 (10).
   69 Oakland vs. Hou. 1967 (4).

Fewest Yards Penalized, Game

   15 Los Angeles vs. Hou. 1960 (3).
   18 Boston vs. S.D. 1963 (1).

Most Yards Penalized, Both Teams, Game

  174 San Diego (106) vs. Hou. (68) 1961 (15).
   92 Houston (50) vs. Dall. (42) 1962 (12).

Fewest Yards Penalized, Both Teams, Game

   48 Boston (18) vs. S.D. (30) 1963 (7).
   49 Oakland (23) vs. N.Y. (26) 1968 (6).

FUMBLES

Most Fumbles

   9 Houston 4gs.
   8 Dall./K.C. 3gs.

Most Fumbles, Game

   5 Houston vs. S.D. 1961.
      Kansas City vs. Oak. 1969.
   4 Houston vs. Oak. 1967.

Fewest Fumbles, Game

   0 By six teams.

Most Fumbles, Both Teams, Game

   7 Houston (5) vs. S.D. (2) 1961.
   6 Kansas City (5) vs. Oak. (1) 1969.

Fewest Fumbles, Both Teams, Game

   0 Buffalo vs. S.D. 1965.
   1 Buffalo vs. S.D. (1) 1964.

RECOVERIES

Most Fumbles Recovered

   9 Houston 4gs (6-own, 3-opp.).
   7 Oakland 3gs (1-own, 6-opp.).

Most Fumbles Recovered, Game

6 Houston vs. S.D. 1961 (4-own, 2-opp.).
5 Oakland vs. K.C. 1969 (1-own, 4-opp.).

Most Fumbles Lost, Game

4 Kansas City vs. Oak. 1969 (5).
2 San Diego vs. Hou. 1961 (2).
   Buffalo vs. K.C. 1966 (3).
   Houston vs. Oak. 1967 (4).
   Oakland vs. N.Y. 1968 (2).

YARDAGE

Most Yards Gained

See following category

Most Yards Gained, Game

21 Kansas City vs. Buff. 1966 (2).
 7 Oakland vs. Hou. 1967 (2).

Longest Gain

21 Kansas City vs. Buff. 1966.
 6 Oakland vs. Hou. 1967.

TOUCHDOWNS

Most Touchdowns

None.

CHICAGO ALL-STAR GAME RESULTS

(Pro teams won 25, lost 9, tied 2)

1969—New York Jets 26, All-Stars 24
1968—Green Bay 34, All-Stars 17
1967—Green Bay 27, All-Stars 0
1966—Green Bay 38, All-Stars 0
1965—Cleveland 24, All-Stars 16
1964—Chicago 28, All-Stars 17
1963—All-Stars 20, Green Bay 17
1962—Green Bay 42, All-Stars 20
1961—Philadelphia 28, All-Stars 14
1960—Baltimore 32, All-Stars 7
1959—Baltimore 29, All-Stars 0
1958—All-Stars 35, Detroit 19
1957—New York 22, All-Stars 12
1956—Cleveland 26, All-Stars 0
1955—All-Stars 30, Cleveland 27
1954—Detroit 31, All-Stars 6
1953—Detroit 24, All-Stars 10
1952—Los Angeles 10, All-Stars 7

1951—Cleveland 33, All-Stars 0
1950—All-Stars 17, Philadelphia 7
1949—Philadelphia 38, All-Stars 0
1948—Chi. Cards 28, All-Stars 0
1947—All-Stars 16, Chi. Bears 0
1946—All-Stars 16, Los Angeles 0
1945—Green Bay 19, All-Stars 7
1944—Chi. Bears 24, All-Stars 21
1943—All-Stars 27, Washington 7
1942—Chi. Bears 21, All-Stars 0
1941—Chi. Bears 37, All-Stars 13
1940—Green Bay 45, All-Stars 28
1939—New York 9, All-Stars 0
1938—All-Stars 28, Washington 16
1937—All-Stars 6, Green Bay 0
1936—Detroit 7, All-Stars 7, tie
1935—Chi. Bears 5, All-Stars 0
1934—Chi. Bears 0, All-Stars 0, tie

MIAMI PLAYOFF BOWL

(Western Conference won 8, Eastern Conference won 2)

1970—Los Angeles Rams 31; Dallas Cowboys 0
1969—Dallas Cowboys 17, Minnesota Vikings 13
1968—Los Angeles Rams 30, Cleveland Browns 6
1967—Baltimore Colts, 20; Philadelphia Eagles, 14
1966—Baltimore Colts, 35; Dallas Cowboys, 3
1965—St. Louis Cardinals, 24; Green Bay Packers, 17
1964—Green Bay Packers, 40; Cleveland Browns, 23
1963—Detroit Lions, 17; Pittsburgh Steelers, 10
1962—Detroit Lions, 28; Philadelphia Eagles, 10
1961—Detroit Lions, 17; Cleveland Browns, 16

NFL PRO BOWL AT LOS ANGELES

(Western Conference won 13, Eastern Conference won 7)

1970—West 16, East 13
1969—West 10, East 7
1968—West 38, East 20
1967—East 20, West 10
1966—East 36, West 7
1965—West 34, East 14
1964—West 31, East 17
1963—East 30, West 20
1962—West 31, West 30
1961—West 35, East 31

1960—West 38, East 21
1959—East 28, West 21
1958—West 26, East 7
1957—West 19, East 10
1956—East 31, West 30
1955—West 26, East 19
1954—East 20, West 9
1953—West 27, East 7
1952—West 30, East 13
1951—East 28, West 27

AFL ALL-STAR GAME

1970—West 26, East 3
1969—West 38, East 25
1968—East 25, West 24
1967—East 30, West 23
1966—All-Stars 30, Buffalo 19

1965—West 38, East 14
1964—West 27, East 24
1963—West 21, East 21
1962—West 47, East 27

Chicago's Dick Butkus (51) lines up his man in the NFL Pro Bowl game.

1969 CHICAGO ALL-STAR GAME

(Soldier Field, Chicago, August 1, 1969)
(Attendance: 74,208)

NEW YORK JETS (26)	Offense	COLLEGE ALL-STARS (24)
George Sauer	WR	Jim Seymour (Notre Dame)
Winston Hill	LT	Dave Foley (Ohio State)
Randy Rasmussen	LG	Mike Montler (Colorado)
John Schmitt	C	Jon Kolb (Oklahoma State)
Dave Herman	RG	John Shinners (Xavier)
Sam Walton	RT	George Kunz (Notre Dame)
Pete Lammons	TE	Bob Klein (Southern California)
Don Maynard	WR	Jerry Levias (Southern Methodist)
Joe Namath	QB	Terry Hanratty (Notre Dame)
Emerson Boozer	RB	Altie Taylor (Utah State)
Matt Snell	RB	Paul Gipson (Houston)

	Defense	
Gerry Philbin	LE	Bill Stanfill (Georgia)
Paul Rochester	LT	Rich Moore (Villanova)
John Elliott	RT	Rolf Krueger (Texas A & M)
Verlon Biggs	RE	Fred Dryer (San Diego State)
John Neidert	LLB	Ron Pritchard (Arizona State)
Al Atkinson	MLB	Bill Bergey (Arkansas State)
Ralph Baker	RLB	Bob Babich (Miami, O.)
John Sample	LCB	Jim Marsalis (Tennessee State)
Randy Beverly	RCB	Bill Thompson (Maryland State)
Bill Baird	LS	Gene Epps (Texas-El Paso)
Jim Hudson	RS	Roger Wehrli (Missouri)

SUBSTITUTIONS

NEW YORK—Offense: Receivers—Bill Rademacher, Bake Turner, Wayne Stewart, John Dockery. Linemen—Pete Perreault, Frank Peters, Gary Roberts, Paul Seiler. Backs—Babe Parilli, Al Woodall, George Nock, Lee White, Bill Mathis. Kickers—Jim Turner, Steve O'Neal.
  Defense: Linemen—Karl Henke, Ezell Jones, Steve Thompson, Ray Hayes. Linebackers—Mike Hall, Paul Crane, Jimmy Jones. Backs—Cornell Gordon, Cecil Leonard, Mike Battle, Mike D'Amato.

ALL-STARS—Offense: Receivers—Ed Hinton (Oklahoma), Bob Miller (Southern California), Mike O'Shea (Utah State), John Spilis (Northern Illinois), Gene Washington (Stanford). Linemen—Dave Bradley (Penn State), Al Jenkins (Tulsa), Rufus Mayes (Ohio State), Jack Rudnay (Northwestern). Backs—Greg Cook (Cincinnati), Bobby Douglass (Kansas), Bill Enyart (Oregon State), Carl Garrett (New Mexico Highlands), Calvin Hill (Yale), Ed Podolak (Iowa), Ron Sayers (Nebraska, Omaha). Kickers—Roy Gerela (New Mexico State), Bill Bradley (Texas).
  Defense: Linemen—Bob Heinz (U. of Pacific), Julian Nunamaker (Tennessee), Ed White (California). Linebackers—Craig Bozich (Brigham Young), Ernie Calloway (Texas Southern), Ted Hendricks (Miami, Fla.), Mike McCaffrey (California). Backs—Terry Brown (Oklahoma State), Tom Maxwell (Texas A & M), Rudy Redmond (U. of Pacific).

COACHES

NEW YORK—Weeb Ewbank, head coach. Assistants—Walt Michaels, Buddy Ryan, Joe Spencer, Ken Meyer.
ALL-STARS—Otto Graham, head coach. Assistants—Mike Scarry, Walt Corey, Lionel Taylor, Leon McLaughlin, Pete Elliott, Stan Springer.

Referee—Jack Vest (AFL). Umpire—Walt Parker (AFL). Field Judge—Charlie Musser (AFL). Head Linesman—William Makepeace (Big Ten). Back Judge—Richard Walterhouse (Big Ten).

SCORING

NEW YORK	6	7	10	3—	—26
ALL-STARS	0	0	17	7—	—24

NY—FG J. Turner 43. NY—FG J. Turner 16. NY—Snell 3 run (J. Turner kick). NY—FG J. Turner 42. AS—Washington 17 pass from Cook (Gerela kick). AS—FG Gerela 28. NY—Snell 35 run (J. Turner kick). AS—Klein 12 pass from Cook (Gerela kick). NY—FG J. Turner 18. AS—Levias 19 pass from Cook (Gerela kick).

TEAM STATISTICS

	NEW YORK	ALL-STARS
Total First Downs	28	8
First Downs Rushing	9	0
First Downs Passing	13	7
First Downs by Penalty	6	1
Total Net Yardage	463	260
Yards Gained Rushing	181	16
Yards Gained Passing	282	244
Passes Attempted	36	31
Completed	18	13
Had Intercepted	3	1
Punts	1	7
Average Distance Punts	38.0	41.7
Punt Returns	2	0
Punt Return Yardage	6	0
Yards Interceptions Returned	13	0
Fumbles	2	0
Opponents' Fumbles Recovered	0	1
Penalties	3	8
Yards Penalized	47	93
Total Offensive Plays	82	44

NFL PLAYOFF BOWL

Orange Bowl, Miami, Fla.   January 3, 1970
Attendance: 30,824

Quarterback Roman Gabriel threw touchdown passes of 35 yards to Les Josephson and 67 yards to Jack Snow the first two times Los Angeles had the ball and the Rams went on to defeat Dallas 31-0 and register the only shutout in the 10-year history of the Playoff Bowl. Gabriel, who completed 12 of 17 passes for 224 yards and was named the game's Most Valuable Player, hit Bob Klein and Snow again for second half touchdowns.

SCORING

DALLAS COWBOYS	0	0	0	0——0
LOS ANGELES RAMS	14	0	7	10——31

LA—Josephson 35 pass from Gabriel (Gossett kick). LA—Snow 67 pass from Gabriel (Gossett kick). LA—Klein 16 pass from Gabriel (Gossett kick). LA—Snow 49 pass from Gabriel (Gossett kick). LA—FG Gossett 42.

INDIVIDUAL STATISTICS

DALLAS   **LOS ANGELES**

Rushing

	Atts.	Yds.	LG		Atts.	Yds.	LG
Garrison	9	47	11	L. Smith	10	29	6
Staubach	6	41	19	Studstill	1	22	22
Hill	8	36	13	Bass	6	17	12
Reeves	5	24	17	Ellison	6	8	7
Shy	1	—1	—1	Josephson	8	8	8
Morton	1	—11	—11	Gabriel	2	—6	—3

Passing

	Atts.	Comp.	Yds.	Int.	TD		Atts.	Comp.	Yds.	Int.	TD
Morton	17	9	120	1	0	Gabriel	17	12	224	0	4
Staubach	7	1	16	1	0	Josephson	1	0	0	1	0
						Sweetan	1	0	0	0	0

Receiving

	No.	Yds.	TD		No.	Yds.	TD
Hayes	3	50	0	Snow	5	144	2
Norman	2	24	0	Josephson	4	55	1
Rentzel	1	25	0	Klein	2	23	1
Hill	1	17	0	L. Smith	1	2	0
Homan	1	16	0				
Garrison	1	4	0				
Welch	1	0	0				

TEAM STATISTICS

	DALLAS	LOS ANGELES
Total First Downs	13	13
First Downs Rushing	6	4
First Downs Passing	7	8
First Downs by Penalty	0	1
Total Net Yardage	222	297
Yards Gained Rushing	136	78
Yards Gained Passing	86	219
Rushing Attempts	30	33
Avg. per Rush	4.5	2.4

	DALLAS	LOS ANGELES
Passes Attempted	24	19
Passes Completed	10	12
Had Intercepted	2	1
Punts—Number and Avg. Distance	4–44.0	4–42.5
Punt Returns and Yardage	2–(−1)	3–37
Kickoff Returns and Yardage	4–96	1–17
Fumbles and Opponents' Recovered	2–1	3–2
Penalties and Yardage	2–25	2–37
Total Offensive Plays	60	53

Mel Renfro isn't enough as Dallas loses to the Rams in NFL Play-off Bowl.

PRO BOWL

Memorial Coliseum, Los Angeles   January 18, 1970
Attendance: 57,786

EAST (13)	Offense	WEST (16)
Paul Warfield (Cleveland)	WR	Gene Washington (Minnesota)
Bob Reynolds (St. Louis)	LT	Grady Alderman (Minnesota)
John Niland (Dallas)	LG	Tom Mack (Los Angeles)
Len Hauss (Washington)	C	Mick Tingelhoff (Minnesota)
Gene Hickerson (Cleveland)	RG	Gale Gillingham (Green Bay)
Ralph Neely (Dallas)	RT	Charlie Cowan (Los Angeles)
Roy Jefferson (Pittsburgh)	TE	Charlie Sanders (Detroit)
Jerry Smith (Washington)	WR	Carroll Dale (Green Bay)
Bill Nelsen (Cleveland)	QB	Roman Gabriel (Los Angeles)
Larry Brown (Washington)	RB	Gale Sayers (Chicago)
Leroy Kelly (Cleveland)	RB	Tom Matte (Baltimore)

	Defense	
Tim Rossovich (Philadelphia)	LE	Carl Eller (Minnesota)
Walter Johnson (Cleveland)	LT	Merlin Olsen (Los Angeles)
Bob Lilly (Dallas)	RT	Alan Page (Minnesota)
George Andrie (Dallas)	RE	Jim Marshall (Minnesota)
Chris Hanburger (Washington)	LLB	Dave Robinson (Green Bay)
Dave Lloyd (Philadelphia)	MLB	Dick Butkus (Chicago)
Chuck Howley (Dallas)	RLB	Dave Wilcox (San Francisco)
Pat Fischer (Washington)	LCB	Lem Barney (Detroit)
Mel Renfro (Dallas)	RCB	Bob Jeter (Green Bay)
Jerry Stovall (St. Louis)	LS	Rick Volk (Baltimore)
Larry Wilson (St. Louis)	RS	Paul Krause (Minnesota)

SUBSTITUTIONS

EAST—Offense: Receiver—Harold Jackson (Philadelphia). Linemen—Jake Kupp (New Orleans), Ernie McMillan (St. Louis). Backs—Fran Tarkenton (New York), Tony Baker (New Orleans), Andy Livingston (New Orleans). Kickers—Tom Dempsey (New Orleans), Bobby Walden (Pittsburgh). Defense: Linemen—Jack Gregory (Cleveland), Joe Greene (Pittsburgh). Linebacker—Jim Houston (Cleveland). Back—Willie Williams (New York).

WEST—Offense: Receivers—Gene Washington (San Francisco), Tom Mitchell (Baltimore). Linemen—Ed Flanagan (Detroit), Elmer Collett (San Francisco), George Kunz (Atlanta). Backs—Bob Berry (Atlanta), Jim Butler (Atlanta), Ken Willard (San Francisco). Kicker—Bob Etter (Atlanta). Defense: Linemen—Gary Larsen (Minnesota), Dave Jones (Los Angeles). Linebacker—Greg Brezina (Atlanta). Backs—Willie Wood (Green Bay), Ken Reaves (Atlanta).

HEAD COACHES

EAST—Tom Fears (New Orleans). **WEST**—Norm Van Brocklin (Atlanta).

OFFICIALS

Referee, Harry Brubaker. Umpire, Joe Muha. Headlinesman, Burl Toler. Field Judge, Armen Terzian. Back Judge, Grover Klemmer. Line Judge, Bob Frederic.

SCORING

EAST	7	6	0	0——13
WEST	0	7	0	9——16

East—Kelly 10 run (Dempsey kick). East—FG Dempsey 46. West—Gabriel 1 run (Etter kick). East—FG Dempsey 27. West—Safety, Brezina tackled Walden in end zone. West—Dale 28 pass from Gabriel (Etter kick).

INDIVIDUAL STATISTICS

Rushing

EAST	Atts.	Yds.	LG	WEST	Atts.	Yds.	LG
Brown	8	46	10	Butler	5	8	8
Baker	6	19	8	Gabriel	3	5	4
Kelly	8	45	12	Matte	6	34	11
Livingston	3	8	3	Sanders	1	−3	−3
Tarkenton	1	2	2	Sayers	9	75	41
Warfield	1	3	3	Willard	6	23	9

Passing

	Atts.	Comp.	Yds.	Int.	TD		Atts.	Comp.	Yds.	Int.	TD
Nelsen	21	12	98	1	0	Gabriel	24	13	212	0	1
Tarkenton	8	3	67	0	0	Berry	4	2	1	1	0

Receiving

	No.	Yds.	TD		No.	Yds.	TD
Brown	4	26	0	Dale	3	50	1
Jackson	1	55	0	Matte	1	6	0
Jefferson	1	7	0	Sanders	1	4	0
Kelly	3	14	0	Sayers	4	66	0
Livingston	1	8	0	Washington (SF)	2	50	0
Smith	3	40	0	Washington (Minn)	1	16	0
Warfield	2	15	0	Willard	3	21	0

TEAM STATISTICS

	EAST	WEST
Total First Downs	14	16
First Downs Rushing	5	7
First Downs Passing	8	8
First Downs by Penalty	1	1
Total Net Yards	238	315
Yards Gained Rushing	123	142
Yards Gained Passing	115	173
Rushes	27	30
Average per Rush	4.6	4.7
Passes Attempted	29	28
Passes Completed	15	15
Had Intercepted	1	1
Punts	5	6
Average Distance Punts	42.8	39.3
Punt Returns	5	3
Punt Return Yardage	24	7
Kickoff Returns	3	4
Kickoff Return Yardage	48	62
Interceptions By	1	1
Interception Return Yardage	31	0
Fumbles	4	3
Opponents' Fumbles Recovered	1	3
Penalties	4	7
Penalty Yardage	31	46
Total Offensive Plays	60	66

AFL ALL-STAR GAME

Astrodome, Houston

January 17, 1970

Attendance: 30,170

The West limited the East to a third-period field goal in scoring a 26-3 victory in the final American Football League All-Star Game. John Hadl completed 18 of 26 passes, including 7 to his San Diego teammate, Lance Alworth, and was voted the game's Most Valuable Player. Jim Turner's 44-yard field goal saved the East from the only shutout in the game's history. Three leading quarterbacks, Joe Namath for the East and Daryle Lamonica and Len Dawson for the West, were unable to play because of injuries.

East (3)	Offense	West (26)
George Sauer (New York)	WR	Fred Biletnikoff (Oakland)
Winston Hill (New York)	LT	Jim Tyrer (Kansas City)
Billy Shaw (Buffalo)	LG	Ed Budde (Kansas City)
Jon Morris (Boston)	C	Jim Otto (Oakland)
Dave Herman (New York)	RG	Walt Sweeney (San Diego)
Glen Ray Hines (Houston)	RT	Harry Schuh (Oakland)
Alvin Reed (Houston)	TE	Billy Cannon (Oakland)
Ron Sellers (Boston)	WR	Lance Alworth (San Diego)
Mike Taliaferro (Boston)	QB	John Hadl (San Diego)
Carl Garrett (Boston)	RB	Dick Post (San Diego)
Matt Snell (New York)	RB	Robert Holmes (Kansas City)
	Defense	
Gerry Philbin (New York)	LE	Rich Jackson (Denver)
Jim Hunt (Boston)	LT	Curley Culp (Kansas City)
John Elliott (New York)	RT	Buck Buchanan (Kansas City)
Elvin Bethea (Houston)	RE	Steve DeLong (San Diego)
Garland Boyette (Houston)	LLB	Bobby Bell (Kansas City)
Nick Buoniconti (Miami)	MLB	Willie Lanier (Kansas City)
Larry Grantham (New York)	RLB	Gus Otto (Oakland)
Miller Farr (Houston)	LCB	Jim Marsalis (Kansas City)
Butch Byrd (Buffalo)	RCB	Willie Brown (Oakland)
Ken Houston (Houston)	LS	Kenny Graham (San Diego)
Don Webb (Boston)	RS	Dave Grayson (Oakland)

SUBSTITUTIONS

EAST—Offense: Receivers—Jim Beirne (Houston), Haven Moses (Buffalo). Linemen—Larry Little (Miami), Tom Goode (Miami). Backs—Jack Kemp (Buffalo), O. J. Simpson (Buffalo), Jim Kiick (Miami). Defense: Lineman—Bill Stanfill (Miami). Linebacker—Harry Jacobs (Buffalo). Back—Zeke Moore (Houston). Kicker—Jim Turner (New York).

WEST—Offense: Receivers—Al Denson (Denver), Willie Frazier (San Diego). Linemen—Mike Current (Denver), George Goeddeke (Denver). Backs—Mike Livingston (Kansas City), Floyd Little (Denver), Paul Robinson (Cincinnati). Defense: Lineman—Dave Costa (Denver). Linebacker—Bill Bergey (Cincinnati). Back—George Atkinson (Oakland). Kicker—Jan Stenerud (Kansas City).

HEAD COACHES

EAST—George Wilson (Miami). **WEST**—Lou Saban (Denver).

OFFICIALS

Referee, Walt Fitzgerald. Umpire, Walt Parker. Head Linesman, Al Sabato. Line Judge, Jack Steffen. Back Judge, Dick Eichhorst. Field Judge, Frank Kirkland.

SCORING

EAST	0	0	3	0—	3
WEST	13	0	3	10—	26

West—Post 1 run (Stenerud pass failed). West—Alworth 21 pass from Hadl (Stenerud kick). West—FG Stenerud 38. East—FG Turner 44. West—FG Stenerud 30. West—Livingston 11 run (Stenerud kick).

INDIVIDUAL STATISTICS

East   **West**

Rushing

	Atts.	Yds.	LG		Atts.	Yds.	LG
Garrett	8	22	7	Hadl	1	9	9
Kiick	4	21	11	Holmes	10	55	12
Simpson	4	21	16	Little	8	—11	3
Snell	3	11	7	Livingston	1	12	12
				Post	12	27	6
				Robinson	6	42	15

Passing

	Atts.	Comp.	Yds.	Int.	TD		Atts.	Comp.	Yds.	Int.	TD
Kemp	16	7	31	1	0	Hadl	26	18	224	3	1
Taliaferro	19	4	69	1	0	Livingston	1	1	10	0	0

Receiving

	No.	Yds.	TD		No.	Yds.	TD
Garrett	2	26	0	Alworth	7	85	1
Kiick	2	—9	0	Biletnikoff	3	34	0
Reed	2	50	0	Cannon	1	17	0
Sauer	1	6	0	Denson	3	47	0
Sellers	1	4	0	Frazier	1	18	0
Simpson	3	23	0	Little	2	11	0
				Post	1	17	0
				Robinson	1	5	0

TEAM STATISTICS

	EAST	WEST
Total First Downs	8	22
First Downs Rushing	3	8
First Downs Passing	4	13
First Downs by Penalty	1	1
Total Offensive Yardage	162	334
Total No. of Offensive Plays	56	69
Avg. Gain per Offensive Play	2.8	5.0
Net Rushing Yardage	75	134
Total Rushing Plays	19	38
Avg. Gain per Rushing Play	4.3	3.8
Net Passing Yardage	87	200
Gross Yards Gained Passing	100	234
Times Thrown and Yards Lost Attempting to Pass	2-13	4-34
Passes Att.-Comp.-Int.	35-11-2	27-19-3
Avg. Gain per Pass Play	2.0	6.5
Punts—Number and Average	8-37.6	3-43.0
Had Blocked	0	0
Fumbles—Number and Lost	1-1	2-1
Penalties—Number and Yards	6-73	2-10
Total Return Yardage	180	110
No. & Punt Returns	2-10	4-20
No. & Yards Kickoff Returns	5-128	2-59
No. & Yards Interception Returns	3-28	2-15
No. & Yards Miscell. Returns	1-14	1-16

1970
National Football League
Team Directories And Schedules

(All times Local, Daylight or Standard)

BALTIMORE COLTS

Address: 600 N. Howard Street, Baltimore,
   Maryland 21201
Telephone: 301-685-6400
President: Carroll D. Rosenbloom
Ass't to President: Steve Rosenbloom
General Manager: Don Klosterman
Head Coach: Don McCafferty
Assistant Coaches: Dick Bielski, Bobby Boyd, Ed
   Rutledge, John Sandusky, John Idzik, Lou Rymkus
Director of Player Personnel: Upton Bell
Publicity Director: Ernie Accorsi
Ass't Publicity Director: Chip Campbell
Trainer: Ed Block
Stadium: Memorial Stadium (60,238)
Stadium Address: 33rd Street, Baltimore,
   Maryland 21218
Colors: Royal Blue, White, Silver

Sept. 20	at San Diego	1:00
Sept. 28	KANSAS CITY	9:00
Oct. 4	BOSTON	2:00
Oct. 11	at Houston	1:00
Oct. 18	at New York Jets	1:00
Oct. 25	at Boston	1:00
Nov. 1	MIAMI	2:00
Nov. 9	at Green Bay (Mil)	8:00
Nov. 15	BUFFALO	2:00
Nov. 22	at Miami	1:00
Nov. 29	CHICAGO	2:00
Dec. 6	PHILADELPHIA	2:00
Dec. 13	at Buffalo	1:00
Dec. 19	NEW YORK JETS	3:00

BOSTON PATRIOTS

Address: 78 Lansdowne Street, Boston,
  Massachusetts 02215
Telephone: 617-262-6363
President: William H. Sullivan, Jr.
Vice President-Head Coach: Clive Rush
General Manager: George H. Sauer
Assistant Coaches: John Mazur, Bruce Beatty,
  Jerry Stoltz, Bill Elias, Jesse Richardson, John
  Meyer
Director of Player Personnel: Rommie Loudd
Director of Public Relations: Jack Nicholson
Ticket Manager: John J. Fitzgerald
Trainer: William Bates
Colors: Red, White, Blue

Sept. 20	MIAMI	1:00
Sept. 27	NEW YORK JETS	1:00
Oct. 4	at Baltimore	2:00
Oct. 11	at Kansas City	1:00
Oct. 18	NEW YORK GIANTS	1:00
Oct. 25	BALTIMORE	1:00
Nov. 1	BUFFALO	1:00
Nov. 8	at St. Louis	1:00
Nov. 15	SAN DIEGO	1:00
Nov. 22	at New York Jets	1:00
Nov. 29	at Buffalo	1:00
Dec. 6	at Miami	1:00
Dec. 13	MINNESOTA	1:00
Dec. 20	at Cincinnati	1:00

BUFFALO BILLS

Address: 69 West Mohawk Street, Buffalo, New York 14202

Telephone: 716-856-1567

President: Ralph C. Wilson, Jr.

Vice President-General Manager: Robert T. Lustig

Head Coach: John Rauch

Assistant Coaches: Marvin Bass, Ralph Hawkins, Lew Engelberg, Ray Malavasi, Bobby Hunt, Chuck Gottfried

Vice President: Patrick J. McGroder, Jr.

Vice President-Public Relations: Jack Horrigan

Director of Player Personnel: Harvey Johnson

Ticket Director: Jim Cipriano

Trainer: Ed Abramoski

Stadium: War Memorial Stadium

Stadium Address: Jefferson and Best Streets, Buffalo, N.Y.

Colors: Scarlet Red, Royal Blue, White

Sept. 20	DENVER	1:00
Sept. 27	LOS ANGELES	1:00
Oct. 4	NEW YORK JETS	1:00
Oct. 11	at Pittsburgh	1:00
Oct. 18	MIAMI	1:00
Oct. 25	at New York Jets	1:00
Nov. 1	at Boston	1:00
Nov. 8	CINCINNATI	1:00
Nov. 15	at Baltimore	2:00
Nov. 22	at Chicago	1:00
Nov. 29	BOSTON	1:00
Dec. 6	at New York Giants	1:00
Dec. 13	BALTIMORE	1:00
Dec. 20	at Miami	1:00

CINCINNATI BENGALS

Address: 1804 Carew Tower, Cincinnati, Ohio 45202
Telephone: 513-621-3550
President: John Sawyer
General Manager-Head Coach: Paul E. Brown
Assistant Coaches: Vince Costello, Jack Donaldson, Bill Johnson, Chuck Studley, Bill Walsh, Chuck Weber
Ass't General Manager: Michael Brown
Business Manager: John Murdough
Director of Public Relations: Allan Heim
Director of Player Personnel: Pete Brown
Ass't Director of Player Personnel: Doug Hafner
Ticket Manager: Roger Noble
Trainer: Marv Pollins
Stadium: Riverfront (55,000)
Stadium Address: Riverfront—Downtown, Cincinnati, Ohio
Colors: Orange, Black, White

Sept. 20	OAKLAND	1:00
Sept. 27	at Detroit	1:00
Oct. 4	HOUSTON	1:00
Oct. 11	at Cleveland	1:00
Oct. 18	KANSAS CITY	4:00
Oct. 25	at Washington	1:00
Nov. 2	at Pittsburgh	9:00
Nov. 8	at Buffalo	1:00
Nov. 15	CLEVELAND	1:00
Nov. 22	PITTSBURGH	1:00
Nov. 29	NEW ORLEANS	1:00
Dec. 6	at San Diego	1:00
Dec. 13	at Houston	1:00
Dec. 20	BOSTON	1:00

CLEVELAND BROWNS

Address: Tower B, Cleveland Stadium, Cleveland, Ohio 44114
Telephone: 216-696-5555
President-Treasurer: Arthur B. Modell
Vice President-General Manager: Harold Sauerbrei
Head Coach: Blanton Collier
Assistant Coaches: Howard Brinker, Dick Modzelewski, Eddie Ulinski, Fritz Heisler, Bob Nussbaumer, Nick Skorich, Howard Keys
Director of Player Personnel: Paul Bixler
Ass't Director of Player Personnel: Mike Nixon
Business Manager: Ben Flieger
Director of Public Relations: Nate Wallack
Controller: Bob Brodhead
Ticket Director: Ed Greulich
Trainer: Leo Murphy
Stadium: Cleveland Stadium (79,282)
Stadium Address: West Third Street, Cleveland, Ohio 44114
Colors: Orange Trim, White with Silver

Sept. 21	NEW YORK JETS	9:00
Sept. 27	at San Francisco	1:00
Oct. 3	PITTSBURGH	9:00
Oct. 11	CINCINNATI	1:00
Oct. 18	DETROIT	1:00
Oct. 25	at Miami	1:00
Nov. 1	SAN DIEGO	1:00
Nov. 8	at Oakland	1:00
Nov. 15	at Cincinnati	1:00
Nov. 22	HOUSTON	1:00
Nov. 29	at Pittsburgh	1:00
Dec. 7	at Houston	8:00
Dec. 12	DALLAS	1:15
Dec. 20	at Denver	2:00

DENVER BRONCOS

Address: 5700 Logan Street, Denver, Colorado 80216
Telephone: 303-623-8778
Chairman of Board: Gerald H. Phipps
President: Allan R. Phipps
General Manager-Head Coach: Lou Saban
Assistant Coaches: Joe Collier, Whitey Dovell, Hunter Enis, Stan Jones, Dick MacPherson, Sam Rutigliano
Director of Public Relations: Richard (Moon) Mullins
Ticket Manager: Earl Hartman
Director of Player Personnel: Fred Gehrke
Associate Ticket Manager: Carroll Hardy
Trainer: Allen Hurst
Stadium: Denver Mile High Stadium (50,000)
Stadium Address: West 19th and Eliot, Denver, Colo.
Colors: Burnt Orange, Royal Blue, White

Sept. 20	at Buffalo	1:00
Sept. 27	PITTSBURGH	2:00
Oct. 4	KANSAS CITY	2:00
Oct. 11	at Oakland	1:00
Oct. 18	ATLANTA	2:00
Oct. 25	at San Francisco	1:00
Nov. 1	WASHINGTON	2:00
Nov. 8	at San Diego	1:00
Nov. 15	OAKLAND	2:00
Nov. 22	at New Orleans	1:00
Nov. 29	at Houston	1:00
Dec. 6	at Kansas City	1:00
Dec. 13	SAN DIEGO	2:00
Dec. 20	CLEVELAND	2:00

HOUSTON OILERS

Address: 6910 Fannin, Houston, Texas 77025
Telephone: 713-748-2780
President: K. S. "Bud" Adams, Jr.
Executive Vice President: John P. Collins
Vice President-Treasurer: L. Wayne Fisher
Head Coach: Wally Lemm
Assistant Coaches: Joe Childress, Hugh Devore, F. A. Dry, Bud McFadin, Fran Polsfoot, Walt Schlinkman
Director of Public Relations: John W. Breen
Publicity Director: Jim McLemore
Ass't to Head Coach & Community Relations: Tom Williams
Director of Player Personnel: Charlie Hall
Business Manager: Lewis Mangum
Ticket Manager: Dan Downs
Trainer: Bobby Brown
Stadium: Astrodome (50,000)
Stadium Address: Loop 610, Kirby & Fannin Streets, Houston, Tex.
Colors: Scarlet, Columbia Blue, White

Sept. 20	at Pittsburgh	1:00
Sept. 27	MIAMI	1:00
Oct. 4	at Cincinnati	1:00
Oct. 11	BALTIMORE	1:00
Oct. 18	PITTSBURGH	1:00
Oct. 25	at San Diego	1:00
Nov. 1	at St. Louis	1:00
Nov. 8	at Kansas City	1:00
Nov. 15	SAN FRANCISCO	1:00
Nov. 22	at Cleveland	1:00
Nov. 29	DENVER	1:00
Dec. 7	CLEVELAND	8:00
Dec. 13	CINCINNATI	1:00
Dec. 20	at Dallas	1:00

KANSAS CITY CHIEFS

Address: 5605 East 63rd Trafficway, Kansas City, Missouri 64130
Telephone: 816-924-9300
President: Lamar Hunt
Executive Vice Pres.-Gen. Manager: Jack Steadman
Head Coach: Hank Stram
Assistant Coaches: Bill Walsh, Pete Brewster, Tom Bettis, Tom Pratt, John Beake, Tommy O'Boyle
Ass't General Manager: Jim Schaaf
Business Manager: Ron Combest
Ticket-Stadium Manager: Bob Wachter
Promotions Director: Lee Derrough
Publicity Director: Bill Hamilton
Trainer: Wayne Rudy
Stadium: Kansas City Municipal Stadium (49,002)
Stadium Address: 22nd and Brooklyn Avenue, Kansas City, Mo.
Colors: Red, Gold

Sept. 20	at Minnesota	3:00
Sept. 28	at Baltimore	9:00
Oct. 4	at Denver	2:00
Oct. 11	BOSTON	1:00
Oct. 18	at Cincinnati	4:00
Oct. 25	DALLAS	3:00
Nov. 1	OAKLAND	3:00
Nov. 8	HOUSTON	1:00
Nov. 15	at Pittsburgh	1:00
Nov. 22	ST. LOUIS	3:00
Nov. 29	SAN DIEGO	1:00
Dec. 6	DENVER	1:00
Dec. 12	at Oakland	1:00
Dec. 20	at San Diego	1:00

MIAMI DOLPHINS

Address: 330 Biscayne Boulevard, Miami, Florida 33132
Telephone: 305-379-1851
Managing General Partner: Joseph Robbie
Head Coach-Vice President: Don Shula
Assistant Coaches: Bill Arnsparger, Mike Scarry, Tom Keane, Howard Schnellenberger, Monte Clark, Carl Taseff
Director of Player Personnel-Executive Ass't: Joe Thomas
Publicity Director: Charlie Callahan
Controller: William Jackson
Promotion Director: Earl Truax
Ticket Director: Jack McGowan
Promotion and Sales: Charles Gesino
Administrative Ass't: Doug Lang
Trainer: Bob Lundy
Stadium: Orange Bowl (75,000)
Stadium Address: 1501 N.W. Third Street, Miami, Fla.
Colors: Aqua, Orange

Sept. 20	at Boston	1:00
Sept. 27	at Houston	1:00
Oct. 3	OAKLAND	8:00
Oct. 10	at New York Jets	8:00
Oct. 18	at Buffalo	1:00
Oct. 25	CLEVELAND	1:00
Nov. 1	at Baltimore	2:00
Nov. 8	at Philadelphia	1:00
Nov. 15	NEW ORLEANS	1:00
Nov. 22	BALTIMORE	1:00
Nov. 30	at Atlanta	9:00
Dec. 6	BOSTON	1:00
Dec. 13	NEW YORK JETS	4:00
Dec. 20	BUFFALO	1:00

NEW YORK JETS

Address: 595 Madison Avenue, New York, New
York 10022
Telephone: 212-421-6600
President: Philip H. Iselin
General Manager-Head Coach: Weeb Ewbank
Assistant Coaches: Walt Michaels, Joe Spencer,
Buddy Ryan, Ken Meyer
Director of Public Relations: Frank Ramos
Ass't Director of Public Relations: Jim Trecker
Director of Player Personnel: Homer Edington
Ass't Director of Player Personnel:
Clyde Washington
Business Mgr.-Traveling Secretary: John Free
Ass't to Gen. Mgr: Mike Martin
Ticket Manager: Leo Palmieri
Trainer: Jeff Snedecker
Stadium: Shea Stadium (60,000)
Stadium Address: Flushing, New York
Colors: Kelly Green, White

Sept. 21	at Cleveland	9:00
Sept. 27	at Boston	1:00
Oct. 4	at Buffalo	1:00
Oct. 10	MIAMI	8:00
Oct. 18	BALTIMORE	1:00
Oct. 25	BUFFALO	1:00
Nov. 1	NEW YORK GIANTS	1:00
Nov. 8	at Pittsburgh	1:00
Nov. 15	at Los Angeles	1:00
Nov. 22	BOSTON	1:00
Nov. 29	MINNESOTA	1:00
Dec. 6	OAKLAND	1:00
Dec. 13	at Miami	4:00
Dec. 19	at Baltimore	3:00

OAKLAND RAIDERS

Address: 7811 Oakport Street, Oakland, California
  94621
Telephone: 415-562-5900
General Partners: Edward M. McGah,
  Wayne Valley, Al Davis
Managing General Partner: Al Davis
Executive Assistant: Al LoCasale
Head Coach: John Madden
Assistant Coaches: Ollie Spencer, Tom Dahms,
  John Polonchek, Richie McCabe, Sid Hall, Dick
  Wood, Marv Marinovich
Director of Player Personnel: Ron Wolf
Director of Administration: Del Courtney
Business Manager: Ken LaRue
Director of Public Relations: Tom Grimes
Publicity Assistant: Ken Bishop
Ticket Manager: George Glace
Trainer: George Anderson
Stadium: Oakland-Alameda County Coliseum
  (53,825)
Stadium Address: Hegenberger Road and Nimitz
  Freeway, Oakland, California
Colors: Silver, Black

Sept. 20	at Cincinnati	1:00
Sept. 27	at San Diego	1:00
Oct. 3	at Miami	8:00
Oct. 11	DENVER	1:00
Oct. 19	WASHINGTON	6:00
Oct. 25	PITTSBURGH	1:00
Nov. 1	at Kansas City	3:00
Nov. 8	CLEVELAND	1:00
Nov. 15	at Denver	2:00
Nov. 22	SAN DIEGO	1:00
Nov. 26	at Detroit	12:00
Dec. 6	at New York Jets	1:00
Dec. 12	KANSAS CITY	1:00
Dec. 20	SAN FRANCISCO	1:00

PITTSBURGH STEELERS

Address: Three Rivers Stadium, 300 Stadium
  Circle, Pittsburgh, Pa. 15212
Telephone: 412-323-1200
President: Arthur J. Rooney
Vice President: John R. McGinley
Vice President: Daniel M. Rooney
Head Coach: Chuck Noll
Assistant Coaches: Max Coley, Walt Hackett,
  Charlie Sumner, Bob Fry, Lionel Taylor
Director of Player Procurement:
  Arthur J. Rooney, Jr.
Director of Public Relations: Ed Kiely
Ticket Manager: Joseph H. Carr
Traveling Secretary: James A. Boston
Publicity Director: Joe Gordon
Personnel Scout: William Nunn, Jr.
Trainer: Ralph Berlin
Stadium: Three Rivers Stadium (50,000)
Stadium Address: North Side, Pittsburgh,
  Pennsylvania
Colors: Black, Gold

Sept. 20	HOUSTON	1:00
Sept. 27	at Denver	2:00
Oct. 3	at Cleveland	9:00
Oct. 11	BUFFALO	1:00
Oct. 18	at Houston	1:00
Oct. 25	at Oakland	1:00
Nov. 2	CINCINNATI	9:00
Nov. 8	NEW YORK JETS	1:00
Nov. 15	KANSAS CITY	1:00
Nov. 22	at Cincinnati	1:00
Nov. 29	CLEVELAND	1:00
Dec. 6	GREEN BAY	1:00
Dec. 13	at Atlanta	1:00
Dec. 20	at Philadelphia	1:00

SAN DIEGO CHARGERS

Address: 2223 El Cajon Boulevard, San Diego, California 92104

Telephone: 714-297-4461

President: Eugene V. Klein

Chairman of Board: Samuel Schulman

General Manager: Sid Gillman

Head Coach: Charlie Waller

Assistant Coaches: Joe Madro, John (Red) Cochran, Jim Phillips, O. A. Phillips, Hal Herring, Jackie Simpson

Business Manager: Irv Kaze

Director of Public Relations: Jerry Wynn

Director of Player Personnel: Tom Miner

Ticket Manager: Phil Barile

Ticket Promotions Director: Emil Karas

Controller: Frances Beede

Ass't Director of Public Relations: Walter Hoye

Special Assignments: Bob Hood

Trainer: Jimmy Van Deusen

Stadium: San Diego Stadium (50,000)

Stadium Address: 9449 Friars Road, San Diego, California

Colors: Blue, Gold, White

Sept. 20	BALTIMORE	1:00
Sept. 27	OAKLAND	1:00
Oct. 4	at Los Angeles	1:00
Oct. 12	GREEN BAY	6:00
Oct. 18	at Chicago	1:00
Oct. 25	HOUSTON	1:00
Nov. 1	at Cleveland	1:00
Nov. 8	DENVER	1:00
Nov. 15	at Boston	1:00
Nov. 22	at Oakland	1:00
Nov. 29	at Kansas City	1:00
Dec. 6	CINCINNATI	1:00
Dec. 13	at Denver	2:00
Dec. 20	KANSAS CITY	1:00

ATLANTA FALCONS

Address: 521 Capitol Avenue S.W., Atlanta, Georgia 30312
Telephone: 404-688-8684
Chairman of Board: Rankin M. Smith
President: Frank E. Wall
General Manager-Head Coach: Norm Van Brocklin
Assistant Coaches: Fred Bruney, Marion Campbell, Harry Gilmer, Bob Griffin, Duane Putnam, Walt Yowarsky
Director of Player Personnel: Tom Braatz
Business Manager: Richard Hull
Ticket Manager: Bill Brokaw
Ass't Ticket Manager: Hank Clay
Public Relations Director: Jan Van Duser
Ass't Public Relations Director: Tom Bennett
Trainer: Jerry Rhea
Stadium: Atlanta Stadium (58,850)
Stadium Address: 521 Capitol Avenue S.W., Atlanta, Ga.
Colors: Red, Black, White, Old Gold

Sept. 20	at New Orleans	1:00
Sept. 27	at Green Bay	1:00
Oct. 4	SAN FRANCISCO	1:00
Oct. 11	at Dallas	1:00
Oct. 18	at Denver	2:00
Oct. 25	NEW ORLEANS	1:00
Nov. 1	CHICAGO	1:00
Nov. 8	at Los Angeles	1:00
Nov. 15	at Philadelphia	1:00
Nov. 22	LOS ANGELES	1:00
Nov. 30	MIAMI	9:00
Dec. 6	at San Francisco	1:00
Dec. 13	PITTSBURGH	1:00
Dec. 20	MINNESOTA	1:00

CHICAGO BEARS

Address: 173 West Madison, Chicago, Illinois 60602
Telephone: 312–332–5400
Chairman of Board: George S. Halas
President-General Manager: George Halas, Jr.
Vice President: Ed McCaskey
Vice President: J. W. McMillen
Secretary: Ralph Brizzolara
Head Coach: Jim Dooley
Assistant Coaches: Ed Cody, Abe Gibron, Sid Luckman, Jim Ringo, Bob Shaw, Don Shinnick
Business Manager: Rudolph Custer
Traveling Secretary: Frank Halas
Director of Research & Planning: Luke Johnsos
Director of Public Relations: Dan T. Desmond
Director of Player Personnel: Bobby Walston
Trainer: Ed Rozy
Stadium: Wrigley Field (45,000)
Stadium Address: N. Clark and W. Addison, Chicago, Ill.
Colors: Orange, Navy Blue, White

Sept. 19	at New York Giants	8:00
Sept. 27	PHILADELPHIA	1:00
Oct. 5	at Detroit	8:00
Oct. 11	MINNESOTA	1:00
Oct. 18	SAN DIEGO	1:00
Oct. 25	DETROIT	1:00
Nov. 1	at Atlanta ·	1:00
Nov. 8	SAN FRANCISCO	1:00
Nov. 15	at Green Bay	1:00
Nov. 22	BUFFALO	1:00
Nov. 29	at Baltimore	2:00
Dec. 5	at Minnesota	12:15
Dec. 13	GREEN BAY	1:00
Dec. 20	at New Orleans	1:00

DALLAS COWBOYS

Address: 6116 North Central Expressway, Dallas, Texas 75206
Telephone: 214–EM 9-3211
Chairman of Board: Clint W. Murchison Jr.
President-General Manager: Texas E. Schramm
Head Coach: Tom Landry
Assistant Coaches: Ermal Allen, Bobby Franklin, Jim Myers, Dan Reeves, Ray Renfro, Ernie Stautner, Jerry Tubbs
Ass't General Manager: Al Ward
Director of Public Relations: Curt Mosher
Business Manager: Tom Hardin
Ticket Manager: Kay Lang
Director of Player Personnel: Gil Brandt
Ass't Player Personnel Director: Bob Griffin
Trainers: Don Cochren, Larry Gardner
Stadium: Cotton Bowl (72,000)
Stadium Address: Fair Park, Dallas, Texas
Colors: Royal Blue, Metallic Blue, White

Sept. 20	at Philadelphia	1:00
Sept. 27	NEW YORK GIANTS	1:00
Oct. 4	at St. Louis	1:00
Oct. 11	ATLANTA	1:00
Oct. 18	at Minnesota	3:00
Oct. 25	at Kansas City	3:00
Nov. 1	PHILADELPHIA	1:00
Nov. 8	at New York Giants	1:00
Nov. 16	ST. LOUIS	8:00
Nov. 22	at Washington	1:00
Nov. 26	GREEN BAY	2:30
Dec. 6	WASHINGTON	3:00
Dec. 12	at Cleveland	1:15
Dec. 20	HOUSTON	1:00

DETROIT LIONS

Address: 1401 Michigan Avenue, Detroit, Mich. 48216

Telephone: 313–965–6644

President: William Clay Ford

Vice President-General Manager: Russell Thomas

Executive Vice President: Edwin J. Anderson

Head Coach: Joe Schmidt

Assistant Coaches: Bill McPeak, Jim Martin, Jim David, Chuck Knox, John North

Secretary-Legal Counsel: Fred C. Nash

Treasurer: Newton S. Peters

Director Public Relations-Business Manager: Lyall Smith

Chief Talent Scout: Jerry Neri

Ass't Publicity Director: Elliott Trumbull

Ass't Treasurer: Magda Kende

Ticket Manager: Maurie Schubot

Special Staff Assistant: Richard Lane

Trainers: Kent Falb, Dave Smith

Stadium: Tiger Stadium (54,082)

Stadium Address: Michigan and Trumbull Avenues, Detroit, Michigan

Colors: Honolulu Blue and Silver

Sept. 20	at Green Bay	1:00
Sept. 27	CINCINNATI	1:00
Oct. 5	CHICAGO	8:00
Oct. 11	at Washington	1:00
Oct. 18	at Cleveland	1:00
Oct. 25	at Chicago	1:00
Nov. 1	MINNESOTA	1:00
Nov. 8	at New Orleans	1:00
Nov. 15	at Minnesota	1:00
Nov. 22	SAN FRANCISCO	1:00
Nov. 26	OAKLAND	12:00
Dec. 6	ST. LOUIS	1:00
Dec. 14	at Los Angeles	6:00
Dec. 20	GREEN BAY	1:00

GREEN BAY PACKERS

Address: 1265 Lombardi Avenue, Green Bay, Wisconsin 54305
Telephone: 414–494–2351
President: Dominic Olejniczak
Vice President: Richard Bourguignon
Secretary: John Torinus
Head Coach-General Manager: Phil Bengtson
Assistant Coaches: Zeke Bratkowski, Forrest Gregg, Dave Hanner, Wayne Robinson, Bob Schnelker, Ray Wietecha
Ass't to General Manager: Tom Miller
Director of Player Personnel: Pat Peppler
Ticket Director (Green Bay): Merrill Knowlton (Milwaukee): Milt Wittig
Public Relations Director: Chuck Lane
Trainer: Dominic Gentile
Stadiums: Lambeau Field (56,161) (Green Bay) Milwaukee County Stadium (47,823) (Milwaukee)
Stadium Addresses: 1265 Lombardi Avenue, Green Bay, Wis. 54305
Hwy. 1–94, Milwaukee, Wisconsin
Colors: Green, Gold

Sept. 20	DETROIT	1:00
Sept. 27	ATLANTA	1:00
Oct. 4	MINNESOTA (Mil)	3:00
Oct. 12	at San Diego	6:00
Oct. 18	LOS ANGELES	1:00
Oct. 25	PHILADELPHIA (Mil)	1:00
Nov. 1	at San Francisco	1:00
Nov. 9	BALTIMORE (Mil)	8:00
Nov. 15	CHICAGO	1:00
Nov. 22	at Minnesota	1:00
Nov. 26	at Dallas	2:30
Dec. 6	at Pittsburgh	1:00
Dec. 13	at Chicago	1:00
Dec. 20	at Detroit	1:00

LOS ANGELES RAMS

Address: 10271 W. Pico Boulevard, Los Angeles, California 90064

Telephone: 213–277–4700

President-General Manager: Daniel F. Reeves

Ass't to President: Jack Teele

Ass't Gen Mgr.-Director of Player Personnel: John R. Sanders

Head Coach: George Allen

Assistant Coaches: Ray Prochaska, Tom Catlin, Ted Marchibroda, LaVern Torgeson, Marv Levy, Boyd Dowler, Joe Sullivan

Business Manager: William H. John

Controller: Don Canning

Directors of Public Relations: Jerry Wilcox, Jack Geyer

Director of Scouting: Normal Pollom

Trainers: George Menefee, Cash Birdwell

Stadium: Los Angeles Memorial Coliseum (76,000)

Stadium Address: 3911 S. Figueroa Street, Los Angeles, Calif.

Colors: Royal Blue, White

Sept. 18	ST. LOUIS	8:00
Sept. 27	at Buffalo	1:00
Oct. 4	SAN DIEGO	1:00
Oct. 11	SAN FRANCISCO	1:00
Oct. 18	at Green Bay	1:00
Oct. 26	at Minnesota	8:00
Nov. 1	at New Orleans	1:00
Nov. 8	ATLANTA	1:00
Nov. 15	NEW YORK JETS	1:00
Nov. 22	at Atlanta	1:00
Nov. 29	at San Francisco	1:00
Dec. 6	NEW ORLEANS	1:00
Dec. 14	DETROIT	6:00
Dec. 20	at New York Giants	1:00

MINNESOTA VIKINGS

Address: 7809 Southtown Center, Bloomington, Minnesota 55431
Telephone: 612–866–3601
President: Max Winter
Board of Directors: H. P. Skoglund, Bernard H. Ridder, E. Wm. Boyer, Ole Haugsrud
Vice-President-General Manager: Jim Finks
Head Coach: Bud Grant
Assistant Coaches: Neill Armstrong, Bob Hollway, John Michels, Jack Patera, Jerry Burns, Bus Mertes
Business Manager: Harley Peterson
Ticket Manager: George Arneson
Player Personnel Director: Jerry Reichow
Director Public Relations and Promotion: Bill McGrane
Ass't Public Relations and Promotion: Sherm Pinkham
Trainer: Fred Zamberletti
Stadium: Metropolitan Stadium (47,900)
Stadium Address: Cedar Ave. at Freeway 494, Bloomington, Minnesota
Colors: Purple, White, Gold Trim

Sept. 20	KANSAS CITY	3:00
Sept. 27	NEW ORLEANS	1:00
Oct. 4	at Green Bay (Mil)	3:00
Oct. 11	at Chicago	1:00
Oct. 18	DALLAS	3:00
Oct. 26	LOS ANGELES	8:00
Nov. 1	at Detroit	1:00
Nov. 8	at Washington	1:00
Nov. 15	DETROIT	1:00
Nov. 22	GREEN BAY	1:00
Nov. 29	at New York Jets	1:00
Dec. 5	CHICAGO	12:15
Dec. 13	at Boston	1:00
Dec. 20	at Atlanta	1:00

NEW ORLEANS SAINTS

Address: 944 St. Charles Avenue, New Orleans, Louisiana 70130
Telephone: 504-524-1421
President: John W. Mecom, Jr.
General Manager: Victor E. Schwenk
Head Coach: Tom Fears
Assistant Coaches: Ed Biles, Brad Ecklund, Don Heinrich, Billy Ray Barnes, Ed Khayat, Jerry Smith
Ass't Gen. Mgr.-Director of Public Relations: Harry Hulmes
Director of Player Personnel: Jack Faulkner
Chief Scout: Henry Lee Parker
Business Manager: Eddie J. Jones
Ticket Manager: Henry Simoneaux
Publications Director: Patricia L. Cross
Trainer: Warren Airail
Stadium: Tulane Stadium (80,997)
Stadium Address: 6401 Willow Street, New Orleans, La. 70118
Colors: Old Gold, Black, White

Sept. 20	ATLANTA	1:00
Sept. 27	at Minnesota	1:00
Oct. 4	NEW YORK GIANTS	1:00
Oct. 11	at St. Louis	1:00
Oct. 18	at San Francisco	1:00
Oct. 25	at Atlanta	1:00
Nov. 1	LOS ANGELES	1:00
Nov. 8	DETROIT	1:00
Nov. 15	at Miami	1:00
Nov. 22	DENVER	1:00
Nov. 29	at Cincinnati	1:00
Dec. 6	at Los Angeles	1:00
Dec. 13	SAN FRANCISCO	1:00
Dec. 20	CHICAGO	1:00

NEW YORK GIANTS

Address: 10 Columbus Circle, New York, N.Y. 10019

Telephone: 212–JU 2–7272

President: Wellington T. Mara

Vice President-Treasurer: Timothy J. Mara

General Manager-Secretary: Raymond J. Walsh

Head Coach: Alex Webster

Assistant Coaches: Norb Hecker, Jim Katcavage, Emlen Tunnell, Joe Walton, Roosevelt Brown, Ken Kavanaugh, Jim Garrett

Controller: Meyer Berger

Director of Personnel: Jim Lee Howell

Director of Pro Personnel: Jim Trimble

Director of Public Relations: Don Smith

Director of Promotions: Ed Croke

Trainers: John Johnson, John Dziegiel

Stadium: Yankee Stadium (64,892)

Stadium Address: 161st Street and River Avenue, The Bronx, N.Y.

Colors: Red, White, Blue

Sept. 19	CHICAGO	8:00
Sept. 27	at Dallas	1:00
Oct. 4	at New Orleans	1:00
Oct. 11	PHILADELPHIA	1:00
Oct. 18	at Boston	1:00
Oct. 25	ST. LOUIS	1:00
Nov. 1	at New York Jets	1:00
Nov. 8	DALLAS	1:00
Nov. 15	WASHINGTON	1:00
Nov. 23	at Philadelphia	9:00
Nov. 29	at Washington	1:00
Dec. 6	BUFFALO	1:00
Dec. 13	at St. Louis	1:00
Dec. 20	LOS ANGELES	1:00

PHILADELPHIA EAGLES

Address: 30th and Market Streets, Philadelphia, Pennsylvania 19104
Telephone: 215–EV 2–5000
President: Leonard H. Tose
Vice President: Joseph A. Donoghue
Vice President-General Manager: Pete Retzlaff
Vice-President: Sydney Forstater
Head Coach: Jerry Williams
Assistant Coaches: Irv Cross, Jim Carr, Charlie Gauer, Joe Moss, Dick Stanfel, Jack Zilly
Business Manager-Ticket Manager: Leo Carlin
Director of Public Relations: James A. Gallagher
Public Relations Ass't: James Murray
Traveling Secretary-Entertainment Director:
  William A. Mullen
Trainer: Moose Detty
Stadium: Philadelphia Veterans Stadium (65,000)
Stadium Address: Broad and Pattison Streets, Philadelphia, Pa.
Colors: Kelly Green, White

Sept. 20	DALLAS	1:00
Sept. 27	at Chicago	1:00
Oct. 4	WASHINGTON	1:00
Oct. 11	at New York Giants	1:00
Oct. 18	ST. LOUIS	1:00
Oct. 25	at Green Bay (Mil)	1:00
Nov. 1	at Dallas	1:00
Nov. 8	MIAMI	1:00
Nov. 15	ATLANTA	1:00
Nov. 23	NEW YORK GIANTS	9:00
Nov. 29	at St. Louis	1:00
Dec. 6	at Baltimore	2:00
Dec. 13	at Washington	1:00
Dec. 20	PITTSBURGH	1:00

ST. LOUIS CARDINALS

Address: 200 Stadium Plaza, St. Louis, Missouri 63102
Telephone: 314–GA 1–0777
President: Charles W. Bidwill, Jr.
Vice President: William V. Bidwill
Secretary-Business Manager: Arch Wolfe
Treasurer: Charles H. Shea
Head Coach: Charley Winner
Assistant Coaches: Chuck Drulis, Bob (Red) Miller, Dick Voris, Ken Shipp, Ken Blue
Director of Player Personnel: Emmett (Abe) Stuber
Director of Public Relations: Joe Pollack
Public Relations Ass't: Lori Greenstein
Ticket Manager: Jim Cash
Trainers: Jack Rockwell, John Omohundro
Stadium: Civic Center Busch Memorial Stadium (50,492)
Stadium Address: 200 Stadium Plaza, St. Louis, Mo. 63102
Colors: Cardinal Red, White, Black

Sept. 18	at Los Angeles	8:00
Sept. 27	WASHINGTON	1:00
Oct. 4	DALLAS	1:00
Oct. 11	NEW ORLEANS	1:00
Oct. 18	at Philadelphia	1:00
Oct. 25	at New York Giants	1:00
Nov. 1	HOUSTON	1:00
Nov. 8	BOSTON	1:00
Nov. 16	at Dallas	8:00
Nov. 22	at Kansas City	3:00
Nov. 29	PHILADELPHIA	1:00
Dec. 6	at Detroit	1:00
Dec. 13	NEW YORK GIANTS	1:00
Dec. 20	at Washington	1:00

SAN FRANCISCO 49ERS

Address: 1255 Post Street, Suite 300, San Francisco, California 94109
Telephone: 415-771-1149
President: Louis G. Spadia
Ass't to President: Art Johnson
General Manager: Jack White
Head Coach: Dick Nolan
Assistant Coaches: Ed Hughes, Ernie Zwahlen, Doug Scovil, Paul Wiggin, Mike Giddings, Jim Shofner
Public Relations Director: George McFadden
Promotions Director: Dick Berg
Controller: Nate Scardigli
Ticket Manager: Pete Giannini
Trainer: Lincoln Kimura
Stadium: Kezar Stadium (59,000)
Stadium Address: Golden Gate Park, San Francisco, Calif.
Colors: 49er Scarlet & Gold

Sept. 20	WASHINGTON	1:00
Sept. 27	CLEVELAND	1:00
Oct. 4	at Atlanta	1:00
Oct. 11	at Los Angeles	1:00
Oct. 18	NEW ORLEANS	1:00
Oct. 25	DENVER	1:00
Nov. 1	GREEN BAY	1:00
Nov. 8	at Chicago	1:00
Nov. 15	at Houston	1:00
Nov. 22	at Detroit	1:00
Nov. 29	LOS ANGELES	1:00
Dec. 6	ATLANTA	1:00
Dec. 13	at New Orleans	1:00
Dec. 20	at Oakland	1:00

WASHINGTON REDSKINS

Address: 1835 K Street, N.W.,
   Washington, D.C. 20006
Telephone: 202-296-1455
President: Edward Bennett Williams
Exec. Vice President-Head Coach: Vince Lombardi
First Vice President: Jack Kent Cooke
Vice President-Treasurer: Milton W. King
Assistant Coaches: Bill Austin, Lew Carpenter,
   George Dixon, Harland Svare, Mike McCormack,
   Don Doll
Secretary: Bernard I. Nordlinger
Executive Ass't: David D. Slattery
Publicity Director: Joe F. Blair
Publicity Ass't: George Christophel
Business Manager: Col. O. C. Krueger
Personnel Director: Tim Temerario
Ticket Manager: Bill Lally
Administrative Ass't: Chester Minter
Trainer: Joe Kuczo
Stadium: Robert F. Kennedy Stadium (50,366)
Stadium Address: East Capitol Street, Washington,
   D.C.
Colors: Burgundy, Gold

Sept. 20	at San Francisco	1:00
Sept. 27	at St. Louis	1:00
Oct. 4	at Philadelphia	1:00
Oct. 11	DETROIT	1:00
Oct. 19	at Oakland	6:00
Oct. 25	CINCINNATI	1:00
Nov. 1	at Denver	2:00
Nov. 8	MINNESOTA	1:00
Nov. 15	at New York Giants	1:00
Nov. 22	DALLAS	1:00
Nov. 29	NEW YORK GIANTS	1:00
Dec. 6	at Dallas	3:00
Dec. 13	PHILADELPHIA	1:00
Dec. 20	ST. LOUIS	1:00

NFL 1970 REGULAR SEASON SCHEDULE

(All times Local, Daylight or Standard)

FRIDAY, SEPTEMBER 18 (First Week)

1. St. Louis at Los Angeles   8:00

SATURDAY, SEPTEMBER 19

2. Chicago at New York Giants   8:00

SUNDAY, SEPTEMBER 20

3. Atlanta at New Orleans   1:00
4. Baltimore at San Diego   1:00
5. Dallas at Philadelphia   1:00
6. Denver at Buffalo   1:00
7. Detroit at Green Bay   1:00
8. Houston at Pittsburgh   1:00
9. Kansas City at Minnesota   3:00
10. Miami at Boston   1:00
11. Oakland at Cincinnati   1:00
12. Washington at San Francisco   1:00

MONDAY, SEPTEMBER 21

13. New York Jets at Cleveland   9:00

SUNDAY, SEPTEMBER 27 (Second Week)

14. Atlanta at Green Bay   1:00
15. Cincinnati at Detroit   1:00
16. Cleveland at San Francisco   1:00
17. Los Angeles at Buffalo   1:00
18. Miami at Houston   1:00
19. New Orleans at Minnesota   1:00
20. New York Giants at Dallas   1:00
21. New York Jets at Boston   1:00
22. Oakland at San Diego   1:00
23. Philadelphia at Chicago   1:00
24. Pittsburgh at Denver   2:00
25. Washington at St. Louis   1:00

MONDAY, SEPTEMBER 28

26. Kansas City at Baltimore   9:00

SATURDAY, OCTOBER 3 (Third Week)

27. Oakland at Miami   8:00
28. Pittsburgh at Cleveland   9:00

SUNDAY, OCTOBER 4

29. Boston at Baltimore   2:00
30. Dallas at St. Louis   1:00
31. Houston at Cincinnati   1:00
32. Kansas City at Denver   2:00
33. Minnesota vs. Green Bay at Milwaukee   3:00
34. New York Giants at New Orleans   1:00
35. New York Jets at Buffalo   1:00
36. San Diego at Los Angeles   1:00
37. San Francisco at Atlanta   1:00
38. Washington at Philadelphia   1:00

MONDAY, OCTOBER 5

39. Chicago at Detroit	8:00

SATURDAY, OCTOBER 10 (Fourth Week)

40. Miami at New York Jets	8:00

SUNDAY, OCTOBER 11

41. Atlanta at Dallas	1:00
42. Baltimore at Houston	1:00
43. Boston at Kansas City	1:00
44. Buffalo at Pittsburgh	1:00
45. Cincinnati at Cleveland	1:00
46. Denver at Oakland	1:00
47. Detroit at Washington	1:00
48. Minnesota at Chicago	1:00
49. New Orleans at St. Louis	1:00
50. Philadelphia at New York Giants	1:00
51. San Francisco at Los Angeles	1:00

MONDAY, OCTOBER 12

52. Green Bay at San Diego	6:00

SUNDAY, OCTOBER 18 (Fifth Week)

53. Atlanta at Denver	2:00
54. Baltimore at New York Jets	1:00
55. Dallas at Minnesota	3:00
56. Detroit at Cleveland	1:00
57. Kansas City at Cincinnati	4:00
58. Los Angeles at Green Bay	1:00
59. Miami at Buffalo	1:00
60. New Orleans at San Francisco	1:00
61. New York Giants at Boston	1:00
62. Pittsburgh at Houston	1:00
63. St. Louis at Philadelphia	1:00
64. San Diego at Chicago	1:00

MONDAY, OCTOBER 19

65. Washington at Oakland	6:00

SUNDAY, OCTOBER 25 (Sixth Week)

66. Baltimore at Boston	1:00
67. Buffalo at New York Jets	1:00
68. Cincinnati at Washington	1:00
69. Cleveland at Miami	1:00
70. Dallas at Kansas City	3:00
71. Denver at San Francisco	1:00
72. Detroit at Chicago	1:00
73. Houston at San Diego	1:00
74. New Orleans at Atlanta	1:00
75. Philadelphia vs. Green Bay at Milwaukee	1:00
76. Pittsburgh at Oakland	1:00
77. St. Louis at New York Giants	1:00

MONDAY, OCTOBER 26

78. Los Angeles at Minnesota	8:00

SUNDAY, NOVEMBER 1 (Seventh Week)

79. Buffalo at Boston	1:00
80. Chicago at Atlanta	1:00

81. Green Bay at San Francisco	1:00
82. Houston at St. Louis	1:00
83. Los Angeles at New Orleans	1:00
84. Miami at Baltimore	2:00
85. Minnesota at Detroit	1:00
86. New York Giants at New York Jets	1:00
87. Oakland at Kansas City	3:00
88. Philadelphia at Dallas	1:00
89. San Diego at Cleveland	1:00
90. Washington at Denver	2:00

MONDAY, NOVEMBER 2

91. Cincinnati at Pittsburgh	9:00

SUNDAY, NOVEMBER 8 (Eighth Week)

92. Atlanta at Los Angeles	1:00
93. Boston at St. Louis	1:00
94. Cincinnati at Buffalo	1:00
95. Cleveland at Oakland	1:00
96. Dallas at New York Giants	1:00
97. Denver at San Diego	1:00
98. Detroit at New Orleans	1:00
99. Houston at Kansas City	1:00
100. Miami at Philadelphia	1:00
101. Minnesota at Washington	1:00
102. New York Jets at Pittsburgh	1:00
103. San Francisco at Chicago	1:00

MONDAY, NOVEMBER 9

104. Baltimore vs. Green Bay at Milwaukee	8:00

SUNDAY, NOVEMBER 15 (Ninth Week)

105. Atlanta at Philadelphia	1:00
106. Buffalo at Baltimore	2:00
107. Chicago at Green Bay	1:00
108. Cleveland at Cincinnati	1:00
109. Detroit at Minnesota	1:00
110. Kansas City at Pittsburgh	1:00
111. New Orleans at Miami	1:00
112. New York Jets at Los Angeles	1:00
113. Oakland at Denver	2:00
114. San Diego at Boston	1:00
115. San Francisco at Houston	1:00
116. Washington at New York Giants	1:00

MONDAY, NOVEMBER 16

117. St. Louis at Dallas	8:00

SUNDAY, NOVEMBER 22 (Tenth Week)

118. Baltimore at Miami	1:00
119. Boston at New York Jets	1:00
120. Buffalo at Chicago	1:00
121. Dallas at Washington	1:00
122. Denver at New Orleans	1:00
123. Green Bay at Minnesota	1:00
124. Houston at Cleveland	1:00
125. Los Angeles at Atlanta	1:00
126. Pittsburgh at Cincinnati	1:00
127. St. Louis at Kansas City	3:00
128. San Diego at Oakland	1:00
129. San Francisco at Detroit	1:00

MONDAY, NOVEMBER 23

130. New York Giants at Philadelphia   9:00

THURSDAY, NOVEMBER 26 (Eleventh Week)
(Thanksgiving)

131. Oakland at Detroit   12:00
132. Green Bay at Dallas   2:30

SUNDAY, NOVEMBER 29

133. Boston at Buffalo   1:00
134. Chicago at Baltimore   2:00
135. Cleveland at Pittsburgh   1:00
136. Denver at Houston   1:00
137. Los Angeles at San Francisco   1:00
138. Minnesota at New York Jets   1:00
139. New Orleans at Cincinnati   1:00
140. New York Giants at Washington   1:00
141. Philadelphia at St. Louis   1:00
142. San Diego at Kansas City   1:00

MONDAY, NOVEMBER 30

143. Miami at Atlanta   9:00

SATURDAY, DECEMBER 5 (Twelfth Week)

144. Chicago at Minnesota   12:15

SUNDAY, DECEMBER 6

145. Atlanta at San Francisco   1:00
146. Boston at Miami   1:00
147. Buffalo at New York Giants   1:00
148. Cincinnati at San Diego   1:00
149. Denver at Kansas City   1:00
150. Green Bay at Pittsburgh   1:00
151. New Orleans at Los Angeles   1:00
152. Oakland at New York Jets   1:00
153. Philadelphia at Baltimore   2:00
154. St. Louis at Detroit   1:00
155. Washington at Dallas   3:00

MONDAY, DECEMBER 7

156. Cleveland at Houston   8:00

SATURDAY, DECEMBER 12 (Thirteenth Week)

157. Dallas at Cleveland   1:15
158. Kansas City at Oakland   1:00

SUNDAY, DECEMBER 13

159. Baltimore at Buffalo   1:00
160. Cincinnati at Houston   1:00
161. Green Bay at Chicago   1:00
162. Minnesota at Boston   1:00
163. New York Giants at St. Louis   1:00
164. New York Jets at Miami   4:00
165. Philadelphia at Washington   1:00
166. Pittsburgh at Atlanta   1:00
167. San Diego at Denver   2:00
168. San Francisco at New Orleans   1:00

MONDAY, DECEMBER 14

169. Detroit at Los Angeles   6:00

SATURDAY, DECEMBER 19 (Fourteenth Week)

170. New York Jets at Baltimore   3:00

SUNDAY, DECEMBER 20

171. Boston at Cincinnati	1:00
172. Buffalo at Miami	1:00
173. Chicago at New Orleans	1:00
174. Cleveland at Denver	2:00
175. Green Bay at Detroit	1:00
176. Houston at Dallas	1:00
177. Kansas City at San Diego	1:00
178. Los Angeles at New York Giants	1:00
179. Minnesota at Atlanta	1:00
180. Pittsburgh at Philadelphia	1:00
181. St. Louis at Washington	1:00
182. San Francisco at Oakland	1:00

NFL POST-SEASON GAMES

Saturday, December 26	American Conference Divisional Playoff
	National Conference Divisional Playoff
Sunday, December 27	American Conference Divisional Playoff
	National Conference Divisional Playoff
Sunday, January 3	American Conference Championship Game
	National Conference Championship Game
Sunday, January 17	Super Bowl Championship Game at Miami, Fla.

NATIONALLY TELEVISED GAMES

REGULAR SEASON

Monday, Sept. 21—New York Jets at Cleveland (night, ABC)
Monday, Sept. 28—Kansas City at Baltimore (night, ABC)
Monday, Oct. 5—Chicago at Detroit (night, ABC)
Monday, Oct. 12—Green Bay at San Diego (night, ABC)
Monday, Oct. 19—Washington at Oakland (night, ABC)
Monday, Oct. 26—Los Angeles at Minnesota (night, ABC)
Monday, Nov. 2—Cincinnati at Pittsburgh (night, ABC)
Monday, Nov. 9—Baltimore vs. Green Bay at Milwaukee (night, ABC)
Monday, Nov. 16—St. Louis at Dallas (night, ABC)
Monday, Nov. 23—New York Giants at Philadelphia (night, ABC)
Thursday, Nov. 26 (Thanksgiving)—Oakland at Detroit (day, NBC)
                      —Green Bay at Dallas (day, CBS)
Monday, Nov. 30—Miami at Atlanta (night, ABC)
Saturday, Dec. 5—Chicago at Minnesota (day, CBS)
Monday, Dec. 7—Cleveland at Houston (night, ABC)
Saturday, Dec. 12—Dallas at Cleveland (day, CBS)
                      —Kansas City at Oakland (day, NBC)
Monday, Dec. 14—Detroit at Los Angeles (night, ABC)
Saturday, Dec. 19—New York Jets at Baltimore (day, NBC)

POST-SEASON

Saturday, Dec. 26—Conference Divisional Playoffs (day, NBC & CBS)
Sunday, Dec. 27—Conference Divisional Playoffs (day, NBC & CBS)
Sunday, Jan. 3—American Conference Championship Game (day, NBC)
              —National Conference Championship Game (day, CBS)
Sunday, Jan. 17—Super Bowl at Miami (day, NBC)

TV DOUBLEHEADER GAMES

(The following games will be seen in most market areas as part of television doubleheaders):

Sept. 20—Kansas City at Minnesota (NBC)
Sept. 27—Oakland at San Diego (NBC)
Oct. 4—Minnesota vs. Green Bay at Milwaukee (CBS)
Oct. 11—San Francisco at Los Angeles (CBS)
Oct. 18—Dallas at Minnesota (CBS)
　　　　—Kansas City at Cincinnati (NBC)
Oct. 25—Dallas at Kansas City (CBS)
Nov. 1—Oakland at Kansas City (NBC)
Nov. 8—Cleveland at Oakland (NBC)
Nov. 15—New York Jets at Los Angeles (NBC)
Nov. 22—St. Louis at Kansas City (CBS)
Nov. 29—Los Angeles at San Francisco (CBS)
Dec. 6—Washington at Dallas (CBS)
Dec. 13—New York Jets at Miami (NBC)
Dec. 20—San Francisco at Oakland (CBS)